Thomas Aquinas's
Summa Theologiae

Thomas Aquinas's *Summa Theologiae*

A Guide and Commentary

BRIAN DAVIES

OXFORD
UNIVERSITY PRESS

OXFORD
UNIVERSITY PRESS

Oxford University Press is a department of the
University of Oxford. It furthers the University's objective
of excellence in research, scholarship, and education
by publishing worldwide.

Oxford   New York

Auckland   Cape Town   Dar es Salaam   Hong Kong   Karachi
Kuala Lumpur   Madrid   Melbourne   Mexico City   Nairobi
New Delhi   Shanghai   Taipei   Toronto

With offices in

Argentina   Austria   Brazil   Chile   Czech Republic   France   Greece
Guatemala   Hungary   Italy   Japan   Poland   Portugal   Singapore
South Korea   Switzerland   Thailand   Turkey   Ukraine   Vietnam

Oxford is a registered trade mark of Oxford University Press
in the UK and certain other countries.

Published in the United States of America by
Oxford University Press
198 Madison Avenue, New York, NY 10016

Library of Congress Cataloging-in-Publication Data
Davies, Brian, 1951–
Thomas Aquinas's Summa theologiae : a guide and commentary / Brian Davies.
pages   cm
Includes bibliographical references and index.
ISBN 978-0-19-938062-6 (cloth : alk. paper)—ISBN 978-0-19-938063-3 (pbk. : alk. paper)
1. Thomas, Aquinas, Saint, 1225?–1274. Summa theologica.   2. Catholic
Church—Doctrines.   3. Philosophy, Medieval.   I. Title.
BX1749.T6D38   2014
230'.2—dc23   2013043444

For Christopher Arroyo, with love, and for
Paul Kucharski, for his friendship
and sense of direction.

Contents

Preface

THE *SUMMA THEOLOGIAE* is one of the most impressive and influential treatises on Christian theology ever written. Even its critics would admit this. It is also Thomas Aquinas's best-known and most studied work, and it can be thought of as expressing his views after a time of much reflection since it was what he was working on just before he died. But it is very long, with later sections building on earlier ones, and its author presupposes that his readers are familiar with writings and terminology of which most people today are largely ignorant.

Experts on medieval theology and philosophy will know how to make sense of the *Summa Theologiae* in general, even if they disagree among themselves when interpreting parts of it. What, however, of those wanting to read it with little or no familiarity with Aquinas or medieval thinking in general? Such people need detailed guidance on how to appreciate the ways in which its various sections connect with one another. They also need help when it comes to understanding its vocabulary and the traditions of thought that it takes for granted. In short, nonspecialists turning with interest to the *Summa Theologiae* need a comprehensive and extended running commentary on it.

Such a work might take different forms. It might consist only of summary or paraphrase. It might concentrate on historical matters, such as context and sources. Its approach might be critical, or it might be primarily concerned with praising what Aquinas has to say. In this book I try to explain what Aquinas argues in the *Summa Theologiae* while providing more than a mere paraphrase of it, and I do so while presuming that the reader has the *Summa* (or sections of it) in hand when following what I say. I also try to locate the *Summa* historically and to note the extent to which Aquinas was influenced by people writing before him and by traditions that he inherited, and I write while hoping to prod readers into thinking about it critically. A full-scale philosophical or theological evaluation of the *Summa Theologiae* would need many volumes. In this book, though, I intend to provide some help when it comes to reflecting about it both with respect to some of its details and with respect to it as a whole.

I begin with an account of Aquinas's life and the circumstances in which he started to write the _Summa Theologiae_. Why did Aquinas write it? Did he intend it for people well advanced as students of philosophy and theology? Or did he intend it for people other than these? Did he think of it as a treatise on theology or philosophy? Such questions need to be raised if we want to know what we are dealing with when it comes to the _Summa Theologiae_.

I then proceed in detail through the entire text of the _Summa_. I explain what it is arguing, what its structure is, how its key technical terms are to be understood, and how bits of it relate to other bits. People turning to the _Summa Theologiae_ often seem to be more interested in some of its parts than in others. My aim, however, is to consider the _Summa_ as a whole. Commentators on it often highlight certain sections of it while ignoring others, and their doing so is understandable. If we want to understand what the _Summa Theologiae_ is, though, we need to plow through it while noting all that it has to offer.

I am presuming that most readers of this book will be reading Aquinas while working with English translations of his works. The best available English edition of the _Summa Theologiae_ currently available is, I believe, the sixty-one-volume Blackfriars one published by Eyre and Spottiswoode and the McGraw-Hill Book Company (1964–1981), now reprinted by Cambridge University Press (2006). It has its flaws, but it provides generally reliable translations together with the Latin original as presented in the critical (Leonine) edition of the _Summa_. It also offers a wealth of useful explanatory material. All of its many volumes were reviewed by the distinguished Anglican theologian Eric Mascall (1905–1993) in _New Blackfriars_ between 1964 and 1976. Mascall helpfully corrected their renditions of Aquinas's Latin at some points, but he was very supportive of the Blackfriars edition, and I think that he was right to have been so. For this reason, my English quotations from the _Summa Theologiae_ come from this edition, though sometimes with emendation by me.

When it comes to sections of the _Summa Theologiae_, there are many English translations. When it comes to the _Summa Theologiae_ as a whole, however, the only current rival to the Blackfriars one is the 1948 edition published as coming from "the Fathers of the English Dominican Province." In fact, this translation was the work of only one greatly unacknowledged English Dominican friar named Laurence Shapcote (1864–1947), and it is a good translation. You can buy it for a small fraction of the cost of the Blackfriars volumes, it is available for free online, and you will be able to use the present book while having it in hand. It is, however, the work of someone whose English will seem slightly old-fashioned to many contemporary readers, and it sometimes errs on the side of literalness when a more colloquial rendition might have been appropriate.

The appendix to this book (a visual breakdown) is presented so that you might get a sense of what Aquinas was interested in while writing the *Summa Theologiae*. It will give you a useful picture of its contents, the space that Aquinas devotes to various topics, and, therefore, a sense of what Aquinas thought to be significant when writing it.

Translations from the Bible in what follows come from the New Revised Standard Version. Books that appear in my bibliography, but are not mentioned in notes to chapters of my text, are there because I think of them as texts that those with interests in the *Summa Theologiae* would benefit from consulting. I should also note that, though I am not presuming that readers of this book are able to read Latin, I frequently indicate, for those who might be interested, which Latin terms Aquinas sometimes uses, and I occasionally comment on possible alternative translations of them.

For advice on earlier versions of what follows, or on parts of it, I am, with the usual disclaimer, much indebted to Christopher Arroyo, David Burrell, James Claffey, John Drummond, Samuel Kampa, David Kovacs, Paul Kucharski, Timothy McDermott, Jon McGinnis, Turner Nevitt, Adriano Oliva, Zita Toth, and Joseph Trabbic. I would also like to express thanks to Cynthia Read, of Oxford University Press, for being a most gracious in-house editor for this book, and for performing the same role for previous publications of mine.

Thomas Aquinas's
Summa Theologiae

I

Setting the Summa Theologiae

AQUINAS ONCE WROTE that, having learned that something exists, it seems sensible to ask what the thing is.[1] Now we know *that* the *Summa Theologiae* exists. But what is it? And where did it come from? With these questions in mind, my intention in this chapter is to provide some background setting. First, I offer a brief account of Aquinas's life. Then I say something about how the *Summa Theologiae* came to be written and how it should be classified.

1.1 Aquinas Himself

1.1.1 Early Years

Aquinas was born around 1224–1226.[2] His family was aristocratic, and his birth took place at the castle of Roccasecca, midway between Naples and Rome. So Aquinas was a southern Italian. His father was Landulph d'Aquino.[3] His mother was named Theodora. His baptismal name was Thomas.[4]

At about the age of five or six, Aquinas was sent to study at the Abbey of Monte Cassino, with which his family had special connections (one of Aquinas's relatives was its abbot).[5] Here he received an education in grammar and writing. He also studied the Bible and patristic authors such as St. Augustine of Hippo (354–430) and St. Gregory the Great (ca. 540–604).

Around 1239, however, Aquinas's time at Monte Cassino ended for political reasons. The emperor Frederick II (1194–1250) and Pope Gregory IX (d. 1241) were at that time seriously in conflict with each other. Early in 1239 Frederick's soldiers were preparing to occupy Monte Cassino on strategic grounds. Likely forewarned of a military presence at the abbey, Aquinas's family arranged for him to continue his education at the University of Naples.

The University of Naples was the first European university established as a distinct entity by civil, as opposed to ecclesiastical, charter.[6] It still exists and bears an image of Frederick II on its crest. Frederick founded his university in 1224 chiefly to train people to work for him as lawyers, judges, and administrators, but the curriculum taught there ranged widely. According to Frederick's charter, it comprised "the arts and all disciplines," including, presumably, logic, metaphysics, philosophy in general, and theology. Based on the report of one of Aquinas's early biographers, William of Tocco, it has often been said that Aquinas was taught in Naples by someone called Peter of Ireland (*Petrus de Hibernia*). We have reason to doubt that claim, however, since the presence of Peter at the University of Naples is not attested to before 1250.[7]

1.1.2 Naples to Paris

During his student time at Naples, Aquinas entered the Order of Preachers (the Dominicans) founded by St. Dominic Guzman (1170–1221). He probably took the Dominican habit in 1242 or 1243. His family objected to this decision and detained him under a form of house arrest until 1245 or 1246.

Why so? Possibly because the Dominican Order was then relatively new and did not conform to established patterns for religious life as exemplified by Benedictine and Cistercian monks. We should also note that Aquinas's joining the Dominicans would have been perceived by his family as probably dashing any hopes of his acquiring ecclesiastical preferment.

Why did Aquinas choose the Dominicans? He left no written explanation of his reasons. Indeed, he hardly ever writes explicitly about his order and never refers to St. Dominic by name. However, the way in which he prizes a commitment to preaching, study, and poverty might suggest why he was drawn to the Dominicans.[8] And in the *Summa Theologiae* he explains why a religious order that looks like the Dominicans would be the best possible order. In 2a2ae,188,6, he writes, "Religious institutes dedicated to teaching and preaching have the highest place (*summum gradum*)."

Around 1246 Aquinas was probably living in Paris and may have spent time studying in some way in, or in connection with, the Faculty of Arts there.[9] He was almost certainly working under the direction of St. Albert the Great (*Albertus Magnus*), then one of the Dominicans' intellectual stars.[10] In 1248, however, Albert moved to Cologne to establish a Dominican house of studies, and Aquinas went with him.

At Cologne, Aquinas worked as Albert's secretary and student. He might also have written his *De Principiis Naturae* (*On the Principles of Nature*), a short treatise presenting some ideas derived from the *Physics* of Aristotle.[11] Also in Cologne, Aquinas may have delivered some lectures on the Bible.[12] If so, this was the beginning of a lifelong teaching career.

In 1251 or 1252, Aquinas was sent by the Dominicans to teach at the University of Paris. His move came at the suggestion of Albert. The idea was that Aquinas should prepare to become a Master of Theology. On arriving in Paris, however, his primary teaching obligations were first to give lecture commentaries on biblical texts as a *baccalaureus biblicus* ("Biblical Bachelor") and then to give lecture commentaries on the *Sentences* of Peter Lombard (1095–1160) as a *baccalaureus Sententiarum* ("Bachelor of the *Sentences*"). Lombard's *Sentences*, written in the 1150s, became the standard textbook for students and teachers of theology in the years following the Fourth Lateran Council (1215). Commentaries on it by those preparing to be Masters of Theology proliferated during the Middle Ages, and continued to be produced until the time of the Reformation. Even Martin Luther (1483–1546) lectured on the *Sentences*.[13]

While he was teaching in Paris, Aquinas wrote a short treatise called *De Ente et Essentia* (*On Being and Essence*), in which he develops arguments that resurface in the *Summa Theologiae*. He also became involved in some ecclesiastical controversy at the University of Paris. A lively (not to say acrimonious) dispute had broken out between the mendicant orders (the Dominicans and Franciscans) and the "secular masters," who were opposed to allowing mendicants to teach in the university. The secular masters were teachers at Paris who, though clerics, did not belong to a religious order. The presence in Paris of Masters of Theology who were members of the two mendicant orders was, for various reasons, perceived by the secular masters as threatening. Also, there was considerable opposition to the very existence of these orders in the Church, an opposition led by William of Saint-Amour (ca.1200–1272).[14] Aquinas became involved in this controversy and in 1256 defended the mendicants in a work called *Contra Impugnantes Dei Cultum et Religionem* (*Against Opponents of the Worship of God and Religion*). In later years, he followed up this defense in two other texts: *De Perfectione Spiritualis Vitae* (*On the Perfection of Spiritual Life*) and *Contra Doctrinam Retrahentium a Religione* (which I freely translate as *Against the Teaching of Those Who Belittle the Life of Friars*).[15]

Following a delay occasioned by the quarrel between secular masters and mendicants, Aquinas became a Master of Theology in 1256 largely, it seems, because of intervention by Pope Alexander IV prompted by the head or "Master" of the Dominicans. This advancement left him with two main teaching duties.[16] First and foremost, he had to lecture on the Bible.[17] He was also expected to preside over "Disputations." These were events in which matters of theological significance were focused on with arguments being given for and against various positions and with a master giving his view or "determination" of them. The minutes of these events were sometimes written up for publication by the presiding master. The collected works of Aquinas contain a number of "Disputed Questions."[18] His *Disputed Questions on Truth* (*De Veritate*) date from the first time he taught at Paris.[19]

I use the phrase "first time" here because Aquinas had two teaching periods in Paris. His first ended in or around 1259.[20] But he returned to Paris in

1268, leaving again in 1272. During what is commonly referred to as his second "Parisian Regency," Aquinas again lectured on the Bible. He also wrote a number of commentaries on the writings of Aristotle, and his *De Aeternitae Mundi* (*On the Eternity of the World*) dates from this period. In this work, Aquinas argues that it cannot be proved by reason alone that the universe had a temporal beginning. He also argues that this fact does not mean that we lack reason for thinking of God as creator of the universe.

1.1.3 Later Years

Around 1261, Aquinas was appointed by his religious superiors to become a Conventual Lector in the Dominican priory at Orvieto in Italy. In this context, he was not teaching university students. He was working with Dominican friars assigned to the Orvieto house. He was now dealing not with academics but chiefly with people going out into the day-to-day world while trying to do some good as preachers and pastors.

While he was at Orvieto Aquinas again continued to write. He drafted a commentary on the book of Job.[21] He also forged ahead with his *Summa Contra Gentiles* (*Summary Against the Pagans*), a work that he began during his first Parisian Regency and finished around 1265.[22]

Aquinas's purpose in composing the *Contra Gentiles* has been a matter of much academic speculation. It has been suggested that the work was produced as a handbook for Dominican friars working in Islamic territory. Yet the *Contra Gentiles* does not read like a missionary manual, and it is not especially critical of Islam. Much of it amounts to a sustained philosophical case for believing that God exists and that certain truths can be affirmed of God on the basis of human reason. Specifically Christian doctrines are also addressed in the *Contra Gentiles*, but only in its last book, though the teaching of this book is in line with things that Aquinas argues in the *Summa Theologiae*.[23]

The Dominican Order comprises provinces established on a regional basis. It works in a democratic way with superiors elected by their brethren. Each province of the order regularly elects delegates to attend and vote at the order's General Chapters, which legislate for the order as a whole. In September 1265, the Provincial Chapter of the Dominican Roman province, to which Aquinas belonged, directed him to establish a house of studies for Dominican students coming from all over the Roman province. It was set up in the priory of Santa Sabina in Rome and was something new in the Dominican world. The order then had five official houses of studies (*studia*) in Paris, Bologna, Cologne, Montpellier, and Oxford, and all the Dominican provinces sent a limited number of promising students to them. The Santa Sabina *studium*, however, seems to have been created by the order's Roman province simply for Aquinas to run with a curriculum of his choosing and with students handpicked by him; it ceased to exist when he returned to Paris in 1268.

It was while he was teaching in Rome that Aquinas began work on his *Summa Theologiae*.[24] And he continued writing it throughout his second Parisian Regency. Indeed, he was still engaged with it when he died. The *Summa Theologiae* was never completed by Aquinas. For all its length, it comes to us as a work in progress. Some printed editions of it "complete" it by noting where Aquinas seemed to be heading by inserting sections from his *Commentary on the Sentences* (these sections are commonly referred to as the "Supplement" to the *Summa Theologiae*). The motive behind this "completion" of the text is understandable, though it should not be assumed that Aquinas agreed with everything he said in his *Sentences* commentary by the time of his death. The "Supplement" may well derive from Reginald of Piperno (ca.1230–1290), a Dominican and the longtime friend and secretary of Aquinas.

In 1272, Aquinas was assigned to found a provincial *studium* in Naples. Actually, the Dominicans asked him to found a *studium* anywhere in Italy, and he decided on Naples. Here he continued to work on the *Summa Theologiae* and on commentaries on Aristotle.[25] At this time he was also being paid (at the rate of one ounce of gold each month) to teach theology at the University of Naples. But his health was clearly failing by early 1274, the year of his death.

Aquinas was well versed in matters to do with what is now called "ecumenical theology," and in 1274 was asked to attend the Second Council of Lyons to advise about differences between Greek and Latin Christians. He set out for the council but died on the way—in a guest room at the Abbey of Fossanova. This we know. But speculations concerning the cause of his death are, indeed, just speculations.[26]

1.2 *The* Summa Theologiae

Speculations, of course, are frustrating. For we naturally want answers to our questions rather than guesses. Unfortunately, however, we are left with speculation not only concerning the cause of Aquinas's death but also with respect to the question "How did Aquinas conceive of his *Summa Theologiae*?" We can read this work and form various impressions of it. What, however, was Aquinas trying to do while writing it? He worked steadily on it for many years, yet with what aim in mind? What kind of treatise did he take himself to be composing? Is there some genre into which we can place it? These questions are not easy to answer.

1.2.1 Why Did Aquinas Write the *Summa Theologiae*?

Well, why *did* Aquinas write it? And what was its intended readership? I have noted that Aquinas started work on it while at Santa Sabina presiding over what was effectively a "personal *studium*."[27] But for whom did he take himself to be writing, and to what purpose?

It has been suggested that Aquinas embarked on the *Summa Theologiae* so as to assist gifted students aiming to become Masters of Theology in places like the University of Paris.[28] A problem with this suggestion, however, seems to be presented by what he writes in his prologue (*Prooemium*) to the *Summa*. Here he says:

> Since the teacher of Catholic truth has not only to build up those who are advanced (*non solum provectos*) but also to shape those who are beginning (*incipientes*)...the purpose we have set before us in this work is to convey the things which belong to the Christian religion in a style serviceable for the training of beginners (*ad eruditionem incipientium*). We have considered how newcomers to this teaching are greatly hindered by various writings on the subject, partly because of the swarm of pointless questions, articles, and arguments, partly because essential information is given according to the requirements of textual commentary or the occasions of academic debate, not to a sound educational method, partly because repetitiousness has bred boredom and muddle in their thinking. Eager, therefore, to avoid these and other like drawbacks, and trusting in God's help, we shall try to pursue the things held by *sacra doctrina* ('sacred teaching', i.e., the Bible and those who interpret it correctly) and to be concise and clear, so far as the matter allows.[29]

This passage hardly seems to indicate that Aquinas started writing the *Summa* with an eye on people on the verge of becoming Masters of Theology at Paris or anywhere else. It seems to suggest that he was concerned to write for people much lower down on the academic pecking order. So could it be that this was actually his intention? We have some reason for thinking that it might have been since a case can be made for viewing the *Summa Theologiae* as having its beginnings in concerns about the education of Dominicans.

1.2.2 Aquinas and Dominicans Trying to Study

Aquinas's assignment to set up his Santa Sabina study house came when he had already begun to be actively involved in the system of studies in his province.

In 1260, the Roman province's chapter promoted him to the rank of *praedicator generalis* ("Preacher General"). This meant that he became, for life, someone with an automatic right to vote at all the Roman provincial chapters, and, surely not accidentally, the Roman province of the Dominican Order started to become serious about studies from around the time that Aquinas became a Preacher General.[30]

Aquinas attended all of his province's provincial chapters from 1261 to 1268, and he had a hand in the progress of Dominican studies even before 1261. In 1259, he was a member of a committee that presented a *ratio studiorum* ("plan of studies") for the whole Dominican Order at its general chapter at Valenciennes.[31] Prior to this chapter, and notwithstanding the traditional reputation of the Dominicans for having a concern with study, learning seems not to have been given great priority in its Roman province. However, that province's chapters start to attend to learning in 1263 and 1264. The 1263 chapter decreed that all Dominicans of the province should attend classes to be set up for them. The 1264 chapter lamented a neglect of study in the Roman province and insisted that all of its houses should provide serious study opportunities for the Dominicans living in them.

Remember that Aquinas was deputed to organize his study house in Rome in 1265. Given what I have just reported, a natural inference is that the Santa Sabina venture was an experiment conducted by a province trying to get its act together on studies with the help of someone distinguished and already seriously committed to the education of Dominicans. And it is evident that Aquinas was so committed. Hence, for example, his work at the Orvieto priory. Here his explicit brief was to teach Dominicans.

What would these Dominicans have been like, intellectually speaking? The overwhelming majority of them, as in the Dominican Order as a whole at that time, were not people who had pursued courses in universities. They were not academic stars like Albert and Aquinas. They were mostly working friars who needed help when it came to their primary tasks—preaching and hearing confessions.[32] It is also worth bearing in mind that their teacher (i.e., Aquinas) was someone who, though nowadays commonly thought of as a university professor, spent only around seven years of his Dominican life working in a university.

He spent the majority of the other twenty-four or twenty-five years of it teaching Dominicans in Dominican priories. The students that Aquinas would largely have taught in such places came to be known as *fratres communes* ("regular brothers" or "common brothers").[33] Regardless of their age, they were sometimes referred to as *iuniores* ("juniors"), *incipientes* ("beginners"), and *simplices* ("simple").[34] They were also all required to attend classes. As

Leonard Boyle puts it: "In this sense, the *fratres communes* were forever *iuniores*."[35] When Aquinas was teaching at Orvieto, these Dominicans were chiefly working from moral manuals and manuals of concern to confessors.

Famous among these was Raymond of Penafort's 1224 *Summa de Casibus Poenitentiae* (*Summary Concerning the Cases of Penance*), followed by many other comparable texts. Aquinas may very well have lectured on the Bible while he was living in Orvieto, yet the teaching of practical theology would have taken up a great deal of his time, with the *Summa de Casibus* being a major work of reference. So could it be that trying to improve on such works, with an eye on Dominican students, was Aquinas's intention as he began his *Summa Theologiae*? That such is the case has been argued by Boyle, whose position on the "setting of the *Summa*" has been received with much critical acclaim.

1.2.3 Leonard Boyle on the Origins of the *Summa Theologiae*

Boyle (1923–1999) taught at the Pontifical Institute of Mediaeval Studies in Toronto and subsequently became prefect of the Vatican Library and president of the Leonine Commission.[36] His area of expertise was paleography, but (perhaps because he was a Dominican) he had interests in the biography of Aquinas and in 1982 gave the Etienne Gilson Lecture in Toronto with the title "The Setting of the *Summa Theologiae*."[37] In this lecture, he suggested that the *Summa Theologiae* was intended by Aquinas for "run of the mill" Dominicans charged with the *cura animarum* ("care of souls") and was designed to improve on manuals then available to them so as to place practical or moral theology into a full theological context. Boyle's conclusion was that the *Summa* was Aquinas's attempt to provide "his own very personal contribution to a lopsided system of theological education in the order to which he belonged."[38]

There is a case to be made for this conclusion. For one thing, it perfectly coheres with what Aquinas says in his prologue to the *Summa*, in which he declares himself to be writing for those "who are beginning" rather than those who are advanced. He goes on (alluding to 1 Corinthians 3:1) to call them "babes in Christ" to whom he is offering milk rather than meat. "Novices" in *sacra doctrina*, he adds, are much hindered by various writings that do not proceed from a sound educational method. Aquinas, as we have seen, concludes by saying that his aim in what follows is to provide a helpful alternative to the writings to which he has just referred. His intention, he observes, is to be as concise and clear as possible. The *Summa Theologiae* was written over a number of years, and it may be that, as he proceeded with it, he had given up on the sentiments and intentions expressed in its prologue. That prologue, however, must surely be given serious weight when trying to decide what Aquinas took the pages that follow it to be.

One might read it as saying that the *Summa Theologiae* is intended for absolutely anyone not an expert in *sacra doctrina* but interested in it. Yet it is unlikely that Aquinas could ever have had such a hugely general readership in mind. He must have been thinking more precisely when it comes to his "target audience," and if this was not a body of theological experts or would-be Masters in Theology, it seems plausible to suggest that it was Aquinas's own brethren, whether students in formation, or those engaged in an active ministry, or those who had retired from such ministry but were still obliged, as far as they were able, to continue with studies.

This thought is supported by the fact that what Aquinas writes in his prologue to the *Summa Theologiae* strongly resembles what Humbert of Romans (d. 1277) says in his *Liber de Instructione Officialium Ordinis Praedicatorum* (*Book of Instructions for Officials of the Order of Preachers*). Humbert was the Master General of the Dominican Order from 1254 to 1263.[39] In the work to which I have just referred, he talks about how he thinks that Dominican teachers of Dominicans should proceed, and his recommendations seem to be very much echoed by Aquinas when embarking on the *Summa Theologiae*.[40]

Again, Boyle's conclusion is attractive given that Aquinas began work on the *Summa* in Rome and after teaching at Orvieto. He was then, for the first time in his life, able to teach Dominicans as he pleased and must, therefore, have been thinking about how Dominicans should be taught. Also, there is reason to believe that, while he was teaching at Rome, Aquinas embarked on a new commentary on Lombard's *Sentences*, that he lectured on Lombard in Rome, and that he abandoned work on Lombard in order to begin the *Summa Theologiae*.[41] All of this could be interpreted along these lines: (1) Aquinas, with a free hand concerning the education of Dominicans, lectures on the *Sentences* at Santa Sabina; (2) he comes to think that complicated works such as familiar commentaries on texts and editions of Disputed Questions are not what regular Dominicans need in order to help them to do their work; (3) Aquinas, therefore, stops writing a new commentary on Lombard and begins a work designed to simplify while giving Dominicans an A–Z when it comes to Christian theology.[42]

A third point worth noting is that while he was at Rome Aquinas began to write his *Compendium Theologiae* (*Compendium of Theology*). Unfinished at the time of his death, it covers the range of Christian doctrine in roughly the same manner as does the *Summa*, and it does so in a wholly introductory way. It begins by reflecting on how God incarnate provided, as it were, a brief account of what God is about and of the truths that people need to help them to union with God. It goes on to describe the *Compendium* as "a summary instruction in the Christian religion." The *Compendium* indicates that Aquinas was thinking about how to present an introductory and not an academically oriented work of theology when he started work on the *Summa Theologiae*.

So there is good circumstantial evidence favoring the conclusion drawn by Boyle. Yet the evidence *is* circumstantial, and there are reasons for being cautious about it.

One is that the Roman province of the Dominican Order did not adopt the *Summa* as a textbook for Dominican students in the years following its composition. As Boyle himself agrees: "There is no sign even that any of the annual Provincial chapters ever recommended Thomas or any of his works in the way in which, a shade unrealistically, the Chapter of 1284 at Aquila ordered that 'lectors and others of the brethren in their lectures and disputations' should use the formulary book of papal and other letters compiled by Marinus of Eboli, lately archbishop of Capua."[43] As Boyle also notes, as late as 1308 we find another provincial chapter of the Roman province stating: "We wish and order that all lectors and bachelors lecture on the *Sentences* and not on the *Summa* of Thomas." Aquinas may have given up writing a commentary on the *Sentences* in Rome so as to work on a text to be read by Dominican students.[44] But his Dominican province does not seem to have supported him in this venture so as to make his text a standard one for Dominican students to read.

Another point to be made against Boyle's thesis is that, in spite of the *Summa*'s prologue with its reference to "those who are beginning," the text as a whole seems to presuppose a lot of philosophical background on the part of its readers. From the outset it makes use of a lot of Aristotelian terminology without providing explanations for it.

It might well have been the case that in the course of their previous studies, Dominicans in the thirteenth century normally acquired a rudimentary knowledge of Aristotle's thinking of the kind imparted by Aquinas in works such as *De Principiis Naturae*, *De Ente et Essentia*, and his commentary on Aristotle's *Physics*, and perhaps Aquinas was well aware of this while attempting to write the *Summa Theologiae*. Some readers of this text might, however, and understandably, suspect that Aquinas was writing it with a more academically advanced audience in mind. They might, for example, think that the beginners Aquinas seems to be targeting are people proceeding from a degree in Arts to studies in *Sacra Doctrina*.

Yet the circumstantial evidence in favor of Boyle's suggestion remains.[45] That Aquinas's province did not promote it as a text for Dominicans to study might tell us more about people in power in that province than it does about Aquinas.[46] And, though knowledge of Aristotelian notions seems to be presumed in the *Summa*, the inference should not be from "Aquinas was writing for Domini-cans engaged in study" to "Aquinas did this successfully." Gifted academics often talk past their students and do not manage sufficiently to meet them where they are. Aquinas may have been such an academic himself and might, therefore, have failed to write for his intended audience as well as he should have if he was trying to do what Boyle suggests that he was.

If I am right here, of course, there are implications for the way in which we should read and try to evaluate the *Summa*. It has sometimes been ap-proached as a philosophical treatise aimed at a highly educated philosophical audience. If what I say above is correct, however, Aquinas never intended readers of the *Summa Theologiae* to think of it like this. He was not even writ-ing for people with a huge theological background. He was writing in sum-mary fashion for an audience that took for granted the truths of Christianity as he took them to be. He was not writing a text on the philosophy of religion for people with no prior religious beliefs. Nor was he writing for the edifica-tion of Masters of Theology in his day. Rather, he was trying to help his Do-minican colleagues to get a sense of how to think about the Christian religion while paying attention to what might be said about it with an eye on the his-tory of theology and with an eye on how reason, as distinct from revelation, might help one to approach it.

Here, of course, I am saying that the *Summa Theologiae* is both a theolog-ical and a philosophical work. In what sense, however? To what extent is it a work of theology? To what extent is it a work of philosophy?

1.2.4 The *Summa Theologiae* as a Work of Theology

Its title would naturally suggest that it is primarily a theological treatise.[47] The Latin word *summa* means "summary" or "compendium." One might even trans-late it as "manual," "handbook," or "textbook."

A medieval *summa* was (or eventually came to be) a systematic and wide-ranging discussion of a particular topic or range of topics presenting arguments for and against a collection of conclusions. Both Aquinas's *Summa Theologiae* and his *Summa Contra Gentiles* well qualify as *summae* (the plural of "summa") on this understanding.[48] And the former is obviously a work of theology. For one thing, it is presented to believing Christians on the assumption that the author and the reader agree from the outset that texts like the Nicene Creed (325) and that promulgated by the First Council of Constantinople (381) express true beliefs.

The *Summa Theologiae* comes in three parts, the second of which is divided into two. So we have the *Prima Pars* (the First Part), the *Prima Secundae* (the

First Part of the Second Part), the *Secunda Secundae* (the Second Part of the Second Part), and the *Tertia Pars* (the Third Part).

Each of these parts is broken down into questions divided into articles, all of which typically reflect the usual structure of articles in disputed questions of Aquinas such as the *De Malo* (*On Evil*) or the *De Potentia* (*On the Power of God*). The structure of such articles is as follows. First a question is raised. Then objections to the position that Aquinas wants to defend are listed. Then comes a brief summary of the position that Aquinas defends followed by an explanation of why he defends it. Finally, replies to the initial objections are provided.[49] In Aquinas's disputed questions, objections at the beginning of articles are usually numerous, as are the corresponding replies. In the *Summa Theologiae*, however, Aquinas usually confines himself to only three initial objections.[50]

The *Summa Theologiae* begins with a firm insistence on the need for divine revelation followed by reflections on how Christians can profitably think about their faith and the biblical basis for it. With this matter providing the context to what follows, Aquinas then proceeds to talk about the existence and nature of God, the doctrine of the Trinity, the notion of God as creator, the nature of angels, human nature, and God's governing of the world.

In the *Secunda Pars*, Aquinas turns to human happiness that, he says, is only to be found in union with God. The discussion then moves to human actions and the factors that govern them (with some focus on emotions), virtue, the gifts of the Holy Spirit, sin, grace, faith, hope, and charity. As he approaches the end of the *Secunda Pars*, Aquinas writes about topics such as superstition, prophecy, the active and contemplative life, and the pastoral and religious life.

In the *Tertia Pars*, Aquinas homes in on Christ. He talks about what is involved in God becoming human and goes on to discuss the life, death, and resurrection of Jesus of Nazareth and what is effected by this. He then moves on to the sacraments of the Catholic Church. Having written on baptism, confirmation, and the Eucharist, he began on a discussion of the sacrament of penance but died before finishing it.

It is often suggested that when writing the *Summa Theologiae*, Aquinas was working with an *exitus-reditus* design—the idea being that he starts with the coming forth (*exitus*) of creatures from God and ends with an account of their return (*reditus*) to God. This way of thinking about the *Summa* is most associated with the Dominican author Fr. Marie-Dominique Chenu (1895–1990), who did an enormous amount to help contemporary scholars working on Aquinas with serious interests in approaching him historically.[51]

The *exitus-reditus* reading of the *Summa Theologiae* makes sense since Aquinas (once he is done with its first question) writes about the existence and nature of God while going on to talk about human nature, grace, and the Incarnation. Yet the *Summa Theologiae* does not display a clear and sharp *exitus-reditus* structure. Instead, we seem to have Aquinas (1) talking about revelation and the need for it; (2) moving on to reasons for believing that the proposition "God exists" can be shown to be true given certain understandings of the word "God"; (3) proceeding to an account of what might be said of our knowledge of God after our death (the "beatific vision"); (4) moving next to a discussion of how we should think about our talk of God and to a treatment of the doctrine of the Trinity and what it means to say that God is the creator and why we should suppose that there is a creator; (5) engaging in a discussion of what people are and how we should think about various ways in which they are; (6) talking about the Incarnation, the mother of God incarnate (Mary), the life of Christ, and the sacraments.

I am not saying that it is absolutely wrong to think of the *Summa* as having an *exitus-reditus* structure. My point is that we can easily read it without thinking of Aquinas as having such a fixed schema in mind. It can also be read as coming from someone concerned to write about God and God's products (some of which never "return" to God since, being material, they just perish) with a long account about things of which we know little (i.e., angels), followed by long discussions of human nature with and without grace, followed by a treatment of Christology, an account of the life, death, and resurrection of Jesus of Nazareth, and a series of remarks on sacramental theology. And some of the topics discussed in the *Summa* do not seem to fit into a master *exitus-reditus* plan. Here I think, for example, of the passages that discuss the active and contemplative life, the offices to which people are appointed in the Catholic Church, what bishops are and how they should behave, and what those who have entered religious life (monks or friars or nuns) should be doing.

There is a lot about this kind of thing in 2a2ae. Taken as a whole, and incomplete as it is, the *Summa Theologiae* reads mostly like a series of discussions of a large range of traditional theological topics, some of them especially controversial in Aquinas's day. Aquinas certainly turns to the question of God's existence early in the work (in 1a,2), and many questions later (in 1a,44, and long after a discussion of the "beatific vision") he discusses the coming forth of things from God as creator. One may, however, wonder whether Aquinas would have been happy to say "Please consider my *Summa Theologiae* as something to be, from start to finish, read with a view on the *exitus-reditus* scheme sometimes invoked by those who have read it." On the other hand,

Aquinas did think that we come from God and (if graced) are united with God, and this thought is very evident in the *Summa Theologiae*.

1.2.5 The *Summa Theologiae* and Philosophy

The *Summa Theologiae* is obviously a work of theology, but it also contains a lot of tight philosophical reasoning, as do many of Aquinas's writings.[52] The distinguished British philosopher Bertrand Russell (1872–1970) once complained that Aquinas lacked a true philosophical spirit since he wrote while convinced of the teachings of the Catholic Church.[53] The philosophical climate, however, seems to have changed somewhat since Russell's day. In 1990, an editorial comment in the British Royal Institute of Philosophy journal *Philosophy* asserted that "St Thomas Aquinas is a genius whose claim to that accolade is barely debatable." Anticipating such a verdict, the prolific analytical philosopher Anthony Kenny (not someone believing in God) has declared that Aquinas is "one of the dozen greatest philosophers of the western world."[54] It is now two decades since the Royal Institute of Philosophy gave Aquinas his philosophical Oscar, but philosophers continue to study Aquinas as someone of significance to them. And, with good reason, they often do so when turning to the *Summa Theologiae*.

With all of that said, however, it is best to think of this work as primarily a theological one. Aquinas was certainly interested in writing what we nowadays think of as philosophy.[55] He produced commentaries on philosophical texts, and some of his writings just have to be categorized as philosophical essays, as is the case with, for example, *De Principiis Naturae* and *De Ente et Essentia*. When it comes to the *Summa Theologiae*, however, Aquinas's intentions seem to be theological right from the start, even though he goes on to offer many philosophical arguments. In the *Summa Contra Gentiles*, he begins by reflecting on what a "wise man" should be doing, going on to say that he wishes to explain how it is that a "wise man," as Aristotle understood that phrase, can end up believing in God as Aquinas took God to be. So it is easy to see how the *Summa Contra Gentiles* has a serious philosophical focus from the outset. Not so, however, when it comes to the *Summa Theologiae*. Anyone reading the *Summa Contra Gentiles* ought to be struck by the way in which it seems to begin while having a philosophical audience in mind even though it makes copious reference to the Bible. By contrast, the *Summa Theologiae* starts with a serious consideration of the Bible and the importance of divine revelation.

We shall probably never know what exactly Aquinas thought he was up to when writing the *Summa Theologiae*. Nor are we likely to be able to decide with certainty whether his aim in composing this work always remained the same. I hope, though, that what I have said above will give you some sense of the possibilities. The good news is that the text of the *Summa* is not a purely possible being but an actual one. We can pick it up and read it even if we are not Dominican students or prospective Masters of Theology. So let me now start to embark on the main purpose of this book, which is to provide you with a walk through it with some commentary from me.[56]

2

Sacred Teaching (1a,1)

THAT AQUINAS WROTE the *Summa Theologiae* for believing Christians is clear from its outset, for its first question is devoted to the topic of *sacra doctrina* ("sacred teaching"), which Aquinas takes to be equivalent to divine revelation as provided in the Bible. Aquinas offers the *Summa* as an extended treatment of the truths of Christianity based on the Bible. He sometimes discusses matters that are hardly central to Christian belief, and the *Summa* contains a number of sections that might readily be thought of as straightforwardly philosophical (its discussion of emotions in 1a2ae,22–30 would be a case in point). But Aquinas's focus throughout the *Summa* is on what he takes to be the core of Christian belief, which he will sometimes refer to as the "articles of faith" (*articuli fidei*)—meaning what we find in texts like the Apostles' Creed and the Nicene Creed.[1]

The phrase *sacra doctrina* in 1a,1 has sometimes been translated into English as "theology." This translation is, however, somewhat misleading. It is justified in that Aquinas does think of *sacra doctrina* as what Masters of Theology such as himself were supposed to be offering in places like the University of Paris. Yet Aquinas also thinks that there is theology that is not inspired by what he takes to be divine revelation.

Hence, for example, in 1a,1,1 he can refer to the "theology which is ranked as a part of philosophy," by which he means any reflection on God not taking its start from belief in Christianity. The Blackfriars edition of the *Summa* renders *sacra doctrina* by "Christian theology," and this is a respectable rendering. It should not, though, be taken to imply that for Aquinas *sacra doctrina* is just *anything* offered as theology by people calling themselves Christian theologians. Aquinas thinks of it as equivalent only to the *correct* passing on of revelation. His view is that the Bible provides us with revealed teachings about God, and he takes *sacra doctrina* to be the accurate presentation of *these*. So in 1a,1 he sometimes uses *sacra scriptura* ("sacred scripture") as equivalent to *sacra doctrina* (cf. 1a,1,2, ad.2).

The *Summa Theologiae* is, in effect, an attempt by Aquinas to continue (at length and in a way suitable to his target audience) what he took himself to be doing as a Master of Theology at Paris. We can see what this was by looking at the inaugural lecture he gave in 1256, which reflects on what the teacher of *sacra doctrina* is supposed to do with reference to Psalm 103:13: "Watering the earth from his things above, the earth will be filled from the fruit of your works." The focus of the lecture is "the communicating of spiritual wisdom," that is, the handing on of *sacra doctrina*. The wisdom in question here, says Aquinas, is "elevated" since it comes from God, since it transcends human reason, and since it is there to help us to eternal life.[2] This is the wisdom with which Aquinas is chiefly concerned in the *Summa*. Hence we find him talking about it in general in Question 1, the title of which is "Sacred Teaching: What It Is and What It Covers" (*de sacra doctrina, qualis sit et ad quae se extendat*).

2.1 The Need for Sacra Doctrina *(1a,1,1)*

Aquinas takes *sacra doctrina* to be first and foremost what God has revealed or taught us in the Bible. But you may wonder whether there is any need for such revelation or teaching. After all, cannot we at least in principle arrive at all truth relevant to us by means of our reason, by means of "philosophical disciplines" as Aquinas calls them?

Aquinas's answer is no. He notes that Scripture teaches what we need to be informed of but cannot come to know by purely rational inquiry or reflection. Yes, he thinks, there are truths about God that we can come to know by thinking philosophically, albeit with difficulty and much labor. Yet the revelation provided by God informs us of what reason cannot. So, Aquinas concludes, we need divine revelation. "We are," he says, "ordered to God as an end beyond the grasp of reason.... So, it was necessary for the salvation of human beings that truths surpassing reason should be made known to us by divine revelation."[3] This conclusion sets the tone for all that follows.

2.2 Sacra Doctrina *as* Scientia *(1a,1,1–7)*

As I have noted, for Aquinas *sacra doctrina* is basically what Scripture teaches concerning what we might call "the hidden things" of God. If it is going to be handed on in a systematic manner, however, people have to hand it on, and it can, presumably, be thought of as a discipline of which someone might be thought to be a teacher. If it is a discipline that someone might profess, though, what kind of discipline is it? Thinking with a view to what Aristotle and most of Aquinas's contemporaries thought, Aquinas turns to this question (1a,1,2) by asking whether *sacra doctrina* can be thought of as a *scientia* ("science").

People today sometimes protest that theology should not be taught in universities. The idea here is that theology has to do with personal faith and that universities are concerned to hand on *knowledge* rather than *faith*. This is a somewhat naive view since, to avoid an infinite regress of justifications, when trying to expand our knowledge we always have to start with beliefs that we take for granted, many of them being ones that we hold simply on someone's say so.[4] And with that said, I should note that in Aquinas's view teachers of *sacra doctrina* are indeed concerned to transmit knowledge, insofar as "knowledge" means "that which is true."

He makes his point by saying that *sacra doctrina* is a science (*scientia*). By *scientia* he means "a branch of knowledge." He recognizes, however, that *sacra doctrina*, unlike other branches of knowledge, does not proceed from premises the truth of which can be recognized by us while using the rational faculties with which we are endowed. So, he thinks, it is not as though your average chemist might stumble upon that with which the professor of *sacra doctrina* is concerned. But might *sacra doctrina* still not be thought of as a science in some sense?

Aquinas argues that *sacra doctrina* is a *scientia* since it proceeds from what God knows and has revealed and since those who impart it can be thought of as starting from what God knows while arriving at conclusions that are true. Some sciences, Aquinas thinks, work from principles known by the natural light of reason. He takes arithmetic and geometry as examples. Yet, he notes, some sciences "work from principles known by the light of a higher science."[5] Those who specialize in optics, he argues, presume and do not try to prove certain geometrical premises, and those concerned with music rely on arithmetical premises. By the same token, he reasons, teachers of *sacra doctrina* rely on premises supplied by God and work from these.

In this sense, *sacra doctrina* is a *scientia*, and Aquinas makes it clear that he understands *scientia* to mean what we have as we rightly deduce conclusions that follow from what is already given or known.[6] He takes the teacher of *sacra doctrina* to impart knowledge, though not knowledge that rests on premises the truth of which is evident to us. He thinks that the teacher of *sacra doctrina* draws on God's knowledge shared with us by divine revelation.

Readers of Aquinas today might wonder why we should suppose that any divine revelation has been given. The *Summa* takes it for granted, however. You might ask how we can prove philosophically or empirically that there is such a thing. Aquinas would reply that of necessity we cannot do this for, if we could, we would know what only God can know, while the truth is that when it comes to the articles of faith we have to proceed on the basis of faith. This is what Aquinas is arguing in 1a,1,1. Allowing for what he says in texts other than 1a,1, however, you should realize that he does not take himself to be proceeding on the basis of faith in what might be considered an arbitrary or purely "fideistic" way.

Aquinas does not suppose that acceptance of what he thinks of as divine revelation is wholly unsupportable by reason. He draws a sharp distinction between reason and revelation so as to assert, for example, that the doctrine of the Trinity is demonstrably indemonstrable (cf. 1a,32,1). But he also suggests that orthodox Christians do not believe what they do with no reason at all.

Here we need to recognize that Aquinas takes *sacra doctrina* to be primarily handed on to us by the Bible, and, in particular, in the teachings of Jesus of Nazareth recorded in the New Testament. We also need to recognize that Aquinas thinks that the Bible provides us with a reliable account of what Jesus did and said. Some biblical scholars since the early nineteenth century have expressed doubts about the historical accuracy of the New Testament and of the Bible in general, and debates about the historical value of biblical texts continue to this day. For present purposes, however, I need to stress that, rightly or wrongly, Aquinas thinks that we have accurate access via the Bible to the life and sayings of Jesus, whom Aquinas takes to be divine in the sense taught by the Council of Chalcedon, according to which Christ is literally both divine and human—one subject having two natures, one human and one divine. So Aquinas, for whom the Bible is authoritative, thinks that we have, in the teachings of Jesus, a divine endorsement of the idea that the Old Testament provides us with teaching from God. He also thinks that the teachings of Jesus in the New Testament provide us with God's final word on what God is and what God is doing.

Assuming that Aquinas is right on this point, the next question would seem to be "Shall we believe what Jesus says and start to think from that?" Given that Aquinas takes the teachings of Jesus largely to be declaring what we cannot know to be true by means of anything that we might think of as a watertight philosophical or empirical proof, he thinks that the answer to this question is yes.

For him, everything here depends on faith (which he turns to directly in the *Secunda Pars*). Yet as we can also see from a telling passage in his *Summa Contra Gentiles*, Aquinas does not think that we lack reasons when believing what is believed by those who have faith. In *Summa Contra Gentiles* I,6, Aquinas says that those who assent to the truths of faith do not believe foolishly (*non leviter*) even though these truths are above reason. He speaks of revelation being given with "fitting arguments" and accompanied by what he takes to be miracles (including, I presume, the miracles attributed to Christ in the New Testament) that he thinks confirm its divine origin. His idea seems to be "If you believe Christ and what Christ taught, then you will not do so without reason" (a point also made in 3a,43,4). At the same time, though, he does not think that the articles of faith are demonstrable.[7]

With all of that said, however, the main point to latch onto when it comes to trying to follow Aquinas in 1a,1 is that for him teachers of *sacra doctrina* can be thought of as imparting knowledge since they are teaching what is true. And *sacra doctrina*, Aquinas adds, is a single science—meaning that it has a single focus: what God has revealed (1a,1,3).

Since Aquinas takes the Bible to contain teachings that instruct us how to behave, one might wonder whether he takes *sacra doctrina* to be a science that tells us what to do. The truth of the matter is that he does, but not unequivocally. He argues (1a,1,4) that *sacra doctrina* is primarily "theoretical" insofar as it is concerned with what is true of God and not just concerned with how we should behave, though it is, indeed, concerned with this. *Sacra doctrina*, Aquinas adds (1a,1,5), should be thought of as superior to other sciences since its source is God's own self-knowledge and since it teaches us what cannot be arrived at by human reasoning. It should be thought of as wisdom since it proceeds from God whose self-knowledge conveyed in revelation excels anything that we can arrive at by trying to think straight given our natural abilities (1a,1,6).

In 1a,1,7, Aquinas raises the question "Is God the subject (*subjectum*) of *sacra doctrina*?" Here he is asking whether or not teachers of *sacra doctrina* are focused on one thing, and his answer is that they are focused on God and nothing else. God is the one interest in mind when it comes to *sacra doctrina* and everything else is discussed only insofar as it relates in some way to God. "Sacred doctrine deals with all things in terms of God, either because they are God himself or because they are related to God as their origin and end."[8] It will be obvious from the way the *Summa Theologiae* proceeds how strictly Aquinas adheres to this understanding of *sacra doctrina*.

2.3 *Argument and Language in* Sacra Doctrina *(1a,1,8–10)*

Given that Aquinas takes *sacra doctrina* to be revealed truth, one might wonder whether he thinks of it as merely declarative rather than argumentative. Texts like the Apostles' Creed and the Nicene Creed do not present any arguments: they just profess the truth of certain beliefs. So does Aquinas take himself, when concerned with *sacra doctrina*, to be doing nothing but saying something like "Just believe A, B, C..."? Is he engaging in what we might call an "Open your mouth and shut your eyes" approach?

In one sense he is. For him, *sacra doctrina* is revealed by God and is what God declares. Yet Aquinas also thinks that the teacher of *sacra doctrina* can employ arguments. *Sacra doctrina*, he says (1a,1,8), does not argue to establish its "first principles," which are the articles of faith. But it can argue *from* them so as to explicate the truths of Christianity. I might not be able to establish by argument that there is a physical universe, but with the assumption that there is such a thing (together with a number of other assumptions) I might be able to argue that water is H_2O. By the same token, thinks Aquinas, the teacher of *sacra doctrina* can proceed to argue for various conclusions, advancing from belief to proof.

Here Aquinas seems to be viewing the teacher of *sacra doctrina* as reflecting on the Bible and on the teachings of the Church so as to develop a systematic and reasonable account of revelation and what it amounts to. Since Reformation times Christians have taken sides on the question "Is Christian faith based only on Scripture?" Some (Protestants) have said that it is, while some (Roman Catholic and Orthodox Christians especially) have said that Christians should also pay attention to or defer to the teachings of the Church, to "Tradition" as well as Scripture. Is Aquinas presenting a position on this question in 1a,1?

One sentence of the text here could be read as indicating that he is and that his leanings are toward an emphasis on the primacy of Scripture. For in 1a,1,8 we find Aquinas saying that when *sacra doctrina* "argues conclusively," its "own proper authority is canonical Scripture." He continues: "It has other proper authorities, the doctors of the Church, and it looks to these as its own—but for arguments that carry no more than probability. For our faith rests in the revelation made to the prophets and apostles who wrote the canonical books, not on a revelation, if such there be, made to any other teacher."[9] One could well be forgiven for reading these words as an endorsement of the *Sola Scriptura* ("Scripture Alone") slogan defended by people like Martin Luther.

Yet one should also bear in mind that Aquinas was not familiar with the Scripture-Tradition debate as that has been conducted since the sixteenth century. It would, therefore, be anachronistic to suppose that he takes sides on it in 1a,1. Yes, he emphasizes the authority of Scripture, but he also has time for what has come to be called Tradition. He regards the Apostles' Creed and the Nicene Creed as authoritative, and these, of course, are not part of what Aquinas takes to be Scripture. Again, he does not think that the New Testament was delivered to people on a cloud from God with the label "Divine Revelation" attached to it. He knows that Christians existed for a long time before the Canon of the New Testament was settled upon by Western Christians. As we shall later see, in the *Secunda Secundae* he declares (a) that the Church in drawing up "symbols" of faith (creeds) has authority to decide what the articles of faith amount to, and (b) that popes have the right to promulgate new editions of the creeds in the face of heresies that may arise (cf. 2a2ae,1,8 and 10). In none of his works, though, does he offer a treatise on the value of Tradition versus Scripture. The word *traditio* ("tradition") occurs only fifty-six times in the writings of Aquinas.[10] And none of these occurrences come in the context of what might be thought of as a post-Reformation Scripture versus Tradition discussion.

It has been suggested that Aquinas explicitly defends post-Reformation Roman Catholic teaching on Tradition in *Summa Theologiae* 2a2ae,5,3 and 3a,25,3, and one can understand why some people think that this is so. 2a2ae,5,3 speaks of the importance of holding to the "formal object of faith" that is the "first truth handed down in Scripture and Church teaching." 3a,25,3 speaks of how it can be right to adhere to "traditions" handed down by the apostles. Even these texts, however, do not seem to amount to a full-blown defense of Tradition as opposed to *Sola Scriptura* as understood with Reformation thinking in mind. The first is assuming that the Church hands down what Scripture declares. The second is arguing that certain Christian observances, such as paying worship to images of Christ, can be justified by referring to oral tradition, as opposed to written tradition, deriving from apostolic times. Aquinas certainly takes ecclesiastical teaching dating from postbiblical times seriously. But he never explicitly targets the *Sola Scriptura* notion for criticism in the way in which many post-Reformation Catholics have done.

With that said, however, in 1a,1 Aquinas seems chiefly to presume the authority of a tradition culminating in texts like the Apostles' Creed and the Nicene Creed, which he believes to be based on the New Testament. Some Roman Catholic readers of Aquinas have taken him to be saying that anything ever proclaimed by the Roman Catholic Church is true, yet Aquinas actually denies some things proclaimed by the Catholic Church (albeit after his lifetime). In 1854, Pope Pius IX declared that the mother of Jesus was conceived without original sin. In his *Compendium of Theology* (1,224), however, Aquinas argues explicitly against this teaching.[11] He does the same in 3a,27,3. So one would be mistaken to cite Aquinas as a friend of Tradition as opposed to Scripture alone while reading him as a participant in debates about these since the Reformation. In 1a,1, he takes his stand on the Bible, the Apostles' Creed, and the Nicene Creed, while allowing for discussion concerning their meaning and implications.

This, of course, is what most Christian theologians since the appearance of these creeds have tried to do. Some of them have criticized Aquinas while saying that he places more trust in human reasoning than he should. Their argument is that it is God, not human reasoning, that determines what we should believe about God as Christians receiving divine revelation. A particularly famous exponent of this argument is Karl Barth (1886–1968).[12] As we shall see, however, Aquinas is at one with Barth in the conclusion that human reasoning always leaves us without a knowledge of what God is, though Aquinas develops this position by appeal to philosophical argument in a way that Barth does not. And the *Summa Theologiae*, like Barth's later writings, takes its cue from the Bible considered as God's revelation in words. So Aquinas can say in 1a,1,8 that "sacred Scripture, which has no higher science over it, disputes the denial of its first principles."[13] Yet he does not take this position to be incompatible with the idea that the teacher of *sacra doctrina* can engage in argument. Such a teacher, he thinks, can argue with those who accept Christian revelation while seeming to misconstrue it somehow. Here Aquinas is thinking of those whom he would have called "heretics," that is, people accepting the authority of Scripture while using it to defend positions that are contrary to what Aquinas regards as Church teaching solidly grounded in Scripture.

And, Aquinas adds, there is nothing to stop the teacher of *sacra doctrina* from arguing philosophically that critics of Christianity have not proved their case. It is often said that key Christian doctrines, such as the doctrine of the Trinity and the doctrine of the Incarnation, are demonstrably self-contradictory (that, to put things crudely, three into one does not go, and "___is human" and "___is divine" are mutually exclusive predicates that cannot both be applied to one subject). Since he believes that truth cannot contradict truth, however, and since he believes in the truth of Christian doctrines, Aquinas takes the view that objections such as these are, at least in principle, answerable by argument. Hence, in 1a,1,8 we find him saying: "Since faith rests on infallible truth, and since the contrary of truth cannot be demonstrated, it is clear that alleged proofs against faith are not successful demonstrations but charges that can be refuted."[14]

In 1a,1,8 ad.2, Aquinas also maintains that teachers of *sacra doctrina* can rightly employ human reasoning considered as able to assist faith in something like the way that our natural desires can serve us as we engage in acts of charity (which, as we shall see when we come to the *Secunda Secundae*, Aquinas takes to be directly brought about in us by God alone). "Sacred doctrine," he observes, "uses the authority of philosophers who have been able to perceive the truth by natural reasoning."[15] As you might now find unsurprising, Aquinas immediately backs up this claim by appealing to the Bible. He alludes to a passage in Acts 17 in which St. Paul, preaching in Athens, commends the Athenians for recognizing that God is that in which "we live and move and have our being."[16] Aquinas here clearly takes the Bible to support the idea that there is some knowledge of God to be obtained by human reasoning, and in 1a,1,2 he will begin to explain what he thinks can be known of God by this means.

Starting in 1a,1,2, Aquinas embarks on a series of arguments that would nowadays be referred to as exercises in natural theology. By "natural theology" I mean the attempt to reason philosophically to certain conclusions concerning the existence and nature of God while not relying on premises that might be thought of as deriving from Christian revelation. And Aquinas is very "into" natural theology. He started to present his contribution to it in *De Ente et Essentia*. He developed his thinking at length in the *Summa Contra Gentiles*, and a good bit of the *Summa Theologiae* is devoted to natural theology. Should we think of Aquinas as misguided to take this seriously as something to engage a teacher of *sacra doctrina*? It has been argued that, whatever philosophers might have to say, we should presume Aquinas to be wrong in his approval of what natural theologians are about since the Bible is opposed to natural theology.

Here I am again thinking of Karl Barth, who (in spite of the similarity between his thinking and that of Aquinas) wrote an emphatic critique of natural theology as a whole. According to Barth:

> Natural theology does not exist as an entity capable of becoming a separate subject within what I consider to be real theology—not even for the sake of being rejected. If one occupies oneself with real theology one can pass by so-called natural theology only as one would pass by an abyss into which it is inadvisable to step if one does not want to fall.[17]

Strong words, indeed! And Barth supports them by saying that biblical authors reject natural theology. As I have noted, Aquinas takes the speech of St. Paul in Acts 17 to favor the idea that there is knowledge of God even without Christian revelation. Barth, however, takes Paul's speech to be a critique of those who think that they know anything of God apart from revelation. The First Vatican Council (1869–1870) views St. Paul as being favorable to the idea that we can know something about God by reason alone. It cites Romans 1:20: "Ever since the creation of the world his eternal power and divine nature, invisible though they are, have been understood and seen through the things he has made"—a text quoted more than once by Aquinas in favor of the view that there is knowledge of God apart from Christian revelation.[18] Barth's reading of this biblical passage, however, has St. Paul saying that human reason actually leaves us alienated from God.

Yet Barth's exegesis of these biblical texts is open to criticism, as James Barr has, I believe, decisively shown in his book *Biblical Faith and Natural Theology*.[19] Barr notes all the passages in which Barth argues against the suggestion that texts such as Acts 17 and Romans 1 seem favorable to the idea of there being knowledge of God apart from Christian revelation. He then explains why, though these texts do not present sustained philosophical essays in natural theology, they do seem to presume that there is some philosophical knowledge of God.[20] And Barr tellingly adds: "If you thoroughly reject natural theology, and if natural theology underlies the Bible to any significant degree, then you must judge that the Bible is inadequate as a theological guide."[21]

Whether or not Barr is right on this matter, and whether or not Barth is right to take natural theology to be a route to theological death, Aquinas is most definitely a natural theologian, and in 1a,1,8 he is preparing the ground for a long and favorable treatment of natural theology starting at 1a,2. In 1a,1,8, Aquinas can also be thought of as paving the way for ideas he wants to defend from 1a,13 onward—these having to do with how we should understand the language used by the Bible when talking about God. Does *sacra doctrina* use metaphorical or figurative language? Can we read one passage of Scripture in different senses? These are the questions with which 1a,1 concludes.

Aquinas's answer to the first one defends the claim that *sacra doctrina* uses metaphors. You might think that Aquinas obviously has to say this since various passages in Scripture must be construed metaphorically—since we cannot, for instance, presume that talk about God's mighty arm should be taken to imply that this arm is something bodily, unless we think of God as being a body, a notion that Aquinas rejects in 1a,2. But there is a big question in the background when it comes to the topic of God and metaphor. For some Christians would say that the Bible is inerrant and should be read literally. In that case, however, are we not committed to thinking of God as having a bodily arm? And should we not suppose that Scripture tells us nothing about God that cannot be thought to be literally true?

Aquinas is generally keen on preferring a literal reading of the Bible. In 1a,1,9, he seems to be so without arguing for his position, though he does say a lot about it later. On the other hand, Aquinas takes it for granted that the Bible is full of metaphor when it talks about God. Yet he is grateful for this since, he observes, we are physical beings whose thoughts depend on what our senses deliver to us, and since our attempts to think about God naturally employ images that we use when thinking about things in the world, even if we can go on to talk about God without understanding God in physical terms. Aquinas notes that speaking of God without thinking of God materially is something that the teacher of *sacra doctrina* must try to do. But, he adds, there is something to be said for talk about God that crudely takes God to be something in the world. For since such talk obviously cannot be taken to be literally true, it serves to remind us of the difference between God and creatures. This is the force of 1a,1,9, ad.3, and Aquinas follows up on this thought in 1a,1,10.

Indeed, he says, we can read Scripture as if it were all literally true, but we can read texts without treating them as understandable only at such a level, and this is so when it comes to the Bible. The Bible, thinks Aquinas, though readable in literal terms, can also be read as teaching us what is not just conveyed by taking it literally verse by verse. There are, Aquinas argues, senses in which various texts of Scripture can be read that go beyond what they appear literally to assert.

1a,1 composes but a small portion of the *Summa Theologiae*. So you might think that I have devoted more space to it than I should have. But 1a,1 needs to be read as showing the hand that Aquinas is going to play with as he continues. Indeed, 1a,1 is, in effect, a *summa* of the *Summa*. One needs seriously to bear its contents in mind when proceeding to what follows. As I have said, in 1a,1 Aquinas is warning us that the *Summa* comes from a teacher of *sacra doctrina*, not a philosopher who doubts what Christians believe. But he also makes it clear that, though he relies on the Bible and certain Christian creeds, he thinks that human beings can arrive at some knowledge of God independently of Christian revelation. Why does he think this? He begins to explain himself in 1a,2.

3

Knowing That God Exists (1a,1,2)

SUMMA THEOLOGIAE 1A,2 is titled *de Deo, an Deus sit* ("Does God exist?"). Consisting of only three much-quoted articles, it gives us the start of the *Summa*'s treatment of natural theology.[1] Aquinas believes that before embarking on a "scientific" study of anything we need to know that the thing in question exists, and this is the thought that governs what he says in 1a,2. Aquinas distinguishes between the questions *an est* ("Does it exist?") and *quid est* ("What is it?"), and he will turn to the question "What is God?" in 1a,3. In 1a,2, however, his focus is on what we might call "the mere existence" of God. Does this mean that 1a,2 is offered by Aquinas as a help to people with no belief in God? Not quite, given 1a,1. Even in 1a,2, Aquinas is writing for Christians. Yet Aquinas does think that a good philosophical case can be made in defense of the truth of the proposition "God exists," and in 1a,2 he aims to indicate what that case amounts to.

3.1 Per se Notum *(1a,2,1)*

Aquinas's position is that we can only know that God exists by means of causal inference from God's effects.[2] He is, however, aware that some people have taken "God exists" (*Deus est*) to be known to be true without reference to causal reasoning. He discusses this way of thinking in 1a,2,1, where he raises the question "Is it self-evident (*per se notum*) that God exists?"

Per se notum literally means "known through itself," and Aquinas takes the claim that "God exists" is *per se notum* to hold that the truth of "God exists" is something we can arrive at by virtue of some understanding we have of God not grounded in causal reasoning—that "God exists" is known by us in some basic way just because we are thinking things that we are.[3] More specifically, in 1a,2,1 he takes it to amount to three arguments: (1) Knowledge of God is implanted in us by nature; (2) Once we understand what the word "God" means, we can see that it would be self-contradictory to deny that God exists; (3) Since God is Truth, and since we cannot consistently assert that it is true that there is no truth, God evidently exists. Aquinas is partly sympathetic to these arguments. He agrees, for example, that everyone has a desire for God since everyone naturally desires happiness and since our ultimate happiness is to be found only in God. He also agrees that if we could understand what God is we would immediately see that God cannot but exist. And he accepts that there evidently is such a thing as truth. At the same time, however, he rejects (1) to (3) just noted. Vaguely to desire God is not, he says, to know that God exists any more than to recognize that *someone* is coming is to know *who exactly* it is that is coming. And there being truth in general does not imply that there is anything to be dignified by the title "First Truth" (i.e., God).

Argument (2) is today, perhaps, the best known version of what Aquinas has in mind when thinking of the claim that *Deus est* is *per se notum*. That is because, as Aquinas presents it in 1a,2,1, it reads like a famous argument (usually referred to as the "Ontological Argument") first presented by St. Anselm of Canterbury (1033–1109) in his *Proslogion*.[4] This argument is defended by some philosophers today, so there is a lot of contemporary literature on it.[5] As Aquinas presents the argument (without citing Anselm as its source), it runs: "Once we understand the meaning of the word 'God,' we immediately see that God exists. For the word means 'that than which nothing greater can be signified.' So, since what exists in thought and fact is greater than what exists in thought alone, and since, once we understand the word 'God,' God exists in thought, God must also exist in fact."[6]

Anselm says more than this in defense of his ontological argument, but Aquinas seems unconcerned with the details of Anselm's argument or with Anselm's defense of himself to one of his contemporaries.[7] Rather, he focuses on the general idea that we have an understanding of God that leaves us being inconsistent should we go on to deny that God exists. He writes:

> Even if someone thinks that what is signified by 'God' is 'that than which nothing greater can be thought', it does not follow that the person in question thinks that what is signified by 'God' exists in reality rather than merely as thought about. If we do not grant that something in fact exists than which nothing greater can be thought (and nobody denying the existence of God would grant this), the conclusion that God in fact exists does not follow.

Critics of versions of the Ontological Argument have often suggested that we cannot conclude from the meaning of the word "God" that there is anything in reality corresponding to it, and Aquinas seems to support this line of thinking, though he does agree that a knowledge of what God actually is would leave us with an understanding that God has to be. In 1a,3, he will argue that it is God's nature to exist. So Aquinas does think that God *cannot but* exist. In 1a,2,1, however, he is criticizing approaches defending the truth of *Deus est*, which seem to presume a knowledge concerning God that, in Aquinas's view, we lack. He makes a distinction between what is *per se notum* in itself (per se) and what is *per se notum* to us (*quoad nos*). He thinks that *Deus est* is "self evident in itself" in that it is God's nature to exist. But, as we shall soon see, he denies that we have a God's-eye view of what God is.

3.2 Demonstrating That God Exists (1a,2,2–3)

Some philosophers have said that we come to know that God exists by employing what they call "intuition." The idea here is that, with no reliance on inferential argument, we know that God exists by just seeing all at once that this is so.[8] Such is not Aquinas's view, however, and in 1a,2,2 and 3 he maintains that we can demonstrate that God exists. Yet what does Aquinas mean by "demonstrate" and "demonstration"?

He takes a demonstration to be an argument that, starting with true premises, entails its conclusion formally or validly. Here Aquinas is drawing on Aristotle's *Posterior Analytics*. He takes a demonstrative argument to have the form: (1) "All X is Y" (e.g., "All human beings are mammals"); (2) "All Y is Z" (e.g., "All mammals breathe air"); (3) "Therefore, All X is Z" (e.g., "Therefore, all human beings breathe air"). Given (1) and (2), (3) follows necessarily. This is not to say, as some would, that (1) to (3) erroneously "beg the question" since (3) seems to be somehow "contained" in (1) and (2). All valid deductive arguments beg the question inasmuch as all of their conclusions are implied by their premises.[9] But a good demonstrative argument, as Aquinas understands it, still leads us from known truth to yet more truth. So he thinks of it as an especially forceful kind of argument, and he holds that such argument is available to those who conclude that God exists.

As I noted in chapter 2, some theologians have resisted this conclusion of Aquinas, a prominent example being Karl Barth. And some of their objections to it seem to be anticipated by Aquinas in 1a,2,2.[10]

How, one might ask, can it be demonstrated that God exists since it is an article of faith that this is so? And is it not absurd to seek to demonstrate that God exists given that God and creatures are incommensurable (God being infinite and creatures being finite)? Also, what about the (1)–(3) pattern of argument that I have just noted? Does it not seem to rely on an understanding of what Y stands for (mammals in my examples)? Yet should we not accept that we do not know what God is? If we cannot know what God is, however, how can we proceed to a demonstration that God exists?

In 1a,2,2, Aquinas raises all of these questions while proceeding to argue that there is nothing wrong in principle with the idea that it is possible to demonstrate that God exists.[11]

In doing so, he denies that "God exists" is an article of faith (1a,2,2 ad.1). Here he is thinking in terms of the Nicene Creed, and his point is that the creed *presupposes* that God exists and does not explicitly *proclaim* that this is so. Readers of 1a,2,2 will perhaps grasp what Aquinas is saying about "God exists" not being an article of faith by noting what he observes in 2a2ae,1,8. There he says that the articles of faith are properly formulated and that the first article of faith is that there is but *one* God—not that it is true to say that God exists. By contrast to what some philosophers have argued, Aquinas in 1a,2,2 asserts that there is "nothing to stop people from accepting on faith some demonstrable truth that they cannot personally demonstrate."[12] He does not, however, take this thought to imply that there cannot be a demonstration of the claim that God exists.

In true Barthian fashion, Aquinas agrees that God and creatures are seriously different from each other. He suggests, however, that we need to distinguish between a *comprehensive* knowledge of God and *some* knowledge of God. We can know that God exists even if we lack a comprehensive knowledge of what God is (1a,2,2, ad.3). Here Aquinas is saying that a demonstration of the truth of "God exists" does not have to be thought of as including an understanding of what God is. Yet how does Aquinas take himself to be able to argue that it can be demonstrated that God exists, given that we do not know what God is, while providing an argument of the kind (1)–(3) noted above?

Anticipating this question, Aquinas distinguishes between demonstration *propter quid* (literally, "on account of the whatness") and demonstration *quia* ("that"). He says (1a,2,2): "There are two kinds of demonstration. One kind, *propter quid*, argues from cause to effect and proceeds by means of what is unqualifiedly first. The other, demonstration *quia*, argues from effect to cause and proceeds by means of what is first so far as we are concerned."[13] Here Aquinas is thinking of a *propter quid* demonstration as an argument that proceeds from an understanding of what something is.

Consider the following argument: (1) Cats are mammals; (2) Smokey is a cat; (3) therefore, Smokey is a mammal. We get to (3) here, Aquinas thinks, on the basis of an understanding of what cats actually are and on the basis of knowing what some particular cat (Smokey) is. Given that we know that cats are mammals, and given that we know that Smokey is a cat, we can readily conclude that Smokey is a mammal.

But now consider this scenario: We try to push a door open but encounter resistance. We shall presumably conclude that something accounts for the door not opening, but we might not know what the something in question is. Nevertheless, we might do our best to say something about the cause of the door not opening based on our knowledge that the door is meeting resistance.

Here we might argue along these lines: "Well, something is blocking the door." And we might then speculate about what the thing in question is based on what we are observing. Here, Aquinas is thinking, we would be engaging in a demonstration *quia*. We would be arguing from an effect we know well to a cause that we do not know as well. Aquinas thinks that such a demonstration *quia* might be possible when it comes to arguing philosophically for the truth of "God exists" even though we do not know what God is (something on which he will say more in 1a,1,3).

Note, however, that in taking this line Aquinas holds that we need some initial understanding of the word "God." I might not know what X actually is; I might not, as Aquinas would say, know what its essence is. But in arguing that X is the cause or explanations of something I am familiar with, I have to work with some nominal definition of X. By "nominal definition" I mean an explanation of what a word means as opposed to an account of what some actually existing thing is by nature. There may be no wizards, but I can explain what the word "wizard" means (as dictionaries do). Thus, for example, suppose I argue that E, which I take to be an effect, is to be accounted for in terms of C, which I take to be the cause of the effect. Suppose, for instance, I argue that a human being with abilities X, Y, and Z accounts for there being a human corpse before me. To prove this I shall have to proceed by working the understanding of C as "human being with abilities X, Y, and Z" into my argument. Accepting this point, Aquinas, in 1a,2,3 goes on to argue for the truth of "God exists" by employing a series of nominal definitions of the word "God" and by using them in a set of causal arguments.

3.3 *Arguing for God Causally (1a,2,3)*

Aquinas uses the Latin word *causa* to mean more than we typically signify by "cause."[14] When we are asking what caused what, we are, so to speak, normally looking for a *culprit*. Hence, for example, a doctor might wonder what virus is causing the symptoms of a patient. However, and as is indicated by our use of the word "because," causes might not just be things in the world (like viruses) that act so as to bring about changes in other things (such as healthy human beings). Also, they might not be things in the world that bring about the persistence of some state of affairs. For example, a crystal glass that I drop might shatter *because* it is made of crystal as opposed to plastic. My cat might meow *because* of what it is by nature, and I might be racing to the railway station *because* I need to catch a particular train. Aquinas has these uses of "cause" or "because" in mind when he distinguishes in 1a,2,2 between demonstrations *propter quid* and demonstrations *quia*. In moving to 1a,2,3, however, he is concerned with what I am calling the "culprit" sense of cause. Suppose that I feel a tap on my shoulder. I will react and turn around while looking. Here I am reacting to what Aquinas would have called an "agent cause" or "efficient cause." I am looking for some particular thing whose action is the tap I feel on my back. Similarly, Aquinas's *Summa Theologiae* arguments for the truth of "God exists" are all arguments for the existence of God considered as an agent cause.[15]

You may wonder why I have so far spoken of Aquinas as looking to show that "God exists" is true. Should I not have instead said that Aquinas seeks to prove or demonstrate the existence of God? The answer is no since, as we shall see, Aquinas thinks that God's existence (*esse*) is not to be distinguished from God's essence (*essentia*), which he thinks we cannot know. Yet Aquinas thinks that he can show that "God exists" is a true proposition defensible with an eye on agent causation. This is what 1a,2,3 is chiefly about.

3.4 The Five Ways

1a,2,3 presents what Aquinas calls "five ways in which one can prove that there is a God." These arguments are famous and have given rise to a huge amount of literature both expository and critical.[16] I cannot here offer a detailed analysis and discussion of them. I shall, therefore, (1) make some general expository points concerning the Ways as a whole, (2) present the text of each Way with brief explanatory notes designed to help you to understand what Aquinas is arguing in them, and (3) briefly draw attention to some familiar criticisms of the Ways while offering some comment on these criticisms.

3.4.1 The Ways as a Whole

As I have noted, Aquinas turns to the business of arguing that "God exists" is true with an eye on certain *nominal* definitions of the word "God." In the Five Ways these are: (1) "God" means "an uncaused agent cause of change not itself changed by anything"; (2) "God" means "an uncaused agent cause not itself having an agent cause, that is, a first agent cause"; (3) "God" means "a source of the existence (*esse*) of all things that can be thought of as necessary beings"; (4) "God" means "the cause of the existence of things displaying perfection to any degree"; and (5) "God" means "one who directs things lacking awareness to their ends." Presuming that we do not know what God is essentially, Aquinas uses these nominal definitions in the Five Ways so as to provide demonstrations *quia* of the truth of "God exists."

This point leads me to stress another directly related to it, one concerning what Aquinas takes himself to have established in his Five Ways. These have sometimes been criticized as "arguments for the existence of God" on the ground that they do not establish that God exists as having *all* the "attributes" ascribed to God by those who profess belief in God. As I have noted, however, there is a sense in which it would be wrong to read Aquinas as taking himself to be making the *existence* (*esse*) of God clear in the Ways, and, as we shall see, Aquinas, in a serious sense, denies that God has any attributes. Also, though sometimes wrongly read as such, the Ways are not Aquinas's last word in the *Summa Theologiae* when it comes to what he thinks can be known of God by reason as opposed to revelation. That is why he follows them up with a series of separate arguments for conclusions such as "God is perfect," "God is good," "God is eternal," "God is one," "God knows," "God loves," and "God has power." Insofar as the *Summa Theologiae* can be thought of as offering a de- fense of "God exists," the defense is not over until 1a,26—actually, it is not really over until the end of 1a,45. The Five Ways are but an attempt to get a certain ball rolling.

A third point worth noting when it comes to the Ways is that none of them are arguing in what we might think of as chronological terms. Theists have sometimes maintained that we can know that God exists since the universe must have had a beginning and since we can reason to God as accounting for the beginning of the universe.[17] Yet Aquinas does not think it possible to dem- onstrate that the universe had a beginning (as we shall see when we come to 1a,46), and it would be wrong to read the Ways as claiming that God must be responsible only for something arising in the past while not being active in what is happening presently. In 1a,2,3, Aquinas denies that there can be an infinite regress of agent causes, but his denial here presupposes a distinction that he wants to make between a series of causes ordered *per accidens* and a series of causes ordered per se.

For Aquinas, a causal series *per accidens*, which he thinks might proceed to infinity, would be referenced by noting, say, that Abraham begat Isaac who begat Jacob who begat Joseph. On this scenario, Abraham is certainly causally related to Joseph by being his great-grandfather. Of course, though, Abraham, being dead at the time, was doing nothing to bring about the conception of Joseph. In the Five Ways, however, the causal series with respect to which Aquinas denies the possibility of an infinite regress is a per se one—a series in which a first cause's activity runs through a series of effects all of which depend equally on there being such a first cause.[18]

Consider the flame on the cooktop of a gas stove, which is heating a pot sitting on it, which, in turn, is heating the water it contains, which, in turn, is heating some spaghetti placed in it. Here the temperature of the pot and the water and the spaghetti can all be traced to the action of the flame, and

Aquinas would say that in this case we are dealing with a per se causal series. In the Five Ways, Aquinas starts by noting certain phenomena the occurrence of which at any time, he thinks, depends on the activity of God. He agrees that particular instances of these phenomena might be explicable in terms of things other than God, things that are like them as displaying what they display. He agrees, for example, that a moving ball might cause another ball to move, and that the second ball might cause yet another to move. His point, though, is that there being such phenomena at all cannot be accounted for in terms of something that displays what they exactly display as we seek to account for them. He thinks, for example, that nothing caused to change by something can account for there being things caused to change by other things.[19]

Finally, and given what he goes on to say after 1a,2,3, Aquinas takes the Five Ways to be arguing for what cannot be part of the scientifically observable world, the world considered as an object of scientific research. The Ways do not present a series of scientific hypotheses. Aquinas takes them to be suggesting that things with which we are familiar ought to lead us to suppose that there is something that is quite distinct from the world considered as something to be explored scientifically.

3.4.2 The First Way

It is certain, and clear to our senses, that some things in the world undergo change. But anything in process of change is changed by something else. For nothing can be undergoing change unless it is potentially whatever it ends up being after its process of change—while something causes change in so far as it is actual in some way. After all, to change something is simply to bring it from potentiality to actuality, and this can only be done by something that is somehow actual: thus fire (actually hot) causes wood (able to be hot) to become actually hot, and thus it changes and modifies it. But something cannot be simultaneously actually x and potentially x (something actually hot, for instance, cannot also be potentially hot, though it can be potentially cold). So, something in process of change cannot itself cause that same change. It cannot change itself. Necessarily, therefore, anything in process of change is changed by something else. And this something else, if in process of change, is itself changed by yet another thing; and this last by another. But there has to be an end to this regress of causes, otherwise there will be no first cause of change, and, as a result, no subsequent causes of change. For it is only when acted upon by a first cause that intermediate causes produce change (if a hand does not move the stick, the stick will not move anything else). So, we are bound to arrive at some first cause of change that is not itself changed by anything, which is what everybody takes God to be.[20]

Here note:

(a) The second sentence quoted above reads in Aquinas's Latin *Omne autem quod movetur ab alio movetur*, which can also be translated as "Anything *changed* is changed by something else." Because of ambiguity concerning Latin usage when it comes to the verb *movere* ("to move"), scholars have asked whether the First Way is starting from the fact that some things are passively acted on as they change (are *changed*) or starting from the fact that things just go through a process of change (are *changing*). You might think that "everything changed is changed by something else" is so obviously true that Aquinas cannot go on to argue for its truth as he does in the First Way. But, of course, something can be changed by itself, as when I cut myself. And one might well construe the First Way as starting from the fact that things are changed (passive) and not from the fact that things change (intransitive).

(b) Like each of the Five Ways, the First Way begins with what we might call an observational premise. This is that some things in the world undergo change (*motus*). By *motus* Aquinas means real change in general.[21] The First Way has often been described as an argument for there being an unmoved mover. "Motion," however, is commonly taken these days to refer only to local motion, and we need to realize that Aquinas takes *motus* to include not just change of *place* but also change of *quantity*, as when I put on weight, or *quality*, as when I acquire a suntan.[22] The First Way is arguing that instances of change in these senses depend on something bringing the change about.

(c) At the center of the First Way's argument is the claim that *motus* occurs as something comes to be what it is not to start with because something that is actually able to account for this is actually doing so. In making this claim, Aquinas distinguishes between something being *potentially* thus and so and something being *actually* thus and so. Here he is distinguishing between (1) something now thus and so though able to be different, and (2) something just being real (*aliquid ens actu*—"some real thing"). He would say, for example, that, though I am actually sitting at a desk I could be standing in my kitchen. Then he would say that my coming to be standing in my kitchen is brought about by something real.[23] He would also say that something potentially thus and so coming to be actually thus and so is not explicable in terms of what the thing is to start with, that X coming to be F is not explicable with reference to a description of what X is before it comes to be F. He certainly thinks that a description of X as being F can be a genuine description of X. But he does not think that it accounts for X coming to be F having previously been not F. Here he looks for something distinct from X as not F, and, we should realize, in spite of the heat example he uses in the First Way, he does not thereby commit himself to the principle that whatever accounts for X coming to be F must itself be F in the way X is F once it has come to be F. He does not, for example, think that if I break your arm I must myself have a broken arm. What he thinks is that if you end up with a broken arm, that will be because of something (or maybe more than one thing) that actually exists and has the power to bring it about that your arm is broken.

(d) In the First Way, Aquinas denies that there can be an infinite regress of changers. We should remember that the infinite series that he is here denying is a series ordered per se.

3.4.3 The Second Way

> We find that there is an order of efficient causes in the observable world. Yet we never observe, nor ever could, something efficiently causing itself. For this would mean that it preceded itself, which it cannot do. But an order of efficient causes cannot go back infinitely, for an earlier member in it causes an intermediate, and the intermediate causes a last (whether the intermediate be one or many). If you eliminate a cause, however, you also eliminate its effects. So, there cannot be a last cause, nor an intermediate one, unless there is a first. If there is no end to the series of efficient causes, therefore, and if, as a consequence, there is no first cause, there would be no intermediate efficient causes either, and no last effect, which is clearly not the case. So we have to posit a first cause, which everyone calls "God."[24]

Here note:

(a) When talking about efficient causes in the Second Way, Aquinas starts from the premise that there are agent causes in the world, causes that, just by being so, have effects. He is alluding to the fact that, for example, we can be clearly aware that the pages of a book I am reading are being turned over by me, or that barbers cut people's hair. Since examples such as these evidently involve instances of what Aquinas would call *motus*, the concern of the Second Way clearly overlaps with what the First Way talks about, though, by contrast to the First Way, the Second Way proceeds by reference to observable causality taken itself as an effect to be explained by reference to a further cause, and not from a non-causal effect to a cause.

(b) Aquinas takes it to be obvious that there is agent causation in the world. You should realize, however, that he would not take all such causation to involve the bringing about of a change in something. You might think that a picture on a wall stays in position because it is supported by what it is hanging on, and you may think that what it hangs on stays there because it is supported by the wall into which it is driven. And Aquinas would think the same. So the Second Way is not just concerned with causes of change but also with causes of a *status quo* obtaining by virtue of something else.

(c) In the Second Way, Aquinas is arguing for a "first cause," and it has been suggested that he is, therefore, arguing that there has to be a cause for the sheer existence (*esse*) of anything that exists, as he does in *De Ente et Essentia*,4. There he argues (1) that understanding what existing things are by nature does not come with the understanding that some particular things exist (that, for example, understanding what cats are does not guarantee that one understands that *my cat* or *any particular cat* exists), and (2) that we need to account for there being things that do not exist by nature. But Aquinas is not arguing along these lines in the Second Way, though he is evidently concerned with things coming to be somehow, if only because he would take it that coming to be thus and so because of an agent cause is always a matter of something coming to a way *of being* or having its way *of being* maintained. Like all of the Five Ways, the Second Way begins with an observational premise and is not concerned, as is the *De Ente et Essentia*, with maintaining (without critical reference to an observational premise) that the existence of things other than God can be distinguished from their natures and that there has to be a cause of such things existing on pain of an infinite regress of causes. What he claims in the Second Way is that we observe agent or efficient causes to be ordered to effects.[25] In other words, thinks Aquinas, there evidently are effects of efficient or agent causes and, therefore, efficient causes of effects.

(d) Given the observational nature of the start of the Second Way, and given that Aquinas takes observable agent or efficient causation to include cases where change in one thing comes about by virtue of something else, the Second Way can be read as parallel to the reasoning of the First Way while concentrating (though not exclusively) on causes of *motus* rather than on *motus* considered as an effect.[26]

(e) In the Second Way, Aquinas appears to presume that nothing can be its own efficient cause without being prior to itself. As John Wippel observes, he seems to be thinking that "for something to cause itself efficiently, it would have to exist in order to cause (itself), and yet would not exist, insofar as it was being caused."[27] The reasoning here is comparable to or, indeed, exemplified by that of "Nothing can itself account for the warmth it is getting from something else." You might, perhaps, think that something can be or can come to be while lacking what Aquinas thinks of as an agent or efficient cause. In the Second Way, however, Aquinas is not arguing otherwise; indeed, he is arguing that something can be while lacking an agent cause. His point about nothing being its own efficient cause amounts to a claim concerning what has to be the case only of what *is* efficiently caused (a change in something owing to something, or the maintaining of something's physical position owing to something, and so on). When it comes to this, he thinks, an *other* is required.

(f) In the Second Way, Aquinas denies that there can be an infinite regress of efficient causes. We should remember, however, that the infinite series that he is here denying is a series ordered per se.

3.4.4 The Third Way

Some of the things we encounter are able to be or not to be, for we find them generated and perished (and, therefore, able to be or not to be). But not everything can be like this. For something that is capable of not being, at some time is not. So, if everything is able not to be, at some time there was nothing in the world. But if that were true, there would be nothing even now, for something that does not exist is only brought into being by something that does exist. Therefore, if nothing existed, nothing could have begun to exist, and nothing would exist now, which is patently not the case. So, not everything is the sort of thing that is able to be or not to be. There has got to be something that must be. Yet a thing that must be either does or does not have a cause of its necessity outside itself. And just as we must stop somewhere in a series of efficient causes, so we must also stop in the series of

> things which must be and owe this to something else. This
> means that we are forced to posit something which is intrin-
> sically necessary, owing its necessity to nothing else, something
> which is the cause that other things must be.[28]

Here note:

(a) The observational premise in the Third Way is "Some things come
to be generated and some things perish." Aquinas's reference to generation and perishing here seems to imply that he is thinking of examples
such as "People come to be as other people mate" or "People die."

(b) The coming to be and passing away to which Aquinas refers in his
Third Way involves what he would call "substantial change." For him, a
substantial change occurs when a genuine substance ceases to exist because of the activity of something other than it, as when a cat is put to sleep
by a vet.[29] Strictly speaking, Aquinas thinks, a substantial change is not a
change undergone by something that exists throughout the course of the
change in question—it is not an "accidental change." He recognizes, for
instance, that, while my cat exists through the changes it undergoes when
I clip its claws, it does not exist before its generation and after its demise.
Yet he also thinks that some changes in the world amount to a coming to
be and a passing away. There are, he believes, more changes in the world
than what he would call "accidental changes." When I have clipped my
cat's claws, it has undergone a change, but it has survived as the cat that it
is. What if I kill it, however? It would seem that a change of some sort has
occurred, but not one of which my cat can tell the tale. And what if my cat
breeds and produces kittens? Again, it would seem that a change of some
sort has occurred, but not a change in the kittens, for this is a change
amounting to their coming to exist. It is with an eye on such examples that
Aquinas quite generally in his writings refers to "substantial change,"
which he takes to occur as genuine substances come into being and pass
away in the context of the material world.

(c) Some readers of Aquinas have taken his Third Way to argue that
God, considered as the *one and only* necessary being, has to exist in view of
the fact that contingent things exist. These readers have interpreted the
Third Way as holding: (1) some things are contingent things; (2) all contingent things require a cause to account for their existence; (3) so there has
to be a single non-contingent necessary thing accounting for the existence
of all contingent things; (4) so God exists. This argument seems dubious
since each contingent thing might have a cause of its existence without

there being a single cause of the existence of all contingent things.[30] Be that as it may, the argument I have just noted is not that of the Third Way. Aquinas does not use the word "contingent" in the Third Way. He focuses on things able to be or not to be in that they come to be and perish.[31] And he clearly accepts that there might be more than one necessary being.

(d) In the Third Way, Aquinas says, "Something that is capable of not being at some time is not (*quandoque non est*). So if everything is able not to be, at some time there was nothing in the world." Interpreters of Aquinas have disagreed about how to understand his reasoning here. Some have taken him to be arguing that if everything is perishable, then everything would have perished by now.[32] Others have read him as claiming that if everything is a generated thing, there would be nothing now since a series of generated things has to be accounted for with respect to what is not itself generated. The first reading here seems dubious for two reasons. First, it leaves us supposing that Aquinas is fallaciously arguing that if everything is perishable, there has to be a single time at which everything has perished—while we might reasonably suppose that the fallacy involved here would have been obvious to someone of Aquinas's intellectual stature.[33] Second, the reading appears to attribute to Aquinas the view that things able to be or not to be have existed from an infinite past time, while Aquinas does not articulate this view in the Third Way, and we know that he did not think it possible to establish philosophically that the world has existed for an infinite past time.[34] So it seems more likely that in the Third Way Aquinas is focusing on generation rather than perishing and arguing (a) that things that are generated come to be having not existed before they came to be, and (b) that if everything is a generated thing, there would be nothing now. On this reading Aquinas would be saying that anything generated depends on a cause of its coming to be and that there could not be any generated things unless there were something acting causally while not itself being something generated. In support of this reading we might note that in the Third Way, and as part of his argument to the effect that not everything is able to be or not to be, Aquinas insists that "something that does not exist is only brought into being by something that does exist."

(e) Unlike some philosophical texts, the Third Way, as I have already noted, is not arguing that God exists as the *only* necessary being there is. Having maintained that not everything is able to be or not to be, Aquinas turns to things *not* able to be or not to be (things that are, in his terminology, necessary) while clearly presuming that there might be more than one of them. And, apart from what he says in the Third Way, we know that Aquinas believed that there were *many* necessary beings, that is, beings not generated or perishable in the course of nature—such as angels and human souls. So Aquinas does not take himself in the Third Way to have arrived at the conclusion that God exists merely by establishing that not everything is able to be or not to be. And he goes on in the Way to ask whether a series of things *not* able to be or not to be can exist without there being something *both* not able to be or not to be *and* existing uncaused. He argues that a series of things not able to be or not to be has to depend on something that exists uncaused. As he puts it: "Just as we must stop somewhere in a series of efficient causes, so we must also stop in the series of things which must be and owe this to something else."[35]

3.4.5 The Fourth Way

We find some things to be more or less good, more or less true, more or less noble, and so on. But we speak of various things as being more or less F in so far as they approximate in various ways to what is most F. For example, things are hotter and hotter the closer they approach to what is hottest. So, something is the truest and best and most noble of things, and hence the most fully in being. For, as Aristotle says, the truest things are the things most fully in being. But when many things possess some property in common, the one most fully possessing it causes it in the others. To use Aristotle's example, fire, the hottest of all things, causes all other things to be hot. So, there is something that causes in all other things their being, their goodness, and whatever other perfection they have, and we call this "God."[36]

Here note:

(a) The observational premise of the Fourth Way might strike some readers as not being any such thing. For do we *observe* that some things are more or less good, true, noble, and so on? In the Fourth Way, Aquinas seems to begin with a premise with an evaluative component built into it. Some people, though, have wanted to distinguish sharply between facts and values so as to suggest that none of our descriptions of observable things in the world entail that these things should be evaluated in some particular way. They have suggested, for example, that, from what we know of John by watching him, we cannot conclude that he is a good man. Aquinas, however, never employs such a fact-value distinction. When speaking of things in the world he always takes them to be gradable (in principle, anyway, and albeit with qualifications) with an eye on what we can see them to be empirically. He would say, for example, that a good cat is not just well behaved (by some standards of being well behaved that we might have), but objectively healthy.[37] And Aquinas thinks of health as something detectable by our senses. So he takes the first premise of his Fourth Way to be an observational one. He regards it as, for example, truly asserting that we can literally see that some things display more goodness than other things.

(b) To understand the Fourth Way one needs to realize that Aquinas regularly takes being, truth, and goodness to be related in a serious way.[38] For him, something that has being is always to some extent good. He also thinks that things that exist and are, therefore, good in some way can be thought of as true in that they possess what our minds can latch onto as intelligible. With these thoughts in mind, Aquinas can say, as he does in the Fourth Way, that things are good and true. We would not naturally assert that a cat, say, is true, though we readily refer to true propositions or statements. But taking truth to amount to a "conformity" of thing and intellect, Aquinas has no problem in supposing that we grasp truth as we latch on to what is. And he would have no problem in supposing that to latch onto the truth about some cat (or whatever) is to be presented not just by a true proposition or statement but by something that exists and can, therefore, be said to be true (and good).[39] Aquinas will also say that something can be better (more good) than something else, more true than something else, and more in being than something else. For Aquinas, something is good insofar as it exhibits actual perfections in some way— this amounting to it having being to a certain extent—and with this thought in mind he will say that if X is better than Y, then there is *more* present (more being) in X than in Y. Since he holds that truth and being can be thought of as seriously coinciding, Aquinas will assert that something can be more true than another thing insofar as it possesses more than another thing does and is, in this sense, better than it. In the Fourth Way, Aquinas is drawing on all of these notions, odd or obvious as you might take them to be.

(c) The Fourth Way starts from the claim that things in the world display different degrees of perfection. Given what I have just noted, we should not take it just to be noting that we can grade things within a certain class. We obviously do exactly this. We say, for example, that cat 1 is healthier than cat 2 and that cat 3 is healthier than cats 1 and 2. As the example of heat that he gives indicates, Aquinas is allowing for this kind of comparative evaluation in the Fourth Way. But the Fourth Way is also working with the thought that comparisons when it comes to perfections can be made with respect to things of different kinds. In particular, it is assuming that goodness, which can be had in different degrees by things of one kind, can be had to a greater degree by something not belonging to that kind. Since Aquinas thinks that something is good insofar as it possesses reality, insofar as it exists as it does, he thinks that where we have more that is real we have more goodness. He does not take "good" to signify a distinct property as, for example, does "plastic" in "plastic bag." Nor does he take "exists" ("has being") to signify such a property. But he does think that being good involves being or being actual. So he holds that even though two things, an angel and a mouse, for instance, might not belong to one kind, they can be comparatively graded when it comes to perfection. Aquinas would say that there is more (being) in angels than in mice. He would therefore say that angels are more perfect than (better than, more good than) mice. This means that the Fourth Way should not be construed as, for example, arguing that if some cat is good, and if another cat is better than it, there has to be a cat that is the best cat of all.

(d) Like all the Five Ways, the Fourth Way presents a *causal* argument for the existence of God as an agent or efficient cause, and its crucial causal move comes in the words "When many things possess some property in common, the one most fully possessing it causes it in the others." What does Aquinas mean when saying this? He does not mean that, for example, if A, B, and C are green, then they are all caused to be green by something that is supremely green. He means that if different things can be thought of as being thus and so, their being thus and so has to be accounted for in terms of something that has in it the wherewithal to bring it about that they are thus and so, something whose nature is reflected in what it brings about. As we can see from texts like his *De Principiis Naturae*, Aquinas holds that the effects of agent causes resemble their causes, but he does not think that they have to *look* like their causes. Rather, he maintains, agent causes account for what they produce by being what they are and, accordingly, *explaining* the coming to be of what they account for. I might ask "Why did my cat get sick?" Research might show that my cat licked up some disinfectant that I spilled on my kitchen floor. Given this scenario we would say "Well, of course, given that the cat consumed disinfectant, it is only to be expected that it would get sick." But why would we say this? I presume that we would do so because of our knowledge of disinfectant and the changes it brings about in different things, and Aquinas would agree with us. He would, however, add that our knowledge of disinfectant would here

have to amount to a knowledge of what it essentially is and not just a recognition that disinfectant has often produced thus and such effects in things.
To note that cats who drink disinfectant regularly become sick does not
explain why any cat becomes sick having drunk disinfectant. It merely reports what we have become used to experiencing, and Aquinas would say
that understanding why an agent cause has the effect it does depends on
understanding the *nature* of the cause (not to mention the things on which
it is acting). Only when one has developed this kind of understanding,
thinks Aquinas, does one know why certain effects show their causes in
action and why the effects in question are only to be expected. When saying
that effects resemble their agent causes and vice versa, he means that agent
causes are somehow reflected in their effects. Aquinas thinks that agent
causes sometimes produce what looks just like them, and in the Fourth
Way he gives the example of fire being hot as things affected by it are hot.
But he does not think that this is always the case, as you need to recognize
when reading the Fourth Way.

(e) As I have noted, the Fourth Way starts with reference to degrees of
goodness or perfection, and it concludes by saying that goodness and
being in things we encounter require a cause. The goodness and being
of things in the world, Aquinas thinks, have to be efficiently caused by
something the goodness and existence of which are not derived from any
agent cause. Given the way in which he thinks that to be good is to be
somehow, what this means is that, in the Fourth Way, Aquinas is effectively asking "How come something rather than *nothing*?" while maintaining that there is an answer to this question, albeit one that we cannot
understand. As we shall see, this thought dominates the reasoning given
in the *Prima Pars*.

3.4.6 The Fifth Way

> *The Fifth Way is based on the guidedness of things. For we*
> *see that some things that lack intelligence (i.e., material ob-*
> *jects in nature) act for the sake of an end. This is clear from*
> *the fact that they always, or usually, act in the same way so*
> *as to achieve what is best (and therefore tend to a goal and do*
> *not reach it by chance). But things lacking intelligence tend*
> *to a goal only as directed by one with knowledge and under-*
> *standing. Arrows, for instance, need archers. So, there is a*
> *being with intelligence who directs all natural things to ends,*
> *and we call this being "God."*[40]

Here note:

(a) Some people have argued that the world contains designed objects that demand explanation with reference to a celestial designer not itself part of the world. An especially famous example of someone thinking along these lines is William Paley (1743–1805). In *Natural Theology*, he compares various naturally occurring things to watches while arguing that they are made up of parts that seem put together to achieve a definite result. "Every indication of contrivance" and "every manifestation of design" that can be found in a watch, he says, "exists in the works of nature; with the difference, on the side of nature, of being greater and more."[41] Though some readers of it seem to have thought otherwise, however, the Fifth Way is not an "argument from design" in Paley's sense. It does not appeal to vast cosmic evidence of design not produced by any human being while produced by a nonhuman designer. Nor is it saying that the world is a single, huge designed object. Rather, it is noting that some, and *only some*, things in the world "act for the sake of an end." Aquinas is saying that, forgetting about anything we might know about human behavior, there are some things in the world that can be thought of as goal-directed in their activity, and his argument is that the goal-directed activity of these things has to be due to a directing (nonhuman) intelligence of some kind.

(b) Why does Aquinas say that certain things "act for the sake of an end"? The answer to this question can be found in his claim that some things that lack intelligence "always, or usually, act in the same way so as to achieve what is best" without doing so "by chance." Aquinas believes that chance events occur since (as he says in 1a,116 and 2a2ae,95,5) an event might have no single cause accounting for just that event. My happening to be killed by the branch of a tree that falls on me as a gust of wind strikes it just as I pass under it would, for Aquinas, be an instance of a chance event. But what about the fact that female cats regularly and instinctively suckle their newborn kittens and thereby help them to become healthy cats? Or what about the fact that my heart regularly functions so as to circulate my blood and, accordingly, keep me alive? These are the kinds of examples that Aquinas seems to be thinking of in the Fifth Way. In instances like these, he perceives goal-directed activity, but not activity that is goal-directed because a human being is at work.

(c) When we seek to account for what we encounter, thinks Aquinas (and if we read him as though he were speaking English), we are always looking for an account that begins with the word "because," as in "This can be accounted for *because* of that." In other words, we are looking for causes in some sense. As I have noted, the Latin word for "cause" is *causa*. As I have also noted, however, *causa*, for Aquinas, signifies more than what most of us these days would mean when referring to a cause. I presume that when we look for causes we are normally looking for what Aquinas calls an "agent" or "efficient" cause (as in "Who killed Fred?"). Following Aristotle, however, Aquinas says that there are four kinds of cause: efficient, material, formal, and final, and it is final causality that is the focus of the Fifth Way. Although it concludes with reference to God as an agent cause, the Fifth Way is also much concerned with final causation in that it begins with the claim that there is goal-directed activity even on the part of things different from John in that they are not reasoning or thinking individuals. Such things, Aquinas holds, have goal-directed tendencies, albeit ones that are sometimes frustrated. In this sense, he thinks, there are non-reasoning things that aim at certain goods, and, he maintains, such aiming is derivative from what has knowledge or understanding. Hence, the example he uses of an arrow shot by an archer.

3.5 Critical Responses to the Five Ways

How cogent is Aquinas's reasoning in the Five Ways? I cannot note all that has been said in criticism of them (of which there is a lot), but here are some arguments that have often been leveled against them:

(a) The arguments fail because they do not succeed in showing that God exists. At best, they only show that there is an unchanged changer, an uncaused agent cause, a necessary being not caused to exist by anything, a source of there being things with degrees of perfection, and a cause accounting for things in nature acting for ends. But arguments purporting to show that God exists must establish that God is, for example, one, omnipotent, omniscient, and any number of other things. Since the Five Ways do not do this, they fail as arguments for the conclusion that God exists.

(b) All of the Ways rest on dubious claims. The First Way, for instance, asks us to believe that anything undergoing change so as to become F is being changed by something else that is F. But this principle is obviously false since, for example, one does not need to be dead to commit murder. Again (so it has been argued), the First Way was in effect refuted by Isaac Newton (1642–1727) whose first law of motion states that, because of the principle of inertia, an object will just continue to move in a straight line in absolute space unless interfered with.

(c) We have no good reason to think that any causal series has to have something uncaused at the start of it.

(d) All of the Five Ways depend on a logical fallacy that can be illustrated by the example "All roads lead somewhere; so there is some (one) place to which all roads lead"—a fallacy sometimes referred to as "the quantifier shift fallacy." For instance, the First Way fallaciously argues that since each instance of *motus* has an agent cause, there is one agent cause accounting for each instance of *motus*. And the Second Way argues in a comparable way with an eye on agent causality, while the Third Way fallaciously maintains that, since everything perishes at some time, there must be a time at which everything has perished. With respect to the Fourth and Fifth Way, one can object to them since they fallaciously maintain that (1) if the perfection exhibited by one thing depends on a cause, there is one thing that accounts for all things exhibiting degrees of perfection, and (2) if something accounts for the tending to an end of something lacking awareness, there is some one thing accounting for the tending to an end of all things lacking awareness.

(e) In the Five Ways, Aquinas always seems to assume that we should be looking for agent causes. But why should we not take various things we know about to be "just there" with no causal questions arising from them being so? Why not suppose, for instance, that something undergoing change is *just changing*? Or why not suppose that something in the world can *just exist* without us having to look for a cause of its existing? And why not settle for the conclusion that things lacking awareness tend to an end because that is *just what they do*?

In response to these criticisms I can imagine Aquinas saying:

(1) The Five Ways do not purport to establish that God exists as being all that those who believe in God take God to be. They purport to establish only that there is something unchanged accounting for change, some uncaused agent cause, something necessary the existence of which is underived, something accounting for there being things that exist and are good, and something accounting for goal-directed activity on the part of things lacking intelligence.

(2) The First Way does not invoke the premise that only what is F can bring it about that something comes to be F, that, for example, one needs to be dead in order to commit murder. And the principle of inertia should not be thought to refute the point that something coming actually to be what it was before only potentially does not bring itself into the state of actuality at which it arrives.

(3) While a *per accidens* series of agent causes might proceed to infinity, this cannot be so when it comes to a per se series.

(4) None of the Five Ways displays a quantifier shift fallacy. Their concern is to argue that, given certain things we encounter, we need to suppose that there is something accounting for them that is distinct from them.

(5) The quest for an agent cause (or for several agent causes) is legitimate when we are concerned with what does not have to be the case considered as what it is, what it does, or what is happening to it.

At least, I *suspect* that Aquinas would make these points and go on to develop them in response to the criticisms of the Five Ways noted above. Whether or not he might ultimately be successful in pressing them, however, is not a question that I can try to discuss now. Instead, I must content myself with noting that, having arrived at the end of 1a,2, Aquinas takes himself to have said enough to show that we have good philosophical reason to think that God, understood in the senses specified in the Five Ways, exists. As he moves on, he proceeds to ask what God actually is and how our talk about God can be thought of as latching on to God's nature. Let us see what he has to say about this.

4

The Divine Nature: Part 1 (1a,3–13)

SUMMA THEOLOGIAE IA,3 comes with a short introduction that should be noted by anyone trying to understand Aquinas as he moves on from his defense of "God exists" in 1a,2. If one accepts *that* something exists, he observes, it seems natural to go on to consider *what* it is. Yet, so Aquinas immediately declares: "We cannot know what God is, only what God is not" and must, therefore, "consider the ways in which God does not exist rather than the ways in which God does."[1]

Between 1a,3 and 1a,26 Aquinas says a lot about how to think of God in positive terms, but even as he starts on 1a,3, he is quite clearly warning us that we are seriously ignorant when it comes to God's nature and need to focus on what God cannot be. The *Summa Theologiae*'s treatment of the divine nature is very much an essay in what is sometimes called *negative* or *apophatic* theology—theology that strongly distinguishes between God and things in the world of which we can have what Aquinas called *scientia*. We can have a pretty good understanding of what, for example, dogs, cats, people, planets, and parrots are. Yet we cannot, Aquinas believes, have a corresponding understanding of what God is, since God is not material, not an individual, and not something created—the main points made in 1a,3, where Aquinas talks about divine simplicity.

4.1 Divine Simplicity (1a,3)

Aquinas holds that God is simple in that God lacks "composition" (*compositio*) of certain kinds. His meaning here is best grasped by noting that he thinks that a substance can be "composite" in one or more of several ways.[2]

First, it can be composite by being a body with measurable parts, as a human being is composite since it is made up of arms, legs, and various distinguishable organs.

Second, a substance can be composite insofar as it is made up of *matter* and *form*. For Aquinas, a substance's form is what is actually intelligible in it, such as the feline nature had by a cat, and a substance's matter is what allows it to occupy space and be distinguished (and distinguishable) from other substances, particularly other substances of the same kind. So Aquinas would say that my cat has a form in that it possesses a feline nature, and he would say that it is material in that it can be picked out with respect to its dimensions as the particular cat that it is.[3] He would also say that a substance's matter is its potentiality for change, that anything material is essentially changeable. Note that Aquinas does not think of matter here as stuff of some sort, as when we say that the matter of which something is made is plastic or lead or wood. For Aquinas, to speak of something as plastic or made of wood would be to draw attention to a formal aspect of it.

A third kind of *compositio* that Aquinas acknowledges is that between essence (*essentia*) and individual (*suppositum*). Julius Caesar was an individual human being. Since he was a human being, he was exactly what the rest of us are: human. But he was Julius Caesar and not anybody else. Aquinas would make this point by distinguishing between the essence, the human nature, of Julius Caesar and his *suppositum*, the individual being that Caesar was. The assassination of Julius Caesar, he would have said, did not result in the end of all human beings, the end of human nature as such.

In the fourth place, Aquinas distinguishes between *compositio* of essence (*essentia*) and existence (*esse*). You and I are human beings. So we are essentially the same; we share a way of being or existing. Someone who understands what we are essentially or by nature, however, will not thereby understand that you or I exist. We certainly cannot exist as what we are without being human, yet to understand what it is to be human is obviously not thereby to understand that some particular human being (e.g., Brian Davies) exists. Aquinas therefore thinks that something can be composite in that what it is does not amount to it actually existing and can, therefore, be conceptually distinguished from this.

So Aquinas notes a number of senses in which something can be thought of as composite, and in 1a,3 he denies that God is composite in any of them.

To start with, he claims that God is not a body with parts (1a,3,1). His arguments are: (1) God causes change while being unchanging, but bodies causing change undergo change themselves; (2) Bodies are always potentially different from what they are at any given time, but God lacks potentiality; (3) God surpasses all things when it comes to excellence, but a body is not the most excellent thing conceivable. And, Aquinas adds (1a,3,2), God is, therefore, not composed of form and matter.

In 1a,3,3–4 Aquinas denies that God should be thought of as something the *suppositum* of which can be distinguished from its nature or as something the nature of which can be distinguished from its existence. We can, he argues, distinguish between two individuals sharing a nature because of their matter rather than their form. Since God is immaterial, however, God is pure form and is what God's nature is. God is the individual that God is solely because of the divine nature, and the divine nature (i.e., God) is not something deriving its existence from anything extrinsic to it. Rather, it is God's nature to exist and God is, therefore, *ipsum esse subsistens* ("subsisting being itself"). According to Aquinas, essence and existence amount to the same thing in God.

Because of all this, Aquinas infers the following: (a) God is not a member of a genus, (b) God is not a substance with accidents, (c) God is entirely simple, and (d) God does not enter into composition with anything. What Aquinas chiefly wants to stress in making these claims is that God is not something *classifiable*, that God transcends the world of our experience (the world containing things of which we can have what we might call a scientific understanding), that God and the world cannot be added up to make 2 in any intelligible sense.

4.2 God's Perfection and Goodness (1a,4–6)

In 1a, 4–6 we find Aquinas explaining why he thinks that, even without reference to divine revelation, it is possible to hold that God is perfect and good.[4] Given what he has written in 1a,3, he cannot say that God is a perfect or good *such and such* as someone might be said to be a perfect husband or a good singer. However, Aquinas does want to speak of God as perfect and good in the light of the fact that "perfect" and "good" are words that we can understand without thinking of particular ways in which specifiable things that we know of can be rightly described as being perfect or good. For "perfect" at the most general level means "not able to undergo improvement" and "good" means "desirable" or "attractive."

Aquinas holds that "perfect" and "good" are normally to be construed as what Peter Geach calls "logically attributive" rather than "logically predicative" adjectives.[5] Aquinas thinks that, for example, we know exactly what "red" means in "X is red" and "Y is red," while we do not know exactly what is being said when it is said that X is perfect/good or that Y is perfect/good unless we know what X and Y stand for. The words "perfect" and "good" normally make sense to us when we are thinking of a noun to which these adjectives are applied. Hence, while "X is perfect" might strike us as puzzling, "X is a perfect parent" will not, and neither will "X is a good singer." In this sense, and as Aquinas believed, "perfect" and "good" are relative or context dependent in their meaning in that what makes for perfection and goodness in one thing might not make for perfection and goodness in another. We might commend someone for being a perfect or good parent while agreeing that he or she is a bad singer, and so on. Yet, so Aquinas also thinks, "perfect" and "good" are general terms of commendation and can be understood as such. He does not think that all perfect or good things share a particular empirical property, as, for example, do all plastic things, but he does think that all things that are perfect or good have *something* in common.

Aquinas therefore argues for God being perfect in the light of the thought that anything that is perfect is not subject to improvement (1a,4,1). "We call things perfect," he says, "when they have achieved actuality (a perfect thing being that in which nothing required by its particular mode of perfection fails to exist)."[6] The meaning here is: "God is perfect since God contains no potentiality (is not able to be other than God eternally is); God is not something capable of improvement."[7]

As for the notion of divine goodness, Aquinas's main argument is that God is good and *essentially* so in that God is desirable (1a,1,5–6).[8] To call something good, he maintains, is normally to say that it is what we look for when we want the kind of thing it is—that it is, in this sense, desirable or attractive.[9] In his view, for instance, a cat can be said to be good insofar as it is a fit and healthy cat, or singers can be good insofar as they easily hit high notes. This is usually what we would look for if we wanted to adopt a cat or hear a singer. Given his notion of divine simplicity, however, Aquinas does not want to say that God is a good *such and such* and that God is desirable because of this fact. But he does think that the goodness of creatures must reflect what God is as the cause, albeit the entirely simple cause of their existence. So Aquinas argues that God somehow contains the goodness of creatures. "We attribute goodness to God," he observes, "as being the first source of every perfection that things desire."[10] According to Aquinas, the goodness of creatures is in God in some sense before it is in them (otherwise God could not have caused it), which means that created things, in seeking their good, can be thought of as seeking God who, on this account, turns out to be the *omega* or end because the divine nature is the *alpha* or beginning. "All things," says Aquinas, "are good by God's goodness, which is the pattern, source and goal of all goodness."[11]

4.3 God as Limitless and as Existing in All Things (1a,7–8)

Having said what he thinks that he presently needs to say on God's perfection and goodness (topics to which he returns later in the *Summa*), Aquinas next moves to the idea that God is unlimited and present in all creatures. Is God unlimited? Is *only* God unlimited? Is God in everything? Is God everywhere? Is God *wholly* everywhere? In 1a,7–8, Aquinas gives reasons for answering all of these questions affirmatively. He argues: (1) God is unlimited since God is subsisting *esse* itself and the source of all things that can be thought of as limited; (2) Nothing other than God is unlimited in this respect; (3) God (and only God) is in everything in that God is creatively present to all existing things that have their continued existence because of God; (4) God is everywhere as creatively making all places to be; (5) God is *wholly* everywhere since God is not something composed of parts.

Aquinas devotes eight articles in defense of these claims. They do not, I think, call for much commentary from me since they rely on philosophical notions used by Aquinas that I have already tried to explain. It might be helpful, however, if I note the following points.

(1) The discussion in 1a,7 recognizes different senses in which a thing can be thought of as limited, one being "limited by matter." Aquinas thinks that something is limited by matter insofar as it is packed up in a parcel, so to speak. He would say, for example, that my cat is limited in that its nature, which is shared by other cats, is present in a particular material thing and, in this sense, is limited or circumscribed by it. Aquinas thinks that Plato held that things in the world share in separately existing forms corresponding to them—that cats, for instance, share in a separately existing "form" of cat—and he disagrees with Plato on this score.[12] In 1a,7, therefore, he is not suggesting that corresponding to some particular cat there is a separately existing form of cat. Instead, he claims that all individual cats have a nature had by other cats and, in this sense, display form as limited by matter that, thinks Aquinas, God does not do.[13] He also thinks that something material can be thought of as limited by form in that anything material is potentially different from what it actually is at any given time and, in this sense, is limited as (so to speak) dependent on forms to be acquired by it.

(2) Since he believes in the existence of angels, which in his view are nonmaterial, Aquinas (1a,7,2) acknowledges that angels are, in a sense, unlimited as not "composed" of form and matter. But, he argues, even angels are limited in that their being what they are depends on God, who is unlimited and whose nature is to be rather than something whose being is had by the agency of something else.

(3) 1a,7,4 does not directly bear on the question "Is God unlimited?" In this article, however, Aquinas seems to be concerned to make a point about limits on which he will draw later in the *Summa Theologiae*. Can there be an unlimited number of things? Is there a limit when it comes to things that have existed in the past? Is the universe something with a beginning, or has it existed for an infinite time and therefore in an unlimited

way? When thinking that one can always continue the series 1 + 1 + 1, some people have suggested that there could be an unlimited number of things and that there is no philosophical objection to the idea of the universe never having had a beginning. Aquinas effectively agrees with this suggestion in 1a,7,4, in which he appeals to the distinction I have already noted concerning causal series per se and *per accidens*. But, and with an eye on just this distinction, he also (1a,7,4) notes a sense of "unlimited" as meaning "requiring an unlimited number of things for its existence," and he denies that anything can be unlimited in this way. He argues that, while there might be a *potential* infinity of things, an infinite series of things causally ordered *per accidens*, the things that actually exist at any given time have to add up to a definite and, therefore, limited number.

(4) The argument of 1a,8,1 and 2 relies heavily on Aquinas's notion that the action of the agent lies in the patient. So while denying that God is *dimensively* in everything or *dimensively* everywhere, Aquinas holds (a) that God is causally present in the existence of all creatures and is therefore *in* all creatures and (b) that, by making all places to be in virtue of making the things that constitute places, God is everywhere. Something, of course, might be causally active in something else or in a place while being distant from it or by acting upon it only with a part of itself. You, for example, might act on something through many intermediaries, or you might act on something with, say, nothing but your hand or your foot. Drawing on the claim that God accounts directly for all that has *esse* (existence), and drawing on the claim that God is entirely simple, 1a,8 concludes in articles 3 and 4 by saying that God is everywhere *as a whole* and not by an intermediary or a part of God. All of this means that Aquinas thinks that being everywhere, as God is everywhere, is God's prerogative and not something of which any creature is capable. I might add that, in many ways, 1a,8 presents the essentials of Aquinas's notion of God as creator in a particularly sharp way.

4.4 *God, Change, and Eternity (1a,9–10)*

Is God unchangeable? Is God eternal? 1a,9–10 argues that the answer to both of these questions is yes. The questions are connected to each other in Aquinas's mind, since he takes God to be eternal because God is unchangeable.

That God undergoes change is a view that has strongly appealed to many theologians, and understandably so. After all, the Bible frequently depicts God as something that changes—as being like a human person first doing or thinking this and then doing or thinking that, or even as being like an animal going through various processes. Again, Christians want to insist that God loves creatures, which, one might suppose, has to mean that God reacts to things or is affected by them—implying that God somehow undergoes change.[14]

Yet Aquinas firmly resists the notion that God is changeable or changing, and you will, by now, realize why he does so. He denies that God is changeable or changing for the reasons that he gives in 1a,2 and 3 for concluding that God is the non-composite (simple) first cause of change—reasons that Aquinas again draws attention to in 1a,9,1 while adding (in 1a,9,2) that only God is unchangeable since only God transcends the world in which things do or can come to be, whether substantially or accidentally. Even an actually unchanging creature is able to be other than it is in that it is subject to alteration or annihilation by God. And from these thoughts Aquinas moves approvingly to the claim that God is eternal.

To say that God is eternal has sometimes been understood as meaning only that God never began to exist and will never cease to exist. Yet such is not Aquinas's view of eternity. He takes time to be the "numbering of before and after in change." We have the notion of things being in time, he holds, only because we think of them as undergoing change, which allows us to speak of there being a *before* and *after*. Aquinas, therefore, takes unchangeable existence to be non-temporal existence and as such "eternal existence." Drawing on the writings of Boethius (ca. 476–ca. 525), Aquinas (1a,10,1) takes eternity to be "an instantaneous whole, lacking successiveness."[15] He argues that God is eternal in that God, and only God, is not only everlasting by lacking a beginning and end but also something lacking what we can take to be a history or biography—something never varying in its mode of existence.

Aquinas acknowledges that biblical authors use tensed verbs when talking of God, but he does not think that this should force us to conclude that God is literally something whose life is spread out over time. Biblical talk of God as having a lifetime should, Aquinas argues, be construed as metaphorical just like biblical talk of God being bodily. He does not deny that God endures or has duration.[16] He is not arguing that God is timeless as, say, numbers might be thought of as being so. He takes God to be a real, living, and subsisting thing, something he would never take a number to be. However, Aquinas firmly wants to deny that God should be thought of as living a life through time—a life during which God loses a past state while enjoying a present state and looking forward to what is to come.

In 1a,10,5 and 6 Aquinas (using terminology he inherited) introduces the term "aevum" while alluding to the time in which nonmaterial things other than God might be thought of as living. If something is wholly immaterial, then should it not be thought of as unchangeable and therefore "eternal" in Aquinas's sense? Aquinas agrees that a nonmaterial thing cannot undergo material or physical change; but it would not, he thinks, thereby be eternal as God is. It would, Aquinas holds, possibly be subject to nonmaterial change and, like everything other than God, would be actually or potentially subject to *motus*—as God, thinks Aquinas, is not (cf. the first of the Five Ways). In his own words: "Time has a before and an after; aeviternity has no before nor after in itself but can be accompanied by it; eternity possesses neither a before nor an after."[17]

4.5 *God as One (1a,11)*

Deuteronomy 6:4 reads: "Hear, therefore, O Israel: The Lord is our God, the Lord alone." Aquinas quotes this verse in Latin as *Audi, Israel, Dominus Deus tuus Deus unus est*, which we can translate as "Hear, Israel, that the Lord your God is one God," and he takes the verse to be asserting that God is one or that there is only one God. But how is "one" to be understood in "God is one"? Aquinas's answer to this question in 1a,11 draws on what he says in 1a,3, so you will not now be surprised to learn that he does not take "God is one" to mean that God is one individual among many of the same kind or even one of a kind.

We would not normally describe something as being *one*. Thinking of some particular thing, we might say that it is the individual that it is and not something else, or we might describe it as being unique in the sense of "unusual" or "the only instance of its kind." However, we would not, for example, say without qualification that a cat is *one*. We are dealing with a numerical word when we use the word "one" (as in 1 + 1 = 2), and if we think of "one" with this in mind, we might well want to say that "___ is one" does not tell us what anything actually is, does not describe it as, for example, "is made of stone" describes something.

In his *Foundations of Arithmetic*, Gottlob Frege (1884–1925) argues that statements of number are relative in that one single thing that we pick out for discussion can, in fact, be thought of numerically in different ways. I have one desk in my study, yet my desk can be thought of as amounting to one writing space, two drawers, and the four feet that hold it up. So is my desk one or two or four? Depending on what we are interested in when describing it, it can be thought of as being one, two, or four—so Frege thinks. Now I want to stress that Aquinas is of the same mind as Frege here, as we can see from 1a,11,1, in which he argues that to be one is not to have some property that other things lack, but is just to be something that exists in its own right and not as subdivided somehow.

Aquinas does not take "one" to be an adjective like "metallic." He takes it to signify existing as a *whole*. The existence of something, he observes, is a matter of its being one thing and not another, meaning that "being one" and "existing," though not synonymous terms, are really equivalent in that for something to have *esse* is for it to be one.[18]

Yet why suppose that God is one in this sense? Because, Aquinas answers, God is simple and cannot be thought of as something whose *esse* is shared by anything. If God's existence (*esse*) and God's essence (*essentia*) are indistinguishable as Aquinas has argued that they are, then God can no more be multipliable than can some particular human being. One may speak of there being many men, but it would be nonsense to speak of there being many Socrateses, even though there might be many men called Socrates. And, Aquinas adds, God can be said to be one (a) because God is perfect and (b) because God's oneness is indicated by the fact that there is a unity among all of God's effects.

If there were two Gods, thinks Aquinas, they would have to differ from each other in that one would lack a perfection had by the other or in that one would have a perfection not had by the other. If, however, "God" signifies that which is unreservedly perfect, Aquinas maintains, there can be no question of God lacking a perfection had by another God or having a perfection not had by another God.

Developing the second point, Aquinas notes that, though the activity of many things can result in order of a certain kind, a single order displayed by something suggests the work of a single orderer. Here Aquinas again draws on his distinction between a per se causal series and a *per accidens* one. The causality of God, he thinks, runs through the causal operations of all agent causes other than God and is not like the causality of a multitude of agent causes just happening to result in some particular effect. So the effects of God as agent cause need to be thought of as deriving from what is one and not many.

4.6 Knowing God (1a,12)

As we have seen, 1a,3–11 amounts to a discussion of what God is (or is not), and in 1a,14–26 Aquinas will go on to consider a number of assertions typically made by believing Christians, Jews, and Muslims such as "God has knowledge" and "God has power." In 1a,12, however, he breaks off from a treatment of questions of the form "Is God X?" in order to reflect in general about human knowledge of God both in this life and in the life to come. In doing so he makes it clear that he is thinking about our knowledge of God as someone who believes in divine revelation, which Aquinas thinks of as assuring us that we shall indeed exist so as to have knowledge of God after we have died.

The discussion that ensues in 1a,12 presupposes much that Aquinas has already put on the table in the questions of the *Summa* leading up to it—questions employing terminology and arguments that I have tried to explain in previous sections of this book. At this point, therefore, I would simply like to note the main conclusions defended by Aquinas in 1a,12 and to provide some help when it comes to understanding them. I shall do so in a numerical order corresponding to the articles of 1a,12.

1. Given Aquinas's claim that we cannot know what God is, one might expect him to end up taking the position that we can never have a direct awareness of God's essence, that we cannot, as Aquinas puts it, "see" the divine essence. But, and with 1 John 3:2 in mind, Aquinas argues otherwise (1a,12,1).[19] Holding to belief in what is commonly referred to as the beatific vision, Aquinas maintains that after death we *can* see God. Since God is pure form, Aquinas reasons, God is intelligible and, therefore, knowable. And, he adds, since our being happy involves us in understanding, which Aquinas takes to be our highest activity, knowledge of God's essence must be something of which we are capable—at least in principle. Note, though, that Aquinas is not here trying to provide a demonstrative proof that anybody does attain the beatific vision. He is not offering an argument for there being life after death that includes a knowledge of God's essence. The reality of the beatific vision is something that Aquinas accepts on faith and in 1a,12,1 he argues only that it is not impossible for us to get to it, though its reality is taught by Scripture and believed in faith, and though it fits with the notion that people naturally desire to know.[20] According to Aquinas, the beatific vision occurs as the very form of God is united to human beings as knowers (1a,12,2). Aquinas wants to stress that God, and not something else, really is in the minds of those who enjoy the beatific vision. When I see something bodily, thinks Aquinas, the thing I see is not literally (i.e., materially) in me: I see it by means of a likeness of the thing in me. But, he suggests, seeing God's essence (this being *ipsum esse subsistens* and not something bodily) occurs as that essence itself becomes the means by which it is seen. So, Aquinas concludes, in the beatific vision God is both that which is seen and that by which God is seen. Aquinas's idea here is that people enjoying the beatific vision are quite seriously in-*formed* by what God is.

2. Laboring this point, Aquinas goes on to insist that God cannot be seen by bodily eyes (1a,12,3). In doing so he draws on the conclusion that God is incorporeal.

3. In 1a,12,4, Aquinas wants to stress that nothing created is naturally able to see God's essence—that no creature with intellect is, just by being intellectual, something that enjoys the beatific vision. Unless we are maimed or afflicted in some way, we naturally see various physical objects and can come to understand what they are. In Aquinas's view, however, the beatific vision is not automatically had by any creature with understanding. One's having the beatific vision depends on God freely sharing the knowledge of what only God is, which amounts to the very essence of God—on God *granting* the beatific vision to something that could exist as what it is without the beatific vision, even though, as doing so, it might naturally know God indirectly (as it were).[21]

4. The purpose of 1a,12,5 is to argue that the beatific vision depends on divine assistance that helps creatures with understanding to arrive at an understanding of God's essence. Aquinas refers to this assistance as "light" by which some creatures are made to resemble God, whose form is in them as they see God's essence (cf. 1a,12,2).

5. Do some of those who see God's essence see it better than others? Aquinas thinks that they do. I might understand what penguins are better than you do—even if you have more than a passing understanding of penguins. Similarly, thinks Aquinas, one creature might have a better understanding of God's essence than another in that God illumines it more. Aquinas does not provide much argumentative defense for this conclusion in 1a,12,6. All he says is that there is a greater share in "the light of glory" for those with more charity than others. Given what he goes on to say about charity later in the *Summa Theologiae*, however, I suspect that the condensed reasoning of 1a,12,6 might be expanded along the lines: (1) Charity is a gift of God that (allowing for various qualifications) makes people like what God is essentially; (2) some people have more charity than others; (3) so some people are more like God than others; (4) so being like God can admit of degrees; (5) so there can be degrees when it comes to being in-formed by the form that God is; (6) so there can be degrees of being in-formed by the form that God is when it comes to the beatific vision.

6. But now for a crucial qualification. In 1a,12,7, Aquinas makes it clear that he does not want to say that creatures with understanding can *comprehend* God's essence—that they can understand God as perfectly as God does, that they can have in them what God actually is.[22] God, for Aquinas,

cannot be contained as a whole in any creature, even a creature knowing God's essence because God is present to it as something known and as that by which what is known is known.

7. 1a,12,7 leads to 1a,12,8, which is largely concerned to deny that a knowledge of what God is comes with a knowledge of everything owing its existence to God. You might think that if God and God's knowledge are not distinguishable (as is implied by 1a,2,3), to know God must involve knowing all that God knows, yet Aquinas rejects the inference here. He holds that one can know or see what God is essentially without knowing all that God can do, has done, or will do. Aquinas does not think that God is *essentially* the cause or maker or creator of anything. As we shall see, in 1a,19,3 Aquinas denies that God is by nature compelled to create. Assuming (traditionally) that God is not so compelled, in 1a,12,8 Aquinas is saying that to know what God is by nature, to "see" God's essence, does not automatically come with a knowledge of God's effects, even if these spring from God's essence (i.e., God).

8. Could it be that God's essence is seen not directly but by a likeness, as we see our image in a mirror that contains a likeness of ourselves when we look into it? Aquinas thinks not. Seeing God's essence, he argues, is to see God's essence, not something like it (1a,12,9).

9. One can, however, come to know various things successively. So is there successiveness in the beatific vision? In 1a,12,10, Aquinas denies that there is. For him, the beatific vision is not something in which those who enjoy it go through a process of seeing God's essence in stages.

10. Can the beatific vision be enjoyed by people in the present life? One might, Aquinas notes, think that the answer to this question is yes because of biblical passages that seem to refer to a direct awareness of God on the part of various human beings—passages like Genesis 32:30, in which Jacob declares that he has seen God "face to face." In response to this line of thinking (and some others), however, Aquinas argues that the ability to know as had by human beings in their present state does not allow them to see God's essence. Rather, it enables them to know material things, things that we come to know by means of our physical senses. Not being part of the material world, thinks Aquinas, God is not naturally knowable by us as God is known by those enjoying the beatific vision.[23]

11. Aquinas does not, however, conclude without qualification that God cannot be known by people in this life. As we have seen, he thinks that we can know by reason that "God exists" is true. He also thinks that we can come to know by reason that various statements traditionally made about God are true. In 1a,12,12, he returns to these thoughts in the light of what

he has said about the beatific vision. Yes, he agrees, our knowledge of things has its source in our senses. And yes, he agrees, our natural way of knowing does not extend to an unmediated knowledge of what God is. But this is not to say that reason does not lead us to some knowledge of God. By reason, thinks Aquinas, we can know, for example, that God is an agent cause, one distinct from things in the world, one to be thought of as surpassing everything else.

12. Aquinas concludes 1a,12 by echoing what he says in 1a,1,1 and anticipating what he will go on to say in the *Secunda Pars* when he turns directly to the topic of faith. By reason, he says, we can know that certain propositions concerning God are true. This, however, does not mean that God cannot come to the assistance of our natural knowledge so as to build it up in some way (1a,12,13).

4.7 De Nominibus Dei *(1a,13)*

Along with 1a,2,3, the text of 1a,13 is one of the most quoted and discussed in the whole of Aquinas's writings. Here I am going to try to introduce you to it by first providing a short overview of it and by then noting some passages in it that you might find puzzling and in need of explanation.

4.7.1 1a,13: The Big Picture

The title of 1a,13 is *de nominibus Dei*. We can translate this title literally as "On the Names of God," but we would need to note that, in the context of 1a,13, *nomen* ("name") has the general meaning of "word," on the understanding that a word can be thought of as a noun, adjective, or verb.[24] We should also note that, in the context of 1a,13 (and especially in the light of 1a,13,8), *nomen* is not to be thought of as meaning "name" in what, I suppose, is the most common English use of "name"—as meaning "proper name" as in "My name is Brian." Clearly working with the fact that *theology* literally means "words about God," the Blackfriars edition of the *Summa Theologiae* translates *de nominibus Dei* as "Theological Language," which is perhaps a more helpful rendition than "On the Names of God." Or we might just translate *de nominibus Dei* as "Talking About God"—since that is really the concern of 1a,13. This topic is obviously a general one. It is not about how particular statements about God (e.g., "God is an agent cause," "God is perfect," or "God is good") latch onto God and can be thought to be true. Rather, 1a,13 is a question discussing "God talk" in general. More precisely, it is concerned with what is going on when we speak of God literally and not just metaphorically.

Aquinas clearly feels the need to address this matter because (a) he wants to deny that everything we say about God is to be understood figuratively and (b) because he takes our language to have its natural home in discourse about things in the world and, so, he thinks it worth asking how this language can be used to speak truly and literally about what is not part of the world but its maker or creator. Quite generally, Aquinas has the idea that the words we use when talking about God amount (as it were) to ill-fitting and secondhand clothes in which we try to dress God.[25] In that case, however, how can we think of them as truly telling us about God? Aquinas's answer to this question is that some words familiar to us from our use of them in our talk of what is not divine are to be understood as employed *analogically* as opposed to *univocally* or *equivocally* in our talk of God.

He notes that one and the same word can be used in two different sentences while meaning exactly the same in each—as "car" does in "John owns a car" and "Mary owns a car." Here we have what Aquinas thinks of as *univocal* usage.

He also notes that one and the same word can be used in two different sentences while having no meaning at all in common—as in "I keep my pen in my pocket" and "I keep my pigs in a pen." And here we have what Aquinas thinks of as *equivocal* usage.

When it comes to words used literally to talk of both God and creatures, however, Aquinas thinks we are dealing with *analogy*—the use of the same words without the result being a matter of either univocity or equivocation.

According to Aquinas, *analogical* use of a word occurs as one word is employed on two occasions without meaning exactly the same but without meaning something entirely different. Consider "I love my wife," "I love my job," and "I love spaghetti bolognese." Does "love" mean exactly the same in each of these sentences? Surely not, since love of a spouse presumably amounts to more than what love of one's job or a spaghetti bolognese can amount to and since love of one's job can amount to something different from what love between spouses amounts to and what love of spaghetti bolognese can amount to. On the other hand, "love" in the three sentences now in question is hardly to be thought of as employed purely equivocally. There are threads of connection here, or, as Aquinas would say, in the three sentences now in question, "love" is to be understood analogically. And he thinks that some words used when speaking of both God and creatures can be construed as instances of analogy or analogical predication.

Why not construe them as signifying univocally? Why, for instance, not conclude that in, say, "The President of the United States is powerful" and "God is powerful" the word "powerful" is to be understood as meaning exactly the same? With questions like this in mind, Aquinas replies by saying that when we say that something other than God is thus and so we are always thinking of it as being thus and so because it has an attribute or property while being distinguishable from the attribute or property that it has—that, for example, the power had by the U.S. president is not to be identified with the president, that it is something different from the individual whom the president is. And, Aquinas adds, the way in which something other than God is thus and so cannot be exactly the way in which God is thus and so. We may say that my cat is something with life and that God is something with life, but, Aquinas holds, what is involved in my cat being alive is different from what is involved in God being so—just as what is involved in being alive differs when it comes to things in the world that belong to different genera.

One might, of course, want to suggest that all words used of God and what is not God should be construed as employed equivocally. In 1a,13, however, Aquinas rejects this suggestion in the light of what he has already taken himself to have shown in the *Summa*. As we have seen, he thinks that he has given good philosophical reasons for accepting certain propositions concerning God. He goes on to argue that this could not have been the case if all words used when talking of creatures and God are employed equivocally. If I were to argue (1) baseball players use bats; (2) bats are furry mammals with wings; (3) therefore, baseball players use furry mammals with wings, my argument would not be valid because of the shift of sense it employs for the term "bat." By the same token, Aquinas holds, there could be no good argument for God being X, Y, or Z, if all words used of God and creatures should be construed as employed equivocally.

So Aquinas ends up saying that some words can be used with respect to God and creatures analogously. Which words does he have in mind? He is chiefly thinking of words signifying perfections—like "good" and "powerful." We can, he holds, employ such words literally when talking about God. As we have seen, Aquinas holds that some talk of God should be construed figuratively or metaphorically. When thinking of analogical predication and God, however, he is working with the view that to predicate of God and creatures analogously is not to engage in figurative discourse but in discourse that is literally true. So even though he is eager to stress the difference between God and what is not God, he thinks, for example, that to say that God is good is to say what God really is.

Aquinas concedes that some have claimed that no positive statements about God tell us what God is. Hence, he alludes in 1a,13,2 to the view that apparently positive statements about God are really disguised denials—that, for example, "God is good" should only be understood as affirming that God is not bad. He also refers to the view that apparently positive statements about God are just statements to the effect that God causes in some way—that, for example, "God is good" should be understood only along the lines "God is the cause of good things." Aquinas, however, rejects both these positions. He agrees that when speaking of God we certainly need to note what God is not, yet he also denies that all true talk of God is just a matter of negation, whether explicitly or by implication, and he denies that it should always be construed as saying that God causes something to be thus and so. He argues, for example, that "God is good" does not just mean "God is not bad." He also argues that it does not just mean "God causes good things." Rather, he holds, the goodness of what is not God depends on God being good to start with.

In developing this line of thinking, Aquinas maintains that certain things said of God can be thought of as literally true because they draw attention to perfections that exist in God, perfections displayed by various effects of God. As I have explained, Aquinas holds that our philosophical knowledge of divinity is always indirect and based on inference from our knowledge of what is not divine—inference employing the thought that effects of an agent cause must resemble it somehow. When thinking about talk about God in general, Aquinas pushes this idea so as to argue that God can be named from what is not divine since what is not divine can be thought to reflect what God is as its cause. He maintains, for example, that the goodness displayed by things derives from God, who can, therefore, be said to be good.

This, of course, is not a position coming to us in the *Summa Theologiae* for the first time. Aquinas has effectively already defended it before he gets going on 1a,13, and this, I think, means that in a serious sense 1a,13 is not adding much to what precedes it. In this connection I like to say that 1a,13 can be read as something like a State of the Union address presented each year by the president of the United States. In giving this address, the president is (among other things) trying to answer the question "Where have we got to now?" and in 1a,13 Aquinas is doing something similar. Standing back from what he has argued in previous questions of the *Summa*, Aquinas is here asking "How should we think of talk about God in the light of this?" So, and drawing on much that he has already argued before 1a,13, he says: (a) We cannot take all that is said of God and what is not God univocally; (b) We cannot take it to be purely equivocal; (c) It seems as if we should view it as analogical since it has to be regarded as literally true even though, in acknowledging this fact, we need to remember how God and creatures must differ. Before he embarks on 1a,13, Aquinas has been arguing that certain things can be said both of God and what is not God analogically. In 1a,13, Aquinas is generalizing when it comes to what he has previously been saying. In this sense he is offering a State of the Union address. The notion of analogy emerges for the first time in 1a,13 since this question is concerned with language in a way that previous questions in the *Summa* have not been. However, 1a,13 is drawing on what precedes it so as to argue:

"Well, given what we have seen, we ought to conclude that certain words used of God and what is not God need to be understood analogically."

It has sometimes been said that 1a,13 presents us with a "theory of analogy," which Aquinas takes to generate a series of propositions of the form "God is X," "God is Y," and so on. In one sense it does, since in 1a,13 Aquinas commits himself to the idea that perfections had by creatures can be thought of as reflecting what God is. In another sense, however, it does not, since it amounts to a reflection on how we should think of talk of God and talk of what is not God *in general* and since it evidently concedes that *particular* things that we say of God using the language we have derived from our talk of creatures can be or, indeed, needs to be defended instance by instance. Aquinas clearly does not think of 1a,13 as his final answer to what we can take ourselves literally to be saying when speaking about God. If he did, he could have saved himself the trouble of writing 1a,2–12. He could also have saved himself the trouble of writing 1a,14–26.

4.7.2 1a,13: Some Details

1. In 1a,13,1, Aquinas asserts that God can be spoken of both concretely and abstractly—that we can as well say, for example, "God is good" and "God is goodness." Aquinas's reasoning here depends on what he has already argued concerning God's simplicity (see 4 below).

2. 1a,13 employs a distinction between the literal and the figurative use of language while arguing that some of the things that we say of God can be taken to be literally true. How, though, does Aquinas distinguish between the literal and the figurative? He seems to think that we have a figurative use of language if (while not wanting to give up on figurative discourse in general) we can reply no to the question "Is that really true?" Suppose I say that God is a mighty fortress, and suppose that you ask me "Is that really true?" I might stand by my statement but might also want to say "No, it is not really true since God is not a physical object made of bricks and mortar." Here, Aquinas would take me to be speaking figuratively when saying that God is a mighty fortress (and to be saying something that is true in some way). But what about "God is good"? Aquinas holds that this is not a statement that admits of the follow-up "No, it's not really true because . . ." One needs to bear this fact in mind when reading 1a,13. Here Aquinas is thinking that to use a word analogically of both God and creatures is to be speaking literally, not figuratively.

3. 1a,13,3 invokes a distinction between "thing signified" (*res significata*) and "manner of signification" (*modus significandi*). In making this distinction,

Aquinas is saying that God and what is not God do not possess perfections in the same way. Yes, Aquinas agrees, we might say that an elephant is powerful and that God is powerful, and we are therefore ascribing power to both God and the elephant. In "This elephant is powerful" and "God is powerful," the word "powerful" signifies one and the same property or attribute. But Aquinas also denies that God and elephants exhibit any property or attribute in the same way—that, for example, while elephants have power as material objects whose strength can be distinguished from the individuals they are, such is not the case when it comes to God having power. Given God's simplicity, Aquinas thinks, our ways of talking about what is not God will always fail to mirror the reality of which we are speaking when trying to talk about God. Why? Because, thinks Aquinas, our ways of talking about God (our saying things like "God is powerful" or "God is good") have their origin in our attempts to capture in language what things other than God are—an origin that Aquinas does not think of as abolished just because we start talking about God.

4. It is with this thought in mind that in 1a,13,1 Aquinas says that the use of abstract language is as appropriate when speaking of God as is the use of concrete language. God, he observes, "is both simple, like a form, and subsistent, like something concrete." So, Aquinas adds, "we sometimes refer to God by abstract nouns to indicate God's simplicity while at other times we refer to God by concrete nouns to indicate God's subsistence and completeness—though neither way of speaking measures up to God's way of being."[26] One of the main things that Aquinas is doing in 1a,13 is to remind us that when talking positively about God, when trying to say what God is, we are using words and stretching them almost to the breaking point—that we are, if you like, trying to say more than we can understand, that, in a sense, we do not know what the word "God" means.[27]

5. This point is further developed in 1a,13,4, in which Aquinas argues that the words we predicate of God are not all synonymous even though we use them to latch on linguistically to what is entirely simple. Consider "good" and "powerful" in the sentences "God is good" and "God is powerful." Are they synonymous? Aquinas thinks that they are obviously not, since "good" and "powerful" do not have the same meaning. Yet given what he thinks about divine simplicity, Aquinas goes on to say that what words like "good" and "powerful" signify when we try to talk about God is not something complex, that God's goodness and God's power are not distinct parts or different aspects of God. In the case of God, therefore, "good" and "powerful" must signify the same thing, that is, God. As P. T. Geach notes, there is an analogy to what Aquinas seems to have in mind here. "'The square of___' and 'the double of___' signify two quite different functions,

but for the argument 2, these two functions both take the number 4 as their value."[28] In the same way, words can have different meanings while signifying the same thing in certain cases. Now Aquinas is clear that things that are not divine may be thought of as having attributes or properties that are truly different from one another. Yet God, he maintains, cannot be thought of as being like them in this respect. So, he concludes, our words always "signify imperfectly" when we put them to work in talking about God.

6. In 1a,13,5, Aquinas distinguishes between two kinds of analogical uses of language. He illustrates the distinction he wants to make by means of the word "healthy." We may, he says, speak of both medicine and urine as healthy since health-giving medicine and healthy symptoms like urine can be related to health in general. Or, Aquinas adds, we may think of medicine and urine as healthy in that health in what has taken medicine can be thought to reflect what the medicine is as a cause of health. So which of these senses of analogical use is Aquinas trying to highlight in 1a,13? At the end of 1a,13,5 he draws attention to the first one. Before doing so, however, he dwells on the second one while saying that we can say certain things about God because of God's producing or causing certain effects in creatures. This, I think, indicates that in 1a,13,5 Aquinas is thinking of analogy only in highly general terms—as a linguistic phenomenon in which one and the same word is used to speak of different things with connections of meaning that can be traced in each use of the word. One might suppose that, in what he wants to say about speaking analogically of God and creatures, Aquinas has to be thinking only in terms of the medicine/urine example in which two things seem to be related to a third thing. But, of course, Aquinas does not think that, say, in "John is good" and "God is good" the goodness of John and the goodness of God can be thought of as related to a third goodness existing apart from John and God. He would not, therefore, want to press the idea that when analogically talking of God and creatures, we are relating them to a third thing. In 1a,13, however, he repeatedly says that God can be said to be X, Y, or Z because of the fact that something not divine being X, Y, or Z can be thought of as being caused by God and, therefore, as reflecting what God is essentially. In 1a,13, Aquinas is out to reject the view that if God is not exactly like things that God produces, then God cannot be truly spoken of as we speak of them. This is what his "doctrine of analogy" as presented in 1a,13 really amounts to.

7. In 1a,13,7, Aquinas talks about language that tries to say that one thing is related in some way to another. The main thing to note about this discussion is that it is chiefly concerned to defend talk about God that employs tensed language. As we have seen, Aquinas thinks of God as unchanging and

unchangeable. So what about statements like "God brought about the conquest of England by the Normans in 1066"? Should statements like these not be thought of as telling us what, in the course of a life lived in time, God has produced? In 1a,13,7, Aquinas argues that they should not be understood in this way. He argues that such statements are true only because events in the world can be dated and because God's causal activity can be dated accordingly. Aquinas has no problem when it comes to statements like "William the Conqueror was led to victory by God in 1066." But, he thinks, this can only mean "In 1066 William was victorious, by God's doing," not that God, thought of as a spatio-temporal individual, or even a non-spatial but temporal one, was around doing anything at a date in God's life corresponding to our 1066.

8. People often seem to take "God" to be a proper name—the name, perhaps, of the best person of which they can think. In 1a,13,8, however, Aquinas begs to distinguish himself from such people. He argues that "God" is the name of a nature (*nomen naturae*) like "cat," and not a proper name, like "Smokey." He takes *Deus* ("God") to refer to the divine nature. Here again, Aquinas's thinking on divine simplicity is at work, as in 1a,13,9–11, in which Aquinas does three things. First, in 1a,13,9 he argues that the word "God" applies, strictly speaking, to God alone since the divine nature is not something multipliable. Aquinas allows that we may use the word "God" when talking about what is not divine, but the usage here, he says, is nothing but a case of metaphor. Second, he argues that when the word "God" is used to talk of something other than the divine nature, its use is to be understood with reference to its proper application to the divine nature (1a,13,10). Finally, in 1a,13,11 Aquinas (drawing, so he thinks, on Exodus 3:13 and 14) claims that God can be most appropriately named or referred to by the phrase *Qui Est* ("He who is").[29] This phrase, he observes, signifies existence itself, and is, therefore, especially suited for talking about God. Aquinas adds that the phrase is appropriate when employed to talk of God (a) because it does not suggest that God is something belonging to a natural kind and (b) because it does not pin God down so as to suggest that God is something with a past or a future.

9. In 1a,13,11, we find a very telling sentence that sharply highlights the fact that in 1a,13 Aquinas is concerned to stress that our language can never really capture the reality of God. I noted above that he speaks of words as signifying imperfectly when used to talk of God. In 1a,13,11, he reaffirms this point in the sentence "In this life our minds cannot grasp what God is; whatever way we have of thinking of God is a way of failing to understand God as God really is."[30] The extent to which the *Summa Theologiae* is shot through with this conclusion cannot be overemphasized.

10. If 1a,13 as whole can be thought of with respect to what precedes it as comparable to a U.S. presidential State of the Union address, 1a,13,12 can be thought of similarly with respect to 1a,13,1–11. In 1a,13,12, Aquinas repeats the point that, even though God's simplicity stands as an obstacle to our effectively expressing what God is in human language, it is also true that we can speak affirmatively of God so as to note what really is true of God and not just what might be thought to be metaphorically true.

11. I have noted how in 1a,13 Aquinas thinks that some statements about God can be thought of as using words we employ when talking of creatures, yet without doing so univocally or equivocally. I have also noted how Aquinas appeals in this connection to the notion of analogical predication, which he takes to be a literal mode of speaking. Readers of 1a,13 should, however, also be aware that Aquinas is here working with the view that analogical predication in sentences like "John is F" and "God is F" has, so to speak, a "whiff" of equivocation about it. In 1a,13,5, he says that when using words analogically as we speak of God and what is not God, we are not "merely" or "purely" equivocating. He goes on to observe that employing words used with respect to creatures in order to speak about God "lies somewhere between pure equivocation and simple univocity" (*est inter puram aequivocationem et simplicem univocationem*). Here Aquinas seems to be accepting that when speaking of God non-metaphorically, we always have to bear in mind that the language we use to talk about God, without taking it to be metaphorical, is always language whose ordinary meaning (whose *modus significandi*) fails to capture or express what God is.

1a,12 and 13 can be thought of as something of an interruption in the flow of thought that Aquinas embarks on in 1a,3. The preceding questions, 1a,3–11, amount to the first part of a treatise on the divine nature dealing with God's simplicity, perfection, goodness, limitlessness, existence in things, unchangeableness, eternity, and oneness. 1a,12 presents us with Aquinas writing about creaturely knowledge of God and about the beatific vision in particular, while 1a,13 is devoted to talk about God in general. It is not obvious to me why Aquinas chose to discuss the matters that he turns to in 1a,12–13 at this particular place in the *Summa Theologiae*. A friendly editor of the *Summa* might, indeed, have suggested to Aquinas that 1a,12–13 would have been better placed after 1a,26 or 1a,43. Be that as it may, the flow of thought from 1a,3–11 gets picked up again by Aquinas in 1a,15–26, in which he returns to what can be said philosophically in reply to the question "What is God?" So let us now see what else he has to say on that question.

5

The Divine Nature: Part 2 (1a,14–26)

1A,14–26 TURNS TO the following questions: (1) Does God know, and if God does know, what does God know? (2) Are there ideas in God? (3) Is God alive? (4) Is there will in God, and if God is something with will, how should we think of God as having will? (5) Can love be ascribed to God? (6) Can justice and mercy be ascribed to God? (7) Does God care for things? (8) Can power be ascribed to God? (9) Can beatitude be ascribed to God, and, if so, in what sense?

5.1 God's Knowledge (1a,14)

Aquinas does not infer that the universe as a whole indicates that it is evidently the product of something with intelligence. Nor does he think of God acquiring knowledge as time goes on. Nor does he take God's knowledge to be an effect that arises in God because of things somehow causally interacting with God. His line, quite simply, is that there must be knowledge in God because God is immaterial (1a,14,1).

Aquinas's thinking here rests on the Aristotelian view that to know is to have in one the form of something else but without being what that something else is.[1] Aquinas's view is that if I know what, for example, dogs are, then my intellect contains the substantial form of dogness but without me being a dog. Though he will go on in 1a,14,11 to speak of God knowing individuals, Aquinas most commonly construes knowledge in universal terms—as knowledge of what any X, Y, or Z is substantially. He also thinks that the presence in a knower of a substantial form that belongs to something known by the knower amounts to that form existing in the knower without being confined by matter—since the forms of what we can know are always confined by the matter of the things in which they exist naturally. According to Aquinas, my knowledge of dogs is knowledge of what is material, but my knowledge of dogs is not itself something material—it is the existence in me of the dog form liberated from matter. So, Aquinas argues, knowledge is always existence unconfined by matter.

Indeed, he thinks, existence is either confined by matter, as is the existence of a dog or any other material thing, or it is existence unconfined by matter and, therefore, existence in something that is knowing. This is why Aquinas concludes that, since God is immaterial, God is existence unconfined by matter and is, therefore, something with knowledge or, given the notion of divine simplicity, "knowledge as such." For Aquinas, intelligibility actualized without matter (form without matter) is what knowing is, from which it follows that God, being form without matter, is intelligibility actualized and is something with knowledge.

In trying to understand Aquinas here, it is crucial to recognize that his view is that human knowledge arises only as we receive the forms of material things immaterially, having first encountered them as material objects (more on this when we come to 1a,85). His main reason for ascribing knowledge to God rests on this notion and on the idea that the material/knowing distinction is an exhaustive one when it comes to what exists. Aquinas thinks that things are either purely material or the bearers of knowledge. If they are the bearers of knowledge, then that is because of existence unrestricted by matter in them, and this, with an eye on God, is what 1a,14,1 is arguing.[2]

1a,14,2,3, and 4 go on to suggest that since God is simple, there can be no distinction between God and what God knows and no restriction when it comes to God's knowledge of God. We may come to know forms as exemplified empirically by things other than ourselves, but the knowledge of form had by God essentially cannot, thinks Aquinas, be the result of a coming to know or a coming to know of something other than God. So God's knowledge essentially has to consist in a knowledge of God and all that God is and cannot, indeed, be distinguished from God.

One might think that Aquinas should consider the possibility of God coming to know what is not divine accidentally, as I might come, in time, to know what dogs are, or coming to know what God is in the same way, as I might come, in time, to understand what I am. Yet Aquinas's thinking on divine simplicity prevents him from going down that road. God and God's knowledge, he thinks, have to be indistinguishable. That Aquinas thinks this should, of course, be taken as a clear indication that, when ascribing knowledge to God in the *Summa Theologiae*, he is not thinking of God as having knowledge in the way people have it, even though he makes the connection between people and God knowing insofar as they both exemplify form without matter.

Does God know what is not divine? Aquinas takes 1a,14,1–4 as explaining why God, with or without reference to what God has brought about, can be thought of as knowing. Yet he does think that God has produced or created things. So what about God's knowledge of these? In 1a,14,5 and 6, Aquinas argues that God knows them and knows them individually, that is, as things that can be distinguished from one another. He does not, however, suggest that God knows what is not divine by, as it were, *peering* at it and acquiring what we might think of as a scientific understanding of it. He thinks that God unchangeably and essentially knows creatures just by knowing the divine nature that is not distinguishable from God—this involving a knowledge of what God eternally wills to produce by virtue of being the creator of all things visible and invisible. You might ask whether this conclusion commits Aquinas to the view that what is not God cannot *not* be since God and what God knows cannot *not* be—a view at odds with much that Aquinas has been arguing up to 1a,14. As we shall see, though, Aquinas is aware that there is a matter for discussion here.

The remaining articles of 1a,14 do not, I think, need much explanatory comment given what I have already said about Aquinas's thinking. 1a,14,7 denies that God's knowledge is discursive by resulting from a process of reasoning, and it does so on the ground that God is immutable. 1a,14,9 holds that God knows what does not exist because God is the maker of what *does* exist and, therefore, knows what might have been but is not, in that God knows what God can make and not make to be. 1a,14,10 argues that God knows evils in that God, knowing what is not divine, knows that some things are bad in some way or other in that they fail in goodness in some way.

1a,14,11, titled "Does God Know Individuals?" is worth pausing over since Aquinas is rather famous for denying that even we know individuals. In fact, he alludes to his position here in 1a,14,11 itself (in objection 1 and in the reply to it). It amounts to the view that material things are the individuals that they are because they are physically distinct—a view that Aquinas takes to imply that we do not know material individuals *as individuals* by understanding what they are essentially (by understanding their forms) but only by being acquainted with them at a sensory level.

Aquinas thinks that there is a big difference between sensation and understanding and that our encounter with material individuals is sensory, not intellectual (more on this in chapter 9). Yet he does think that God knows individuals as individuals insofar as God accounts for the existence of material individuals (this including their forms and their matter) and insofar as God fully understands the divine essence and what it is that God is doing by bringing it about that various individual things exist. "Since," he observes, "God is the cause of things through God's knowledge, God's knowledge has the same extension as God's causality."[3] God's knowledge of God is again appealed to by Aquinas in 1a,14,12, in which he holds that God knows infinites by understanding the divine nature and the unlimited range of things it can in principle produce or the unlimited range of things that can, in principle, be produced by creatures.

1a,14,13 turns to an especially famous question: Does God know contingent future events?[4] Aquinas is here taking a contingent future event to be an event in the future that does not have to come about, one that might not have occurred even if it does occur, and he draws attention to three reasons for supposing that God cannot know such events.

According to the first, future events will be caused to occur by God, whose knowledge, being identical with God, is necessary since God is not even potentially nonexistent—this seeming to imply that the objects of God's knowledge are necessary and, therefore, not contingent.

According to the second, if God knows that such and such will occur, then such and such cannot fail to occur since God's knowledge is what it is from eternity and is necessary as God is.

According to the third, everything that God knows must necessarily be, since what is known must always be necessarily, but no contingent event is something that just has to be.

In replying to these arguments, Aquinas stresses that God's knowledge of future events is not something that springs up and is established before they come to pass. If I know on Tuesday that you will buy a book on Wednesday, then there seems to be little that you can do on Wednesday to make me to have been wrong on Tuesday when it comes to your book buying.[5] But, argues Aquinas, God does not have *fore*-knowledge of future events.

God's knowledge, says Aquinas (drawing on 1a,10), is eternal and does not occupy a moment of time. So it can encompass past, present, and future, but without determining the future. Yes, says Aquinas, God knows what is caused by God, but, he adds, God is not just the cause of things determined by causes. God is also the cause of things that are not so determined. Yes, Aquinas concedes, God's knowledge cannot not be, but, says Aquinas, this does not mean that what God knows is something that cannot not be. Yes, Aquinas agrees, if God knows that something will happen, then it will happen, but, he reasons, it does not follow from this that what God knows is going to happen is going to happen necessarily, just as it does not follow that if I know that you are playing the piano, you are playing the piano necessarily.[6]

In 1a,14,13 Aquinas, of course, is thinking that God does not know as we know (as things in time caused to exist by God, things that come to know in a human way), and he continues with this thought to the end of 1a,14. Hence, in 1a,14,14 he maintains that God knows what can be expressed by true propositions, but not by constructing propositions as do users of language by connecting linguistic subjects and predicates so as to conclude, for example, that "___has left the building" should be predicated of "Elvis" for some reason. In 1a,14,15, Aquinas (for reasons familiar to you now) argues that

God's knowledge is not changeable, as if God were to know *this* without knowing *that* while going on to know *something else*. And, in 1a,14,16, Aquinas ends his discussion of God's knowledge with an eye on his view (developed later in the *Summa*) that we can distinguish between human theoretical reasoning and human practical reasoning.

Aquinas takes theoretical reasoning to be reasoning by which we come to know what is true, what is the case, and why it is the case. So, he thinks, we would be engaging in theoretical reasoning when arguing, for example, that lung cancer is a disease of the respiratory system sometimes caused by smoking. But Aquinas also notes that we sometimes reason with an eye on action. I might reason as follows: (1) I want to get home by 9:00 p.m.; (2) The 8.30 train will get me home by 9:00 p.m.; (3) So I should catch the 8:30 train. This, for Aquinas, would be an instance of practical reasoning, reasoning with an eye on action.

Aquinas does not think of God as being able to go through any processes of reasoning. In 1a,14,16, however, and drawing on what he has already said in 1a,14, he argues that God has both theoretical and practical knowledge insofar and only insofar as God eternally knows what God is and insofar as God eternally knows what God has eternally chosen to make to exist. God's theoretical knowledge can be compared to some limited extent to our knowledge of what things in the world are. God's practical knowledge, Aquinas goes on to argue, can be compared to an even more limited extent to our knowledge as displayed by us in acting for an end. I should, perhaps, add that the argument defended in 1a,14,16 employs the premise (frequently invoked in 1a,14) that God cannot be thought of as lacking any perfection had by the creatures God brings about. In 1a,14, Aquinas is not asking us to think of God as a knower or reasoner in the sense that we are. He is arguing that our being knowers or reasoners has to reflect in some way what God is and that God's knowledge can be thought of by finite things as being in some way comparable to what we think of as knowledge in human beings—even if, so Aquinas thinks, it is seriously different, since God is not something in the world (or any world that we can imagine to exist).

5.2 God's Ideas (1a,15)

Suppose I say, "I have thought of a good idea to help our company make a lot more money." You will understand what I am saying (roughly, anyway), though, of course, I might be quite wrong when it comes to whether or not my idea here is going to work. In 1a,15, Aquinas argues that there are ideas in God. By now, however, you will realize that God's ideas cannot, for Aquinas, be thought of like bright ones that occurred in a company board room. They amount to what God knows insofar as God knows God as the cause of creatures, and, since Aquinas thinks that all that is in God *is* God, he holds that God's ideas are God.

In 1a,15,1, Aquinas explains that he takes the word "idea" (*idea*) to be the Greek term corresponding to the Latin word *forma* ("form"). As we have seen, Aquinas thinks that forms can be in a knower. In 1a,15,1, he goes on to argue that the forms of various things are in God as God knows what God brings about. In knowing God's effects, says Aquinas, God has their forms immaterially. He also argues that the forms of God's effects can be likened to patterns in the mind of human makers and, therefore, amount to exemplars. Here Aquinas uses the example of architects who conceive of the buildings they intend to construct and who build with a view to their conception. Like architects, God has a conception of something to be produced and this, in God, is an idea.

How many ideas are there in God? Since he takes God to be the producer of many things, Aquinas argues that there are many ideas in God (1a,15,2). He says:

> If the whole universe's order is the direct object of God's creating, and if it is intended by God, God must have an idea of it. But a plan governing a whole has to involve knowledge of what is special to the parts which make it up (as, for example, builders can only plan a house while knowing what its parts amount to exactly). So, the natures of all things, including what belongs exactly to each of them, must be in God's mind.[7]

Is this argument compatible with Aquinas's teaching on divine simplicity? Aquinas argues that it is, since the forms of things produced by God, while existing as a collection in the realm that God has brought about, exist in God in a simple act of understanding that is God. When it comes to God's ideas, Aquinas argues, the multiplicity to be associated with them exists in what God produces, not in God, even though, as Aquinas argues in 1a,15,3, God has ideas of everything God knows.

What Aquinas says in 1a,15 is pretty much contained in or can be inferred from what he writes in 1a,14. So why do we have a separate question dealing with divine ideas? The answer probably lies in the esteem that St. Augustine of Hippo enjoyed in the intellectual world in which Aquinas worked. Augustine was aware of a Platonic line of thinking (to which I have already referred) according to which there are subsisting, immutable, and eternal forms corresponding to the natures of particular things in the world. Given his Christianity, Augustine maintained that these forms are ideas in God, not something existing independently of God. Aquinas is aware of this fact and in 1a,15 he seems to be trying to incorporate it into his account of God's knowledge. He does so by arguing that many ideas can exist in God as the exemplars and objects of God's knowledge and that they can do so as being God's subsisting, simple, immutable, and eternal act of understanding.

5.3 Truth and Falsity (1a,16–17)

Since he has just been talking of God's knowledge, Aquinas thinks it natural to move in 1a,16 to a discussion of the object of knowledge in general, which he takes to be truth. This, in turn, leads him to a discussion of falsity (1a,17). 1a,16 and 17 might seem to you to interrupt the flow of Aquinas's reasoning in the questions immediately preceding and following them, all of which are concerned with God's nature. Yet since, as we shall see, Aquinas wants to identify truth with God (1a,16,5), the interruption is more apparent than real. Its theological motivation for Aquinas lies in John 14:6, which reports Jesus as saying that he is the way, the truth, and the life, and in Psalms 19 and 57, which use "true" as an adjective to describe God

In 1a,16 Aquinas argues as follows:

1. Truth is what is arrived at by us because we have the ability to think and reach conclusions. We seek to know, and knowledge can only be of what is true (1a,16,1).
2. Truth exists primarily in knowers (1a,16,1), though it can also be thought to exist in what is known in that we can speak, for example, of "true gold" or our grasp of the truth of things.
3. Truth "lies in the conformity between intellect and thing" (*per conformitatem intellectus et rei*). Here Aquinas means that we have truth in us insofar as we latch on to the way things are by having what they are formally in our minds. In this connection, Aquinas speaks of truth in our minds as bearing a likeness to what we know (1a,16,1).
4. Truth is expressed by true propositions that express what a knower actually knows (1a,16,2).
5. In knowing that a proposition is true, one always knows what is the case, so "being true" and "being the case" are related (though distinguishable) notions in that one can only know that-p by knowing what is the case. To call something good is to draw attention to what it is, and, in this sense, being good and being true are related. But in knowing what is true, one

connects first and foremost with being (that which exists) rather than with being good, since one can lay hold of truth without knowing that something is good (1a,16,3 and 4).

6. God is Truth since God knows all that is the case, since truth is in God as a knower, and since God's knowledge is not something other than God (cf. 1a,3).

7. What we know to be the case when it comes to our knowledge of creatures (and remembering that we do not know what God is) derives from God and comes from the first Truth that God can be thought to be (1a,16,6). Might there be truths existing independently of God, such as those expressed in logical laws like "A statement cannot be both true and false at the same time and in the same respect"? Aquinas's answer is no, since statements asserting what is necessarily true are ones that we arrive at on the basis of our knowledge of what God has produced and on our understanding of what can and cannot be based on this (1a,16,6).

8. Truth is unchangeable insofar as God is unchangeable. But this does not mean that we cannot first think truly and then think falsely.

And in 1a,17 Aquinas argues thus:

1. Like truth, falsity is in the intellect (1a,17,1). Abstracting from the thought that truth, being, and goodness can be intellectually connected, things in themselves are neither true nor false. They are true or false only insofar as they are truly or falsely grasped by our minds—though we can, with qualification, speak of things being false in that they do not measure up to some standard or are in some way fake, like "false teeth."

2. Falsity can exist in sensation insofar as our ability to sense can malfunction for medical reasons (1a,17,2).

3. One cannot know what is not the case since what does not exist is not there to be known, though one's knowledge of what is the case might be deficient in some respect (1a,17,3).[8]

4. "It is not the case that John weighs 140 lbs." contradicts the statement "John weighs 140 lbs." The assertion of one of these statements entails the denial of the other. Propositions A and B are contradictory if the truth of A implies the falsity of B and vice versa and if the truth of B implies the falsity of A. But one can have propositions that, while not contradicting each other, cannot both be true but can both be false, as, for example, "That wall is white all over" and "That wall is black all over." With this distinction in mind, Aquinas argues in 1a,17,4 that true and false are contraries and not contradictories. His argument (drawing on Aristotle's *Metaphysics*, IV,2) is

that to say what is false is not necessarily to contradict what someone says when speaking truly, even though to speak falsely is not to state what is true. Aquinas is of the view that a statement can be false even if, so to speak, there is nothing for it to be about; that, for example, "John is bald" can be false just because there is no such person as John and not because an actual John has hair. So he thinks that the contradictory of this statement, namely, "It is not the case that John is bald," is true, whereas its contrary, namely, "John is non-bald,"that is, "John has a full head of hair," is false.

5.4 God as Alive (1a,18)

One might think that if God exists then God is something living. Yet Aquinas does not think that "God is alive" follows explicitly from anything that he has said prior to 1a,18. His arguments for asserting that God exists are causal ones. But they do not, he thinks, show that God has to be something alive, and it is not surprising that he thinks in this way since some causes (or in Aquinas's terminology, some *agent causes*) are not living things. Why, therefore, suppose that God is alive? This is the question that Aquinas turns to in 1a,18.

Aquinas's argument for God being alive rests on the view that a living thing has a principle of movement within itself (that it is, in a literal sense, an automobile). Since that is what something alive is, says Aquinas (1a,18,1 and 2), we can attribute life to God in the highest degree since God acts without being moved by anything else at all (1a,18,3). Aquinas adds that since God is simple, it would seem that God and God's life amount to the same thing.

5.5 God's Will and Providence (1a,19)

Aquinas holds that will can be ascribed to God essentially, and not just because God has chosen to produce certain things, because of what he takes will in general to be. In the case of what has intellect, he thinks, will is a tending to a perceived good and a delight in such a good when it is obtained. Since Aquinas takes God essentially to know what is perfectly good (i.e., God), he quickly concludes (1a,19,1) that there is will in God.

You should notice that in presenting this argument Aquinas is understanding will and knowledge of what is good to be more connected than some people do. It is sometimes said that one can first know what is good and then decide whether or not to seek goodness one knows—as if the judgments "X is good" and "X is desirable" were quite separate from each other. In Aquinas's view, however, to judge that X is good is always somehow to desire (will) X. He thinks that we always at some level will or desire what we take to be good.

Since we are fallible, Aquinas concedes that we might often desire what is not really good. In God's case, however, Aquinas holds that there is no room for intellectual error. So he thinks that God infallibly and essentially knows the perfect good that God is, and therefore desires (wills) it with nothing to impede God embracing and delighting in it.

It remains true, though, that Aquinas does think that will can be ascribed to God because of what God has brought about. Aquinas thinks that there is goodness in everything produced by God simply insofar as it exists (cf. 1a,5,3). This goodness, Aquinas argues in 1a,19,2, is willed by God and reflects the goodness of God who is, therefore, willing the goodness that is God when willing the goodness of what is not God. This conclusion might seem to suggest that God has to will or produce what is not divine just because, as it exists, it reflects the goodness that God is. In 1a,19,3, however, Aquinas insists that God does not have to will all that God wills. He agrees that God cannot but will the absolute good that God is, but he goes on to say that there are things God has willed or produced that do not have to exist, absolutely speaking, and that are therefore not willed by God of necessity. Yes, Aquinas agrees, in tending to their good, creatures are tending to goodness as it exists in God, and God is, therefore, willing the divine goodness when willing the goodness of creatures. And yes, Aquinas also agrees, if it is true that God does will something that is not divine, it follows that God, being immutable, cannot not will the something in question. But God, Aquinas argues, does not have to will the good of what is not God in order to will the perfect good that God is, just as we do not have to will to take a train to get to a desired destination that we can equally well arrive at by means of a bus or a taxi cab. In this connection, Aquinas draws on the distinction (already invoked in 1a,14,13) between "Necessarily if p, then p" and "If p, then p is necessarily true." He reasons that while it is necessarily true that if God wills such and such, then God wills such and such, it does not follow that if God wills such and such, then such and such is absolutely necessary. The distinction that Aquinas has in mind here is clearly a valid one since, for example, as Aquinas says in 1a,19,3, while "It is necessarily true that if Socrates is sitting, then Socrates is sitting" cannot be denied, it does not follow that if Socrates is sitting then Socrates is sitting of necessity.

Still, Aquinas thinks, God's will does cause what is not divine. In 1a,19,4, he briefly defends this conclusion (a) by repeating a version of the fifth of the Five Ways, (b) by arguing that God's nature, as pure being, is not the nature of a cause whose effects have to be like this as opposed to like that as, say, the effects of something belonging to a natural kind have to reflect its nature as a thing of the kind it is rather than of some other, and (c) by suggesting that what is produced by God proceeds from God as willing—God as an agent cause being just God as willing. And these lines of argument lead Aquinas in 1a,19,5 to deny that God's willing is caused by what is not God. One might produce X be*cause* one has a motive for doing so. But Aquinas denies that any creature can causally act on God so as to make God will anything. Relatedly, Aquinas also denies that anything can interfere with God's will so as to frustrate it (1a,19,6).

Aquinas's main line of argument here rests on positions that he has already defended in the *Summa Theologiae* when speaking of God as accounting for the *esse* (existence) of creatures. However, he has an unusually long reply (by *Summa Theologiae* standards) to one of the objections in 1a,19,6.

In 1 Timothy 2:4 St. Paul says that God wills everyone to be saved. You might think (Aquinas did) that not everyone is saved, that not everyone ends up with the beatific vision. So what sense can be made of what St. Paul says, if it is true (as Aquinas thinks) that God's will is inevitably fulfilled? Aquinas suggests that St. Paul's statement can be understood in three senses: (1) "God wills all those who are saved to be saved"; (2) "God wills people from every class to be saved"; (3) "God wills all to be saved antecedently, but not consequently."

Although he draws on St. Augustine and John Damascene while noting (1) and (2) here as possible readings of the Pauline text, Aquinas is much more taken with (3) as a way of reading it. He elaborates on (3) by noting the case of a judge who might condemn someone to death while not actually wanting anyone to suffer the death penalty.[9] A judge might say, "Obviously, I want all people to be well behaved, to never be convicted of crimes, and never to end up being condemned to death," yet the same judge might pronounce a death sentence. So says Aquinas: "We can speak of a justice that *antecedently* wishes every human being to live but *consequently* pronounces the capital sentence. By analogy, therefore, God antecedently wills all people to be saved, yet consequently wills some to be damned as God's justice requires."[10]

The obvious objection to this line of argument is that if, as Aquinas maintains, God is the cause of the existence of all creatures, then God is responsible for creatures being what they are and as such has no business condemning or punishing them. Judges in courts do not account for the being of the people who come up before them and can excuse themselves for condemning people found to be guilty. Can God be excused in this way, however? Though he does not say so in 1a,19,6, his response (as we shall see from what he says in 1a,19,8) would be (a) that God creates people as free in the context of the existing universe, (b) that people who freely choose wrong are people accountable for their actions, and (c) that God is no more unjust than a human judge in treating people with respect to the choices they have made, even though all that is real in them derives from God's causality as the source of the *esse* (existence) of things.

But is the causality of God that of a cause with a will that undergoes change? Let us assume that you and I are individuals who can act for reasons and do not always behave because of a physical constitution that compels us to go through various motions. Let us say that we act willingly or freely. It still remains that our will can be thought of as changeable in that we can change our minds. Today I might book a Caribbean cruise, while tomorrow I might decide to cancel the booking. So is being changeable in this sense an aspect of God's will?

One might think that it is, because of biblical texts that speak of God regretting having done something.[11] Or one might think of God's will as changeable in that God first commands this while then requiring something different. One might also think that God's will is changeable since God does not will what God wills of necessity and must, therefore, be open to change. But Aquinas rejects these lines of argument. If God is immutable, he reasons, then God's will, which is not something different from God, is immutable. God may, Aquinas agrees, will different changes to occur. This, however, does not entail that God's will undergoes change, and biblical language suggesting otherwise has to be construed as being metaphorical.

If God wills a change to come about, however, must it not follow that God's will imposes necessity on what God wills? If God wills that such and such comes about, does it not *have* to come about? Aquinas thinks that the answer to this question is no, because he thinks that God can will into existence both things that do not have to be as they are and things that have to be as they are (1a,19,8). His argument is: (1) Some things that come about are things that do not have to come about (free human choices, for instance); (2) Some things come about inevitably because they are the effects of things in the world whose effects are necessitated by their causes (I take it that Aquinas is here thinking of examples such as skin burning because acid has been poured on it or milk boiling when left over heat for too long); (3) God's willing extends to the production both of what comes about without having to do so and to what comes about while having to do so.[12]

Aquinas's reasoning here is that what we might think of as coming about contingently (non-necessarily) is not something that comes about contingently *in spite of* God but *because of* God—that the contingent/necessary distinction as we apply it to events in the world positively depends on God willing there to be this distinction when it comes to events in the world. As Aquinas writes: "Since God's will is the most effective of all causes, those things come about which God wills, and they also come about in the manner that God wills them to....The reason why effects willed by God come about contingently is not because their proximate causes are contingent, but because God has prepared contingent causes for them because God willed that they come about contingently."[13] Yes, thinks Aquinas, all of God's effects are willed by God and nothing can hinder God's will from taking effect, but not all of God's effects are things that are, absolutely speaking, inevitable.[14] Here Aquinas is evidently thinking of "necessary" and "contingent" as signifying different ways of being had by different things, all of which are God's effects.

Yet is evil not one of God's effects? And if it is, should we not conclude that God wills evil? In 1a,19,9, Aquinas argues that God does not will evil directly since God's willing is primarily a matter of God willing (desiring) what is good. That things fall short of being as good as we might like them to be seems obvious, but Aquinas does not take this to mean that God wills evil as such and directly anymore than he thinks that we can desire what we take to be evil. Aquinas *does* think that evil can be thought of as willed by God *indirectly* insofar as God wills certain goods that depend on it rather as we might will to undergo certain painful medical treatments for the sake of our health. Yet Aquinas finds it absurd to suppose that God could ever directly will evil (for its own sake, as it were). As we shall see, this line of thinking is later pursued by Aquinas in 1a,48 and 49, in which he considers what evil should be thought to be and how God can be related to it causally.

1a,19,10–12 does not add much to what Aquinas has already said about God's will in 1a,19. In 1a,19,10, Aquinas argues that freedom of choice can be ascribed to God since, though God wills the goodness that God is of necessity, God does not have to will to produce things that are not divine (cf. 1a,19,3). 1a,19,11 and 12 are asking whether one can think of us having "signs" of God's will as one might think of different things that people do as indicating what their willing in general amounts to. With some subtle qualifications, Aquinas answers that we can think of ourselves as having signs of God's will as long as we bear in mind what has already been said in the *Summa Theologiae*, especially with regard to what can be thought to be true of God literally and what can only be thought to be true of God metaphorically.

5.6 Love in God (1a,20)

We read in the New Testament that God is love (1 John 4:16), and we will, therefore, not expect Aquinas, the teacher of *sacra doctrina*, to deny that there is love in God. Readers should not, however, think of 1a,20 as Aquinas's final word on the love of God in the *Summa*. Rather, they should read 1a,20 as an introduction to the notion of God as loving, one that sets the scene for what

Aquinas goes on to say about the love of God. And what are the main points that Aquinas wants to emphasize in this introduction? There are five of them.

First, Aquinas argues (1a,20,1) that there is love in God since there is will in God and since will is a matter of desire (or love). Here Aquinas is ascribing love to God as belonging to what God is by nature. He is not offering an argument for God loving based on what God has brought about (us being happy, for example). You might conclude that Fred and Mary love their children because of what they do for them, but Aquinas is not thinking along these lines in 1a,20,1. Here his point is that God, whom he takes not to have to produce anything, can be thought to love just because God can and must delight in the goodness that is God.

Yet Aquinas goes on to argue that God can be thought to love even what is not divine. This is so, Aquinas thinks, because to love something can be thought of as willing good for it and because God wills good to every creature in that everything that exists is somehow good (remember what I have previously said about Aquinas's view that being and goodness are interconnected notions). In willing the existence of what is not divine, God is willing good to all that is not divine and, therefore, loves it by being the cause of its existence (1a,20,2). Aquinas goes on to argue (1a,20,3 and 4) that this conclusion does not entail that God loves all things equally. For Aquinas, there are degrees of goodness when it comes to creatures, and God must, therefore, be thought to love some things more than others just by bringing it about (willing) that some things are better than others.[15]

5.7 Justice, Mercy, and Providence (1a,21–24)

In 1a,21 and 22, Aquinas maintains that there is both justice and mercy in God and that God provides for creatures.

When it comes to God being just, Aquinas (as you will now probably expect) denies that God can be just in the familiar sense of "just" according to which one is just insofar as one pays what one owes ("commutative justice" as Aristotle calls it).[16] He argues that God cannot be commutatively just because God is not in debt to anyone or anything, because when it comes to God and creatures, the debt is entirely on the side of creatures since their entire being derives from God.

But Aquinas recognizes a sense of "just" other than that to be found in the notion of commutative justice, for he also thinks that there is such a thing as distributive justice, and he thinks that God can be thought of as just with an eye on this. Here Aquinas is thinking that justice can be ascribed to one, such as a ruler, who distributes goodness justly on the basis of merit or appropriateness. God does this, Aquinas thinks, insofar as God distributes goodness to creatures in a way that befits what they are and how they are related to God as their maker and as the source of their natures and goodness.

Aquinas goes on to add (1a,21,2) that God's distributive justice is truth in that the goodness produced by God in creatures is goodness that conforms to God's will, which can be thought of as measuring or being the standard of goodness to which the goodness of creatures conforms. As we have seen, Aquinas takes truth to consist in a matching of mind and reality. So he thinks that we grasp truth insofar as our minds conform to the ways things are. But what if a mind accounts for the way something is by being responsible for it being what it is? Then, Aquinas thinks, truth can be thought to exist insofar as the something in question conforms to the mind responsible for it as we might speak of "a true Picasso" being something actually painted by Picasso and conforming to his intentions. And, Aquinas argues, that which conforms to the mind of God, and hence to God's justice, expresses the mind of God and allows us to speak of God's justice, reflected in what God produces, as being truth.

As for mercy, Aquinas thinks (1a,21,3 and 4) that it too can be ascribed to God since God provides goodness for things as a pure act of generosity. One might think that God's justice must require that God cannot, for instance, pardon offenses against God, that, in this sense, God can only be just and not merciful. Thinking of pardon as a kind of gift, however, Aquinas holds that God can pardon offenses against God without this implying that God is not just. He goes on to say that all of God's works display both justice and mercy. They display God's justice in that they show God to be providing what is good for what God governs. They display mercy since all goodness in creatures derives from God as a gift to them.

Since Aquinas thinks of God's justice and mercy very much in terms of what is produced by God, and especially in terms of goodness produced by God, 1a,22 (on God's providence) seems to follow on fairly naturally from 1a,21, which is also concerned with what God produces and with goodness produced by God. Aquinas takes "providence" to signify an ordering or governing or caring for something, a looking after something, a providing for it. So he asks whether providence can be ascribed to God—the question being "Does God care or govern or look after or provide for creatures?" His answer is that God does this since God accounts for the goodness had by creatures. Aquinas also thinks that God leads things to goods that they do not already possess at different times and ultimately, in the case of some things, to the goodness of the beatific vision.

Providence, Aquinas suggests in 1a,22,1, can be thought of as a kind of plan for creatures, existing in God from eternity, and as that with reference to which God acts as the maker of all things. He also suggests (1a,22,2) that everything is subject to divine providence. God, considered as the first efficient cause, "has a causality reaching to everything, both immaterial and mortal, and it reaches not only to the sources of their species but also to their sources as individuals."[17]

One might think that some events happen by chance. As we have seen, Aquinas does not deny the occurrence of chance events, since he thinks that some occurrences can be understood as not being the result of some one cause geared to them. It would not, he thinks, be a matter of chance that you die when I cut your throat. But what if we both bump into each other somewhere without either of us intending to meet each other? Then Aquinas would think of us bumping into each other as a chance event. He does not, however, think that chance events are, absolutely speaking, events that lack causes, and, since he takes God to be the universal cause acting in all creatures, he concludes that even chance events fall within the scope of divine providence.

One might think that some events come about of necessity, like your dying when you consume cyanide, and that this implies that God's providence does not extend to everything. Yet Aquinas takes the view that even that which happens of necessity in the natural world happens by virtue of God's causality (1a,19,8).

One might think that not everything is subject to divine providence since people can act freely. But, says Aquinas, even the free choices of people are caused to exist by God and, therefore, do not fall outside God's providence. Many philosophers and theologians have thought of human freedom as arising as God stands back from people and allows them to act in causal independence of God. Aquinas has a very different view. He observes: "Because the very act of free choice goes back to God as its cause, whatever people freely do on their own must fall under God's providence."[18]

So Aquinas takes God's plan (and causality) when it comes to creatures as extending to all that is real in them, even what is real in lowly things that we might suspect God to be unconcerned with, as Aquinas argues in 1a,22,3. Does this view of providence not imply that everything that happens *has* to happen because it is eternally willed by God? In 1a,22,4, Aquinas discusses this question in pretty much the same way as he discusses the question he raises in 1a,19,8, where he asks whether God's will imposes necessity on what God wills.

He argues: "The effect of God's providence is for something to come about not just anyhow but in its own proper style, necessarily or contingently as the case may be. What the plan of providence has arranged to result necessarily and without fail will so come about. What it has arranged to result contingently will likewise so come about."[19] Aquinas's point here is that "determined by a cause" and "not determined by a cause" is a distinction applicable to things in the world (the created order), not to the world as a whole viewed as deriving its existence from God. For Aquinas, God's causality extends to making things to be just as they can be truly thought to be even if we have no belief in God. Let us suppose that X is something that cannot be other than it is because something is interfering with it and compelling it to be as it is, and let us suppose that Y is something that is not interfered with or compelled in this way. Let us also suppose that we are right in our suppositions about X and Y here. Noting our suppositions, Aquinas would say that both X and Y are effects of God— implying that some of God's effects come about of necessity while others do not. Aquinas does not think that God's causality renders things either determined or not determined. Rather, it makes them to exist as what they are, whether determined or not determined. For Aquinas, God's causality primarily accounts for things existing (period, and whether or not they are things like *this* or things like *that*)—a point that (as we shall soon see) surfaces strongly in the discussion of God's power in 1a,25.

Before he turns explicitly to the topic of God's power, however, Aquinas winds up his discussion of providence by talking about predestination and what he calls "the book of life" (1a,23–24). In doing so he introduces a number of questions that he has not previously raised and goes in for a number of new distinctions. What he says in 1a,23–24, however, basically reiterates what he has said in 1a,22 and you should be able to get a sense of it from what I have already said with respect to that question. Some additional explanatory observations might, however, help you to get an even better sense of 1a,23–24. These I now present in list form.

1. One needs to remember that Aquinas wrote before the numerous theological debates about predestination that occurred during the Reformation period (before the existence of theologians such as Martin Luther and John Calvin).[20] So readers of 1a,23 who know something about these Reformation debates are, perhaps, best advised to forget what they know lest they read into the text what is not actually there.

2. Aquinas certainly thinks that predestination is included in divine providence. His primary reason for doing so lies in St. Paul's Letter to the Romans. Here we read: "We know that all things work together for good for those who love God, who are called according to his purpose. For those whom he foreknew he also predestined to be conformed to the image of his Son, in order that he might be the firstborn within a large family. And those whom he predestined he also called; and those whom he called he

also justified; and those whom he justified he also glorified."[21] It is obvious from this text that St. Paul thought that God predestines people somehow, and Aquinas, unsurprisingly, follows St. Paul on this matter, though he is also influenced by St. Augustine, who is, perhaps, the most significant defender of belief in divine predestination between St. Paul and Aquinas.[22]

3. Aquinas takes predestination to be the predestination of people to eternal life with God. He does not speak of God predestining people to hell. Aquinas also takes predestination to involve the (planned by God) raising of people to what they cannot achieve by their own natural abilities.

4. The word "predestination" seems to involve a temporal reference. It seems to imply that one who *predestines* is doing something at some time *before* something else occurs. As we have seen, though, Aquinas does not think of God as undergoing any process in time. But he does (cf. 1a,23,1) think of predestination as being in God in that he takes God to predestine. So Aquinas evidently does not think of divine predestination as an event prior to others. He takes it to be identical with the eternal will of the simple God.

5. One might think that if someone is predestined, then the person in question possesses a distinct property or attribute in addition to others possessed by that person—that "predestined" can be added to a description of someone along with terms like "jovial" or "right-handed" or "intelligent." Yet Aquinas does not think of "predestined" in this way. His view is that predestination is in God, not in anything else. He means that predestination only exists in the eternal will of God (this, of course, implying that we are in no position to examine people empirically so as justifiably to conclude that some of them are predestined to eternal life while others of them are not).

6. Some theologians have spoken of there being such a thing as double predestination—meaning that God actively decrees to save some people and to damn others. Aquinas, as I have noted, does not speak in these terms. He says that God predestines some people to the beatific vision. He also agrees that God does not predestine all people, and he takes the beatific vision and the deprivation of this to derive from God's eternal will. But he also thinks (the thought is developed in 1a,23,3) that those who end up falling short of enjoying the goodness of God in a blessed state do so not because God is leading them to what is bad but because God is not leading them to a good. Aquinas wants to distinguish between (a) God causing X to be good and (b) God not causing X to be good. He thinks that (a) involves God making something to exist and that (b) is just an absence of God

making something to exist. For now I shall express this distinction as one between (a) "actively willing" and (b) "permitting," while asking you to await more clarification of what Aquinas is driving at in 1a,23,3 until I come to talk about what he says in 1a,48 and 49 (though when reading 1a,23,3 think back to what Aquinas says in 1a,5,1 and 4).

7. One might suppose that God predestines some people to glory because their merits cause God to do so. An analogy might be: "Romeo cannot take his eyes off Juliet because of her beauty." In 1a,23,5, though, Aquinas rejects this view of predestination. That is because he does not take anything in God to be caused by anything distinct from God.

8. We often use the word "predestined" as if it meant "determined" or "unavoidable" or "necessary" in the way in which people sometimes speak of our "fate" as being our inevitable "destiny." As is obvious from 1a,23,6, Aquinas does not understand "predestined" in this way when he is talking about divine predestination. That is because, as we have seen, he does not think that "God wills (or knows) that such and such is the case" entails that the such and such is something that cannot not be.

9. In 1a,23,8, Aquinas asks whether prayer makes a difference when it comes to predestination. He obviously thinks that the answer to this question is no, if it is construed as meaning "Can I bring about a change in God's eternal will just by asking God for something?" But Aquinas also thinks that God, from eternity, can will to bring something about as a response to a request, just as he thinks that God, from eternity, can will to bring it about that you get something from me for which you have asked. So he argues that God's pre-ordaining, though not something causally influenced or determined by people praying (i.e., asking God for this, that, or the other) can be thought of as taking account of prayer, just as it can take account of someone doing what he or she can manage to do when trying to teach children about the truths of Christianity. My use of the phrase "taking account" here is possibly misleading since it might suggest that, for Aquinas, God or God's will can somehow intelligently respond to what God observes as being the case at some time or other, which Aquinas does not allow. The point to note, however, is that, for Aquinas, prayer, considered as asking God for what we want, is something that God brings about with a view to the entire course of history as willed by God. He also thinks that nothing that happens can be thought of as a *response* to a prayer if there is no prayer, as my receiving a *reply* to an email presupposes my having sent one to start with. But we shall need to arrive at 2a2ae,83 in order to get a serious sense of what Aquinas takes "prayer" (*oratio*) to be by the time he is writing the *Summa*.

10. I am guessing that readers of Aquinas with little knowledge of his writings and their theological background will be perplexed when it comes to what Aquinas takes himself to be thinking about in 1a,24—the title of which is *de libro vitae* ("On the Book of Life"). What is the book of life supposed to be? And why does Aquinas include a discussion of it when talking about God's will and providence? References to the book of life can be found in a number of Old and New Testament texts. In Exodus 32:33, God is reported as saying to Moses, "Whoever has sinned against me I will blot out of my book." Again, in Psalm 69:28, the author asks that the unrighteous should "be blotted out of the book of the living." In Philippians 4:3, St. Paul refers to fellow Christians "whose names are in the book of life." And references to there being a book of life appear several times over in the book of Revelation (cf. Revelation 3:5 and 20:15). The idea in these passages is that God has recorded the names of all those to be saved—these names being thought of as contained in a book. Aquinas was familiar with this idea and turns to it in 1a,24 because it can obviously be connected with the idea that some people are predestined to union with God. He considers talk about the book of life to be metaphorical and as referring to God's knowledge of those predestined to eternal life (a record of predestination in God's mind, as it were). His discussion of the book of life in 1a,14,3, however, adds nothing of substance to what he says in the question preceding it.

5.8 God's Power and Beatitude (1a,25–26)

Aquinas's treatment of the divine nature in the *Prima Pars* concludes with respect to two questions: "Is there power in God?" (1a,25) and "Is God blessed?" (1a,26). The question devoted to God's blessedness is fairly short and, like 1a,24, adds little to what precedes it. In 1a,26, Aquinas takes the words "beatitude" or "blessedness" to signify the perfect good for something with understanding, something knowing what it is as having this good, and he quickly argues for God having beatitude by appealing to what he has already said concerning God's perfection and knowledge. So I shall say nothing more about 1a,26 now. 1a,25, however, calls for a more detailed discussion.

In a serious sense, of course, 1a,25 also draws on earlier discussions in the *Prima Pars*. We shall not, therefore, be surprised to find Aquinas saying in it that there is power in God since God brings things about as an agent cause. But we should note that in 1a,25,1 Aquinas distinguishes between two kinds of power: active power as in "I can cook lasagna" and passive power as in "I can be burned." In 1a,25,1, his main point is that active power can be ascribed to God and that passive power cannot. He argues that God has active power as being the source of the *esse* (existence) of all that is not divine, and he denies that God has passive power since he thinks that God, considered as the source of the *esse* of things, cannot be acted on or modified by any agent cause distinct from God. Nothing very new here, perhaps, and nothing very new really in 1a,25,2, in which Aquinas says that God's power is infinite, and in which he draws on the ideas (a) that God and God's nature amount to the same simple reality and (b) that God is infinite. But how should we think of God's power given what 1a,25,1 and 2 have to say?

Aquinas's answer (1a,25,3) is that we should think of God as *omnipotent.* Yet how should we understand the word "omnipotent" (*omnipotens*)? Some philosophers have taken "omnipotent" to mean "can do anything that can be done." They have thought that "X is omnipotent" means that "X can φ" where any mentionable activity can be substituted for φ, and they have argued that God cannot be omnipotent in this sense since there are millions of things that God cannot do. For example, what about eating ice cream? If God is incorporeal, then God cannot eat ice cream. Or what about riding a bike? Again, if God is incorporeal, God cannot ride a bike.[23] Yet Aquinas does not take "God is omnipotent" to mean that God can engage in any action one might care to mention.

Aquinas's understanding of divine omnipotence is grounded in his notion of God as being the source of the *esse* of creatures, his notion of God as making things to exist and, therefore, as being *able* to make things to exist. His approach to divine omnipotence is really rather straightforward. His idea is that if something can be thought without contradiction to exist, then God can make it to exist.

In 1a,25,3, he refers to the suggestion that God can do all that something made to be by God might be able to do (e.g., eat ice cream) only to dismiss it, while noting that power can be understood with respect to what is possible *absolutely.* It is possible these days to get from the United Kingdom to the United States within around nine hours if one takes a plane flying nonstop from London to New York. Let us call the possibility now in question "conditional or relative possibility" because of the presence of the word "if" in my last sentence. But there is no "if" lurking around in sentences like "It is possible for cats to purr" since purring is what cats do naturally. So let us call the possibility here in question "absolute possibility," and let me now (again) note that Aquinas takes God's omnipotence to amount to God being able to make to exist anything that is possible absolutely speaking.

He writes: "God's being, on which the notion of his power is based, is infinite existing, not limited to any kind of being, but possessing in itself the perfection of all existing. So, whatever can have the nature of being falls within the range of things that are absolutely possible, and we call God omnipotent with respect to these."[24] Aquinas is here thinking that, say, "God can make a square triangle or a feline dog to exist" has to be false while, say, "God can make it to be the case that someone is sitting" is true. He writes: "Whatever does not imply a contradiction is included in the class of possible things with respect to which we call God omnipotent."[25]

This conclusion of Aquinas is illustrated by him in 1a,25,4, in which he asks whether God can make the past not to have been. Yes, he replies, the past could, absolutely speaking, have been different from what it was. God, for example, could have made a world in which Abraham Lincoln was not assassinated. But, Aquinas would add, *given* that Lincoln was assassinated, God cannot bring it about that he was not assassinated since that would involve God trying to bring it about both that Lincoln was assassinated and that he was not, which is impossible.

Aquinas thinks that "It is the case that-p" and "It is not the case that-p" are contradictories and, therefore, cannot both be true. So he does not think that God's power extends to making both of them true. He takes God's power to extend to making it to be the case that what can exist actually does exist. When reading 1a,25, you should bear in mind that, when writing about omnipotence, Aquinas is firmly focusing on there being things made to exist by God, while arguing that anything that can be can be made to be by God. The notion of God as the source of the existence of creatures is central to Aquinas's understanding of divine omnipotence, which is why objections to the notion of omnipotence derived from the thought of God not being able to eat ice cream simply talk past what Aquinas says about divine omnipotence and do not engage with it.

One might wonder whether God's omnipotence extends to producing what God has not actually produced. This is the question with which 1a,25,5 is concerned, and you will now, I hope, be able to anticipate how Aquinas goes on to answer it. His thinking is that God can make to be what God has not made to be since God is not compelled in any way by an external force in producing what is not divine. And, he argues, God, considered as making things just to exist, is able to make anything that can be. You and I are remarkably constricted when it comes to what we can bring about, since we are things belonging to a natural kind and are, therefore, restricted. Yet, Aquinas holds, God is not so constricted, since God is not something belonging to a natural kind and is that by virtue of which anything other than God exists or could exist. In 1a,25,6, Aquinas adds that God can make things to be better than they are just because there is no contradiction involved when thinking of something other than God as being better than it is. Yes, says Aquinas, God cannot make something to be better than it is *essentially*—God cannot make a cat that is, so to speak, a Supercat and, therefore, not really a cat at all, as Superman is not really a man. But, Aquinas thinks, (a) God can make things that are superior to cats or anything else you care to mention apart from God and (b) God can bring it about that things come to be better than they are at some particular time.

With 1a,26 we come to the end of what Aquinas has to say in the *Summa Theologiae* about what can be truly said of God independently of divine revelation. 1a,2–26 is often, and with good reason, referred to as a treatise *De Deo Uno* ("On the One God")—a treatise on the divine nature abstracting from what Christians believe about God in the light of the doctrine of the Trinity and the doctrine of the Incarnation.[26] Yet Aquinas, of course, was not just a monotheist. He recognized that there are beliefs about God shared by Jews, Muslims, and Christians, and in 1a,2–26, he is concerned with some of these beliefs and with philosophical reasons for supposing that God exists in accordance with them. But Aquinas also believed that God is somehow three and that God became human. He starts to turn to these beliefs (and others) at 1a,27. Let us now follow him as he does so.

6

The Divine Trinity (1a,27–43)

SOME THEOLOGIANS HAVE criticized Aquinas for embarking on a discussion of the Trinity as late in the *Summa* as 1a,27. They have said that when Christians identify themselves as those who believe in God, they are proclaiming belief in the Trinity (in God the Father, the Son, and the Holy Spirit, considered as three *persons*).[1] They go on to argue that Aquinas should not have spent some twenty-five questions talking about God without grounding everything said in them in the doctrine of the Trinity. He should not have written anything that suggests that one can seriously distinguish between a discussion of God's one nature (*De Deo Uno*) and a discussion of God as Trinity (*De Deo Trino*). The distinction between God's nature and God as Trinity is untenable.

This quite common criticism of Aquinas can, however, be faulted on a number of fronts.

For one thing, Aquinas does not deny that God is from eternity Father, Son, and Spirit—three persons in one substance, as classical Trinitarian texts put it. Only a superficial reading of the *Summa Theologiae* could lead one to conclude that Aquinas views the doctrine of the Trinity as an appendage to an otherwise perfectly well-constructed account of what God is.

Then again, the criticism seems to forget that the doctrine of the Trinity historically arose as a bit of a surprise to those thinking of God only in Old Testament terms. Christian theologians have often read various Old Testament texts in Trinitarian terms, but they have done so retrospectively while taking both the New Testament and the Old Testament to present divine revelation. Read without reference to the New Testament, the Old Testament has nothing in it that looks explicitly like what Christians have in mind when they speak of the Trinity. Christian talk of God as Trinity has a background in talk about God that is not explicitly Trinitarian (Old Testament talk of God)—which would seem to imply that one can talk about God without explicitly talking of God as Trinity.

Finally, consider what the Christian doctrine of the Trinity asserts. It says that the Father is God, the Son is God, and the Holy Spirit is God. The word "God" in this profession of belief clearly has a life of its own (so to speak) apart

from the profession—otherwise there would be no point in making the profession, as Aquinas is well aware. He recognizes that "God" is a word shared
by Jews, Muslims, and Christians. But only one of these groups goes so far as
to say that God is "three persons in one substance." Since he takes Jews,
Muslims, and Christians not to be equivocating when they use the word
"God," Aquinas thinks that the doctrine of the Trinity expresses a truth about
God that is not captured by what orthodox Jews and Muslims say about God.

What, then, does Aquinas teach concerning the Trinity? Though he talks
about it in many places, 1a,27–43 is his most systematic treatment of it. The
discussion here draws heavily on authors that Aquinas admired, while also
dissenting from some of what they say. In what follows, I am not going to try
to explain how Aquinas's discussion of the Trinity agrees with or differs from
what people writing before him (or even in his lifetime) thought about the
Trinity. Nor am I going to try to relate what Aquinas says about the Trinity in
the *Summa* to what he says about it elsewhere.[2] Instead, I aim to guide you
through 1a,27–43 in order to give you a sense of its main conclusions.

6.1 Reason and the Trinity (1a,32,1)

So that you do not misunderstand what is going on in 1a,27–43 as a whole, it
helps at this point to jump forward to 1a,32,1. Given what Aquinas does in
1a,2–26, you might assume that when turning to the Trinity, he is presenting
further philosophical arguments for the truth of certain statements about
God. As 1a,32,1 shows, however, he is not doing that.

In 1a,32,1, Aquinas asks whether the divine persons of the Trinity can be
known by natural reason (*utrum per rationem naturalem possint cognosci divinae
personae*), and his answer is no.[3] Drawing on 1a,2–26 he says that one can know
something about the divine nature through natural reason only on the basis of
what God creates. Yet, he adds, the doctrine of the Trinity is revealed by God
and can only be embraced in faith and not on the basis of a philosophical demonstration. Yes, he agrees, there is knowledge of God that does not derive only
from divine revelation. Such knowledge, however, is knowledge of what Father,
Son, and Spirit equally are (i.e., God), not knowledge of any kind of plurality
within God. "The creative power of God is shared by the whole Trinity," Aquinas observes. So, he says, "it goes with the unity of nature, not with the distinction of persons."[4] Yes, one can philosophize about the Trinity, having accepted
orthodox teaching about it on the basis of faith. But in doing so one will only
be defending "the position that what faith upholds is not impossible."[5]

If 1a,27–43 does not offer a philosophical case for the doctrine of the Trinity,
then, what is Aquinas trying to do when writing this text? The answer to this

question is that he is seeking to show how the doctrine is thinkable without contradiction, and he is doing so largely with an eye on what he has already said concerning divine simplicity.

To hold that God is Father, Son, and Spirit seems on the face of it to conflict with the claim that there is no composition in God and the claim that God is one. As he starts writing 1a,27, Aquinas takes the claim that God is somehow three to be nonnegotiable. As he proceeds, therefore, he spends a lot of time trying to explain how the claim can be thought of and expounded in light of the conclusion that God is simple.

That is a point that readers coming fresh to 1a,27–43 should keep firmly in mind.[6] And they should do so because it is easy to read 1a,27–43 as an attempt by Aquinas to make God comprehensible, to explore the insides of God with a flashlight (so to speak). But Aquinas is not trying to do anything like this in what he says about the Trinity. He does not believe that anyone in this life really knows what God is. His view is that we are, at present, stuck with a limited grasp of what God is, one that we always have to articulate by means of analogies, using familiar words to mean more than they commonly do, and this stance of Aquinas is as much present when he talks about the Trinity as when he speaks of God as the source of the existence of creatures. One might even assume that it is more present in what he says about the Trinity than in what he says about the one divine nature. For, given that he takes the doctrine of the Trinity to be revealed by God, must not he take it as helping us at a point where our reason breaks down? In a sense, of course, he does so. We need to remember, though, that, for Aquinas, our reason has already seriously broken down as soon as we begin to talk positively about God at all.

6.2 Processions (1a,27)

1a,27 is working from the belief that distinction in God arises because of procession, because of a "coming from." That there is procession in God is affirmed by the Athanasian Creed (late fifth century A.D.), which is a touchstone of orthodox Trinitarian theology among Western Christians, and "procession" language about God occurs in the New Testament. In John 8:42, for instance, Jesus speaks of himself as proceeding or coming forth from God. John's Gospel takes Jesus to be the "Word" that was "with God" in "the beginning" and that "was God" (John 1:1–2). The Gospel goes on to speak of this "Word," the "father's only son," as becoming flesh in the birth of Jesus.[7] In John 15:26, the evangelist speaks of "the spirit of truth" to be sent by the Father while proceeding or coming from the Father. With this notion of procession in mind, 1a,27 affirms that we can think of there being procession in God since we can think of God the Son (the second person of the Trinity) eternally proceeding from God the Father (the first person of the Trinity) and of there being procession in God accounting for God the Holy Spirit (the third person of the Trinity). But how can we think in these terms if we also suppose that God is entirely simple?

Aquinas turns to this question in 1a,27,1. Here he says that procession in God is not a "coming from" as creatures might be thought to come from other creatures or even as creatures might be thought of as coming from God. Aquinas thinks that "coming from" in the Trinity cannot amount to what we have when, say, physical things in the world give birth to something other than them, and he denies that procession in God can be thought of as a matter of God making something to exist that is not God. So he ends up appealing to a notion of "coming from" that is not that of the coming of one physical thing from another and not that of a creature coming to exist from God—a notion that depends on a distinction Aquinas draws between what we might call transitive and intransitive action or activity.

Some actions involve a coming about in something other than the agent whose actions they are. If I clean my apartment, for example, then a change comes about not just in me as I sweep and dust but in my apartment as well. I have an effect on my apartment when I clean it. Let us call actions like cleaning an apartment "transitive actions" (or collections of them). But what if I come to understand or love something or someone? Here we have a coming about, but it is a coming about that is only in me. My coming to understand or love X is not a modification by me of something other than me; it is a matter of understanding or loving arising in me. Let us call actions like coming to understand or love something "intransitive actions." In 1a,27,1, Aquinas argues that procession in God can be thought of as such intransitive action.

For what if God understands God or forms a concept of God? When we understand something, says Aquinas, there comes to be in us a "word in the heart" (*verbum cordis*), a concept of what is known, and when we come to love something, there comes to be in us a desire or attraction to the something in question. Now, Aquinas holds, God does not *come to* understand or love. God *eternally* knows and loves, and God's knowledge and love are identical with God. But God's own knowledge of God can, says Aquinas, be compared with our knowledge of ourselves (our concept of ourselves in us) and our love of ourselves. Such concepts and desires are, he thinks, ascribable to God and are in God.

The Word of which St. John's Gospel talks, says Aquinas, is what in God corresponds to a *verbum cordis* in us, and the Holy Spirit is what in God corresponds to an act of love in us. Aquinas speaks of it as what is in God as God knows and loves what God is, and, since Aquinas takes God to have no accidents, God's knowledge of what God is, and God's love of what God is, he believes, have to be identified with God.

So there can be procession in God as God knows God and loves God. From eternity, says Aquinas, there is the changeless coming forth in God of God's understanding of God and God's loving of God. Objects of knowledge and objects of love, Aquinas argues, are distinguishable in the case of human knowledge (meaning that we might know what something is without loving it). Yet, says Aquinas, we should think of this distinction as breaking down when it comes to what God knows and loves in knowing God and in loving God. He argues that we can think of there being distinction in God without supposing that God is composite.

That is what Aquinas chiefly suggests in 1a,27. He writes:

> In speaking of divine realities holy Scripture makes use of words applicable to procession.... Procession [in God] should not be taken as it is in corporeal realities....It should be taken like an issuing in the mind....God's Word (*verbum*) of necessity is perfectly one with its source....In God procession corresponds only to an action which remains within the agent itself, not to one bent on something external. In the spiritual world the only actions of this kind are those of the intellect and will. But the Word's procession corresponds to the action of the intellect. Now in us there is another spiritual process following the action of the will, namely the coming forth of love, whereby what is loved is in the lover, just as the thing expressed or actually understood in the conceiving of an idea is in the knower.[8]

For this reason, says Aquinas, in addition to the procession of the Word, another procession is posited in God, namely the procession of love.[9] As we try truly (albeit inadequately) to say what God is, Aquinas suggests, we can speak of God as bringing forth or generating God the Son in knowing God. And in loving God, Aquinas suggests, God can be thought of as bringing forth the love between God the Father and God the Son, this being the Holy Spirit. Since Aquinas takes all that is in God to be God, however, Aquinas also suggests that Father, Son, and Holy Spirit are not aspects or parts of God; they are each God.

At this point I want to stress again that nothing that Aquinas is saying here should be read (a) as an attempt to work out a philosophical defense of belief in the doctrine of the Trinity or (b) as a description of God to be placed alongside descriptions that we might be able to give of things in the universe. 1a,27 comes from a teacher of *sacra docrina* recognizing that the Bible (as interpreted by the Christian Church in his day) speaks of God as Father, Son, and Spirit. Still speaking as a teacher of *sacra doctrina*, Aquinas tries to suggest comparisons to be used when thinking how there can be a "coming forth" in God without God's simplicity being compromised. He is well aware, however, that these comparisons limp when used to speak about something that exceeds human understanding, as he thinks that the Trinity does. Indeed, he highlights the ways in which they limp even as he proposes them.[10]

6.3 *Relations (1a,28)*

If X proceeds from Y, then X and Y presumably stand in a relationship to each other—not "relationship" as in "John and Mary are now in a relationship," but "relationship" as in "If Fred is Jane's father, then Fred and Jane are related to each other," or "If my parrot is to the left of me, then I am related to it by being on its right." Aquinas sometimes says that, while creatures are really related to God, God is not really related to creatures—by which he seems to mean that statements relating God to creatures that appear to suggest that God undergoes change should not be taken to mean that God really changes (cf. 1a,10,2). I might be said to be related to you if you come to love me. But your coming to love me is something in you, something of which I might be quite unaware and unaffected by. Yet, thinks Aquinas, we can think of there being relations in God that are real in God and that constitute the identity of the persons of the Trinity. He says that there can be such a thing as a subsisting relation, and that God the Father, God the Son, and God the Holy Spirit are, from eternity, subsisting relations.

The argument here rests on Aquinas's previous insistence that there is procession in God. If, he thinks, God the Son and God the Holy Spirit proceed, and if procession in this case is grounded in God the Father, then there is genuine distinction in God and, therefore, genuine relation. So he says, for example, "'Father' is named from fatherhood, and 'son' from sonship. If then fatherhood and sonship are not real relations in God, it follows that God is not Father or Son in reality, but only because our minds conceive God so."[11] But, since God is entirely simple, distinctions or relations in God cannot be like what we refer to when distinguishing between different things of the same kind and relating them to one another as distinct things having the same nature—as when we speak of there being three distinct human beings or three distinct dogs related in some way. Aquinas therefore argues that distinction or relation in God has to be distinction established *only* by relation, since "only in the category of relation do we find terms which express what is conceptual and not real."[12]

Here Aquinas is drawing on what we find in a work of Aristotle known as the *Categories*.[13] In this text, Aristotle dwells on ways in which we speak about things. Sometimes, he notes, we pick them out as individual substances and we say what they are as such (or "essentially" as Aquinas would say)—as when we say "Fred is a human being." But what kinds of things can we say about substances besides just noting what they are essentially? Aristotle claims that we might speak of them as being somehow related to something else. Aquinas picks up on this notion of relation so as to argue that to speak of X as related to Y need not be construed as saying what X or Y are by nature, but can be understood only as connecting X and Y under certain descriptions. "Relative terms," he observes, "by their very meaning indicate only a reference to something."[14] Again, in relation, "the specific character is thought of with regard to something other, not the subject in which it is."[15] Aquinas argues, however, that Trinitarian relations in God really exist and are not just in our minds. So, given his notion of divine simplicity, he also holds that such relations have to be what God essentially is.[16]

Relations in God, thinks Aquinas, are not accidents (i.e., accidental forms arising in God, as my becoming someone's political supporter would amount to the coming to be of an accident or change in me). Relations in God, Aquinas says, have to be God. In Aquinas's words: "A real distinction in God is in reality identical with nature and differs only in our mind's understanding, inasmuch as relation implies a reference to a correlative term, which is not implied by the term 'nature.' Therefore it is clear that in God relation and nature are not two things but one and the same."[17]

One might think that if the divine nature really is simple, one cannot seriously entertain the notion of there being distinct relations in God. Anxious to avoid the suggestion that there is no real distinction in God, however, Aquinas insists on there being distinct relations corresponding to Father, Son, and Spirit. He argues that relation implies reference to another "according to which the two things stand in relative opposition to each other" while maintaining that since there is real relation in God, "relative opposition must also be there." He goes on to say, "There must be real distinction in God, not indeed when we consider the absolute reality of God's nature, where there is sheer unity and simplicity, but when we think of God in terms of relation."[18]

Aquinas's point here is that a real relation has to involve distinction between the things related, and in God, he thinks, real relations follow from procession. Yet he also thinks that Father, Son, and Spirit cannot be three gods. Indeed, says Aquinas, (1) all that constitutes God the Father as Father is the relation implied by the Father being Father of the Son proceeding from the Father, (2) all that constitutes God the Son as Son is the relation implied by the Son being generated by the Father, and (3) all that constitutes the Spirit as Spirit is the relation implied by the Spirit being what is loved as God loves what God is. For Aquinas, Father, Son, and Spirit are just three relations that can be thought to exist as distinct.

6.4 Persons (1a,29–30)

What if we are looking for a common noun to use when speaking of what Father, Son, and Spirit are? Aquinas obviously cannot suggest that we should use the noun "god." We cannot speak of Father, Son, and Spirit as "three gods." So what noun can we use? Aquinas employs the word "person" (*persona*) since this is the word traditionally used by Christian theologians when distinguishing between Father, Son, and Spirit. Indeed, in 1a,29,3, Aquinas defends his Trinitarian use of "person" by invoking the Athanasian Creed. He recognizes that "person" is never used in the Bible when referring to God (cf. 1a,29,3 ad.1). But, he says, there is nothing to stop us using non-biblical language so as to hand on biblical teaching and to do so in a way that rules out misunderstandings of what the Bible teaches. And, he maintains, "person" is appropriately used when talking about the Trinity because of what it signifies.

What does it signify? Aquinas takes "person" to signify "that which is most perfect in the whole of nature, namely what subsists in a rational nature."[19] And he takes Father, Son, and Spirit to be appropriately referred to as three persons since he takes God and all that is in God to be perfect (in general) and perfect in knowledge (in particular). Aquinas recognizes that, like all words used by us to say what God is, "person" is inadequate (cf. 1a,13). We speak of human beings as persons, he notes, but the divine persons (unlike human beings), cannot be thought of as existing materially or as having a nature distinct from the individuals they are. And if "rational" is taken to mean "able to reason by going through processes of thought," then Aquinas denies that the divine persons are rational. The divine persons and only the divine persons, says Aquinas, are distinct or individual as relations. "It is," he observes, "one thing to look for the meaning of 'person' in general and another to look for that of 'divine person.'"[20] The phrase "divine person," he argues, "signifies relation as something subsisting."[21] Again, Aquinas is thinking that Father, Son, and Spirit are not three things of a kind whose natures can be distinguished from what God is.

6.5 Father, Son, and Spirit (1a,33–43)

In 1a,31, Aquinas argues that God can be thought of as Trinity (as both three and one), that the Trinity consists of distinct persons (to be thought of as

"other" than each other), and that the word "alone" when applied to God (as in
1 Timothy 1:17), should not lead us to conclusions such as "The Father alone
is God" or "The Son alone is God."[22] And, as I have said, in 1a,32 he strongly
maintains that the Trinity of persons cannot be known by means of purely
philosophical inquiry.[23] But Aquinas's treatment of the Trinity goes on, in
1a,33–43, to devote attention to the persons of Trinity considered individually,
and in this section of his text Aquinas's main conclusions (those seriously distinguishable from what he has already argued for in 1a,27–32) are as follows.[24]

1. God the Father is the "principle" (principium) of God the Son and God the Holy Spirit (1a,33,1)

Here Aquinas wants to resist saying that the Son and the Holy Spirit are caused
to exist by God the Father and are other than the Father as, say, two kittens are
other than their parent cats. Aquinas understands the word "principle" as
meaning "that from which something proceeds." So he finds it appropriate to
say that God the Father is the principle of the Son and the Spirit. At this point
he is obviously relying on his notion of there being procession in God.

2. The word "father" as applied to God the Father does not imply reference to creatures (1a,33,3)

Here Aquinas is saying that, when thinking of the Trinity, to ascribe fatherhood
to God is to talk about what God is, not what God has brought about (things
distinct from God). Christians speak of God as being their father, and Aquinas
is perfectly happy with this, but he also wants to insist that God the Father is
that from which God the Son and God the Holy Spirit eternally proceed and that
what God is eternally is something in God and not something deriving from any
way in which God might be thought to be related to creatures. So he concludes
that "the term 'fatherhood' applies to God first as connoting the relation of the
one [divine] person to another, before it applies as connoting the relation of God
to creatures."[25] When used to speak about human beings, Aquinas adds, "father"
can be understood as a common noun (like "cat"); in the context of talk about
the Trinity, however, it can be thought of as a proper name (like "Felix").

3. God the Father knows all creatures while generating God the Son (1a,34,3)

Here Aquinas seems to be denying that creatures are some kind of afterthought on God's part. We have seen Aquinas saying that God, in knowing

God, can (albeit inadequately) be thought of as forming a concept or under-standing (a *verbum cordis*) of what God is. In 1a,34,3, Aquinas argues that God, therefore, knows creatures while knowing God, that the Word (God the Son) "contains" creatures as God knows God eternally (and therefore knows God's unchangeable power, will, and so on).

4. God the Holy Spirit proceeds from God the Father and God the Son (1a,36,2)

When trying to explain what Aquinas says about the Trinity, I have to some extent managed to avoid noting that Aquinas takes the Holy Spirit to proceed *both* from the Father and the Son. But he says so explicitly in 1a,36,2 while being aware of some theological controversy prior to and during his lifetime.

The Nicene-Constantinopolitan Creed (A.D. 381) in its Latin version pro-claims that the Holy Spirit proceeds from the Father *and* the Son (*filioque*). This version of the Creed, though accepted by St. Augustine and many others, was disputed by Eastern Christians, who argued that the Holy Spirit proceeds *only* from the Father, and not from the Father *and* the Son. But in 1a,36,2, Aquinas defends the idea that the Spirit proceeds both from the Father and the Son.

He does so because he thinks that if there is procession in God, it has to be along the lines he has already tried to suggest. According to Aquinas, distinc-tion in the Trinity can only exist as a matter of being at opposite ends of a re-lation based on a procession of origination.[26] And, he argues, "if the Holy Spirit does not proceed from the Son there is no such relation between them and therefore no distinction between Son and Holy Spirit."[27] The Word pro-ceeds from the Father as God forms the *verbum cordis*, which is God's act of self-understanding, and so Father and Son are distinct, says Aquinas. But, Aquinas adds, there is another procession than that of understanding in God. This is the procession of God's act of self-love (willing, delight), and it constitutes the Holy Spirit, which must, therefore, proceed distinctly from Father and Son.

5. God the Holy Spirit proceeds from the Father through the Son (1a,36,3)

Here Aquinas makes some concession to the notion that God the Holy Spirit proceeds from the Father by upholding it insofar as it is understood along the lines "the Spirit proceeds from the Father *through* the Son." The Spirit would not be were it not for the Son, he says (in accordance with 1a,36,2). He adds, however, that the Son would not be were it not for the Father, and the Spirit, therefore, proceeds from the Father as proceeding from the Father through the Son. In this connection, Aquinas invokes the analogy of something being made by someone using a tool. If I make a desk using a saw, the desk comes to be from me by means of the saw. In something like this way, Aquinas suggests, the Spirit can be thought of as coming from the Father by means of (through) the Son, though Aquinas is perfectly aware that the analogy here limps, since he does not want to say that the Son is a tool used by God to bring about the Holy Spirit.

6. God the Son and God the Holy Spirit can be thought of as sent (1a,43)

Aquinas realizes that some New Testament texts speak of Jesus and the Holy Spirit as being sent by God. He is aware, for example, that in John 20:21 Jesus says, "As the Father has sent me, so I send you," and in John 14:26 declares, "The Advocate, the Holy Spirit, whom the Father will send in my name, will teach you everything." Since Aquinas thinks of Jesus as God the Word incarnate, and since he thinks of the Holy Spirit as a person of the Trinity, he concludes that God the Son and God the Holy Spirit can be thought of as sent.[28]

You might naturally suppose that if X sends Y, then Y is somehow inferior to X, as a messenger sent by a king might be thought of as inferior to the king. You might also naturally suppose that if X sends Y, then Y is distinct from X, as the king's messenger is distinct from the king. Now Aquinas, as we have seen, does not take any divine person to be unequal to another, and he thinks that all the divine persons are the one God and not three gods. But, working with what he takes to be biblical revelation, Aquinas thinks it appropriate to speak of divine persons being sent since he takes the Son and the Spirit both to proceed from God immanently and to be a presence in the world of space and time.

The Son, says Aquinas, comes to be in the world because of the Incarnation, and the Spirit comes to be in the world as divine grace raises people to union with God. Contemporary theologians sometimes distinguish between "the immanent Trinity" and "the economic Trinity." The word "economic" derives from a Greek term signifying "management of a household," and in discussions of the Trinity the distinction between the "economic" and "immanent" Trinity is meant to correspond to a distinction between what the Trinity is in and of itself from eternity and what the Trinity is at work in the world (God's household, as it were). Aquinas does not use these contemporary terms when writing about the Trinity, but his talk of divine persons as sent seems to presuppose something like the distinction they signify. And, indeed, his talk about the Trinity springs from what he takes to be revealed about God in the Bible concerning Jesus as God's son and the Holy Spirit as sent into the world by God.

6.6 Some Concluding Points Concerning 1a,27–43

It is not easy to understand what Aquinas is saying in 1a,27–43. But it is easy to misunderstand it. So, and at the risk of repeating myself, let me conclude by emphasizing the following points, which are mostly concerned to stress what Aquinas is *not* saying in 1a,27–43.

1. Aquinas does not take the doctrine of the Trinity to be provable philosophically. Philosophical arguments concerning God do not, he thinks, oblige us to think of God as Father, Son, and Spirit. One might assume that if God knows, then there has to be an "other" in God, but Aquinas does not think this. His reflections on God the Son are sparked off by the idea presented, so he thinks, in the Gospel of John, that there is a Word in God that is God. Aquinas does not think that we are philosophically compelled to think of there being any Word or Son in God just because we can think of God as having knowledge. Nor does he think that we are philosophically compelled to think that there is a Spirit in God that is identical with God but distinct from God the Father and God the Son. Like his talk about God the Son, Aquinas's talk about God the Holy Spirit is always grounded in biblical texts.

2. Aquinas does not maintain that what he says about the Trinity should be thought of as providing us with an understanding of what God, as Trinity, actually is any more than he thinks that what he has said in 1a,2–26 provides us with an understanding of what God is. In 1a,27–43, he takes himself to be struggling to express in words what really cannot be captured by them, on the assumption (a critical one for him) that when talking about God, and doing so even as believing in the Trinity, we are not positively talking nonsense or contradicting ourselves in some way. As Herbert McCabe says, Aquinas holds that "we cannot understand how God could be both Father, Son, and Spirit as well as utterly one and simple, but we do understand that this does not involve the kind of contradiction that would be involved in saying, say, that God is three Fathers as well as being one Father, or three Gods as well as being one God."[29]

3. When it comes to the Trinity, Aquinas wants to insist that there are *real* relations *in* God. You might think that if God is my creator, various different relations arise between God and me as I live my life, and Aquinas agrees that

this is so in the sense that, for example, yesterday I was related to God as the cause of my cleaning my apartment while today I am related to God as a creature trying to type the words you are now reading. But Aquinas does not think that there is any change in God arising from the fact that I do something one day by virtue of God and then do something else another day by virtue of God. As we have seen, Aquinas holds that God is simple. He does not, however, think it absurd to speak of distinction *in* God based on relation. That is because he thinks it possible to conceive of there being a real relation in God quite apart from ways in which God might be thought of as related to what God makes to be. Here again I think that McCabe captures Aquinas well. He writes: "We should not expect to form a concept of the triune God, or indeed of God at all; we must rest content with establishing that we are not breaking any rules of logic, in other words that we are not being intellectually dishonest."[30]

4. If you pick up on nothing else in what Aquinas says about the Trinity, please note his teaching (cf. chapter 4 above) that there are no accidents in God and that, therefore, *all that is in God is God.* This teaching informs all that Aquinas says in 1a,27–43. If you do not pay attention to this fact, you will just miss what Aquinas is driving at in his teaching concerning the Trinity.

5. Aquinas's discussion of the Trinity in the *Summa Theologiae* may well seem to contemporary readers to be dry and academic, as it is. It is not an exercise in rhetoric or poetry. It is the work of a philosophically trained Scholastic theologian concerned to press against the boundaries of reason. You should not, however, allow this fact to lead you to conclude that Aquinas takes what he says about the Trinity to be of what we might call "merely academic interest."

The revelation that God is three in one is, for him, central to Christian belief and something that is given to us so that we might enjoy eternal life with God. Aquinas really does think that God is a Trinity, that it is the Trinity from which all creatures come, that it is the triune God who is at work in the life, death, and resurrection of Jesus and in the lives of Christians. And Aquinas holds that it matters that we should believe all of this. He makes this clear in 1a,32,1, ad.3. Here we read:

> To know the divine persons was necessary for us for two reasons. One in order to have a right view of the creation of things. For by maintaining that God made everything through God's Word we avoid the error of those who held that God's nature compelled God to create things. By

affirming that there is in God the procession of love we show that God made creatures, not because God needed them nor because of any reason outside God, but from love of God's own goodness....The other and more important reason is so that we may have the right view of the salvation of human beings, accomplished by the Son who became flesh, and by the Gifts of the Holy Ghost.[31]

Once again, the doctrine of the Trinity is, for Aquinas, the life blood of all good Christian teaching. It is not of merely esoteric interest to him and it is not a dispensable appendix to his treatise on God. On the other hand, as 1a,27–43 makes clear, Aquinas does think that the doctrine of the Trinity can be approached seriously by someone concerned to explain that it is neither philosophically impossible nor philosophically provable.

7

Creation, Good, and Evil (1a,44–49)

AS I HAVE noted, Aquinas has been criticized for providing a treatise on God in the *Summa Theologiae* before he starts talking about the Trinity. Yet in 1a,44–49, as he moves on from his discussion of the Trinity, Aquinas provides a discussion that echoes a lot that he has been saying in 1a,2–26. That indicates that there is no hard and fast distinction in Aquinas's mind between there being one God as discussed in 1a,2–26 and God who is Father, Son, and Spirit as discussed in 1a,27–43. He embarks on 1a,44 because he thinks of creatures as coming from God and because, having spoken of God as Trinity in terms of God's immanent action, he wants next to talk about God's transitive action. He makes the move between 1a,43 and 44 by saying, "After the coming forth of the divine Persons there now remains that of creatures from God."[1] How is God to be thought of as the source of creatures? What kinds of creatures are there? And what should we take certain creatures to be? These are the questions that Aquinas is concerned with as he begins to write 1a,44. They are ones that occupy him right up to the end of the *Prima Pars*.

7.1 God as Cause (1a,44,1–4)

Obviously, there are many people who just do not think that there are any creatures since they do not think of there being a creator that causes the existence of everything other than God. As we have seen, however, Aquinas thinks that everything other than God has its *esse* (existence) by virtue of God's activity and that, apart from what the Bible says about God as Creator, we have positive philosophical reasons for taking this to be so. Aquinas's line of thinking here is represented in 1a,44,1–4—a text that reiterates much that he says in 1a,2–26. It focuses largely on God as agent cause and maintains that everything other than God is from God (*a Deo est*).

Hence, 1a,44,1 calls to mind what Aquinas says in 1a,3 about God as subsisting *esse* lacking all potentiality. "All things other than God are not their own existence but share in existence."[2] Aquinas's meaning here is that in creatures existence is something derived, not something belonging to them by nature. He agrees that one can think of something whose existence is not caused, for one can think of God. So "existing," he concedes, is not equivalent to "being caused." Yet he thinks that the existence of something that does not exist by nature has to be caused.

This thesis (like it or not) is at the center of everything that Aquinas says when distinguishing between creatures and God. For Aquinas, creatures are what God makes to be by causally accounting for their *esse*. The words "creator" and "create" actually do not feature much in 1a,2–26. Yet Aquinas draws on them heavily from the outset of 1a,44. He does so not only because he thinks that he has already shown that what is not divine has its being from God but also because of biblical texts speaking of God as standing to what is not God as its creator.

What, though, shall we list under the heading "what is not God"? You might reply, "Anything we can think of that is not divine," and you might invoke as examples angels (if they exist), people, dogs, planets, and so on, and Aquinas would agree with you here, as we shall soon see. But he also thinks that we can speak of what he calls "prime matter" (*materia prima*) as being other than God, and in 1a,44,2 he argues that prime matter must also be thought of as caused by God.

Aquinas takes prime matter to be a material thing's potentiality for substantial change. It is not, he thinks, a substance. Nor, as I have noted, does he equate it with some kind of stuff of which material things are made. He certainly holds that material things can be thought of as being composed of what we might call "stuff" (as when we speak of the stuff of which something is made—the stuff of which a jug is made up, for instance). But this is not what Aquinas is thinking of when referring to prime matter.

He takes this to be nothing but the potential that a material thing has for undergoing substantial change. He does not think that it is something having a form. So it is not, in his view, something intelligible. However, he thinks, it is real enough, if it is true that things have a genuine potentiality for substantial change, and if it is right to say there is unformed materiality underpinning all substantial change.[3] If that is so, he concludes, the reality of this materiality must depend on God as the cause of the *esse* of things. Or, as Aquinas himself puts it:

> To be the cause of things in that they are beings is to be the cause of all that belongs to their existence in any way whatsoever, not merely as regards what they are like by the properties which shape them or what kind they are by their substantial forms. So we have to lay down that even primary matter is caused by the all-embracing cause of beings.[4]

It is the notion of agent causality that is in the forefront of this conclusion, but Aquinas also wants to say that we should think of God as an exemplar cause of creatures and as their final cause (1a,44,3 and 4). His reference to exemplar causation here needs to be understood in the light of what he says in 1a,15 concerning God's ideas. His point is that the forms of creatures exist in God immaterially and can be thought of, so to speak, as blueprints of creatures in God's mind. And the reference to final causation picks up on what Aquinas says in 1a,6 and in 1a,19,1–2, where he speaks of God being good, as having will, and as willing creatures as directed to goodness that is in God before it is in them. God's causation, says Aquinas in 1a,44,4, extends to God willing creatures as tending to or aiming at God's goodness. "Each and every creature," he observes, "stretches out to its own completion, which is a resemblance of divine fullness and excellence. Thus, then, divine goodness is the final cause of all things."[5]

7.2 Creation (1a,45)

When it comes to the notion of God as creator, Aquinas thinks that God makes the difference between there being a world of things and there being nothing at all, that God is what accounts for there being something rather than nothing. He defends this conclusion in 1a,45,1, where he is working with the traditional view that for God to create is for God to make something to be *but not out of anything*.

If I produce a fine wine, I do so while using things that I have at hand (grapes, say). When Michelangelo painted the *Last Judgment* in the Sistine Chapel, he was working with brushes, paint, and a wall to decorate. According to Aquinas, however, for God to create is not for God to work on or with anything. God creates things *ex nihilo* (out of nothing). The idea here is not that there is something rightly to be called "nothing" on which God acts when creating. Aquinas's point is that God makes things to be, *but not out of anything*. In his words, "Creation, the introduction of being entirely, is out of the non-being which is nothing at all."[6]

This notion of God as creator leads Aquinas in 1a,45,2 to argue that God can create any genuine substance, anything having *esse*, or anything whose existence depends on a genuine substance. The discussion in 1a,45,2 relies on what Aquinas has already argued in 1a,25. Notice, however, that it highlights a point not previously stressed by Aquinas, although it is implied—this being that in creating something God is not modifying or changing anything.

In Aquinas's view, if God creates something, then God is not, so to speak, tinkering with something that preexists God's act of creating as we tinker with or modify things on which we act. He writes:

> Were God to work only on something presupposed the implication would be that it was not caused by God. . . . Creation, whereby the entire

substance of things is produced, does not allow of some common subject now different from what it was before, except according to our way of understanding, which conceives an object as first not existing at all and afterwards as existing.[7]

Being created, says Aquinas (1a,45,3), is being related to God as deriving being or existence from God. It is not being related to God as being changed by God. As Aquinas also puts this point (in the ad.3 to 1a,45,2): "Since there is no process of change in creation, a thing is simultaneously being created and is created."[8]

An implication of this conclusion, one noticed by Aquinas in 1a,45,3, is that something created by God is never something interfered with by God. For a creature to be *now* like *this* and *then* like *that* is not for it to change from one state of being to another induced in it by God as manipulating it somehow. God's act of creating anything at any time it exists is, says Aquinas, "the production of existence entire by the universal cause of all beings, which is God."[9] This remark indicates that when Aquinas thinks of God as creating things, he is not just concerned with them beginning to exist by virtue of God, but also with them continuing to exist. His view is that God creates things by accounting for their existence whenever and for as long as they exist.[10] It is also his view that only God should be thought of as creating things.

As he indicates in the first sentence of the *corpus* of 1a,45,5, Aquinas takes the conclusion that only God creates to be obviously true given what he has previously said. "In the light of what has been established," he says, "a glance is enough to show that creation is the proper activity of God alone."[11] Why, therefore, does Aquinas bother writing 1a,45,5, which asks the question "Is it exclusively for God to create?"

He does so because he is aware that some people have thought that certain creatures can create while somehow being instruments of God, and because he wants to reject their view explicitly. If God's creating something is for God to account for all that is real in the thing, then creating is an activity in which only God can engage, and this activity, Aquinas argues in 1a,45,6, can be ascribed to each of the persons of the Trinity since each of them is equally divine (cf. 1a,32,1). "Creative action," he says, "is not peculiar to any one person, but is common to the whole Trinity."[12] In 1a,45,6, Aquinas shows himself prepared to accept that, as an artist works "through an idea conceived in his mind and through love in his will bent on something," the Father can be thought to bring creatures about through the Son, God's Word, and the Holy Spirit, God's love. In 1a,45,7, Aquinas goes on to suggest that the persons of the Trinity are reflected in creatures insofar as rational creatures (and only these) reflect what God is as processions come forth in God as knowing and loving.[13] But Aquinas is quite clear that it is the Trinity as a whole that creates.

7.3 The Beginning of Creatures (1a,46)

As I noted when turning to 1a,2, it is often said that to speak of God as the Creator is just to say that God made the universe to exist some time ago. As you will now recognize, however, Aquinas takes God as creator to account for the existence of anything at any time. Yet the book of Genesis speaks of God making heaven and earth *in the beginning* (Genesis 1:1). So how should one think about God and the beginning of the universe? This is the question that Aquinas turns to in 1a,46.[14]

His answer is that it cannot be proven philosophically either that the world began to exist at some time in the past or that it did not. Yes, says Aquinas, we should believe that the world had a beginning because of what the book of Genesis says and because of what other biblical texts say.[15] But that the world had a beginning has to be thought of as an article of faith. There is, Aquinas believes, no impossibility in the world never having begun even though God is the creator of the world. In Aquinas's view, one cannot demonstrate that the world had a beginning or that it did not, since God, being free and constrained only to will the divine goodness, could have made a world with a beginning and could have made a world without one.

Aquinas is aware that Aristotle seems to have taught that the universe never began to be.[16] However, says Aquinas (1a,46,1), there is nothing to stop God from making a world with a beginning. God is eternal, Aquinas accepts, but he does not therefore concede that God is forced to create something lacking a beginning. Aquinas's discussion here refers his readers to 1a,19,4.

On the other hand, Aquinas also denies that one can demonstrate that the world had a beginning (1a,46,2). He argues (a) that the world can be consistently thought of as never having begun, that it is not part of the meaning of the word "world" that it has a beginning, and (b) that our knowledge of God does not come with the knowledge that God had to create a world with a beginning. Yes, says Aquinas, things were created at the beginning of time (1a,46,3), but, he declares, it does not therefore follow that the world had a beginning.

7.4 Distinctions in Creation (1a,47)

The world contains things of different kinds. Are these things distinct because of God or something else? In 1a,47,1, Aquinas unsurprisingly says that the existence of distinctions in creatures derives from God. As creator, it is God who primarily accounts for the distinctions between them, and this, Aquinas thinks (1a,47,2), has to mean that God is also primarily responsible, in some sense of "responsible," for inequalities between them. Variety and inequality in the world, he adds, can be thought of as desirable and as expressing God's goodness. "What good would it be," he asks, "for an animal were every organ to be an eye with the special excellence of sight?"[17]

7.5 Evil (1a,48–49)

Can we think of a distinction between things that is especially pervasive? One might say that we can since it is obvious that some things are good and that other things are bad. With this thought in mind, Aquinas proceeds in 1a,48 and 49 to consider evil and what accounts for it. In 1a,48, he is chiefly out to argue that evil, though real, lacks *esse* (existence). In 1a,49, he is chiefly concerned to deny that God creates evil.

How is Aquinas understanding the word "evil" in these questions? You will see how by reading 1a,48, though I should note that "evil" for Aquinas means something much broader than what it usually means in contemporary English.

We normally think of "evil" (used both as a noun and as an adjective) in what I would call "extreme" terms. I mean that, when asked to cite instances of evil (noun), we are most likely to give examples of really horrendous things like the Holocaust, and when asked to cite individuals who are evil (adjective), we are most likely to cite moral monsters such as people responsible for genocide. However, the Latin word equivalent to the English word "evil" is *malum*, which signifies badness of any kind.

To put this in concrete terms: While you might not think of a mild headache as being an evil, Aquinas, writing in Latin, would call it a *malum*. Again, while you might think that, say, telling a lie does not make you evil, Aquinas would say that it involves *malum* since it is bad for you to be lying. In accordance with Aquinas's understanding, there is *malum* wherever there is any badness or deficiency. So, he would say, for example, that there is *malum* in a cat that is sick, that there is *malum* when something fails to be what we can reasonably want it to be, like a non-working computer, and that there is *malum* even when people are merely impolite to each other. As we have seen (cf. 1a,4–6), Aquinas takes "good" (*bonum*) to mean "attractive" or "desirable" in general. Corresponding to this understanding of *bonum*, he takes *malum* to mean "not attractive" or "not desirable" in general.

Aquinas clearly takes goodness to be real, since he takes it to be present in something insofar as the thing possesses some form that perfects it somehow, a form by which it has being as flourishing in some way (cf. 1a,5,1).[18] Goodness, for Aquinas, is a matter of actuality (*esse*), but he thinks differently when it comes to badness. To be sure, he thinks, something can be bad only if it exists to start with, and badness is not so opposed to goodness as to wipe it out entirely. This is the argument of 1a,48,2–4. Here Aquinas suggests (a) that badness is found in existing things, (b) that all bad things (all things bad in some way) are real things, and that badness can therefore be thought of as grounded in what has *esse*, and (c) that something bad or defective in some way still has to be something existing and therefore in some way good (cf. 1a,5). In 1a,48,1, however, Aquinas resolutely insists that badness itself is a lack or privation of being.

He means that *malum* is not a distinct substance or a positive or actual form in such a substance, that things we can think of as bad always lack being in some way. The idea here is not that evil or badness is an illusion or hallucination. The idea is that there is badness only insofar as things lack being or goodness appropriate to them.

One can certainly say that there is badness or that badness exists, says Aquinas, since one can truly speak of various existing things as being somehow defective. But, he thinks, to be defective is to lack a form needed for perfection—as to be blind is just to lack the power of sight (a perfection in things like people). More precisely, Aquinas thinks, badness is the absence in something of a form that it needs in order to flourish as the thing it essentially is. He observes:

> Like night from day, you learn about one opposite from the other. So you take good in order to grasp what evil means. Now we have accepted the definition that good is everything that is desirable. Well then, since each real thing tends to its own existence and completion, we have to say that this fulfils the meaning of good in every case. Therefore evil cannot signify a certain existing being, or a real shaping or positive kind of thing. Consequently, we are left to infer that it signifies a certain absence of a good (*quaedam absentia boni*).[19]

The qualification "certain" in the last sentence here is important for Aquinas. He does not think that *any* absence of a good makes for evil. He would not say, for example, that human beings are bad or defective because they cannot fly like birds. They are bad or defective, he thinks, insofar as they lack goods that they need to flourish as human beings.

So Aquinas thinks of evil or badness as a matter of privation, as an absence of being in some sense. For him, something bad or evil lacks a good of some kind and the reality of evil is the lack of such a good. Evil, he thinks, always amounts to something failing to be good or desirable in some way. However, he also thinks it possible to distinguish broadly between two kinds of evil. In 1a,48,5, he refers to these two kinds of evil as *malum poenae* and *malum culpae*.

The phrase *malum poenae* can be literally translated as "evil of penalty" or "evil of punishment," and *malum culpae* can be rendered as "evil of fault." The distinction intended by Aquinas here is basically that which many philosophers have made while distinguishing between "physical evil" and "moral evil," or "evil suffered" and "evil done."

Some evils strike people without anybody positively choosing to bring them about, like natural disasters. Other evils amount to the badness we have as people freely choose to act badly—meaning that they amount to the badness of people *being immoral*, not the badness *brought about* by the immoral actions of bad people.[20] This is the thought that Aquinas has in mind when making his *malum poenae*/*malum culpae* distinction.

Is he thereby suggesting that pain or suffering or injury that we endure due to nobody's decision is a case of *punishment* from God? To some extent he is. He does not think that all instances of physical evil or evil suffered can be matched one to one with particular choices made by people. He does not suppose, for example, that if I catch a cold this week that is because I lied to you last week. Nor does he ever say anything corresponding to the (unhappily now familiar) claim that people with AIDS are enduring punishment inflicted on them by God because of what they have done. As we shall see, however, he thinks that human beings derive from Adam and Eve (as in the Genesis account) and that their naturally occurring woes come as a consequence of what Adam and Eve did when disobeying God. Hence the phrase *malum poenae*. In Aquinas's view, all naturally occurring evils afflicting people should be thought of as coming about because of God's providence and justice. But it is *malum culpae* that worries him more than *malum poenae*. This, he says (1a,48,6), is the greater evil. Why so? Because, Aquinas argues, (a) people become evil because of what they do, not because of woes that afflict them in the course of nature (even if these woes bring about privations), and (b) because moral evil is directly opposed to the goodness that God is while *malum poenae* falls under God's providence and justice and is, in fact, brought about by God.

Brought about by God in what sense, however? This is the question that Aquinas turns to in 1a,49, where he begins by saying that all evil must have an efficient cause since it is, in a sense, anomalous. There must, he thinks, be some created agent cause accounting for something falling short when it comes to what is naturally good for it. He thinks, for example, that some natural causal explanation is called for if my friend starts to develop fits or becomes comatose. Since such a cause must be something that exists or used to exist, and given his views about the connection between being and goodness, Aquinas reasons that evil is always efficiently caused by what is in some way good. He does not mean that evil is a positive substance or form brought into existence by the activity of an agent cause. His point is that evil, considered as privation, is to be indirectly accounted for with respect to what actually exists, as, for example, when something flourishing causes something else to become defective, or as when something fails to act well because something in its makeup is impeding its successful activity.

What, though, of God's causal relation to evil? In 1a,49,2, Aquinas maintains that God cannot be thought to cause evil creatively by making it to have *esse* (existence) since evil is a lack of *esse*. Yet he does not therefore think that God and the "existence" of evil are causally unconnected. He agrees that God cannot causally bring about the evil in evil done, since that is just a failure in action (a failure to act well) leading to no good at all (except, perhaps, incidentally).[21] Yet *malum poenae*, he argues, is indirectly caused by God insofar as God makes and continues to make things that flourish at the expense of other things—that, for example, the evil of an animal being eaten by a lion goes back to God causing the well-being of the lion that is now mauling the animal (an example that Aquinas uses in 1a,48,2, ad.3).

In other words, Aquinas's position in 1a,49,2 is that God causally accounts for *malum poenae* indirectly by accounting for things that act in ways that bring about defects in other things. Since Aquinas does not think of evil as having *esse*, he does not think that God *creates* evil as God creates people or tigers. He does not think that God wills evil *as an end in itself* (so to speak), but he is equally sure that various things fall short in many respects. Some of these things, he suggests, do so as God is bringing about a flourishing in something else, and here, Aquinas thinks, there is evil as God is creatively bringing about good.

Sometimes, however, there is moral evil, that Aquinas does not think of as coming with a concomitant good created by God. The cause of this, says Aquinas, is an agent failing in moral goodness, not God as making moral evil to exist as a substance or accident of any kind. And, from this account, Aquinas (in 1a,49,3) draws the conclusion that, while there is a sovereign good (i.e., God) that directly causes all that is good to exist, there is no comparable cause that brings about everything evil.

So in 1a,44–49, Aquinas has commented on the notion of creation in general and on the distinction in created things between that which is good and that which is bad, and he has ended his discussion of good and evil with an analysis of what he takes to be God's causal role with respect to evil. But Aquinas also thinks that creatures display more than just a distinction between what is good and what is bad. For, he believes, there are things of different kinds that come from God—things that are substantially distinct from one another, and as he moves on from 1a,49, Aquinas proceeds to talk about these while focusing on a distinction between things that are essentially incorporeal and things that are not so. In the next chapter we shall consider what he has to say about certain purely incorporeal things, which he calls angels.

8

Angels and the Days of Creation
(1a,50–74)

QUESTIONS 50–74 OF the *Prima Pars* are today, I suspect, among the least
read sections of the *Summa Theologiae*. The issues they raise and comment on
are just not at, or even close to, the forefront of contemporary theological discussion.[1] And they hardly feature at all in recent philosophical literature. They
also frequently rely on assumptions that many people today (and not just
theologians and philosophers) would find incredible, arcane, or of merely historical interest.

Aquinas, of course, was a thirteenth-century thinker and should not be
thought of as writing in the present intellectual climate. He took for granted a
lot of things that many people now do not, and we should not be surprised to
see such things surfacing as they do in 1a,50–74, where Aquinas first offers a
rather detailed treatise on angels and then proceeds to a fairly lengthy discussion of the account of the six days of creation offered in Genesis 1, which he
assumes should be read as literally true. What Aquinas says in 1a,50–74, if
read with its historical context in mind, is somewhat impressive. 1a,50–64 is
the most systematic discussion of angels coming from any historical period.[2]
And 1a,65–74, which reflects many comparable treatises coming from authors
earlier than Aquinas, can be thought of as every bit as distinguished as any of
them. Still, 1a,50–74 may seem somewhat alien to you.[3]

For this reason I am not going to try to talk you through it in detail. Instead,
I aim to give a brief sense of what Aquinas is saying in this section while
drawing attention to some conclusions found in the text, ones that connect
with things of more contemporary interest in the *Summa Theologiae*.

8.1 Angels (1a,50–64)

Angels are referred to in a number of biblical texts (especially in the New Testament), where they are taken to be intelligent nonhuman beings. Sometimes
they are said to be messengers used by God to convey important truths to
people. Sometimes they are taken to be things that help or hinder people.
Sometimes they are described as servants of God.

The Bible, however, is decidedly vague when it comes to the nature of angels, and Christian declarations of faith that mention angels have followed the Bible in this respect. The Nicene Creed speaks of there being creatures both "visible" and "invisible." The Fourth Lateran Council (1214) talks of God making out of nothing both corporeal and incorporeal things, the "angelic and the terrestrial" (*angelicum videlicet et mundatum*) and goes on to say that some angels are bad ones. The First Vatican Council repeats what Lateran IV says, but the Bible and what many would take to be official ecclesiastical sources of teaching have little to say about what it is to be an angel. In 1a,50–64, however, Aquinas tries to explain what, in his view, we should take angels to be.

Why does he do so? Primarily because he takes belief in the existence of angels for granted and because at this point in the *Summa* he is turning his mind to differences between things in the order created by God. The discussion of angels is there because Aquinas, taking himself to be a teacher of *sacra doctrina*, wants to say something about creatures believed in by the theological tradition he inherits—individual things that are wholly immaterial. The treatment of angels is also there because Aquinas has in mind the distinction between (a) "purely spiritual creatures," (b) creatures that are "only corporeal," and (c) "the creature called the human being, composed of spirit and body."[4] He is beginning to work his way from (a) to (c) as he writes about angels in 1a,50–64.

Is his discussion of angels a philosophical or a theological one? It is theological, since Aquinas obviously takes it to contribute to a biblically grounded account of God and God's doings. Yet it is also philosophical since it tries to explain what it means to say that angels exist, and since it does so by drawing on philosophical arguments. The treatise on angels is an attempt to philosophize about what Aquinas takes to be a matter of revelation, an attempt to understand philosophically what is believed on the basis of faith.[5] From some things he says about angels you might think that Aquinas believes that he can demonstrate that they exist.[6] He does not, though.[7] He thinks that there being angels would contribute to the goodness of a universe that an omnipotent God can create and that angels, if they exist, would fill a gap between things that are both corporeal and partly incorporeal (as Aquinas takes people to be) and God (whom Aquinas takes to be wholly incorporeal and also uncreated). But he does not hold that the existence of angels can be proved philosophically. Drawing on what he takes to be divine revelation, his discussion of them is an attempt to try to say something sensible about them—an attempt that turns out mostly to be one saying what angels *cannot* be (and for this reason resembles much that Aquinas says about God earlier in the *Prima Pars*).

Above all, Aquinas denies that angels are in any way corporeal (1a,50,1) and composed of matter and form (1a,50,2).[8] Angels, for Aquinas, are subsisting immaterial forms—pure intelligences who, because they have understanding, are also able to act freely.

In that case, however, and given that, as Aquinas supposes, there are many angels, what makes one angel distinct from another? As we have seen, Aquinas thinks that distinction of individuals within a species consists in material difference. So what of distinction among angels, if they are entirely non-material? Aquinas suggests (1a,50,4) that each angel amounts to a species in itself, that distinction among angels, rather than being distinction between members of a species, is a matter of distinction between species. "If," he observes, "the angels are not composed of matter and form…it is impossible that there should be more than one angel in a species."9

Are angels immortal? Aquinas thinks that they are (1a,50,5). Angels, he reasons, cannot perish as parts of the material world do. Yes, Aquinas agrees, angels depend for their existence on God and would "fall out of existence if God did not uphold them."10 But, he argues, angels are by nature not subject to what we mean by death, that is, ceasing to exist because of the decay of physical parts or damage to such parts. Aquinas thinks that this conclusion follows from the thesis that angels are entirely non-material or intellectual.

He is, however, prepared to say that angels can be related to bodies or even assume bodies (1a,51,2 and 3). How so? By forming bodies distinct from themselves, through which they can communicate to human beings, as Aquinas takes certain scriptural passages to imply that they do. One might assume that Aquinas would therefore want to suggest that angels occupy space by having dimensions, that they can be thought of as material, but he does not do this. Instead, he argues that angels can exist in distinct places by accounting for certain spatially identifiable things going on (1a,52,1).11 He also maintains (1a,53) that angels can move from place to place—not by being bodies undergoing local motion, but by acting on what is physical and in different places. "An angel," Aquinas observes, "is in contact with a given place simply and solely through its power there; hence its movement from place to place can be nothing but a succession of power-contacts."12

So Aquinas takes angels to be immaterial. They are, in his view, purely intellectual. Their essence is to know and to will.13 And Aquinas takes all of this to mean that angels resemble God much more than anything that is part of the material world does, including people. Yet he is also at pains (1a,54) to insist on the difference between angels and God.

The former, he argues, lack a composition of *suppositum* or individual and nature.14 But they always have a composition of essence (*essentia*) and existence (*esse*), and their substance is not to be identified with their activity.15 For these reasons, Aquinas maintains, angels contain potentiality and differ from

God who is pure act (*actus purus*). Yet Aquinas also wants to say that there is a kind of potentiality not to be found in angels (in addition to the material potentiality they lack). This he takes to be a potentiality to be ascribed to people as individuals who know.

As we shall see when we come to 1a,79, Aquinas holds that we possess an "agent" (*agens*) intellect and a "potential" (*possibilis*) intellect. His view is that, while we *sometimes* actually understand, we are not *always* understanding—that, for example, we can *now* understand what a mouse is while *later* not even think about mice though still be able to do so—a distinction between understanding as actually occurring versus understanding as merely able to occur on the basis of previous understanding. This twofold nature of understanding in people, thinks Aquinas, derives from the fact that we come to understand and to acquire new knowledge as individuals that are parts of the material world, individuals coming to know because they are capable of sensation. However, so Aquinas argues (1a,54,4 and 5 and 1a,58,1), angels are wholly immaterial and therefore do not come to understand as we do. So there is in them no distinction between agent and potential intellect (1a,58,1), though angels can come to know certain things by divine revelation. Aquinas also holds that angels do not come to know by means of sensation. Nor do they come to reflect on what they have previously come to know. Aquinas does not take this conclusion to entail that their act of understanding is just an understanding of themselves. He thinks that they know both themselves (1a,56,2) and what is not angelic—but not by acquiring knowledge over time as we do (1a,55,1–2). According to Aquinas, angels by nature have a knowledge of what is not angelic (even if they are not omniscient), which would seem to mean that in knowing themselves angels also know things other than themselves—including other angels and God (1a,56,2–3).

Given his exalted view of angels, whom he describes in 1a,57,1 as being more like God than are any other creatures, Aquinas goes on to note other ways in which angels differ from people when it comes to knowing. He argues, for example, that, while we often come to understand by engaging in discursive thinking, angels do not. They know in an "all at once" or immediate way, not by reasoning from premises to conclusions (1a,58,3) or by forming judgments by putting together subjects and predicates (1,58,4). Aquinas also argues that angels, being immaterial, are not subject to anger or lust when it comes to their willing (1a,59,4).[16]

As he winds up his discussion of angels, Aquinas turns to what he obviously regards as a difficult topic: the existence of fallen angels—angels who have rejected God and can be thought of as sinful. That such angels exist is something that Aquinas presumes given his reading of the Bible. How, though, can angels reject God if they are as intellectually excellent as Aquinas takes them to be? His answer is that they do so while falling into line with Satan, originally the greatest of all angels. Yet how could Satan sin? Aquinas replies that Satan first sinned by wanting to be the source of his own beatitude and, in this sense, wanting to be like God. He adds that this first sin of Satan results in Satan also envying (and therefore seeking to undermine) those fixed on union with God while embracing the fact that this is God's gift.[17]

In reaching these conclusions, Aquinas is drawing on what he takes himself to find in the Bible and in the writings of patristic authors such as St. Augustine. Aquinas, however, also elaborates on the conclusions in his own way. He argues (1a,62,1), for example, that angels, like people, fall short by nature of what God is and therefore require God's assistance in order to come to the beatific vision (cf. 1a,12). He also argues (1a,63,1) that angels can display *malum culpae* (evil of fault) just because they are things with understanding and will and are not identical with God (in whom, says Aquinas, understanding and will are identical with the unlimited goodness that God is).

To be sure, Aquinas agrees, angels cannot sin by wrongly desiring what leads to bodily satisfactions, for angels are not physical things. But, Aquinas holds, they can sin at the level of non-corporeal or spiritual desire (1a,63,2), and Satan's sin, he maintains, was at this level (1a,63,3). It consisted first of all in wanting to be as God (*esse ut Deus*).

Aquinas accepts that Satan could not have desired absolute equality with God (to be literally divine), since he always knew the unbridgeable gulf between creatures and God. Also, says Aquinas, Satan could not have wanted literally to be God, since that would have meant that he would have wanted to cease to exist as what he naturally was (an angel).[18] But, Aquinas argues, it is not absurd to think that Satan could have wanted the good of his beatific vision to be something due to him by right, or something deriving from what he was by nature and not as a matter of God's free gift.[19]

In effect, Aquinas argues, the first sin of Satan, from which all of his other sins follow, can be thought of as the sin of pride (1a,63,2). Aquinas holds that Satan is not wholly bad since to be created is to be made to be good in some way (1a,63,4; cf. 1a,5,1). Aquinas also thinks that Satan's sin should not be thought of as coming about following a time after his creation (1a,63,6). He holds that Satan's sin followed hard upon his coming into being just as "he brought his free will into action." Yet Aquinas indeed thinks that Satan *fell* into sin and that it is not incoherent to think of him as having done so. He also finds it coherent to think of other angels *falling* into sin together with Satan (1a,63,8). The greatest of angels can, thinks Aquinas, induce inferior angels to side with him (the first sin of angels other than Satan amounting to the same sin of pride as his, so Aquinas thinks).

8.2 The Days of Creation (1a,65–74)

Genesis 1 speaks of God creating various things in six days and resting on the seventh. This biblical account of creation, often referred to as the "Hexameron" from the Greek words for "six" and "day," occupied a number of Christian thinkers in the East and West from New Testament times to the time of Aquinas, and it led to many commentaries, discussions, and sermons. St. Augustine of Hippo effectively wrote three commentaries on Genesis 1. Other notable figures writing at some length on this text include St. Bede (d. 735), Vincent of Beauvais (1149–1265), St. Albert the Great, Peter Lombard, and St. Bonaventure.

How should the six days of creation be understood? What exactly was God doing on this or that day? How should various words used in Genesis 1 be interpreted, words like "light," "firmament," and "water"? Patristic and medieval commentators on the Hexameron tried to deal with questions like these, and often did so while appealing to certain philosophical authors, especially Plato and Aristotle. In 1a,65–74, Aquinas does the same. This text is his commentary on the Hexameron, one that he presents as part of his account of divisions or differences among created things. It frequently draws on patristic writers and on certain medieval scientific views, many of which are false by contemporary scientific standards. It is a text primarily of interest to specialists in medieval cosmology, so I am not now going to talk about it in detail.[20] Instead, I shall simply note that it proceeds (1a,65) by emphasizing that what is not divine is made to be by God and by God *alone*—a thesis not just of interest to those concerned with medieval cosmology.

Why should Aquinas want to highlight this thesis? Has he not already defended it previously? Why go back to it again? Though Aquinas has already said much in support of the claim that only God creates, he highlights this claim in 1a,65 with an eye on certain views not explicitly discussed by him earlier in the *Summa Theologiae.* One of these views is that material things, by contrast to nonmaterial ones, derive from a quasi-divine being. This view was defended by people following the teachings of Mani (ca. 216–276), people who came to be known as Manicheans. The view became very influential in Persia, Egypt, and the Roman Empire. St. Augustine seems to have subscribed to it at one period of his life and describes his conversion from it to Christianity in his *Confessions.*[21]

In 1a,65, Aquinas is out to resist Manicheism and comparable teachings. So in 1a,65,1 he writes: "Certain heretics take the position that these visible things [i.e., material creatures] have not been created by a good God, but by an evil principle." He goes on to say, "Their position, however, is completely untenable."[22] Why untenable? Because, Aquinas says (drawing on much that we have already seen him arguing), only God can make the difference between there being something and nothing. One might wonder whether angels can create things, since they are so like God in Aquinas's view. With a question like this in mind, however, Aquinas argues (1a,65,3 and 4) that angels cannot make things to exist and to be what they are essentially. "Creation," he says, "is the production of anything in the totality of its substance, presupposing nothing that is either uncreated or created by another."[23]

Contemporary theologians often go about their business by focusing on what should be said about people in relation to God, but such theologians are, of course, not writing texts comparable to what Aquinas was producing with the *Summa Theologiae*. With rare exceptions (and the only serious one I can think of is Karl Barth, who is now hardly contemporary), their aim is to do theology without offering a huge treatise that aims to talk about anything and everything that might be thought of in relation to God. Aquinas, by contrast, wrote the *Summa Theologiae* as someone concerned to do exactly this, which is why this work stands out among Christian theological writings. For people with an interest in God and Christianity, it amounts to a kind of theme park through which to roam (whether or not one likes what one finds along the way), and it is a systematic work in that Aquinas moves with a perceptible logic in mind as he proceeds from one topic to another, a logic that I have tried to flag as we go along. As we have seen, Aquinas turns from the topic of God, considered as the one and triune creator of the universe, to an account of what creatures are. Some of them, he thinks, are good or bad (1a,44–49). Some, he believes, are wholly incorporeal, things with intellect and will (1a,50–64). But he also thinks that some of God's creatures are neither divine nor angelic but human. So, having said what he wants to about angels, Aquinas proceeds to talk about what human beings are. This is his concern in 1a,75–102, which I shall turn to next.

Human Beings and Divine Government (1a,75–119)

AQUINAS BRIEFLY INDICATES what he will be doing in the questions that immediately follow 1a,74. "After created spirits and created bodies," he writes, "human beings must be considered, viewed as compounds whose substance is both spiritual and corporeal."[1] As he begins 1a,75, Aquinas is following through on his previously stated promise to consider what various creatures are. In 1a,50–64, Aquinas has already offered an account of creatures that are entirely immaterial (angels) and of creatures that are entirely physical (the universe deriving from God according to Genesis 1). Now he moves on to consider human beings, whom he takes to be both immaterial in some sense *and* material. As he explains what he takes human beings essentially to be, this being the subject matter of 1a,75–89, Aquinas has a lot to say about the human soul, which is a topic he takes to be of special theological significance.[2]

The "Treatise on Human Nature," as 1a,75–89 is sometimes called, is something that many contemporary readers might easily misunderstand because of some assumptions that they may bring to it regarding the word "soul." So, in turning to 1a,75–89 now, my aim is chiefly to try to indicate what might be called its "big picture"—this being the idea (for which Aquinas is much indebted to Aristotle) that human beings are ensouled bodies with certain distinguishable powers.[3] Having tried to indicate how Aquinas thinks of people in 1a,75–89, I shall briefly draw attention to the main points he makes when speaking of people as made in God's image (1a,90–102), and to what he says about God's government of the world (1a,103–119) as he concludes the first part of the *Summa Theologiae*.

9.1 Soul and Body (1a,75–76)

In 1a,75–89 Aquinas argues that human beings are things with souls—things with bodily functions and sensations, things with the ability to move, and things with the ability to understand and choose. In 1a,78,1, he expresses this conclusion by saying that the human soul has five kinds of *potentiae* ("abilities" or "powers" or "capabilities"): vegetative, sensitive, appetitive, locomotive, and intellective.

Something has vegetative powers, he thinks, if it is able to feed or nourish itself, if it is able to grow, and if it is able to reproduce (1a,78,2). Sensitive powers, thinks Aquinas, lead things to be able to latch onto the world by touch, sight, taste, hearing, or smell (1a,78,3). Something with appetite is an individual that is naturally drawn to goods of various kinds that it senses, while something capable of locomotion is just able to move around under its own steam (as it were). As for being intellective, Aquinas takes something with intellect to be an individual that is able to understand the world in which it lives. One might truly think of a cat as having vegetative, sensitive, appetitive, and locomotive abilities, but cats cannot give you a lecture on what cats are; they are not things with understanding expressible linguistically.

One might, of course, say that my cat understands perfectly well that I usually get home from work at 7:00 p.m., since at that time he is always waiting at my door looking expectantly for me. I do not think that Aquinas would reject that observation if "understands" is construed analogically (cf. 1a,13). Here, though, we need to remember that Aquinas takes *scientia* primarily to be a grasp of what created things in the material world essentially are and of why these things are as they are. A cat may look at a king. It may even look at a king expectantly. Does it, however, understand what the word "king" means, or what some particular king is considered as a human being? Aquinas thinks not.

How, though, is Aquinas understanding the word "soul"? The Latin for "soul" is *anima*, and Aquinas thinks that anything *living* has a soul (as we might appreciate given our use of the words "animate" and "inanimate"). People sometimes speak of souls as ethereal incorporeal entities distinct from anything bodily, and they sometimes say that only human beings have souls. Such people will often go on to speak of human souls as being able to escape their existence as attached to human bodies or as being able to come to inhabit different human bodies. In order to understand Aquinas on soul, however, it is important to realize that he does not think in quite these terms.

He does not, for a start, think that only human beings have souls. He believes that plants and nonhuman animals also have souls. That is because of the connection he makes between the words "soul" and "living." According to his philosophical vocabulary (derived in great part from Aristotle, though also owing much to St. Augustine), anything alive has a soul just because it is alive. And how does Aquinas distinguish between what is alive and what is not alive? He thinks that something alive is something able to move or operate of its own accord and not just as pushed around by something else.

My desk is not alive. It moves only if I drag it or push it. A stone is not alive. It moves only if something acts on it so as to change its position. But what about my cat? He moves around a lot and employs various powers while doing so.

He is, Aquinas would say, something with life, something animate and, therefore, something with a soul. When trying to understand Aquinas on soul, you need to bear in mind that his use of the word "soul" is one that, from beginning to end, is meant to flag a distinction between things such as desks and cats—the distinction being one between "not being alive" and "being alive." So Aquinas will happily speak not only of you and I as having souls, but of my cat and my house plants as having souls.

When it comes to the souls of human beings, Aquinas is concerned with the question "What makes human beings different from other living things?" That is really the main question Aquinas seeks to answer in 1a,75–89. His primary aim is to explain *what it is to be alive* as a human being, as opposed to *what it is to be alive* as, say, a cat or a cabbage. As I have said, Aquinas distinguishes between the vegetative, sensitive, appetitive, locomotive, and intellective powers of living things. In 1a,75–89, he explains what can be said about human beings with these distinctions in mind.

Aquinas believes that human beings have all of the powers just noted. People, he thinks, are alive precisely because they have them. So they have souls. You should recognize, however, that Aquinas does not think of human souls as distinct from human beings considered as parts of the material world. Some people do think of human souls in this way. On their account my soul is something that exists quite independently of my body—is a thing or substance to be distinguished from what my body is in something like the way in which the driver of a car is to be distinguished from the car. One driver plus one car makes two individuals, you might say.[4] And, so it has been suggested, my soul and my body are two distinct things. This point has sometimes been made by saying that you and I are souls or spirits attached to a body. Aquinas, though, does not think of human souls (or any souls) in this way.

According to him, anything alive has a soul, but the word "has" here is not to be understood as signifying possession—as in "I have a cat." It is to be construed somewhat along the lines of "has" as in "John has a cheerful disposition" or "Mary has keen eyesight." John's cheerful disposition and Mary's keen eyesight are not objects that either of them possess in the way that they can possess a cat. To speak of John's cheerful disposition is to draw attention to what kind of thing John is. And to speak of Mary as having keen eyesight is to do the same; it is to speak of her as something that sees very well. When saying that all living things have souls, Aquinas means that they are alive (animate), and are to be thought of differently from nonliving things.

As we have seen, Aquinas distinguishes between a living and a nonliving thing by saying that a living thing moves of itself. So he thinks that to speak of people as having souls is primarily to say that they move of their own accord.

His idea is that to have a human soul is to be a living and material thing of a certain kind. But, says Aquinas, living things vary largely because of what they are and because of the different powers that they have on account of what they are. He thinks, for example, that the soul of a plant differs from the soul of a dog, since plants lack sensation, which dogs have. And he thinks that the soul of a human being differs from the soul of a dog, since people act with understanding rather than merely on the basis of sensation and instinct like dogs. When it comes to soul, Aquinas recognizes a kind of hierarchy in terms of which some things can be thought of as being more in control of themselves than other things and as, so to speak, being more alive than other things. He argues that human beings are things with souls that enable them to live in ways that other things in the world cannot, as things having not just the ability to feed and move around and sense, but as things also able to understand.

Aquinas draws a sharp distinction between sensation and understanding. He takes sensation to occur as a felt physical change is brought about in the relevant bodily organs of a sensing thing—as when we come to feel pain because we have cut ourselves. Sensation, for Aquinas, is something material: a perceived change in a body (though see what I say below concerning 1a,78,3). When it comes to understanding, however, Aquinas thinks we are dealing with something that is not a bodily process or a change in a body. He certainly believes that you and I are bodily things that understand, but he denies that understanding itself is something material or that its occurrence essentially involves people undergoing a physical change in a bodily organ. In this connection we need to note a distinction Aquinas draws between two ways of being.

Consider the case of my cat Sweetie. What is he? Aquinas would say that Sweetie is a cat and that his being a cat is what his existence amounts to. He would say that for Sweetie to exist is just for him to be a cat, to have the substantial form of cat (cf. chapter 4 above). And what is it for Sweetie to exist as such? Aquinas would say that it is for him actually to be a living cat (an obvious conclusion, you might think).

Yet what if I come to understand what Sweetie is? Then, says Aquinas, I must have Sweetie's substantial form *in my mind*. Sweetie's substantial form is something that Sweetie (a particular physical individual) has just by being a cat, but Aquinas also holds that I can have that form in me insofar as I understand what Sweetie is essentially.

In effect, Aquinas thinks that understanding what something is involves having the form of something without actually being what the thing whose nature one understands is. As Herbert McCabe observes: "This doctrine will be totally misunderstood if it is not recognized to be *obvious*. It is not a description of a process by which we understand, if there is any such process. It is a platitude; it says 'What I have in mind when I know the nature of a cow is the nature of a cow and nothing else.'"[5]

In Aquinas's view, understanding what a cow is amounts to having what it takes for something to be a cow *in mind*, having the nature of a cow "intentionally," as he puts it. So Aquinas thinks that human beings have souls as individuals able to "take in" the natures or forms of other things. Since we obviously cannot take these natures in as naturally possessing them (since, for example, I cannot literally become a cow), Aquinas concludes that human understanding of forms is not a physical process or a physical object. Indeed, on his account form is always to be distinguished from matter.[6] A dandelion, say, is obviously something material—or, as Aquinas would say, it is something in the world able to undergo substantial change. But Aquinas does not think that the form of dandelion is a material thing (even though he does not agree with the view that the forms of material things exist as individuals in some spiritual realm). And this form/matter distinction is important for Aquinas as he proceeds to talk about human souls, since he thinks that the human soul is the form of the human body (1a,76,1).

He means that human beings are what they are because of their substantial form, which he takes to be what makes people to be alive as the things that they essentially are. This principle of life for people is what Aquinas calls their *souls*. He does not mean that human bodies are somehow connected to independently existing substances called "souls." He means that human beings, which he takes to be things in the physical world able to be examined and classified with respect to other comparable things, are things with a substantial form, which enables them to understand, and so does not leave them being totally material (as, say, the form of a dandelion does to a dandelion).

As we have seen, Aquinas thinks that form can exist while being purely immaterial. He takes God to be form without matter, as he takes angels to be. He does not, though, want to say that people are *wholly* immaterial like angels. He thinks that people are evidently things with bodies—things that are generated and corrupted, things that can be pushed, killed, kicked, and kissed (another unsurprising conclusion).

So he thinks that people are essentially material, but he does not take them to be purely material, since he thinks that they are able to grasp the forms of material things immaterially, and therefore he thinks that what makes them to be what they are and able to do what they do, their substantial form, cannot be wholly material. People, in Aquinas's view, straddle the realm between cats and angels. Like cats, they are essentially material, but, like angels, they are things that operate at a non-material level because they have understanding, because their substantial form, what makes them what they are, includes being able to function immaterially.

This view of Aquinas will seem nonsensical to someone who thinks that people are nothing but physical. Aquinas, however, holds that a purely physical account of what people are is just unbelievable given that people, when understanding, can receive the forms of intelligible things. For him, matter is always the big obstacle when it comes to understanding. A physical thing, he thinks, is always a physical thing and is confined by what it is physically. It is, and is only, a particular material individual. But, thinks Aquinas, intelligibility is not something physical and neither is understanding. In his view, material things come to be intelligible as they are, so to speak, liberated from their individual material confinements so as to become universal objects of understanding. According to Aquinas, a stone is an individual material thing and nothing else unless someone understands what a stone is, what it takes for a stone to exist—which is universal in the sense that it is true of all stones whatsoever. He does not, of course, mean that a stone undergoes a change when someone comes to understand what it is. He means that there can be an understanding of stones that amounts to the occurrence in someone of what a stone is essentially—this, for him, not being identical with the existence of any material object (or series of material events) precisely because it is true of many material objects.

So Aquinas takes human beings to be somehow both material and immaterial. Yet he also holds that human souls are distinct and immaterial, capable of existing on their own apart from human bodies. He does this because he takes my soul to be a substantial form that exists in its own right and as what we might loosely call a "thing."

Aquinas does not generally think that substantial forms exist as things. He typically thinks of things as what has a substantial form. He typically holds that, for example, Fred's cat and my cat are what they are essentially because they share the same form, because they are both cats. When speaking along these lines he does not mean that what cats are essentially is some object that is divided up among all cats that come to exist. He means that cats share a nature (not "share" as in "share a bed," but "share" as in "share a trait or feature"). According to Aquinas, you and I share our human nature because we are both human beings and because the "what it is to be human" about us is not something that distinguishes us from one another in the way that the sound of my voice distinguishes me from you and the sound of your voice distinguishes you from me. In general, thinks Aquinas, substantial forms are what individuals have as indistinguishable from other members of the same species having the same substantial form.

Could it be that a substantial form exists just in its own right and not as something that can be attributed to an individual? With an eye on human beings, Aquinas argues that it could. Indeed, he says, the human soul *is* an immaterial subsisting substantial form. This is the argument of 1a,75,2. Here Aquinas observes: "The principle of understanding which is called mind or intellect has its own activity in which body takes no intrinsic part. But nothing can act of itself unless it subsists in its own right. For only what actually exists acts."[7]

Aquinas agrees that since a human soul is the form of a human body, it does not exist "in the full integrity of its nature" when considered as existing apart from a human body. But it is still, he thinks, an existing thing, since it is that by which people understand. Aquinas does not mean that the human soul is a substance distinct from a human organism. His position is that the whole human being has one soul that cannot be thought to be a physical object (though he is quite clear that people are physical objects).

The idea here is that all that makes a human being to be a living thing derives from the existence of the human soul, which can be thought of as one thing, albeit not one *physical* thing. For Aquinas, being alive as a human being involves being ensouled in a way unique to human beings. To be alive as a human being, he thinks, is to be something essentially material, but it is also to be alive as understanding or as capable of understanding, which he takes to be immaterial. Aquinas thinks that an account of soul in humans has to involve reference to what is bodily (to being essentially mammalian, for example), but that the human soul is not itself a physical thing. The human soul is that by which some physical things (people) have their existence and live as what they essentially are. The human soul as something able to sense but also able to understand. Considered as such, the human soul is the really existing but immaterial principle of the life of a human being: really existing, since it can be distinguished from a particular human body, and immaterial since one of the activities it enables humans to carry out is not carried out with a bodily organ.

When it comes to the human soul, Aquinas is arguing, we are dealing with form (as with angels), but with form that is configuring or informing something material. This is the main point made in 1a,75,7 in which Aquinas denies that the human soul is an angel. It is natural, says Aquinas, for the human soul to configure a human body (to animate what is physical), but it does not, he thinks, follow that the human soul is something physical. It is, in his view, more natural to think of the soul as something able to exist in some sense apart from a human body.

Indeed, says Aquinas, it has to do so because body and soul are not just one thing even though the human soul is incomplete when the body it animates perishes. When I die, thinks Aquinas, it does not follow that my soul dies.

Indeed, so he reasons, though my soul would cease to exist if God ceased to maintain it in being (cf. 1a,75,6 ad.2), the thought of my soul dying makes no sense. Aquinas takes my soul to be a form and since perishing is always a case of something losing a substantial form, not of a substantial form perishing as such.

This is the argument of 1a,76,6. Aquinas accepts that the soul of someone who dies does not exist as a substance in its own right, for what it is in its own right is the form of a human substance. Still, he thinks, the souls of the dead are subsisting things in the sense of being things that can exist on their own.

In short, Aquinas's treatment of the human soul in 1a,75–83 resolutely steers a middle course between the extremes of concluding (a) that people are simply and wholly material and (b) that people are non-corporeal substances related to bodies as substances in their own right.

That people are material things seems obvious to Aquinas (as it might seem to us), but it also seems to him that they are not wholly material. That by which human beings are the living things that they are (their soul) exists in and animates them at all levels of their being—from their being able to feed, walk, and sense to their being able to acquire knowledge or understanding, which, for Aquinas, are not physical processes. Aquinas is aware that some of his predecessors and contemporaries argue that people have several souls, one that informs them at a vegetative level, one that informs them at a sensory level, and one that informs them at an intellectual level. Aquinas is convinced, however, that people are individual things (even though they have parts) that must therefore live as the individuals that they are by virtue of a single principle of life, a single substantial form. So he argues in 1a,76,3 and 4 that human beings have a single substantial form or soul. Since he takes this soul to be something non-material and existing in its own right, he thinks of the human soul as able to survive the death of the body it informs (cf. 1a,76,6).[8]

Notice, though, that Aquinas does not think that our souls are us once we have died. He thinks that the human soul cannot perish, since it is a subsisting substantial form, but he also holds that a human soul surviving the death of a human being is not that human person. He believes that the separated soul is what remains of a human person it once informed, that it is the surviving part of what is properly a matter-form composite (cf. 1a,76,1).

He has to think this given his view that a human being is essentially something composed of matter and form. In 1a,75, he asks whether the soul of a human being is that human being. His answer is that it is not, in that Fred's soul is not Fred but something that informs the body we identify as Fred. For Aquinas, Fred is something material, so his immaterial soul is not Fred. Or, as Aquinas himself writes in 1a,75,4, "Man is no mere soul, but a compound (*compositum*) of soul and body."⁹ In the same article he observes that a human soul is no more a human person than is a human hand or foot.¹⁰ For this reason, Aquinas takes the soul of someone who has died to be ailing until it animates a human body again. "It belongs to the very essence of soul," he writes, "to be united to a body.... The human soul, remaining in its own existence after separation from the body, has a natural aptitude and a natural tendency to union with body" (1a,76,1, ad.6).¹¹

9.2 Human Abilities (1a,77–79)

In Aquinas's view, we should distinguish between a human soul and the powers or abilities that human beings have as ensouled. According to him, we (unlike God) are not our own life and activity. What we are differs really from what we are able to do and what we actually do (1a,77,1).

So what powers or abilities does Aquinas take us to have? Although he takes all of our abilities to depend on the fact that we have souls that enable us to understand, Aquinas thinks of people as having powers or abilities at both a bodily and an intellectual level. He says that we can move around, reproduce, feed ourselves, grow, and sense.¹² He also says that we can understand, reason, and act accordingly.¹³

Some "powers of the soul" depend on our being bodily and come into effect because of bodily change. Other powers do not (77,2). These powers are connected in that the more perfect ones depend on the less perfect ones (1a,77,4–7). Here Aquinas is thinking that our exercising intellectual powers, which Aquinas ranks highly, depends on our exercising powers of nutrition and sensation, which he ranks less highly, although he takes them to be essential to human existence. As we have seen, Aquinas thinks that the human soul can survive the destruction of the human body, so he thinks that not all the powers of the human soul in its natural state remain in the souls of people once they have died (1a,77,8). Understanding and will, he argues, are not bodily processes and can therefore be had by the human soul apart from a body (1a,78,1). Not so, however, when it comes to sensation and nutrition, which are essentially bodily processes (1a,78,2–4).

Some readers of Aquinas have taken him to suppose that human sensing, though dependent on bodily change, is a non-bodily affair. That is because he speaks of sensation occurring as the forms of material things come to be in us without being as they are in the things that we sense. I might sense a dog by sight or hearing or smell or touch—these amounting to bodily changes in me. So, thinks Aquinas, a dog can enter into my animate life at a sensory level because of what it is and because of its effect on my senses. He also thinks that my sensing a dog does not mean my having either the substantial or accidental forms that a dog has considered as a dog. Yet Aquinas does not seem to think of sensation as an instance of form without matter. In 1a,78,3, he speaks of sensation as involving a "spiritual" change, but he does not construe such change as the coming about of what is not material. Rather, he thinks that, in sensation, a material form can come to exist in a different material way—in bodily organs by which we sense.[14] In 1a,78,4, Aquinas talks about what he calls "interior senses." You might find this notion an odd one since you might naturally think that we sense what is outside us, not what is inside us, that our senses have to do with things other than ourselves insofar as we see, hear, taste, smell, or touch them. As well as holding that people have these five "exterior" senses, however, Aquinas believes that we have "interior" senses, of which he acknowledges five: the *sensus communis* (common sense), the *phantasia* (phantasy), the *imaginatio* (imagination), the *sensus aestimativus* (estimative sense), and sense *memoria* (memory).

In making these distinctions, Aquinas is holding that, as well as sensing objects that impinge on them physically in the world by the external senses, people can (1) co-ordinate the sensory impact coming to them from external things, (2) form impressions of what impacts on them physically and retain what it was like to sense these things, (3) evaluate the significance for them physically of what impacts their exterior senses, and (4) retain what it was like to have such significant sensory experiences. These "interior senses" are things that Aquinas takes to be different from the "exterior" ones, but he thinks that they go to make up what we are as sensing human beings.

So, he argues, for example, that as well as sensing things as they impinge on us physically, we must have some ability to relate to them—some capacity to coordinate, evaluate, and remember them in their impact on us. For Aquinas, "interior senses" are what allow us to interpret the input provided by our exterior bodily senses and to eventually find meaning in it.[15]

As we have seen, though, Aquinas takes people to exist as ensouled not only at a sensory level. He thinks of them as having understanding, an idea that he returns to in 1a,79, in which he talks about what he calls our "intellectual powers." In most of this question Aquinas teases out explicitly what he takes to be implied by what he has previously said about human beings. So, for example, he says that understanding is a power of the human soul, not its essence (1a,79,1), and that human understanding (unlike that of God and angels) arises as people are acted on by their physical environment (1a,79,2). In 1a,79,3, Aquinas also says that people have an "agent intellect" (*intellectus agens*).

What does he mean by this phrase? In speaking of us having an agent intellect, Aquinas is thinking that we have an active power by which we are able to proceed from sense experience to an interpretation of the world as meaningful, an interpretation that allows us to recognize what things are and to form true judgments accordingly. Unlike philosophers such as Plato, Aquinas denies that people are born with an innate understanding of forms. In Aquinas's view, we arrive in the world without any knowledge at all, and since he thinks of us as essentially material beings, he concludes that all our knowledge arises as a result of our encounter with the world at a sensory level. However, he also thinks that sensory experience is of material things that, considered only as objects extended in space, are not intelligible.

As I noted in chapter 4, for Aquinas it is form, not matter, that is intelligible. So, he argues, our minds must be able to deal with sensory input so as to form concepts. This ability of our minds is what Aquinas is referring to when speaking of the agent intellect. For him, this can be compared to a flashlight that illumines what we might bump into in the dark.

Our agent intellect, thinks Aquinas, is what allows us, on the basis of our sensory experience, to form concepts or language.[16] His idea (expressed in linguistic terms) is that our agent intellect is a power we possess by which we make language, by which, in a sense, we create it. Meanings, he thinks, are not actually there in objects we encounter at the sensory level (not there as, say, their physical parts are). Before people existed there were dinosaurs with heads and tails, and Aquinas, though knowing nothing about dinosaurs, would have agreed that they were real things with parts. He would not, however, have said that dinosaurs had parts that included a head and a tail *and a meaning*. He would have said that a dinosaur was something with parts and that it was not actually intelligible to anything in its environment since nothing was around to understand it as we can understand things in our environment. He would have added, though, that we can understand things in our environment on the basis of our sensory acquaintance with them.

Why? Because, Aquinas says, our minds can get to work on them and turn what is only potentially intelligible in them into actual understanding, into actual meanings. This is what he is saying when he speaks in 1a,79,3 of the agent intellect. This, he thinks, is an agent in that it accounts for actual understanding occurring.[17] He does not mean that my agent intellect is something in me working as, say, my heart does. He means that I am something with an ability to make things in the material world actually understood, that (unlike stones or cats) I am able to think, able to proceed from sensation to reflection and argument. Aquinas also holds that I can retain ideas and conclusions once I have arrived at them. For, he says, as well as having an agent intellect we also have a "possible" or "receptive" intellect (*intellectus possibilis*)—effectively, the ability to retain and draw on what we have learned (1a,79,6 and 7).[18]

9.3 Reason and Will (1a,79–83)

In his Treatise on Human Nature, Aquinas, as we have now seen, pays a lot of attention to the notion of understanding, but he does not want to suggest that people are just intellectual beings able to know. He thinks of them as things that employ understanding in order *to act*.

Hence the distinction he draws in 1a,79,11 between "speculative intellect" (*intellectus speculativus*) and "practical intellect" (*intellectus practicus*). As human beings, he thinks, we can to some extent come to know what is what in the world, which is the achievement of speculative intellect, but we can also draw on this knowledge when acting, and thereby display practical intellect, intellect as employed when deciding what to do in specific contexts.

This theoretical/practical distinction is of great importance to Aquinas. He draws on it frequently. For now, however, the main point to note about it is that it is acknowledged by him in 1a,79,11, in which he also claims that speculative and practical intellect should not be thought of as two distinct powers of the mind but as one power in that, when knowing and acting on the basis of knowledge, people are acting as individual knowers and agents. "The speculative intellect," he says, "knows but does not relate what it knows to action. It merely considers the truth. But we speak of the intellect as practical when it orders what it knows to action."[19]

At this point Aquinas has begun to embark on an account of people as *behaving* as well as *knowing*—a topic that will seriously engage him in one way or other right up to the end of the *Secunda Pars*. That is why I am now flagging its first serious emergence in 1a,79,11. The distinction is a natural one to note since there is obviously a difference between knowing that such and such is the case and proceeding to act on the basis of such knowledge.[20] What one might not find so natural is the distinction that Aquinas draws between *synderesis* and *conscientia* in 1a,79,12 and 13.[21] He regards these as things to mention as we consider ourselves as doers and not just knowers, but the difference between them that he wants to note needs some explaining.

There is no English word that corresponds to Aquinas's *synderesis*.[22] I am, therefore, going to leave the word untranslated. Aquinas takes *synderesis* to be a natural tendency or disposition we have that inclines us to what is good, an infallible grasp of right and wrong at a basic level, of fundamental moral principles that are per se *nota quoad nos* ("self-evident to us").[23] It is, he says, a *habitus* ("tendency" or "disposition"), not a power.[24] When deciding what to do, he holds, we automatically move toward what we take to be good and we naturally recognize that evil should be shunned, or that we should live according to reason. This natural way of thinking is what he calls *synderesis*.

Our speculative intellect, says Aquinas, instinctively adheres to certain intellectual principles when it gets to work on the basis of our sensory experience—such principles as that a whole is greater than its parts or that contradictory statements cannot both be true at the same time and in the same respect. In a similar way, Aquinas argues, our practical intellect naturally adheres to what we take to be good. Effectively, it tells us to seek what is good and avoid what is evil as an inbuilt instinct to gravitate to what is good.[25] This instinctive way of thinking with a view to action is what Aquinas calls *synderesis*.

Medieval authors sometimes take *synderesis* and *conscientia* to be equivalent, and, unlike *synderesis*, the word *conscientia* has an obvious English equivalent in the word "conscience." Albeit with some qualification, Aquinas does not regard *synderesis* and *conscientia* as synonyms. In 1a,79,13, he accepts that what he thinks of as *conscientia* springs from *synderesis* in that it relies on it or draws on it, but he takes *conscientia* to be distinguishable from *synderesis* since he thinks that *conscientia* is a matter of acting on the basis of *synderesis*. We cannot, thinks Aquinas, set aside our natural awareness of what is good, but we can, he thinks, act contrary to conscience.

"Conscience," of course, is something of a weasel word since people have understood it to mean quite different things. Some have taken it to be an intuitive ability to recognize the difference between good and bad in concrete situations. This understanding has led to talk about acting or not acting according to conscience and to the suggestion that one should always "follow" one's conscience, considered as a moral guide almost talking to one, or even as the "voice of God." A classic philosophical text to note in this connection comes in the *Sermons* (1726) of Joseph Butler (1692–1752). He writes:

> There is a superior principle of reflection or conscience in everyone, which distinguishes between the internal principle of our heart, as well as our external actions: which passes judgment upon ourselves and them; pronounces determinately some actions to be in themselves just, right, good; other to be in themselves evil, wrong, unjust.[26]

This quotation (taken by itself and without reference to other things that Butler says) seems to suggest that by virtue of conscience we can always know, without argument, what it is good to do in particular situations and how right differs from wrong when it comes to them. Aquinas, though, does not think of conscience (*conscientia*) in this way.

He takes conscience to be a potentially fallible process of reasoning concerning the goodness and badness of particular actions. When evaluating a particular action, one starts, thinks Aquinas, with a general moral principle grasped by virtue of *synderesis*, and one then applies the principle to the action one is evaluating. The pattern of reasoning that Aquinas has in mind has this form: (1) To φ is good/bad; (2) this action is a case of φ-ing; (3) so I should/ should not do this action. In other words, *conscientia*, for Aquinas, is a matter of applying general principles to cases to hand and making an *inference*. So in 1a,79,13, Aquinas denies that conscience is a power and prefers to describe it as an act (*actus*) since it is a matter of "applying knowledge to something."[27] Frequently, thinks Aquinas, conscience is concerned with what we are doing or are about to do (or not doing or are about not to do). Yet he also argues that it can sometimes be concerned with what we have done or not done in the past.

Yet do we really ever act at all? If you fling a chair from a tall building it will fall to the ground and break into pieces. Is it, however, *acting* as it goes through the business of falling and breaking up? In one obvious sense it is not, since it is not *choosing* its fall and its decomposition; it is going through processes over which it has no control, and some philosophers have suggested that you and I are no more in control of ourselves than is the chair in my example. They have claimed that our history is determined and that there is no such thing as human choosing. Yet Aquinas rejects this conclusion. He argues that people have "will" (*voluntas*) and "freedom of choice" (*liberum arbitrium*)— these being his focus in 1a,82 and 83.

Immediately prior to1a,82, however, Aquinas considers what he calls "appetite" (*appetitus*) and "sensuality" (*sensualitas*). We have appetite, he argues, since we are able to assimilate the forms of things outside ourselves and are drawn to what we find good in things (1a,80,1). He thinks we can think of appetite on our part as twofold: sensitive appetite that arises as we sense things, and intellectual appetite that arises as we understand them (1a,80,2). Aquinas regards sensuality as attraction that arises at the sensory level as a matter of sense appetite, but, he notes, our senses can lead us to revolt against what we sense as well as to pursue it. So, he says, sense appetite can amount to a leaning to some objects we sense and a backing away from others. It can also lead to a complicated interaction of leaning to and avoiding as, for example, when we tolerate what we recoil from at a sensory level because of what we seek at another level.[28] Sensory desire can sometimes be controlled by reason, thinks Aquinas.

This notion of reason as playing a role when it comes to what we are drawn to at the sensory and intellectual level is what leads Aquinas to his discussion of will (*voluntas*) in 1a,82. He takes willing to be a rational power, a matter of being drawn to a good as *understood*. He also views it as incompatible with coercion, since he takes coercion to involve forces acting on us to prevent us from moving toward what we want as understood, which is what he takes us to be doing when acting by will, when acting voluntarily. When we act voluntarily, thinks Aquinas, we are, so to speak, "doing our own thing"—something that he takes to be different from acting when being forced to act (1a,82,1). Yet Aquinas also recognizes that we can be subject to necessity of a kind when acting voluntarily. I might want to get from New York to Madrid in less than twenty-four hours. As we know, I can only achieve my goal by taking a plane. In this sense, thinks Aquinas, voluntary action can be constrained by factors beyond one's control, and, he adds, one cannot but will what one's absolute good is if and to the extent that one is aware of what that amounts to (1a,82,1).

Do we inevitably will in the way that we do? Aquinas thinks not (1a,82,2). His view is that, just as we do not have to assent intellectually to propositions that are not necessarily true, we do not have to will what we do not perceive to be necessary for our ultimate or complete happiness. It would surely be reasonable to think that a human being can be happy without, say, watching a particular well-rated movie, and Aquinas argues that there are plenty of good things that one does not have to will. He thinks that to have the beatific vision would leave one unable not to want God or be drawn to God. Failing such certain knowledge of what final happiness amounts to, however, we do not have to will as we do, so Aquinas thinks. In this sense, willing (acting voluntarily) is subject to our understanding what is good for us (the main point of 1a,82,3).

Aquinas clearly thinks that when we act voluntarily, there is a kind of interweaving of intellect and will. Generally speaking, he holds that we are drawn to what we take to be good as we think about things, but he also thinks that how we think about things can be affected by our willing or desiring. Suppose that I am head over heels in love with someone. This fact might well affect my thinking in that it may lead me to ignore certain goods to which I should pay attention. In light of similar facts, Aquinas concludes that our willing can influence our understanding (1a,82,4). He means that what we know can sometimes depend on what we are willing to pay attention to.

Does this conclusion entail that we have something called "free will"? In one sense, Aquinas does not take it to do so, since he does not believe in free will. In saying this I mean that he does not subscribe to the notion that just to be willing is to have free will.

As I have noted, for us to have *voluntas* is, for Aquinas, for us to be "doing our own thing," and, since he takes acting voluntarily to be incompatible with being coerced, he thinks that there is freedom of a sort involved as long as we act voluntarily. But now consider an instance of human voluntary behavior such as brushing one's teeth because one wants to, and ask yourself how many actions are involved.

You might say that there is only one action that I perform when I brush my teeth. You may say that I *just brush my teeth*. But, of course, one goes through many distinct motions when brushing one's teeth. So my cleaning my teeth might also be described as me choosing to perform a great number of actions as I first move the toothbrush *this* way and then move it *that* way.

We can therefore distinguish between doing something voluntarily (e.g., brushing our teeth) and making discrete choices or decisions when it comes to what we do. When we brush our teeth we do not, in fact, go through a series of discrete choices or decisions. We *just brush our teeth*. But we sometimes do make particular or discrete choices when acting voluntarily, and it is this fact that Aquinas is concerned with as he turns in 1a,83 to discuss what he calls *liberum arbitrium* ("freedom of choice") as belonging to people who act voluntarily. He therefore distinguishes between *voluntas* (voluntary behavior) and *liberum arbitrium* (freedom of choice). He does not have a separate notion of "free will" even though he thinks that all voluntary behavior is uncoerced.

In 1a,83,1,therefore, he asks whether we have *liberum arbitrium*, having already argued that we can act voluntarily, and his answer is yes. As well as acting voluntarily without making a series of particular choices, we can, says Aquinas, sometimes freely decide to do something quite particular—such as hugging someone or paying an invoice.

He notes that stones and the like act simply as their nature and circumstances dictate and that some animals act just by instinct. But, he adds, people can sometimes act with an intelligent eye on what is good and bad and make decisions accordingly. Aquinas thinks that we have *liberum arbitrium* since unlike, say, stones and sheep we can engage in practical reasoning by thinking about what to do in particular circumstances with an eye on various possible outcomes. As he observes: "In contingent matters reason can go either way.... Now particular actions are contingent. And so in regard to particular acts reason's judgement is open to various possibilities, not fixed to one. It is because people are rational that such decisions have to be free."[29] Aquinas notes a number of arguments in defense of the claim that we lack *liberum arbitrium*, some of them based on biblical texts and some of them philosophical, but he resists them while concentrating on what it means to deliberate or reflect on what to do. His reasoning is: (1) We cannot but go through certain bits of behavior because of our bodily natures (for example, we cannot but vomit having swallowed certain bad foods); (2) We cannot but think certain thoughts on some occasions (e.g., we cannot but think that a proposition cannot be simultaneously true and false in the same respect); (3) We are not so forced when it comes to deliberating about what to do on some occasions, because we can sometimes recognize the virtue or viability of different conclusions when it comes to the desirability of an action we are thinking about. So Aquinas concludes that people have *liberum arbitrium*, which in 1a,81,4 he refers to as *vis electiva* ("power of choice") based on desire.[30]

9.4 Human Understanding in This Life and the Next (1a,84–89)

In 1a,84–89, Aquinas expands on the account he has been presenting in 1a,74–83. From what I have already said in this chapter, and from things that I have drawn attention to in previous ones (especially chapter 5), you should be able to see how this is so and should have a sense of the moves that Aquinas is making at this point in the *Summa Theologiae*. Yet some new points made in these questions need to be highlighted, and I am now going to try to meet this need by saying something about each of the questions Aquinas answers in this section of the *Prima Pars*.

> 1. In 1a,84, Aquinas asks how human beings in the present life know material things. Unwilling to accept either that everything in the world is material or that human knowledge depends on access to a world of separately existing immaterial forms or ideas, Aquinas argues that we know things in the world insofar as they impinge on our senses. As we have seen, Aquinas thinks that the world contains material things displaying substantial and accidental forms. In 1a,84, he reiterates this view and the idea of forms coming to be in us immaterially as knowers.

To say that there is an immaterial reception of forms might sound like claiming that to know what something in the world is amounts to being descriptively like the thing in question, but it should be clear from 1a,84,2 and from what I have previously noted that Aquinas's point is not this one. As we have seen, he thinks that to know what a particular cow is amounts to having the intelligibility (or "whatness") of the cow without actually being a cow. In this sense, Aquinas argues, our knowing what something in the world is amounts to us having in ourselves an immaterial likeness of what is known.

As Aquinas develops this point he compares our minds at birth to a collection of pages on which nothing is yet written. Unless we are damaged in some way, we cannot, he thinks, fail to recognize certain necessary truths (such as that a whole is greater than a part), yet knowledge of material things is not innate or worked into our mental "hardware" from the outset. It emerges in us, Aquinas thinks, as we encounter the world at the sensory level and proceed from such encounters to an understanding of things in the world. Notice that in developing this point, Aquinas again distinguishes between sensation and understanding. A cat may sit on my lap and thereby produce sensations (considered as bodily changes) in me. But, we may think, there is a difference between sensing a cat and understanding what it is, and Aquinas wants to flag this difference.

For Aquinas, as emerges clearly in 1a,84,6, knowledge in us arises from sensation but is nevertheless different from it. In his view, human beings have a faculty that allows them to draw on their sense impressions so as to arrive at judgments concerning what exists in the world. In this sense, human knowledge depends on sensory "images" and is impeded if our senses malfunction in some way. Or as Aquinas writes: "If it is actually to understand its proper object, then the intellect has to turn to sense images in order to look at the universal natures existing in particular things."[31]

> 2. In 1a,85, Aquinas aims to fill in some details when it comes to this approach to human understanding, which he thinks of as different from angelic and divine understanding. To begin with, he argues that human understanding arises by "abstracting" a "species" (*species*) from a "sense image" (*phantasma*).

By *species* Aquinas means what he elsewhere refers to as "form." By *phantasma* he means the impressions of sensible things that exist in us physically as we sense them (sensation as occurring). To a certain extent, he thinks, sensation leaves us with a kind of knowing, since it puts us in touch with things in the world considered as imparting their forms to us at a sensory level, as the heat of a cat transmits itself to me when I feel the cat sitting on my lap. Again, though, Aquinas wants to distinguish between sensation and understanding. He thinks that more than sensory acquaintance with things is needed when it comes to understanding what they are since sensation is of particular individuals, like this cat, and understanding is of universal forms, like what it is to be a cat.

In other words, Aquinas takes our knowledge of things in the world to be an ongoing story, so to speak. It arises as we sense particular material objects and then form general concepts on the basis of our sensations. Here, thinks Aquinas, there is a move or progression from the individual to the universal. Knowledge or understanding can also arise, says Aquinas, as one builds on what one already grasps, by reasoning from what one knows to truths implied by this, or by connecting separate items of knowledge and bringing them together in some way. In this sense, as Aquinas maintains in 1a,85,3 and 1a,85,5, human knowledge comes about in stages and is not an "all at once" affair, as he takes the knowledge of God and angels to be. As Aquinas puts it, "The human intellect knows by combining, separating, and reasoning."[32]

3. Aquinas goes on to argue that human knowledge extends not only to what things in nature are (substantially or accidentally) but also to things that are contingently so and to future things. We can know contingent things, he reasons, since their existence is what allows us to build up an understanding of things in the world that come about and pass away. These things are contingent because they come to be and cease to be (cf. 1a,2,3). As we have seen, Aquinas holds that the object of understanding is essentially form, not the matter that makes one physical thing to be the individual that it is and not another, and he takes contingency in the world to be ascribable to individual physical things. He does not, therefore, think that the contingency of a particular physical thing, though sensible, is understood directly in the way that its substantial form can be. But it can, he thinks, be understood indirectly.

He means that one can understand that there are contingent beings, since one can understand what they are even though their contingency, considered as had by each of them individually, is not in itself something intelligible, since matter is not in itself something intelligible (cf. chapter 4 above). As for the future, Aquinas thinks that, though we cannot know it in the way that God knows it, we can have some knowledge of it insofar as we can know that certain things, left to themselves, are going to go through certain processes.

Can we also know ourselves? Aquinas thinks that we can be aware of ourselves as operating at an intellectual level. We can know ourselves by being present to ourselves as thinking. Aquinas, however, does not take such knowledge to amount to a knowledge of what we are essentially. This knowledge, he argues, has to be the result of "diligent, subtle inquiry." In short, Aquinas does not think that we can know what we are as knowers simply by introspection (1a,87,1). As Robert Pasnau puts it, Aquinas holds that "we understand the mind only indirectly, from the outside in."[33] And, Aquinas maintains (1a,87,2), diligent and subtle inquiry is needed if we are to understand our dispositions, the ways in which we are inclined to behave. In other words, Aquinas's view is that someone other than me might have a better knowledge of my character than I do. If we think of character as a matter of disposition to behave in this or that way, it is not, in Aquinas's view, something known by introspection at a certain time. Rather, character is recognized for what it is as it plays itself out in particular actions observable in principle to anyone.

4. Much of 1a,88 reiterates points that we have already seen Aquinas defending earlier in the *Prima Pars*. So, for instance, we find him again maintaining that human knowledge of God derives from knowledge of creatures by way of causal reasoning (1a,88,3). But in 1a,88, Aquinas provides a background for this conclusion that draws on what he has been arguing in 1a,84–86. In 1a,88,1, he does so by distinguishing his view of human knowledge from what he takes to be that of Plato and the Arabic philosopher Averroes (ca. 1126–1198).

Aquinas takes Plato to have thought that true human knowledge is always knowledge of what is immaterial—a view that Aquinas takes to be wrong given his claim that we come to know what is in the world as we live in it and acquire knowledge on the basis of sense perception.

Aquinas takes Averroes to have thought that there is an immaterial thing on which we depend for all of our knowledge, an independently existing and single agent intellect. Against Averroes, however, Aquinas maintains that there is no agent intellect existing apart from human knowers.[34] In 1a,88,2, Aquinas denies that we can understand what is not material while understanding what is material, but he believes that we can make inferences concerning what is not material based on our understanding of various material things. On the other hand, he says, we cannot understand what is not material as we can understand what is material.

For Aquinas, our knowledge of what something is depends on our being acquainted with it as something in the world with which we can interact at a sensory level—a familiar story to you by now. In his view, I can know what a cat is since I can interact with it at a sensory level, but not know, say, what God is. Indeed, says Aquinas, our knowledge of what is not material is best thought of as knowledge by negation, as knowing what it is not. "In the theological and philosophical sciences," he observes, "things of a higher order are treated for the most part in terms of what they do not have." He goes on to say that treatises on immaterial substances "are given to us in the theological and philosophical sciences in negative terms of what they are not, or by relationship to material things."[35] Here, of course, is the thinking at work in what Aquinas says in his introduction to 1a,3, where he says that we cannot know what God is and must therefore consider what God is not.

5. In 1a,89, Aquinas considers what knowledge might amount to when it comes to people who have died.[36] As we have seen, he thinks that our souls can exist independently of our bodies, but can they know anything

while doing so? And if so, what do souls know when separated from their bodies?

This, says Aquinas, "is a very difficult question by reason of the fact that the soul, while joined to the body, cannot understand anything except by turning to sense images."[37] He thinks this, of course, because of the way in which he ties human understanding to having a human body with sense organs. But what he is now concerned with is the survival of the human soul considered as something immaterial, and he succinctly identifies the problem: "If we hold that the soul, by its very nature, has to understand by turning to sense images, then, since the nature of the soul is not changed by the death of the body, it would seem that the soul, naturally speaking, can understand nothing, for there are no sense images at hand for it to turn to."[38]

Elaborating on this, Aquinas effectively grants that a human soul separated from the body of the person whose soul it is has to be in a bad way, since it exists in a state that is not natural for it. He is convinced that even a "separated soul" is a human soul, but he is equally convinced that it cannot acquire knowledge as a human being in the world does. So he argues that our souls after death and before they are reunited with our bodies at the resurrection (as Aquinas believes that they will be) can have knowledge by virtue of God's direct action.

His idea here is that God directly causes separated souls to have knowledge, that God, just by fiat, brings it about that they understand in some way. Aquinas is clear that this action of God results in knowledge that arises in a way that differs from that by which living human beings acquire knowledge, yet he evidently takes it to be possible knowledge. He sees it as God's knowledge shared with human souls by the creative activity of God. He also argues (1a,89,5) that knowledge acquired in the present life can remain in separated souls insofar as it is not tied to the knower being in a particular physical state at a particular time. He means that, for example, if we have acquired an understanding of what lions are in general, this understanding can remain in us after death even though we are not then in any position to acquire knowledge of what some particular lion is doing as it goes about its business. Or, as Aquinas himself puts it, "By means of species acquired here, the separated soul can understand the things it understood before, though not in the same way (by turning to sense images)."[39]

The words "though not in the same way" in this last quotation need to be taken very seriously. In 1a,89, Aquinas is not purporting to provide a detailed description of separated souls and their way of existing. Nor is he claiming to prove that there are separated (human) souls. In 1a,89, Aquinas frequently notes that such souls are peculiar and somewhat beyond what philosophy can fathom. On the basis of what he takes to be revelation, he supposes that we are not entirely extinguished at death, that something of us survives even before our bodies are raised (which resurrection of our bodies he takes to be something to believe in only as revealed by God), and he does his best to suggest that this supposition is not obviously incoherent, that it is thinkable even if not provable.[40]

That Aquinas does not believe the life of a separated soul to be seriously comparable to the life of a living human being comes out fairly strongly in what he says about whether the dead know what is going on in the world now (1a,89,8). He says that they cannot. You may think that your deceased relatives are gazing down on you and taking note of what you are up to, but Aquinas does not. As he drily observes: "In terms of natural knowledge…the souls of the dead do not know what happens here, and the reason for this can be learned from what has been said."[41] In this connection, Aquinas also appeals to St. Gregory the Great and St. Augustine of Hippo. However, he also (somewhat vaguely) maintains that a case can be made for supposing that the souls of the dead enjoying the beatific vision see what goes on in the world insofar as they see God.

9.5 Human Beings as Made to God's Image (1a,90–102)

1a,75–89 can be read as an attempt by Aquinas to note what human beings are from a philosophical point of view. His discussions in these questions are shot through with appeals to divine revelation and to ecclesiastical authorities, and sometimes (as in 1a,89) they do not amount to purported proofs but, rather, to the claim that something that Aquinas takes to be part of Christian belief is not impossible or is not inconsistent with what a philosopher can establish. Nevertheless, 1a,75–89 largely amounts to a philosophical discussion and can hardly be read as nothing but an exposition of Scripture.

When writing 1a,90–102, however, Aquinas has biblical texts firmly in mind. For these questions focus on the Genesis account of the origin of human beings and raise questions that Aquinas takes to be worth asking about that account. Many contemporary readers will find what Aquinas says in this section of the *Summa* to be dated, since Aquinas is evidently assuming that the book of Genesis, and specifically what we read in it about Adam and Eve, should be read literally.[42] Even if we disagree with his assumption here, though, some of the things he has to say in 1a,90–102 can, perhaps, still be thought of as contributing to an enduring theological understanding of human beings. In this section of the present chapter I shall concentrate on what I take these things to be.

First, then, there is what he has to say about the production of human souls. Are they made up out of what God is, as a cake is made up of ingredients used by a chef? Aquinas thinks not because of the huge difference between God and human beings (1a,90,1).

But we cannot, he adds, deny that human souls are created by God. In saying this, Aquinas means his reader to understand that human souls do not come into being because of causes existing in the world. He is saying that they are directly caused to exist by God. Our bodies, he agrees, come to be because of the activity of other physical things. But not our souls. Why so? Because human souls are subsisting things (1a,75,2) but are not material objects. So, Aquinas reasons, they cannot come to exist from what is material, or even from the agency of non-material beings other than God. They must be created directly and, therefore, made to exist by God and nothing else (1a,90,2 and 3).

In 1a,92, Aquinas talks about Eve, whom he takes to be the first woman. He takes it as given that sexual differences between people (that X is born male and that Y is born female) spring from God's will that there should be more people as time goes on (1a,92,1). Because of antiquated views that he inherited, Aquinas also thinks that women are somehow inferior to men (1a,92,1, ad.1). We should note, however, that, considered as human beings, Aquinas takes men and women to be equal as sharing the same nature. His thinking on this matter becomes clear in 1a,92,3, in which he turns to Genesis 1:21, which says that Eve was made from Adam's rib. Commenting on this verse in very much the manner of a typical medieval exegete, Aquinas notes that ribs, unlike heads or feet, signify companionship rather than domination or subservience.

In 1a,93, Aquinas turns to Genesis 1:26, which says, "Then God said, 'Let us make man in our image, according to our likeness.'" He asks how we should understand this passage. Scholastic to the bone, Aquinas distinguishes between "image" and "likeness" (1a,93,9).

He says that something can be *like* another thing because it resembles it in *some* way. But an *image* of something resembles it fairly *precisely*, and, thinks Aquinas, human beings resemble God in quite precise ways even though they are unequal to God, and are therefore imperfect images of God.

But how so? Because, says Aquinas (1a,93,1), people derive from God causally and must therefore resemble God as their maker (on the now-familiar principle that the effects of agent causes show forth the nature of their causes). Yet Aquinas thinks that all of God's effects somehow show forth God's nature. So what makes people rightly to be singled out as being in God's image?

Here Aquinas appeals to the fact that human beings have understanding and will. "While all creatures bear some resemblance to God," he observes, "only in a rational creature do you find resemblance to God in the manner of an image…[and]…what puts the rational creature in a higher class than others is precisely intellect or mind."[43] Aquinas is not, you will now realize, saying that God is like us since God is a thinking thing that reasons as time goes by, but he does hold that we resemble God, and do so more than anything else in the material world, insofar as we are able to understand and to act on the basis of our understanding. He even suggests (1a,93,7) that people can be thought to resemble God considered as Trinity insofar as they know and love what they know (cf. chapter 6 above). As should be obvious from what Aquinas has said earlier in the *Prima Pars*, he takes the distinction between people and God to be a serious one. However, and reflecting on Genesis 1, he finds reasons for making limited comparisons between God and human beings.

As he proceeds through 1a,94–102, Aquinas raises a number of questions while presupposing that the biblical account of Adam and Eve should be read historically. Did Adam understand everything? Could he see angels? Could he have been mistaken? Was he created in a state of grace? Did he have all virtues? Did he have dominion over animals and all other creatures? Was he immortal? Did he suffer? Did he need food? Did he procreate? And so on. I shall not dwell on what Aquinas says about these questions, but I do want to make one point in connection with them.

Aquinas thinks of Adam at two levels: first, before he sinned; then after he sinned. Aquinas says that before he sinned, Adam was graced by God in what Aquinas calls "the state of innocence" and that as such Adam had all the virtues, was lord of all animals, was immortal and immune from suffering. After Adam sinned, however, he lacked all these benefits. In other words, Aquinas's view, based on his reading of Genesis, is that God created human beings to be in union with God and in a state of great and unending happiness. That they are not now in that state derives, thinks Aquinas, from the sin of Adam.

Once again, this conclusion of Aquinas comes in a text that is assuming the historicity of the Adam and Eve story. It can, though, presumably be read without a commitment to such historicity, since its emphasis seems to fall on the idea that there is a bodily state of perfection available to people were it not for the fact of them being separated from God by sin. As he continues, Aquinas will represent this idea without special reference to what he takes to be the historicity of the Adam and Eve story, and it is, I suspect, not unlikely that he would stand by it even if he came to be unpersuaded that the Adam and Eve story should be read as an accurate historical account.

In other words, Aquinas's reading of the Adam and Eve story in 1a,94–102, which may strike us as somewhat dated, can be read at two levels. At one level we can read Aquinas as writing in his historical context and, unsurprisingly, as reading Genesis 1 as historically accurate. At this level we would be reading Aquinas as only preoccupied with Adam and Eve as historical individuals. At another level, though, we can read him as taking the book of Genesis to teach us important truths about human possibilities in relation to God's will and about the nature and effects of sin. Read at this level, 1a,94–102 is talking about what human life might be apart from sin and with the grace of God— the basic topic of the *Secunda Pars*.

9.6 God's Governance (1a,103–119)

As we have seen, quite a bit of the *Prima Pars* is concerned with what God has created: with the varieties of things in the created order, with goodness and evil, with the material universe, with angels, and finally with human beings. In 1a,103–109, Aquinas keeps very much to the same topic and repeats much that he has already said. This is especially so when it comes to 1a,103–105, which adds little to what we find already in 1a,2–26. Here Aquinas is arguing that creatures are made to exist by God, who operates in all of their operations (1a,103). Here, too, Aquinas is saying that creatures need God in order to exist (1a,104). And in 1a,106–114, Aquinas returns to the topic of angels, both good and bad.

But Aquinas presents some new ideas in 1a,103–119. For instance, we find him adding to his account of divine omnipotence by turning to the topic of miracles. We also find him turning to questions about the activities of certain creatures that he has not so far discussed.

When it comes to miracles, Aquinas argues that they are possible since God can bring things about without using any created cause. For Aquinas, a miracle is, strictly speaking, an event that comes to pass that can *only* be brought about by God (1a,105,6). God, he says, sometimes brings events about by means of the activity of creatures, but God is not beholden to the powers of created things when it comes to what happens in the world. Aquinas thinks that God can bring about what is not within the power of a creature to bring about. One may, he notes, think something to be a miracle if it strikes one as unexpected or surprising, but Aquinas takes a miracle to be more than this. He says, "The word 'miracle' connotes something altogether wondrous, i.e. having its cause hidden absolutely and from everyone. This cause is God."[44]

When it comes to the activities of certain creatures, Aquinas spends quite a long time at this stage of the *Summa Theologiae* considering the activities of angels. He talks about the extent to which they can be reasonably thought of as communicating with one another and with God (1a,106–107). He also talks about how they can be ranked hierarchically in some sense (1a,108) and how we might think of their action on things in the world (1a,110). I am not going to try to summarize his discussion of these matters partly for reasons of space, but also because I doubt that it is something of major interest to contemporary readers of the *Summa Theologiae* who are not especially concerned with the influence on Aquinas of certain texts, not much read today, which he took to be authoritative—in particular, the writings of Dionysius the Areopagite.[45] However, Aquinas's line of thinking at this point in the *Summa* should be intelligible to you given my account of 1a,50–64. For the record, though, his main conclusions are: (1) Angels can communicate with one another and with God and can have influence on one another (1a,106–107); (2) Angels can be ranked (1a,108–109); (3) Angels can have a limited causal effect on things in the world (1a,110); (4) Angels cannot work miracles (1a,110); (5) Angels can enlighten human beings intellectually, but cannot act on their will (1a,111); (6) Angels are sent by God to help some human beings (1a,112–113).

In what he says about angels at this point, Aquinas is manifestly not writing as a pure philosopher. He is trying to make sense of various beliefs about angels familiar to people of his day. In doing so, he draws on his philosophical expertise, but 1a,106–114 is strikingly different from, say, 1a,2–26 or 1a,75–89 when it comes to the employment of philosophical arguments. While 1a,2–26 and 1a,75–89 rest firmly for Aquinas on what he can take to be true independently of divine revelation, 1a,106–114 is assuming a number of ideas that Aquinas thinks of as ultimately grounded in biblical texts and in the authority of certain other authors.

Matters are different, however, when it comes to 1a,115–119. For here we find Aquinas touching on matters to do with scientific explanation, causality in the material world, and certain kinds of causality associated with human beings. Hence, for example, 1a,115, 1–2 reiterates the notion that there are physical things that exercise genuine causal power. Again, in line with medieval cosmology according to which what happens on earth partly derives from movements of the heavenly bodies, Aquinas asks whether these bodies cause what comes to pass on earth. Following Aristotle, he argues that they do so to some extent, even if they cannot determine human free choices (1a,115,3–4), and even though they do not impose necessity on everything they influence (1a,115,6).[46]

His discussion of causation on the part of material things leads Aquinas to turn to the topic of fate in 1a,116. With an evident eye on Boethius's *The Consolation of Philosophy*, Aquinas argues that fate is real, not in the sense that everything that happens is bound to happen because of mindless causes working away inexorably, but because the world is governed by divine providence, which Aquinas takes to be operating even in chance events lacking a single natural cause.

What though of human causation? As we have seen, Aquinas touches on human beings and the results of their actions earlier than 1a,117, but in 1a,117–119 he singles out four questions for brief discussion and follows them up with an account of what he takes to be involved as people generate other people.

The four questions are: (1) Can people teach each other? (2) Can they teach angels? (3) Can they affect physical things by sheer "will power"? (4) Can human-separated souls move things around physically? Aquinas answers (2)-(4) in the negative while drawing on points he has previously made in the *Prima Pars*. He thinks, though, that the answer to (1) is yes. If we think of learning as the occurrence in a person of understanding, then, Aquinas concedes, this is not something that one human being can directly bring about in another, since it is not the occurrence of something material. Understanding is a change in a human mind, an illumination of the agent intellect. However, Aquinas still maintains that people can teach one another by taking positive steps to bring them to a state of understanding, by leading them from what they know to what they can learn with some prompting, by drawing their attention to what they already know and to its implications.[47]

The discussion of human generation in 1a,118–119 owes a great deal to Aristotle's *De Generatione Animalium* (*On the Generation of Animals*) and *De Anima* (*On Soul*), and like much of 1a,66–71 it contains many elements that will seem false to most people today given developments in science since the thirteenth century. I am not, therefore, going to dwell here on 1a,118–119. Instead, I shall try to pave the way to the following chapter in which I turn to the Second Part of the *Summa Theologiae*.

In his *Prima Pars*, Aquinas begins by reflecting on *sacra doctrina* and its scope (1a,1). Continuing to write as a doctor of *sacra doctrina*, he then considers what can be known of God independently of divine revelation. Thus we have the long account of how we can know that *Deus est* is a true proposition (1a,2–11) and of what we can say truly of God and God's doing as creatures who understand God only imperfectly (1a,12–26). From an account of the divine nature, Aquinas then turns to God as Trinity and creator (1a,27–49) while moving on to consider different things that exist in God's created order, from angels to people to non-thinking material objects (1a,50–119).

From what I have reported Aquinas to be saying in the *Prima Pars*, you will doubtless have gathered that he takes human beings to exist at a level that makes them greater than purely material things, though inferior to God and even, in some respects, to angels. However, you will also, I hope, have taken on board the fact that Aquinas takes people to be capable of union with God and to have received divine revelation. Like any Christian theologian, Aquinas is concerned to note how we might come to union with God. In his view, the incarnation of the second person of the Trinity is what throws light on this issue, and he talks about it in detail in the *Tertia Pars*. Anticipating that discussion, however, he moves in the *Secunda Pars* to a discussion of what our happiness lies in and how we can be thought of as moving toward it given the grace of God and given how we live our lives. His "big picture" is that we can only be fully happy while enjoying the beatific vision and that we can be brought to this only by God's grace and not just because of our own merits or efforts.

So when proceeding from his *Prima Pars* to his *Secunda Pars*, Aquinas shifts the focus from God and God's creation to human beings as created by God for union with God. I shall now try to help you see how he proceeds. He does so in his typical fashion, by bringing together thoughts that he takes us to be able to arrive at by philosophical reasoning and thoughts based on what he takes to be divine revelation.

Happiness, Human Action, and Morality (1a2ae, 1–21)

IN HIS FOREWORD to 1a2ae,1 Aquinas writes: "Human beings are made to God's image, and since this implies...that they are intelligent and free and in charge of themselves, now that we have agreed that God is the exemplar cause of things and that they issue from God's power through God's will, we go on to look at this image, that is to say, at human beings as the source of their own actions, ones that fall under their responsibility and control."¹ So, the *Secunda Pars* is concerned with human beings as directed to God. Its focus is on what they are considered as such and how they can be thought to be brought to union with God.

As we have seen, in 1a Aquinas says a lot about human beings at a philosophical level (without relying on divine revelation), and he draws on this material and sometimes repeats himself as he carries on. From 1a2ae,1, though, his theological understanding of people increasingly emerges. Early in 1a2ae, he dwells again on the notion that people are destined for the beatific vision (1a2ae,3,8). In 1a2ae,68–70, he works on the supposition that special gifts come to those whom God draws toward this vision, and as 1a2ae concludes he concentrates on what he calls grace, the effects of which he dwells on in 2a2ae. By "grace" Aquinas means God's empowering of people to share in the divine life. People with grace, he thinks, are aided by God to arrive at a state that they cannot get to simply by being human beings in the sense that philosophers might think of them. At the same time, however, Aquinas does not think of grace as turning people into something that they are not essentially, given that they are human beings, and he devotes quite a bit of 1a2ae to discussing people, considered as able in principle to move toward the happiness with God that he takes to be possible. He does so even as he embarks on 1a2ae while devoting four questions to the topic of human happiness.

10.1 Happiness (1a2ae,1–4)

The discussion here starts with reflection concerning ends. Aquinas takes union with God to be something we should aim for. But do we act with aims in mind? Do we act with a view to ends? Aquinas suggests (1a2ae,1,1) that we sometimes do not, since we often act unthinkingly—as, for example, when we stroke our chins when talking to someone while focused on what we are saying and not at all on our chins (1a2ae,1,1). One might, of course, deliberately stroke one's chin to relieve an itch, but we often pass our hands over ourselves and go through other bits of bodily behavior without deliberation. Aquinas therefore holds that we should distinguish between "acts of a human being" (*actiones hominis*) and "human acts" (*actiones humanae*). He thinks that we certainly go through various quasi-automatic movements like stroking our chins while concentrating on what we are saying to someone, these being "acts of a human being." He also maintains that we sometimes deliberately act with a view to particular and precise goals, as, for example, when we nowadays decide to press "Send" having drafted an email. He argues that as well as there being "acts of a human being" there are also "human acts," actions deliberately chosen by people aiming at an end.

This acting for an end is, Aquinas says, peculiar to human beings considered as things in the world with rational faculties. He thinks, of course, that the world contains non-thinking things that act so as to achieve various ends (1a,2,3). He thinks, for example, that tigers are truly acting for an end as they seek prey. But, he insists, there is a difference between tigers acting and people doing so, because people, unlike tigers, can think or reflect about what they are doing or are about to do and *deliberately* act for ends (1a2ae,1,2). Moreover, thinks Aquinas, there has to be a final end aimed at by people as they act (1a2ae,1,4). He means that when we aim for an end we have to be aiming at something specific and not at some collection of ends proceeding to infinity. He denies that one might ad infinitum aim to do such and such in order to a-chieve such and such. Human acting for an end, he thinks, has to amount to acting for some particular end even if it involves a series of intermediate actions for an end. He holds that "Act for an infinite series of ends" amounts to an impossible command even though there might be an infinite number of desirable things.

Do we, though, always act with a view to one and only one particular end? Apparently not. I might act so as to arrive at goal X while you might act so as to arrive at goal Y, and Aquinas accepts this point. Yet he also thinks that nobody can fail to desire what they take to be good (1a2ae,1,6–7). We might, he allows, be wrong when it comes to what is good for us, but he also thinks that we naturally gravitate to what we take to be good. In this sense, he argues, we always aim at goodness and have an innate tendency to desire what is good.

In what does our good lie? What makes for our fulfillment? Aquinas's answer is "beatitude" (*beatitudo*), by which he means union with God after death, the beatific vision. The word *beatitudo* can be translated into English as "happiness," as can the Latin word *felicitas*, so Aquinas holds that our good ultimately lies in being happy. When he uses the term *felicitas*, however, he is thinking of what we might call "earthly happiness," and it is not this that he has in mind when saying that our fulfillment lies in *beatitudo*. This becomes clear in 1a2ae,2, in which Aquinas lists possible answers to the question "In what does our happiness lie?" while rejecting all of them in favor of the answer "beatitude." The reasoning goes as follows:

1. *Does ultimate happiness lie in riches?* Riches can satisfy our natural or basic needs—food, drink, and shelter would be "natural riches." Riches can also be artificial as, for example, is money. Yet ultimate happiness lies in neither kind of riches, since both are merely means to other ends. We seek food and the like because we aim at keeping ourselves alive. We desire money and the like since they help us to obtain certain other desirable things. Also, riches can be had by both good and bad people, yet perfect happiness is incompatible with evil of any sort (1a2ae,2,1).

2. *Does ultimate happiness lie in honors?* No, because honors, even if they make us happy, go to those who have achieved something and therefore cannot be the cause or aim of these achievements in the sense that we cannot think of ultimate happiness as consisting in present achievements for which we are already honored. And, like riches, honors can be had by people who are bad (1a2ae,2,2).

3. *Does ultimate happiness lie in fame or glory?* No, since fame and glory can be illusory in the sense that one might be famous and deemed praiseworthy for achievements that are not real (1a2ae,2,3).

4. *Does ultimate happiness lie in power?* No, since power is what *enables* activity while ultimate happiness is an *achievement*. Also, power can be used well or badly, while ultimate happiness involves no possible badness. Furthermore, power, like riches, honors, fame, and glory, can be had by people who lack other sources of happiness, which is not the case with those who enjoy ultimate happiness. Note also that riches, honors, fame, glory, and power can all sometimes lead to the harm of those who have them, which is inconsistent with a source of ultimate happiness. Also note that riches, honors, fame, glory, and power come from sources outside ourselves and do so often by luck or chance, whereas ultimate happiness lies within us and fulfills what is intrinsic to us (1a2e,2,4).

5. *Does ultimate happiness lie in bodily well-being?* Human bodily qualities cannot make for people's ultimate happiness since such qualities are often found to a greater degree in nonhuman animals. For example, elephants

tend to live longer than we do, and lions are stronger than we are. Also, since we are essentially intellectual beings, our ultimate happiness cannot lie in physical well-being alone, nice though that can often be (1a2ae,2,5).

6. *Does ultimate happiness lie in bodily (sensory) pleasures?* No, for these are not the only sources of enjoyment. They are also temporary, while ultimate happiness depends on our sustained intellectual grasp of what goes well beyond these (1a2ae,2,6).

In short, Aquinas finds it hard to believe that ultimate happiness (*beatitudo*) can lie in anything creaturely. He says:

> For humans to rest content with any created good is not possible, for they can be happy only with complete good which satisfies their desire altogether: they would not have reached their ultimate end were there something still remaining to be desired. The object of the will, that is the human appetite, is the Good without reserve, just as the object of the mind is the True without reserve. Clearly, then, nothing can satisfy the human will except such goodness, which is found, not in anything created, but in God alone. Everything created is a derivative good.[2]

The goodness that Aquinas is thinking of here is the enjoyment of the beatific vision, which he takes to be a direct knowledge of God together with a delight in it, and he thinks the joy of this vision is only perfected in us when our bodies are raised to life. In his words: "There can be no complete and final happiness for us save in the vision of God" (1a2ae,3,8).[3]

This account of our final happiness may strike you as austerely cerebral, and you may well think that Aquinas is looking forward to something lacking what we might call "the joy of life." You need to remember, though, that Aquinas thinks of people as being above other things in the material world precisely because of their ability to understand, and he therefore takes human happiness ultimately to consist in understanding. At the same time, however, he recognizes that people are essentially corporeal. So he also insists that our final happiness (*beatitudo*) requires our bodily well-being even if we can be happy merely by virtue of seeing God (1a2ae,4,5 and 7). Here, of course, Aquinas is trying to bring together the views (a) that we can be happy with God after death and before our bodies are raised and (b) that we are essentially bodily individuals to whom are promised in Scripture a bodily life after death. And, Aquinas adds, our final happiness once gained cannot be lost (1a2ae,5,4). Happiness gained in this life, he says, can be lost, but not the happiness of beatitude, since this involves us in directly knowing the perfect good that is God as God raises us to do so—something from which, as good-loving things, we cannot pull away. Beatitude, says Aquinas, amounts to "seeing God just as God is." However, "to gaze on God and to will not to see God is impossible.... For a good that is possessed and is nevertheless relinquished is either found insufficient, so that something more satisfying is sought instead, or else has something wearisome about it, so that it becomes distasteful. Now by seeing God just as God is, the soul is filled with every good.... Manifestly nobody could give up such brimming happiness of their own accord."[4]

How can people come to enjoy this happiness? Can they, for instance, do so by using their wits and natural abilities? Aquinas thinks not. We can act smartly and arrange to have a happy Christmas, but we cannot, in Aquinas's view, act so as to bring about beatitude for ourselves (1a2ae,5,5). And yet, so Aquinas also thinks (1a2ae,5,7), what we do plays a role in us achieving beatitude. One cannot arrive at union with God, he argues, if one does not want what is good, if one does not desire the good that God is, and Aquinas thinks of such wanting on the part of the blessed as starting in their earthly lives. If we come to enjoy the beatific vision in the next life, that is because we already want God in this life.

10.2 Human Action, Will, and Choice (1a2ae,6–17)

What, though, is human action? This is Aquinas's next question, and what he wants chiefly to note is that human action is voluntary. In arguing to this effect, Aquinas is suggesting that our actions can sometimes proceed from ourselves in that they can amount to a moving toward what we can know to be desirable in some way. For Aquinas, voluntary action involves noting an end as good and pursuing it while (in principle) being able to answer the question "With a view to what are you doing that?" As I have said several times, Aquinas notes that some non-rational things can be thought of as aiming at ends. But, he observes, they do not intentionally set themselves to the ends they pursue and therefore do not act voluntarily (1a2ae,6,1). Those things "which have some grasp of what an end implies," he says, "are said to move themselves because within them lies the source not only of acting but also of acting with a purpose."[5] Voluntary activity can, Aquinas concedes, be attributed to certain nonhuman animals to a degree, since they can be thought of as sometimes moving in the light of what they perceive. Properly speaking, though, voluntary activity in the full sense is, Aquinas argues, the prerogative in this world of people who apprehend ends as good, deliberate about ways to achieve them, and act accordingly (1a2ae,6,2).

In Aquinas's view, voluntary activity comes with responsibility. We are responsible for what we do voluntarily. But Aquinas also takes us to be responsible for what we voluntarily do not do, since he thinks that we can will not to act as well as to act (1a2ae,6,3). With that thought expressed, Aquinas again goes on to hold that voluntary activity has to be incompatible with compulsion. When wanting to do something we may, he thinks, suffer from compulsion in that our bodies might be constrained in some way, in that, for example, we may find that our limbs are unable to move (1a2ae,6,4). Yet, he maintains, "as to its proper act…the will cannot be exposed to violence" and violence renders an action involuntary (1a2ae,6,5).

One might wonder just what Aquinas has in mind by "violence" here. He obviously thinks that if, say, you push me down a flight of stairs, my tumbling down them does not amount to voluntary activity on my part. Yet what if I act out of fear or lust or ignorance? In response to this question, Aquinas argues that fear, lust, or ignorance do not necessarily render an action involuntary. He agrees that they can be forceful influences on us. If we act out of fear, he thinks, we are confronted by what we take to be repugnant and contrary to what we want, but he also believes that we can still be acting voluntarily insofar as we act so as to avoid something we take to be terrible and wish to avoid (1a2ae,6,6). And lust, he thinks, actually renders an action voluntary rather than involuntary because the action springs very much from the desire of the lustful agent doing just what he or she wants to do (1a2ae,6,7). As for ignorance, Aquinas thinks that this can render an action involuntary but does not necessarily have to do so. Suppose that I want to kill you and manage to do so while mistakenly taking myself to be killing someone else who looks like you. Do I kill you voluntarily? Aquinas thinks that in such a case what comes about is not willed by me even if it amounts to what I desire. On the other hand, he also thinks that I can be thought of as responsible for something that happens if I act in a state of ignorance that I positively will or could have avoided. He denies, however, that I act voluntarily (when it comes to an end willed by me) if I end up doing something that has a consequence that I could not foresee or do not have an obligation to foresee (1a2ae,6,8).

He also thinks that what he calls "circumstances" (*circumstantiae*) can be significant when it comes to what is going on in particular actions (1a2ae,7).[6] You may be inclined to say that an act is an act and that it can only be described in one way, and Aquinas agrees with this verdict in a sense. He would say, for example, that praising a person is always just praising a person regardless of context. Yet he also thinks that there might be a difference between, say, praising someone who commits genocide and praising a figure like Florence Nightingale—the difference lying in the person being praised. Again, he thinks that there might be a difference between a recovering alcoholic taking a drink and someone doing so who is not a recovering alcoholic, or between me drinking alcohol to relax after a busy day and a surgeon drinking alcohol before performing an operation. In this sense, Aquinas thinks that circumstances can be important when it comes to figuring out what is actually going on when people act in particular ways in particular contexts. Aquinas has a mind to questions such as "Who is doing this?" "Where?" "When?" "Why?" and "By what means?" He takes these questions to be relevant when it comes to deciding what is going on in particular actions done by particular people at particular times. So he denies that an act is just an act and that there is no more to be said of it apart from noting that it is just an act of doing such and such—this description being applicable to actions that can be thought of as the same while abstracting them from the circumstances attaching to them, while, for example, focusing on the notion "drinking alcohol" without reference to who is doing this and in what context.

In general, though, Aquinas takes a voluntary action to be one that always aims at what is perceived to be good (2a2ae,8,1). One may think that someone might voluntarily aim for what is not good, and Aquinas does not deny that people can will what is objectively bad. He thinks, though, that when we act voluntarily we always aim at what we, for whatever reason, *think of* as good, even if it is not objectively so. Here he again invokes his notion that good is what everything desires (cf. 1a,5). On the other hand, Aquinas does not think of voluntary action as only concerned with good *ends*. He thinks that it can also be performed with an eye on *means* (1a2ae,8,2 and 3). I may want to lose weight, but in voluntarily trying to achieve my goal I will also have to decide on the means to achieve it. Shall I just starve myself? Or shall I go on a diet that will reduce my weight without injuring me? Aquinas observes: "If willing bears on an end it also bears on that which is for it."[7]

What leads us to act voluntarily? Can we speak of there being causes of actions that we will? Aquinas thinks that voluntary action has to proceed on the basis of understanding of some kind, so he argues that will is set in motion by understanding. We would not will without some understanding of a possible good to be achieved. In this sense, will is "moved" (*movetur*) by "intellect" (*intellectus*) (1a2ae,9,1). It can also, Aquinas suggests, be sparked off by our emotions, by what Aquinas calls our "sensitive appetite" (1a2ae,9,3). And yet, Aquinas thinks, we are seriously to be thought of as self-movers when we act voluntarily (1a2ae,9,2). That is because he takes voluntary action to be incompatible with external compulsion. In his view, to act voluntarily is to do what *we* want to do, not what something *else* makes us do. We can, he thinks, be moved to will because of something apart from us that we desire (considered as an object of thought, so to speak). He does not, however, take such external objects of the will to be things that compel us as we act as, say, my forcing your arm upward compels your arm rising.[8] Yet, so he argues, voluntary action is something real in the world, something that does not exist of necessity. So he takes it as somehow arising from a cause or causes to be distinguished from it. My voluntarily doing such and such is not, Aquinas thinks, only explicable by the fact that I am able to act voluntarily. There remains the question "How come any voluntary human behavior?" which Aquinas does not take to be adequately answered by replying "Because people can act voluntarily."

What might be the final answer to the question "How come any voluntary behavior?" Aquinas, with an eye on certain medieval astrological theories, denies that heavenly bodies account for all that takes place on earth (1a2ae,9,5; cf. 1a,115,4). On the other hand, and in keeping with what he teaches about divine causality in 1a, he maintains that God moves us as we act willingly (1a2ae,9,6). In 1a2ae,9,4, he argues that, on pain of an infinite regress, there has to be a first extrinsic principle of our willing, and in 1a2ae,9,5, he denies that this can be a heavenly body. He is clear that to act voluntarily is to act "from within" (*ab intrinsico*) and is incompatible with compulsion undergone by us because of the activity of creatures on us. But voluntary action, thinks Aquinas, has to derive from God working in us (a) since we will because of a power of our rational soul, which is created by God and (b) since to will is to be moved by goodness as such, which is nothing other than God.

Do we, however, will anything naturally? Aquinas thinks that we must since to will is to be drawn to goodness in general, and since we are naturally attracted to this and to what makes for our good as the human beings that we are (1a2ae,10,1). But, he adds (1a2ae,10,2), we do not necessarily will particular goods since we can choose between different goals when acting voluntarily. Indeed, we can choose not to think about certain possible objects of willing unless we are presented with "what is universally good and good from every point of view," this being God alone.[9] Our willing, Aquinas continues, is not even moved of necessity by our "lower appetites." Passion tends to influence us when it comes to what we pursue and may be powerful enough to prevent us from acting on the basis of reason, though not necessarily so (cf. 1a2ae,6,6 and 7). Even when in the grip of passion one might be able to reason and to decide what to do on the basis of this. Yet does God acting on us necessitate our willing what we do? In line with what he has now said several times (cf. 1a,19,8), Aquinas argues in 1a2ae,10,4 that God's creative activity in us does not render our acts involuntary. God moves our will, he says, "in such a way that it is not predetermined to one object; its motion remains contingent and not necessary, except for the things on which it is set by the burden of its nature."[10] It is, thinks Aquinas, *because* and not *in spite of* God that we act voluntarily.

In his thinking about human willing Aquinas holds that "enjoyment" (*frui*) plays a part, since he thinks that we are always at some level pleased when we are engaged in voluntary activity, that to act voluntarily is always to be drawn to what we are doing, that it is somehow to savor what we are about. In this sense of "enjoyment," he holds, enjoyment is something of which nonhuman things are incapable, even if they act for ends, as he supposes. Yet he thinks enjoyment is something that nonhuman animals can achieve to some degree, though not as fully as people. "The full meaning of enjoyment," he says, "applies to rational creatures, something short of this to animals, but nothing of the sort to other creatures."[11] On the other hand, Aquinas is clear that our ultimate enjoyment (enjoyment without any qualification) can only be had by us in the beatific vision. "Rest is not utter and complete," he claims, "except in our ultimate end."[12]

Aquinas also regards intention as part of what is in play when we act voluntarily (1a2ae,12). In his view, to will something is to desire it, but acting voluntarily can also involve desiring an end and taking steps to achieve it. For Aquinas, this means that willing presupposes knowledge of an end to be desired and can amount to selecting means by which the end might be obtained, and this selecting of ends and means is what he has in mind when speaking of intention as part of willing. Such ends or goals need not, he thinks, be ultimate ones, since we can intend stages on the way to them (intermediate goals, so to speak), and we can, he argues, intend various intermediate goals simultaneously and with an eye on various different purposes. Aquinas also notes that when willing an intermediate goal as a means to an end we are willing both the intermediate goal and the end that we take it to lead to when achieved. He means that if, say, I pick up the phone in order to talk to you, I am willing both the talking to you *and* the picking up of the phone in a single intention. He therefore thinks that intention to act is not just to be defined by what I end up doing by various actions. I can be intending what I do as a means to what I end up doing. In practice, this means that Aquinas is committed to the view that my dentist, for example, cannot say that he was not intending to drill one of my teeth but only intending to free me from pain.

Other aspects of voluntary action that Aquinas highlights are "choice" (*electio*), "deliberation" (*consilium*), "consent" (*consensus*), "application" (*uti*), and "command" (*imperium*).[13] In doing so, he presents the following account of voluntary activity in 1a2ae,13–17:

1. To act voluntarily involves identifying a desirable goal (ultimate or intermediate) and being drawn to it.[14]

2. It also involves deciding on possible means to attain it and on the particular ones we use for doing so.
3. It also involves wanting or consenting to certain decisions to act with respect to various possible means, implying that acting voluntarily involves us in using our ability to reason in getting what we want and in wanting to get what we want by certain means.[15]
4. One may sometimes act voluntarily without thinking too much, as when jumping out of the way of an oncoming car, but voluntary activity can sometimes be, and most frequently is, the product of weighing up the pros and cons (even if briefly) of various means by which a desired end can be achieved.

As he develops these thoughts, Aquinas presents an account of what he calls "practical reasoning," which he distinguishes from "theoretical reasoning."[16] Given that I think all material things are divisible, and given that I think that my desk is a material thing, I will naturally conclude that my desk is divisible, and in doing so, says Aquinas, I would be engaging in theoretical reasoning—reasoning about what is the case based on premises concerning what is the case. But Aquinas also thinks that I might reason concerning what I should do on some occasion, which is what he has in mind when referring to practical reasoning, which he takes always to be involved (at least implicitly) in voluntary action and always to include reference to what I desire or want to avoid.

Aquinas does not mean that when we act voluntarily we are always doing so after having gone through a lengthy process of argumentation. He is well aware that voluntary action can be instantaneous and almost unreflective, as when one avoids an oncoming car suddenly bearing down on one. He does, however, think that where we have a voluntary action, we always have action that can, as it were, be analyzed in terms of an agent's goals and in terms of means noted and intended by the agent. I may quickly avoid an oncoming car by jumping backward. Yet I am definitely aiming to avoid an oncoming car by choosing what strikes me (whether rightly or wrongly) as a good means to do so (whether or not I am aware of all the means open to me). And, thinks Aquinas, when we decide to act in more usual cases, we are engaging in what, in retrospect on our part or on that of others, can be thought of as a process of reasoning that differs from that involved in theoretical reasoning.

Aquinas believes that theoretical reasoning has a kind of inevitability attached to it.[17] If I agree that anything material is divisible, and if I agree that desks are material, then I have to conclude that desks are divisible. But what if I want to get home by 9:30 p.m. and agree that the 8:00 p.m. train will get me there on time? Should I conclude that I should catch the 8:00 p.m. train? It would be reasonable for me to do so, though here we should note that additional premises might reasonably lead me *not* to do so. For what if I learn that the 8:00 p.m. train has a bomb on it planted by terrorists, or that someone I hate to meet is on it? In that case, I might reasonably conclude that I should stay well away from it. Aware of this fact, Aquinas thinks of practical reasoning as being defeatable by premises in a way that theoretical reasoning is not.[18]

Aquinas holds that practical reasoning is central to acting voluntarily.[19] And he takes it to proceed from a premise (or several premises) reflecting my desire for something together with premises concerning how to obtain what I desire.[20] He is aware that additional premises might change what I end up choosing to do after having first thought of doing something else, but he is clear that such choosing is related to noting the means by which certain results that I desire can be achieved. As he puts it: "Choice (*electio*) follows the decision or verdict (*judicium*) which, as it were, is a conclusion of a practical syllogism. It is this which offers the object of choice."[21] For Aquinas, voluntary action proceeds by a combination of desire, attention to ends, attention to means, decision to act, and choice of how in detail to act with an eye on means as recognized and desired with respect to ends that we have. "The meaning and nature of our action," he says, "comes from the end."[22]

10.3 Good and Evil in Human Action (1a2ae,18–21)

Having commented on what he takes to be involved in true human action, and having noted that some of our behavior does not amount to human action (*actio humana*) but is rather something instinctive and without thought (*actio hominis*), Aquinas proceeds in 1a2ae to consider what is involved in willed human actions being good and bad. Or, so we might say, he turns to what he takes moral goodness and badness to amount to when it comes to human action.[23]

Aquinas is clear that some human actions can be bad (1a2ae,18,1). We speak, he notes, of various objects being good and bad, and we can speak similarly when it comes to human actions. Given his understanding of goodness as a matter of what is desirable and as having to do with being (cf. 1a,5), he argues that human actions can fail when it comes to goodness in that they can lack what is desirable for them considered as human actions. Any human action is real and is, to that extent, good, he thinks. On the other hand, not all existing human actions are as good as they might be. They can, Aquinas thinks, be defective.

How so? Aquinas thinks that human actions can be good or bad because of that at which they aim (1a2ae,18,2 and 4). He also thinks that goodness and badness in human actions can depend on their circumstances (1a2ae,18,3).[24]

In Aquinas's view, some actions are good or bad because of being of a certain kind, as we might say that stealing is a bad kind of action or repaying debts is a good kind.[25] What, however, might be a good or bad kind of action can, he thinks, take its individual shape from how it is performed and by whom and in what circumstances, though he also thinks that the ends we intend when acting are critical when evaluating our actions. So he concludes that an action may be thought to be good in one respect (with respect to being real or good as a kind of action, say) and not good in another (with respect to motive, say). At the same time, however, Aquinas maintains that the basic notion to be held in mind when calling human acts good or bad is whether or not they accord with what, on reflection, is objectively good when it comes to the people whose actions they are, whether or not they are perfective of these people.[26] He argues that an act can be good or bad because of the intention we have when performing it (1a2ae,18,7). He also suggests that, for example, an action, though of a good kind under one description, might be described another way as a bad kind of action. Suppose I steal Fred's money so as to distribute it to the poor. What am I doing here? Aquinas would say that I am stealing from Fred, which is bad, even if I am thereby doing something that can be thought of as good, providing money for those in need (cf. 1a2ae, 18,1).[27]

Some actions, thinks Aquinas, can be morally neutral (1a2ae,18,8). Good kinds of actions, he says, are actions that accord with right reason, and bad kinds of actions are ones that do not. But some kinds of acts are neither good nor bad kinds of acts. As an example, Aquinas cites plucking a blade of grass, something that one might unthinkingly do on a country walk. On the other hand, he also says that, considered in context, a morally neutral act can be good or bad as performed by an individual in a particular context. He thinks that, considered as actions in the life of an individual, there are no morally neutral human actions proceeding from deliberation. If we act on the basis of deliberation, then our actions have moral significance.[28]

In this part of 1a2ae, Aquinas is clearly not trying to provide a list of things we should do and things we should not do, a list to be consulted as we act in various contexts. One reason why he is not doing so is because he is conscious of how circumstances can make a difference when it comes to whether what we are doing is good or bad. That this is so should be clear from what I have already reported him as saying, but it is highlighted by 1a2ae,18,10, in which he argues that the goodness or badness of what one is doing on some occasion might even depend on where and when one is doing what one does.[29] Generally, though, Aquinas takes good acts of willing to amount to willing what is good (1a2ae,19,1) and concludes that, when it comes to willing, moral good and evil "derive from the objective alone, not from circumstances" (1a2ae,19,2).[30]

He means that we will well when we will what is good, even if whether or not we do this depends somehow on circumstances. He also thinks that to will what is good is to will in accordance with reason, "good as intelligently perceived" as he puts it[31] as opposed to sensory desire. Willing badly, he goes on to say, is to will contrary to God's wisdom governing things to their ends (1a2ae,19,4,9 and 10). This he calls the Eternal Law, something to which he returns later in 1a2ae.[32]

What, however, if conscience directs us to do what is objectively wrong? In 1a2ae,19,5 and 6, Aquinas adds to what he says about conscience in 1a,79,13 while arguing that it is always wrong to act contrary to conscience even though acting according to conscience might sometimes amount to one doing what is objectively bad. Conscience, he observes, is a matter of applying knowledge with respect to action, and he admits that one might be mistaken when it comes to what one takes oneself to know. But he also thinks that one should always act on the basis of what one takes oneself to know and that, therefore, an erring conscience is still binding. In other words, Aquinas holds that if I am honestly convinced that I ought to do or not do such and such, then I should do or not do such and such even if I am wrong in my conviction (1a2ae,19,5). He therefore bluntly declares that "every act of will against reason, whether in the right or in the wrong, is bad."[33] At the same time, though, Aquinas is equally clear that this does not make what I do or do not do in the light of conscience a good or bad kind of action. Convinced that action should be governed by what one takes to be true, Aquinas concludes that conscience (even erring) is binding when it comes to action, but, also convinced that one can be wrong when it comes to what one takes to be true, he asserts that acting on the basis of intellectual error can involve one in acting badly (doing something that is objectively bad). In other words, he thinks that an erring conscience, though binding, might not excuse one (even if it sometimes does), because ignorance can sometimes be culpable (cf. 1a2ae,6,8).[34] Involuntary actions, he observes, lack moral good and evil, though ignorance does not always render an action involuntary since the ignorance in question might be willed directly as such or indirectly because of negligence.[35]

With that point made, Aquinas argues that the goodness of a human act depends on the end intended even though this end might be aimed at as one performs a number of different actions with an eye on it (1a2ae,19,7). He means that good willing when willing *this* with a view to *that* can depend for its being good on what *that* happens to be. On the other hand, he also accepts (1a2ae,19,8) that one might have an intention when acting that is better than what one actually wills. I might, he thinks, act while aiming for a great deal of good, but I might thereby fail to produce a great deal of good. What we actually do might not match what we want to do when we act, which Aquinas takes to imply that we may not always be as deserving as we take ourselves to be, that we cannot declare that what we have done is good just because we were trying to will what is good.

In other words, Aquinas holds that we can act and will well or badly depending not only on what we manage to bring about by our actions but also on what we intend as we act—intention, for him, being something that can precede a particular action while also running through it, or a series of actions, as performed. Yet Aquinas also holds that good intentions might be present even in bad actions, which can even become worse as intentions get better. So he denies that the goodness of an action can be determined by the goodness of its intention, even though he accepts that good intentions can be commended and that their goodness can, as it were, overflow into the action thereby preserving it in goodness insofar as it springs from a desire for what is objectively good.

Does Aquinas think that the goodness of human actions depends on the extent to which they conform to God's will? 1a2ae,19,10 makes it clear that he does, because he holds that to will is to desire what is good (even if one fails on some occasion to be willing what is really good) and because he takes God's will to be for what is supremely good (God). He does not, however, think that goodness in human actions depends on them being explicitly willed as conforming to God's will considered as generally willing the goodness that all created things display (1a2ae,19,10). Voluntary action, he observes, proceeds on the basis of reason, which can regard ends under different descriptions (good from one point of view, say, and bad from another). It is wanting something as good (and not wanting it as evil) that renders someone's willing good.[36] And, Aquinas argues, one might will a particular good without willing the universal good that God wills as making and ruling the universe. One should, he says, have an eye on the goodness common to all things whenever one is willing, but one does not have to be willing this explicitly when willing a particular good, even though to will what is good is always to be somehow conformed to God's will. To will what contributes to a common good is to will in correspondence to God's will insofar as God wills the common good. To will what one takes to be good is the result of God's agent causality operating in the action of all creatures (cf. 1a,105, 4 and 5).

Aquinas thinks that goodness in human action can be approached from several different perspectives. We can focus on goodness and badness in human acts in general (the topic of 1a2ae,18). We can also concentrate on goodness and badness in human acts considered with an eye to what is involved in good and bad willing as such (the topic of 1a2ae,19). But we can also pay attention to human actions with a view to the physical activity involved in carrying out what we will well or badly—"outward acts" as Aquinas calls them. This is what he turns to in 1a2ae,20, in which he reasons similarly to the way in which he does in 1a2ae,18 and 19, albeit that he takes himself to be turning to conceptually different issues. Thus, for example, he insists that the goodness or badness of outward acts depends on the kind of acts they are and on the end we have when intending them (1a2ae,20,1). Again, he holds that good intention alone does not make what we do good (1a2ae,20,2) and that being physically thwarted as one tries to do something does not mean that one is not willing badly (1a2ae,20,4). In 1a2ae,20,5, Aquinas's non-consequentialist temperament emerges as he maintains that what results from our actions need not render them either good or bad actions, though in 1a2ae,20,5 Aquinas is clear that the badness of what we do can be increased if we act in the knowledge of various bad consequences likely to arise from what we do.

As he concludes the section of 1a2ae on which I have just been commenting, Aquinas briefly offers a series of what we might think of as terminological remarks bearing on "good" and "bad" as adjectives applied to human actions. Do the words "good" and "bad" mean what "right" and "sinful" mean? Is a sinful act nothing but a blameworthy act? Is a human act meritorious or otherwise just because it is good or bad? Is a human action meritorious or otherwise just in virtue of its being good or bad in God's eyes (*apud Deum*)? These are the questions discussed in 1a2ae,21.

When reading Aquinas's treatment of these questions, one needs to remember that Aquinas always thinks of human actions as those of reasoning creatures able in principle to live a life resulting in them enjoying the beatific vision. Much of 1a2ae can be read as presenting philosophy of action or moral philosophy as many contemporary secular philosophers would think of this. Aquinas, though, was not a secular philosopher. He took human action to be properly and finally evaluated with respect to the end of people considered as ordered toward union with God. So, in 1a2ae,21 he is concerned with the notion of falling short of God's goodness while reflecting on good and evil in human action.

His basic position is that what we do voluntarily should be thought of either as bringing us closer to God or as alienating us from God (even if only temporarily since we can change when it comes to what we want). He presents this conclusion while speaking in terms of "merit" and "sin."

Aquinas holds that when human beings act well, they are meritorious or deserving before God since they are willing what God wills. Meritorious people, thinks Aquinas, are, in a sense, divine. Correspondingly, he says, not to will in accordance with God's will is to sin, to be un-Godlike.[37]

Both merit and sin are topics on which Aquinas has things to say after 1a2ae,21, but he introduces them in this question while arguing that "good" and "bad" are broader concepts than those of "sin" (*peccatum*) and "right" (*rectum*).[38] He also argues that a human action can be meritorious or sinful depending on its objective goodness or badness and that, in the end, all our actions are to be judged as according or not according to the goodness that is the divine nature and will.

Now, though, consider the question "On what basis do we do what we do?" In 1a2ae,18–21, Aquinas frequently refers to us acting on the basis of reason. Yet we often seem to act on the basis of our feelings or emotions and on how we are disposed to behave while not actually going through an explicit process of reasoning. Does Aquinas have something to say about these obvious facts? As we shall see in the next chapter, he certainly does.

Emotions (1a2ae,22–48)

IN IA2AE,22, AQUINAS turns to what he calls *passiones animae*, and he continues to discuss these up to the end of 1a2ae,48. The phrase *passiones animae* can be translated into English as "emotions," and it is commonly so translated.[1] From the amount of space that he devotes to them in 1a2ae one can infer that emotions are important for Aquinas as he develops his account of what human beings are and what is involved in them acting. As he continues with this account from 1a2ae,62, he increasingly speaks of human beings in the light of what can be thought of as theological premises, but in 1a2ae,22–48 (and beyond these questions to some extent) Aquinas proceeds in a largely philosophical manner, notwithstanding his various citations from Scripture and theological authorities. Indeed, the 1a2ae treatment of emotions is one of the most sustained and sophisticated philosophical treatments of emotions coming from any period, and it finds strong echoes in some recently published non-theological work on emotion.[2]

Why does Aquinas the Christian theologian feel the need to philosophize about emotions? He does so because he aims to note what can be known insofar as it has a bearing on our lives considered as ordered to the beatific vision and because he thinks that we live our lives as creatures experiencing emotions. Aquinas also thinks that truth cannot contradict truth and that teachers of *sacra doctrina* ought to be noting truths that are relevant to understanding what human beings are, whether or not these truths derive from divine revelation. He obviously believes that there are truths about human beings that are not particularly relevant when it comes to understanding people as ordered to final happiness that can lie only in union with God. So, for instance, he has nothing to say about the fact that we cannot hold our breath for twenty-five minutes. But that people have emotions, he maintains, is something we need to take account of as we consider human action in general and as we go on to think of people as being drawn to what is good and, ultimately, to God, who is goodness itself.

11.1 1a2ae,22–48 as a Whole

Aquinas holds that people undergo emotions as they are acted on or, perhaps better, as they *react to* what they are aware of around them. As we have seen, his general approach to human understanding takes it to arise because of what we encounter at the sensory level given our ability to assimilate the forms of what exists in the world, and his account of emotions is grounded in this approach to human understanding. We have emotions, Aquinas holds, because we are physical things existing in a physical world that impinges on us and to which we react as things capable of understanding. Some people would say that emotions are purely non-material occurrences going on in our minds or souls considered as non-material things. Aquinas, though, does not think of emotions in this way since, as we have seen, he thinks of human souls as informing human bodies. To be sure, he refers to emotions as "passions of the soul," yet he does not believe that people are purely immaterial substances or, for that matter, souls.

We can, thinks Aquinas, react to the world or be affected by it at different levels. We might simply note what water is, and here we would just be understanding it. What, however, if we are stranded in a desert? Then, and given that we understand what water is, we might *strive to obtain it*. Understanding what water is would, for Aquinas, be a theoretical business, while taking steps to get water would involve practical reasoning. So, roughly speaking, he thinks that we can react to the world by understanding it or by trying to use our knowledge of it so as to act. What, though, of cases where we find ourselves loving or hating, desiring or being repelled, being joyful or sorrowful, hoping or despairing, being confident or fearful or angry? Aquinas takes note of these states in what he says about emotions or "passions of the soul."

Aquinas regards the occurrence of such passions as bound up with physical changes in us.[3] Purely intellectual beings such as God and angels cannot, in his view, undergo emotion, considered as a reaction resulting from physical contact, since they are not material. For Aquinas, we are prone to emotions since we are animals of a certain kind. In this connection, he has no problem agreeing that nonhuman animals can to some extent be thought of as having emotions—as being afraid or desiring, for instance. I might panic in fear when I recognize that a bear is sniffing at my tent on my walk along the Appalachian Trail, and Aquinas accepts that a sheep might also panic in fear when coming across a bear. Yet he recognizes a distinction to be drawn here. In his view, the difference between me and a sheep as both panicking lies in the fact that I, unlike a sheep, can have some explicit or intellectual understanding of what it is that I find before me, so that I can react to what is around me on the basis of something more than instinct. Aquinas also thinks that I might even be able sometimes to control my emotions so as to act contrary to ways in which my natural instinct inclines me to act. In a dentist's chair we might automatically incline to knock the dentist aside and run away in fear. But we might also just sit tight and grip the chair. Why so? Aquinas would reply "Because reason, or rational appetite, can sometimes overcome emotion."

The notion of reason is important for Aquinas as he treats emotion in human beings. I do not mean that Aquinas implausibly thinks that we are always going through some process of argument as we have various emotions. He does, however, hold that emotions arise in us because of what we take to be the case intellectually.[4]

For Aquinas, human emotions arise as people recognize what is around them, even if they can overcome the resulting emotions by thinking in different ways about what they regard as the case. Can people be frightened by what they do *not* believe to be dangerous for them? Aquinas thinks not. Can they love or be averse to what they do *not* think of as falling under some description as desirable or repulsive? Aquinas thinks not. Can they be angry with *no* knowledge of anything or anyone to rail against? Again, Aquinas thinks not. So he views human emotions as springing from ways in which the world appears to us as we encounter it as beings with understanding. He does not think of them as pure feelings recognized for what they are by introspection. According to Aquinas, there is an intellectual or cognitive element lying behind all human emotions, which he therefore distinguishes from effects that we feel as things in the world act on us just so as to produce sensations in us. In Aquinas's opinion, emotions also arise in us as reactions to things or situations in the world, so they are reactions that are *passive* to what brings them about. They amount to us being *moved* in some way, either by attraction or aversion. But, as I have said, Aquinas also thinks that we can sometimes control our emotions, and he thinks that emotions can sometimes be causally effective, as, for example, when fear leads us to run away from a potentially threatening object.

He also thinks that emotions need not necessarily be triggered by what is presently before us, which is a further indication that Aquinas distinguishes between emotion and sensation. We might, he suggests, be sorrowful about some past event or fearful of some possible future event. At the same time, however, Aquinas, as I have said, takes human emotions to have a physiological aspect, to involve a change in our bodily states deriving from the fact that we are drawn or repelled by things in the world as beings that have sensory desires and aversions as well as intellectual ones.[5] He is here, for example, thinking of the fact that, while one might dispassionately acknowledge that bears can kill people, one's being in the grip of fear when confronted by a bear comes with a racing pulse, rapid breathing, sweating, and so on. And why might one be fearful when faced by a bear? Because, thinks Aquinas, one might see a bear, know what bears are, and perceive them *as* a threat to one's well-being and therefore as relevant and meaningful to one's sensory desires and aversions.[6] Perceiving *as* is important for Aquinas as he reflects on emotions as had by people and other animals.[7] He thinks that what we perceive something *as* can make a difference to how we react to it emotionally.

My cat Sweetie nearly always seems to see me as a good thing. He often jumps on my lap, and he sleeps on my bed once I am in it. But Aquinas would think of Sweetie's emotions when it comes to me (attraction rather than fear) as instinctive. Had I treated Sweetie badly in the past, he would doubtless react to me differently than he does now, and perhaps I might be able to train him to react to various things in different ways (though cats, unlike dogs, are pretty untrainable). Yet Sweetie has natural desires and he immediately reacts to the world around him with a view to his needs, and Aquinas can make sense of this fact (and its implications for nonhuman animal behavior in general). He thinks, though, that emotion in people is more complicated than it is in things like Sweetie. He believes that people can be influenced by reason, imagination, or what they are attracted to as they act voluntarily, and that they can bring these things into play when it comes to their immediate emotional reactions and might therefore influence the extent to which certain emotions affect them and how they act when in the grip of them.

Aquinas, working from Latin translations of Aristotle, maintains that there are two basic types of emotion: "concupiscible" (*concupiscibilis*) and "aggressive" (*irascibilis*).[8] He goes on to sub-distinguish among each of these general kinds. His concupiscible/aggressive distinction is intended to acknowledge that some human emotions arise as we desire or dislike certain things, while others arise as we find obstacles in our way as we go about desiring or disliking things. Aquinas thinks that concupiscible emotions are responses to what we take to be nice or desirable. He thinks of aggressive emotions as arising in us as we confront what we take to be nice or desirable *considered as difficult or hard to attain*. Hence, for example, he takes love and hate to be concupiscible emotions, since I may just love or hate someone, but hope and despair to be aggressive ones, since I may exult as I think that what I love is within my grasp or go to pieces as I recognize that I am never going to obtain it.

In Aquinas's view, there are six concupiscible emotions coming in contrary pairs (though he makes subdivisions of a kind even among these). The concupiscible emotions are "love" (*amor*) and "hate" (*odium*), "desire" (*desiderium*) and "aversion" (*fuga*), and "joy" (*gaudium*) and "sorrow" or "pain" (*tristitia* or *dolor*). The aggressive emotions are "hope" (*spes*) and "despair" (*desperatio*), "confidence" (*audacio*), "fear" (*timor*), and "anger" (*ira*). Anger, Aquinas supposes, is unique since it has no contrary emotion. We may, he thinks, be consumed by love as opposed to hate, but there is no state that we can switch to from anger so as to be in a contrary state, even though we might just cease to be angry.

You might suppose that emotions are always bad. In concluding the present "Big Picture" of 1a2ae on emotions, however, I should stress that Aquinas would not agree with you. He is clear that emotions can overwhelm us and lead us to act badly, but he also thinks that they can help us to act well and to become good human beings. Indeed, he argues, some emotions are positively needed in order to act well (though this point is developed more in what follows 1a2ae,22–48).[9]

11.2 1a2ae,22–48: Some Details

1. In 1a2ae,22, Aquinas argues that human beings can undergo "passions of the soul." You might think that he should not, since (a) "passion" suggests suffering undergone by a physical thing as it is acted on by some other physical thing, and since (b) Aquinas has already argued that the human soul is not a material object (cf. 1a,75,1 and 5). Aquinas, however, defends the thesis of 1a2ae,22 while arguing that people can undergo passion or emotional reaction as they are affected by various things, whether good or bad for them. As we have seen, Aquinas insists that human souls are not physical objects to be interfered with by other physical objects, but, as we have also seen, neither does he think of human beings as purely incorporeal substances. He thinks that people are soul-body composites and are therefore able to be affected by the physical world in various ways, even though he also conceives of there being *passiones animae* that are not purely physiological events or the result of physical agent causes.

2. Aquinas takes human emotions to arise because of what we are drawn to or averse to. He thinks of them with an eye on what he calls our "appetites." In 1a2ae,22,2 and 3, he argues that emotion derives from appetite rather than understanding, that having emotions can be distinguished from knowing what things are, even if they might also involve this.[10] He is thinking, for instance, that I do not need to have a grasp of the essence of a bear in order to be frightened by one looming up in front of me with its jaws open, and even though my fear of a bear might spring from my knowing just what it is that confronts me when I meet it.

3. The distinction noted above between concupiscible and aggressive *passiones animae* is presented by Aquinas in 1a2ae,23, where he also classifies the different kinds of concupiscible and aggressive emotions. He makes the distinction between concupiscible and aggressive emotions because he takes them to have different objects. He means that, as the object of

sight (what is visible) is formally different from the object of hearing (what is audible) even though you may be seeing and hearing one and the same thing, the object of love is different from the object of fear even though you may love and hate one and the same thing (cf. 1a,77,3).[11]

4. In 1a2ae,24,1, Aquinas argues that emotions can be morally good or bad depending on whether or not they accord with what we will. His idea here is that, though emotions can arise in us because of feelings uncontrolled by reason (and, considered as such, are neither morally good or bad), we might deliberately try to acquire a particular emotion or to nurture it in ourselves, in which case emotions become morally significant because they are, as Aquinas puts it, "commanded by our reason," and as such become things with respect to which blame or praise can be ascribed to us.

5. Notice that in 1a2ae,24,2,3, and 4, Aquinas does not take emotions to be morally bad just because they are emotions. Some people have seemed to suggest that emotion is always a sign of moral weakness and always something that we should try to be rid of, yet this is not Aquinas's view. His position is that emotions can sometimes positively contribute to our flourishing as human beings and can, therefore, be thought of as morally good if willed by us in the light of reason.[12] Here, of course, Aquinas is presupposing what he says in 1a2ae,24,1.

6. As 1a2ae,25,1 makes clear, Aquinas regards concupiscible and aggressive emotions as relatable to each other in different ways. In this text, however, he also seems to favor the conclusion that we can only make sense of aggressive emotions in the light of concupiscible ones, since the latter provide the context in which we can understand the former. He thinks, for example, that we might love or be drawn to such and such and exult and rest in it having acquired it. Between loving X and resting in or enjoying it, however, we might be striving for it considered as something hard to achieve (we might be hoping for it).

7. 1a2ae,25,2 argues that love (*amor*) is the primary concupiscible emotion, since everything is drawn to good rather than evil, which, as we have seen, Aquinas takes to be a certain privation of goodness and being, and since hating is parasitic on somehow being drawn to a good, since we only hate or are averse to what we take to conflict in various ways with what we regard as good. In 1a2ae,25,3, Aquinas argues that hope (*spes*) is the first aggressive emotion. This claim may seem odd to you since you might think that hope is hardly an emotion at all and that it is not in any way aggressive. To understand Aquinas here, though, one needs to bear in mind his general understanding of the aggressive emotions as I have tried to explain it. He takes them to spring from us recognizing certain goods as

hard to achieve, goods with respect to which we are, as it were, halfway between desiring and enjoying (1a2ae,25,1). We might be angry or despairing if goods such as these elude our grasp, but, Aquinas argues, our anger or despair here is secondary to our hope of achieving them and is parasitic on it. He seems to be working with this scenario in mind: (1) We are naturally drawn to what we take to be good; (2) So we hate or are averse to what we take to be bad; (3) We sometimes note that goods are hard to achieve, and we react to them as hoping to achieve them; (4) Sometimes we fail to achieve them and give up, though our giving up makes no sense apart from our hoping. Aquinas is also thinking that on the basis of what we might have or hope for, we might also be fearful because of some good that we do not have or cannot hope to enjoy.

8. If we grant that our emotions proceed from what we take to be good for us, we might ask, "Can we hate ourselves?" Aquinas turns to this question in 1a2a,29,4 and argues that in one way we cannot hate ourselves but in another way we can. He suggests that people cannot hate themselves in the sense that they cannot will what they unreservedly take to be bad for themselves. He accepts, though, that one can hate oneself (a) insofar as one ends up willing what (unbeknownst to one) is bad for oneself and (b) insofar as one ends up willing only with respect to one's body and senses and not with respect to reason.

9. Can one hate truth? In 1a2ae,29,5, Aquinas considers this question in the light of his belief that good, being, and true are "convertible" (cf. 1a,2,3). He replies that, though one cannot explicitly hate goodness or being or truth in general, one can hate truth if one finds it unpleasant for some reason. One might hate the fact that something one would like not to be the case is the case, or one might wish that one did not know some truth that one takes oneself to know. Or one might hate a truth about oneself known by someone else, a truth that one would like to keep secret. One can also, Aquinas goes on to argue (1a2ae,29,6), hate "universals" and not just particulars. His idea here is that hatred can extend to universal objects of understanding and not just to individual things we interact with at the sensory level. I might hate the individual mosquito biting my arm right now, but I might also hate mosquitos *as such*. To be sure, says Aquinas, universals are not things in the world that we are drawn to or repelled by on the basis of our senses. And universals cannot provoke anger (*ira*) in us, since this always arises in response to particular actions of particular things that affect us as the individuals that we are. But we can still, Aquinas maintains, hate with a view to what we might think of as a general description true of many things of a single kind. So as well as hating the

mosquito biting my arm now, I might abstractly hate mosquitos considered as a certain general kind.

10. We have seen that Aquinas distinguishes between concupiscible and aggressive emotions, but he also thinks that there is a distinct emotion of concupiscence or desire (*desiderium*) bound up with sensory appetite or attraction (1a2ae,30,2). He takes this emotion to be had by us as body-soul composites (1a2ae,30,1), so he distinguishes it from mere instinctive or animal attraction, and thinks of it as peculiarly human and as a matter of us desiring goods that we sense and want as bodily satisfying to us. Note, though, that the desiring that Aquinas has in mind here is, specifically, craving or desiring physical goods that we do not presently possess. He therefore distinguishes between concupiscence, on the one hand, and love (*amor*) and pleasure (*delectatio*), on the other. We manifest love, he thinks, as various goods elicit desire on our part, and we manifest pleasure as we rest in various goods as obtained by us. Concupiscence, he holds, is our desiring particular bodily goods that we have not yet obtained. Aquinas takes some of these goods (food and drink, for instance) to be naturally or inevitably desired by us in that they are bound up with our very survival. But he also thinks that some of them are goods that appeal to us even though our existence does not depend on them and even though we do not have to desire them (1a2ae,30,4). We cannot but desire to eat sometimes. What, though, about desiring to live in London as opposed to Paris? If we desire to live in some particular place, that is because something about the place strikes us as agreeable, even though desiring to live there is not something built into us by nature. In this connection, Aquinas distinguishes between "natural" and "nonnatural" desires while arguing (1a2ae,30,5) that there can be any number of nonnatural desires. Such desires are, he holds, as infinite as the possibilities that reason can suggest to us. We can only naturally desire so much food or drink at a given time (though once our hunger and thirst have been satisfied we can later become hungry and thirsty and then go on to desire more food and drink). Yet, thinks Aquinas, some desires might be ones the object of which is unlimited (like an unlimited supply of money).

11. Aquinas's 1a2ae discussions of pleasure (*dilectatio*) and of pain (*dolor*) and sorrow (*tristitia*) display almost identical structures. Aquinas considers these emotions generally. Then he proceeds to talk about their causes, their effects, and their moral standing. His account of pain and sorrow, however, has a therapeutic aspect lacking in his treatment of pleasure, since it contains remarks about how to overcome these emotions (1a2ae,38), which he takes to be basically about the same thing even though he draws a distinction between them (1a2ae,35,2).

12. Aquinas thinks of pleasure (*delectatio*) as people's reaction to agreeable sensible states in which they find themselves while, unlike other animals, *recognizing* themselves to be doing so and delighting in the fact that they are doing so. So he regards pleasure as a kind of achievement, as a resting in the enjoyment of what is desired at a physical level (1a2ae,31,1).

13. In 1a2ae,31,2, Aquinas asks whether pleasure is in time. The question may seem odd to you since people exist in time, but Aquinas wants to argue that the concept of pleasure excludes the concept of occupying time since occupying time can be thought of as *essentially* involving movement and succession while the concept of pleasure does not. Pleasure, thinks Aquinas, does not *essentially* involve movement or successiveness. What pleasure essentially amounts to is the possession and enjoyment of a good, even though some particular occurrence of pleasure might be the result or terminus of some movement and succession, and even though it might be obliterated by some movement or succession.

14. In 1a2ae,31,3, Aquinas distinguishes between pleasure (*delectatio*) and joy (*gaudium*). The distinction he makes reflects his view (noted above) that even nonhuman animals can somehow be thought of as undergoing *passiones animae*. Aquinas thinks that nonhuman animals can enjoy certain bodily states and can, therefore, be said to experience pleasure, though they cannot enjoy such states as beings who are able to reason (cf. 1a2ae,30,3). So, he says, we can ascribe pleasure to them but not joy, which he takes to be pleasure that arises in us insofar as we are able to understand. There is, in Aquinas's view, pleasure that arises from bodily states. There is also pleasure that arises from our perception of bodily states with a view to their significance to us considered as thinkers. And, Aquinas says, one might have pleasure in the first sense without having pleasure in the second. Hence his distinction between *delectatio* and *gaudium*.

15. Might bodily pleasure be greater than pleasure arrived at on the basis of intellect or understanding? You might think so since (a) many people seem to prize bodily pleasures above any other kind, (b) bodily pleasures seem to have very strong effects on us, and (c) bodily pleasures are intense and need to be controlled in a way that intellectual enjoyment does not. In 1a2ae,31,5, however, Aquinas argues that intellectual (or as he also says "spiritual") pleasure is greater than sensory or bodily pleasure. He agrees that bodily pleasure is more intense than pleasure deriving from understanding. He also accepts that pleasures of touch are greater than those of other senses, since pleasures of touch are more useful to us than are those of other senses (1a2ae,31,6).[13] But he thinks that understanding is more to be prized than what we can obtain at the sensory level. He says, for

instance, that nobody would trade being able to "see" intellectually for being able to see with physical eyes (that "people would rather lose their sight than their sanity").[14]

16. 1a2ae,31,7 argues that some pleasures are "nonnatural" (*contra naturam*). Here Aquinas is presupposing that "natural" pleasures in human beings are (a) pleasures arising from the fact that people are rational beings or (b) pleasures arising from what people have in common with nonhuman animals (bodily pleasures of food, drink, and the like). Aquinas assumes that people are generally prone to enjoy these pleasures, so he thinks of them as being natural. On the other hand, he notes that some people find pleasure in what most people do not find appealing, and with this point in mind he accepts that there can be nonnatural pleasures. He regards these as springing from a disorder in that they arise because of exceptions in particular people from what is common or usual for people considered in general. Thus, for example, he cites taking pleasure in food that people would normally find unappealing to be unnatural. Another example he gives is taking pleasure in homosexual intercourse. There can, he thinks, be pleasure here, but it is "against nature" since it is abnormal and only comes about insofar as certain people are ailing or disordered in some way. I presume that Aquinas's point here is that people who enjoy what people in general do not enjoy are anomalous and that one should look for some factor explaining their tastes. He seems to think that while, for example, no special explanation is needed for people liking to eat standard fare or to have sex with people of the opposite sex, some special explanation is called for when certain people like to eat sand or to have sex with people of the same sex. Given what we know of people in general, it is not, thinks Aquinas, surprising to find someone who likes eating meat or vegetables, and not surprising to find someone who likes heterosexual sex. However, he thinks that it is surprising (and in need of explanation) to find someone who likes to eat sand or to have homosexual sex. To this thought he adds the idea that what is surprising and in need of explanation here amounts to a deficiency of some kind when viewed in the light of a norm. In short, Aquinas takes what he calls "unnatural pleasures" (viewed by him as what we might call "pathological") to arise from what threatens human well-being.[15]

17. Aquinas's account of the causes of pleasure follows naturally from what he has said about the nature of pleasure in 1a2ae. He argues, as we might expect, that pleasure involves us acting in some way (exercising knowledge, for instance) and that it arises because of changes of some kind (1a2ae,32,1 and 2). He also argues that other people's actions can cause us pleasure (1a2ae,32,5), that pleasure can arise because of hopes

and memories (1a2ae,32,3), and that doing good to others can cause us pleasure (1a2ae,32,6).[16] In 1a2ae,32,4, he cites sorrow or sadness (*tristitia*) as a possible source of pleasure, which might seem an odd thing to do. But Aquinas's point in this article is that sadness can prompt pleasure of a kind in the sense that, for example, even thinking about a beloved dead friend can come with a measure of pleasure. Again, Aquinas suggests, sadly remembering a bad state one was once in might lead one, as they say, to "count one's blessings." You might well find 1a2ae,32,7 puzzling since it asks whether or not "similarity" (*similitudo*) is a cause of pleasure and since you might wonder what Aquinas means by "similarity." He means that similarity can be present when two things are, as we might say, "in tune" with each other by being like each other. Things like each other in this sense might, Aquinas thinks, account for there being pleasure in each of them even if they might also account for each of them being in a bad way.

18. In 1a2ae,32,8, Aquinas introduces the notion of wonder (*admiratio*), and you should realize that this notion is something of a key to Aquinas's thinking in general. I mean that Aquinas has a great deal of time for *admiratio* and that his respect for it governs much that he says even when not talking about it explicitly. What does he mean by *admiratio*? I have just rendered it as "wonder," but that word does not quite bring out what Aquinas seems to mean by it. "Puzzlement" might be a better word to use. That is because Aquinas thinks that we may wonder in two senses. Suppose that we find ourselves displaying certain medical symptoms. We might then, so Aquinas would say, wonder (have *admiratio*) concerning them. We might wonder or be puzzled about what is causing them. So Aquinas thinks of wonder as amounting to a desire for a causal account, as a desire to understand why what we perceive is there or is happening. But we might wonder why what we perceive is there or happening because we do not expect it to be. We might, for example, say, "I am surprised that Fred went for a holiday in Greece given what he has said about that country," and Aquinas's use of *admiratio* also encompasses this fact. Generally, therefore, Aquinas takes *admiratio* to amount to a desire for explanation. You might say that such desire for explanation rests on the unprovable assumption that the world is intelligible. You may say, for example, that looking for causes of what happens in the world is fundamentally unjustifiable since things can just happen without there being a cause of them happening.[17] Yet this is not Aquinas's view. He agrees, as we have seen, that there can be chance events lacking a single presiding cause (1a,22,2). At the same time, however, he also presumes that we are justified in looking for causes of various kinds unless there is something intrinsically silly

about doing so. Some causal questions seem to be intrinsically silly, for example, "What accounts for Thursday being prouder than Friday?" But some causal questions are not intrinsically silly, and Aquinas thinks that we should be struck by them. This "being struck by" is what Aquinas has in mind as he talks about *admiratio*, and in 1a2ae,32,8, he argues that *admiratio* can be a source of pleasure since it can come with the prospect of finding out what is going on. One may be puzzled when it comes to what is going on and might be very frustrated because of this. But Aquinas offers another scenario in 1a2ae,32,8. Here he says that *admiratio* can (emphasis on "can" as opposed to "must") be a source of satisfaction. I take him to be thinking that, for example, scientists might be *excited* as they find themselves moving toward the answers to questions that they have been struggling with for some time.[18]

19. In 1a2ae,33, Aquinas talks about the effects of pleasure. In 1a2ae,33,1, he argues that coming to have pleasure can amount to us coming to have what we did not enjoy before at either an intellectual or sensory level and can, therefore, add to whatever enjoyment we had beforehand. He goes on (1a2ae,33,2) to argue that pleasure can result in a desire for more pleasure. For example, he says, one might enjoy what one possesses while possessing it imperfectly and therefore go on to desire more of that in which one already takes pleasure. He also argues that on the basis of some pleasure remembered one might be moved to seek more of the same, and pleasure as enjoyed, Aquinas also suggests, can interfere with the use of reason (1a2ae,33,3). This need not always be so, he says, since it might be the exercise of reason itself in which one takes pleasure. Immersion in bodily pleasure, however, can impede reason's exercise, Aquinas thinks, since it can lead one partly or wholly to ignore what reason might suggest, since it can lead one to act imprudently, and since it might just mess up one's ability to reason well, as, for instance, in the case of excessive pleasure indulged in with respect to alcohol. On the other hand, Aquinas is not of the view that pleasure inevitably results in those enjoying it ending up in a bad way. Insofar as one takes pleasure in what is good, he argues, pleasure positively completes one's being drawn to the good in question and can make one even more focused on it (1a2ae,33,4).

20. Unsurprisingly, therefore, Aquinas argues that pleasure is not necessarily evil and to be shunned (1a2ae,34,1). Some pleasures are good, he says, even if some are not, and there is pleasure that consists in the enjoyment of God in the beatific vision (1a2ae,34,3; cf.1a,12).[19] At the same time, though, Aquinas also thinks that one can be judged morally good or evil in terms of what one finds pleasurable, good deeds or evil ones.

21. Aquinas takes pain (*dolor*) to be an emotion. He also takes sorrow
or sadness (*tristitia*) to be one. We have seen that in 1a2ae,31,3, Aquinas
distinguishes between pleasure and joy. Correspondingly, in 1a2ae,35,2, he
distinguishes between pain and sorrow by arguing that sorrow results
from understanding or imagination of some kind rather than from what
impacts us at a sensory level and might therefore cause us pain. As pleasure
stands to joy, Aquinas argues, pain stands to sorrow or sadness. Both pain
and sorrow are, he thinks, contrary or opposite to pleasure since good and
evil are contraries or opposites (and even though sorrow can sometimes
lead one to pleasure).[20] On the other hand, Aquinas denies that every
sorrow is contrary to every pleasure. Being sorrowful about and taking
pleasure in one and the same object, he agrees, are contraries, but, he suggests, one might be sorrowful about one thing while rejoicing in another.
Emotions, says Aquinas, can be distinguished in terms of genus and species with respect to their objects, what they focus on generally or in particular. In general, he observes, emotions amount to either attraction or recoil
and can therefore be generically contrary to each other. Yet emotions taken
specifically might have different objects (one might grieve over one thing
and be pleased about another). So not every sorrow is contrary to every
pleasure. Yet Aquinas accepts (with reservations) that there is no sorrow
that is contrary to contemplation (*contemplatio*), by which he means
roughly "joyfully resting in or enjoying understanding." One may understand what is harmful and distressing. One may also understand what is
agreeable and pleasurable. The pleasure of contemplation, says Aquinas,
can, therefore, have a contrary sorrow because of its object at different
times. Considered in itself, as an object of pleasure, however, Aquinas
thinks that the pleasure of contemplation does not have a contrary since
there is no such thing as the pleasure of not understanding. We might
lament that we do not understand, but, thinks Aquinas, we do not and
cannot take pleasure in this—that there is no such intelligible pleasure as
the pleasure of not understanding.[21]

22. What causes sadness and pain? Given his view that evil is a privation of being in some sense (cf. 1a,48), Aquinas can hardly say that sadness
and pain are caused (in the "agent cause" sense of "cause") by substances
or independently existing and naturally occurring things. In 1a2ae,36, "On
the Causes of Sorrow or Pain," however, he distinguishes between what
evil is when understood as a privation and what evil is as perceived by us.
He argues (1a2ae,36,1) that evil can, considered as perceived by us, cause
us pain since we may sorrow because of goodness lost or evil present. Evil
may be no existing thing (something having *esse*), but this does not mean

that I cannot end up coming to be pained or saddened by evil since even a privation can be thought of and recognized for what it is (whether present or past). He goes on to suggest (1a2ae,36,2) that desire (*concupiscentia*) can cause sadness insofar as sadness can arise because one's desire is thwarted. It may be thwarted, thinks Aquinas, because one has never managed to obtain some good that one desires. It may also be thwarted since a good obtained might be taken away from one. In 1a2ae,36,3, Aquinas adds that the desire for unity (*appetitus unitatis*) can cause sorrow. Drawing on his conclusion that one, good, and being are "convertible" (cf. 1a,5,1 and 11,1), he suggests that wanting goodness that comprises a perfection in oneself always involves wanting what is one or unified in some sense, and that sorrow can therefore be causally related to the wanting of good. In 1a2ae,36,4, Aquinas concludes his discussion of the causes of sadness or pain by arguing that these can be caused by a power one cannot resist. Sadness or pain can, he thinks, be traced to the effects of what accounts for there being evil or badness (these being contrary to desire) unless what accounts for there being evil manages to work on our desires so as to bring it about that they gravitate toward what is bad. Here Aquinas is effectively saying that if something acts so as to bring our will or inclinations within its sway, we do not have pain or sorrow because of it. Rather, we are in tune with it.

23. What are the effects of sadness or pain? In 1a2ae,37, Aquinas says that they include an inability to learn, depression (literally "a heaviness" or "aggravation" of soul), and a weakening of one's activity. Pain, he thinks (1a2ae,37,1), can sometimes affect one to the extent of leaving one hardly able to think about anything else, including what might be learned. And pain or sorrow, he argues (1a2ae,37,2), can weigh us down or depress us since it can deprive us of enjoying what we want to enjoy and sometimes leave us helpless. Pain or sadness might prompt us to act positively in various ways, thinks Aquinas, though it generally impedes us from action (1a2ae,37,3).[22] And it especially impedes us at a bodily level (1a2ae,37,4). As we have seen, Aquinas does not think of people as purely immaterial. He thinks that we are essentially material, and his account of human emotion is shot through by this thought. So he argues that pain or sadness seriously afflict us and can grind us down insofar as they strike us at the bodily level.

24. Are there remedies for sorrow or pain? In 1a2ae,38, Aquinas, putting on his therapist hat, as it were, suggests that there are. Pleasure (*dilectatio*), he says, can generally be thought of as an antidote to pain and sadness (1a2ae,38,1). And then, he observes, there is weeping (*fletus*). People sometimes say, "Have a good cry; it will help." Aquinas seems to be of the same mind (1a2ae,38,2) while also noting that one can be aided in

pain and sorrow by the sympathy of friends (1a2ae,38,3), by contemplating truth (1a2ae,38,4), or even by sleeping or having a hot bath (1a2ae,38,5).

25. How should we think of sadness or pain when it comes to good and evil? This is the topic of 1a2ae,39. Here Aquinas first argues (1a2ae,39,1) that sorrow is always evil insofar as it amounts to someone being distressed in some way and failing to rest in a good of some kind. But, he adds, it might sometimes be good for people to be sorrowful, as when, for instance, they are sad because they have done something bad. And sorrow, he says, can sometimes be useful to us insofar as it prompts us to seek and achieve what is good for us (1a2ae,39,3). As he indicates in 1a2ae,39,4, however, Aquinas does not regard bodily pain as the worst conceivable evil. Evil done (*malum culpae*) is worse than evil suffered (*malum poenae*), he thinks, and it is worse not to recognize and reject what is bad than to be affected by it.

26. When turning to the aggressive emotions, Aquinas first deals with hope (*spes*) and despair (*desperatio*)—thereby indicating that he does not take aggressive emotions to be simply hostile reactions on our part. He takes hope to involve desire for a future good that is hard to obtain but still obtainable. As he puts it: "Hope is a movement of appetite aroused by the perception of what is agreeable, future, arduous, and possible of attainment. It is the tendency of an appetite towards this sort of object" (1a2ae,40,2).[23] Aquinas, therefore, denies that hope can be had with respect to what is somehow perceived as impossible to obtain. In addition, Aquinas thinks that hope is ascribable to nonhuman animals: "If a dog sees a hare or a hawk spies a bird that is too far away it does not go after it, as though it had no hope of catching it. But if the prey be nearby it makes a try for it, as though it hoped to capture it" (1a2ae,40,3).[24] And despair, thinks Aquinas, is the contrary or opposite of hope since it amounts to a giving up on a desired goal rather than a moving toward it with some confidence of obtaining it (1a2ae,40,4). Since he holds (1a2ae,40,5) that hope arises in us on the basis of experience, including knowledge arrived at by various means, he concludes that it abounds in the young and the inebriated (1a2ae,40,6). Young people and those who are drunk, he observes, frequently look confidently to the future while not being able correctly to judge what is and what is not possible for them. Yet, though he thinks that it can sometimes be misplaced, Aquinas takes hope to be an aid to action rather than a hindrance (1a2ae,40,8). That is because he views hope as able to spur us on to good objectives considered as obtainable.

27. Aquinas's discussion of fear (*timor*) nicely illustrates the role that he thinks our bodies can have when it comes to emotions, for he stresses

that fear involves a strong physiological element (1a2ae,41,1).[25] Aquinas takes an object of fear, like an object of hope, to be future and not present. You may think that Aquinas is just wrong here since, you might reasonably say, one can be as frightened as can be by a real bear looming up before one, even if one can also be afraid because one thinks that a bear might be about to appear. But Aquinas does not seem to be denying this obvious fact. His point seems to be that fear essentially has to do with what is *going to happen* rather than with what is happening *now*. He seems to be thinking, for example, that bears do not always incite fear in us, since they might be a source of delight when observed in a zoo, but that they do so insofar as we perceive them as likely to inflict harm on us in certain ways. It is harms as perceived as coming our way that Aquinas takes to be the objects of fear, among which, in 1a2ae,42,2, he includes death.

28. What causes fear? Aquinas's answer is "love and defect" (*amor* and *defectus*). We perceive objects of fear, he argues, as able to take away what we somehow want. Fear's object, he says, "is something regarded as disagreeable, future, threatening, and not easily resisted" (1a2ae,43,1).[26] So, Aquinas reasons, love enters into the picture causally when it comes to fear since our desires make us subject to fear when it comes to certain things. It comes in as "a quality which disposes one to be affected by" what we perceive to be evils of various kinds.[27] As for defect, Aquinas takes this to be a cause of fear since he takes it to be inadequacy on our part to stand up to and resist objects of fear (1a2ae,43,2). We do not fear physical damage from people who are considerably weaker than ourselves, but we might well fear such damage as possibly coming to us from someone much more powerful than we are. In this sense, thinks Aquinas, ways in which we are adversely mismatched in relation to things, as defective by comparison to them in various ways, can cause fear in us.

29. What are fear's effects? In 1a2ae,44, Aquinas argues that they are contraction (*contractio*), deliberation, and trembling. He takes contraction to be a bodily change that occurs to help those in danger (1a2ae,33,1). He associates it with a "concentration of heat and vital spirits in the internal organs" and compares it (a) to the way in which the strength of dying people homes in on mere matters of survival and (b) the way in which people in towns under siege regroup at their centers.[28] Aquinas also associates fear with trembling, which he also describes in physiological terms (1a2ae,44,3). Deliberation enters into Aquinas's account of fear's effects since he thinks that when confronted by what is potentially harmful to us we naturally try to figure out how to withstand it, though Aquinas also thinks

that fear can distort our perception so as to obstruct good deliberation. Passion or emotion, he observes, can hinder our capacity to deliberate wisely. And yet, he adds, the emotion of fear does not necessarily interfere with action. Fear, he notes, can certainly render us incapacitated in certain ways, but it can sometimes positively spur us to act in our best interests (1a2ae,44,4).

30. What might be thought of as the passion of the soul contrary to fear? Aquinas says that it is boldness or daring (*audacia*), which he turns to in 1a2ae,45. Fear leads us to shrink from a danger, he says, but boldness amounts to facing up to it, to meeting it head on (1a2ae,45,1). So Aquinas thinks that the bold also have hope (1a2ae,45,2), and, he adds, while fear springs from "defect," boldness springs from a kind of self-confidence in one's ability (1a2ae,45,3).

31. Aquinas's 1a2ae treatment of emotions concludes with a discussion of anger and follows roughly the same format as his discussions of pleasure, pain, and fear. First Aquinas asks about the nature of anger. Then he turns to its motives and effects. When it comes to anger's nature, he argues that anger is the product of different emotions since we are angry because of sorrow combined with desire and hope (1a2ae,46,1). Aquinas distinguishes between degrees or kinds of anger (1a2ae,46,8), all of which he takes to be species of reactions to what we take, rightly or wrongly, to be injustices.[29] When angry, he thinks, we might immediately rail against something or someone and thereby display wrath (*fel*). Again, we might brood negatively and over time on some past cause of anger and thereby display ill will (*menis*). Or we might be angry and seeking revenge. So Aquinas thinks that there is an intellectual component to anger since we are angry with respect to what we take to be the case.[30] But he also thinks that anger arises because of what we like and because of what we hope for. You might instinctively presume that Aquinas would think of anger as inevitably a bad thing. He does say that anger can arise without good reason, yet he does not think that it is necessarily bad. He thinks that it can be triggered by what is truly deserving of contempt. An angry person, experiencing anger and acting on it, might be thoroughly justified, he holds, since anger can arise because of goods rightly understood to be such and evils rightly understood to be such. And anger, thinks Aquinas, is "aggressive" in the sense that it amounts to a reaction infecting our attempts to deal with certain difficulties that we perceive with an eye on what we take to be good and evil—evils that we take to be instances of injustice to ourselves that we want made up for in some way by goods.

Aquinas's account of emotions is obviously offered by him so that we might be able to understand something about ourselves as we react and act. It focuses on feelings and on action resulting from them. But our feelings, you might think, have to arise in us because of what we are disposed to like or dislike. You might also think that our feelings and actions must derive from what we are disposed to think and from ways in which we are disposed to behave. You might say that our personality, and the tendencies we have because of it, have to enter into an account of what we are actually doing at any given time, and Aquinas would agree with you. That is why he moves in 1a2ae,49 to a consideration of the notion of disposition (*habitus*). In the next chapter we shall see how he thinks of this and how he goes on to connect it to the notions of virtue and vice.

Dispositions, Virtues, Gifts, Beatitudes, and Fruits (1a2ae,49–70)

THE SECUNDA PARS is mostly concerned with what goes on as people become united to God. It continually looks forward to beatitude, and considers how people come to this both in general, considered simply as people, and in particular, considered as people in different walks of life. That is why the *Secunda Pars* begins with a discussion of human happiness.

As we have seen, though, Aquinas distinguishes between two kinds of happiness: that which we can enjoy in this life and that which amounts to something beyond it. This distinction obviously raises the question "What do we need in order to obtain happiness of each of these kinds?" Aquinas's basic answer to this question is "To be happy in this life we need virtues that we can bring about in ourselves; to be happy in the next life we need virtues or gifts that only God can bring about in us." He thinks that virtues always make for well-being of those who have them, and he holds that some virtues can be cultivated by us—these, with qualification, being "cardinal" or "moral" ones. But he also thinks that there are virtues that are beyond our natural powers to obtain—these being "supernatural" virtues that are essential for beatitude.

Virtues in the second sense here are dealt with in detail by Aquinas in 2a2ae. Virtues in the first sense are chiefly discussed by him in 1a2ae,55–67. There is, however, a certain amount of overlap between 1a2ae and 2a2ae when it comes both to "natural" and "supernatural" virtues, since in 1a2ae,68–70 Aquinas discusses "the gifts of the Spirit," which he takes to be supernatural, and in 2a2ae,47–62 he discusses prudence and justice, which he thinks of as perfective of us in this life and, with certain qualifications, able to be acquired by our effort.

Yet what should we take a virtue to be? Aquinas thinks that a virtue (and a vice as well) is a *habitus*, and in 1a2ae,49–54 he works up to his treatment of virtues and vices by first reflecting on the notion of *habitus*.

12.1 Habitus (1a2ae,49–54)

The connection between virtue and habit goes back to ancient philosophy. Aristotle, whom Aquinas frequently quotes in 1a2ae,49–54, says that virtue is a habit "involving rational choice, consisting in a mean relative to us and determined by reason."[1] He does not, of course, say that virtue is a *habitus* (the plural of which is *habitus*) since he wrote in Greek and not in Latin. He says that virtue is a *hexis*. But *hexis* came to be translated into Latin as *habitus*, and *habitus* came to be translated into English as "habit." For this reason we can say that Aristotle and Aquinas both took a virtue to be a habit.[2]

What, though, did Aristotle mean by *hexis*? Did he mean the same by it as Aquinas does by *habitus*? And are *hexis* and *habitus* best rendered into English as "habit"? By *hexis* Aristotle seems to mean a state or disposition (whether good or bad) that people might be in as they go about acting. And, though differences have sometimes been noted between Aristotle's understanding of *hexis* and Aquinas's understanding of *habitus*, Aquinas's understanding of *habitus* in 1a2ae,49–54 frequently corresponds to what Aristotle says about *hexis*.[3] Both of them think that our acting well or badly can derive or spring from settled ways of behavior that we have built up over time—some of them good (virtues) and some of them bad (vices). For this reason, we might translate *habitus* as employed by Aquinas with the words "disposition" and "dispositions." In 1a2ae,49–54, Aquinas gives a variety of examples of what he takes to be *habitus*. He cites health, sickness, virtues, vices, knowledge of facts, and even knowledge of languages. So a precise English equivalent to his use of *habitus* is, perhaps, not available. But although Aquinas has at hand and sometimes uses the Latin word *dispositio* distinctly from his use of *habitus*, "disposition" seems to cover a lot of what he seems to have in mind when speaking of *habitus*.[4] And the Latin rendering of *hexis* by *habitus* is arguably fortunate, since both terms are built up around the idea of "having" and since both construe *having* as a matter of *how we are doing*.[5]

With those points in mind we still need to note that there are reasons for distinguishing between what we now tend to mean by "habit" or "habits" and between what Aquinas means by *habitus*. He thinks of a *habitus* (whether good or bad one) as making it easy or natural for us to do something. For Aquinas, a *habitus* indicates what we *want*. By contrast, of course, a habit, for us, can often conflict with our wants and be hard to shake off, as when we speak of a cocaine habit or the habit of smoking. We often tend to associate habits with *addictions*. For Aquinas, though, a *habitus* puts our activity more under our control than it might otherwise be, since it reflects our desires, since it can lead us easily or spontaneously to pursue goals that reflect what we are about as the people we are.

Anthony Kenny has suggested that a *habitus* for Aquinas is "half-way be-tween a capacity and an action, between pure potentiality and full actuality."[6] I think that Kenny is right here, even though Aquinas sometimes speaks of physical states like being beautiful as amounting to the possession of a *habitus*. Aquinas's discussion of *habitus* in 1a2ae,49–54 clearly has its sights on dispositions that enable us to act well or badly and, therefore, seems to be chiefly concerned with *habitus* as governing or accounting for what we do voluntarily.

Consider the case of someone disposed to pay his or her bills. Such a person might be so disposed without actually paying any bill since, perhaps, he or she currently has no incoming bills to pay. But this does not mean that he or she is not a "bill-paying person," that he or she is not someone disposed to pay bills. So one can have a disposition when it comes to action without actually acting on it, and this is what Aquinas thinks as he talks about us having a *habitus* (cf. 1a2ae,50,4). Our actions, he says, can spring from our dispositions even though our dispositions do not amount to a series of already achieved actions (albeit that dispositions might be built up in us on the basis of such actions). So in 1a2ae,55,4, Aquinas claims that a virtue, which he takes to be a *habitus*, is "a good quality of mind by which one lives righteously, of which no one can make bad use."[7] Aquinas does not think of a *habitus* as hard to overcome. If I am disposed to act in certain ways, it does not follow that I *have* to act in these ways. But, so you might think, my being disposed to act in certain ways indi-cates my character, and character is important for Aquinas when it comes to *habitus* since he thinks of virtues and vices as displaying and springing from character. He does not suppose that virtuous Fred is guaranteed always to remain virtuous. He does, however, think that Fred as virtuous is displaying his current character, just like vicious John. He also thinks that virtues are disposi-tions that serve us well in the business of living and that vices serve us badly.

Aquinas's point here is that virtues and vices are what we have as we develop settled ways of acting that can be thought of as good or bad. So when approach-ing virtues and vices he wants to stress that these amount to more than lip service paid to a set of conclusions offered by sound moral philosophers. The general discussion of *habitus* in 1a,2ae,49–54 is arguing that living well in-volves developed skills just as does playing certain games well. I might read a book on how to play tennis, but I will not actually end up playing tennis well just by reading about it. I will need to *play* tennis and *to work at* doing so well. I will need to acquire abilities needed for playing tennis, and to do this I will need to practice. In a similar way, Aquinas thinks, I will need to acquire abili-ties or developed instincts required for living well. Such abilities or instincts are what he takes virtues to be.

In 1a2ae,50, Aquinas notes that there are dispositions of both intellect and will. He means that dispositions can be involved in how we think and choose. We can, he thinks, have tendencies to think in certain ways and tendencies to act in certain ways, the former often being influenced by the latter and vice versa. Later in 1a2ae, Aquinas will elaborate on this idea when talking about particular virtues and vices to be distinguished as intellectual and moral ones. In 1a2ae,51, however, he settles for noting that not all dispositions are innate, that they can sometimes be caused by repeated actions, and that they can sometimes be "infused" in us by God.

12.2 Virtue (1a2ae,55–67)

In 1a2ae,55–67, Aquinas directly applies to the notion of virtue what he has previously been saying about dispositions. His claim is that virtues are dispositions, that they are tendencies in us to act well, that they are character-revealing and are shown forth by our behavior over time. In 1a2ae,55,1 and 2, therefore, we find him saying that a human virtue is a *habitus* while stressing that virtues are displayed in good actions and that "an act of virtue is nothing other than free choice well applied."[8] A virtue, he suggests, is an "operative disposition" (*habitus operativus*), one geared to doing rather than being. He adds (1a2ae,55,3) that virtues are always good dispositions since "the virtue of anything has to be judged in reference to a good" because "virtue implies a perfection of a power."[9]

Aquinas was aware of the definition of "virtue" that I quoted above, but I did not quote it fully. Altogether, it reads: "Virtue is a good quality of mind by which one lives righteously, of which no one can make bad use, which God works in us without us."[10] This definition was attributed to St. Augustine in Aquinas's day, and it does not sound very Aristotelian since Aristotle did not refer to virtues as coming to us *from God without us*. Aquinas, however, likes it and says that it "comprises perfectly the whole notion of virtue."[11]

Virtue, he observes, belongs to the genus of quality.[12] He adds that virtue is a quality of mind since it is we who have human virtues, and that virtue (unlike vice) is always directed to what is good. Evidently aware that Aristotle says nothing about virtue as brought about in us by God without us, Aquinas notes that the definition of virtue of which he himself approves also covers what he thinks of as infused or theological virtues such as he will go on to discuss in 1a2ae,63. But he thinks that it applies well enough to non-theological virtues such as he will go on to discuss in 1a2ae,57–61. It has sometimes been suggested that Aquinas did not think of non-theological virtues as really being virtues, and, as we shall see, there is something to be said for that suggestion.

On the other hand, as 1a2ae,55,4 seems to indicate, Aquinas is perfectly happy to think of non-theological virtues as being genuine virtues (just as he is happy in the *Prima Pars* to consider knowledge of God derived from human reasoning to be genuine knowledge of God, albeit that it falls short of the beatific vision). So he observes that, shorn of the phrase "which God works in us without us," the definition of "virtue" noted above "will be common to all virtues, whether acquired or infused."[13]

Virtues, says Aquinas, belong to the human soul and arise from powers that the human soul has (1a2ae,56,1). But virtues can be ascribed to different powers of the soul, even if only to different degrees (1a2ae,56,2), and, for a start, they can reside as a *habitus* in our intellect or mind, meaning that they can be intellectual (1a2ae,56,3).[14]

In saying so, Aquinas does not mean that we are necessarily virtuous because we are clever or because we have any and every intellectual skill that might be mentioned. He obviously thinks that such is not the case. But he does think that when willing correctly (having a good will, aiming at what is good) we can be aided at the level of understanding or intellect, whether speculative or practical (whether engaged in theoretical or practical reasoning).

Aquinas's view is that good habits of mind can help us when it comes to good ways of acting. We might, he thinks, have intellectual skills (*habitus*) that do not lead us to act well and that cannot, therefore, be strictly thought of as virtues. After all, he observes, intellectual skills can be misused in one way or another, as with very clever thieves and so on. They can, however, also be employed when reasoning rightly with respect to action, in which case they become important for the notion of virtue since they can enable us to use our powers well. Aquinas takes this fact to mean that, in the right hands (so to speak), intellectual skills can lead to full-blown virtues. As governed by right willing, he says, faith (a virtue to do with speculative reason) and prudence (a virtue to do with practical reason) are definitely virtues. In this sense, Aquinas concludes, there can be virtue in the intellect.

In 1a2ae,56,4, Aquinas goes on to argue that there can be virtues located in our irascible and concupiscible powers. Our aggressive and concupiscible emotions, he observes, are not virtuous or vicious considered simply as such, but they can be thought of as leading to virtue if they are rightly governed by reason, with an eye to what is truly fulfilling for human beings. As Aquinas writes: "The irascible and concupiscible powers considered in isolation, as parts of the sensitive appetite, are common to us and non-reasoning animals. But insofar as they are rational by participation, as obeying reason, they are proper to human beings, and in this way can be a seat of human virtue."[15] In 1a2ae,56,5, Aquinas adds that there is no virtue proper to our interior senses (for which see 1a,78,4), since virtues depend on the right use of our intellectual abilities, although this might depend on *habitus* that we have formed on the basis of our interior senses. So in 1a2ae,56,6, he ends up maintaining that human virtue lies in the will. We are virtuous or not, he argues, because of the ways in which we act voluntarily. Working on the assumption that to will is to be drawn to what is good, Aquinas holds that we are virtuous insofar as we positively will what is objectively good.

The distinction between intellectual and moral virtues comes very much into play in 1a2ae,57–60. There are, Aquinas argues (1a2ae,57,1), intellectual virtues insofar as some *habitus* of mind "make us capable of good activity."[16] Seemingly following Aristotle, the *habitus* Aquinas is thinking of here (cf. 1a2ae,57,2) are "wisdom" (*sapientia*), "science" (*scientia*), and "understanding" (*intellectus*), each of which involves a latching on to truth and each of which can be distinguished theoretically from the others.[17] None of these *habitus*, Aquinas thinks, automatically render us good people just by having them since they can all be used in a bad way (1a,2ae,57,1). But, Aquinas insists, they aid us in acting well and are virtues in this sense, and, he goes on to suggest, we can add "art" (*ars*) to the three intellectual virtues just mentioned. That is because he takes art to be "right judgment about things to be made" that can aid us in acting well, even if our *habitus* of art need not actually lead us to want to act in a way that is truly good.[18] Aquinas adds that there is the intellectual virtue of "prudence" (*prudentia*), which he turns to in 1a2ae,57,4 and discusses at greater length in 2a2ae,47–56.

Consider the case of someone who knows a lot. We might admire such a person, but we will also need to remember that knowledge can be used to do evil. Yet consider the case of someone whose knowledge is put to good effect. Such a person knows, but also acts well because he or she *wants* to do so, and, for Aquinas, prudence is the virtue that enables one to act well on the basis of good ways of thinking. Prudence is "right reason displayed in doing" (*recta ratio agibilium*), as Aquinas says in 1a2ae,57,4. Contemporary speakers of English often think of prudence as a matter of not taking risks or as a matter of counting costs or being penny-pinching, but this is not how Aquinas thinks of *prudentia*. He thinks of it as the virtue of acting well from knowledge while wanting what is really good, as being able to put knowledge to good practical effect in one's life and, perhaps, in the lives of those with whom one is engaged. You will remember that in 1a2ae,56,3, Aquinas claims that human virtue can be seated in the intellect. His notion of *prudentia* is bound up with this claim, which is, in turn, bound up with his distinction between theoretical and practical reasoning.[19] A cunning person we might say is a clever one. For Aquinas, though, someone with *prudentia* has a real human virtue and not just a skill. So in 1a2ae,57,5, he can roundly declare that prudence is "a virtue of utmost necessity for human life."

Can we, though, say how moral and intellectual virtues differ? Aquinas thinks that we can, and he tries to explain why he does so in 1a2ae,58. Given what I have been saying, you will not be surprised by what Aquinas argues in defense of himself in this question, for it springs naturally from the discussions immediately proceeding it. Thus, in 1a2ae,58 we find Aquinas holding that not every virtue is a moral one, that moral virtues differ from intellectual ones, that not all intellectual virtues are required for moral virtue (though *prudentia* is one that is), and that people can have intellectual virtues without having moral ones. Perhaps again unsurprisingly, Aquinas argues in 1a2ae,59 that moral virtue can be distinguished from emotions even though it is compatible with emotions of certain kinds.

By now you may be wondering what kind of list of moral virtues Aquinas would offer us. Generally (1a2ae,60), he takes moral virtues to be virtues we display as we voluntarily seek to live a life that truly fulfills us as human beings. And he thinks that moral virtues admit of distinction, and do not all amount to one virtue, since we have different desires or appetites (cf.1a2ae,54,2) and since different virtues come into play as we set about acting in different ways and in varying contexts. As I have noted, Aquinas speaks of there being both "natural" and "supernatural" virtues. He takes the first group to include the Aristotelian "cardinal" virtues of prudence, justice, temperance, and courage.[20] He takes the second group to include faith, hope, and charity, a list that he derives from the teaching of St. Paul in the New Testament.

Given what I have reported him to think about *prudentia*, you might suppose that Aquinas would reduce all "natural" virtues to one, that is, *prudentia*, and he does seriously think of prudence as a governing virtue since he takes it to be present in all right action.[21] But he also thinks (1a2ae,61,2–4) that one can be prudent in different matters, and he supposes that these matters might lead us to speak of there being different cardinal virtues. One can be prudent with respect to what one owes. This, says Aquinas, is where the virtue of justice comes in. Again, one can be prudent with respect to one's bodily desires. This is where Aquinas takes the virtue of temperance to come in. And one can be prudent with respect to what threatens one. This is where Aquinas takes the virtue of courage to come in.

The human need for cardinal virtues is acknowledged by many non-Christian authors writing prior to Aquinas, and, given what they say, one might think that there is no need to have recourse to the notion of supernatural virtues. One might even, perhaps, add that if supernatural virtues are had by human beings, then they have to be natural after all since they are there in people and since people exist in nature. Given his distinction between *felicitas* and *beatitudo*, however (cf.1a2ae,2–3), Aquinas finds it necessary to speak of virtues that we cannot acquire by our natural abilities, these being what he takes supernatural or *theological* virtues to be. He is clear that they exist in people and are, in this sense, part of the world of nature. Yet he is also clear that human beings naturally lack the ability to acquire theological virtues by their own efforts.

Perhaps I can illustrate his main idea here by focusing on his view of the theological virtue of faith and anticipating what he says about it in 2a2ae,1–7. Aquinas takes someone with faith to be someone who *firmly* assents to certain propositions, the articles of faith mentioned in 1a,1, without *knowing* them to be true. The propositions in question are not, in Aquinas's view, ones that we can know to be true; they are not demonstrable, but they are as firmly as-sented to by those having faith as are any conclusions held on the basis of demonstration. So, says Aquinas, those with faith firmly assent as if they had knowledge, though they lack knowledge, and, he thinks, the firm assent of those with faith is not naturally explicable as is that of those who assent to certain conclusions based on a demonstration of them. Assent to demon-strable conclusions is naturally explicable since it inevitably arises once the force of the demonstrations is recognized. If I see that p, and if I see that if p then q, and I conclude that q, then my assent to q can be accounted for in terms of my human power of understanding and reasoning. But, Aquinas argues, such human power does not and cannot come into play when it comes to the articles of faith. My conviction concerning the articles of faith amounts to God directly working in me to bring me to assent. In this sense it is super-natural, not natural. Aquinas, of course, is aware that we might be convinced about truths other than those proclaimed in the articles of faith. He is also aware that we might be convinced about the truth of what is not actually true, and he recognizes that our ending up in these states might be naturally expli-cable. Holding the articles of faith to be true, however, and noting that some people firmly assent to them, Aquinas takes faith to be brought about by God and, therefore, to be a theological virtue leading people to beatitude. And this is the line he takes with all the theological virtues.

As we shall see, Aquinas discusses these virtues at length in 2a2ae. What he says about them in 1a2ae,62 is intended as an introduction and, as such, it sets the scene for what we find in 2a2ae. In 1a2ae,62,1, Aquinas briefly explains why he thinks that people need theological virtues in order to reach beatitude. In 1a2ae,62,2, he argues that theological virtues are different from natural intellectual and moral ones, since they cannot be acquired by human effort. In 1a2ae,62,3, while drawing on 1 Corinthians 13:13, he specifies that the theological virtues are faith, hope, and charity.[22] Faith, says Aquinas, involves assent to believable truths, and therefore engages the mind. Hope follows from faith and involves confidently longing for a future promised in the articles of faith. Charity amounts to us being conformed to the goodness that is God.

As I have noted, Aquinas speaks of theological virtues as "infused" in us by God. I take "to infuse" to mean "to introduce into something," which is how Aquinas uses the verb. He regards theological virtues as infused since they are brought about and directly instilled in us by God. But does Aquinas think that only theological virtues can be so instilled? As 1a2ae,63 makes clear, he does not. Yes, he thinks (1a2ae,63,1 and 2), virtues typically arise in us because of what we naturally are, considered as human beings able to think about what is good for us and able to develop patterns of behavior and inclinations that enable us to arrive at what is good for us. And, Aquinas notes, some people are just naturally virtuous in various ways because of their bodily constitutions. But, he argues (1a2ae,63,3 and 4), this does not mean that God cannot work "in us without us" so as to bring us to have naturally acquirable virtues that order us toward union with God by disposing us to receive the theological virtues.

In 1a2ae,64, the notion of "mean" (*medium*) comes into play. If you know something about the moral philosophy of Aristotle, you will not be surprised by this. Aristotle taught that excellence of human character involves a judicious balancing act. He thinks that we need to act appropriately in the circumstances in which we find ourselves. Sometimes, thinks Aristotle, we should, for example, just boil with anger and express this anger as strongly as possible, but, he also thinks, there are times when we should express our anger differently based on what it might be reasonable to do when and where we are. In chapter 2 of Book II of the *Nicomachean Ethics*, Aristotle says that virtue consists in acting in accordance to a mean, though he does not think that it consists in trying to aim for a mathematical halfway house between extremes of behavior. His idea is that our emotions can lead us to extremes in action and that reason needs to be invoked when we decide how to act appropriately in particular circumstances.[23] Aquinas accepts this Aristotelian teaching on the mean. That he does so is clear from what he says in 1a2ae,64,1 and 2, in which he argues that reason has to be thought of as the yardstick against which to measure moral virtues. Aquinas thinks of what he takes to be natural or acquired virtues as governed by reason and, therefore, as striking a mean between extremes. When it comes to theological virtues, however, he casts the notion of the mean aside. He argues (1a2ae,64,4) that when it comes to theological virtue there can never be too much. There can be no limit, he says, in what is appropriate when striving to gain God since God is infinite and infinitely desirable.

Yet how do theological virtues relate to natural ones, and do those who have them in this life continue to have them in the next? These are questions that Aquinas turns to in 1a2ae,65–67, in which (drawing on what he takes to be the teaching of authors such as St. Paul and St. Augustine) he makes the following points, some of which he develops further in 2a2ae.[24]

1. There can be dispositions to act well in various ways without there being complete virtue. One can, for example, be disposed to act in a generous way without also being disposed to be chaste. But perfect moral virtue involves wanting what is good and pursuing it effectively. So it always involves prudence, which itself presupposes other virtues (1a2ae,65,1). In this sense, human virtues are inseparable from one another (cf. also 1a2ae,65,4).

2. One can have moral virtues without the theological virtue of charity. But the ultimate good is God, with whom we are only finally united by means of charity. So perfect virtue involves the possession of prudence together with charity (1a2ae,65,2), and charity is had only by those who have all the moral virtues, which disappear with the loss of charity since without charity comes a settling for something less than what is ultimately good (1a2ae,65,3).

3. Faith and hope can exist without charity, but only as incomplete virtues, not virtues in the full sense. Aristotle (*Nichomachean Ethics* II,6) says that to be virtuous is to do what is good and to do it well. When it comes to human perfection, doing well means acting on the basis of charity, as being just means acting on the basis of prudence (1a2ae,65,4). On the other hand, though (1a2ae,65,5), there is no charity without faith and hope since charity springs from faith and hope. Charity, which, as 1 John teaches, is primarily love of God, is a kind of friendship with God. Therefore, just as our faith and hope in human beings is grounded in our friendship with them, faith and hope considered as theological virtues are grounded in friendship with God, which is charity.

4. One can rank virtues. One can say, for example, that prudence is greater than any other moral virtue since it informs all of them and amounts to right practical reasoning. Or one can say that justice is greater than temperance since to be just is to be right intellectually and not just right in matters of bodily control and concupiscible appetite. Also, one can think of people as having different virtues to different degrees whether by nature or by the grace of God (1a2ae,66,1–2).

5. Intellectual virtues are greater than moral virtues since the latter depend on the former. Yet moral virtue is found in those who apply reason to action and, in this sense, is greater than intellectual virtue (1a2ae,66,3).

6. Justice is the most excellent of moral virtues "as being most closely allied to reason."[25] It is found in the will of just people and in actions done by those who are well ordered in relation both to themselves and to others. Other moral virtues can be graded in terms of excellence insofar as they show forth the work of reason, so courage, on which human life depends, ranks highly, though below the virtue of justice. Among the intellectual virtues, the greatest is wisdom since it amounts to the consideration of the highest cause, which is God (1a2ae,66,5).

7. The greatest theological virtue is charity, as St. Paul says in 1 Corinthians 23:13. That is because charity actually unites us to God, while faith and hope involve some distance from God insofar as faith is concerned with what is not seen and hope is concerned with what is not yet possessed.

8. Moral virtues are bound up with our bodily lives and with actions of ours that involve and affect us at a material level. For this reason, they do not remain in the life to come, in which we will not be concerned with bodily goods, bodily dangers, or the distribution and exchange of worldly things. But the right will involved in moral virtue will remain in the blessed (1a2ae,67,1). Intellectual virtues will also remain in the blessed because the "receptive intellect" (cf. 1a,79,6) remains in the soul after death, even if the soul can then learn nothing by means of its agent intellect working on the basis of sensory experience (1a2ae,67,3).

9. In the life of the blessed there is no faith, since beatitude brings with it a knowledge of God that abolishes the need for faith (1a2ae,67,3 and 5). This knowledge also abolishes the need for hope in the blessed, since it amounts in them to happiness with God (1a2ae,67,4). But charity remains in the blessed because of what it essentially is—perfect love of God and the goodness that God is (1a2ae,67,6).

12.3 The Gifts of the Holy Spirit (1a2ae,68)

Aquinas's thinking on virtues and human beings has frequently been compared to that of Aristotle, and the comparison is a fair one since Aquinas frequently agrees with Aristotle about virtue and human nature and frequently cites him as an authority when writing about these things. In a serious sense, however, Aquinas is no Aristotelian. He believed all sorts of things that Aristotle did not, and, unlike Aristotle, he writes as someone believing that human fulfillment lies in union with God as revealed by Jesus of Nazareth.

Aquinas clearly admired Aristotle's philosophy and thought of it as potentially helpful to teachers of *sacra doctrina*. In the end, though, his thinking
relies more on the Bible and the writings of Christian authors than it does
on Aristotle, whom Aquinas tends to bring in more as an aid to thinking
than as a final guide to truth. By now, I hope, you will have begun to see how
this is so. The doctrine of God that informs 1a is not Aristotelian, even
though it is defended by Aquinas with reference to him. The notion of moral
and theological virtues infused in us by God so as to lead us to the beatific
vision is not Aristotelian, nor is the view that we have divine revelation as
Aquinas conceives of it. And Aquinas's non-Aristotelian approach to human
well-being again becomes evident in what he says about the gifts of the Holy
Spirit in 1a2ae,68–70. Drawing on biblical texts, Aquinas claims that God
enables some people to be good in ways that lead them to God or lead them
to mirror what God is in ways that cannot be acquired by human effort. His
main idea is that, distinct from cardinal virtues and theological ones, there
are dispositions (*habitus*) given to some people by God, gifts by which people
live in a Godly way.

Aquinas holds that there are seven such gifts: wisdom, understanding,
knowledge, counsel, piety, fortitude, and fear (1a2ae,68,4). You might feel
somewhat confused (or just annoyed) by the extent to which Aquinas goes in
for arithmetic as he adds up processions and relations in God when talking
about the Trinity, as he lists the number of cardinal and theological virtues,
and as, in 1a2ae,68, he adds up the gifts of the Holy Spirit, while in 1a2ae,69
and 70 carefully enumerating "beatitudes" and "fruits." One needs to remember, though, that, for Aquinas, what is simple enough in itself might
admit of distinction for purposes of intellectual analysis, not to mention exposition of the Bible. So the numbers he introduces in his talk of the Trinity are
not intended to suggest that God is something composed of numerically
different parts. And his distinction between virtues is not intended to suggest
that there is in someone, say, a "justice"considered as something to be plucked
out of the person and able to stand on its own (hence his account of the relationship between virtues in 1a2ae,65 and 66). The same goes for the ways in
which Aquinas distinguishes between gifts of the Holy Spirit. His account of
these gifts is offered as an analysis of what God brings about in certain people
so as to make them oriented toward God as revealed in Christ, and not to
anything else.

Aquinas gets to the number seven when counting gifts of the Holy Spirit
mostly because of his reading of Isaiah 11:2–3, although New Testament talk
about the Holy Spirit also lies behind Aquinas's treatment of the gifts.[26]
So Aquinas does not believe in the gifts of the Holy Spirit on the basis of

philosophical argument. He takes their reality and significance to be biblically grounded. At the same time, though, he thinks that they can be spoken of using certain philosophical notions. Hence, for example, he discusses them in relation to the notion of virtue and disposition.

The gifts of the Holy Spirit, he observes, perfect people when it comes to right action, as do virtues (1a2ae,68,1), and they are *habitus* that stand to union with God somewhat as moral virtues stand to our embracing of reason (1a2ae,68,3). On the other hand, Aquinas prefers, mostly on biblical grounds, to speak of the gifts as inspirations from God rather than as virtues and as perfecting people in ways that naturally acquired virtues do not. The gifts of the Holy Spirit, he says, are higher perfections than moral and intellectual ones. They even excel infused moral virtues in that they lead us to follow God's promptings well (1a2ae,68,1).

Aquinas also notes that the gifts of the Holy Spirit even add to the three theological virtues (1a2ae,68,2). The latter, he notes, presuppose a kind of imperfection, since they are had by people who lack in some way—people who lack a natural knowledge of God (and therefore need faith), people who lack a natural possession of what they desire (and therefore need hope), and people who lack a natural ability to love as God loves (and therefore need charity). By contrast, says Aquinas, the gifts of the Holy Spirit lead us to be amenable to God. Excellent students are ones best disposed to how their teachers are leading them.[27] Those with the gifts, says Aquinas, are especially well disposed to how God is leading them to the beatific vision. "The gifts," he observes, "are *habitus* that perfect people so that they will follow the prompting of the Holy Spirit readily, just as the moral virtues perfect the faculties of appetite in their obedience to reason."[28] In 1a2ae,68,8, Aquinas makes it clear that he takes the theological virtues to unite us to God. But he also makes it clear that he takes the gifts of the Holy Spirit to be needed even by those graced with the theological virtues.

12.4 Beatitudes and Fruits (1a2ae,69–70)

Aquinas's account of the gifts of the Holy Spirit in 1a2ae,68 rests, as I have said, on a biblical foundation. The same goes for what he teaches in 1a2ae,69–70, in which he discusses "beatitudes" and "fruits." In these questions, Aquinas is presupposing that his readers are familiar with Matthew 5:3–11 and Galatians 5:22–25. In the first text, Jesus is described as delivering the "Sermon on the Mount," an address given on a mountain in which he proclaims various kinds of people to be "blessed." In the second, St. Paul notes what he takes to be "the fruit of the Spirit." Drawing on these passages,

Aquinas holds that there are eight beatitudes and twelve fruits (1a2ae,69,3 and 1a2ae,70,3), and he takes them to be states in which people can be drawn close to God. Aquinas distinguishes between beatitudes and gifts since, for example, in the Sermon on the Mount we find that the poor in spirit are said to be blessed, while poverty is not mentioned in Isaiah 11 (1a2ae,69,1). And Aquinas distinguishes between beatitudes and fruits since he takes the notion of fruit to be conceptually connected to delight, but the notion of beatitude to be a matter of perfection and excellence (1a2ae,70,2). In general, though, he takes both the beatitudes and the fruits to be gifts of God that lead us to become attuned to God in the present life. In this sense, he assimilates them to the gifts of the Holy Spirit.

But what does Aquinas take as preventing us from being attuned to God? His answer is "Vice and Sin," which is the topic he turns to in 1a2ae,71–89. In the next chapter we shall see what he has to say about this.

Sin (1a2ae,71–85)

IA2AE,55–70 IS AN account of ways in which people live good Christian lives. 1a2ae,71–85, however, is an account of how they might fail to do so, how they might somehow fall short, given what Aquinas takes to be the articles of faith. In brief, 1a2ae,71–85 is Aquinas's treatise on sin. People reading it without having noted what Aquinas says earlier in the *Summa Theologiae* are likely to find it largely incomprehensible, but those who have attended to what comes before it in the *Summa* will find much of it unsurprising and even predictable. To be sure, 1a2ae,71–85 focuses on a topic on which Aquinas has not concentrated previously, so it covers new ground. But it does so in a way that presupposes and applies thinking that Aquinas has already presented. In this chapter, therefore, I shall turn to it only by highlighting and briefly explaining some of its main points.

13.1 Sin and Vice in General (1a2ae,71)

Picking up on a teaching of St. Augustine, Aquinas accepts that sin is "a word, deed, or desire which is against eternal law."[1] By "eternal law" Aquinas means "God as governing and directing all creatures" (cf.1a2ae,91,1 and 93,1–6). So he takes sin to be a turning away from the goodness that God is, a goodness that Aquinas, as we have seen, thinks of as reflected in creatures, and he takes a vice to be a disposition (*habitus*) when it comes to sinning, as he takes a virtue to be a disposition aimed at action that is good and reflective of God. So he views vice as contrary to virtue, and he takes sin to be opposed to virtue since it is action contrary to that to which virtue is directed (1a2ae,71,1). He also makes a connection between vice and nature (1a2ae,71,2). Vice, he argues, is contrary to nature (*contra naturam*) since it is contrary to reason.[2] His idea here is that it befits people to act according to reason and that vice comes about insofar as they fail to do so. Aquinas's view of what is and what is not a vice, therefore, is parasitic on his view of what is and what is not reasonable when it comes to human action.

Aquinas distinguishes between a vice and a sin (1a2ae,71,3). It is, he thinks, one thing to be badly disposed and another and worse thing to act badly, to sin. We saw in chapter 12 that a *habitus*, for Aquinas, is halfway between a capacity and an action. Drawing on this conclusion, Aquinas takes sin to be an action and, therefore, to be worse than a tendency to sin. Habits, he observes, are good or evil because the acts they tend toward are good or evil. One can be blamed more for acting badly than one can be blamed for having an unengaged *habitus* to act badly. Indeed, Aquinas adds, one might continue to possess a virtue even if one commits a sin that is contrary to that virtue (1a2ae,71,4). He means that, say, doing one unjust action need not render someone entirely lacking the virtue of justice. At the same time, however, Aquinas also believes that sin can sometimes destroy virtue at a stroke. For, he says, there can be a sin so radical (or "mortal") that it can place someone beyond the pale when it comes to infused virtues.[3] Here he is thinking of grave sins contrary to charity, like, for example, deliberate murder.

But how does Aquinas think of action as he turns to the topic of sin? Does he, for example, hold that to sin is always to do something in particular? He does not. Edmund Burke (1729–1797) is commonly quoted as saying, "The only thing necessary for the triumph of evil is for good men to do nothing." Burke actually never said this, but one can see why he might have wanted to, and in line with this, Aquinas holds that one can sin by omission as well as by commission, that is, by refusing to act as well as by acting. One might, he says (1a2ae,71,5), choose not to do something one ought to do, or one might just fail to do what one ought to do because one is set on other matters. Aquinas accepts that there is always some doing (some willing) bound up with what we do not do. He thinks, for example, that, even though I am doing nothing today when sound asleep because I stayed up late last night, my choosing to stay up late last night is connected with my doing nothing while asleep today. But Aquinas also thinks that one can be responsible for deliberately not taking action of a certain kind, in which case, he thinks, one might sin.

13.2 *Differences Among Sins (1a2ae,72–73)*

There are distinctions among sins, says Aquinas (1a2ae,72,1), since sinners can be doing different things at different times and with different intentions. For example, it is one thing to murder people and another to rob them. According to Aquinas, sins should be distinguished according to their "objects"—what one has in mind or is aiming at when choosing to act in a sinful way (even by not doing something). He also thinks that sins can be distinguished from one another insofar as they are "carnal" or "spiritual" (1a2ae,72,2). By "carnal" Aquinas means "pertaining to bodily desires." By "spiritual" he means "pertaining to intellectual desires." One might, he thinks, want sexual gratification (carnal) or the pleasure of being praised by one's peers (spiritual).

Either way, he believes, one might (though not inevitably) be wanting a good that one should not be wanting in the circumstances in which one finds oneself. As we have seen, Aquinas thinks that our voluntary action always amounts to us aiming at what we take to be good in some way and at what can indeed be thought of as somehow good, and he upholds this view even when thinking about sin. His claim is that sinners are always oriented to goodness. He thinks, however, that they sin by settling for a lesser good than they should as they are acting. "Every sin," he says, "consists in the pursuit of some passing good that is inordinately desired."[4]

Given his notion of evil as privation, Aquinas always thinks of vice or sin as a failure in some sense, as lacking a good that should be there. So he does not think of the evil of sin as having an agent cause and is, therefore, emphatic (1a2ae,79) that God is not a cause of sin. In 1a2ae,72,3, he notes that one might sin for reasons—reasons being causes in Aquinas's thinking. Yet he does not think that one sin differs from another because of its agent causes. In his view, one sin differs from another because of what the sinner is aiming at, the object of his or her action. I might sin on various occasions because I have a specifiable motive like getting rich. However, thinks Aquinas, this motive can run through different sinful acts that I perform such as robbing you or lying to you. In this sense, he argues, sins are not to be distinguished in terms of their causes.

Sins, Aquinas thinks, have it in common that they are all offenses, whether against God or oneself or one's neighbor (1a2ae,72,4). All sin is an offense against God, he says, since it is action that conflicts with right reason, which reflects the truth that God is, and, he adds, some sins can be thought of as offending God, as being against what God is as supremely good. As for sins against oneself and one's neighbor, these, says Aquinas, can arise as reason takes a back seat in behavior. Effectively, one can, without due reason, act so as to damage oneself or others culpably. Aquinas also thinks that a distinction can be made among sins of thought, word, and deed (1a2ae,72,7). He does not take sins of these kinds to differ as individuals belonging to different species differ (as a dog differs from a cat, say). He does, however, think that different sinful actions *arise from* how we think and can *follow from* what we say when expressing our thoughts.

Do people who sin always aim at the same good? Aquinas thinks that virtuous people always aim to act in accordance with right reason, so he thinks of virtuous acts as seriously connected. But, he argues (1a2ae,73,1), there is no comparable connection between sinful actions. These, with respect to their different objects, can be many and various and might have no common element linking them. Moreover, Aquinas adds, sinful actions might differ in gravity (1a2ae,73,2). Aquinas takes all sin to involve straying from right reason, but he is also clear that, just as one can be more or less sick, one can depart from right reason to lesser or greater degrees. Degrees of gravity when it comes to sins, he thinks, depend on their objects (1a2ae,73,3). So, for example, he takes murder to be worse than theft since it aims at a greater evil, and he takes degrees of badness in sin to reflect opposite degrees of goodness in virtue (1a2ae,73,4). "The greatest sin," he observes, "is directly opposed to the greatest virtue from which it differs to the greatest extent possible."[5]

Christians have often seemed to suggest that what Aquinas means by "carnal sins," especially sexual ones, are particularly grave. You might, therefore, be interested to note that Aquinas does not think along these lines, as he indicates in 1a2ae,73,5, in which he says that "spiritual" sins are worse, or involve more guilt, than "carnal" ones (all things being equal). That, he argues, is (a) because carnal sins involve a turning to bodily goods rather than a spiritual turning away from God, (b) because they generally involve us in loving ourselves at the bodily level, which is less grievous than failing to love God and our neighbor, and (c) because they arise from bodily passion that can affect the degree to which we are responsible for such sins. Gravity when it comes to sin, Aquinas goes on to say, can increase (a) depending on how focused we are on willing to sin (1a2ae,73,6), (b) depending on circumstances (1a2ae,73,7), (c) depending on how much harm we intend to do when sinning (1a2ae,73,8), (d) depending on whom, and how many, we harm or offend by our sins (1a2ae,73,9), and (e) depending on how "excellent" we are at the time when we sin (1a2ae,73,10).[6]

13.3 In What Sin Lies and the Causes of Sin (1a2ae,74–80)

If sin is a reality at all, which many would deny insofar as they deny that God exists, then it is people who commit it. In this sense, we might say, the subjects or agents of sin are human beings (and, if we believe in them, angels). In 1a2ae,74, however, Aquinas, while not denying this point, starts to ask whether sin can be thought of with respect to different human faculties, drawing on various distinctions he has so far made between them. If I choose to murder you, what is going on in me? Obviously, I am willing in some way. So does sin derive from or consist in willing? If I choose to murder you, I might be thinking or reasoning in some way. So does sin derive from or consist in thinking or reasoning? It is with thoughts and questions like these in mind that Aquinas drafts 1a2ae,74, which amounts to an analysis of sin in terms of the sinning agent insofar as such an agent can be thought of as, so to speak, bringing sin to birth.

Aquinas argues that since sins, like acts of virtue, can be actions that originate in human willing, they can be attributed to our will. We can, Aquinas thinks, sin *as intending* to act in certain ways (1a2ae,74,1). And, he says, we can sin not just because of will but because of what we might, so to speak, kick-start in ourselves by willing in a certain way. I might sinfully want to harm you, but my really harming you (as opposed, say, to my fantasizing about harming you) depends on my actually doing you harm (1a2ae,74,2). Aquinas also holds that sin can be found in our sensual appetites insofar as these can express the characters that we are and can account for some of the wrong that we choose to do. We can, Aquinas thinks, sin while inordinately and voluntarily desiring what right reason would advise us to refrain from (1a2ae,74,3). So, he observes, "sin can be found in the sensual part of a human being."[7] He agrees, though (1a2ae,74,4), that what he calls mortal sin is not to be found in this part since one can sin at the sensual level even to a high degree without finally turning one's back on God and failing in charity. One *might*, thinks Aquinas, mortally sin while acting on one's sensual appetites. Yet he does not think that one *automatically* sins mortally just because one acts on one's sensual appetites (cf. 1a2ae,73,5).

What about sin and our reasoning powers? Can there be sin in our reason? Aquinas argues that there can be when reason fails to restrain disordered appetite, when one sins in ignorance of what one should and could know but does not, or when one consents to what is wrong (1a2ae,74,5–7). Continuing with the notion of consent, Aquinas argues in 1a2ae,74,8 that consent to delight (*delectatio*) in what is gravely sinful amounts to mortal sin.[8] Here, once again, Aquinas is thinking of sinful thoughts and feelings, and his position is that dwelling with pleasure on the thought of what is gravely sinful can also be gravely sinful insofar as one is positively yearning for what is gravely sinful. He concedes that one might not sin gravely when thinking with some pleasure of what is gravely sinful, but he also thinks that one might sin mortally by delighting in a gravely sinful act even without having decided to commit that act. So while one might enjoy thinking of fornication without sinning gravely, one can sin gravely when thinking of fornication if one's thinking about fornication comes with a consent to or desire for what fornication is about and a delight in the activity of thinking about fornication.

In short, Aquinas thinks that sin can be located in various elements of our makeup. What, though, about the causes of sin? As I have explained, Aquinas denies that God directly causes sin (cf. 1a2ae,79 and 1a,49). He also denies that Satan can directly cause us to sin (diabolical possession notwithstanding), though he thinks that Satan might influence us by somehow prompting us to sin in different ways (1a2ae,80).[9] We sin, thinks Aquinas, because we freely or voluntarily act sinfully. So the cause of sin lies in us, regardless of who might be prompting us to act sinfully.[10] With that thought in mind, Aquinas notes what he takes to be several causes of sin. He says that will, reason, ignorance, sense appetite, sense perception, and malice can all account for sin, though in different ways. This is the argument of 1a2ae,75–78, and it is an argument you would expect to find Aquinas offering, even when it comes to its details, given what we have already seen him saying about human action, emotion, and will.

Aquinas, however, has more to say about the genesis of sin than what I have just noted. For he also talks about the historical origin of sin and the effects of this origin. In short, he has things to say about original sin (*peccatum originale*).

13.4 Original Sin (1a2ae,81–85)

Genesis 3 refers to Adam and Eve disobeying God by eating from "the tree of the knowledge of good and evil" and being punished accordingly. In Romans 5, St. Paul talks about Adam and Christ while drawing attention to certain contrasts. He says that sin, condemnation, and death came into the world through Adam, while grace, rightness with God, and life came into the world through Christ. According to St. Paul: "Just as one man's trespass led to condemnation for all, so one man's act of righteousness leads to justification and life for all. For just as by the one man's disobedience the many were made sinners, so by the one man's obedience the many will be made righteous."[11]

Various interpretations of Genesis 3 and Romans 5 have been given, but these two texts each seem to be saying that woe befell people because of Adam's sin, and by the time of Aquinas, theologians, especially influenced by St. Augustine of Hippo, were commonly teaching that there is such a thing as sin (original sin) passed on to Adam's descendants because of his sin. This, very briefly, is the context for 1a2ae,81–85 (which needs to be read in conjunction with 1a,93–101).[12]

As we have seen, Aquinas thinks of Adam as a historical individual enjoying union with God in Paradise because of God's help and because of his use of right reason. But, says Aquinas, Adam chose to sin and his descendants can be thought of as inheriting sin. "It is," he says, "basic that according to the Catholic faith we are bound to hold that the first sin of the first man passes to posterity by way of origin."[13] Yet how can sin be *inherited*? One might legally inherit a sum of money or genetically inherit a physical weakness. Is sin, though, not something that one personally engages in and therefore something that can only arise as one acts in some way? Is it not just absurd to speak of inheriting sin?

Some theologians have thought that original sin is something that we might now compare to an inheritance based on genes. In 1a2ae,81,1, however, Aquinas (while knowing nothing of genes) effectively rejects this view, noting that sin implies culpability and that culpability implies voluntary action. We cannot, says Aquinas, inherit sin as we can inherit our parents' good looks or their intellectual abilities. So, for Aquinas, original sin is, in a serious sense, not sin on our part at all. We are not, he thinks, responsible for any action of Adam. "The disorder which is in an individual human being, a descendent of Adam," he says, "is not voluntary by reason of his or her personal will."[14]

How, then, is original sin as inherited by us a matter of sin? In turning to this question, Aquinas invokes a comparison. If I murder you by using my hand, it is obviously true that my hand does not murder you. I do. My hand cannot be blamed for your murder in the way that I can. But, as moved by me, my hand is implicated in your murder. My failure to be good, as it were, runs through into my hand considered as a part of me. In a similar way, Aquinas argues (whether plausibly or implausibly), the failure of Adam, considered as sinful, runs through the people that derive from him as his offspring. They can, Aquinas thinks, be said to inherit Adam's falling away from God with all that this implies because they inherit his fallen state insofar as they are Adam's descendants and therefore inherit what he had to pass on to them considered as such. And Aquinas takes this to mean that the descendants of Adam are born in need of God's grace, considered as what raises people to perfect union with God. "Original sin," he argues, "is the sin of the individual person only because he receives human nature from the first parent."[15]

In short, we are, thinks Aquinas, born as what any right-minded analysis of human nature provided *now* would reveal us to be *now*. As we have seen, Aquinas takes such an analysis to indicate that we have will, choice, emotions, and good and bad tendencies. As we have also seen, he takes such an analysis to indicate that we stand in need of special help from God so as to attain the beatific vision. This analysis of human nature is what Aquinas is presupposing when he says that we inherit original sin, that the sin of Adam is causally effective when it comes to our sinfulness.[16] What if God miraculously created a human being not directly descended from Adam? Then, says Aquinas, such a human being would not inherit original sin (1a2ae,81,4). Consistent with this line of reasoning, in 1a2ae,81,3, Aquinas asserts that Christ did not inherit original sin.[17] He also argues that original sin shows itself in our natural inclinations to act in a way that falls short of human perfection as conceived in what Aquinas takes to be New Testament terms (1a2ae,82 and 83).

When reading 1a2ae,81–85, you might wonder why Aquinas thinks that Adam in Paradise could ever have chosen to sin, for, as we have seen, he depicts Adam before his sin as always acting in accordance with reason. In 1a2ae,81–85, however, Aquinas does not really deal with the question "Why did Adam sin?" though he turns to it later in the *Summa Theologiae*. He says, for example, that even in Paradise Adam lacked the beatific vision (cf. 1a,94,1), and he appears to account for Adam's sin by saying that even those who are graced by God can freely (short of the beatific vision) choose a good that is not in accord with God's will. Aquinas is clear that, though Adam was created as graced by God in various ways, he was also created with the ability to choose a good that is less than God, and in 2a2ae,163, Aquinas brings pride into the picture (as he does in 1a,63 when talking about fallen angels). He suggests that, for all his pre-Fall glory, Adam fell short of God and wanted to be like God by his own efforts and not by God's. He says that Adam "sinned principally in wanting to be like God in knowing good and evil...so that he might determine for himself by his own natural powers what was right or wrong for him to do." He adds that Adam sinned "in desiring God's likeness in his own powers of action, so that of his own capabilities he might achieve happiness."[18]

13.5 The Effects of Sin (1a2ae,85–89)

Aquinas clearly takes sin to be bad. He also takes its effects to be so. What, in his view, are these effects? Given what he has said about original sin, Aquinas regards sin as inherited to result in the loss of what Adam had before he sinned ("original justice" as he calls it).[19] Original sin amounts to a "wounding of nature" and results in various ways in ignorance, malice, weakness, and concupiscence (1a2ae,85,3). Aquinas, however, does not think of sin as taking away our human nature with its various God-given powers (1a2ae,85,2, which should be read in conjunction with 1a,75–89). Nor does he think of sin as leaving us unable to become inclined to virtue, though (in accord with his notion of *habitus*) he does think that sin renders us weak when it comes to becoming so inclined (1a2ae,85,1 and 2) and that original sin brings with it the "penalty" of death (1a2ae,85,5).[20]

Aquinas does not think that our dying is a punishment for sins that we have personally committed and for which we are personally guilty. Following what he takes to be the teaching of Romans 5, however, he takes death and "all like defects in human nature" (*omnium hujusmodi defectum in natura humana*) to befall us as inheriting Adam's loss of original innocence, which Aquinas believes to have preserved Adam from death for as long as he persevered in it (1a2ae,85,6). As we have seen, Aquinas thinks that the human soul is not subject to physical corruption. So he thinks that even the soul of Adam did not become subject to such corruption because of his sin, but Aquinas does think that our bodily death, like that of Adam, results from sin, though he also thinks that Adam's body would have perished even in his state of innocence had God not assisted him because of this state (1a2e,85,6 and 1a,97,2).[21]

In 1a2ae,86, Aquinas says that "stain" (*macula*) is an effect of sin. As he notes, though, he is speaking metaphorically. He means that sin, by going against the "light" of reason, stains us rather as something might tarnish a bright object, and the stain of sin, he adds, can continue in the soul after a particular sinful act (1a2ae,86,2). He also argues that sin renders one guilty, responsible, and deserving of or subject to punishment in various ways (1a2ae,87).

Aquinas thinks of "guilt" (*reatus poenae*) as a matter of culpability, with what that might be thought to entail. He is not thinking that we automatically end up feeling guilty when we sin. He means that sin renders us guilty in the way in which a jury in a court of law might take someone to be guilty whether or not that person feels guilty. And sin, Aquinas thinks, naturally incurs "punishment" (*poenae*) insofar as it involves stepping outside the due order of things, whether with respect to reason, the (just) law of a human group, or the law of God (1a2ae,87,1). Sinning as such cannot, he observes, be its own penalty or punishment, since penalty or punishment is contrary to what one wants or wills. On the other hand, he adds, one might by sinning add to one's woeful state as a sinner (1a2ae,87,2), and some sin can leave one intrinsically subject to everlasting penalty or punishment (irretrievably broken, so to speak) unless one is aided by God (1a2ae,87,3). Some sin is, as Aquinas puts it in 1a2ae,88, "mortal" or "fatal" (*mortale*) rather than "venial" (repairable or pardonable).

One needs to remember that Aquinas thinks of sin as a failure to will in accordance with God, as a failure to want perfect goodness, which Aquinas takes to be what God wills and what God is. With this thought in mind, Aquinas accepts that one might just sin in an ultimate sense. One can make culpable or non-culpable mistakes while pursuing a goal. Yet if one rejects the goal as such, then one would seem to have opted out of interest in it, and it is opting out like this that Aquinas seems to have in mind when saying that while some sins are venial, others are mortal (1a2ae,88,1).[22]

Aquinas takes sin to be comparable to illness. Some illnesses are curable; others are terminal. Similarly, thinks Aquinas, some sins can leave one healthy to some degree (not wholly alienated from God) while others might not. If you definitively reject what Aquinas takes virtue to be, then you cut yourself off from God as effectively as you cut yourself off from a medical life-support system by arranging for it to be disconnected from you. Virtue, he says, is the "principle" (*principium*) of the soul's life. Choosing against it definitively, he adds, is like passing a death sentence on oneself—a sentence that Aquinas takes to be reversible only by God's grace.

For Aquinas, one might say (employing an image he does not use), choosing against virtue *definitively* (sinning mortally) is a bit like cheating when playing a game, as opposed to just not being a very good player of the game. One might indeed cheat when seeming to play a game, but one would not *actually* be playing that game. One would be *pretending* to play the game but *actually* opting out of it for reasons of one's own. In a similar way, thinks Aquinas, mortal sin is a root and branch rejection of the goodness of God, a refusal to abide by the goodness of God that sets the rules of the "game" of virtue. That is why he takes mortal sin to be grave. One might, he thinks, act wrongly for various reasons without sinning mortally, without, as Aquinas would say, turning away from the ideal of perfect charity. Yet he also thinks that one might act wrongly while doing precisely this. In Aquinas's view, all sin by definition comes with a penalty attached while some sins incur more penalty than others. This is the line of thinking that Aquinas pursues right up to the end of 1a2ae,89 while drawing on some distinctions that he has noted before concerning human action.

Later he will ask whether or not God can aid us in willing rightly. He will also ask whether, sinners though we are, we can be reconciled to God by God's action in Christ. Having turned directly to sin in general in 1a2ae,71–89, however, Aquinas moves on to talk about law and grace in 1a2ae,90–114, while evidently aiming to build up to what he wants to say about theological virtues and the Christian life in the *Secunda Secundae*. So let me now turn to 1a2ae,90–114.

14

Law, Old Law, New Law, And Grace (1a2ae,90–114)

GOOD OPERATIC OVERTURES can stand alone. We can listen to them and enjoy them as the individual compositions that they are. An overture to an opera, however, can also incorporate themes or melodies that reemerge in the opera and are developed in detail. What is musically touched on or hinted at in an operatic overture can, so to speak, have flesh and bones put on it in the course of the opera itself.

1a2ae can be viewed as a kind of operatic overture, for it is intended by Aquinas to present questions and answers that allow us to move on to consider what he is most concerned with—this being the way in which God draws people to salvation by acting in them as individuals and by becoming one of them through the Incarnation. 1a2ae (like 1a) can be read on its own and evaluated accordingly. Indeed, it can be broken into sections presented for separate study and discussion (as it often has been), but it is intended by Aquinas as part of a greater whole and is best read as such. More precisely, it is offered by Aquinas as a (admittedly detailed) workup to his account of what he refers to as "the New Law."

As we have seen many times now, Aquinas has a tendency to find words to bear more than one sense without taking them to be equivocal in their meaning. His approach to the word *cause* is indicative of this tendency, which becomes evident, for example, as Aquinas suggests that God can be thought of as a cause even though God's primary causality (the bringing about of the *esse* of creatures) does not amount to God being a part of the world or an individual such and such or operating on it as one thing in the world operates on another (cf. 1a,3). And the same tendency on Aquinas's part can be seen at work when he speaks about law.

The word *law* has a familiar non-theological life in phrases like "law of the state" or "law passed by Parliament." When he comes to speak of "the New Law," however (the "law of the gospel" as he sometimes calls it), Aquinas is using "law" to speak about something that is in his view much more significant and in various ways very different from human legislation. He takes the

New Law to be what we are talking about insofar as we believe that God is at work to bring people to *beatitudo* and not just *felicitas*. He takes the New Law to be God acting in Christ to lift us to levels of virtue not acknowledged in the writings of philosophers such as Aristotle. And it is the New Law that Aquinas is chiefly concerned with in 2a2ae. Here he turns to theological virtues and gifts of the Holy Spirit in more detail than he has so far done in the *Summa Theologiae*, and in 3a he goes on to focus on the person of Christ, to try to say what it might mean to call Christ divine, and to explain (as far as he thinks that he can) what the Incarnation amounts to when it comes to the benefit of human beings.

As I have said, though, the word *law* has a non-theological use and, as he moves to 2a2ae, Aquinas feels the need to reflect on law in general while working up to his account of the New Law, which he takes to be the work of grace in us.

14.1 Law in General (1a2ae,90)

We are all familiar with the notion of there being laws since we live in societies that have them, societies that can punish people for disobeying them. You might well think (as Aquinas did) that not all laws are good laws and that some laws ought to be rejected. But law seems to be a fact of life in human society, whether for good or ill, and Aquinas begins his treatment of law while assuming that this is so and being optimistic about it. He does not disapprove of there being human-made laws governing our behavior. Indeed, he thinks of law as necessary for people to live together in a way that contributes to their flourishing. He thinks that regulation of some kind is needed in any society for the benefit of its inhabitants. Yet what would law be all about when considered as correctly promoting this benefit?[1]

"The burden of law," says Aquinas, "is to prescribe or prohibit." "Law," he claims, "is a kind of direction or measure for human activity through which a person is led to do something or held back."[2] Considered as such, Aquinas argues, law (good law) is grounded in reason and is set on ends or purposes. In fact, he says, "Law is nothing else than an ordinance of reason for the common good made and promulgated by an authority who has care of the community."[3] When it comes to law, the notions of common good and promulgation arise for Aquinas (a) because he thinks of laws as intended to benefit groups and not just individuals (even though groups of people are, of course, composed of individuals) and (b) because he thinks that laws have to be set forth or declared or presented to societies in some way (1a2ae,90,2 and 4). And, so Aquinas also thinks, not just anyone can issue laws. Why not? Because, says Aquinas, if law is directed to a common good it can only proceed from one whose business this is, someone representing and caring for those being governed by the law (1a2ae,90,3).[4]

14.2 Varieties of Law and Effects of Law (1a2ae,91–92)

In 1a2ae, Aquinas distinguishes between eternal law, natural law, human law, and divine law. He will turn to the first three of these in some detail in 1a2ae,93–97. In 1a2ae,91, however, he briefly notes how he takes there to be varieties of law. So 1a2ae,91 sets the scene for 1a2ae,93–97.

Working with the idea that law springs from a ruler, Aquinas identifies eternal law with God. "The whole community of the universe is governed by God's mind," he says (1a2ae,91,1).[5] This divine mind, Aquinas thinks, is God, who is simple and eternal. The idea seems to be that what is good for God's creatures can be thought of as a rule of measure in God's mind before it is in creatures as governed by divine providence. Here, you will note, Aquinas is already (helpfully or unhelpfully) stretching the usual meaning of the word *law*. He does not think of eternal law as being laid down in a printable list of prescriptions or prohibitions. He identifies it with God, considered as that from which all good law can be thought to derive. "The eternal concept of divine law," he observes, "bears the character of a law that is eternal as being God's ordination for the governance of things God foreknows."[6]

Aquinas thinks that acting in accordance with God's intentions for creatures can occur at two levels. On the one hand, creatures lacking intelligence display God's providential guidance and thereby reflect the "mind" of God (cf. 1a,2,3). They are governed by God, the eternal law. What, though, of intelligent creatures? These, Aquinas thinks, can "join in and make their own the eternal reason through which they have their natural aptitudes for their due activity and purpose," and, he adds, "this sharing in the eternal law by intelligent creatures is what we call 'natural law.'"[7] He appears to mean that we act in accordance with natural law insofar as we choose to act in accordance with what is good for us considered as human beings.[8] This conclusion is, of course, a very general one and lays down no specific guidelines when it comes to how we should behave in concrete situations.[9] It cries out for elaboration with respect to what is and is not good for us considered as human beings and with respect to what is and is not natural for human beings. In 2a2ae, Aquinas will go on to offer some such elaboration, but in 1a2ae,91,2 he settles for saying that "the light of natural reason by which we discern what is good and what is evil is nothing but the impression of the divine light on us."[10] Natural law, he says, is a participation (*participatio*) in eternal law. Right practical reasoning, he adds, always derives from a recognition of what we are by nature; and, he goes on to say that human law (drawn up by people) can be thought of as true and good insofar as it accords with natural and eternal law.

In 1a2ae,91,4, Aquinas singles out divine law as a separate category of law. Here he has in mind the idea that, think as well we can philosophically about what is good for us to do, we might yet need to be instructed by God when it comes to what we should and should not do. He means that we should be instructed (and should abide) by what the Bible declares God to decree when it comes to our behavior. When it comes to divine law, therefore, Aquinas thinks that the Bible should be read in a literal sense—that what it says should be believed and acted on unless there are biblical grounds for not doing so.[11] He also thinks of the Bible as providing numerous teachings concerning what we should and should not do.[12]

When it comes to law's effects, Aquinas argues that good law makes people good since, properly speaking, law derives from sound reason and leads people to live virtuously (1a2ae,92,1). Aquinas concedes that some lawmakers might issue bad laws that do not lead people to be good, but bad laws, he thinks, are not true laws and only serve to make those who obey them good subjects or servants of those who promulgate them (1a2ae,92,1, ad.4). And how do laws bring about their goal? By, says Aquinas, permitting, commanding, prohibiting, and punishing (1a2ae,92,2).

14.3 Eternal Law and Natural Law (1a2ae,93–94)

Elaborating on what he writes in 1a2ae,91, Aquinas compares eternal law with an artist's idea or blueprint of a work he or she is about to produce. As an artist has in mind a work of art to be brought forth, so God has in mind the good of things ruled by God. "As being the principle through which the universe is created," Aquinas argues, "divine wisdom means art, or exemplar, or idea, and likewise it also means law, as moving all things to their due ends." So "the eternal law is nothing other than the exemplar of divine wisdom as directing the motions and acts of everything" (1a2ae,93,1).[13]

The eternal law, Aquinas continues, comes to be recognized by us as we acquire knowledge of how to act well. Aquinas is quick to point out, however, that since the eternal law is, in fact, God, it cannot be comprehended for what it is by people in this life since they do not see the essence of God (cf. 1a,12,4), but it can still be grasped by them to some extent and to varying degrees insofar as people can be aware of general moral principles and of more specific ones falling under them. Indeed, says Aquinas, all just laws derive from the eternal law (1a2ae,93,3) just as do the operations of all things governed by divine providence (1a2ae,93,5 and 6). Since the eternal law is God, the only thing not subject to eternal law is God (1a2ae,93,4).

Aquinas, of course, is clear that God knows the eternal law even without being subject to it, yet how do we come to know it? We come to know the eternal law, he says, by having it promulgated to us as reasoning creatures reflecting on how to act well—by recognizing natural law. We come to know what natural law is, Aquinas thinks, as we come to know the difference between good practical reasoning and bad practical reasoning. "Natural law's commands," says Aquinas, "extend to all doing or avoiding of things recognized by the practical reason of itself as being human goods" (1a2ae,94,2).[14] So Aquinas thinks that all virtuous actions, insofar as they are virtuous, accord with natural law in that they benefit us because of what we are by nature (1a2ae,94,3). He also thinks (1a2ae,94,4) that natural law governs the activity of everyone in the same way, since everyone is human. Just as everyone is subject to truth as acknowledged by sound theoretical reasoning, so everyone is subject to truth as arrived at by good practical reasoning. People will determine how they ought to act in the circumstances in which they find themselves, and what one person rightly concludes that he or she ought to do need not be what another person in different circumstances ought to decide to do. Aquinas does not, therefore, think that all conclusions based on right practical reason are binding on everyone. He does, however, hold that everyone (whether aware of this or not) is bound to act in accordance with right practical reasoning, with respect to what he calls "common principles."[15] And he regards these principles as unchangeable (1a2ae,94,5).

14.4 Human Law (1a2ae,95–97)

Aquinas thinks that people have a natural leaning to virtue since they have a natural leaning to what is good for them. As we have seen, though, he also recognizes that people are flawed and frequently behave in ways contrary to virtue. We are not, he believes, as subject to reason in our actions as Adam was before he sinned, and he takes this conclusion to afford the basic rationale for there being human laws set up so as to teach and compel where natural leaning to virtue gives out. Some people, thinks Aquinas, need to be held back from wrongdoing by fear and force, and, one hopes, such people may come in time to act well of their own accord by being truly virtuous (1a2ae,95,1).[16] "This schooling through the pressure exerted through the fear of punishment," says Aquinas, "is the discipline of human law."[17] When it comes to what good human law is, Aquinas is especially impressed by the teaching of St. Isidore of Seville (560–636), according to whom "Law will be honorable, fair, possible, according to nature and the custom of the country, befitting place and time, necessary, serviceable, also clearly stated lest some point, through obscurity, should be harmfully caught at, composed for no private gain but for the common benefit."[18]

In 1a2ae,96, Aquinas homes in on the notion that human laws should be framed with an eye on the common good. "For law," he declares, "the end is the common good" and "human law should be proportioned to the common good" (1a2ae,96,1).[19] So, he adds, human law should "cover all manner of personalities, occupations, and occasions" (1a2ae,96,1).[20] But he does not think that human laws should always be framed so as to outlaw every activity that he believes to amount to a failure in virtue. Rather, he says, they should be framed so as to outlaw grave vices "which the average person can avoid; and chiefly those which do harm to others and have to be stopped if human society is to be maintained, such as murder and theft" (1a2ae,96,2).[21] Reasoning along similar lines, Aquinas argues that human laws need not be framed so as to prescribe all virtuous actions but should legislate in favor of "those acts only which serve the common good" (1a2ae,96,3).[22] As for unjust laws, these, Aquinas maintains, are not really laws at all, so they should not be thought of as binding people in conscience. If just, he thinks, human laws are ordered to the common good, come from people with the right and duty to impose them, and place burdens on everyone equally. If human laws are unjust, however, they are more like acts of violence than laws, he says, and do not bind people in conscience (1a2ae,96,4). On the other hand, Aquinas accepts that laws that are generally just and well-intentioned might sometimes be legitimately suspended or contravened for prudential reasons, both by legislators and by people subject to the law, if circumstances suggest that they should be (1a2ae,96,6).[23]

To what extent does Aquinas in 1a2ae seem open to the idea that laws can be changed? As 1a2ae,97,2 indicates, Aquinas has a somewhat conservative approach to changes in human laws. Just laws, he thinks, need time to achieve their aims and change in them should be motivated by strong reason to suppose that such change will contribute significantly to the common good. Yet he also recognizes that even the best-intentioned lawmakers are fallible and that changes can properly occur in societies governed by them. So he accepts that laws might sometimes need to be refined or altered (1a2ae, 97,1), and he thinks that custom can sometimes rightly lead to a change in law since custom (some custom, anyway) can be thought of as the emergence over time of right practical reason that can trump what might be on the law books of certain societies. Aquinas holds that all human law proceeds from reason and will and that good laws promulgated by human legislators do exactly this, but he also thinks that some human laws promulgated by legislators might be abolished or interpreted by right reason and will as displayed over time in custom (1a2ae,97,3), which Aquinas seems to conceive of as catering to the common good. Custom (*consuetendo*), he says, has the force of law, can rightly lead to the abolition of certain positive human laws, and can interpret laws to be found in statute books.[24] In 1a2ae,97,4, Aquinas also accepts that even laws promulgated by a lawful ruler or governing body might be dispensed as circumstances deem fit. In circumstances of what kind? In this context, Aquinas instances cases when a precept for the benefit of most people does not help someone in particular or is not helpful in some particular case if it stops something better from happening or brings in some evil (1a2ae,96,6).

14.5 The Old Law (1a2ae,98–105)

Aquinas's discussion of law in 1a2ae,90–97 does not dwell on what he calls "the Old Law." It alludes to it occasionally but does not elaborate on it. Aquinas, however, evidently takes it to be important and worthy of some discussion. Hence 1a2ae,98–105.

Aquinas takes the Old Law to be law in accordance with his account of law in 1a2ae,90. He takes it to spring from understanding, to be geared to the common good, and to be promulgated by one with authority.[25] In fact, he takes it to amount to divine law. As perhaps you might be surprised to learn, though, he also takes it to be something that has been superseded.

The word *old* in Aquinas's use of the expression "the Old Law" should be read with an eye on the familiar Christian distinction between the Old Testament and the New Testament. The Old Testament contains many commands, precepts, and prohibitions (the majority of which are to be found in the Pentateuch, the first five books of the Bible), and, as a Christian theologian, Aquinas sets great store by the Old Testament. He takes it to contain divine revelation. On the other hand, he regards it as an account of God's actions and instructions prior to the incarnation of God in Jesus of Nazareth. In his view, the Incarnation marks a turning point both with respect to what God wants people to do and with respect to how God acts in people. So he holds that Old Testament law only prefigures what he calls the law of grace, and he thinks that God is doing something new and different in the lives of those who live as subject to the law of grace. Aquinas allows that various Old Testament figures such as Moses were wholly united to God, but he does so in light of what he thinks that grace can accomplish and in light of the Incarnation.

In short, Aquinas's view of the Old Law is determined by his view of the New Law. He takes the New Law to be God acting in Christ's followers so as to sanctify them and instruct them. He takes the Old Law to be law given by God to the people from whom Christ came, the Jewish people, to prepare the human race for the coming of Christ and the grace of God imparted through this coming.

To a large extent, Aquinas thinks of the Old Law as legislating much of the natural law, as summarizing what is required by right practical thinking or as stating conclusions to which right practical thinking could arrive. This, for example, is how he regards the Ten Commandments in Exodus 20:2–17 (cf. 1a2ae,99,2 and 100,3–8). People, Aquinas holds, are capable in principle of rightly recognizing how to act in accordance with natural law just as they are capable in principle of arriving at the right conclusions concerning the existence and nature of God that occupy so much of 1a. However, Aquinas also holds that our ability to reason well can be hampered by various factors like sin or muddled thinking, for example, and that God can declare, and in the Old Law has declared, what is what concerning God and how people should behave.[26] In this sense, Aquinas thinks of the Old Law as continuous with natural law or as an account of what accords with it.

On the other hand, Aquinas thinks that the Old Law amounts to more than a précis of natural law. Insofar as the Old Law contains "moral" precepts, he says, that is just what it amounts to. Yet he also says that "the Old Law clearly set forth the obligations of the natural law, and over and above these added precepts of its own" (1a2ae,98,5).[27] These added precepts Aquinas refers to as "ceremonial" and "judicial." He takes the ceremonial precepts of the Old Law to be rules concerning divine worship (of which there are many in the Old Testament).[28] He takes the judicial precepts of the Old Law to be precepts legislating fairly precisely for the lives of specifically Jewish people before the time of Christ, and in this sense adding to the dictates of natural law while also including them. In this connection, we need to keep in mind that Aquinas thinks of the Old Law as law delivered to the people of Israel considered as the chosen race from whom the Messiah would spring.[29]

Aquinas's view is that the moral precepts of the Old Law always remain in force but that, in the light of the New Testament, the ceremonial and judicial ones do not (1a2ae,103 and 104,3). The moral precepts are everlasting, he thinks, because they accord with natural law, but Old Testament rules concerning worship and behavior in pre-Christian Jewish society are, he holds, now superseded since we are now obliged to act in accordance with God's revelation in Christ as presented in the New Testament. Aquinas thinks of this revelation as implying a different view of worship than that present in the Old Testament. He also thinks of it as going beyond how Old Testament judicial precepts legislate. The New Law, he argues, is not a law for any particular people; it is a law governing all people, and it is, he says, one written in people's hearts.

Here Aquinas obviously has in mind biblical texts such as Jeremiah 31–33. This passage reads: "The days are surely coming, says the Lord, when I will make a new covenant with the house of Israel and the house of Judah. It will not be like the covenant that I made with their ancestors when I took them by the hand to bring them out of the land of Egypt.... I will put my law within them, and I will write it on their hearts." According to Aquinas, the new covenant of which Jeremiah writes is the New Law that comes about as a consequence of the Incarnation, a law that governs the lives of Christians of whatever race by the indwelling in them of the Holy Spirit. This New Law is a written one in that it contains instructions concerning attitudes and behavior, instructions found in the New Testament. Primarily, though, the New Law is inwardly implanted in our hearts by the "grace of the Holy Spirit" and amounts to God becoming one with people and leading them to the beatific vision so that those with the grace of the Holy Spirit by faith in Christ belong to the new covenant (1a2ae,106,1). By contrast, the Old Law is to a large extent a written code governing the Jewish people prior to Christ. Hence its ceremonial precepts and judicial precepts. So Aquinas says:

> It is the function of divine law to regulate relationships between people, and the relationship of people to God. Now as a matter of general principle both of these relationships are subject to the dictates of natural law to which the moral precepts relate. But both of them require to be applied in the concrete by a further law, either divine or human. The reason for this is that both in the speculative and practical spheres those principles which we are led to recognize by our very nature are universal.... The concrete application of the universal precept concerning divine worship is made by means of the ceremonial precepts. In the same way... The concrete application of the universal principle that justice must be observed among people is made by means of judicial precepts.[30]

The Old Law, Aquinas holds, was given to the Jews so as to restrain appetite working against reason and so as to forbid plainly all sin contrary to reason. So the Old Law was good. It did not, however, lead to the perfection accomplished by means of the New Law, Aquinas thinks, and it was, therefore, lacking in the way that a medicine is lacking that helps but does not cure.[31] It was law in a proper sense, but it did not confer the grace of the Holy Spirit. In this context Aquinas quotes John 1:17: "The law indeed was given through Moses; grace and truth came through Jesus Christ."

14.6 The New Law in General (1a2ae,106–108)

Aquinas views the New Law as a matter of grace, the topic that he immediately turns to once he has outlined his general view of the New Law and the relation between the Old Law and the New Law. And as he moves from the start of 2a2ae to the end of 3a, Aquinas's understanding of grace and the New Law emerges in more and more detail.[32] Indeed, his account of grace and the New Law is not complete until the very last article of 3a. So his general account of the New Law (1a2ae,106–108) and of grace (1a2ae,109–114) needs to be kept in mind when reading what follows it.

When it comes to 1a2ae,106–108, Aquinas mostly defends what I have already noted him to have thought. But let me now summarize some teachings of this text in point form.

1. The New Law is the gift of the Holy Spirit to those who believe in Christ and is primarily implanted in people's hearts.[33] "It is the grace of the Holy Spirit, given through faith in Christ, which is predominant in the law of the new covenant, and that in which its whole power consists. Before all else, therefore, the New Law is the very grace of the Holy Spirit, given to those who believe in Christ.... Hence the New Law is first and foremost an inward law, and secondarily a written law" (1a2ae,106,1).[34]

2. The New Law, understood as the grace of the Holy Spirit given to us, justifies (1a2ae,106,2). That is to say, it puts us in good standing with God.[35]

3. The New Law was given only with the coming of Christ; it was not given from the beginning of the world. This, though, was appropriate since the New Law springs from what the life and death of Christ was all about, since it presupposes a preparation for it given in the Old Law, and since it makes sense for what it is in the light of people coming over time to recognize their need of divine grace (1a2ae,106,3).

4. The New Law will last until the end of the world and we should not look forward to an age in which the grace of the Holy Spirit will be received more perfectly than it has been until now (1a2ae,106,4).[36]

5. The New Law is like the Old Law in that its aim is the same: that people should be subject to God. But the New Law differs from the Old Law by uniting people more intimately with God, by being more perfect than the Old Law (1a2ae,107,1).

6. The New Law amounts to a union with God that was anticipated by the Old Law but not brought about by it. So it fulfills the Old Law (1a2ae,107,2) and can be thought of as contained in the Old Law insofar as it completes what is incomplete (1a2ae,107,3).

7. The New Law imposes a lighter burden than the Old Law since it dispenses with many ceremonial commands laid down in the Old Law. On the other hand, its burden is heavier since it calls for us to be wholeheartedly disposed to certain virtuous ways of acting—this being difficult for some people (1a2ae,107,4).[37]

8. The grace of the Holy Spirit, which is what the New Law first and foremost is, shows itself in people having faith in Christ, comes about by certain external observances (the sacraments of the church), and is also a matter of grace that bears fruit in behavior and is therefore manifest in what we do (1a2ae,108,1 and 2).[38] "It is fitting that the grace which overflows from the incarnate Word should be carried to us by external perceptible realities; and also that certain external perceptible works should be brought forth from this interior grace, by which flesh is made subject to spirit."[39]

9. "In Christ's words we find everything to do with human salvation set out sufficiently."[40] In particular, Christ instituted the sacraments of the New Law, by which we obtain grace (these sacraments being baptism, confirmation, the Eucharist, penance, extreme unction, holy orders, and matrimony).[41]

10. The requirements for people living under the New Law are effectively set out in the text of the "Sermon on the Mount" (Matthew 5–7), which deals with "interior motions" as well as "exterior" ones, that is, with thoughts and desires that we have even if we do not act on them, as well as with thoughts and desires that result in actions. The Sermon on the Mount directs us to perfect virtue with respect to God, ourselves, and our neighbor, and it directs us to how we should behave and not just what we should say when professing our belief in Christ (1a2ae,108,3).[42]

11. The New Law includes counsels as well as precepts. A "precept" (*praeceptum*) tells one what one must do or not do. A "counsel" (*consilium*) advises rather than positively commands; it offers general advice to be acted on as one thinks fit. The Old Law consisted of precepts, but the New Law offers counsels as well as precepts and, for this reason, can be thought of as a law of freedom, one that respects personal reflection and choice. "The difference between a counsel and a precept lies in this, that a precept implies necessity, while a counsel is left to the choice of the one to whom it is given. And so it is fitting that in the New Law, which is the law of freedom, counsels should be provided as well as precepts, but not in the Old Law, which is a law of servitude."[43] The counsels of the New Law can be regarded as advice when it comes to dealing with external possessions, sensual pleasures, and honors. They can be expressed as "Be poor," "Be celibate," and "Be obedient and not proud."[44]

14.7 Grace in General (1a2ae,109–114)

1a2ae,109–114 is a general discussion of grace. Here Aquinas considers why people need grace (1a2ae,109), what grace is (1a2ae,110), whether there are divisions of grace (1a2ae,111), and what grace's causes are (1a2ae,112). In 1a2ae,113 and 114, Aquinas goes on to consider justification and merit, which he takes to come about by grace. I speak here of 1a2ae,109–114 being a *general* discussion of grace because in 2a2ae Aquinas deals with *particular* theological virtues brought about by grace, and in 3a he turns in some detail to the grace of Christ (grace resulting in people because of the life, death, and resurrection of Christ) and the means by which certain religious practices can be thought of as causes of grace. The *Summa Theologiae*'s account of grace is not complete until 3a,90 (and it can partly be found prior to 1a2ae,109).[45] Yet the main lines of what Aquinas teaches about grace are set forth in 1a2ae,109–114.[46] So, what does this teaching amount to?

One thing worth emphasizing about Aquinas's teaching on grace might come as a surprise to you given his view of the enormous difference between God and creatures. This is that Aquinas insists that grace is a matter of people coming to share in God's life. In 1a2ae,110,1, for example, he speaks of grace as "a special love" by which God "draws the rational creature above its natural condition to have a part in the divine goodness" (*ad participationem divini boni*).[47] In 1a2ae,112,1, he says that "the gift of grace" is "nothing other than a certain participation in the divine nature (*quaedam participatio divinae naturae*).[48] By grace, Aquinas declares, God makes us "godlike, by communicating a share in God's divine nature by participation and assimilation."[49] Even as far back at 1a2ae,62,1, we find him talking about "a happiness surpassing our nature" that "we can attain only by the power of God" by which "we are made partakers of the divine nature."[50]

When talking in this way, Aquinas seems to have in mind 2 Peter 1:3–4. According to this text God has "given to us everything needed for life and godliness, through the knowledge of him [i.e., Christ] who called us by his own glory and goodness...so that through them you may escape from the corruption that is in the world...and may become participants of the divine nature." Aquinas takes the author of 2 Peter to be saying that human perfection involves us somehow coming to share in what God is. In adopting this view, however, Aquinas is not asking us to ignore all that he says in the *Prima Pars* concerning the difference between God and creatures. If anything, he is asking us to remember it, for his point is that by means of grace God lifts people to a state that *only* God can bring them to, a state that reflects what only God is or has by *nature*.[51]

As we have seen, Aquinas has a robust notion of human nature. He takes us to be things of a certain natural kind, things with a range of powers and activities considered as members of that kind (cf. 1a,75–89 and 1a2ae,6–64). As we have also seen, though, he thinks of people after the Fall of Adam as being inadequate in various ways when left to their own devices. We are, he holds (1a2ae,55–61), naturally able to obtain virtues of a kind; but we cannot lift ourselves up to beatitude by means of our human abilities (cf.1a,12,4 and 13, 1a2ae,5, 1a2ae,62,1–2, and 1a2ae,68–70). For beatitude, we need the help of God, and Aquinas takes this help in us to reflect what God is by nature rather than what we are, again presuming the principle that effects of agent causes reflect their causes. The more we are what God alone can make us to be, the more like God we are (even though the fundamental disparity between God and creatures remains). And our becoming more like God than we can by our own efforts is what Aquinas takes to be the work of grace. As he says in 1a,62,1:

> People are perfected by virtue towards those actions by which they are directed towards happiness....Yet human happiness or felicity is two-fold....One is proportionate to human nature, and this people can reach through their own resources. The other...they can attain only by the power of God. Because such happiness goes beyond the reach of human nature, the inborn resources by which people are able to act well according to their capacity are not adequate to direct them to it. And so, to be sent to this supernatural happiness, they need to be divinely en-dowed with some additional sources of activity; their role is like that of their native capabilities which direct them, not, of course, without God's help, to their connatural end.[52]

The phrase "not, of course, without God's help" here is evidently intended to remind us of Aquinas's constant teaching that God operates in every opera-tion. He does *not* think that God is *not* acting in those *without* grace, but he *does* think that God is doing *more* in those with grace than those without it. In this sense, grace makes us "participants of the divine nature," albeit that it does not make us to be literally all that God is. This idea is something that Aquinas elaborates on in 2a2ae and 3a as well as in 1a2ae,109–114.

14.8 The Need for Grace (1a2ae,109)

It is with these thoughts in mind that Aquinas writes 1a2ae,109, while some-times moving back and forth from a consideration of Adam to that of Adam's descendants. He argues: (1) While people can know some truth without grace, there are truths to which only grace can lead them to assent (1a2ae,109,1); (2) While people can do some good without grace, they need grace to act perfectly (1a2ae,109,2); (3) While people considered as human are naturally drawn to the goodness that is God, the descendants of Adam need grace in order to love God above all things (1a2ae,109,3); (4) We now need God's grace in order to be morally perfect and to act in accordance with ways in which God has taught us by revelation to behave (1a2ae,109,4);[53] (5) Nobody can merit eternal life without grace (1a2ae,109,5); (6) People cannot prepare themselves for grace without the assistance of grace (1a2ae,109,6); (7) Nobody can "return from the state of guilt to the state of justice" without grace (1a2ae,109,7);[54] and (8) The descendants of Adam, unlike Adam himself, cannot refrain from sinning mortally without grace and need grace in order to persevere in good even after they have already received grace (1a2ae,109,8 and 10). In short, 1a2ae,109 teaches that grace is indispensable for human perfection, and, notice, Aquinas takes grace to make a difference to people. One might be well disposed to someone, one might even shower that person with gifts, without the object of one's benevolence being affected or seriously changed in any way. Aquinas, however, thinks that grace positively improves people, that it makes them better than they were before they received it. "When someone is said to have God's grace," Aquinas observes, "something supernatural is referred to, issuing in the person from God" (1a2ae,110,1).[55] Grace is "a certain quality" (*quaedam qualitas*) in the soul (1a2ae,110,2), though it does not amount to any one of the theological virtues but is, rather, that which leads people to have them (1a2ae,110,3 and 4).

14.9 Divisions of Grace (1a2ae,111)

Aquinas does not think that grace is like cheese. He does not think of it as a genus containing a number of different species. There is cheese, and there is Brie, Edam, cheddar, Gorgonzola, and cheese of many other kinds. In the sense that cheese can be divided into kinds, however, Aquinas does not think that grace can be divided. Rather, he thinks of it as we might think of the effects of a good teacher. The best teachers inspire, instruct, encourage, and correct their students. In doing so they are, in a sense, doing different things. They are, however, really only doing one thing: teaching well. We can distinguish between a teacher inspiring or instructing or encouraging or correcting, but we can also think of teaching as something single and whole in and of itself. In a similar way, Aquinas thinks of grace as something single, though in some ways divisible. Considered as single, he takes grace to be God's action in people leading them to the beatific vision. Considered as divisible, he views it as something that we can classify in six ways.[56]

To be precise, Aquinas distinguishes between (1) "sanctifying grace" (*gratia gratum faciens*), (2) "freely bestowed grace" (*gratia gratis data*), (3) "operating grace" (*gratia operans*), (4) "cooperating grace" (*gratia cooperans*), (5) "prevenient grace" (*gratia praeveniens*), and (6) "subsequent grace" (*gratia subsequens*). And the breakdown here amounts to the following conclusions:

1. Sanctifying grace is grace by which God makes people holy or directed to God or united to God.
2. Freely bestowed grace is grace by which God supernaturally helps people who help *others* to become holy. Here Aquinas is thinking that, for example, someone might be given the gift of prophecy and thereby aid someone else to will what God wills.
3. Operating grace is the grace by which God moves us to *start* willing what God wills.
4. Cooperating grace is the grace by which God *continues* to move us to will what God wills.
5. Prevenient grace is grace that comes to people *before* what they go on to do by means of grace.
6. Subsequent grace is grace that comes *after* what God has previously brought about in them by grace.

14.10 The Cause of Grace (1a2ae,112)

It should be obvious to you now that Aquinas holds that God is the only agent cause of grace, but he reinforces this conclusion in 1a2ae,112. It is impossible, he declares, "that a creature should cause grace" (1a2ae,112,1).[57] We are the recipients of God's grace right from where we start even as we come to be attracted to what God is all about (1a2ae,112,2 and 3), and the degree to which people are graced depends on God (1a2ae,112,4). Can we know that we have grace? Aquinas argues that we cannot. God, he thinks, might inform us by private revelation that we are graced, and we might inductively, as opposed to deductively, conclude with some reason that God is gracing us. By our natural understanding, however, we cannot know that God has given us grace.

You might think that Aquinas's emphasis on God as the agent cause of grace leads him to suppose that grace overrides human freedom, and some people think that Aquinas is committed to exactly this conclusion. Aquinas, however, does not see things that way, as you might appreciate from what we saw him arguing in 1a,19,8, where he maintains that God's will does not impose necessity on things. Yes, Aquinas believes, people depend on God's causality from beginning to end when it comes to grace; but he does not think that grace renders us un-free. His view is that it empowers us freely to desire God and act accordingly. Or, as we find Aquinas saying in 1a2ae,113,3, "No one comes to God by justifying grace without a movement of free choice."[58]

14.11 Justification (1a2ae,113)

What, though, does Aquinas here mean by "justifying grace"? He does not use this phrase when listing the divisions of grace in 1a2ae,111, but he invokes it in 1a2ae,113 as he proceeds to talk about justification, which he takes to be a matter of operative grace.[59] For Aquinas, we are justified as God gives us sanctifying grace, as we have faith in Christ by God's grace, and as God draws us to beatitude while forgiving our sins. For Aquinas, justification is primarily the "justification of the unrighteous" (*justificatio impii*). It is what occurs as people repent of their sins, place their trust in Christ, and act as such repentance and trust requires.

The term "justification" has a long and varied history in the thinking of Christians. Its origins lie in Old Testament talk about God's justice or righteousness. In the New Testament, the notion of justification features prominently in the writings of St. Paul, who says that human beings are "justified" by God's grace "as a gift, through the redemption that is in Christ Jesus."[60] In the sixteenth century, the Protestant reformers (chiefly Luther and Calvin) appealed to their understanding of justification as a corrective to what they took Roman Catholic thinking about it to be, and at the Council of Trent the Roman Catholics responded to the reformers. And discussions of justification abound in theology even today. What, though, does Aquinas take justification to involve?

His thinking on justification takes it to be more than a matter of God forgiving our sins. He does take it to involve that, but he also regards it as a matter of us acting in accordance with God's will. That he should hold this view is not surprising given how he thinks of God's action as present in its effects (given what he says concerning the principle "the action of the agent is in the patient"). For Aquinas, it is impossible to dissociate being forgiven by God and striving to act in accordance with God's will. His whole notion of God as eternal and immutable prohibits him from thinking that God forgiving someone is nothing but an event in God's ongoing life—a mental event, as it were. In his view, to be forgiven involves one repenting. So he thinks that we are forgiven by God as we repent and as we lead lives that square with such repentance. In this sense, he takes justification to be an ongoing process in people. It has been said that God justifies people by treating them as good even though they are sinful. But this idea does not occur to Aquinas. He thinks it obvious that being holy means being holy and not being *taken* to be holy even if one is *not*.

So, in 1a2ae,113, Aquinas says that justification is effected by grace and amounts to the forgiveness of sin, brought about by repentance, and the strength in people, given to them by grace, to persevere on the road to perfection. The essentials of this teaching emerge in 1a2ae,113,6 in which we read:

> Four requirements for the justification of the unrighteous may be listed: namely, the infusion of grace; a movement of free choice directed towards God by faith; a movement of free choice directed towards sin; and the forgiveness of sin. The reason for this distinction lies in the fact that...justification is a kind of movement, in which the soul is moved by God from the state of sin to the state of justice. Now in any movement in which something is moved by something else, three elements are required; firstly, the motion given by the mover; secondly the movement of that which is moved, and thirdly, the completion of the movement, that is, the arrival at an end. As regards the divine motion, then, we have the infusion of grace; as regards the free choice set in movement, however, we have two movements, in the sense of a departure from the initial term and of an approach to the end-term; the completion of the movement, or its arrival at its term, is implied in the forgiveness of sin, for in this justification is completed.[61]

Justification, in this sense, is "the greatest of God's works" (*maximum opus dei*).[62] This verdict of Aquinas might seem surprising since one might naturally think that justification, as Aquinas understands it, pales somewhat by comparison to, say, the creation of the universe from nothing and the guiding of it by divine providence, and in 1a2ae,113,9, Aquinas acknowledges the force of such thinking. But he also argues that the creation and governance of the universe results in the existence or continued existence of what can pass away while those who continue to receive the grace of God until death never pass away as graced but remain forever joined to God.

14.12 Merit (1a2ae,114)

Can grace be thought of in terms of merit? This is the last question raised by Aquinas in 1a2ae, and his answer is that it can.

How should we construe the word *merit*? We normally take it to mean that our behavior can sometimes be thought of as worthy and, therefore, as praiseworthy or deserving of reward. "John behaved meritoriously" means that John is to be commended. "This book has many merits" means that it is good in many ways and should be valued accordingly. To say that people should be treated according to their merits is to say that they should be treated well because of what they are or have done. We think of merit with respect to the notion of desert. Those who are meritorious are deserving in some way.

In 1a2ae,114, Aquinas broadly works with this understanding of merit in mind, though he modifies it to suit his understanding of God and grace. Hence, for example, in 1a2ae,114,1, he argues that, while certain people might rightly claim a reward from others for what they have done, nobody can claim a reward from God absolutely speaking. He thinks this because he takes human beings not to be equal to God, because he denies that God and people each belong to a society in which rules concerning dues are equally binding on each of its members. "Justice holds simply between those who are related by simple equality," he observes. And "there can be no justice between human beings and God in the sense of absolute equality."[63] You and I might enter into an arrangement in terms of which it is mutually agreed that if I do such and such, then you have to reward me in some specified way. In such a case, if I do my part then I have a right to a reward from you, given our arrangement. Aquinas, however, does not think that people can be thought of as related to God in terms of a transaction like this. Rather, he thinks that we can earn a reward from God, that we can merit from God, only on terms laid down by God rather as a monarch might deem someone to be meritorious given the monarch's published decrees concerning what is worthy of reward. "The mode and measure of human capacity," he claims, "is set for human beings by God. And so human beings can only merit before God on the presupposition of a divine ordination, of such a kind that by their work and action people are to obtain from God as a sort of reward that for which God has allotted them a power of action."[64] We have no claim in justice to anything from God, yet God has arranged that we, as freely choosing creatures, can merit from God in terms of God's will and grace.

Unsurprisingly, therefore, Aquinas takes reward from God for human merit to depend on grace and not on human achievements. So, he argues, we cannot merit eternal life (the beatific vision) simply by doing what we can do as human beings without grace (1a2ae,114,2), though by God's decree we can merit eternal life by charity and by virtues springing from it (1a2ae,114,4). Can we merit the coming to be of grace in us? To this question Aquinas replies no. In his view, merit before God is due to what we do as graced by God (1a2ae,114,5), so even perseverance in the good depends on grace "because it depends only on the divine motion, which is the principle and source of all merit" (1a2ae,114,9).[65] And grace, thinks Aquinas, is not a reward for good works. Rather, it is God working in us (considered as freely acting creatures) for our good.[66]

But how does God work in us for our good? Aquinas has tried partially to answer this question in 1a2ae. In 2a2ae, as we shall now see, he elaborates considerably on what he has previously said.

Faith, Hope, and Charity
(2a2ae,1–46)

IN THE FOREWORD to 2a2ae,1, Aquinas indicates his purpose in what follows it. "Having set out the general theory on vices, virtues and other topics related to morals," he says, "we must now turn to specific details about each."[1] Aquinas acts on this self-imposed way of proceeding by first writing more about the theological virtues of faith, hope, and charity (2a2ae,1–46) and then by considering the cardinal virtues of prudence, justice, courage, and temperance (2a2ae,47–80 and 2a2ae,101–170). In 2a2ae,81–100, he turns to "religion" (*religio*), considered as falling under justice, and in 2a2ae,171–189, he considers certain special gifts and the state of life of people devoted to action or to contemplation, and of those who are priests, bishops, or members of religious orders.

15.1 Faith (2a2ae,1–16)

15.1.1 Faith: The Big Picture

Aquinas takes faith to be the chronologically first of the theological virtues since he regards hope and charity as grounded in it. Indeed, Aquinas thinks of faith as presiding over *all* virtues. This is clear from 2a2ae,4,7. Aquinas does not think of faith as the greatest theological virtue (this, for him, being charity) since he regards it as temporary and lasting, if we have it, only for our present lives.[2] But he does, in a sense, take faith to be primary. If we have the theological virtues of hope and charity in this life, he holds, that can only be because we have faith.

Aquinas thinks of faith in fairly precise terms. He takes it to be assent to the articles of faith referred to in 1a,1. For him, faith is explicit belief in a series of propositions, ones that he takes to be suitably formulated in the Apostle's Creed and the Niceno-Constantinopolitan Creed (2a2ae,1,6–9). "The contents of Christian faith," he observes, "are said to be set forth into articles in the sense that they are divided into several parts having an interconnection" (2a2ae,1,6).[3] In 2a2ae,1,8, Aquinas claims that there are fourteen articles of faith: (1) God is one; (2) God is Father; (3) God is Son; (4) God is Holy Spirit; (5) God is the creator of all things; (6) God works for our sanctification; (7) God will raise us from the dead to everlasting life; (8) God became flesh in Christ; (9) God, in Christ, was born of a virgin; (10) God, in Christ, suffered, died, and was buried; (11) Christ descended into hell; (12) Christ was raised from the dead; (13) Christ ascended into heaven; (14) Christ will come again to judge.[4]

Some theologians have disparaged the notion of Christian faith as sub-scription to a set of propositions, while wanting to insist that faith must surely be a matter of living in a trusting relationship with God rather than assenting to verbal formulae. In a serious sense, however, Aquinas is of the same mind. To have faith, thinks Aquinas, is to believe and trust God as revealing to us all that we need to know to achieve beatitude. The object of faith is "the first truth," which is nothing other than God (2a2ae,1,1). One does not need to be educated in order to have faith, he says (2a2ae,2,6), and, so he argues in 2a2ae,1,2, "from the perspective of the reality believed in" the "object of faith is something non-composite, i.e. the very reality about which one has faith."[5] Those with faith respond to God as communicating with us, "and so faith rests upon the divine truth itself as the medium of its assent."[6] In Aquinas's view, those with faith believe God as teaching them, and in this sense have a trusting relationship with God. At the same time, however, Aquinas also thinks that one cannot just *believe* God. One has to believe God *that* certain articulatable truths are indeed true. The command "Just believe" is not one that anyone can act on since it does not specify what one is supposed to be-lieve. Such specification, Aquinas thinks, can only be provided in proposi-tional form. Hence his insistence on the importance of the articles of faith handed down in creeds.

How does one come to have faith? Aquinas holds that one does so by the grace of God and not by any natural human power. He therefore says that faith is not knowledge as one has it when developing a science (*scientia*), when reasoning from evident truths to conclusions that strictly follow from them (2a2ae,1,5). In Aquinas's view, faith is knowledge insofar as those with faith believe what is true and insofar as they share to some extent in God's knowledge, but they do not believe because their intellects are compelled to assent to the articles of faith in the way that the human intellect, when func-tioning properly, is compelled to assent to the stages in a demonstrative argu-ment. Hebrews 11:1 reads: "Faith is the assurance of things hoped for, the conviction of things not seen." Aquinas endorses this definition (2a2ae,1,4 and 2ae2ae,4,1) while connecting it to Aristotelian thinking about demon-strative knowledge and to something that Hugh of St. Victor (d. 1142) teaches—that faith is "mid-way between science (*scientia*) and opinion (*opinio*)."[7] One has *scientia*, thinks Aquinas, when one clearly sees *that* a proposition is true and *why* it is true. One has *opinio* when one inclines to believe a proposition even though one lacks knowledge concerning its truth and so does not see that the proposition is true or why it is true. When it comes to faith, Aquinas concludes, one assents with conviction just as one does when one has knowledge, though what one believes is not known in such a way that one sees why it is true, and so is held rather as opinions are held. "The act of believing," he writes (2a2ae,2,1), "is firmly attached to one alternative and in this respect the believer is in the same state of mind as one who has science (*scientia*) or understanding (*intelligentia*). Yet the believer's knowledge is not completed by a clear vision, and in this respect is like having a doubt, a suspicion, or an opinion."[8]

Aquinas, therefore, thinks that "to be imperfect as knowledge is of the very essence of faith," as he says in 1a2ae,67,3. However, he does not therefore regard faith as something to be denigrated. Some philosophers have argued along different lines. A famous example is W. K. Clifford (1845–1879), who roundly declares, "It is wrong always, everywhere, and for anyone, to believe anything upon insufficient evidence."[9] Clifford seems to require that all beliefs should be solidly grounded in rational, empirical inquiry and that one should be blamed for believing without such inquiry. As other philosophers have pointed out, though, much rational inquiry works from assumptions that are not themselves proved by the inquiry itself. Astronomers and chemists, for instance, take for granted that there is a physical world. Their astronomical and chemical investigations presuppose that the world exists to be studied and do not themselves provide proof of the world's existence.[10] In other words, and as philosophers of a different mind from Clifford have observed, it is not necessarily vicious to believe without being able to formulate a proof that all that one believes is true, and as he turns to the notion of faith, Aquinas shows himself to be in agreement with this view. He thinks that there need be nothing wrong in, and that there may be much that is right in, believing without evidence. In particular, he thinks that it may be necessary to believe people who are teaching one. He quotes Aristotle as saying that every learner must begin by simply believing other people (2a2ae,2,3), and he applies Aristotle's point directly to the virtue of faith. By faith, says Aquinas, we rightly believe God, who teaches us in the words of Christ, the text of the New Testament, and the transmission of these by the Church in the articles of faith.[11] Aquinas does not maintain that study and reflection are of no importance to the life of faith. Quite the contrary (cf. 2a2ae,1,4, ad.2, 2a2ae,1,5, ad.2, 2a2ae,2,1, ad.1, and 2a2ae,2,10). He does, however, think that study and reflection cannot lead us to know the truths of Christian faith. "The things of faith," he says, "surpass people's under-standing and so become part of their knowledge (*cognitio*) only because God reveals them" (2a2ae,6,1).[12] He continues: "Since in assenting to the things of faith people are raised above their own nature, they have this assent from a supernatural source influencing them; this source is God. The assent of faith, which is its principal act, therefore has as its cause God, moving us inwardly through grace."[13]

As I have noted several times, Aquinas does not think of God's causal ac-tivity in us as being a threat to our freedom. This view of Aquinas surfaces again in the claim that faith is voluntary and can, therefore, be meritorious (cf. 2a2ae,2,9). I cannot but accept that all triangles have three sides, if I know what a triangle is, or I cannot but accept that "q" is true, if I know that "p" and "if p, then q" are true and I see their implications. In cases such as these, my assent is involuntary because it is coerced by what I know. Aquinas does not think of faith as coerced in this way, however. We are, he holds, not forced to believe the articles of faith because they are obviously true. We be-lieve them willingly or voluntarily and can, therefore, be held accountable for having or not having faith. In short, we have faith because we want to, be-cause we see good in having it, because it is attractive to us, even though our doing so is only by God's grace. Aquinas's position on the voluntary nature of faith emerges rather sharply in 2a2ae,1,4, in which he discusses the gospel story of doubting Thomas (John 20). Thomas saw the risen Christ and wor-shiped him as God, Aquinas notes. Does this mean that Thomas's confession of Christ as divine was something forced on him by what he saw? Aquinas replies no. "Thomas saw one thing and believed something else. He saw a man; he believed him to be God and bore witness to this, saying, 'My Lord and my God.'"[14]

15.1.2 Faith: Some Details

That is the substance of Aquinas's account of faith in 2a2ae,1–16. That ac-count, however, incorporates some teachings that I have not so far mentioned. The most important amount to the following.

1. Faith is a virtue of the intellect graced by God, who is the first Truth, so nothing false can fall under it. "Nothing false can be the term of faith" (2a2ae,1,3).[15]
2. Faith is not just a vague approval of what is proclaimed by the articles of faith. Nor is it just a matter of acting well. Faith involves believing in the

articles of faith explicitly. "Just as one is obliged to have faith, so too one is obliged to believe explicitly in its primary tenets, i.e. the articles of faith" (2a2ae,2,5).[16] Many Christians are unlettered and unable to talk in a sophisticated theological way concerning the articles of faith, yet even such people attend to what their teachers in the faith have to say insofar as they are teaching correctly, and therefore they believe explicitly at a remove, so to speak (2a2ae,2,6).[17]

3. Salvation depends on holding explicitly to the articles of faith (2a2ae, 2,7 and 8). These, of course, were not proclaimed before the time of Christ as they were following his resurrection, but Jewish people in Old Testament times shared in the Christian faith insofar as they adhered to the Old Law, which prefigured the New Law and served to make the way for Christ's coming.[18]

4. The articles of faith have increased over time, not with respect to their substance but with respect to how that substance has been spelled out. Elaborations of the articles of faith amount to drawing out implications of what was previously taught (2a2ae,1,7). "All the articles of faith are implicit in certain primary ones, namely that God exists and has providence over the salvation of human beings....As to what the articles stand for, there has been no increase in the course of time, because all the things that later generations have believed in were contained, though implicitly, in what those who went before believed in. As far as explicitness is concerned, the number of articles has grown, because certain matters have been known explicitly by later ages that were not explicitly known earlier."[19]

5. Faith needs to be expressed by people formally confessing what they believe. This is its "outward act" and is necessary for salvation (2a2ae, 3,1 and 2). "Witnessing to the faith...is not a matter of salvation at every instant and in every situation, but only where and when failure to do so would jeopardize the honour due to God or a chance to serve one's neighbour."[20]

6. There is no faith without the theological virtue of charity (2a2ae,4,3). Faith is believing God as drawing us to our end in love and it therefore involves loving our neighbor and ourselves. "Faith's act is pointed as to its end towards the will's object, i.e. the good. This good, the end of faith's act, is the divine good, the proper object of charity. That is why charity is called the form of faith."[21]

7. We can distinguish between dead faith and living faith (2a2ae,4,4 and 6,2). Dead faith, which even the devils have, is a matter of mere assent lacking love in what is being assented to. Living faith, on the other hand, is faith had by those who love God and all that God loves.

8. Faith admits of degrees insofar as some people can adhere to God in faith more firmly than others and insofar as some people can be more articulate about matters of faith than others. All with faith have a single virtue whose object is God. Yet "one person can believe more things explicitly than another does," and faith can be greater in some than in others "as being more certain and steadfast" and "as being more prompt, devout, or trusting."[22] A careless reading of Aquinas on faith would lead one to think that he takes it only to be had by enthusiasts like St. Paul, whose adherence to Christ seems to have been engrossing, wholehearted, and joyfully pursued even to the point of embracing martyrdom. Aquinas, though, is not so demanding when it comes to the possession of faith. As a Dominican he was familiar with the business of hearing confessions, many of which might have expressed weakness in faith or uncertainty of some kind. I strongly suspect that his hearing of confessions influenced his account of faith considerably.

9. Those with faith enjoy the gifts of the Holy Spirit (2a2ae,8 and 9). In particular, faith brings with it understanding (*intellectus*) and knowledge (*scientia*). In this context, understanding and knowledge do not, of course, amount to a full grasp of what God is essentially or of all that God does for us as leading us to beatitude. They do, however, amount to help from God so as to think and act well when it comes to the revealed mysteries of God.

10. There is faith, but there is also (2a2ae,10–13) "unbelief" (*infidelitas*). This is always sinful in that it is contrary to the virtue of faith and separates the unbeliever from God. While being as voluntary as faith is, unbelief can manifest itself in different ways. One might disbelieve just because one is someone who, for whatever reasons, happens to lack faith.[23] Again, one might disbelieve as someone positively set on denying the articles of faith or even railing against them. When it comes to disbelief, one needs to bear in mind who is not believing and why, and one can rightly think of those who explicitly reject the articles of faith as being more culpable than those who just do not have faith, even though "by disbelief most of all a person departs from God" (2a2ae,10,3).[24]

11. Unbelief is bad, but it does not follow that unbelievers cannot act well even though they lack grace. So unbelievers do not sin in all that they do, and they might well be able to reason successfully and, therefore, grasp truth in different ways (2a2ae,10,4).

12. Christians should be willing to debate with unbelievers (2a2ae, 10,7). "To debate in order to refute error or for theological practice is praiseworthy."[25]

13. One should not try to force unbelievers to believe in Christianity since belief is essentially voluntary and cannot, therefore, be the result of

compulsion (2a2ae,10,8). One might, however, oppose unbelievers and try to prevent them from influencing people away from the truths of faith or from persecuting people because of their faith, and physical compulsion is appropriate when it comes to heretics insofar as it amounts to trying to make them abide by what they once rightly professed.[26]

14. Christians should resist the coming about of a situation in which unbelievers govern the lives of the faithful since this would endanger the faith of those who believe in Christianity. On the other hand, given a society in which unbelievers already rule, their rule is not against human law based on reason, even though it might conflict with divine law. There can, albeit regrettably, be legitimate government of believers by unbelievers (2a2ae,10,10).

15. Christians should tolerate the religious rites of unbelievers since not doing so might lead to evil consequences (2a,2ae,10,11). "Although infidels sin in their rites, they may be tolerated on account of some good that results or some evil that is avoided."[27] And it would be absolutely wrong to try to baptize the children of Jews and other unbelievers against the will of their parents. Baptism is a sacrament of the Christian Church (see 3a, 66–69) and is a means by which people are brought to God. But "injury should be done to no one," and to force parents of children to baptize them would be to inflict injury against them.

In what he says about unbelievers Aquinas is writing very much as a churchman of his day. We are aware that the world now (and for centuries past) has contained billions of people who are not Christian. We know about Buddhism, Hinduism, Jainism, and other religions. Aquinas did not. He knew about paganism in its Greco-Roman form, and he knew about Judaism and Islam. He also knew about self-professing Christians who challenged what he took to be sound Christian teaching. But he lacked a knowledge of what contemporary scholars dealing with religious traditions now take for granted (a knowledge of religious belief considered globally and historically). So his discussion of unbelief in 2a2ae is clearly affected by ignorance and might be compared with things that he has to say relating to certain antiquated scientific views to which he was heir. On the other hand, you might note that in 2a2ae Aquinas seems to be tolerant and conceding to unbelievers. He never says anything like "They should all be consigned to hell." Instead, while never giving up on his idea that final union with God depends on Christian faith, he seems to leave room for the idea (not developed by him, but developed by many theologians since his time) that God's governance of creatures is not necessarily thwarted by unbelief and can even be thought of as compatible with it. I may be mistaken, but it seems to me that, were he alive today, Aquinas would likely be conceding to many people the dignity and grace that he accords to those Jews in Old Testament times who did not believe explicitly in what he calls "the articles of faith."

15.2 Hope (2a2ae,17–22)

I noted in chapter 11 that in 1a2ae, Aquinas discusses hope, fear, and despair under the heading "passions of the soul" or "emotions." In 2a2ae,17–22, he returns to them and also has something to say about "presumption" (*praesumptio*), which he contrasts with despair. However, while the teaching on hope, fear, and despair in 2a2ae,17–22 echoes what we find Aquinas saying about them previously, in 2a2ae,17–22, he is thinking of hope as something given to us or infused in us by grace, and not as explicable in terms of our human nature and our interaction with the world. His treatment of fear, despair, and presumption in 2a2ae,19–22 is correspondingly geared to human beings thought of as having or lacking divine grace.

According to Aquinas, the theological virtue of hope amounts to trusting that God will lead us to beatitude. "We should," he says, "hope for nothing less from God than God's very self; God's goodness, by which God confers good upon creatures, is nothing less than God's own being. And so the proper and principal object of hope is indeed eternal blessedness" (2a2ae,17,2).[28] The theological virtue of hope is hope for what *only* God can provide. In 2a2ae,17,5, Aquinas concedes that one may place trust in what is not divine as instrumentally helping us to beatitude, so he has no problem with us hopefully invoking the help of the saints in heaven. But, says Aquinas, hope, strictly speaking, is for goodness bestowed by God. He therefore holds that hope springs from or depends on the theological virtue of faith. "Simply speaking," he observes, "faith precedes hope.... The object of hope is eternal beatitude, and in a somewhat distinct way, the divine assistance, both of which are made manifest to us by faith, whereby we know that we can attain to eternal life and that the divine help lies open to us for this very purpose" (2a2ae,17,7).[29] Again, he writes: "Faith is an attachment of someone to God as God is the source of knowing truth—we believe to be true those things spoken to us by God. Hope, in turn, is a cleaving to God as the source of absolute goodness, since hope is reliance on God's help to bring us to blessedness" (2a2ae,17,6).[30] Considered in this way, Aquinas takes hope to be primarily hope for oneself, yet he also thinks it proper to hope for the eternal happiness of others (2a2ae,17,3).

Hope, Aquinas goes on to say, lies in the will. It is a striving or leaning based on knowledge but not identical with it (2a2ae,18,1). Aquinas takes this fact to mean that, as with faith, there is no need for hope among the blessed. They have arrived at beatitude and have nothing further to which to look forward. "Thus hope will pass away in heaven, just as faith will, and so neither of them is to be found in the blessed" (2a2ae,18,2).[31] Nor is there hope in the damned, Aquinas adds. The damned have separated themselves definitively from God and can have no realistic hope of beatitude. "It is no more possible for the damned to consider blessedness as still open to them than for the blessed to conceive of it as not already possessed" (2a2ae,18,3).[32]

In 2a2ae,19, Aquinas moves to a discussion of fear, which he takes to be one of the gifts of the Holy Spirit, and which he discusses in connection with hope since he takes it to be related to hope and to be had by those with hope (and faith and charity). Perhaps the main point to note about Aquinas's discussion of fear is that most of it consists of noting different senses of the word *fear* so as to argue that the fear that is the gift of the Holy Spirit is the fear of being separated from God and of falling short of divine goodness. We fear what is bad, says Aquinas, so we obviously cannot properly fear God since God is good. But we can fear the loss of God (2a2ae,19,1). Some fear is "servile fear" (*timor servilis*)—fear of punishment, and it is not inappropriate for us to have such fear of God. Yet fear as inspired by God comes to perfection as "filial fear" (*timor filialis*), and this is a gift of the Holy Spirit. Filial fear amounts (a) to a love of God for what God is and (b) to the inclination to avoid anything that alienates us from God (2a2ae,19,9). Filial fear and hope, says Aquinas, are "interrelated and perfective of one another."[33] And filial fear increases as charity increases.

> The more people love God, the less they fear punishment: first of all, because they are less solicitous about their own welfare, to which punishment is a threat; and secondly, because being more securely attached to God, they have a greater confidence of reward and consequently less fear of punishment.... Fear of punishment is diminished with the increase of hope, but filial fear is thereby rendered more intense (2a2ae,19,10, corpus and ad.2).[34]

Filial fear, unlike servile fear, remains in the blessed, Aquinas adds, since charity motivates it and since charity never passes away (2a2ae,19,11).

So Aquinas praises and values hope and filial fear, but he disparages despair and presumption. To despair, he says, is to lack the theological virtue of hope since it amounts to giving up on beatitude:

> The mind's true appraisal about God acknowledges that God grants pardon to sinners and brings people to salvation.... Contrariwise, false

opinion envisions God as denying pardon to the repentant sinner, or as not converting sinners to God through justifying grace. And so the act of hope, squaring with true judgment, is praiseworthy and virtuous; while the opposite attitude, which is despair, reflecting as it does a false view of God, is vicious and sinful (2a2ae,20,1).[35]

Those who despair when it comes to beatitude effectively act as if it were true that what those with hope believe in shall never come to pass, and it is bad for them to do so not only because despair is bad in itself but since it can lead them into sin. Despair itself is sinful, thinks Aquinas, but it can lead to yet more sin. And Aquinas takes presumption to be comparable to despair in this regard, for he takes it to amount to mistakenly supposing that God will bring us to beatitude regardless of what we do. Or, as he writes: "Just as it is erroneous to believe that God refuses to pardon those who repent or that God does not turn sinners to repentance, it is equally erroneous to imagine that God gives pardon to those who persist in their sins or leads those to glory who shirk from an upright life" (2a2ae,21,2).[36]

15.3 Charity (2a2ae,23–46)

Faith and hope pass away, Aquinas holds. He takes the opposite line, however, when it comes to charity, which he regards as the greatest theological virtue. For Aquinas, it is charity that most unites us to God since it amounts to loving God for God's sake and to loving those whom God loves. The discussion of charity in 2a2ae is a long one (longer than the discussion of faith and hope put together) and it represents what Aquinas has been working toward all along in 2a2ae.

15.3.1 Charity: The Big Picture

Aquinas's treatment of charity draws on his reading of the New Testament and on the tradition of post-biblical theology he inherited, the writings of St. Augustine being a key example. The Latin word *caritas* is frequently used by the Vulgate translation of the Bible to translate the Greek word ἀγάπη (*agape*), which can be rendered as "love," and Aquinas is working from this fact as he develops his account of charity. So he is thoroughly influenced in his discussion by texts such as 1 Corinthians 13, in which St. Paul speaks of himself being "a noisy gong or a clanging cymbal" without love, and in which he ends up saying that "faith, hope, and love abide; these three; and the greatest of these is love." Another Pauline text governing Aquinas's teaching on charity is Romans 5:5, which says: "God's love has been poured into our hearts through the Holy Spirit that has been given to us."

For Aquinas, we have charity not just because we are actively concerned with the welfare of other people, but because we love what God loves and as God loves it. As we have seen (chapter 6), Aquinas thinks that God is essentially loving because of the love between God the Father and God the Son. He thinks that God from eternity loves the supremely lovable and that the life of God consists of this love even without reference to creatures. Aquinas thinks of charity in people as a sharing in this eternal divine love. Aquinas always lays stress on the difference between God and creatures, but, he holds, God has miraculously graced people with a way of being like or at one with the divine nature, a way that involves them living as divinely as any creature can do. As he puts it: "The divine essence itself is charity even as it is wisdom and goodness. Now we are said to be good with the goodness which is God, and wise with the wisdom which is God, because the very qualities which make us formally so are participations in the divine goodness and wisdom. So, too, the charity by which we formally love our neighbour is a sharing in the divine charity" (2a2ae,23,2, ad.1).

Primarily, therefore, Aquinas thinks that the theological virtue of charity enables us to love God, and he represents this love in terms of the notion of friendship with God.[37] Generally speaking, Aquinas takes friendship to be a relationship between equals. "It makes no sense," he says, "to talk of somebody being friends with wine or a horse" (2a2ae,23,1).[38] One might, therefore, reasonably expect Aquinas to recoil from the thought that God and human beings can be friends with each other. Instead, though, he takes his lead from John 15:12–15, in which Jesus, after having washed the feet of his disciples, declares: "I do not call you servants any longer, because the servant does not know what his master is doing; but I have called you friends, because I have made known to you everything that I have heard from my father." Because of charity, says Aquinas, we have "friendship" (*amicitia*) with God. Charity, he asserts, is friendship (*Caritas est amicitia*). Why? Because "there is a sharing of human beings with God by God sharing divine happiness with us, and it is on this that a friendship is based" (2a2ae,23,1).[39]

Aquinas's main idea here is that charity amounts first of all to a full and proper love of God, and then, based on this, to a full and proper love of what we ought to love in the realm of creatures. And in agreement with what we have seen him to think about the New Law, Aquinas takes charity to be "instilled within our hearts" since it derives from God working directly in us by grace so as to make us God-like in our thinking and acting.

"Charity...is our friendship for God arising from our sharing in eternal happiness....Consequently charity is beyond the resources of nature and therefore cannot be something natural, nor acquired by natural powers....Hence we have it neither by nature, nor as acquired, but as infused by the Holy Spirit, who is the love of the Father and the Son; our participation in this love...is creaturely charity itself" (2a2ae,24,2).[40]

Charity, says Aquinas, is the greatest of all virtues since it amounts to a sharing in God's life. He argues:

That which more fully attains to God is the more important. Now always a being through itself is fuller than a being through another. But faith and hope attain to God according as from God comes knowledge of truth or possession of good, but charity attains God so as to rest in God without looking for any gain. This is why charity is higher than faith and hope, and consequently than all the virtues (2a2ae,23,6).[41]

Indeed, Aquinas adds, there can be no true virtue without charity since true virtue directs us to God and since charity directs us to God perfectly (2a2ae, 23,7). Charity "directs the acts of all the other virtues to our final end. Accordingly, it shapes all these acts and to this extent is said to be the form of the virtues" (2a2ae,23,8).[42] Charity impresses its form on other true virtues. It supports and nourishes them. It directs them to its own end.[43] This is so, Aquinas holds, even though charity can grow in people over time (2a2ae,24,4) and even though charity can be lost by mortal sin (2a2ae,24,11 and 12).

Is charity simply a matter of loving God? Aquinas clearly thinks that love of God lies at the heart of charity, but he also insists that it has other objects. Pet lovers will, perhaps, be disgruntled to find that Aquinas denies that charity can extend to "irrational creatures." He does not think that we can seriously be friends with them—friendship demanding equality and common purpose (2a2ae,25,3). He is clear, though, that human beings are proper objects of charity and he argues that charity includes loving our neighbor (2a2ae,25,1), loving charity itself (2a2ae,25,2), loving oneself (2a2ae,25,4), loving our bodies (2a2ae,25,5), loving sinners (2a2ae,25,6), loving our enemies (2a2ae,25,8), and loving angels (2a2ae,25,10), though not devils (2a2ae,25,11). In sum:

The friendship we call charity rests on a fellowship of eternal happiness. Now in this fellowship we can distinguish three elements. One which actively communicates this happiness to us, namely God; another which directly shares in it, people and angels; and a third, to which eternal happiness comes by a kind of overflow, namely the human body. Now what communicates happiness to us is lovable because it is the cause of our happiness. But what shares in happiness can be lovable for two reasons: either because it is identified with us, or because it is associated with us. And in this way we have two things to be loved by charity, according as people love both themselves and their neighbour (2a2ae,25,12).[44]

15.3.2 Charity: Some Details

1. With an eye on the notion that human action is freely willed by the agent whose action it is, Aquinas stresses that charity is exercised freely even though it arises in us by the grace of the Holy Spirit (2a2ae,23,2). "To be an act of will," he says, "is of the very nature of loving. Likewise it cannot be said that the Holy Spirit moves the will as if it were merely an instrument which, although it is the source of its act, has no power of itself to act or not.... The will must be so moved by the Holy Spirit to the act of love that it must itself also produce it."[45]

2. Aquinas's teaching on virtue accords with his view that true virtue unites people to God and does not just amount to a tendency to right practical reasoning. So he argues that even though there can be virtues distinct from charity, the possession of true virtue requires the possession of charity (2a2ae,23,7). The principal good for people, says Aquinas, is the enjoyment of God, for which charity is essential. "Without charity there cannot be true virtue in an unqualified sense."[46]

3. Charity can grow in us, says Aquinas, by becoming more intense (2a2ae, 24,5), and it "can always increase more and more during this life" since "it is a sharing in that infinite charity which is the Holy Spirit" (2a2ae,24,7 and 8).[47] That being said, though, Aquinas thinks that charity can be perfect in this life insofar as people are wholly intent on God and insofar as they will nothing "contrary to and incompatible with divine love" (2a2ae,24,8).[48]

4. Charity is extinguished by mortal sin (2a2ae,24,12), but not by venial sin, which only weakens it. Sick people can be said to want health even if they sometimes fail to do everything they need to do to ensure their well-being. By the same token, Aquinas argues, one can be set on the goodness that God is, and therefore remain in charity, even if one sometimes falls short in doing what this requires of one (2a2ae,24,10).

5. In 2a2ae,26, Aquinas (largely, though not exclusively, drawing on a range of biblical texts) argues that there is "order" (*ordo*) in charity. He means that we should love some things more than others. We should, he says, love God more than our neighbor or ourselves (2a2ae,26,1–3), and we should love ourselves (though not our bodies) more than we love our neighbor since we should prefer not to sin than to help our neighbor to avoid sin by sinning ourselves (2a2ae,26,4). Aquinas also thinks it right (all things being equal) that, for example, we should love our parents and children more than other people, and that we should love our kin more than strangers (2a2ae,26,6–8).[49]

6. Stressing the outward-going nature of charity as a matter of loving rather than being loved (2a2ae,27,1), Aquinas also argues that the love informed by charity is more than a matter of willing someone well. Rather, it involves "a certain affective union between lover and loved, inasmuch as lovers, seeing the beloved as one with themselves or as part of themselves, is thereby attracted. Therefore love, as an act of charity, includes goodwill, but adds to it a union of the affections" (2a2ae,27,2).[50]

7. As with faith and hope, charity, for Aquinas, comes with gifts of the Holy Spirit, so, its effects include joy and internal peace (2a2ae,28 and 29) together with wisdom (2a2ae,45). Those with charity, Aquinas adds, are merciful and kind to others (2a2ae,30 and 32). In 2a2ae,33, he discusses "brotherly correction" (*fraterna correctio*) and argues that correcting or reproving sinners (ideally in private) can often, though not always, be charitable.

8. In 2a2ae,34–43, we find Aquinas, with much appeal to biblical texts, commenting on things at odds with charity. Under this heading he includes "hatred" (*odium*) of God and neighbor, "spiritual apathy" (*acedia*), "envy" (*invidia*), "discord" (*discordia*), "contentiousness" (*contentio*), "schism" (*schisma*), "war" (*pugna*), "quarreling" (*rixa*), "sedition" (*seditio*), and "scandal" (*scandalum*).

9. Hatred of God is, Aquinas thinks, possible (2a2ae,34,1), though reprehensible (2a2ae,34,2).[51] Hatred of our neighbor, he argues, springs from envy and is condemned in Scripture, though it is less damaging than theft, murder, and adultery (2a2ae,34,3–6).

10. The Latin word *acedia* is not easily translatable into English, though it is sometimes unhappily rendered as "sloth." "Spiritual apathy" would be a better rendition. *Acedia* derives from the Greek word ἀκηδία, which occurs quite a bit in Latin monastic literature, in which it signifies a baleful condition to which monks especially can be prone.[52] For Aquinas, *acedia* is "a bored indifference towards religious and spiritual matters."[53] It amounts

to a kind of depression, sadness, or weariness when it comes to God and what the goodness of God requires of us. So, says Aquinas, *acedia* is contrary to charity even though its presence in someone need not cut that person off from God entirely since it can vary depending on its intensity and its manifestation in behavior.[54]

11. Aquinas distinguishes envy from unhappiness that one experiences because someone else possesses what might threaten one. He takes envy to be grieving over the fact that someone else flourishes in a way that takes away from one's good standing or reputation (2a2ae,36,1). More precisely, he takes it to be "discontent over another's blessings" (2a2ae,36,2).[55] He also thinks that it offends against charity since charity requires one to rejoice in genuine goodness had by others. Does envy cut us off from God? Aquinas replies that it can, though need not. He holds that everything here depends on the presence of full knowledge and consent (a point that he makes several times when discussing what offends against charity).[56]

12. Discord and contentiousness are coupled by Aquinas in 2a2ae,37 and 38. He takes discord to be a matter of being averse to harmony between people because of pride or self-glorification. He takes contentiousness to be a matter of acting or speaking on the basis of such aversion. He comments: "To contend is to tend against someone. Now just as discord implies a contrary will so contentiousness implies contrary speech."[57] Aquinas is not here suggesting that one should never contradict someone or speak against them. He is not against maintaining that someone is somehow in the wrong (he manifestly believes that it can sometimes be thoroughly proper to do so). His point seems to be that it is wrong to be contentious if one's contentiousness amounts to attacking another in an intemperate way. Aquinas is in favor of attacking falsity, but even when it comes to this he looks for respect or "a judicious amount of acrimony."[58] Indeed, he is prepared to criticize the disciples of Jesus recorded in Luke 22:24 as disputing with one another with what Aquinas takes to be "some intemperateness."[59]

13. Aquinas does not equate schism and heresy. He does not think that schism is just a matter of rejecting orthodox Christian belief. Rather, he says, "schismatics properly so called are those who of their own free will and intention separate themselves from the unity of the Church" (2a2ae,39,1).[60] He goes on to say that this unity is represented by "Christ, in whose place the Sovereign Pontiff acts in the Church. So then schismatics are those who refuse obedience to the Sovereign Pontiff and who refuse to communicate with the members of the Church subject to him."[61]

Schism, Aquinas argues, offends against charity since it is at odds with the unity that he thinks Christians should display.

14. When it comes to war, Aquinas is no pacifist (as many Christians have been and still are). He holds that going to war is sometimes permissible, even if regrettable. He is, though, opposed to *unjust* war. On what conditions does he consider a war to be just? In 2a2ae,40,1, he lists three. First, that it be waged on the command of a governing authority (not a "private person").[62] Second, that it be waged in a just cause, that "those who are attacked are attacked because they deserve it on account of some wrong they have done."[63] Third, that it be waged with "right intention," that it must be waged by those who "intend to promote the good and to avoid evil," people acting for "the common good" or even the good of their opponents.[64] Note that these criteria for just war are presented in 2a2ae,40,1 in highly general terms. Aquinas does not here discuss who or what constitutes a legitimate governing authority or what counts as just or unjust in particular war-going circumstances. This, of course, means that anyone wishing to invoke Aquinas to justify the legitimacy of some particular war will have to mine his writings as a whole and not just rely on 2a2ae,40.[65]

15. Aquinas understands "quarrelling" (*rixa*) to signify physically lashing out in anger against someone else, "an antagonism extending to deeds, when one person intends to hurt another" (2a2ae,41,2).[66] This, he thinks, can sometimes be justified and in accord with charity, as in the case of legitimate self-defense. But he also thinks that it can sometimes be against charity if "moved by vengeance or hatred" or if it "goes beyond the restraint called for."[67] His objections to *rixa* (a word that we might also translate as "fighting") accord with those that he has against discord and contentiousness.

16. Aquinas distinguishes between war and *rixa*, on the one hand, and sedition, on the other. He takes sedition to be "between mutually dissident sections of the same people, when, for example, one part of the state rebels against another" (2a2ae,42,2).[68] His objection to sedition is that it conflicts with the common good, so he does not regard rebelling against a tyrannical government as seditious (2a2ae,42,2 ad.3). "Disturbing such a government," he observes, "has not the nature of sedition, unless perhaps the disturbance be so excessive that the people suffer more from it than from the tyrannical regime."[69]

17. Aquinas takes scandal to be speech or action that leads others to be disposed to sin or actually to sin. Effectively, Aquinas sees scandal as setting a bad example, the opposite of brotherly correction. When reading 2a2ae,43, one can forget about the word *scandal* in contemporary references to

"a political scandal" and the like. Aquinas is thinking in New Testament terms according to which a scandal is an obstacle or stumbling block to someone pursuing their good (cf. Matthew 16:23 and Matthew 18:7). Given his view of sin, Aquinas does not think that anyone can actually cause someone else to sin. He does, however, think that people might lead others into sin by what they say and do, so he takes scandal to be an evil and contrary to charity.

In 2a2ae,44, Aquinas sums up his teaching on charity by saying that it consists in willingly obeying two commandments or precepts: to love God and to love our neighbor for God's sake (cf. Matthew 22:40). To do this, he thinks, is to be united with God. Yet as we have seen, Aquinas is aware of ways of talking about human action as good or bad that do not come from his biblical tradition—the ethical teachings of Aristotle, for example. And moving on from his account of the theological virtues, Aquinas proceeds to discuss the goodness or badness of Christians with an eye on what might be called the Greek philosophical tradition (roughly, Socrates to Aristotle) and on what are commonly referred to as the cardinal virtues, together with virtues that Aquinas takes to be allied to them. In the next chapter I shall consider how he does so.

16

Prudence, Justice, and Injustice (2a2ae,47–79)

IN 2A2AE,47–79, WE find Aquinas trying to draw together strands of think-ing that some would never connect to one another. On the one hand, he writes about human virtue in what we might think of as purely philosophical terms. But he also writes about virtue with a Christian audience in mind and there-fore frequently refers to the New Testament and to the teachings of patristic authors such as St. Gregory the Great (ca. 540–604). So 2a2ae,47–79 is the work of a Christian theologian trying to expound what he takes to be *sacra doctrina* while also drawing on good philosophical arguments in the belief that these might help us to understand ourselves insofar as we are (if we are) objects of God's grace. You may suppose, as many have, that Aquinas's efforts in this regard are often unsuccessful—that he gets various things wrong from the viewpoint of sound theology or of good philosophical reasoning. In the present chapter, however, my purpose is not to evaluate what Aquinas says in the *Summa Theologiae* about prudence, justice, and injustice. My aim is to help you to understand what his teaching about these virtues amounts to.

16.1 Prudence (2a2ae,47–56)

2a2ae,47–56 should be read as an elaboration of what Aquinas says about pru-dence in 1a2ae,57–61 (cf. chapter 12). So Aquinas, with multiple references to Aristotle, takes prudence to be an intellectual virtue acquired over time with the benefit of instruction from others, inclining us to right practical reasoning and therefore making its possessor good. Yet the discussion of prudence in 2a2ae,47–56 comes with Aquinas's account of grace preceding it. It therefore considers prudence as a Christian virtue and not just as a humanly acquirable one.[1] Prudence, says Aquinas, involves an intellectual grasp of what is to be done and what is to be avoided not just when it comes to being happy as ra-tional animals but also as those graced by God. There is, he notes, "the gen-uine and complete prudence which, with a view to the final good for the whole of human life, rightly deliberates, decides, and commands" (2a2ae,47,13).[2]

There is (2a2ae,47,14) "prudence of grace" that is "caused by God's imparting." "Prudence, which signifies the rightness of reason," says Aquinas, "is above all helped and completed by being moved and ruled by the Holy Spirit" (2a2ae,52,2).[3] One might, says Aquinas, display prudence to some degree without having the theological virtue of charity. One cannot, however, have charity without having prudence in the full sense—as a disposition that inclines one to think and behave well in conformity with the teachings of Christ, prudence "present as an activity concerning the things necessary for salvation" (2a2ae,47,14, ad.3).[4]

Even without respect to salvation, however, Aquinas seems to think that prudence is critical for virtuous (if not divinizing) behavior. We need prudence, he says, in order to apply ourselves to good action (2a2ae,47,3) since "the role of prudence...is to charge our conduct with right reason" (2a2ae,47,4).[5] Indeed, says Aquinas, "prudence holds special place in the enumeration of the virtues" (2a2a,47,5) and can be thought of as helping us to display other virtues in an appropriate manner with respect to a mean (2a2ae,47,7). He writes:

> To be conformed to right reason is the proper purpose of any moral virtue. The intent of temperance is to prevent us straying from reason because of our lusts; of fortitude lest we forsake the judgment of right reason because of fear or rashness. Such an end is prescribed for us by our natural reason, which bids each to act according to reason. Yet how and through what we strike the virtuous mean, this is the business of prudence.[6]

Prudence, thinks Aquinas, is what guides us to decide to good effect (2a2ae,47,8), and it serves the common good as well as the good of individuals (2a2ae,47,10–12). Those with prudence have gifts of memory and understanding. They have shrewdness, an ability to reason well, foresight, circumspection, and caution (2a2ae,49).[7]

In order to understand what Aquinas takes prudence to be it helps to note what he takes to be vices that are contrary to prudence or fake examples of it. He turns to these in 2a2ae,53–55, where we find him defending a number of conclusions that I now note with some comment.

1. Rushing into action without reflection (being foolhardy and hasty) is evidently contrary to prudence. "Since disordered counsel is part of imprudence, it is clear that the vice of being precipitate falls under imprudence" (2a2ae,53,3).[8]

2. "Thoughtlessness" (*inconsideratio*) is contrary to prudence (2a2ae,53,4). "The defect of right judgment goes with the vice of thoughtlessness, inasmuch as a person fails to come to a sound judgment out of scorn or neglect to attend to the evidences on which to base it."[9]

3. "Inconstancy" (*inconstantia*) is opposed to prudence insofar as it amounts to giving up on what one has previously wisely decided upon, insofar as it involves a lack of steadfastness in good resolves (2a2ae,53,5). "Someone is called inconstant when their reason fails to carry out effectively what they have thought out and decided upon."[10]

4. Prudence can be badly affected by a desire for physical pleasure (especially sexual pleasure) since this can interfere with the ability to reason rightly about what to do (2a2ae,53,6).

5. "Negligence" or "carelessness" (*negligentia*) is against prudence insofar as it amounts to not paying attention to what ought to be noted when deciding to act (2a2ae,54,1).

6. "Prudence of the flesh" (*prudentia carnis*) is opposed to prudence since it amounts to taking material goods and pleasures as our final end (2a2ae,55,1). As I noted in chapter 12, Aquinas does not take the virtue of prudence to be what one might have in mind when speaking, say, of penny-pinching as prudent, and what he says about *prudentia carnis* is one indication of this. Someone solely concerned with how to ensure their material goals, he thinks, might be thought of as exhibiting prudence at some level, yet fully fledged prudence rises above this. Note, however, that Aquinas also holds that *prudentia carnis* does not always lead to mortal sin. He writes: "It sometimes happens that people are inordinately attached to some bodily pleasure without thereby turning away from God by sinning mortally: they do not make bodily pleasure the purpose of their life" (2a2ae,55,2).[11]

7. In 2a2ae,55,3–5, Aquinas turns to "cunning" or "craftiness" (*astutia*), which he takes to be directly opposed to *prudentia*. He thinks of it as being such since, as Herbert McCabe puts it, he takes cunning to be "a kind of bogus *prudentia*, the careful rational pursuit of a *bad* end."[12] In Aquinas's view, practical reasoning is governed by logic insofar as it derives conclusions from certain premises, and he takes this logic to be present even when we are reasoning about a bad end. I might think "John should be helped; if I do X, Y, and Z, I shall help John; so I should do X, Y, and Z." I might also think "John should be murdered; if I do A, B, and C, John will end up murdered; so I should do A, B, and C." The logic is the same in both of these arguments. The difference between them is that the first is an argument offered by one who is aiming at a

genuine good while the second is not. So Aquinas thinks that good practical reasoning involves more than mere logical acumen. It involves willing well. It involves *prudentia*, and Aquinas thinks that reasoning logically but with lack of *prudentia* is, therefore, a kind of unreasonable anti-prudence: something that mimics prudence logically speaking while directed to what a prudent person would avoid. As McCabe elsewhere observes, according to Aquinas, *prudentia* "is distinguished from cunning by its aim, which is acting well, pursuing ends which constitute or contribute to what is *in fact* the good life for a human being."[13] Unsurprisingly, therefore, Aquinas takes "guile" (*dolus*) and "cheating" (*fraus*) to be varieties of *astutia*. Guile, he says, amounts to *astutia* put to work so as to try to deceive people (2a2ae,55,4), and cheating or fraud basically amounts to the same thing (2a2ae,55,5).

8. As he winds up his account of what is contrary to prudence, Aquinas touches specifically on two things that he takes to be contrary to prudence considered as a full-blown virtue in Christians who have the theological virtues and the gifts of the Holy Spirit—these being worrying unduly about temporal matters and worrying unduly about the future (2a2ae,55, 6 and 7). Concern about temporal matters, such as how we are going to feed or clothe ourselves, is, he agrees, proper. Not, however, if it becomes an obsession that draws us away from charity and confidence in God's providence and amounts to forgetting about texts such as Matthew 6:31, which says, "Therefore do not worry, saying, 'What will we eat?' or 'What will we drink?' or 'What will we wear?' . . . Your heavenly Father knows that you need all these things. But strive first for the kingdom of God and his righteousness, and all these things will be given to you as well." Aquinas adds that, while planning for the future is good in principle, over-concern with the future or worrying about the future at the wrong time can be bad and in conflict with some teachings of Christ.

Aquinas's account of prudence is a fairly complicated one. You might, however, think that it is lacking in detail when it comes to instructions about how to be prudent. Should Aquinas not have given us a list of things to do whenever we want to be prudent? This question, though, would spring from a misunderstanding of how Aquinas thinks of prudence. Remember that he takes prudence to involve the right exercise of practical reasoning in real-life situations. Now real-life situations can be many and various, so in 2a2ae,47–56 Aquinas is inevitably talking in general terms about prudence as a virtue and not as a set of laws or imperatives. Aquinas takes prudence to be a matter of practical reasoning (albeit inspired by the Holy Spirit's gift of counsel) and it is hard to anticipate what, in various circumstances, might amount to right practical reasoning, even if it is true that one should never contemplate actions of a certain kind.

Having noted that fact, however, I should also note that Aquinas thinks that there is something common to all vices that are contrary to prudence (2a2ae,55,8). For he says that they all spring from "greed" (*avaritia*) and that "the wrong use of reason is most manifest in the vices opposed to justice, the chief of which is greed."[14] Let me now, therefore, turn to what Aquinas has to say about justice.

16.2 Justice (2a2ae,57–62)

Aquinas's account of justice in the *Summa Theologiae* extends to the end of 2a2ae,122 and includes discussion of much that would not appear today in philosophical treatments of justice. It contains, for example, sections on prayer, oath taking, superstition, and idolatry. But the core of Aquinas's account of justice comes in 2a2ae,57–62, which is immediately followed by an account of what is opposed to justice. Here I am concerned with that core.

Aquinas's discussion brings us back to a distinction to which I drew attention in chapter 5—that between commutative and distributive justice. Before returning to that distinction, however, I should note that Aquinas holds that justice has to do with our dealings with others so that a balance or fairness or equality is maintained, so that others end up with what befits them.[15] Justice is all about "what is right" (*jus*), and the just is the right (2a2ae,57,1). Something is just "because it has the rightness of justice.... Right is the objective interest of justice."[16] And what is right, Aquinas adds, can be thought of in two ways. There is a "natural right" (*jus naturale*), as when we pay exactly what we owe to someone, and there is a "conventional right" (*jus positivum*), as when people privately or as a group act in accordance with a contract of some kind (2a2ae,57,2). In addition (2a2ae,57,4), there is "paternal right" (*jus paternum*) and "right of lordship" (*jus dominativum*), that concern what is right and just when it comes to relationships between parents and children and between masters and servants.[17]

Aquinas therefore defines "justice" as the *habitus* that helps one to give everyone what is due to them or rightfully theirs (2a2ae,58,1).[18] He says, "Justice is the disposition whereby a person with a lasting and constant will renders to everyone their due."[19] Justice, therefore, is always toward another (2a2ae,58,2 and 5 and 9) and is a virtue since it amounts to acting in accordance with reason (2a2ae,58,3) by means of the will (2a2ae,58,4), and its mean (as in "the virtuous mean") is fixed in a way different from the way the mean is fixed by virtues that regulate our emotions (2a2ae,58,10). Here Aquinas is suggesting (1) what might amount to the right mean in courage or temperance can depend on the characters of different individuals and the circumstances in which they find themselves; (2) the mean when it comes to justice is not similarly dependent on person and context; (3) the mean in justice has to do with what is quite simply or objectively required of us when interacting with other people and giving them what is due to them (that, for example, if you have borrowed such and such a sum from me, then you are in debt to me for that sum). "The subject matter of justice," Aquinas argues in 2a2ae,58,11, "is what we outwardly do, according as the doing or the thing we employ is proportionate to the other person who lays claim on our justice. Now each person's own is that which is due to them in proportion to making things even. That is why the proper activity of justice is none other than to render to each their due."[20]

We can now return to the distinction between commutative justice and distributive justice referred to above and discussed by Aquinas in 2a2ae,61, which matches what he says in 1a,21,1. Commutative justice, he states, concerns "the ordering of private persons among themselves" and "engages with their mutual dealings one with another" (2a2ae,61,1).[21] Distributive justice, Aquinas adds, "apportions proportionately to each their share from the common stock."[22] So commutative justice is operating when one individual returns to someone what he or she strictly owes that person, as happens in buying and selling (2a2ae,61,2). Distributive justice is operating when a ruler or government (or even the head of a family) shares out goods available in a proper way, which may involve giving more to one person than to another.[23] "Distributive justice governs the apportioning of community goods, whereas commutative justice governs the exchanging that may take place between two persons" (2a2ae,61,3).[24] An example of commutative justice given in 2a2ae,62 is "restitution" (*restitutio*). "Taking away," says Aquinas, "is a wrong done against commutative justice. And so giving back is an act of the same justice which governs exchanges."[25]

> To make restitution appears to be nothing else than to re-establish people in possession of or dominion over a thing which is theirs. Consequently we mark the equality or balance of justice according to the recompense of thing for thing, which is the concern of commutative justice. So, restitution is an act of commutative justice, namely when one person holds that which belongs to another, whether with the owner's consent, as in a loan or a deposit, or against their will, as in robbery or theft.[26]

16.3 Injustice (2a2ae,59 and 63–79)

If there is justice, of course, there can be injustice, as Aquinas is keenly aware. So in 2a2ae,59 and 63–79, with much appeal to biblical texts and the authority of various theologians as well as to what we might think of as philosophical argument, Aquinas spends time noting what he takes injustice to be and discussing examples of it. He will return to justice again in 2a2ae,101, where he embarks on an account of what he takes to be virtues of justice. The main points he makes concerning injustice are as follows.

1. Injustice is opposed to justice in that it scorns or is against the common good. It can be singled out as a particular vice since it is opposed to justice, which is a particular virtue. Rejection of the common good, however, can run through a number of sins, and injustice can therefore be thought of as displayed by any vice that conflicts with the common good (2a2ae,59,1).
2. One may do what is unjust without being unjust oneself, since one may act unjustly because of ignorance and, therefore, unintentionally, or one may act unjustly in a fit of passion, not because one is ruled by a *habitus* of injustice (2a2ae,59,2). What qualifies one as someone having a *habitus* of injustice is doing "something unjust with malice aforethought and by choice."[27]
3. Injustice is opposed to charity, which brings us to share in God's life. So every act of injustice is effectively directed away from union with God and, in this sense, amounts to mortal sin. On the other hand, in practice not every act of injustice renders one effectively dead when it comes to union with God since some acts of injustice (unlike acts such as murder) amount to acts of injustice in small matters (2a2ae,59,4).
4. The vice and sin against distributive justice is "personal preference" (*personarum acceptio*). One may hand out a good—a sum of money, say, or a job—to one person rather than to another because the one deserves it in terms of distributive justice, and in doing so one may be favoring one person more than another. However, one would be doing so justly, since some people deserve more than others. It is different when it comes to favoring people just because they are one's friends or relatives or are rich, which is typical of personal preference (2a2ae,63,1).
5. Killing living things is sometimes opposed to justice and sometimes not. It is not opposed to justice when it amounts to killing nonhuman animals in order to eat (2a2ae,64,1).[28] Nor is it opposed to justice when it amounts to a justly constituted public authority legally executing criminals because they are a threat to the common good (2a2ae,64,1 and 2). Suicide, though,

is sinful since (a) it runs counter to what God has given us by nature, namely a desire for the good and therefore for existing, (b) it is against charity, which calls on us to love ourselves, (c) it damages the community of which we are part, and (d) it is for God to decide who shall live and who shall die (2a2ae,64,5).[29]

6. Unless ordered to do so by God (as Abraham was), it is never permissible to kill an innocent person.[30] "Every person, even the sinner, has a nature which God made, and which as such we are bound to love, whereas we violate it by homicide" (2a2ae,64,6).[31] One may, however, kill another in self-defense if the death of one's opponent is an unintended (even if foreseen) effect of one's attempts to preserve one's life (2a2ae,64,7). "A single act may have two effects, of which one alone is intended, while the other is incidental to that intention."[32] When it comes to self-defense, one may act while intending to protect oneself but not while directly willing the death of someone else. Aquinas's reasoning here is commonly taken to be the introduction into Western philosophy of what is called "the principle of double effect"—the idea that one may licitly do something that has an undesirable consequence if one is not directly intending that consequence, even if one foresees it. Literature on the principle of double effect runs to many volumes. In 2a2ae,64,7, the notion of double effect seems to be invoked by Aquinas only so as to argue that one is not necessarily unjust when only trying one's best to keep oneself alive when attacked by someone else. Note, however, that Aquinas goes on to say that one might try to defend oneself from a life-threatening attacker by using inappropriate means, means that go beyond what is needed in order to save one's life.[33]

7. Other injustices against people include mutilating them, beating them, and unlawfully imprisoning them (2a2ae,65). Mutilation can be just if performed for purposes of therapeutic surgery and with the consent of the person being mutilated, or if inflicted by a public authority in order to prevent someone from damaging others. Otherwise, it is unjust (2a2ae,65,1). Still, it is not unjust for parents to use corporal punishment if their intention is to train their children (2a2ae,65,2), and, though freedom is an intrinsically good thing, it is not unjust for public authorities to detain or imprison people to punish them for breaking laws or to prevent them from harming others (2a2ae,65,3).[34]

8. We can distinguish between "theft" (*furtum*) and "robbery" (*rapina*) since we can distinguish between stealing from someone surreptitiously and doing so by violence (2a2ae,66,3 and 4).[35] Both theft and robbery are sinful and contrary to justice and charity since they amount to taking what belongs to another against that person's will and against God's revealed will

(Exodus 20:15), and since they involve fraud and deceit (2a2ae,66,5). One might want to challenge this view by denying that anyone has a right to own property, but ownership of things is natural to people and accepted by Christian tradition even though private property should be shared in cases of necessity (2a2ae,66,2 and 3). Even though theft can sometimes be justifiable in cases of extreme necessity (2a2ae,66,7), robbery is always wrong when committed by a private individual acting like a brigand, though it can sometimes be justified when it is ordered by one in public authority (2a2ae,66,8).

9. Lawfully appointed judges have a right to judge only within their legal jurisdiction (2a2ae,67,1). Such judges must attend to evidence presented against those they are judging and not to their personal opinion about the guilt or innocence of the accused (2a2ae,67,2). Such judges must also sentence only when the accused has, indeed, been legally accused, and accused by someone other than the judge (2a2ae,67,3). Once a judge has pronounced sentence, appeal to the sentence should be decided by a higher court, not by the judge passing the sentence (2a2ae,67,4).

10. It is right and proper to denounce an evildoer, and evildoers who have been denounced and justly judged should be punished as a way of making them improve their ways or for some benefit of the community to which they belong. In this life "penalties are not sought for their own sake, because this is not the era of retribution; rather they are meant to be corrective by being conducive either to the reform of the sinner or to the good of society, which becomes more peaceful through the punishment of sinners" (2a2ae,68,1).[36] On the other hand, accusation is unjust if it is not properly documented by being drawn up in writing, if it is made rashly, and if it is made by one who cannot prove the charge being made (2a2ae,68,1–4).[37]

11. People accused of crimes are bound in justice to speak truly in their own defense, as are witnesses against them, though they are not obliged to comment on what is not strictly relevant to the evidence presented against them (2a2ae,69,1–2 and 70,4). And advocates or lawyers should never defend people they know to be guilty of the charge against them (2a2ae,71,3). "It is not right for somebody to be an accomplice in doing wrong, whether by advice or active help or consent of any sort, for an advisor and an abettor are in effect doers."[38]

12. Lawyers are not always obliged to aid people who cannot pay them, just as people with money are not obliged to help everyone who is poor, since nobody can possibly help out all those in need. Yet lawyers in certain circumstances are bound to help those who cannot help themselves and have no other help at hand (2a2ae,71,1), and even lawyers who accept payment

from their clients, as they are entitled to do since they are normally rendering a service that they are not bound to render, should charge fees that accord with the social status of their clients and what is customary where they work. To do otherwise would be to offend against justice (2a2ae,71,4).

13. "Defamation" (*contumelia*) is dishonoring good people verbally by wrongly and publically speaking in a way that seeks to undermine or damage them when it comes to the respect that others pay them (2a2ae,72,1). It seems to proceed from anger (2a2ae,72,4), and it amounts to a sin against justice (2a2ae,72,2). We should "observe discretion and pick our words carefully, for an insult could be so serious that, if uttered incautiously, it could take away the character of the person against whom it is uttered."[39]

14. "Detraction" (*detractio*) is the attempt to sully people's deserved reputation not by speaking openly against them, as defamers do, but by going behind their backs. Detraction pursued intentionally stands to defamation as theft stands to robbery, and one who detracts another should make restitution (2a2ae,73,1 and 2).

15. We can distinguish between detraction and "whispering" (*susurratio*), which amounts to vicious gossip designed to do harm to good people by trying to get others to take action against them and which is contrary to justice (2a2ae,74,1). "The whisperer... wants to split friends."[40]

16. "Ridicule" (*derisio*) is another sin against justice insofar as it amounts to mocking or making fun of people because they lack what they cannot help lacking, insofar as it amounts to dismissing their misfortunes "and treating them as a joke," which conflicts with charity (2a2ae,75,2).[41] Also in conflict with charity is "cursing" (*maledictio*) insofar as it amounts to vocally expressing the desire that somebody should be struck by evil just because it is evil, insofar as it amounts to verbally wishing people ill (2a2ae,76). Cursing may be in order if it is done by someone who is wishing that someone at fault should obtain what is due to them as a penalty, but it is sinful if it amounts to vocally wishing that people should be inflicted by evil as such, if it amounts to an offense against charity.

17. "Fraud" or "cheating" (*fraudulentia*) when it comes to buying and selling is unjust and stands condemned by Matthew 7:12, which says, "Do to others as you would have them do to you." Sellers should charge what their goods are genuinely worth; they should not pass off imitation goods for the real thing; and they should be selling what is genuinely theirs (2a2ae,77,1). Honesty should govern selling and buying. So sellers of goods who know them to be flawed are acting unlawfully, as are those who short-change those who buy from them or pass off goods as being of better quality than they are (2a2ae,77,2). Sellers are not obliged to draw attention to defects in what they

sell if the defects are obvious, but they are so obliged if the defects are not obvious and can lead an unwary buyer into loss or even danger (2a2ae,77,3). And sellers are obliged not to overcharge, even though it is right for them to sell something for more than they paid for it since their work as vendors meeting demands adds to the value of what they sell (2a2ae,77,4).

18. It is unjust to charge for lending someone money (2a2ae,78,1). That is to say, "usury" (*usura*) is sinful. It has been wrongly thought to be commended in some biblical texts and goes legally unpunished in many places. But it is intrinsically unjust since it amounts to charging for what does not exist or charging twice for the same thing. Some things we use by consuming them (food and drink are obvious examples), and the use of these things is not something over and above them to be charged for in addition to them. So it would be wrong to charge someone for a bottle of wine and then add a charge for drinking the wine. By the same token, it would be wrong to give someone money and charge for the use of it. Having money and using it amount to the same thing. The value of money lies in its use or usability. So lending money at interest is charging for more than one is handing over and effectively amounts to theft, which requires restitution. Civil or human law can justifiably refrain from punishing those who practice usury only because punishing them would lead to hardship for many people, but not because usury is just or unsinful. Charity might well lead us to loan people money, yet we cannot in charity charge people for lending them money. Nor can we charge them in kind, by demanding something valuable other than money (though cashable in terms of money) by way of interest, though there is no harm in accepting a gift given by someone to whom we have loaned money. And it would not be wrong for lenders of money to seek compensation from those they have loaned it to if their giving of a loan results in loss for them that they might have made with the money they loaned (2a2ae,78,2). On the other hand, one is not bound to restore to a borrower a gain that one might make on what one has unjustly acquired by usury. If the interest I have charged you on a loan is used by me in a just way so as to increase what I have extracted from you by way of interest, I am not obliged to refund to you the gain I have made. What I earn by using the interest I have charged you is distinct from what I have loaned you, and I might be entitled to this since it amounts to what I have earned over and above what I have loaned to you (2a2ae,78,3).[42]

With these points made, Aquinas goes on to discuss "religion" (*religio*), which he thinks of as a matter of justice because he thinks of it as owed to God. In the next chapter we shall see how his discussion proceeds.

Religion and Other Matters to Do with Justice (2a2ae,80–122)

AQUINAS TURNS TO the topics discussed in 2a2ae,80–122 while considering them relevant to the virtue of justice. You may find this surprising since people who write about justice normally do not deal with all that Aquinas is talking about in 2a2ae,80–100, especially the virtue of what he calls religion. Aquinas, though, takes what he means by "religion" (*religio*) to be a moral virtue had by people who pay God what they owe God. "The good to which religion is directed," he says, "is giving due honor to God; and honor is due on account of excellence. Since God infinitely surpasses and completely transcends all other things, God's excellence is unparalleled. Therefore God should receive a special kind of honor" (2a2ae,81,4).[1] For Aquinas, religion has to do with what justice requires of us with respect to God, so religion and what offends against it can be dealt with in a treatise on justice, as can other virtues and vices such as piety, gratitude, ingratitude, obedience, and disobedience.

17.1 Religion

What does Aquinas mean by the word *religion?* In Henry Fielding's novel *Tom Jones*, Mr. Thwakum declares, "When I mention religion, I mean the Christian religion; and not only the Christian religion, but the Protestant religion; and not only the Protestant religion, but the Church of England."[2] And, in a sense, Aquinas is rather Thwakumite in his approach to "religion." He does not want to home in on the Church of England (which did not, of course, exist in his time), but neither is he concerned with religion as being exemplified by the beliefs and practices of what we would now take to be non-Christian world religions (Buddhism, Hinduism, and so on). In his discussion of religion, he focuses on what he takes to be owed to God in the light of Christian revelation and in the light of certain Roman Catholic customs. So 2a2ae is written by a Catholic for Catholics, though Aquinas obviously views it as intended for anyone who wants to give God what is due to God.

17.2 Religion as Such (2a2ae,81)

Aquinas notes two etymological accounts of the word *religio*, one from Isidore of Seville and another from St. Augustine, but he does not commit himself to the accuracy of either of them. Instead, he says that religion "implies a relationship to God," one that is expressed in behavior (2a2ae,81,1). He takes someone with the virtue of religion to be religious, and he takes being religious to involve certain practices such as reverencing God, praying to God, and adoring God.[3] And he holds that these practices are virtuous since they lead us to what is good for us and pay "the debt of honor" owing to God (2a2ae,81,2).[4]

Note, however, that Aquinas does not take religion to be a theological virtue. He says, "Religion is not one of the theological virtues, whose object is the last end, but one of the moral virtues, whose objects are the means to the last end" (2a2ae,81,5).[5] He adds that religion excels all moral virtues "because its actions are proximately and immediately directed to God's honor" (2a2ae,81,6).[6] This does not mean that religion should be construed as improving God somehow or as modifying God in some way, since God is eternal and immutable (2a2ae,81,7). So Aquinas notes, "Because God possesses perfect glory to which creatures can add nothing, we do not give honor and reverence to God for God's own sake, but rather for our sake, because when we do so our mind is subjected to God and in this our perfection consists."[7]

Is the virtue of religion expressed by external action? Indeed it is, replies Aquinas. "The human mind needs to be led to God by means of sensible things. . . . Hence, in divine worship the use of corporeal things is necessary so that by using signs, our minds may be aroused to the spiritual acts which join us to God" (2a2ae,81,7).[8] Internal acts of religion such as prayer and adoration, he says, are "principal and essential," but exterior acts, though "secondary and subordinate to the internal acts" are also important given our dependence on the material world when it comes to thinking and understanding in general.[9]

17.3 Devotion, Prayer, and Adoration (2a2ae,82–84)

As pertaining to religion, Aquinas singles out "devotion" (*devotio*), "prayer" (*oratio*), and "adoration" (*adoratio*). Notice, however, that he takes each of these to be distinct, so he does not, for example, confuse prayer with adoration, as many theological writers have done. His discussion of prayer is longer than his discussions of devotion and adoration put together—an indication of how important Aquinas takes prayer to be—and I shall therefore dwell on it longer than I dwell on what he has to say about devotion and adoration. But let us be clear about how he construes devotion and adoration so as to be able to appreciate how he takes prayer to be something different from them.

Devotion, says Aquinas, is a willingness to do promptly what pertains to the service of God (1a2ae,82,1). So one can speak of people as being devout insofar as they love God and spontaneously worship and attend to God. Devotion, says Aquinas, is not itself a virtue. Rather, it is a willingness to practice the virtue of religion (2a2ae,82,2), and it is aided by contemplation and meditation, by reflecting on God's goodness, especially as displayed in the passion of Christ (2a2ae,82,3).

Aquinas takes adoration to amount to reverence for God (2a2ae,84,1), and he thinks that it can be internal and external (2a2ae,84,2). It is internal insofar as one is intellectually geared to be devout. It is external insofar as one expresses one's devotion by engaging in bodily activities designed to express reverence to God or worship of God. One does not, Aquinas holds, have to be doing anything particular or to be present in a particular place in order to adore God, but he thinks that adoration can be properly expressed in particular ways of behaving intended to venerate God and in particular places set aside for such veneration (2a2ae,84,3). He also maintains that one should adore and worship only God. Reverence paid to the saints, he agrees, is a good thing, but it should not be confused with the highest type of religious reverence (adoration), which is owing to God alone.[10]

When it comes to Aquinas's treatment of prayer, I think that it can be best read as an attempt to demystify it. Many volumes have been devoted to prayer, and many of them seem to suggest that prayer is out of the ordinary, difficult, and something with respect to which one needs to develop certain skills or techniques. In 2a2ae,83, however, Aquinas thinks of "prayer" (*oratio*) in fairly simple terms: as *asking God for something that one wants*. In 2a2ae,83, Aquinas takes *oratio* to be petition, as did early Latin-speaking Christians, and as does the New Testament when reporting that in response to the request "Teach us to pray" Jesus gave them the Lord's Prayer (the "Our Father"), which is just a series of petitions.[11]

In his *Commentary on the Sentences*, Aquinas approaches the topic of *oratio* in a more complicated way. He offers an indecisive discussion of parts of prayer and kinds of prayer, and he tries to do justice to a range of ideas about prayer advanced by his theological predecessors, some of whom took petition to be an inferior form of prayer, and some of whom took prayer to amount to any devotional act or every good deed.[12] By the time he is writing 2a2ae,83, though, Aquinas has evidently decided that prayer should be taken as asking for things from God, and as just that.[13] Prayer as a request or petition, he says, is "the primary meaning of prayer" (2a2ae,83,1).[14] So he holds that we should ask for something definite when we pray and cites the Lord's Prayer as an example to us (2a2ae,83,5), and, he argues, it can be right to pray for temporal things, like health and income (2a2ae,83,6). In general, he says, we can pray for what we can rightly desire.

Aquinas regards prayer as an exercise in practical reasoning (2a2ae,83,1). His view is that if we need something, the wish for which does not involve us in being unjust or uncharitable, then we should try to get what we need after having reflected on how to do so, and with this thought in mind he argues that it is reasonable to ask for things from God since God can provide them. If I can ask my plumber to fix my sink, Aquinas effectively claims, then I can ask God to help me with other matters (though Aquinas says nothing to suggest that I should not ask God to fix my sink). Prayer, he explains, is "an act of reason by which a superior is petitioned.... Therefore, one who has reason and a superior whom one is able to beseech is able to pray" (2a2ae,83,10).[15] And the Lord's Prayer, Aquinas argues, is the perfect model of prayer since it teaches us to ask for union with God and for what might lead us to this, and since it teaches us to ask for what we need to be well, happy, and holy in this life, and to ask for forgiveness of our sins and the grace to resist temptation to sin (2a2ae,83,9).

Aquinas's account of prayer presupposes that God is omnipotent and can, therefore, give us what we ask for (presuming that we are not asking for what cannot be thought to exist). In his view, prayer is a natural way to put into practice belief in a God who governs the world providentially. But he is aware of some standard objections to engaging in petitionary prayer and brings three of them up for discussion in 2a2ae,83,2 where the question at issue is whether it is appropriate or "fitting" (*conveniens*) to pray.

According to the first objection, prayer is unnecessary since God knows what we need even without us asking.

According to the second, prayer is an attempt to influence God or to change God's mind, and cannot succeed since God is immutable.

According to the third, prayer is redundant since God is generous and will, therefore, give us what we need even without us asking for it.

In arguing, as he does, that prayer is indeed *conveniens* Aquinas echoes what he says about God's will and providence in 1a,19–22, which should be read as background to 2a2ae,83. He observes:

Divine providence not only disposes what effects will take place, but also the manner in which they will take place, and which actions will cause them. Human acts are true causes, and therefore people must perform certain actions, not in order to change divine providence, but in order to obtain certain effects in the manner planned by God. What is true of natural causes is true also of prayer, for we do not pray in order to change the decree of divine providence, rather we pray in order to obtain by our prayers those things which God has planned to bring about by means of prayers.[16]

Aquinas does not think of prayer as informing God of needs that we have, needs unknown to God without our prayer. Nor does he think of prayer as attempting to change or manipulate God. And he agrees that God gives us many things without our asking for them. But he wants to emphasize that we should recognize our dependence on God for goods that we obtain, and he thinks of prayer as amounting to such recognition. In other words, he thinks (a) that there is a difference between us obtaining a good without prayer and our obtaining a good following prayer, and (b) that only in the second case can the good we obtain be construed as a good given to us because we have asked for it as people who acknowledge their total dependence on God. For our own good, says Aquinas, God "wishes to give us certain things upon our request; in this way we gain confidence in God and acknowledge God as the source of all our blessings."[17] And, of course, Aquinas takes our turning to God in prayer as itself a case of God's action in us.

17.4 Other Exterior Acts of Religion (2a2ae,85–91)

In 2a2ae,85–91, Aquinas talks about exterior acts of religion other than adoration. These are sacrifice (2a2ae,85), making offerings for the support of religion (2a2ae,86 and 87), freely vowing to do something pleasing to God that is not obligatory (2a2ae,88), calling on God to witness that we speak truly or will act as we have promised (2a2ae,89), calling on people to witness in this way (2a2ae,90), and praising God vocally and musically (2a2ae,91). I am not going to linger over the details of Aquinas's discussion of these exterior acts of religion since their substance is readily intelligible. Aquinas approves of all of them and sees all of them as possibly (though not automatically) leading people to display the virtue of religion, though he does not think that all of them are required in order to have the virtue of religion. He does not, for example, think that people cannot display the virtue of religion without taking vows as members of certain religious orders do. In general, though, he finds the external acts of religion just noted to be helpful when it comes to leading a good Christian life.

17.5 From Superstition to Simony (2a2ae,92–100)

In 2a2ae,92, Aquinas proceeds to what he believes to be at odds with religion, starting with "superstition" (*superstitio*). Generally speaking, he takes this to be displayed by (a) worshiping something less than God or (b) worshiping God in an unfitting way (2a2ae,92,1). With a view to (a) he cites the vice of "idolatry" (*idolatria*). With a view to (b) he cites fortune telling. Under the heading "Superstition" he also includes engaging in practices that presuppose the efficacy of magic. One may, he thinks, be a true believer while also having an erroneous view of how one's religious actions work. One may, for example, rightly think it good to pray for those who have died or to make use of physical objects in one's devotions, but one might be wrong about what these practices can achieve. One might, for example, think that saying a *fixed* number of prayers for the dead *guarantees* their beatitude, or that using religious medals *ensures* one's salvation or that of others. But both of these thoughts, Aquinas says, amount to belief in magic and are examples of superstition (2a2ae,93).

Aquinas is very dismissive of idolatry, which he takes to be evil since it disregards the difference between God and creatures (2a2ae,94). Given much that I have reported above concerning Aquinas's theology, I assume that you will find 2a2ae,94 to need no commentary. But perhaps it is worth my noting that, by "idolatry," Aquinas does not simply mean paying worship to a physical object such as a statue. He clearly thinks that it is idolatrous to worship *anything* that is not divine.

"Fortune telling" (*divinatio*) is sinful, says Aquinas, because it takes creatures to be able to know or reveal the future, this being something that only God can do (2a2ae,95,1). He associates *divinatio* with trying to consult devils, with taking astrology too seriously, with relying on dreams as predicting the future, and with other such practices (2a2ae,95,4). These, he says, are foolish since only God can infallibly know what is going to happen and since (apart from divine revelation) human beings are only able to arrive at a reasonable (though falsifiable) belief about what is going to happen based on an understanding of things that operate as they do by nature and that tend to bring about certain effects in the natural world while doing so. Thinking otherwise amounts to wrongly believing in magic and is wrong since belief in magic is contrary to belief in God as the primary cause of all that happens in the created order (insofar as belief in magic amounts to denying that God orders things by virtue of providence).[18]

Aquinas winds up his discussion of sins against the virtue of religion by saying that it is wrong to try to put God to the test by, for example, challenging God to cure someone without taking means one has at hand to cure the person oneself, or by presuming on God as a being guaranteed to work miracles whenever one wants them (2a2ae,97). And, Aquinas argues, it is wrong to call upon God in support of one's lying since this is to invoke God's support when it comes to something that is quite against the divine nature, namely falsity

(2a2ae,98). Again, in 2a2ae,99 and 100, Aquinas disparages "sacrilege" (*sacrilegium*) and "simony" (*simonia*), while spending more time on simony than sacrilege. He takes sacrilege to amount to violating things set aside by the Church for purposes of divine worship. Sacrilege, he says, is "the irreverent treatment of a sacred thing."[19] He takes simony to be the attempt to sell people what pertains to their salvation—a sinful and stupid attempt because it is God alone who brings people to beatitude by divine grace.[20] "You cannot buy your way into heaven, and those who try to persuade you otherwise are sinful." This is Aquinas's basic take on simony. It is, says Aquinas, right to support the ministers of the Church, but not on the understanding that this support amounts to buying and selling (2a2ae,100,3).

17.6 Piety and Other Matters (2a2ae,101–122)

In his discussion of justice so far, Aquinas has been speaking of it in general, noting what can offend against it while dwelling on good or bad actions related to it. In 2a2ae,101–122, he continues to talk about virtues and actions that he takes in one way or another to be relevant to a full-scale treatment of justice. In this connection, Aquinas lists ten virtues and eleven vices or sins. The virtues are "piety" (*pietas*), "respect" (*observantia*), "respectful service" (*dulia*), "obedience" (*obedientia*), "gratitude" (*gratia*), "vengeance" (*vindicatio*), "truthfulness" (*veritas*), "friendliness" (*amicitia*), "liberality" (*liberalitas*), and "equity" (*epieikeia*). The vices or sins are "disobedience" (*inobedientia*), "ingratitude" (*ingratitudo*), "lying" (*mendacium*), "deception" and "hypocrisy" (*simulatio* and *hypocrisis*), "boasting" (*jactantia*), "false modesty" (*ironia*), "flattery" (*adulatio*), "quarreling" (*litigium*), "avarice" (*avaritia*), and "prodigality" (*prodigalitas*).

Here are the main points that Aquinas makes concerning these virtues and vices.

1. Piety amounts to due deference, honor, or veneration to those who are excellent or have conferred benefits on one. So piety is especially owed in justice to God and to one's parents, though it is also owed in principle (and all things being equal) to relatives, to ecclesiastical and political superiors, to one's country and its allies, and to one's friends. When it comes to one's parents, piety should extend to physical support and care (2a2ae,101,2), and piety in general should be viewed as a prudentially governed recompense for what has been given to one by others (2a2ae,101,3).[21]

2. Respect is honor, by word or action, due to those who can be thought of as rightfully in authority over us even though they might not have conferred benefits on us as God and our parents and relatives have (2a2ae,102,1–3).

3. One can honor God both spiritually or mentally by, for example, respectfully meditating on God. One can also honor God externally by engaging in certain bodily behavior. When it comes to honoring people, however, bodily behavior is required since, unlike honor to God, who searches our hearts, honor paid to people is not manifest unless displayed in behavior (2a2ae,103,1). Hence the virtue of respectful service, which is owed to people who might, for various reasons, be rightly deemed to be those to whom we owe respect of some kind, including people who, though not especially virtuous, might still be our superiors in some way because of their role or status (2a2ae,103,2).²² Such honor, which can be named *dulia*, should not, however, be confused with the honor due only to God, which can be named *latria* (2a2ae,103,3).

4. Obedience is acting as instructed by a superior, someone *rightly* in authority over one, such as a parent or political leader. Ultimately, it is acting in accord with God's will since God has arranged that people should be instructed to behave by others (2a2ae,104,1). Obedient people, acting in charity, are acting justly since they are respecting people to whom they owe respect (2a2ae,104,3), and justice especially requires obedience to God (2a2ae,104,4). Yet obedience needs to be practiced prudentially. So, for example, it would be right to disobey a superior who asks one to do what conflicts with God's law (2a2ae,104,5–6). Hence, "when any regime holds its power not by right but by usurpation, or commands what is wrong, subjects have no duty to obey."²³ And insofar as obedience is a virtue, then disobedience is a vice (2a2ae,105).

5. Gratitude consists in justly giving thanks to those who have helped us in some way without having been obliged to do so (2a2ae,106,1). "Benefactors as such stand as cause to the one whom they help. As a consequence, the nature of the cause requires that recipients respond to their benefactor in a way that reflects that relationship" (2a2ae,106,3).²⁴ This is so even when it comes to someone helping one for less than noble reasons, though one might reasonably be less grateful to such a person than to someone wholeheartedly trying to do one good (2a2ae,106,3, ad.2). Gratitude can consist in promptly accepting favors graciously or in repaying the favor given some time after it has been given (2a2ae,106,4), and repayment of favors should be appropriate to the favor bestowed, to the person bestowing it, and to its value to the person receiving it (2a2ae,106,5). Since people to whom we are rightly grateful freely bestow favors not demanded of them, we should generally aim to repay them by trying to give them more than they have given us (2a2ae,106,6). "The recompense of gratitude should as far as possible make a point of giving back something better."²⁵ Since gratitude is a virtue,

ingratitude is a vice, albeit one that admits of degrees depending on the form it takes (2a2ae,107,1–3). However, we should not refuse favors to people who have been ungrateful to us, for in this way we imitate God (2a2ae,107,4).

6. By "vengeance" we can mean "maliciously seeking to pay back evil on another person," and, considered as such, vengeance is sinful. By "vengeance," however, we can also mean "justly punishing wrongdoers so as to help them reform or so as to protect others from them." Considered in this sense, vengeance, which can take various forms, is to be thought of as just if practiced prudently and with attention to the offenders against whom it is inflicted (2a2ae,108,1 and 3). Vengeance as a virtue aims to remove harm and prevent it recurring. So it springs from a desire for justice and should be practiced with charity (2a2ae,108,2). "Vengeance is lawful and virtuous to the extent that its purpose is to check evil" (2a2ae,108,4).[26]

7. Truthfulness is the virtue of matching what one says to what one really believes (2a2ae,109,1). It is trying to make one's thoughts and one's talk agree (2a2ae,109,2), and it falls under the virtue of justice since it aims at a balance of a kind: the matching of what is said and what is known, or, at least, believed (2a2ae,109,3). Truthful people are not necessarily people who declare everything they believe to be the case, but they are people who do not say what they believe to be false (2a2ae,109,4). People who say what they believe to be false, and lying is always wrong even if it is understandable and hard to avoid in some cases.

8. It would be wrong to confuse an intention to deceive with lying. One may aim to deceive with good reasons and with good intentions (to prevent vicious people finding and murdering innocent ones, for instance). However, lying, strictly speaking, and considered as the vice opposed to truthfulness, is positively declaring something to be so that one knows not to be so. So it amounts to an abuse of the gift of speech, which is given to us by God so that we might speak truly. In circumstances in which we take ourselves to be bound to lie we always have other options. We can, for example, seek to evade questions somehow without positively lying. Lying sometimes takes place as people joke and others realize that they are doing so. Lying such as this, however, is not lying that offends against virtue since nobody is taken in by it and since the people who lie in such contexts are as well aware of this as is their audience.[27]

9. Lying is all about trying to present the true as false and the false as true. In this sense, it resembles deception and hypocrisy since these amount to acting so as to make people believe that one is not as one is or that one is as one is not. "Every form of deception is a kind of lie.... Lying is the direct opposite of truth. So therefore are deception or hypocrisy" (2a2ae,111,3).[28]

10. Boasting can be a form of lying, since it can amount to making false claims about oneself on the basis of pride so as to make oneself seem to others to be better than one is (2a2ae,112). So boasting can offend against justice.

11. Irony is pretending that one is better or worse than one actually is.[29] It amounts to pretending with a view to being dishonest. In particular, it means pretending to be worse than one is, and is therefore a kind of lying or boasting in reverse (2a2ae,113,1).

12. Friendliness amounts to affability, to trying to maintain good relations with others, to aiming to keep human relations on an even keel, to maintaining good order among people. It is, therefore, allied to justice (2a2ae,114). Quarreling is the opposite of friendliness insofar as it aims to stir up discord or mess up good relationships (2a2ae,116).

13. Flattery can be thought of as trying to please people by praising them for virtues they do not have or by praising them for what is actually bad in them, and it is usually motivated by wanting something from the one being flattered. Understood in this way, flattery is another kind of lying and can be more or less vicious depending on the intention behind it (2a2ae,115).

14. Liberality, which has mostly to do with money, is found in people who are willing to use their wealth for the benefit of good ends and not just for ends of their own (2a2ae,117,1–2). It should be distinguished from a reckless use of money, which might lead one to be unable to meet one's debts (2a2ae,117,3). Liberality amounts to giving even when one does not owe, which means that it is allied to justice though it is not strictly equivalent to it (2a2ae,117,5).

15. Avarice is "the will to acquire or to hoard material goods excessively" and in a way that goes beyond what is needful when it comes to the acquisition and possession of such goods (2a2ae,118,1). Avarice can be displayed with respect to money, but also with respect to other things (2a2ae,118,2). It is opposed to liberality (2a2ae,118,3) and can lead people to some vicious deeds even though it might not be greatly sinful in itself (2a2ae,118,4–8).

16. Whereas avarice is excessive attachment to material goods, prodigality is excessive disregard or irresponsibility when it comes to them. Prodigal people hand out money more quickly than they should, or do not behave prudently when it comes to acquiring money and keeping it as they should (2a2ae,119,1).[30] Prodigality, though, is less of a fault than avariciousness since it can have an element of liberality to it and is not a matter of grasping for oneself, and at least someone might benefit from it, while nobody benefits from avarice, not even the avaricious. In addition, prodigality can be easily knocked out of one as one ages and finds oneself need-

ing to use one's wealth cautiously. Avarice is not so easily discarded (2a2ae,119,3).

17. *Epieikeia* or "equity" is a virtue that is needed since no law can cover every case that might arise.[31] Laws have to be framed in general terms and with a view to what regularly comes about. For this reason they sometimes need to be prudently interpreted in order to be applied to the many different situations that can arise. Such prudent interpretation of law, which can involve setting the letter of a law aside, is what *epieikeia* amounts to (2a2ae,120,1).[32] Considered as such, it is directed to what is truly just and is, hopefully, in accord with how the person or people drawing up the law would have wished to have it interpreted and applied to respect to certain particular and unusual cases (2a2ae,120,1).

Aquinas concludes his account of justice by drawing attention again to the Ten Commandments found in the book of Exodus. He takes these to be a summary or outline of what justice requires since he views them as regulating religion, piety, and our dealings with other people (2a2ae,122). I use the words *summary* and *outline* here since Aquinas clearly views the Ten Commandments as needing interpretation and reflection of the kind he takes himself to have offered in 2a2ae,57–121, which is his most mature treatment of justice as a moral virtue understood with reference to divine revelation. He recognizes, however, that there are two other cardinal virtues to consider, these being courage and temperance. He turns to them in 2a2ae,123–170, which I shall consider in the next chapter.

18

Courage and Temperance (2a2ae,123–170)

2A2AE BEGINS BY turning to the theological virtues, which Aquinas takes to be virtues in the full sense since only they can lead us to beatitude. As we have seen, however, 2a2ae also considers the classical cardinal virtues discussed by Aristotle, though, unlike Aristotle, Aquinas treats them with an eye on what he takes to be divine revelation. Hence the material on prudence and justice in 2a2ae,47–122. With this material offered, Aquinas next turns to "courage" (*fortitudo*) and "temperance" (*temperantia*). As with his discussions of prudence and justice, the account here goes beyond what we might consider to be mere moral philosophy, and it certainly goes beyond what Aristotle has to say, even though it draws quite substantially on Aristotelian ideas. It is very much directed to Christians holding to a creedal position that Aquinas takes to be of critical importance for understanding human perfection. It also introduces us to certain virtues and vices that feature hardly at all in most contemporary essays in philosophical ethics and which, though mentioned by Aristotle, become somewhat transformed in Aquinas's account of them.

18.1 Courage Itself (2a2ae,123)

In 2a2ae,128, Aquinas embarks on an account of what he calls the "parts" of courage, by which he means distinguishable virtues and vices related to courage or the lack of courage. Before doing this, however, he discusses courage in general terms asking whether or not it is a virtue, what it is concerned with, how it displays itself, and how it compares with other cardinal virtues. What he has to say on these matters presupposes what he says about fear in 1a2ae,41–44[1] That, of course, is because Aquinas takes courage to be, broadly speaking, the virtue by which we cope with fear (not, in his view, an intrinsically bad thing) in a way that builds us up rather than drags us down.

Courage, says Aquinas, can mean "steadfastness of mind" of a kind that is a condition for the exercise of any virtue.[2] More precisely though, it is "firmness of mind in enduring or repulsing whatever makes steadfastness outstandingly difficult; that is, particularly dangers" (2a2ae,123,2).[3] But courage is not, Aquinas adds, simply a matter of rushing headlong into dangers or difficulties. Rather, it amounts to an appropriate or prudential reaction to danger and is not to be confused with recklessness (2a2ae,123,3). It also leads one to face death bravely (2a2ae,123,4). So courage is a virtue in a soldier fighting for a just cause, though it is also found in those who act bravely not just when faced with potentially lethal human combatants. Hence, caring for sick people in spite of the risk of deadly infection can amount to a display of courage (2a2ae,123,5). The chief act of courage, therefore, is "not so much attacking as enduring, or standing one's ground amidst dangers" (2a2ae,123,6).[4] And the steadfastness involved in courage helps us to display other virtues in spite of obstacles (2a2ae,123,11). In short (2a2ae,123,12), courage is a virtue since virtuous behavior aims at what reason shows to be good and since "it is fear of mortal danger which is most powerful to cause a person to draw back from reason's good."[5] Courage, says Aquinas, is not the greatest virtue since it is excelled by prudence and justice, which lead us to pursue goods in a fitting way. Courage, though, helps us to preserve goods that we have since it disposes us to persevere in pursuit of good even in the face of mortal danger.[6]

18.2 Other Matters Relevant to Courage (2a2ae,124–140)

One example of courage to which Aquinas draws special attention is willingness to be killed in defense of one's Christian faith or in defense of something belonging to it. This is the courage of the martyr (2a2ae,124,1). To be sure, Aquinas thinks, martyrs display faith and charity, yet it is their courage, amounting to endurance, that brings their faith and charity to completeness in the face of death (2a2ae,124,2 and 3).[7] Such courage, like all courage, is something that Aquinas takes to be opposed to disordered "fear" (*timor*). He thinks that this can be found in every vice.[8] He also notes, however, that death is what we fear most and that chiefly opposed to courage is a disordered fear of death (2a2ae,125,1 and 2). Such fear, he says, can amount to venial rather than mortal sin. But he also thinks that it can be gravely sinful—as, for example, when it leads people to deny the truths of faith in order to save their skins (2a2ae,125,3). At the same time, though, Aquinas concedes that fear can lead us to act in a way that is partly involuntary and, therefore, to some extent excusable (2a2ae,125,4).

Surprisingly, you might think, Aquinas goes on to note (2a2ae,126 and 127) that two vices opposed to courage are "fearlessness" (*intimiditas*) and "daring" (*audacia*). Given contemporary English usage, to call someone fearless or

daring would normally be taken to commend them. By "fearlessness," however, Aquinas means what seems to amount to insensibility to fear for some
pathological reason, and by "daring" he means acting in a foolhardy way and
without reference to reason. He therefore takes both *intimiditas* and *audacia*
to be contrary to courage. Fearless people are, says Aquinas, incapable of
courage because they are incapable of fear, and foolhardy people act without
respect to reason as danger confronts them, while courageous people face up
to danger in a reasonable way.

In 2a2ae,129 and 134, Aquinas discusses two other virtues that you might
also find odd. These are "magnanimity" (*magnanimitas*) and "magnificence"
or "munificence" (*magnificentia*). To magnanimity, Aquinas opposes the vices
of "presumption" (*praesumptio*), "ambition" (*ambitio*), "vainglory" (*appetitus
gloriae*), and "pusillanimity" (*pusillanimitas*). To magnificence, Aquinas opposes "stinginess" (*parvificentia*).

Aquinas takes magnanimity to be the virtue displayed by people (especially
public figures) who are willing to persevere in the face of difficulty for the sake
of achieving what is of great public worth, something that can win someone
justified public praise. "Magnanimity," he says, "by definition implies a certain
aspiration of spirit to great things" (2a2ae,129,1).[9] "The magnanimous person
strives for objects which are worthy of high recognition" (2a2ae,129,2).[10] Magnanimous people are usually those who depend on their wealth, power, and
influence so as to bring about great goods (2a2ae,129,8). What makes them
magnanimous, though, is their aiming to use what they have in order to bring
about something that is unusually good, something that can be perceived to
be good at a public or large-scale level (an effect that Aquinas does not think
impossible to be brought about even by people lacking money, power, and influence). So good and effective politicians might, for Aquinas, fall into the
category of magnanimous people, as might those who devote themselves to
leading national and international charitable organizations, or people engaged
in other great but difficult works with an impact on many people.[11] And Aquinas argues (1) presumption is opposed to magnanimity since it amounts to
unreasonably taking on a great task that one is not actually able to perform
(2a2ae,130); (2) ambition is opposed to magnanimity since it amounts to a disordered desire for praise itself (disordered since it can amount to seeking praise
without deserving it, to failing to acknowledge one's dependence on God, or to
not wanting good things worthy of genuine praise) (2a2ae,131); (3) vainglory
is opposed to magnanimity since it amounts to a disordered recognition of
what is praiseworthy, since it is a desire to be praised for something one is
not, or a desire to be praised by people of unsound judgment, or a desire for
glory that does not pay heed to the true glory that comes with honoring God

properly (2a2ae,132); (4) pusillanimity is opposed to magnanimity since it amounts to the opposite of the largeness of soul that characterizes people who are magnanimous, since it is a refusal to embark on some difficult and large-scale project that one is able to complete (2a2ae,133).

As for magnificence or munificence, Aquinas (2a2ae,134,1–3) takes this to be a reasonable willingness on the part of people who are financially well-off to spend money, to "splash out," on some grand, difficult, and worthy (if also non-obligatory) scheme of good to the public such as building something spectacular, supporting the arts, or even throwing a grand party.[12] Aquinas takes magnificence to be allied to courage not because it amounts to facing danger well but because it faces up to difficulties and displays an attitude toward possessions that courage displays with respect to survival (2a2ae,134,4). Unsurprisingly, therefore, Aquinas reckons that the vice opposed to magnificence is stinginess or meanness or pettiness (2a2ae,135). The magnificent person is boldly willing, without being foolish or wasteful, not to count the cost when it comes to a great project. By contrast, one with *parvificentia* settles for small goals when greater can be achieved, or concentrates on pinching pennies instead of spending money in a good cause (2a2ae,135,1).[13]

Winding up his discussion of courage, Aquinas turns to "patience" (*patientia*) and "perseverance" (*perseverantia*). He argues that patience is a gift of God displayed by those bearing up against difficulties and not being crushed or dejected by them so as to lose interest in striving for what is good, especially union with God (2a2ae,136,1 and 3).[14] Aquinas ranks patience below the theological virtues and the cardinal ones (2a2ae,136,2), yet he also says that it springs from charity, from friendship with God that allows one to hold firm in the face of difficulty while wanting God and all that this implies (2a2ae,136,3). Aquinas, therefore, takes patience to be a virtue aligned to courage since it is a good reaction to evils that one might encounter (2a2ae,136,4). Though he distinguishes between patience and perseverance, Aquinas effectively takes patience to amount to perseverance, since he thinks of perseverance as patience hanging on over a long time, as steadily keeping God in mind regardless of what is going on (2a2ae,137; cf. 2a2ae,136,5). In opposition to perseverance, Aquinas cites the vices of "weakness" (*mollities*) and "obstinacy" (*pertinacia*). He thinks of weakness as derived from a habit of living pleasurably and as a matter of just caving in when confronted by trials and tribulations and just ceasing to seek what is good because of them (2a2ae,138,1). He thinks of obstinacy as derived from vainglory and as a matter of foolishly supposing that one can conquer the world and that nothing can stop one, as unreasonably persisting to think that one is invincible or not likely to suffer from evils of various kinds (2a2ae,138,2).

As he does with other virtues, Aquinas singles out courage as a gift of the Holy Spirit that we cannot acquire by our own efforts. We can work ourselves up to being courageous, but, says Aquinas, the gift of courage takes naturally acquired courage further and to the point where it persists to the end of life with confidence in God (2a2ae,139,1). Aquinas takes the *gift* of courage to amount to us exercising courage before God easily and readily.

18.3 Temperance (2a2ae,141–170)

18.3.1 Temperance: The Big Picture

The core of Aquinas's teaching on temperance comes right at the start of 2a2ae,141. He says, "We have seen that to set human beings towards the good is of the essence of virtue. And good for human beings…means living according to reason. Human virtue, then, is what sets us towards living reasonably. Clearly temperance does this; its very name expresses moderation or temperateness caused by reason."[15]

The key word here is *moderation*, for Aquinas thinks that temperateness always involves moderation of some kind, that it always represents a mean between extremes, a mean between too much and too little. Too much and too little of what? Aquinas's answer is pleasure with respect to our sensory desires, especially the desire to eat, drink, and have sex. For him, temperance comes about as we satisfy our sensual desires in a reasonable way. Aquinas is most emphatically not against sensual pleasure, which he takes to be a gift from God. He is against giving in to a desire for sensual pleasure in ways that he thinks harm us or other people. As we have seen, he takes courage to amount to fear and aggression as governed by reason. Similarly, he takes temperance to amount to sensual desire governed by reason. So we find him saying, "As the virtue of courage, which makes us steadfast, first nerves us in our fear of bodily evils and then controls as well our boldness in tackling them with confidence of gaining the mastery, so also the virtue of temperance is engaged first with emotions of desire and pleasure about goods of sense, and then as well with emotions of grief arising from their absence" (2a2ae,141,3).[16] Aquinas, therefore, does not equate temperance with avoiding sensual pleasure entirely. He thinks, for example, that too little eating and drinking can be as bad as too much. Nor does he commend people for disliking or fearing sensual pleasure. Here, he thinks, vice can be at work, a vice that in 2a2ae,142 he calls "lack of feeling" (*insensibilitas*). Aquinas views sensual pleasure as necessary for the well-being of individual human beings and for the human species in general. So he regards "lack of feeling" as positively conflicting with temperance.

In general, then, Aquinas takes temperance to be found in people who enjoy sensual pleasure in a reasonable way. What, though, are his standards for reasonableness in the enjoyment of sensual pleasure? They are those that he highlights in his accounts of what he takes to be right practical reasoning conducted with an eye on human happiness under divine providence. More specifically, Aquinas's use of "reason" with regard to temperance homes in on two ideas. The first is that sensual pleasures are given to us by God so that we might live well. The second is that sensual pleasures are given to us by God so that we might preserve the human species.

I suspect that most contemporary readers of 2a2ae,141–170 shall (whether or not they believe in God) have little with which to quarrel when it comes to the first of these ideas since we live in a world in which many people seem very preoccupied with health, which is something that we need in order to be well (in some sense, anyway). Hence, we are constantly advised to watch our diet, to exercise, or to refrain from smoking, and Aquinas would clearly have sympathized with such advice. On the other hand, when attacking things like gluttony and drunkenness, vices that he takes to be against temperance, Aquinas's focus is really on how these things can interfere with us acting as people hoping for union with God by using God's gifts of food and drink in a way that might lead us to fail to possess the cardinal virtues. Aquinas's discussion of temperance, therefore, is not a medieval equivalent to contemporary manuals of health.

People have both agreed and disagreed with the way in which Aquinas employs his idea that sensual pleasures are given to us by God so as to preserve the human species. In modern times, it is Roman Catholics who have tended to agree. People taking a different view have contested the claim, which Aquinas takes for granted and does not really argue for, that sexual pleasure is given to us by God only to be indulged in for the sake of producing children. Aquinas obviously knows that not all sexual acts result in conception, but he insists that sexual appetite should be governed with an eye on procreation. Hence, for example, in 2a2ae,154,11 he holds that homosexual sexual activity "is in conflict with the natural pattern of sexuality for the benefit of the species" and is, therefore, "unnatural" (*contra naturam*), and in 2a2ae,153,2 he condemns the use of contraceptives. He argues that, as food is there so that we might preserve ourselves as living things, sexual intercourse is there so that the human species should survive (2a2ae,153,2). He says, "As the use of food is without sin, if taken in due manner and order for the body's welfare, so also is the use of sex in keeping with its purpose that people should be fruitful."[17] Aquinas thought (reasonably enough given when he lived) that the human race would die out if all heterosexuals engaged in nothing but contraceptive intercourse or if everyone engaged only in homosexual sexual relations. With hindsight, many would suppose that he was wrong about this since, as we now know, there is technology such as in vitro fertilization that enables people to reproduce without engaging in sexual intercourse, and even the possibility of producing a human zygote using a female ovum alone no longer appears fantastical.[18] Even putting aside those points, however, Aquinas does not seem to consider the possibility that sex might be rightly thought to have other possible uses than the production of children, or that homosexual sex might be just as "natural" to homosexuals as is heterosexual sex to heterosexuals notwithstanding the obvious fact that human sexual organs seem to be geared to biological reproduction. Nor does he offer a precise account of what "natural" means when it comes to thinking about sex. If he is thinking that "natural" in this context means "what we can observe if we look carefully at people's behavior," then he needs to explain how it is that many people actually do have contraceptive intercourse and that many people have sex with people of the same sex. In fact, Aquinas seems to be working with a notion of "nature" that is not derived from detailed observation of human behavior (all of which is natural in the sense that it is part of the world, in the sense that it can be documented while reporting how people, like other animals, actually behave). When it comes to sex, Aquinas is clearly taking "natural" to imply "open to procreation," and he thinks that sex that is not so open is unreasonable since it conflicts with human flourishing. But is that really so?

This is not the place for me to engage in a detailed discussion of that question. You might, however, wonder whether Aquinas's account of temperance comes with assumptions grounded more in how he read certain biblical texts, especially ones dealing with marriage, and on a restricted observation of human behavior, than on a developed philosophy of human nature as that might be presented today, one that might reasonably find a place for sexual activity that does not occur in a context in which procreation is always the major goal desired. In short, Aquinas's treatment of temperance, we might say, comes with some fairly notable theological premises (whether true or false).[19]

18.3.2 Temperance: Some Details

1. In 2a2ae,141, Aquinas makes it clear that he takes temperance to amount to moderation with respect to desire for what gives rise to physical pleasure. Thinking of temperance as having to do with moderation, he concedes that temperance must be at work in all virtues (2a2ae,141,2 and 6), but he thinks of it as especially directed to moderation when it comes to "libidinousness and concupiscence,"[20] by which he means sensuous desires.

He takes sensuous desire to be an appropriate thing, yet only when acted on in accord with what he takes to be reason (2a2ae,141,3), and he takes sensuous desire only to be activated by that with which we have bodily contact, especially contact by means of touch (2a2ae,141,4 and 5), which is why he draws attention to food, drink, and sex when writing about sensuous desire.[21]

2. The connection that Aquinas makes between temperance and what is needed to preserve the human species arises in 2a2ae,141,5. He writes: "Temperance works with the main pleasures relating to the preservation of human life, either for the individual or for the species."[22]

3. In 2a2ae,142,3, Aquinas says that intemperance, the vice directly opposed to temperance, is worse than cowardice since it is better to flee mortal danger than to run headlong into sensual vice, and since acting intemperately is more under our control than acting in a cowardly way and can be more easily treated than cowardice. He writes: "The deeper the force which moves us to sin the lighter the fault. And so, looking at the urgency of the objective and matter, intemperance is graver than cowardice, as being more unwarranted by the situation."[23] He goes on to observe that fear can numb one's mind while intemperate actions are things that we can control more than we can control what we do on the basis of fear. Indeed, he suggests, to act intemperately is to do *exactly* what one wants to do.

4. To be temperate, says Aquinas (2a2ae,144), involves having "shame" (*verecundia*). Here Aquinas seems to be thinking of shame as a matter of *feeling* shameful because one is aware that one might be unfavorably judged by others for acting dishonorably or disgracefully when it comes to correct views concerning what is honorable or disgraceful. He does so, I assume, because what he has in mind by a lack of temperance would have been regarded as dishonorable or disgraceful by most of his contemporaries. The list of vices that Aquinas provides in 2a2ae as being against temperance would have been thought of as a thoroughly uncontroversial one in his day. Notice, however, that Aquinas does not take all temperate people to feel shameful for what they are doing. He thinks that intemperate people can wrongly lack a sense of shame, but he also thinks that virtuous people and elderly and temperate people can lack shame since feeling shameful for what they are doing does not occur to them (2a2ae,144,4). One may, he says, lack a sense of shame since one is not tempted to do what might be taken to warrant one feeling shameful. "In this way the old and the virtuous lack the sense of shame, though they are so disposed that if they did anything dishonorable they would be ashamed of it" (2a2ae,144,4).[24]

5. In 2a2ae,146–150, Aquinas concentrates on food and drink. First, he argues that abstaining from food and drink can be virtuous when moderately practiced for religious reasons and while trying to cultivate a mean regarding what we eat and drink (2a2ae,146 and 147).²⁵ In 2a2ae,148,1 and 2, he condemns "gluttony" (*gula*) as an immoderate desire for food and drink that does not pay attention to what we actually need to eat, a desire that is immoderate just because its focus is on temporary sensuous delight and not on that for which food and drink exist (our survival as human beings). In 2a2ae,148,2 and 3, Aquinas holds that gluttony is not usually a grave or mortal sin, though he thinks that it can be a vice that might lead to great sin since it springs from greed. Notice, however, that in 2a2ae,148,1, ad.2 Aquinas distinguishes between (1) eating too much because one is obsessed with the desire to eat just for the pleasure of eating, and (2) eating too much while being wrong about how much one needs to eat in order to survive. He says, "When people eat too much, not from need, but from thinking it necessary, they act from inexperience, not gluttony."²⁶

6. Given his take on gluttony, you will not be surprised to find Aquinas praising "sobriety" (*sobrietatis*) and criticizing "drunkenness" (*ebrietas*). He takes sobriety primarily to be moderation in the use of alcohol, and he applauds it because he thinks that excessive use of alcohol can interfere with one's ability to reason (2a2ae,149,1). On biblical grounds, Aquinas denies that drinking alcohol is intrinsically wrong, though he also thinks it can be wrong in certain contexts "because of the condition of the drinker, when it makes the drinker incapable, or breaks a promise to abstain, or exceeds due measure, or because it proves a stumbling block to others" (2a2ae,149,3).²⁷ And he is harsh when it comes to drunkenness because he views deliberately getting drunk as deliberately depriving oneself of "the control of reason, the power of adopting right and rejecting wrong" (2a2ae,150,2).²⁸ In 2a2ae,150,4, he asks whether being drunk can excuse one for doing wrong and argues that it can if the person doing wrong did not actually choose to become intoxicated. On the other hand, Aquinas thinks that sinning as a result of deliberately choosing to get drunk is blameworthy. If one is drunk, he agrees, one might not realize what one is doing and, in this sense, not be guilty for what one does. If, however, one chose to become drunk, one can be guilty of "acting under the influence" since one decided to be "under the influence" in the first place. Aquinas thinks that something can be sinful because sinful in its cause, sinful as proceeding from what is sinful, and he applies this principle to what one might do under the influence of alcohol. In 2a2ae,154,5, we find a comparable argument applied to male nocturnal emission (ejaculating while

asleep). This, in itself, Aquinas says, is not sinful because we cannot sin when we are asleep and because nocturnal emission can have purely physiological causes beyond any control of the sleeper. What, though, if men or boys go to sleep while having done or thought of something likely to cause them to ejaculate while asleep? Then, concludes Aquinas, some fault may be involved.[29]

7. Questions to do with temperateness and sex come up for discussion in 2a2ae,151–156, where Aquinas turns to "chastity" (*castitas*), "virginity" (*virginitas*), "lust" (*luxuria*), "continence" (*continentia*) and "incontinence" (*incontinentia*).

8. Aquinas defines chastity as acting sexually with a view to what is reasonable, not as abstaining from sex altogether (2a2ae,151,1–3). When it comes to virginity, Aquinas thinks of it as perpetually refraining from sex, and not, say, something that is only possessed by a female human being whose hymen is unbroken (2a2ae,152,1), and, though he applauds engagement in sexual activity that aims at procreation, he is also prepared to say that there is nothing wrong with some people permanently refraining from sexual intercourse, and that there might be great good in someone doing so for religious reasons (2a2ae,152,2–4). You might think that if, as Aquinas believes, sex aims at the propagation of people, then virginity amounts to trying to prevent the continuance of the human species, but, says Aquinas, the future of the human race is not going to be jeopardized by a limited number of people choosing never to have sexual intercourse (2a2ae,152,2).[30]

9. While accepting that one might intelligibly speak of people "lusting" after food, drink, fame, or riches, Aquinas takes lust, strictly speaking, to involve inordinateness when it comes to sexual pleasure (2a2ae,153,1). He denies that sexual intercourse is always a matter of lust since it can, within marriage, be engaged in for the purpose of continuing the human species (2a2ae,153,3) in deference to the fact that "the exercise of sex is of capital importance for the common good, namely the preservation of the human race" (2a2ae,153,4).[31] Aquinas, however, is convinced that lust is a vice and that it can be thought of as a great vice since it can lead to many sins of many kinds (2a2ae,153,4 and 5).

10. What sins come under the heading "Sins of Lust"? In 2a2ae,154,1, Aquinas lists six: "fornication" (*fornicatio*), "adultery" (*adulterium*), "incest" (*incestus*), "seduction" (*stuprum*), "rape" (*raptus*), and "unnatural vice" (*vitium contra naturam*). All of these sins, he says, consist "in people applying themselves to sexual pleasure not according to right reason."[32]

11. Aquinas regards fornication, considered as heterosexual intercourse between people who are not married to each other, as gravely sinful.

Fornication, he bluntly says, "is a mortal sin" (2a2ae,154,2).[33] He thinks this because he believes that fornicators act contrary to the welfare of children (the chief purpose of sex) since the good of children requires that their parents be people of different sexes married to each other. "It is evident that the bringing up of children requires the care of a mother who nurses them, and much more of a father, under whose guidance and guardianship their earthly needs are supplied and their characters developed."[34]

12. When it comes to seduction, Aquinas is thinking of it as what happens when a man encourages and succeeds in getting a young woman who is not his wife to have sex with him (2a2ae,154,6). He takes it to be wrong not only because it offends against what he thinks the purpose of sex to be but also because it offends against justice with respect to the person seduced and with respect to her parents.[35]

13. Aquinas seems to work on the assumption that rape can only occur when a man forces a woman to have sex with him against her will. He does not mention the possibility of a woman raping a man, or a man raping a man, or a woman raping a woman. Given his understanding of rape, however, Aquinas takes it to be wrong not only because it goes against what he takes sex to be for but also because he thinks of rape as involving violence contrary to justice (2a2ae,154,7).

14. Aquinas thinks of adultery as sexual activity engaged in by a single person and a married person, or by two people who are married, though not to each other (2a2ae,154,8). He takes it to be wrong since (a) he regards it as contrary to what he takes chastity to be, (b) it is disadvantageous to what is due for the rearing of children, and (c) it amounts to an act of injustice against the spouse or spouses of the people committing adultery.

15. Aquinas defines "incest" as "intercourse between relatives by blood and affinity" (2a2ae,154,9). So he thinks of it as sex between close relatives, though he does not explain how close is too close.[36] He takes incest to offend against chastity, to dishonor relatives, to interfere with family life, to inhibit people becoming related to people of other families, and to promote lust.

16. Aquinas understands "unnatural vice" to be actions that "are in conflict with the natural pattern of sexuality for the benefit of the species" (2a2ae,154,11).[37] As examples of such action, Aquinas cites masturbation, bestiality, and homosexual sex.[38] And he takes unnatural vice to be the worst form that lust can take, worse than incest, adultery, seduction, and rape (2a2ae,154,12). He says, "Unnatural vice flouts nature by transgressing its basic principles of sexuality" and "is in this matter the gravest of

sins."[39] His reason for so concluding (which should, perhaps, be read alongside his condemnations of incest, adultery, seduction, and rape) lies in the fact that he takes what he calls unnatural vice to be a direct affront to God as having made us as what Aquinas thinks God has made us to be, that is, creatures with sexual appetites to be directed to procreation. He therefore takes unnatural vice primarily or "formally" to be sin against God, and he rates it on a scale of gravity according to which sinning against God is always worse than sinning against another human being. You may agree with him on this point, though you will not, I think, find many contemporary moral theologians arguing, for example, that masturbation is more evil than rape.

17. Since Aquinas takes temperance to be essentially a matter of moderation, in 2a2ae,155–162 he goes on to talk about virtues and vices related to it that do not have to do so with sexual matters. In 2a2ae,157, for example, he talks about "clemency" (*clementia*) and "meekness" (*mansuetudo*) while arguing (a) that it can sometimes be virtuous for people, guided by reason, to curb their anger when dealing with people who have in some way offended against them (clemency), or (b) to restrain anger in themselves (meekness). Again, in 2a2ae,162, Aquinas turns to the topic of "pride" (*superbia*) while arguing that it can amount to (a) falsely making oneself out to be more than one is and (b) wrongly presuming that one is as one is not before God (unless one is proud to be a creature of God). "Right reason," says Aquinas, "requires that people should reach out to what is proportionate to them. Consequently pride clearly implies something adverse to right reason" (2a2ae,162,1).[40] In 2a2ae,163, he develops the notion that pride can amount to an offense against God while turning again to the fall of Adam. In this question, Aquinas says that Adam's sin was pride. It could not have been sin arising from unreasonable desire connected with physical things, he argues, since Adam was free of bodily desire ungoverned by reason. Adam, then, must have sinned by desiring something inordinate (the inordinateness here lying in the object desired, not the manner of desiring). It was desire for something beyond human reach, and was therefore a sin of pride. "The first sin lay in this, that man craved for a non-material good above his measure, which is a function of pride" (2a2ae,163,1).[41] Adam's sin was a matter of wanting what belongs only to God. In particular, it was a matter of wanting to know good and evil as God knows them.[42] And its punishment which is inherited by Adam's descendants was subjection to irrational desire and subjection to death and pain, from all of which Adam was free in Paradise (2a2ae,164,1). According to Aquinas, Adam in Paradise was, by God's grace, such that his

body was perfectly subject to his will as governed by reason. So Adam in Paradise was immune to death and pain and was able to live an endless and unencumbered human life. Life and death, as Adam came to know them after he sinned, was punishment for his sin, a punishment inherited by his offspring (2a2ae,164). Aquinas clearly has a historical cause-and-effect picture in mind here, but notice that he seems also to be trying to suggest that death and physical suffering can be thought of as things that inflict human beings trying to pull away from God and from what consti-tutes human perfection (cf. 2a2ae,164, ad.1). He appears to think that suf-fering and death are to be accounted for in terms of human desire to be equal to God, not in terms of God aiming at suffering and death when creating people for union with God.[43]

18. Winding up his treatment of temperance, Aquinas notes three more virtues and one vice, while concluding that instructions concerning temperance are effectively present in the Ten Commandments. The three virtues are "studiousness" or "devotion to learning" (*studiositas*), "modesty in decorum" (*modestia in exterioribus corporis motibus*), and "modesty when it comes to clothing" (*modestia in exteriori apparatu*). The vice is "curiosity" (*curiositas*).

19. By "modesty in decorum" Aquinas means acting physically in a moderate way in order to be what might be described as "well mannered." He says that "there is a moral virtue at work in composing our physical movements" (2a2ae,168,1).[44] When speaking of physical movements here, Aquinas obviously does not have in mind such physical movements as raping, robbing, or killing someone. He is thinking of how we physically behave with people as we engage with them socially and in public, which is why *modestia in exterioribus corporis motibus* can be translated as "good manners."[45] Aquinas is thinking of decorum in terms of acting in a way appropriate to where we are on the public stage and with an eye to ques-tions like "Should I be polite to my employer?" and "Should I act respect-fully to my female colleagues as well as my male ones?." His answer to these questions is "Yes, as long as there is no sin involved in doing so." So he thinks of modesty in decorum as roughly equivalent to *amicitia* ("friend-liness" or "affability") as described in 2a2ae,114,1, and he seems to think that it might come into play when people play games together, which is why, I suspect, he brings it up while discussing temperance. Aquinas is all for people playing games together, but he is not in favor of game playing that amounts to a failure in virtue (2a2ae,168,2).

20. By "modesty in clothing" Aquinas means a moderate use of cloth-ing. Here, I think, your common sense will allow you to understand what

Aquinas is saying in 2a2ae,169. Note, though, that his critique of a lack of modesty in dress extends (nicely, I think) to a critique of people who cannot be bothered to wash themselves in order to prevent other people from being offended by how they smell.

21. Aquinas believes that people naturally desire to know, and he takes this desire to be a good thing, but he also thinks that it can become immoderate. He singles out *studiositas* as the virtue that leads us to pursue knowledge well, the virtue that prompts us to make an effort to learn in an appropriate way, the virtue that amounts to "controlled devotion to learning" (2a2ae,166).[46] Aquinas regards this virtue as a moral one and as belonging to temperance since it amounts to striking a mean in the pursuit of knowledge: a mean between not seeking knowledge at all or seeking it in a wrong way. As opposed to *studiositas*, therefore, he cites the vice of *curiositas* ("inquisitiveness" or "undue curiosity" or "nosiness"), under which he includes desiring to know about what is bad for us, desiring to know about what is not important when we should be concentrating on other matters, desiring to obtain knowledge from sources we should not become engaged with, seeking to know without reference to God, and seeking to know more than we are able to take in (2a2ae,167).

22. With respect to temperance and the Ten Commandments, Aquinas maintains (2a2ae,170) that the commands to love God and neighbor have a bearing on temperance, as do the command to honor one's parents and the prohibition of murder and adultery.

With 2a2ae,170 written, Aquinas has completed his long account of the cardinal virtues aimed at believing Christians. Before concluding the *Secunda Secundae* as a whole, though, he has further things to add concerning human behavior or activity. Virtues, vices, and matters that pertain to them, he says, are topics to be considered as having a bearing on everybody since we all need to be virtuous and to avoid vice. There are, however, activities and states or walks of life that only pertain to some people, and these are also worth discussing. Here Aquinas has in mind (1) activities that result from special graces or charisms given by God for the building up of the Church, (2) the active and the contemplative life considered generally, and (3) different ways of having a canonical position in the Church, and chiefly, the state of being a bishop or a member of a religious order. Aquinas turns to these matters in 2a2ae,171–189, which I shall consider next.

19

Freely Given Graces, Kinds Of Life, and States Of Life (2a2ae,171–189)

WHILE COMPOSING 2A2AE,171–189, Aquinas has in mind what St. Paul says in 1 Corinthians 12:4–7: "There are varieties of gifts, but the same Spirit; and there are varieties of services, but the same Lord; and there are varieties of activities, but it is the same God who activates all of them. To each is given the manifestation of the Spirit for the common good." Aquinas reads this text and texts like Ephesians 4:11 and Luke 10:38–42 in what we might call an ecclesiological way, as a comment on how the Christian Church is structured under God's grace.[1]

This is not to say that 2a2ae,171–189 is a treatise on ecclesiology—theology concerned to explain what the Church is or ought to be. Aquinas never wrote a systematic treatise on this topic. He has things to say that amount to a developed ecclesiology, but he did not write anything explicitly titled *de ecclesia* ("On the Church").[2] Still, the drift of 2a2ae,171–189 would surely have been included in such a work had Aquinas written it, for it focuses on certain ways in which different members of the Church serve to build it up or support it, and it begins by talking about freely given graces.

19.1 Freely Given Graces (2a2ae,171–178)

We encountered the notion of freely given (or gratuitous) grace in chapter 14, where I mentioned that Aquinas has the notion of *gratia gratis data*, grace given to someone for the benefit of others (cf. 1a2ae,111,1,4, and 5).[3] Aquinas thinks that God sometimes works to help members of the Church by giving special gifts or graces to certain people. In 2a2ae,171–178, and drawing on 1 Corinthians 12:8–10, Aquinas discusses some of what he takes to be the more spectacular ones among them: prophecy, ecstasy, tongues, speech, and miracles.[4]

19.1.1 Prophecy (2a2ae,171–174)

In speaking of prophecy, Aquinas presupposes that his readers know the Old and New Testament passages in which the notion of prophecy surfaces. Although contemporary biblical scholars have much to say about how biblical references to prophecy are best understood, for Aquinas prophecy is primarily a matter of conveying truth revealed to a prophet by God, and he takes a prophet to be someone miraculously able to declare what God knows. He observes:

> Prophecy is firstly and principally a knowledge; prophets in fact know realities which are remote from the knowledge of human beings.... Prophecy secondarily consists in utterance or speech, in so far as the prophets know what they have been divinely taught, and they proclaim this knowledge for the edification of others.... Those truths which surpass all human knowledge and which are revealed from God cannot find confirmation in human reasoning which they transcend, but only in the working of divine power (2a2ae,171,1).[5]

Notice that the Latin word here translated "knowledge" is *cognitio*—a term that Aquinas tends to use in a wide sense and as signifying knowledge broadly construed, though he also allows for there sometimes being defectiveness or falsity in *cognitio*.[6] Aquinas has another word that can be translated by "knowledge." This is *scientia*, which, as we have seen, Aquinas takes to be complete and perfect knowledge with no measure of error. So Aquinas's use of *cognitio* when talking about prophecy, indicates that he is not thinking of prophecy as knowledge in the best sense, knowledge that we have when, say, we recognize that a proposition is true and cannot be otherwise. Rather, he is thinking of it as knowledge analogous to the knowledge that he takes people to have when they have the virtue of faith (cf. 2a2ae,1).

Aquinas regards prophecy chiefly as applying to future events, but he also thinks that it can amount to a knowledge of what is eternal or even of what is past. Thus, he takes Isaiah to have prophesied when declaring what God revealed to him about the divine nature. Aquinas also regards prophecy as ranging over truth in general (2a2ae,171,3). He does not, however, suppose that prophets necessarily appreciate the extent to which their prophetic knowledge goes beyond what they know naturally (2a2ae,171,5). He does not even think that prophets have to be holy people possessing the theological virtues (2a2ae,172,3 and 4). He is, though, clear that there is never any falsity in prophecy (2a2ae,171,6) since it derives from God (2a2ae,172,1).

19.1.2 Ecstasy (2a2ae,175)

"Ecstasy" (*raptus*) is, for Aquinas, a term with several meanings. In 2a2ae,175, however, he takes it to refer to what occurs when "one, by the Spirit of God, is uplifted to a supernatural level, with abstraction from the senses" (2a2ae,175,1).[7]

He therefore thinks of ecstasy as occurring when one is, so to speak, raised out of one's normal sphere of operation so as directly to receive revelation from God. The case of ecstasy that specifically engages Aquinas in 2a2ae,175 is the one he takes to be referred to in 2 Corinthians 12, in which St. Paul says that he was once "caught up into Paradise." Aquinas asks whether in this state Paul saw the essence of God. Drawing on St. Augustine, he argues that Paul indeed saw God's essence, albeit briefly and not while enjoying the beatific vision as do the saints in heaven (2a2ae,175,3). One might wonder why Aquinas takes Paul's ecstasy to be a case of *gratis gratia data* since Paul says that when he was "caught up" it was to hear "things that are not to be told, that no mortal is permitted to repeat" (2 Corinthians 12:4). I presume that Aquinas views Paul's ecstasy as an encouragement to others who believe that God can work wonders in people.

19.1.3 Tongues (2a2ae,176)

In 2a2ae,176, Aquinas is not writing with respect to 1 Corinthians 14, in which St. Paul refers to speaking in tongues while somewhat, though not entirely, discouraging the practice. Paul seems to think of speaking in tongues as a matter of making verbal sounds that nobody understands, and he unfavorably contrasts it with prophecy, which he takes to be talking to people in a way that does them good. He says that "those who speak in a tongue do not speak to other people but to God" while "those who prophesy speak to other people."[8] In 2a2ae,176, however, Aquinas has in mind Acts 2 in which it is said that after the day of Pentecost people preached to by the apostles of Jesus "heard them speaking" in the language they understood, though the people in question spoke different languages.[9] Interpreting Acts 2, Aquinas says that we should understand its sense to be that the apostles were miraculously gifted with the ability to speak languages that they did not naturally speak, not that they spoke the language they commonly used and that others miraculously heard them as speaking the language that they understood (2a2ae,176,1). Like St. Paul, however, Aquinas (though for reasons of his own) regards prophecy as a greater gift than the ability to speak in tongues (2a2ae,176,2). It is, he thinks, greater to have knowledge given by God than to be able to express this in different languages, and he takes prophecy as likely to have more of an effect on people than the mere ability to speak in different languages.

19.1.4 Speech (2a2ae,177)

For Aquinas, "speech" (*sermo*) is the grace of speaking effectively for the enlightenment of Christians, speaking in a way that moves people to become better Christians, even if the speaker does not become a better Christian because of the speaking. Aquinas distinguishes *sermo* from the ability to move an audience. So he is not confusing it with rhetorical ability, and he most definitely distinguishes it from speaking so as to entertain people in order to make them one's fans (2a2ae,177,1). Aquinas thinks of *sermo* as a very good thing—unsurprisingly, given he belonged to a religious order devoted to preaching—yet he confines it to men only (2a2ae,177,2). More precisely, he says that women should not "teach and persuade publicly" in churches. Here Aquinas is drawing on 1 Corinthians 14:34 in which Paul says, "In all the churches of the saints, women should be silent in the churches. For they are not permitted to speak, but should be subordinate." Given his historical context, one should not expect Aquinas to have wanted to speak against this biblical precept, and it is one that he defends by saying that it follows from the fact that women should be thought of as naturally subject to men (cf. Genesis 3:16), that it makes sense because beautiful women speaking in church might entice men to lust, and that "generally speaking women are not perfected in wisdom so as to be fit to be entrusted with public teaching."[10] One can only wonder whether, were he alive today, Aquinas would be defending any of these arguments as establishing the conclusion that he draws in 2a2ae,177,2.

19.1.5 Miracles (2a2ae,178)

The grace of working miracles enters into Aquinas's thinking by way of 1 Corinthians 12:9 in which St. Paul lists "the working of miracles" as a "spiritual gift." Aquinas thinks that a miracle might encourage the faithful, which is why he lists working miracles as instances of *gratia gratis data*. He thinks that miracles can help people to recognize that God is at work in the world. Note, though, that he does not think that human beings can, strictly speaking, perform miracles. In accordance with what he says in 1a,110,4, Aquinas is clear that miracles come about by virtue of God alone, that "their cause is God's power—which cannot be communicated to any creature" (2a2ae,178,1, ad.1).[11] But he also thinks that God can produce a miracle that occurs as some human being is doing something in the name of God, that "the mind of one working a miracle is moved to do something which results in a miracle—which God does by God's own power" (2a2ae,178,1, ad.1).[12] It seems to be Aquinas's view that the grace of miracles is given to those whose lives and actions can be associated with miracles occurring at their behest.

19.2 Active and Contemplative Life (2a2ae,179–184)

Having discussed gratuitous graces, Aquinas turns to what he calls the active and the contemplative life. What, though, is he talking about when doing so?

The distinction between "active" and "contemplative" today tends to flag a difference between certain kinds of religious orders. Those who now make the distinction usually want to recognize that some religious orders are "contemplative" and some are "active," meaning that some contain members entirely devoted to prayer and meditation (as are, e.g., Carthusian monks) while others engage primarily in pastoral work (as do, e.g., congregations of religious women devoted to education or nursing). This active/contemplative distinction is not, however, what Aquinas has in mind in 2a2ae,179–182. He is working with the idea that contemplation and action are different occupations in which anyone might engage.

Authors earlier than Aquinas use the word *contemplation* in a variety of senses, as Aquinas seems to have been aware. Indeed, by Aquinas's time "contemplation" and "contemplative" seem to have become somewhat vague terms. Some authors took "contemplation" to be equivalent to "study," while others took it to mean being pious in an affective or emotional way. St. Gregory the Great speaks of the active life as amounting to works of charity and of the contemplative life as resting from activity to cling solely to the desire for God (implying that the contemplative life is led only by some individuals). Other medieval writers, however, speak of contemplation as something that should inform the lives of everyone, including members of all religious orders, and some speak of it as amounting to particular activities such as reading and prayer.[13]

This somewhat confused notion of contemplation is what Aquinas inherited, and in 2a2ae,179–182 he does his best to do justice to it, though arguably in a way that does not result in a clear and coherent treatise of the kind that he offers on prayer in 2a2ae,83.[14] In his treatment of contemplation, Aquinas bases himself on Luke 10:38–42, in which Mary, who sits listening to Jesus, is described as having chosen "the better part" in comparison with Martha, who is distracted by household chores. In interpreting this text, Aquinas seems to follow traditional ideas to the effect that contemplation is better than activity. As you will realize, however, Aquinas's theology in general prizes charity above everything else.[15]

With all of that said, here are the main points that Aquinas makes in 2a2ae,179–182.

1. Contemplation involves focusing on truth, concerning God, while activity involves behaving so as to bring about certain desirable ends. So contemplation is an intellectual business concerned with understanding rather than one preoccupied with other matters such as obtaining some goal by employing practical reasoning. We can therefore speak of there

being a distinction between "contemplative" and "active" life because some people primarily devote themselves to thinking about truth while others primarily engage in other matters (2a2ae,179,1 and 2).

2. The contemplative life is intellectual since it is devoted to considering truth. It involves attraction and appetite to truth, but contemplation is not a virtue when it comes to willing. Such a virtue can dispose us to contemplate, but contemplation itself is not a matter of willing but of arriving at truth and enjoying it (2a2ae,180,1 and 2).

3. Contemplation can be thought of as an (admittedly feeble) attempt to arrive in this life at what the blessed enjoy in the beatific vision (2a2ae,180,4 and 5).

4. The active life is concerned with doing things, with getting various works accomplished (2a2ae,181,1). At its best, it is governed by the virtue of prudence (2a2ae,181,2). Teaching belongs to the active life because it aims to help people. Yet teachers can be thought of as contemplative insofar as they consider truth and love it (2a2ae,181,3).

5. Our active life ends when we die. After death, everything for us is a matter of contemplation (2a2ae,181,4).

6. The contemplative life is better than the active life because it concentrates on God, though this thesis needs to be qualified. So, for example, we should not wish for everyone to be devoted to a life of contemplation alone because human well-being also depends on practical activity. Luke 10:42 tells us that Mary "has chosen the better part" in comparison with Martha, yet we should not therefore infer that Martha chose to do something bad or unnecessary, and, as needs arise, action should be preferred to contemplation (2a2ae,182,1). One might also rightly refrain from contemplation because of a need to be charitable (2a2ae,182,2). The active life can hinder contemplation, but it might also help us as we try to contemplate since living and acting well can lead us to contemplate better (2a2ae,182,3), and we have no chance of getting to heaven if we do not act well (2a2ae,182,4, ad.1).

19.3 States of Life (2a2ae,183)

The *Secunda Pars* ends on what some readers might find to be a rather anticlimactic note. Having dealt with such difficult topics as human happiness, emotion, sin, law, grace, moral virtues, and prophecy, it concludes with a discussion of some matters concerning bishops and people who have entered religious orders. Instead of rising to some kind of eulogy about the beatific vision, it seems to descend to matters of ecclesiastical organization in the form it took around 1270. One might think that any sense of anticlimax regarding the end of the *Secunda Pars* should be dismissed because Christian perfection amounts to being a bishop or a member of a religious order. But Aquinas does not think that Christian perfection amounts to this. How could he, given what he has been saying throughout the *Secunda Pars*? He is aware of there being something called "the state of perfection," which he takes to be a canonical notion (2a2ae,184,5–8). Yet he certainly does not think that a bishop, say, is automatically more personally perfect before God than anyone else might be, even a layperson. He does not think that episcopal consecration automatically makes one a saint any more than he thinks that all monks or nuns go to heaven and enjoy the beatific vision. These facts might leave one feeling that 2a2ae,183–189 is a bit of a letdown, a descent from the essence of Christian perfection to something else.

One needs to remember, however, that Aquinas never tells his readers that the *Secunda Pars* is intended as a march to a bells-and-whistles finale intended to bring the house down with an ear-splitting round of applause. Scholastic as he is, he typically moves from question to question so as to be all-inclusive rather than aesthetically striking, and 2a2ae,183–189 is just his way of finishing what he said that he was going to do in the foreword that precedes 2a2ae,171. Here he notes that there are matters of vital importance to be touched on when it comes to everyone seeking beatitude. He adds, though, that people differ and should be considered as the different people they are, and it is the difference between people in the Church that leads him to the matters he touches on when concluding the *Secunda Pars*. Having said things about people before God in general, he narrows down, as we have seen, to those with gratuitous graces and to those whose focus is contemplation rather than action. In 2a2ae,183–189, he simply concludes by saying something about people in the Church who have an official ecclesiastical status.

2a2ae,183–189 is yet another bit of the *Summa* that few people study nowadays, and with some reason. It is assuming much that is not assumed these days even by Roman Catholics, who work on the understanding that the Church requires bishops and that religious orders are a good thing in principle. In 2a2ae,183–189, Aquinas is not, for example, anticipating certain later developments in Roman Catholic theology when it comes to what bishops and members of religious orders are about and to what they are obliged.[16] For this reason, I am not going to linger over it in detail. But I shall note some of the conclusions in it that might be recognized as being of some contemporary interest.

    1. We can distinguish broadly between being poor or rich, for example, and more narrowly between people having different sociological statuses

in the human community. So we can distinguish between (a) being poor or rich and (b) being married, or single, or a priest, or a layperson, or a member of a religious order, and we can therefore reasonably speak of there being states of life (2a2ae,183,1).

2. The Church is there to help people get to heaven. So it is fitting that it should contain people in different states of life with differing obligations attached to them (2a2ae,183,2–4).

3. Charity is what most unites us to God (2a2ae,184,1 and 3), though none of us can be perfect as God is perfect (2a2ae,184,2). However, Christ spoke highly of poverty, chastity, and obedience, which are means by which some people might be led to charity. Though these things are not absolutely required for the perfection of people, they are possible aids to human perfection. The Church, therefore, rightly organizes itself in order to allow for people formally embracing a state of life committed to poverty, chastity, and obedience (2a2ae,184,3). Note, though, that someone formally or officially committed to poverty, chastity, and obedience might be a really bad person, just as a layperson might be a truly great saint (2a2ae,184,4).

4. Bishops are a good idea in principle. They help govern the Church if they are doing their job properly. Someone aspiring to become a bishop might do so for base motives such as the comfort and deference that being a bishop normally accords one. One therefore needs to be wary of people seeking episcopal office for reasons of ambition and a congenial lifestyle (2a2ae,185,1).

5. Bishops should be able to instruct Christians and to govern those under their jurisdiction with a view to what is best for them (2a2ae,185,3). They should resign from their office if they lose the ability to do this (2a2ae,185,4).

6. Members of religious orders belong to organizations with different goals. Some are focused on contemplation. Some concentrate on a variety of charitable activities (2a2ae,187,1–2), and some rightly depend on begging rather than on income derived from manual labor (2a2ae,187,3–5).[17]

7. Those aspiring to enter religious orders should, in charity, bear in mind what they might be doing when entering religious life. If they are abandoning parents who need their support, they should not enter religious life. This, though, does not mean that people should not become friars or monks or nuns just because their parents are not happy about them doing so (2a2ae,189,6).

With these thoughts of Aquinas noted, I shall now move on to what he has to say in his *Tertia Pars*.

God Incarnate (3a,1–26)

THE FOREWORD TO the *Tertia Pars* begins with the words "Our Saviour, the Lord Jesus Christ…showed in his person that path of truth which…we can follow to the blessedness of eternal life. This means that after our study of the final goal of human life and of the virtues and vices we must bring the entire theological discourse to completion by considering the Savior himself and his benefits to the human race."[1] Aquinas adds that such consideration means first thinking about Christ in himself and then thinking about the Christian sacraments instituted by him. When it comes to Christ in himself, he observes, we need to focus on what the Incarnation amounted to and what it achieves for us.[2]

3a, 1–26 is Aquinas's account of what the Incarnation amounts to.[3] Some readers of Aquinas have expressed surprise that the discussion of the Incarnation appears so late in the *Summa Theologiae*, yet its contents have been assumed and alluded to by Aquinas from 1a,1. He waits until the *Tertia Pars* to articulate them in detail only because he thinks that a discourse on the Incarnation follows most naturally upon a discussion of those for whose benefit it was intended—these providing the context for the Incarnation. Aquinas does not think that the Incarnation was absolutely necessary. He does not think that God had to become incarnate. He thinks that God became incarnate so as to benefit human beings given what they are with all their various flaws and weaknesses. He therefore finds it appropriate to turn to the Incarnation in detail after having said what he has to concerning human beings.

20.1 Aquinas's Basic Account of the Incarnation

Aquinas takes the Incarnation to amount to God becoming human. Given his view that God is immutable, he does not view the Incarnation as amounting to a change in God. Instead, he views it as a change on the side of what is created, and he thinks that God became human insofar as there came to birth in the world one who, though human, was also divine. In thinking along these lines, Aquinas is presupposing the teaching on the Incarnation delivered by the Council of Chalcedon, according to which:

Following the saintly fathers, we all with one voice teach the confession of one and the same Son, our Lord Jesus Christ: the same perfect in divinity and perfect in humanity, the same truly God and truly human, of a rational soul and body; consubstantial with the Father as regards his divinity, and the same consubstantial with us as regards his humanity; like us in all respects except for sin; begotten before the ages from the Father as regards his divinity....One and the same Christ, Son, Lord, only-begotten, acknowledged in two natures which undergo no confusion, no change, no division, no separation; at no point was the difference between the natures taken away through the union, but rather the property of both natures is preserved and comes together into a single person and a single subsistent being; he is not parted or divided into two persons; but is one and the same only-begotten Son, God, Word, Lord Jesus Christ.[4]

According to Aquinas, the Incarnation amounts to there being a divine subject (God the Son) united with what is human in a way that allows us to say that some human being is both human and divine.

That God became incarnate as taught by Chalcedon is not something that Aquinas takes to be philosophically demonstrable any more than he takes the doctrine of the Trinity to be. He thinks that the divinity of Christ is attested to by miracles performed by him and by his resurrection from the dead as reported in the Gospels, but, though he thinks that only God can produce miracles, he does not argue that since Christ performed miracles Christ is obviously divine. Rather, he believes that the most we can conclude from the miracles associated with Christ is that God was performing miracles, not that Christ was God because of the miracles associated with him (though for more on this see the following chapter). Aquinas holds that someone might miraculously recover from an illness on the occasion of my touching them, yet he does not argue that I am therefore working a miracle and that I am therefore divine. He thinks that God is working a miracle in a certain context of which I am a part. Similarly, he thinks that the miracles associated with Jesus display the working of God while not demonstrating that Jesus is divine. Aquinas's approach to the Incarnation rests on his faith that Christ was divine, not on any inference to be drawn on the basis of empirical investigation. It also rests on what he takes the teaching of Jesus to be as recorded in the New Testament, for he believes this to include a claim to divinity.

As we have seen, Aquinas accords a special respect to New Testament texts. He always takes them to amount to divine revelation. His approach to the New Testament is, however, one that many contemporary thinkers do not share.

These people (hardly unreasonably) take the contents of the New Testament to be a set of writings produced long ago, to be treated and studied as we should treat and study anything in writing that we might encounter as scholars. Academic people today will typically turn to texts like those in the New Testament while confining themselves to questions like "Who wrote them?" "When were they written?" "What were their authors trying to say?" and "What sources were they drawing on?" Authors of academic discussions of the New Testament, sometimes having no religious affiliation themselves, tend to approach the New Testament as an expert on Julius Caesar might approach his account of the Gallic Wars in *Commentarii de Bello Gallico*. Scholars dealing with historical texts today rarely (as pure scholars) take them to amount to divine revelation. They take them to be compositions of human beings and nothing more than that. Rightly or wrongly, however, Aquinas reads the New Testament as inspired by God and, therefore, as containing divine revelation. And not only that, for he also reads the New Testament Gospels as being historically accurate and as giving us a true account of what Jesus did and said.

Was he right or wrong to do so? If you look at what New Testament exegetes have said about the historicity of the Gospels in the last 150 years or so, you will find an astonishing amount of disagreement concerning what is sometimes called "the historical Jesus." Some have argued that the Gospels provide a substantially reliable account of what Jesus did and said. Others have argued that some of what the Gospels say about Jesus might be historically accurate while some of it is either probably not or certainly not. Yet others have been thoroughly skeptical when it comes to the historicity of the Gospel accounts of Jesus, which is a matter of controversy among New Testament specialists and looks likely to remain so. When trying to understand Aquinas on the Incarnation, however, we need to recognize that he, like most of his contemporaries and theological predecessors, took it for granted that the Gospels put us in touch with what Jesus actually said and did. In 3a,5,3, Aquinas notes the suggestion that Christ cannot, contrary to Gospel reports, have been literally angry or sad or tired. The suggestion he is concerned with here holds that references to Christ undergoing bodily changes should be read metaphorically as should Old Testament texts ascribing bodily changes to God. However, Aquinas rejects this suggestion while saying that, should it be accepted, "the reliability of the Gospel account would perish." He goes on: "What is prophetically announced in figurative speech is one thing; what is described in historical terms by the Evangelists in a literal sense is another."[5] That gives you Aquinas's approach to the historicity of the Gospels in a nutshell, and it is one that leads Aquinas to say that the Gospels give us access to Jesus as effectively teaching that he is the second person of the Trinity.

Aquinas's account of the Incarnation is, therefore, grounded in what he takes to be the teaching of Christ, whom he calls "the first and chief teacher of the faith" who knows what is true of God without revelation since he is himself divine (3a,7,7). Since Aquinas takes the teaching of Christ to proclaim (among other things) his equality to God, Aquinas reads it in the light of Chalcedon as allowing us to conclude that Christ is one subject—the Word, the second person of the Trinity—walking around our world and speaking to us as a human being.

Yet how is this conclusion thinkable? As we saw in chapter 6, Aquinas holds that there is a real distinction of persons within God. As we have also seen, though, he thinks that each divine person is God and that there is only one God. How, therefore, can he make sense of the idea that God is a human being? How, for example, can he avoid concluding that if God is a human being then God is not divine but human?

At one level, Aquinas does not pretend to be able to make sense of the Incarnation, if by "make sense" one means comprehending what exactly the Incarnation involves. He thinks that we can obtain a fairly good (if imperfect) understanding of what, for example, cats are and of what goes on with them. As I noted in chapter 4, however, he denies that we can understand what God is, which means that he does not think that we can fully understand what God is even as human.[6] I noted in chapter 6 that Aquinas takes the doctrine of the Trinity to present us with a mystery, though not one more profound than the mystery of God considered without reference to the Trinity, and he takes the same line when it comes to the doctrine of the Incarnation. He thinks that in turning to it we inevitably bring with us our profound ignorance when it comes to what divinity is.

Yet Aquinas insists that the articles of faith can be defended against charges of contradiction and therefore holds that the doctrine of the Incarnation can be expressed in a way that does not leave its defenders talking obvious nonsense. Thinking that the Chalcedonian account of the Incarnation involves logical contradictions, some theologians have settled for an understanding of Christ that has him being inspired by God but not himself divine. Aquinas, though, does not think that the Chalcedonian account of the Incarnation involves contradictions.[7]

In doing so, he works on the assumption that sentences of the form "X is Y" can sometimes tell us what something is by nature and are not always identity statements like "The Morning Star is the Evening Star." And when it comes to ascribing a nature to something, Aquinas is thinking in terms of substantial form. Something has a substantial form, he holds, insofar as it has a nature or essence, and to declare what something's nature is amounts to saying that certain things pertaining to its essence can be truly asserted of it. So in the case of "John is a human being" we are being given notice that we can truly say of John "John is a mammal," "John is a rational animal," "John is mortal," and so on, and when it comes to "Fido is a dog" we are being given notice that we can truly say things like "Fido is a quadruped," "Fido is a carnivore," "Fido hears better than human beings do," and so on. In taking this line, Aquinas is not suggesting that we have a complete knowledge of the essence or nature of everything or of anything. Rather, he is claiming that we know enough to be able to say with respect to some things what naturally belongs to them, how they should be described, and what their abilities are in general, and he draws on this thought when turning to the Incarnation in the light of the Council of Chalcedon.

Aquinas understands Chalcedon to teach that in Christ there is one divine subject—the Second Person of the Trinity—who can be truly spoken of as we might speak both of what is divine and of what is human. So he thinks that of Christ we can truly say things like "Christ walked around" and "Christ was incorporeal," "Christ was born in time" and "Christ is eternal," "Christ is human" and "Christ is divine." In short, Aquinas holds that both "Christ is human" and "Christ is divine" are both literally true. He holds that the Incarnation really amounts to there being one subject with two distinct natures.

An obvious objection to this conclusion is that nothing can simultaneously be both able to eat and incorporeal, or both born in time and eternal, or both human and divine, and Aquinas agrees with this objection if it is understood as ascribing to something with one nature attributes or activities that cannot simultaneously be had by things possessing only that single nature. He would, therefore, have no problem conceding that a cat, say, cannot be both corporeal and incorporeal. In line with Chalcedon, however, Aquinas does not think of Christ as having only one nature. He thinks that Christ is one subject with two distinct natures. He holds that we have two ways of speaking about Christ, based on the two distinct natures in Christ, both of which ways are true since they can both be used when referring to one subject—Christ, considered as the Second Person of the Trinity. The word *Christ* is, for Aquinas, a name. It names the one who is God incarnate (though see below for some qualification of this), and what we truly predicate of Christ is what we can predicate given that Christ has both a divine nature and a human nature.

Aquinas will say, for example, that with respect to his divine nature, Christ was incorporeal, while with respect to his human nature, Christ was able to eat. Or again, Aquinas will say that, with respect to his human nature, Christ was born in time while with respect to his divine nature, he is eternal. Aquinas does not think of the two natures of Christ as being like two essential attributes or two accidental properties that something with one nature might have.

He regards them as completely distinct natures had by one subject. In doing so, he is not saying that humanity is divine or that divinity is human. He is saying that when it comes to the Incarnation, we have one subject with two natures. As he writes in 3a,2,2: "The Word has a human nature united to itself, even though it does not form part of the Word's divine nature...[and]...this union was effected in the person of the Word, not in the nature."[8] In accordance with this conclusion, Aquinas argues that, since Christ is God, everything truly said of Christ with respect to his humanity can be attributed to God. So, for example, we can assert that God died since Christ died, or that God was born since Christ was born. Correspondingly, Aquinas thinks, everything truly said of Christ with respect to his divinity can be attributed to the man Jesus. So, for example, we can assert that Jesus is omnipotent, omniscient, and eternal since God is omnipotent, omniscient, and eternal.

Once again, the key to thinking about the Incarnation is, for Aquinas, the idea that Christ is one subject with two distinct natures. Insofar as Christ has a divine nature, Christ is all that God is. Insofar as Christ has a human nature, Christ is all that is required to be essentially human. Aquinas thinks that *as divine* Christ is all that God essentially is and that *as human* he is all that a human being essentially is.[9] For Aquinas, when it comes to Christ "we have two ways of speaking about him—only one of which we understand. In virtue of his human nature, we speak of him in exactly the same way that we would speak of any other human being. In virtue of his divine nature, we can also say more enigmatic and mysterious things such as that he forgives sins or is our redeemer."[10] When it comes to the subject term "Christ," however, Aquinas sees no problem in saying things like "Christ rode on a donkey," and, since he thinks that "God" can be substituted for "Christ" in this sentence for purposes of signifying a subject, he also has no problem in saying "God rode on a donkey." He does, however, have a problem saying, for example, "Christ, insofar as he is divine, rode on a donkey" or "Christ, insofar as he is human, is omnipotent."

The above account gives you the main thrust of Aquinas's thinking in 3a,1–26 when it comes to what the Incarnation involved (as distinct from his thinking about its effects), but 3a,1–26 goes into a number of details when presenting what I have so far briefly summarized, so let me now note what I take to be the most important of them.

20.2 The Fittingness of the Incarnation (3a,1)

Aquinas holds that it was fitting for God to become human because of our way of understanding, which proceeds by means of sense experience.[11] "It is most fitting to manifest the unseen things of God through things that are seen" (3a,1,1).[12] The Incarnation, Aquinas thinks, shows us God's goodness in a tangible way.

Was the Incarnation necessary for the salvation of people? On biblical grounds, Aquinas thinks that we are saved by the Incarnation, but he does not think that we could not have been saved without it.[13] "The incarnation," he says, was "not necessary for the restoration of human nature since by God's infinite power God had many other ways to accomplish this end" (3a,1,2).[14] On the other hand, Aquinas regards the Incarnation as bringing about our salvation in an especially good way since, among other things, it involves God directly speaking to us as a human being, since it brings us to hope and to charity because of our recognizing (if we do) that God is one who shares our human nature, since it provides us with a perfect and intelligible example of right living, and since it reminds us of the dignity of human nature.[15]

If we agree that the Incarnation somehow rescues us from the effects of sin, should we conclude that God would not have become incarnate had people never sinned? In 3a,1,3, Aquinas notes that theologians have offered conflicting answers to this question. Without vilifying people concluding differently, however, he veers to the view that the Incarnation would not have occurred if it were not for sin since he reads the New Testament as continually presenting the Incarnation as a remedy for sin.

20.3 *Christ as God and Human (3a,16)*

If you think in accordance with the Council of Chalcedon, then you will believe that in Christ there was a union of divinity and humanity in one subject. But what kind of union? This question is what Aquinas deals with in 3a,2–6 and in 3a,16. I have already tried to summarize the reasoning of 3a,2–6, so let me now focus on 3a,16, which reads like a quiz on the contents of 3a,2–6. In 3a,16, Aquinas singles out a series of propositions concerning the Incarnation and asks whether or not they are true. He also raises two questions concerning predication as it relates to the Incarnation. The significance of 3a,16 lies in the fact that it neatly draws together the substance of Aquinas's teaching about the Incarnation in 3a,2–6 in question-and-answer form. Here are Aquinas's questions, together with his answers.

1. *Is this statement true: "God is a human being"?* "God is a human being" is a true statement since Christ is one divine subject with both a human nature and a divine nature. Since this subject is truly and not just apparently a human being, God is a human being. "Since, therefore, the person of the

Son of God, for whom the term 'God' here stands, is a subject subsisting in a human nature, the term 'a human being' may be truly and literally predicated of the term 'God' when the latter stands for the person of the Son of God" (3a,16,1).[16]

2. *Is this statement true: "A human being is God"?* "A human being is God" is true for the same reason as "God is a human being" is true. If one subject is divine and human, that subject is both God and a human being (3a,16,2).

3. *Should we call Christ "a human being of the Lord"?* No. Christ is a human being, but given that he is also God, he is the Lord, and not a human being of the Lord. The second person of the Trinity, being God, is Lord of all (3a,16,3). If one thinks of Christ as a human being who is nothing but a creature, then one might speak of Christ as being a human being of the Lord, just as one might speak of any saintly person being so. Christ, however, was not just a saintly human being. He was the Word incarnate.

4. *Can we predicate of God what we attribute to human nature?* We can, since God incarnate is one subject with two natures, one of which is human. Unlike certain heretics, we should say that "whatever is predicated of Christ, in virtue of either his divine nature or of his human nature, may be predicated both of God and of the human being" (3a,16,4).[17] We need to remember, however, that when predicating of God what is predicable of human nature we should be clear that we are talking of God insofar as God is incarnate, not insofar as God is divine.

5. *Can we predicate of the divine nature what can be attributed to human nature?* Definitely not, for the divine nature and human nature are distinct. So, for instance, we cannot say that the divine nature is essentially corporeal or mortal. We can speak of Christ as divine and as being all that God is. We cannot, however, conclude that what human nature is essentially is true of the divine nature (3a,16,5).

6. *Is this statement true: "God was made a human being"?* The statement is true since the eternal Word, God the Son, became a human being by taking on a human nature, as it says in John 1:14: "The Word became flesh" (3a,16,6).

7. *Is this statement true: "A human being was made God"?* When it comes to the Incarnation, it is false to say that a human being was made God since prior to the Incarnation there was no human being about to be united to God as God is united to human nature by virtue of the Incarnation. The Incarnation does not amount to a change in anything human. It amounts to something human being born that is from the outset divine (3a,16,7).

8. *Is this statement true: "Christ is a creature"?* If by "Christ" we intend to signify the Word incarnate, then it is false to say that Christ is a creature, since the

Word is God, not a creature, and since we should say nothing to imply otherwise. Instead, when speaking of Christ we should do so in terms of Christ's two natures as had by one subject—the Word, God the Son. So "it should not be stated without qualification that Christ is a creature or is subordinate to the Father; such statements should be qualified by the phrase 'according to his human nature.'"[18] It is fine to say that Christ suffered, died, and was buried, but not with respect to his divine nature (3a,16,8).

9. *Is it true to say that Christ, considered as a particular human being, began to exist?* No, it is not, if we take Christ (Jesus of Nazareth) to be the eternal Word who is one subject with two natures. Given this understanding of Christ, Christ never began to exist since God the Son never began to exist anymore than God the Father or God the Holy Spirit began to exist. To be sure, Jesus of Nazareth came on the human scene at a particular time, so the Incarnation came about in time. But the Incarnation is a union of the divine nature with human nature in one person, and this person is eternal. Considered as God, therefore, the Word did not begin to exist, even though Jesus was a human being born in time (3a,16,9).

10. *Is this statement true: "Christ, as a human being, is a creature" or "began to be"?* This statement is indeed true since the Incarnation came about in time. God was not incarnate in, say, the time of Moses. At that time there was no human being who was God. In the time of Jesus, though, there was, since Jesus, born of Mary, was both human and divine. As human, Jesus was not the eternal creator of the universe. As human, he was born of Mary. So, as human, Christ was a creature and began to be, meaning that Jesus was a human being and began to be at some time. As human, Christ, like all human beings, is a creature that has not always existed or that does not exist of necessity (3a,16,10).

11. *Is this statement true: "Christ, as a human being, is God"?* In one sense, it is not. It cannot be true that his being human automatically guarantees Christ being divine because of the difference between what it is to be human and what it is to be divine. However, if we take "Christ" to signify one subject (the Word) having two natures, then Christ, the man, is God since Christ is one subject with two natures, one divine and one human. In the end, though, it might be best to deny that "Christ, as a human being, is God" since such a statement can easily be taken as wrongly asserting that by being human Christ is divine (3a,16,11).

12. *Is this statement true: "Christ, as a human being, is an independent subject or person"?* This statement is false since the Word, even as a human being, is one subject or person—the second person of the Trinity, who exists

eternally, who does not have to become incarnate, and whose nature does not admit of division for various reasons (cf. 1a,2–26).[19] Yet God the Son (the Word) became a particular human being whom anyone around him might have bumped into. Considered as such, God incarnate is a particular person (Jesus), though we should not assume that Jesus had powers open only to human beings, for he was both divine and human, given that he was one subject with two natures (3a,16,12).

20.4 The Grace of Christ (3a,7–8)

As we have seen, Aquinas holds that human beings can receive grace from God, and, since he holds that Christ is what any human being is, he obviously thinks that Christ can receive grace from God insofar as he is human. Indeed, he thinks that Christ was supremely graced. In what way, though?

Aquinas's discussion of this question is, unsurprisingly, governed by the conviction that Christ is a divine subject with two natures. It therefore begins by claiming that Christ's human soul was filled with sanctifying grace and that this grace came to be imparted to others just because Christ was God and, therefore, the source of grace (3a,7,1). As God incarnate, thinks Aquinas, Christ must have had all that we think of as grace considered as uniting us to God. Aquinas also thinks that "since grace was at its best in Christ, it gave rise to virtues which perfected each of the faculties of the soul and all its activities" and that "in this way Christ had all the virtues" (3a,7,2).[20]

In making this claim, Aquinas is asserting that Christ had all the *moral* virtues (theologically construed), not all *possible* virtues, for he denies that Christ had all the *theological* virtues since he thinks that Christ could not have had the theological virtues of faith and hope. Why does he think this? Because, as we have seen, Aquinas regards faith and hope as virtues had only by people who do not have the knowledge of God had by those enjoying the beatific vision, and because he thinks that Christ must have always enjoyed the beatific vision (3a,7,3–4).[21] On the other hand, in 3a,7,5, Aquinas insists that Christ must have had all of the gifts of the Holy Spirit (cf. chapter 12 above). "Clearly," he says, "the soul of Christ was perfectly subject to the movement of the Holy Spirit.... Obviously then he was outstandingly endowed with the gifts."[22] Aquinas also thinks (3a,7,7–8) that Christ had at least some of what falls under the heading of *gratia gratis data* (cf. chapter 19). He observes: "A teacher must have the means to present his or her doctrine.... Now Christ is the first and most authoritative doctor of the faith and of spiritual teaching.... It is clear then that Christ had all the charisms in a surpassing degree, as befits the first and original teacher of the faith."[23]

In 3a,7,10–13, Aquinas elaborates on the grace of Christ in a way that you should be able to understand given what I have written above. In 3a,8, however, he turns to a new notion: Christ's grace as head of the Church.

When he uses the word *church* Aquinas basically means the Catholic Church, which he took to be an authority handing on orthodox Christian teaching, and, based on his reading of the Bible, he takes the Church to have Christ as its head. Ephesians 1:22 says that God has made Christ "head of all things for the church," and Colossians 1:18 declares Christ to be "the head of the body, the church." In view of texts such as these, Aquinas holds that Christ is head of the Church (3a,8,1), and he speaks of Christ having grace as head of the Church not only to insist that Christ was graced in himself but also to stress that the grace had by members of the Church should be thought of as flowing from Christ as God incarnate.[24] As head of the Church, says Aquinas, Christ holds the highest place in the body of Christ that is the Church, and Christ's humanity "acts upon people, on their bodies as well as on their souls."[25] Christ, Aquinas adds, is head of all people and all angels (3a,8,3–4). In teaching along these lines, Aquinas is evidently thinking of texts like John 1:16–17: "From his fullness we have all received, grace upon grace. The law was indeed given through Moses; grace and truth came through Jesus Christ."

20.5 Christ's Knowledge (3a,9–12)

The emphasis that Aquinas places on Christ being truly God and truly human comes into play again when he turns to the topic of Christ's knowledge. Given that he takes Christ to be one subject, the Word, with two natures, he obviously thinks it necessary to affirm both that Christ had knowledge as God has knowledge and that Christ had knowledge as a human being (albeit a perfect one) has it. So in 3a,9–12 he embarks on a delicate balancing act designed to present the knowledge of Christ as both divine and human. How successfully Aquinas manages to produce an account of Christ's knowledge that does not leave his divinity compromised by his humanity, or his humanity compromised by his divinity, is something I must leave you to consider. When talking of Christ's knowledge, however, the main claims he makes are as follows.

1. In general, we have to say that Christ had the knowledge that God has, but also that he had to have knowledge that people have as human beings. "There had to be something other than divine knowledge in Christ. Otherwise the soul of Christ would be less perfect than the souls of other human

beings" (3a,9,1).[26] In 3a,9,1, Aquinas elaborates on this point by arguing that if Christ did not have knowledge that human beings can have, there would not in him have been a genuine union of human and divine natures in one individual.

2. As God incarnate, Christ is as graced as any human being can be, and the grace of all who have grace derives from Christ. Even as human, therefore, he enjoyed the beatific vision (3a,9,2).[27] "Human beings have a potential for beatific knowledge...They are brought to this...by the humanity of Christ...Hence, beatific knowledge, which consists in the vision of God, must be found in its supreme degree in Christ, since the cause must always be superior to what it causes."[28]

3. Colossians 2:3 says that in Christ "are hidden all the treasures of wisdom and knowledge." We should therefore assume that Christ miraculously had innate knowledge of the essences of things (3a,9,3). "Christ, therefore, has to be credited with infused knowledge: intelligible species covering everything to which the passive intellect is in potency have been imprinted by the Word of God on the soul of Christ which is personally united to him."[29] Aquinas's idea here is that Christ's passive intellect was always innately stocked with knowledge of all intelligible objects. So, for example, if asked to do so in his day, Christ could have given lectures on atomic physics.[30]

4. Christ had some knowledge acquired on the basis of sensory experience (3a,9,4 and 12,1–2). That is to say, he gained knowledge by means of his agent intellect (cf. 1a,79,3). "The proper operation of the agent intellect is to activate intellectual species by abstracting them from the data of imagination.... Hence it is necessary to say that some intelligible species were received in the passive intellect of Christ as a result of the action of his active intellect."[31] Again: "Just as by infused knowledge the soul of Christ knew everything to which the passive intellect is in potency in any way whatever, so by acquired knowledge he knew everything that can possibly be known by the exercise of the active intellect."[32]

5. Though Christ's human soul always enjoyed the beatific vision, it did not comprehend the essence of God perfectly any more than the saints in glory do. That is because the divine essence is infinite and cannot be fully comprehended by what is finite (3a,10,1).

6. In knowing the Word by means of the beatific vision, Christ knew "everything that is, was or will be, in any way whatever, be it deed, word, or thought, by anyone, at any time.... Through the Word the soul of Christ knows everything that exists in the entire course of time; and he also knows the thoughts of human beings of whom he is the judge" (3a,10,2).[33]

7. The soul of Christ sees the essence of God more perfectly than any other creature since it is united to the Word in person and is more closely joined to it than any other creature (3a,10,4).

8. "The soul of Christ had to be entirely perfect" (3a,11,1).[34] So Christ knew "everything that can be known by human beings through the enlightenment of the agent intellect" and "everything that is made known to people by divine revelation."[35]

9. Christ's infused knowledge was complete, so he did not need to perform inferences or engage in rational investigation so as to reach conclusions previously unknown to him. On the other hand, he could articulate what he knew by infused knowledge so as to make matters of inference clear to his hearers and to indicate how he could himself see how one item of knowledge is connected to another (3a,11,3). And Christ's infused knowledge was habitual, as is our knowledge—meaning that it was there for him to draw on at will (3a,11,5 and 6).

10. Given that acquired knowledge can be attributed to Christ, it follows that Christ can be thought of as having learned certain things or as advancing in knowledge (3a,12,2). But we should not suppose that Christ was taught anything by another human being or that he was taught anything by angels (3a,12,3 and 4).

20.6 Christ's Human Power (3a,13–15)

Aquinas is clear that Christ, as God, is omnipotent. He is equally clear, however, that Christ, as human, is not. "Since the soul of Christ is a part of human nature," he says, "it is impossible for it to have omnipotence" (3a,13,1). So Christ, as human, cannot create as God creates. He can be God's instrument when performing miracles; but he is not, as human, the final explanation of miraculous occurrences (3a,13,2). In Aquinas's view, we should not even suppose that Christ, as human, had unlimited power over his own body any more than he had unlimited power over other bodies (3a,13,3). As God, Christ indeed had power over his body; but not as human.[36]

This conclusion leads Aquinas to consider the physical disabilities of Christ as human together with his disabilities of soul.

One might think it inappropriate for the incarnate Son of God to have had physical disabilities. One might, for example, think that it would be wrong for Christ to have endured physical pain, hunger, or thirst. Aquinas, however, holds otherwise. His basic line is that if (so to speak) an incarnation of God is to be worth the paper that it is written on, then it involves God actually being human and therefore being subject to bodily woes that can afflict us. This is the drift of 3a,14,1. Given that he thinks of *malum poenae* as inherited by Adam's descendants because of his sin (cf. 1a2ae,81–85), Aquinas does not want to say that the Word incarnate endured bodily hardship because of original sin (3a,14,3). He believes that Christ was born without original sin, yet he also thinks that Christ must have been as subject to physical grief as anyone else. As we have seen, Aquinas maintains that it is possible to be human without undergoing physical disability, for he takes Adam before he fell to have flourished perfectly at the physical level. But Aquinas views the Incarnation as God acting for the benefit of people as they are since the fall of Adam. He therefore finds it appropriate for God, as human, to assume some of the physical limitations that people now typically endure.

As for disabilities of soul, Aquinas insists that Christ did not sin and was not able to sin (3a,15,1 and 2). He also denies that Christ was ignorant in any way (3a,15,3). He accepts that Christ had human emotions, but he thinks that Christ must have dealt with them better than we typically do (3a,15,4). So he denies that Christ's human emotions could have led him to act sinfully or against reason. Aquinas concedes, though, that Christ could suffer pain (3a,15,5) and be sorrowful (3a,15,6), and that Christ could have been fearful as shrinking from pain, though not as failing to know what was to come in its wake (3a,15,7).

In 3a,15,10, Aquinas offers a summary of what he has been saying previously. He asks, "Was Christ, at one and the same time, a pilgrim and a beholder?" (*utrum Christus fuerit simul viator et comprehensor*). His answer is yes. By "pilgrim" Aquinas means someone proceeding to beatitude. By "beholder" he means someone enjoying the beatific vision. And his view is that, while Christ enjoyed the beatific vision, he was also subject to physical pain and death.

20.7 Implications of the Hypostatic Union

Following traditional terminology, Aquinas sometimes employs the phrase "hypostatic union" when referring to the Incarnation. The Greek word *hypostasis* means "what underlies," and it was used by the Council of Chalcedon to refer to the one subject in whom, because of the Incarnation, there were two natures, one divine and one human. Generally, then, by "hypostatic union" Aquinas is referring to the union of human nature and divine nature in God incarnate, and in 3a,16–26 he continues to explore what this union means.

As we have seen, in 3a,16, Aquinas does so by considering a range of statements concerning Christ. Subsequently he turns to what he calls the "unity" of Christ (3a,17–19), Christ's relation to God the Father (3a,20), the prayer of

Christ (3a,21), the priesthood of Christ (3a,22), Christ and adoption (3a,23), the predestination of Christ (3a,24), the reverence due to Christ (3a,25), and the sense in which Christ can be said to be the mediator of God and human beings (3a,26). The conclusions defended by Aquinas in these questions always cautiously abide by the main points concerning the Incarnation that he has already articulated, but they also introduce some new material. Thus:

1. In 3a,17,1, Aquinas observes that Christ is one being, not two, since Christ is one divine subject with two natures, and he takes this conclusion to imply that in Christ there is only one actually existing thing (3a,17,2). In the Incarnation, he says, the Word does not somehow pick up a new existing thing as we might pick up a hitchhiker. Rather, the Word is related to human nature by assuming that nature.

2. Christ, says Aquinas in 3a,18,1, had a human will because he was human and a divine will because he was God. In this connection, Aquinas alludes to Luke 22:42 in which Christ before his crucifixion prays by saying, "If you are willing, remove this cup from me; yet not my will but yours be done." As human, thinks Aquinas, Christ willed as a human being and could, therefore, recoil from pain. As God, though, Christ subjected his human will to the divine will (3a,18,5). Aquinas therefore holds that Christ had animal appetites (3a,18,2), though ones always subject to his reason and therefore to the will of God (3a,18,5 and 6).

3. In 3a,19,1, Aquinas argues that Christ's activity can be thought of as two-fold. As a human being, Christ engaged in human activity; as God, he engaged in divine activity. But, Aquinas adds, Christ's human activity could instrumentally come under the control of divine activity so as to produce what only God can produce, and the natural processes of Christ's human body were subject to his reason and will in a way that they are not when it comes to the rest of us (3a,19,2).[37]

4. We sometimes speak of people being meritorious, meaning that they deserve a reward of some kind because of the way they have behaved. In 3a,19,3 and 4, Aquinas argues that Christ could merit both for himself and for other people. Christ could merit for himself since by always acting in conformity to God's will he could lay claim to certain goods not yet had by him (goods such as being raised from the dead) even though he was always graced by God and always enjoyed the beatific vision. And Christ could merit for others since he is head of the Church and can help its members insofar as they are in solidarity with him.

5. If Christ is God, is he subject to God the Father? In 3a,20,1, Aquinas answers this question in the negative by saying that, being divine, Christ is

not subject to God the Father if "being subject" is taken to imply inferiority. He adds, though, that Christ is a human being who, like all human beings, is, as human, subject to God. "Christ, in so far as he has the form of a servant, is subject to the Father."[38]

6. The New Testament tells us that Christ prayed, that he asked God for certain things (cf. Luke 6:12). Noting this fact, Aquinas argues in 3a,21 that it was "fitting" (*conveniens*) that Christ should have prayed.[39] Aquinas has no doubt that, as God, Christ is the one to whom all prayer should be addressed. Yet Aquinas is also convinced that Christ was human and had a human will as well as a divine will (cf. 3a,18,1). So he says, "As God, Christ could accomplish all that he desired, but not as human."[40] Being divine, thinks Aquinas, Christ was able to answer any prayer made by any human being. As human, though, Christ could fittingly pray for what he could bring about as God. For what it is worth, this conclusion of Aquinas seems odd to me since it effectively seems to amount to the conclusion that Christ could have prayed to himself, and I suspect that Aquinas is aware that this is so since in 3a,21,1 he lays stress on the notion that Christ prayed in order to give us an example of prayer, to teach us to pray. He says that Christ wished to pray not because he lacked any power but "for our instruction."

7. What, then, was Christ doing when praying for himself as reported in texts like John 17:1 and Luke 22:44? In 3a,21,3, Aquinas argues that Christ was expressing his sensuous desires while giving us an example when it comes to our prayer and while asking for what he could not achieve by means of his human nature.

8. Hebrews 4 emphasizes the notion of Christ being a priest and Aquinas picks up on this in 3a,22,1. "The characteristic function of a priest," he says, "is to act as mediator between God and God's people. This implies firstly that he communicates to the people the things of God....It implies secondly that he offers to God the prayers of the people and in some degree makes reparation to God for their sins....These functions are carried out by Christ in an eminent degree."[41] Aquinas, following the Old Testament, also associates priesthood with the offering of sacrifice. So he speaks of Christ as offering sacrifice. Yet he also holds that the sacrifice offered to God by Christ was Christ himself (3a,22,2). In freely accepting suffering and death, Aquinas says, Christ gained for people the remission of sins, continuance in grace, and union with God (3a,22,3).[42] And, Aquinas adds, Christ's priesthood is eternal, not temporary since its effects in people are unending (3a,22,5).

9. Ephesians 1:5 speaks of Christians being adopted children of God, and Aquinas obviously approves of this way of talking (3a,23,1), as long as it is

understood to mean that people adopted by God are adopted by the whole Trinity and not just God the Father (3a,23,2), and as long as it is realized that it is only rational creatures that can sensibly be spoken of as adopted by God (3a,23,3). Should we, therefore, conclude that Christ is God's adopted son? In 3a,23,4, Aquinas argues that we should not. Why not? Because Christ is literally the Son of God (the Word Incarnate) and is so naturally and not by any legal arrangement.

10. As we have seen, Aquinas thinks that some people are predestined to salvation (1a,23). Yet he also thinks (3a,24) that Christ (unique among people) can be thought of as predestined since, from eternity, God willed that Christ should be born in time as one having both the divine nature and a human one. In other words, Aquinas does not take the Incarnation and what he believes to be its effects as an *afterthought* on God's part. He takes it to express God's timeless will for Christ and those united to God in Christ.

11. Should one adore Christ and venerate him as God? Obviously, Aquinas's answer to this question is yes (3a,25,1). As both God and human, Christ is one existing thing (cf. 3a,17,1) and is therefore to be adored as such. Aquinas does not take this conclusion to imply that we should worship Christ's human flesh considered only as human flesh. However, since he thinks of Christ's flesh as belonging to one divine person, he thinks that it should be worshiped because to worship Christ is to worship one who is both divine and human (3a,25,2). He adds that worship of images of Christ and of relics of Christ's cross is appropriate if understood as worship of Christ for whom they *stand* and not as worship of the images or relics *in themselves* (3a,25,3–4).

12. First Timothy 2:5 says that Christ is "one mediator between God and man." Quoting this text in 3a,26,1, Aquinas goes on to argue that Christ is such a mediator because he reconciled people to God by his death, adding that people other than Christ share in his status as mediator insofar as they help to get others to turn to God and insofar as they minister to those who aim for union with God. Following up on this conclusion, Aquinas maintains that it is as a human being that Christ is the mediator between God and human beings (3a,26,2). He says that Christ bridges the gulf between people and God in an unprecedented way. Mediators try to bring differences between parties to a resolution, to an agreement or union, and, says Aquinas, Christ did exactly this because he is both divine and human. As God, Christ was no mediator at all since God is perfect and self-contained and in no need of someone to serve as a representing mediator. But, Aquinas adds, Christ, in his human nature, can be thought

of as mediating for us, as standing on our side as human beings. "As human he is set apart from God in nature and from people in the eminence of his grace and glory. Likewise as human his office is to unite people with God, which he does by setting before them the divine commandments and by atoning and interceding for them with God. It is, therefore, as human that he is, in the truest sense of the word, mediator."[43]

3a,1–26 lays out Aquinas's thinking about the Incarnation as it relates to the question "What should we take ourselves to mean when saying that 'the Word became flesh and lived among us'"? Yet Aquinas believes that the Incarnation was not just a brute fact but something with effects in the life of Christ and in the life of Christians. As we have now seen, 3a,1–26 sometimes alludes to Christ as saving people or uniting them to God in some way. In 3a,27–59, Aquinas begins to follow up on these allusions in quite detailed ways. Let us see how he does so.

The Life, Death, Resurrection, and Ascension of Christ (3a,27–59)

IMMEDIATELY BEFORE HE embarks on 3a,27, Aquinas writes: "Having gone through the matters relating to the union of God and the human and the corollaries that follow from that union, we turn now to the things the incarnate Son of God actually did and suffered in the human nature united to him."[1] This announced agenda indeed corresponds to the contents of 3a,27–59, but Aquinas breaks his discussion into four sections dealing with (1) the conception and birth of Christ, (2) his life between birth and death, (3) his death, and (4) his resurrection and ascension. And since Aquinas takes Christ to have been born of Mary he begins what he has to say about the life of Christ with a discussion of Mary, which amounts to his most mature treatment of her.[2]

21.1 Mary (3a,27–30)

Devotion to Mary was common during Aquinas's lifetime and well before it, and it continues to this day.[3] Yet Aquinas never wrote a systematic treatise on Mariology (theology concerning Mary), and in 3a,27–30 Mary modestly appears only as one to be discussed with reference to Christ. Aquinas is interested in Mary not in isolation but because he takes her to have a special relationship to Christ as his mother. The main points Aquinas wants to make concerning Mary are as follows.

1. Mary, like Jeremiah and John the Baptist, received sanctifying grace before she was born (3a,27,1 and 6).[4] But she was not conceived without original sin (3a,27,2). Here we need to note that Aquinas distinguishes between being conceived and having a rational soul and, therefore, denies that Mary could have been sanctified or freed from original sin at conception.[5] He says that "fault cannot be cleared except through grace, and grace belongs only to the rational creature," adding, "the blessed virgin was not sanctified before the infusion of the rational soul."[6] In 3a,2, therefore, Aquinas denies that Mary was *conceived* without original sin. Instead, he

argues, Mary was *born* without sin and lacked sin from the time she acquired a rational soul.[7]

2. Since Mary was graced before birth, she was always without sin. She was not inclined to sin (3a,27,3), she did not actually sin (3a,27,4), and she was always *full* of grace (3a,27,5). Note that Aquinas is here relying on a mixture of Old and New Testament passages together with reference to St. Augustine. He also appeals to what he takes to be "fitting" (*conveniens*). For example, he argues that as the mother of God it would have been unfitting for Mary to have sinned (3a,27,4). He also argues that, since Mary was closest to Christ in his human nature, it was fitting that she should always be graced above all other people (3a,27,5).

3. Mary remained a virgin in conceiving Christ (3a,28,1), in giving birth to him (3a,28,2), and throughout the rest of her life (3a,28,3). She even took a vow of virginity (3a,28,4). In reaching these conclusions, Aquinas again employs arguments appealing to what he takes to be fitting or suitable for Mary given that her son was divine. He suggests, for example, that "since Christ is the true and natural Son of God it was not appropriate for him to have a father other than God since such a man might be thought of as having divine dignity."[8] Again, he reasons that Christ came to heal damage and could, therefore, hardly have taken away Mary's virginity at his birth. Yet again, he reasons that Mary could not have wanted ever to throw away the gift of virginity that she had when conceiving and giving birth to Christ. As for Mary's vow of virginity, Aquinas infers it based on Luke 1:34 as interpreted by St. Augustine and based on the fact that it was appropriate for her to consecrate her virginity to God by a vow since "works of moral perfection are more worthy of praise if they are done under a vow."[9]

4. It was, for a variety of reasons, fitting for Mary to have been married to Joseph when Christ was born (3a,29,1), and her marriage to Joseph, though never involving intercourse between them, certainly involved a union of mind and a willingness on both their parts to rear the child Jesus (3a,29,2).

5. It was fitting that, as described in Luke 1, Mary should have been solemnly told by an angel that she was to become the mother of God (3a,30,1–2). The Annunciation (1) allowed Mary to receive Christ in faith even before she bore him, (2) made her a witness to the Incarnation by receiving word of it from God, and (3) allowed her to consent freely on behalf of all people to the coming into the world of God as a human being. In 3a,30,3, Aquinas holds that it was right for the angel of the Annunciation to appear visibly to Mary because the angel's message concerned the entering into the physical world of one who is eternally invisible. Aquinas

goes on in 3a,35,6 to add that Mary endured no pain or distress in giving birth to Christ.

21.2 3a,31–59: The Big Picture

In 3a,37,2, Aquinas notes that Christ's proper name was Jesus (cf. Luke 2:21).[10] Since he thinks that "the names conferred upon some by God always signify some gratuitous gift from heaven," he concludes that "Jesus" was right as the proper name of Christ since it implies that he saves. Etymologically, Aquinas seems to have been correct here since the English "Jesus," derived from the Latin form of the Greek *Iesous*, goes back to a name based on the Hebrew verb meaning "to save" or "to deliver." Etymology notwithstanding, however, in 3a,37,2, Aquinas is also clearly drawing on Matthew 1:21 in which Mary is told to call her son Jesus "for he will save his people from their sins."

In a nutshell, therefore, the Incarnation, for Aquinas, is all about the salvation of human beings, the rescuing of them from their alienation from God due to original sin and individual sins, and the drawing of them to the beatific vision. This saving character of the Incarnation comes to the foreground in 3a,31–59. In these questions, Aquinas discusses many aspects of Christ's life, death, resurrection, and ascension, but always with an eye to the notion that all of them bear on closing the distance between people and God caused by sin (cf. 3a,1,3). In theological jargon, therefore, Aquinas's Christology is irreducibly soteriological—focused on the theme of salvation.

But in what way? Reflecting on Christ's saving work in the light of certain New Testament texts, especially Paul's Letter to the Romans, theologians over the centuries have tended to focus on the death of Christ as being of special significance, and Aquinas is no exception.[11] Notice, however, that, in conformity with St. Augustine's *De Trinitate* XIII,10, Aquinas is quite clear that God could have saved or redeemed people without the passion of Christ.[12] So in 3a,46,2 he declares, "Simply and absolutely speaking, God could have freed people otherwise than by Christ's passion, for nothing is impossible with God."[13]

God, Aquinas argues, has eternally decreed to save people by Christ's death, so there is a sense in which this death was hypothetically necessary for human salvation, given that God's decree is eternal. Yet we should not, Aquinas thinks, assume that God could not have saved people without the passion of Christ. His view is that the passion of Christ (and other things concerning the life of God incarnate) amount to a good or very suitable way of saving people.

Aquinas's judgments concerning what is good or fitting or suitable when it comes to what God brings about often strike people as curious, and with some reason, given the way in which he typically distinguishes between God and creatures. I might conclude that you did something very suitable when, say, you decided to buy me a car for my twenty-first birthday. My reasoning might be "You knew me and my tastes, and you knew how special a twenty-first birthday is." No problem here. Talk of God acting fittingly or suitably, however, seems problematic if one denies that God is a creature in the emphatic way that Aquinas does. Where do the criteria for suitability derive from when it comes to what the mysterious maker of all things does? As far as I can gather, Aquinas's talk about suitability or appropriateness when it comes to God saving people should be read (a) in light of his conviction that God actually *has* saved people by certain means (a conviction grounded in his reading of the Bible), and (b) in light of the fact that he thinks that something can be said at the level of philosophical reasoning to the effect that the means in question were good when considered from a human point of view. Something, of course, can be good without being best. Without making the good/best distinction in any sharp way, however, in 3a,31–59, Aquinas seems to conflate "good" and "best" in his discussion of the saving work of Christ. I presume that he does so because he takes all that God has done in Christ to be for the best in some ultimately incomprehensible sense, though also fitting or good in some sense that we can understand to a limited extent.

Many people have said that there is a fairly simple account to be offered of Christ and salvation: Christ saves us by suffering to a high degree, thereby warding off the wrath of God directed to sinners. In terms of this picture, God had to demand the painful death of God's Son in order to forgive sinful people, and God's son obediently complied with this demand—end of story.

But this story is problematic. For how is God forgiving us by demanding the death of anyone? If I say to you, "I forgive you on condition that you or somebody else dies," then I am, surely, not forgiving you but declaring that I will act only if certain conditions are met. Again, how can we reasonably think that we can only be brought to union with God because some human being (even though divine) has suffered greatly? And why should the suffering of one human being be thought of as needed in order to bring others to union with God? Some have said that human sin is an offense against God that demands punishment and that Christ's suffering can be thought of as the punishment required to pay a debt owed to God. This view, though, raises questions like (1) How can Christ be thought of as being punished if he is divine and sinless? (2) Why should we suppose that union with God on the part of human beings requires any punishment at all? (3) Why should God take any pleasure in human suffering? and (4) Why did God require the sufferings that Christ actually endured rather than some other suffering that he might have endured, such as being eaten alive by wild animals?

The story I have just referred to, however, is not that of Aquinas, which is more complex. He certainly thinks of the death of Christ as uniting us to God in a way that is *conveniens*, but he also thinks that the same can be said of the whole life of Christ, from birth to death. He thinks that the mere fact of the Incarnation amounts to God becoming a human being in order to express a solidarity with us that we might not have expected when thinking about God and ourselves from a purely philosophical perspective or even from the perspective of Old Testament theology. In 3a,48,1, ad.2, Aquinas says, "From the moment of his conception Christ merited eternal salvation for us." He does not mean that Christ merits salvation for us just because Christ was conceived, yet he does seem to think that if (and only if) we embrace the Incarnation for what he takes it to be, then the Incarnation saves us insofar as it amounts to God offering salvation to us, insofar as it amounts to God, if you like, miraculously coming to us in peace and forgiveness while looking to be received as such.

When it comes to forgiveness, Aquinas is clear that God can forgive all sins simply by fiat and regardless of the Incarnation because he takes sins to be offenses against God that God can pardon at will. God, says Aquinas, "has no one above" and "violates no one's rights" by forgiving sin "which is a crime in that it is committed against God" (3a,46,2, ad.3). He also thinks that God has provided a *suitable* way for people to be united to God (always assuming that they are happy with this way and wish to embrace it). In expressing this thought, Aquinas speaks of "satisfaction" (*satisfactio*). He says that "Christ by his suffering made perfect satisfaction for our sins" (3a,48,2).[14]

Aquinas takes satisfaction to be made when someone who has wronged another willingly makes up for the wrong, or when a friend of one who has wronged another makes up for the wrong done on behalf of the wrongdoer with the wrongdoer's consent.[15] His view is that, though one I have wronged might simply choose to ignore the wrong done, there still remains the fact that wrong has been done, and though Aquinas thinks that God can forgive people for their acting wrongly, he thinks that the death of Christ amounts to the bringing about of what is lacking in mere forgiveness: satisfaction. Echoing a famous line of thought to be found in St. Anselm's *Cur Deus Homo* (*Why God Became Man*), Aquinas argues: (1) Sin is an offense against God; (2) For this offense to be properly compensated for, restitution is required, just as it is required when anyone wrongs another; (3) Yet human beings cannot properly make restitution to God since an offense against God is offense against infinite goodness and since people and their actions are finite; (4) God cannot make restitution to God since God is no wrongdoer; (5) Ideally, therefore, for sins against God to be compensated for we need one who is both God and human to make restitution or to satisfy for offenses against God. In Aquinas's own words:

> Someone effectively satisfies for an offense when he or she offers to the one who has been offended something which he or she accepts as matching or outweighing the former offense. Christ, suffering in a loving and obedient spirit, offered more to God than was demanded in recompense for all the sins of people, because first, the love which led him to suffer was a great love; secondly, the life which he laid down by way of satisfaction was of great dignity, since it was the life of God and of a human being.... Christ's passion, then, was not only sufficient but superabundant satisfaction for the sins of human beings.[16]

Notice that Aquinas is not here saying that sinners cannot be brought into a right relationship with God without Christ having suffered a bloody and painful death. As we have seen, he thinks that God can simply forgive sin, and he says enough in the *Summa Theologiae* to show that he does not take the crucifixion of Christ to be inevitable or determined. He does not hold that those who crucified Christ were compelled to do so by God or by anything else. He clearly allows for the possibility that Christ's contemporaries could all have welcomed him with open arms. Recognizing that they did not do so, however, Aquinas views Christ's willingly going to his death as a matter of fidelity to his mission of reconciling humanity and divinity in the circumstances in which he found himself.[17]

We might express this fact by saying that Aquinas sees the death of Christ as representing God's ultimate respect for human freedom. He also sees it as making satisfaction for sin, since he takes Christ in his dying to be offering obedience to God as one who is both divine and human. Unlike some people, Aquinas does not think of Christ's death as appeasing an angry deity craving human pain for wrongs done to it. Nor does he think of Christ's death as a process that automatically guarantees a particular outcome. He does not, for example, think that the death of Christ brings people into union with God whether or not they want such union, whether or not they believe the teachings of Christ that brought him to his cross. So in 3a,49,3, ad.3, he states, "Christ's satisfaction brings about its effect in us in so far as we are incorporated into him as members are into the head."[18] But Aquinas does think of Christ's death as, all things considered, a fitting way of rectifying the distance between God and sinners, a way accomplished by one both divine and human, one who, as such, represents and stands as champion for those who embrace what he embraces.

As we have seen (cf. 3a,8), Aquinas makes much of the idea that Christ is the head of the Church, which can be thought of as his body. In his thinking about the satisfaction achieved by Christ's death, therefore, Aquinas takes Christ to be bringing his followers with him before God as one like them, though also divine. As he says in 3a,46,1, ad.3, "The liberation of human beings through the passion of Christ was consonant with both God's mercy and justice. With justice, because by his passion Christ made satisfaction for the sin of the human race, and human beings were freed through the justice of Christ. With mercy, because human beings by themselves are unable to satisfy for the sin of all human nature."[19] Aquinas views Christ's passion as satisfying in justice and mercy since he takes it to amount to Christ, as both God and human, willingly representing his friends before God insofar as they are sinners.

Aquinas, however, does not simply equate Christ's saving work, his uniting people to God, with his dying in pain. That is because, as I have said, he thinks that the mere fact of the Incarnation amounts to God coming to people as loving them and as wanting them to be in union with God. In other words, Aquinas believes the Incarnation *as such* to be a saving initiative on God's part, one designed to bridge the gulf between God and humanity caused by sin. Developing this point, he argues that human salvation is effected (not mechanically but only as freely accepted by people) by all that Christ was and did in his lifetime and also by his resurrection and ascension. In particular, says Aquinas, human salvation is effected (if embraced by sinners) because Christ by his life and death merits grace for his followers. As head of the Church, Aquinas holds, Christ is at one with his followers, who therefore share in his grace as a human being. He writes: "There is the same relation between Christ's deeds for himself and his members as there is between what another person does in the state of grace and his or her self. Now it is clear that if people in the state of grace suffer for justice's sake, they by that very fact merit salvation for themselves.... Therefore, Christ by his passion merited salvation not only for himself, but for all who are his members, as well" (3a,48,1).[20] Notice, yet again, that Aquinas is presuming that Christ's "members" want what he wants. His point is that only those in a union of heart and mind with Christ share by God's grace his status before God.

21.3 3a,31–59: Some Details

1. On biblical grounds, Aquinas holds that Christ was descended from Adam and the Old Testament figures Abraham and King David. In 3a,31,1 and 2, he argues that this fact was fitting since Christ came to rescue the

human race that is derived from Adam and since both Abraham and David were promised that salvation would come to people through one of their descendants. Aquinas also notes that the genealogies of Christ in the Gospels of Matthew and Luke differ in some ways and that both of them trace Jesus's descent through a line leading down to Joseph, the husband of Mary, though not really the father of Jesus. Contemporary New Testament scholars would generally acknowledge that there are serious and irreconcilable differences between the Matthean and Lukan genealogies, and some people would argue that if Christ's genealogy is traced through Joseph, and if Joseph was not the father of Jesus, then Jesus is not descended from Abraham and David. Aquinas, however, claims that both the Matthean and Lukan genealogies are suitably presented since "all scripture is inspired by God" (2 Timothy 2:16) and since the conflicts between the Matthean and Lukan genealogies can be resolved in various ways (3a,31,3). When it comes to the genealogies tracing Jesus back through Joseph, Aquinas says that Mary was related to Joseph and that Christ can therefore be traced back to David (3a,31,2).

2. Was it appropriate for God to be become incarnate as born of a woman? In 3a,31,4, Aquinas argues that it was. He holds that it was appropriate for a woman to be involved in the event of the Incarnation since Christ came for the benefit of everyone. He goes on in 3a,31,5–6 to insist that no man was directly involved in the conception of Christ since Christ was born of a virgin and since Christ is related to Adam only through Mary.

3. Matthew 1:18 says that "Mary was found to be with child through the Holy Spirit." In 3a,32, Aquinas takes these words to mean that Christ was conceived of the Holy Spirit (3a,32,2), and he argues that it was fitting that this should be so. In Aquinas's view, "the whole Trinity brought about the conception of the body of Christ" (3a,32,1).[21] But, he adds, the Holy Spirit is the love between the Father and the Son and to note that Christ was conceived of the Holy Spirit is a way of reminding ourselves that, as John 3:16 says, the Incarnation "was an outcome of God's supreme love."[22]

4. In keeping with the notion of the Incarnation presented previously in the *Summa Theologiae*, 3a,31–59 frequently argues that Christ, even as human, was seriously different from your average human being. So in 3a,33, for example, Aquinas argues that Christ had a rational soul as soon as he was conceived and that his conception was miraculous. Again, in 3a,34, he holds: (1) that Christ as human had sanctifying grace at his conception (3a,34,1), (2) that Christ was perfect in understanding and will when he was conceived (3a,34,2), and (3) that Christ enjoyed the beatific

vision when he was conceived (3a,34,4). In a similar vein: (1) Christ could have obtained any material advantages he desired (3a,40,3), (2) he was never really able to be tempted against his will (3a,41,1), (3) Christ performed miracles (3a,43–44), (4) Christ was never sick (3a,46,5), and (5) even when dead Christ existed as God (3a,50,3). All of these conclusions are ones that Aquinas, rightly or wrongly, takes to be entailed by his account of the hypostatic union and his reading of the Gospels.

5. One notable example of the way in which Aquinas wishes to distinguish between Christ and other human beings comes in his account of Christ's baptism by John the Baptist (cf. Matthew 3:13–17; Mark 1:9–11; Luke 3:21–22; John 1:29–34). This account is notable since Aquinas maintains that Jesus did not need to be baptized (3a,39,1). Why, then, did Jesus undergo baptism by John? Only, says Aquinas, because he wished to set an example for Christians practicing the rite of baptism and to sanctify water used for Christian baptism.

6. Another notable example of the way in which Aquinas wishes to distinguish between Christ and other human beings comes in his account in 3a,41 of the temptation of Christ by Satan (cf. Matthew 4:1–11; Mark 1:12–13; Luke 4:1–13). Unlike some who have commented on the New Testament testimony to Christ being tempted, Aquinas does not for a moment think of Christ as being temptable. What, therefore, was going on in the temptation of Christ as reported in the New Testament?[23] Aquinas's line is that Christ's temptation was largely a matter of Satan trying to determine who Christ really was. Satan suspected that Christ was God, but was not sure. So he strove to tempt Christ in order to pass from suspicion to certainty, and Christ allowed him to do this "to warn us, so that nobody, however holy, may think himself safe or free from temptation" (3a,41,1).[24] Aquinas distinguishes between temptation on the side of the tempter and temptation on the side of the tempted. One may be tempted because someone or something is trying to lead one astray, or one may be tempted because one is actually drawn to what someone or something is wrongly urging one to do. In Aquinas's view, Christ was tempted in the first sense here, but never in the second (cf. 3a,41,1, ad.3).

7. Appealing again to the notion of fittingness, Aquinas argues that it was fitting that (as the Gospels depict) Christ directed his preaching to Jewish people (3a,42,1). The life and death of Christ is, Aquinas believes, of significance for everyone. Yet he also thinks that, in preaching to Jewish people, Christ was, among other things, fulfilling certain Old Testament expectations and starting with those to whom God had first given divine revelation. Though Aquinas acknowledges that Christ sometimes taught

by means of parables, he stresses that Christ's teaching was delivered publicly and in plain terms that anyone willing to listen to him could understand (3a,42,3). One might wonder why Christ seems to have left us no written account of his teaching and one might feel that he ought to have done so. Confronted by the fact that Christ chose not to write his teaching down, however, Aquinas unsurprisingly holds that this was *conveniens*.

8. Drawing on the Gospels, Aquinas attributes miracles to Christ (3a,43–44). In doing so, however, he develops a line of thought that you might take to be somewhat at odds with what he says earlier in the *Summa Theologiae*. As we have seen, Aquinas thinks that the doctrine of the Incarnation, like the doctrine of the Trinity, is an article of faith, not something philosophically demonstrable. In 3a,43,4, though, he claims that Christ's miracles show that he was divine. "Since the power to work miracles is proper to God alone," he argues, "from any single miracle worked by Christ by his own power it is sufficiently shown that he is God."[25] In support of this conclusion, Aquinas starts from the premise that only God can work miracles. Aquinas then goes on to argue based on biblical grounds and patristic authorities that, as is not the case with miracles associated with people other than Christ, he worked miracles "as though by his own power, and not by praying."[26] And Aquinas notes that Christ claimed to be God, "which teaching, unless it were true, would not be confirmed by miracles worked by divine power."[27] This argument seems to be stating that, because of the miracles attributed to Christ in the Gospels, it would be positively unreasonable not to believe that Christ was divine. Notice, however, that in 3a,43,4, Aquinas is not claiming to offer a formal demonstration of Christ's divinity considered, if you like, as a sort of "Sixth Way" of proving God's existence to be added to the Five Ways in 1a,2,3. He does not speak of demonstration at all in 3a,43,4. He does not even employ the verb *probare* ("to prove").[28] Instead, he relies on the verb *ostendere* (to show) and other Latin words with a similar significance, speaking of Christ's miracles as "showing forth" or "manifesting" his divinity or as being an "argument" for it. He does not speak of Christ's miracles as furnishing us with a scientific proof that Christ is necessarily God.[29] His point seems to be that if one concedes that Christ claimed to be God, and if one concedes that Christ performed miracles, and if one concedes that he did this in his own right and not as someone asking God to perform miracles in answer to his prayers, then one ought to conclude that Christ is God. In 3a,43,4, therefore, Aquinas is not going back on his claim that the articles of faith are not subject to demonstration. This reading of 3a,43,4 seems to accord with what Aquinas says in 3a,43,1 in which he claims that human beings can be

empowered by God to work miracles either (a) to provide divine confirmation of their teaching, should this exceed what can be explicitly proved by human reasoning without divine revelation, or (b) to show that God is present in them by grace. When it comes to Christ's miracles, Aquinas argues in 3a,43,1, these indicate that he was teaching truly and that God was at work in him by grace.[30] Notice also that in 3a,43 in general, and in accord with his notion of faith as believing God, Aquinas seems to think that conversion to belief in Christ as God's Son prompted by miracles is inferior to simply believing God as speaking to us in the person of God incarnate.

9. Reflecting further on Christ's miracles, Aquinas argues in 3a,44 that Christ worked miracles involving every kind of creature. His idea is that, since all things are subject to divine power, it was appropriate that Christ should perform miracles in which different sorts of created things feature: spiritual things such as evil spirits (3a,44,1), heavenly bodies (3a,44,2), human beings (3a,44,3), and non-rational things (3a,44,4). Aquinas goes on to argue that it was also appropriate for Christ to have been witnessed by some of his disciples as bodily transfigured and as appearing gloriously before his death (cf. Matthew 17:1–8; Mark 9:2–8; Luke 9:28–36). Aquinas takes Christ's transfiguration to be a preview of what the life of the resurrected body is like (3a,45,2), and he views it as an encouragement to Christ's followers as they face death, by providing them with some foreknowledge of their end (3a,45,1). "Christ wished to be transfigured in order to show human beings his glory, and to arouse them to a desire of it" (3a,45,3).[31] The transfiguration of Christ reveals something of "the splendour of our future glory" (3a,45,4).[32]

10. Aquinas's account of Christ's birth and life in 3a,27–45 continually stresses how it is directed to the salvation of people. It is not offered as a bald biography but as a biblically based reflection on how human beings are brought to God by means of God incarnate. As I have noted, however, when it comes to human salvation, Aquinas lays special stress on Christ's passion and death. He turns to this explicitly in 3a,46–50, in which the main points he makes, in addition to those noted above, are: (1) Christ being crucified, an especially painful and degrading way to die, both displays the extent of God's love for repentant sinners and teaches us never to fear any form our death might take (3a,46,4–6), even though Christ continued to enjoy the beatific vision during his passion (3a,46,8); (2) Jerusalem was an appropriate place for Christ to die because of the presence there of the Jewish temple, in which sacrifice to God was offered (3a,46,10); (3) Christ, by his divine power, could have disabled his executioners but chose not to do so, thereby indicating that his passion and death were

willed by him and not forced upon him (3a,47,1 and 3); (4) Christ's passion can be thought of as a fulfillment of Old Testament sacrifices since it perfectly unites human beings to God (3a,48,3); (5) It can also be thought of as redemptive since it releases us from the imprisonment of sin (3a,48,4); (6) Christ's passion has a medicinal effect as a cure for sin insofar as it is freely received as such by those wishing to avail themselves of it by following Christ and living as members of his Church (3a,49,1).

11. Even in death the body of Christ was hypostatically united to the Word. That is to say, God was incarnate even in the corpse of Christ (3a,50,2). "Christ's body was not separated from divinity at death.... Just as before his death Christ's flesh was personally and hypostatically united to the Word of God, it continued to be united to the Word after death."[33] On the other hand, Christ was not a human being between crucifixion and resurrection since a corpse is not a human being but only what physically remains after a human being has died (3a,50,4). In 3a,51,1, as also in 3a,52,4 and 53,2, Aquinas emphasizes the fact that Christ was buried since he takes this to indicate that Christ really died and that his resurrection was, therefore, a miracle. He adds that Christ's burial serves as hope for all who die and are buried.

12. In 3a,52, Aquinas writes about Christ's descent into hell between his death and resurrection. He does so because (1) he is aware that various Christian creeds, including the Apostles' Creed and the Athanasian Creed (late fifth or early sixth century), speak of Christ descending into hell, and (2) because he is aware of 1 Peter 3:18–19, which says that after he died, Christ was "made alive in the spirit, in which also he went and made a proclamation to the spirits in prison"—this being the text that gave rise to creedal affirmation concerning Christ's descent into hell. In 3a,52, Aquinas is obviously not thinking of hell as a place below the earth to which Christ went down as in an elevator of some kind. Nor is he thinking of it as whatever we might conceive to be the place or state in which human souls exist as definitively separated from God because of mortal sin. By "those in hell" Aquinas has in mind in 3a,52 those who inherited original sin while being predestined to be united to God in the beatific vision, among whom Aquinas includes Old Testament figures such as Moses.[34]

13. Unsurprisingly, we find Aquinas in 3a,53 waxing eloquent concerning the resurrection of Christ as recorded in all of the Gospels. He sees this as God's final endorsement of all that Christ was about in his life and teaching. He also sees it as confirming Christian faith in Christ's divinity, as giving Christians hope for their own resurrection, as instructing them to live as dead to sin in the hope of glory, and as completing the work

of salvation begun by Christ's birth (3a,53,1). Conscious of biblical texts referring to people other than Christ returning to life after being dead (cf.
Lazarus in John 11), in 3a,53,3, Aquinas insists that the people here in question came back to life with the prospect of death still before them, while
Christ rose from the dead never to die again. And in 3a,54, he lays emphasis on the fact that Christ's resurrection (like, he believes, the general
resurrection to come) was a truly material one involving flesh and blood
and bones (3a,54,3). "It was," he says, "necessary for a true resurrection of
Christ that the same body be once more united to the same soul…[from
which it follows that]…the body of Christ after the resurrection was both
a true body and was of the same nature as before" (3a,54,1).[35] He thinks of
this body as "glorified" and as not subject to corruption or to other limitations that we commonly associate with human bodies as we know them
(3a,54,2), but he insists on its material continuity with the body that Christ
had before death. In 3a,54,4, therefore, he has no problem with John
20:29, which describes the risen Christ as displaying the wounds of his
crucifixion to his disciples after his resurrection. In 3a,56, Aquinas holds
that, as Christians are united to God in the death of Christ, they are united
to God in Christ's resurrection. He means that as members of Christ's
body, Christ's followers are saved by his resurrection as they are saved by
his death. So, he observes, Christ's resurrection "is the model for our
own." "The death of Christ, by which he was deprived of mortal life, is the
cause of the destruction of death on our behalf.…His resurrection, which
began his immortal life, is the cause of the restoration of life in us"
(3a,56,1).[36]

14. The New Testament tells us that after his resurrection Christ ascended into heaven (cf. Luke 24:50–53 and Acts 1:6–11). Commenting on
this fact, Aquinas understands the ascension of Christ as fitting since it
definitively took him out of the world in which corruption is the norm
(3a,57,1).[37] Does Aquinas have a recognizably scientific understanding of
the Ascension? Does he offer a topographical or geographical or astronomical analysis of heaven? No. Unfortunately, you might think, Aquinas does
not claim that we are able to provide a "physics" of the Ascension so as to
locate the ascended Christ and understand how he got to be where he is
now. Instead, he settles for stressing that by virtue of his ascension Christ
was mysteriously, by divine power alone, removed from a place in the
world of perishable things and transferred to a better though still material
state, this implying a genuine change in Christ considered as human, one
that amounted to a move from a corruptible state to one of perfect human
fulfillment with no corruption possible. The ascension, says Aquinas,

"brought about our loss of his bodily presence" while at the same time giving Christians an object of faith considered as belief in what is not seen, a ground for hope for themselves, and a reason to love what is more desirable than physicality as we understand it.

15. By virtue of his ascension, says Aquinas, Christ sits at the "right hand" of God the Father (3a,58) and is judge of the living and the dead (3a,59). You may wonder what talk about God's "right hand" can mean coming from someone who, as we have seen, is clear that God is not a body and that talk suggesting otherwise should be taken figuratively. In 3a,58, though, Aquinas clearly *does* think that to speak of Christ sitting at God's right hand *is* to be construed figuratively. He does not think that the persons of the Trinity occupy thrones and that the Son is literally sitting to the right of the Father. He thinks that Christ sits at the right hand of the Father since he abides in the status and happiness that belong to the Father (and the Holy Spirit) as God, and since he rules with the Father (and the Holy Spirit) as God (3a,58,1). "Christ sits at the right hand of the Father," he says, "because by his divine nature he is equal to the Father and by his human nature he surpasses all other creatures in his possession of divine goods" (3a,58,4). And, Aquinas adds, Christ in heaven is judge of the living and the dead because he is God. Notice, however, that, in accordance with what he has previously been saying in 3a, the picture of Christ as judge that Aquinas intends to convey is not one according to which the first image to come to mind is that of Christ as God condemning. So in 3a,59,3, Aquinas connects Christ's role as judge with his role as meriting salvation for people by his life and death. He says that Christ came to resist injustice while suffering from it and dying in order to rescue people from it according to the will of God, who desires people to be united with divinity and not separate from it.

21.4 *Living Christian Lives*

3a,27–59 is concerned with how God comes to people affected by sin so as to woo them to beatitude by a perfect example of what humanity and divinity amount to when they come together in Christ. In developing this theme, however, Aquinas does not want to say that the life and death of Christ provide us with nothing but an example of how to behave. He does not think that God has chosen to save people from sin just by providing a sinless person for them to emulate. For Aquinas, it is important that Christ is truly divine and that, in Christ, God was truly reconciling people to the perfection of the divine nature by laying on more than an instance of someone acting as God wills and as teaching us accordingly. As we have seen, Aquinas does not believe that the Incarnation is something that secures our reconciliation with God regardless of how we react to Christ. Some theologians writing later than Aquinas have claimed that we are saved or damned by a decree of God and regardless of how we behave, but Aquinas is of quite another mind. He thinks that our salvation or damnation has to make sense in terms of what we are about intentionally. Are we aiming at what is good or are we aiming at what is bad?

As we have seen, the *Secunda Pars* offers a detailed analysis of goodness and badness in human behavior, and the *Secunda Pars* is written by Aquinas because he is convinced that human perfection is not established by God while ignoring what we aim at daily and while switching on a green light above a sign labeled "Entry into Beatitude." The *Secunda Pars* offers us a crucial insight into Aquinas's conception of what beatitude means. It shows us that Aquinas takes us to come to beatitude (if we do indeed do so) as human beings with particular goals, not as individuals with respect to which God simply says, "Forget what you are and I shall wave a wand and save you regardless." In various writings, Aquinas holds that grace perfects nature and does not abolish it. He means that we are not saved in spite of ourselves but because by God's grace we want the goodness that God is.

So Aquinas thinks that how we live our lives and what we aim at when doing so is what we bring before God as finally judging us. He also thinks that since we live after the death of Christ, there are certain practices instituted by Christ that help us to conform to what he was about. He takes these to be the sacraments of the Christian Church, to which he proceeds in 3a,60–90, and to which I shall turn next.

The Sacraments of the Christian Church (3a,60–90)

RIGHT BEFORE THE start of 3a,60, Aquinas writes: "Now that we have completed our consideration of the mysteries of the incarnate Word, our next field of investigation is the sacraments of the Church, seeing that it is from this same incarnate Word that these derive their efficacy."[1] By "sacraments" here Aquinas is thinking of the seven sacraments subsequently listed by the Second Council of Basel (1431–1435) and the Council of Trent (1545–1563). These are baptism, confirmation, Eucharist, penance, extreme unction, holy orders, and matrimony. That there are *just* these seven sacraments was not defined by the Church in Aquinas's day, but there was even then a general understanding that there are only these seven sacraments. St. Augustine, whose sacramental theology greatly influenced Aquinas, did not specify that there are exactly seven sacraments. However, theologians later than Augustine, the most influential being Peter Lombard, frequently spoke of there being seven.[2]

Writing before Reformation debates about sacraments, Aquinas assumes that there are seven sacraments and that all of them were instituted by Christ. Why, though, does he think that they should be of interest to Christians in general? What does he mean by the word *sacrament* and what place does he think sacraments should have in the lives of Christians?[3]

22.1 Sacraments in General

The word *sacrament* derives from the Latin term *sacramentum*, which originally meant a "promise," "oath," or "pledge" by which one formally entered into some position, service, or responsibility. By the time of St. Augustine, however, *sacramentum* was being used to refer to Christian rites, which is how Aquinas chiefly employs the word. For him, the sacraments are particular rites or rituals celebrated by believers within the Church. More specifically, they are rites by which Christ's followers are conformed to Christ and benefit from his life, death, and resurrection. By means of them, thinks Aquinas, people grow in grace and benefit from the presence of the Holy Spirit given to dwell in them. In short, sacraments are physical rites or actions by which the saving work of Christ is applied to, or bears fruit in, the lives of his followers considered as members of a society established by him.

Some Christians have taken the view that Christian sacraments are essentially symbolic, that they amount only to an acting out of some Christian truth, and Aquinas frequently refers to sacraments as "signs" (*signa*).[4] But he does not think that sacraments are signs because they simply symbolize something or represent it. He takes them to be signs insofar as they are physical processes that actually effect or bring about the grace they signify, namely the union of people with God, the presence in them of the Holy Spirit.

At one level, Aquinas believes, sacraments certainly symbolize, and do so because of the natural symbolic meaning of the rituals associated with them. Hence, for example, he takes baptism with water to symbolize coming to be cleansed from sin because of the connection we commonly make between water and cleansing. At the same time, however, he also thinks that the sacrament of baptism actually does cleanse people from sin, including original sin, and he thinks something similar about the respective symbolism and efficacy of all the sacraments.[5] His view is that in the sacraments, God shows us what he does and does what he shows us.[6] So he observes, "The very fact that the term 'sacrament' signifies the reality which sanctifies means that it should signify the effect produced" (3a,60,3, ad.2).[7]

Standing behind this idea is the view that the primary sacrament (though not one of the seven) is Christ.[8] As we have seen, Aquinas takes Christ to be literally divine and not something that just reflects what God is in some way. Aquinas will therefore say that "the sacraments derive their power from Christ" and that their being able to play a role in our salvation should be thought to "flow from the divinity of Christ through his humanity into the actual sacraments" (3a,62,5).[9] The incarnate Word is, for Aquinas, part of the physical world drawing us (if we want it) to union with God. In a similar way, thinks Aquinas, sacraments are physical processes by which people are truly brought closer to God, processes through which they acquire grace and head for the beatific vision.[10]

Aquinas is quite clear that one can receive grace without getting involved with the rituals used in the celebration of Christian sacraments. "The Passion of Christ," he bluntly says, "is the sufficient cause of the salvation of people" (3a,61,1, ad.3).[11] But, Aquinas adds, "It does not follow on this account, that the sacraments are not necessary for human salvation, for they produce their effects in virtue of the Passion of Christ, and it is the Passion of Christ which is, in a certain manner, applied to people through the sacraments."[12] Aquinas, of course, believes that, though the saving work of Christ took place in the past, Christ's followers live after his ascension. So, he thinks, God has provided them with means to render Christ's saving work effective in them as time goes on. As Timothy McDermott puts it, Aquinas's view is that "each sacrament is a moment in my human life on this earth, a moment which develops the identification of my individual life with the saving life of Christ, and so at the same time marks my individual life as a continuation of that saving life."[13]

Notice, however, that Aquinas's overall thinking on the sacraments is not individualistic. In 3a, he refers to "the sacraments of the church" rather than "my sacraments" or "the sacraments of Fred or Mary or whoever," and he does so because he takes sacraments to be what Christians have as the Church, considered as the body of Christ. Aquinas's teaching on sacraments in 3a is part of his ecclesiology, his view of the Church. Conscious of the fact that we are human beings who typically flourish best in society, Aquinas thinks of sacraments as being there for Christians to help them to do just that. He takes individual salvation typically to take place in the context of the society that Christ left behind, the Church, and he takes this society to have inherited from Christ certain physical ways by which to be united to God. His view is that, just as the Incarnation was a physical way by which Christ's followers are saved, sacraments are physical ways in which they grow into God or God comes to be in them. According to Aquinas, the sacraments bind Christians together as members of the body of Christ and, in this sense, make the Church to be what it is: God's instrument for bringing human beings to union with God by conforming them to what God is all about.

One may wonder whether there might not be something equivalent for people who do not belong to what Aquinas took the Christian Church to be. For what about people of non-Christian religions such as Buddhism or Hinduism? Questions like these, however, spring from theology as it is engaged in today rather than as it was engaged in by Aquinas. Aquinas was certainly aware of there being non-Christian religions. As I have already said, he was, for example, very aware of Judaism and Islam. As I have also said, though, Aquinas knew little or nothing about Buddhism or Hinduism or Jainism, Shinto, Confucianism, and so on. His approach to sacraments, therefore, is definitely not an exercise in theology of world religions. Its focus is austerely Christian, and its main claim is that, whatever else God chooses to do by virtue of his omnipotence and mercy, God has definitely instituted certain practices by which the followers of Christ can benefit from his saving life and death.

In 3a,61,3, with things like the Old Testament sacrificial system in mind, Aquinas says that there were sacraments before the birth of Christ. He calls these the "sacraments of the Old Law" (cf. 1a2ae,98–105), and he thinks of them as sacraments because he takes them to have signified ways in which God connected with people in order to make them favorable to God. Yet he does not take the "sacraments of the Old Law" to be sacraments in the way that those of the "New Law" are sacraments. He views them as only pointing forward to the genuine article, so to speak, and he takes the genuine article to be the sacraments of the Church, established by Christ for the benefit of those explicitly believing in him.

Just as he regards the Incarnation to involve God speaking to us at a particular time and in a particular way and as bringing people to God on that basis, Aquinas views the sacraments of the Church as God's way of bringing people to God after the death of Christ in a particular way chosen by God from eternity. As far as I can see, Aquinas believes this way to be necessary for human salvation. In saying so, my point is that Aquinas does not seem to conceive of there being serious alternatives to what the sacraments are and effect. I might get myself from England to France by taking a boat or a train or a plane, but Aquinas does not seem to think that I might make use of something other than the sacraments so as to get myself to God. That is because he takes the sacraments to be specific ways that Christ has established for people, as members of his body, to share in his bringing people to the beatific vision.

In other words, insofar as Aquinas's thinking about sacraments in 3a is individualistic, it is so because it is grounded in the thought that the Word of God became incarnate in Christ, an individual man, and that this fact needs to be reckoned with by all Christian theologians, even those eager to accommodate the teaching of religions other than Christianity. Aquinas views the Incarnation as something that occurred in history, and he takes it to be *the* way in which God has revealed to human beings what God is and how to be in union with God. So he takes the Incarnation to have historical implications for those living after the birth of Christ, implications concerning what they should do as followers of Christ, and his teaching on the sacraments springs from this fact. Aquinas's idea is that Christ's obedient followers are, in fact, saved by a particular figure in history and that their relationship to this figure, while believing him to be God, is something to be played out in time sacramentally and with reference to him.[14]

22.2 *What Sacraments Are (3a,60)*

The notion of sacraments as signs is developed in 3a,60, where Aquinas quotes St. Augustine saying that a sacrament is a "sacred sign" of something "invisible."[15] Drawing on the concept of analogy as expounded in 1a,13, Aquinas is happy to think of "sacrament" as a term that can be used analogically to speak of a "sacred secret" or of something related to what is sacred as its cause or sign or in some other way.[16] For the purposes of his discussion of the sacraments of the Church, however, Aquinas settles on the idea that a sacrament relates to the sacred by being a sign.

Presumably with a view to his claim that there were sacraments of the Old Law, Aquinas argues in 3a,60,2 that "every sign of a sacred reality is a sacrament."[17] He says, "The term 'sacrament' is properly applied to that which is a sign of some sacred reality pertaining to people; or...it is applied to that which is a sign of sacred reality inasmuch as it has the property of sanctifying people."[18] However, Aquinas quickly goes on in 3a,60,3 to narrow down the meaning of "sacrament" to specifically Christian celebrations. Christian sanctification, he argues, comes about by virtue of the passion of Christ (the "cause" of sanctification), by virtue of grace and the theological virtues (the "form" of sanctification), and by virtue of eternal life (the "end" of the saved), and the sacraments, as Aquinas is concerned with them, involve this cause, form, and end. "As signs," he says, "the sacraments stand for all of these." He goes on to observe: "A sign as sacrament has a threefold function. It is at once commemorative of that which has gone before, namely the passion of Christ, and demonstrative of that which is brought about in us through the passion of Christ, namely grace, and prognostic, i.e., a foretelling of future glory."[19]

In 3a,60,4–8, Aquinas homes in on the physical aspect of sacraments. He takes sacraments to be rituals involving physical human beings using physical things while employing certain words, and he sees God's wisdom at work in this fact because he thinks that God "provides for each reality according to its condition."[20] In 3a,60,2, Aquinas notes that "it is characteristic of people that they achieve an awareness of things which they do not know through things which they do know."[21] In 3a,60,4, he draws on this notion so as to argue:

> It is connatural to people to arrive at a knowledge of intelligible realities through sensible ones, and a sign is something through which a person arrives at knowledge of some further thing beyond itself. Moreover, the sacred realities signified by the sacraments are certain spiritual and intelligible goods by which people are sanctified. And the consequence of this fact is that the function of the sacrament as signifying is implemented by means of some sensible realities. The case here is similar to that in the holy Scriptures where, in order to describe spiritual realities to us, corresponding sensible realities are used to illustrate them.[22]

So Aquinas thinks it matters which things and words are used in the celebration of sacraments. In his view, sacraments are not just any old way of worshiping God. They are provided by God for our sanctification, and the way they should be celebrated comes from the way in which they have been instituted by God in the teachings of Christ. For Aquinas, therefore, it is important that, say, baptism be celebrated using water and using a linguistic formula meaning the equivalent of "I baptize you in the name of the Father and of the Son and of the Holy Spirit" construed in terms of what Aquinas takes to be orthodox teaching concerning the doctrines of the Trinity and the Incarnation (3a,60,6–8; cf. 3a,66,5).

22.3 The Need for Sacraments (3a,61)

As we have seen, Aquinas thinks that God can bring people to beatitude without the Incarnation, let alone the sacraments of the Church. But in the light of the fact that (as he believes) God saves people through the Incarnation and sacraments, Aquinas thinks that sacraments are necessary.

He is clear that sacraments were not needed before Adam sinned since they amount to a remedy for sin and a means of perfecting human beings, while Adam in Paradise was without sin and fully in tune with God (3a,61,2; cf. 1a,95,3). He is equally clear, though, that sacraments are needed given the fact of sin insofar as they amount to a remedy for sin—insofar as they serve to unite us to God given our sinful nature. Aquinas's position is that of the New Testament—that salvation from sin comes through Christ—and his thinking about the necessity of sacraments springs from this belief. He takes sacraments to be necessary if we are to share in Christ's work of redemption. I say "share in Christ's work of redemption" since, as we have seen, Aquinas does not take the life and death of Christ to have an automatic effect on people when it comes to their redemption. He thinks that we need to accept Christ and repent of our sins in order to benefit from Christ's work. Aquinas believes that I do not teach you unless you learn because of me (cf. 1a,8,1–2). In a similar way, his account of redemption by Christ depends on the idea that the work of Christ only takes effect as people receive it by wanting it and by acting and choosing accordingly.

It is at this point in his discussion of sacraments that Aquinas (3a,61,3) alludes to the sacraments of the Old Law. He writes:

> Sacraments are necessary for the salvation of people inasmuch as they constitute certain sensible signs of invisible things by which people are sanctified. Now, no one can be sanctified after sinning except through Christ....This is why it was right that before Christ's coming there should be visible signs which people could use to attest to their faith in

the future coming of the saviour. Now it is signs of this kind that we call sacraments.[23]

Having said this, however, Aquinas stresses that Old Testament sacraments merely prefigured or anticipated the Christian ones. Following the death of Christ, he argues, Christians are able to identify explicitly with the cause of human salvation (Christ) and to live their lives in the Church he established, whose members have ways of becoming holy through the sacraments of the Church, unknown to the saints of the Old Testament period. He says:

> Just as the fathers of old were saved through faith in the Christ who was to come, so we too are saved through faith in the Christ who has already been born and suffered. Now sacraments are the sort of signs in which the faith by which people are justified is explicitly attested, and it is right to have different signs for what belongs to the past, the present, or the future.... Hence it is right that in addition to the sacraments of the Old Law which foretold realities that lay in the future there are certain other sacraments of the New Law to stand for realities which have taken place in Christ in the past.[24]

Aquinas emphatically asserts that sacraments belong to the present time. The time of the New Law, he says, comes between the time of the Old Law and the state of glory "in which every truth will be made manifest fully and absolutely in itself." So Aquinas thinks that there are no sacraments in heaven (3a,61,4, ad.1). In 3a,61,1, however, Aquinas presents three reasons for thinking of the sacraments as things that we need in this life.

The first amounts to the point that we are physical things. "It is," says Aquinas, "appropriate that in bestowing certain aids to salvation upon people the divine wisdom should make use of certain physical and sensible signs called the sacraments."

The second concerns the fact that, as sinful creatures, we have a yearning for or addiction to physical things. We are lovesick for material realities. So says Aquinas, "It was appropriate for God to apply spiritual medicine to people by means of certain physical signs. For if people were to be confronted with spiritual realities pure and unalloyed, their minds, absorbed as they are in physical things, would be incapable of accepting them."

The third has to do with what we like to do. We like to engage in physical activities, and this need of ours is met by the sacraments of the Church, which provide us with engaging ways to worship God. Here, I think, Aquinas is acknowledging that people in general love rituals or ceremony of some kind and that the sacraments provide us with good and saving rituals rather than ones that lead us away from God.[25]

Aquinas sums up the above line of argument as follows:

> Through the sacraments, therefore, sensible things are used to instruct people in a manner appropriate to their nature. They are humbled by being brought to recognize their subjection to physical things, seeing that they have to rely upon them for the help they need. At the same time they are preserved by the health-giving practices made available to them in the sacraments from various kinds of harm in the physical order.[26]

It is not Aquinas's view that sacraments unite us to God simply considered as physical processes. He agrees with St. Paul that physical activities are of little profit for our salvation, and he agrees that it is only God's grace that makes us holy. He also agrees that the passion of Christ wipes sins away. At the same time, though, he takes the physical processes involved in celebrating sacraments to be more than physical because of their significance, just as he takes the death of Christ to be more than a physical event because of its significance. And while he is convinced that it is by grace given to us by God that we are holy, Aquinas thinks that grace comes to us as we act, think, and live in certain ways. When it comes to the passion of Christ and the sacraments, Aquinas's view is that the sacraments are there precisely to allow us to be graced by the passion of Christ.[27]

22.4 The Sacraments and Grace (3a,62)

The topic of grace and the sacraments comes to the foreground in 3a,62, where Aquinas repeats the point that sacraments bring people to share in the saving death of Christ. "In a special way," he says, "the sacraments of the Church derive their power from the passion of Christ" (3a,62,5).[28] The sacraments bring about grace in those who celebrate them, thinks Aquinas, and do so as related to Christ's passion and the eternal life of Christ's followers. But why should Aquinas think that sacraments cause grace? And how does he think that they do so?

Given what we have seen of his teaching on grace (chapter 14), it seems clear that Aquinas is not bound to conclude that having grace depends on celebrating Christian sacraments. That is because he takes grace (sanctifying grace, at any rate) to be God's drawing people to share in the divine life to some extent, and because there seems to be no logical connection between

God doing this and people engaging in certain rituals. Aquinas, however, does think that the sacraments of the New Law "cause grace in some way," and that is because he thinks of the sacraments historically—as being instituted by Christ as means by which his followers can come to share in his life and death according to their purpose in God's scheme for drawing sinners to beatitude. "Through the sacraments of the New Law," he argues, "people are incorporated into Christ.... But people are not made members of Christ except through grace" (3a,62,1).[29] Adherence to Christ, which Aquinas takes to include celebrating sacraments, is always a matter of acting as the recipient of grace.

Again, though, in what sense can sacraments be thought of as causally efficacious? Aquinas cannot think of them as being agent causes like agent causes in the physical universe. He cannot think that, say, the water used in baptism cleanses us from sin as automatically as it washes away dirt. Such a view would commit Aquinas to a magical or mechanistic view of sacramental rites, one that would appear to suggest that one can ensure grace for oneself just by engaging in certain physical practices. On the other hand, Aquinas does not want to think of sacraments as mere tokens of what God is doing alongside them being celebrated. He thinks that the grace received by celebrating sacraments is connected to their being celebrated, as he thinks that the salvation brought about by Christ's passion is connected to Christ actually dying. In other words, Aquinas denies that sacraments are mere signs of grace.

So he goes on to appeal to the notion of instrumental causality. I might causally bring about an effect by using some tool or instrument. Thus, for example, I might clean my bathtub by washing it with a brush. Here, so we may say, the brush is an instrument of mine in cleaning the bathtub. At one level, of course, it makes sense to say that brushes do not clean anything. Brushes are not capable of intentionally bringing it about that something is clean. It is people who clean bathtubs by means of brushes. Still, brushes are instrumentally causal when people use them deliberately to clean bathtubs, and, Aquinas thinks, sacraments can be thought of as instrumentally causing grace by being particular means by which God has decreed that people should receive grace. So he reasons: (1) God can cause someone to have grace just because God is God and intrinsically has the power to do so, but (2) God can also cause grace by means of the sacraments considered as God's instruments in causing grace. He writes:

> The principal cause produces its effect in virtue of its form, to which that effect is assimilated, as fire warms in virtue of its own heat. Now it

belongs to God to produce grace in this way as its principal cause.... An instrumental cause, on the other hand, acts not in virtue of its own form, but solely in virtue of the impetus imparted to it by the principal agent. Hence the effect has a likeness not to the instrument, but rather to that principal agent.... And it is in this way that the sacraments of the New Law cause grace. For it is by divine institution that they are conferred upon people for the precise purpose of causing grace in and through them (3a,62,1; cf. 3a,62,4).[30]

Yes, thinks Aquinas, sacramental rites cannot on their own bring about grace, but such rites have causal efficacy when considered as instruments of God. Aquinas therefore takes the rites to be necessary for grace given that God is using them to impart grace. On this account, the sacraments are neither merely symbolic nor redundant. They are "causes and signs at the same time."[31]

Do sacraments impart grace over and above the grace that is had by those with supernatural virtues and the gifts of the Holy Spirit? Aquinas thinks that they must, otherwise Christ would not have bothered to institute them. They are there, he thinks, for a purpose given that we live in time and given that Christ's followers live as graced in God's Church. "The sacraments," he says, "are designed to achieve certain special effects which are necessary in the Christian life" (3a,62,2).[32] "Sacramental grace adds something over and above grace as commonly defined, and also above the virtues and the gifts, namely a special kind of divine assistance to help in attaining the end of the sacrament concerned" (3a,62,2).[33] I might generally cherish you, but I would be doing something more, though along the same lines, if I help you to pass an exam or get well from an illness. By the same token, Aquinas seems to think, God, though gracing some people in general, can do more for them as they live their particular Christian lives.

22.5 Character as an Effect of Sacraments (3a,63)

Aquinas's view is that grace is the chief effect of sacraments. However, he also thinks that some (and only some) sacraments confer a "character" (*character*) or "sign" (*signum*) upon people.

A remote source of his thinking here lies in the Roman practice of tattooing or branding slaves and soldiers with a mark indicating that they belonged to or owed allegiance to someone in particular. By their branding, the soldiers or slaves were permanently signed as having a status with respect to someone superior to them. *My* branded soldier or slave was *my* soldier or slave, not *yours*—a notion possibly echoed by New Testament texts such as Ephesians 4:30 and Revelation 7:3.

A less remote source of Aquinas's thinking on sacramental character lies in the view attacked by St. Augustine that sacraments cannot be validly cele-brated by people who are sinful or in some way unworthy. Suppose you have a priest who is not in a state of grace, and suppose that this priest baptizes people and presides over the public celebration of the Eucharist. Are we to think that the sinfulness of the priest means that those he baptized were not really baptized? Are we to think that the sinfulness of the priest means that the Eucharist he presided over was a sham or fake? In answer to questions like these, Augustine replied no. His line was that priests, whether holy or sinful, validly preside over genuine sacraments because they are priests—the impli-cation being that the sacrament of holy orders gives ordained priests a status in the Church that cannot be removed because of faults they commit.[34]

Writing with this background in mind, Aquinas (quoting 1 Corinthians 1:21–22) says that some sacraments impart character considered as "a certain kind of sign." They permanently mark people out in some way. The sacraments of the New Law are, he thinks, "designed to produce two effects, namely to act as a remedy against sin and to bring the soul to its fullness in things pertaining to the worship of God in terms of the Christian life as a ritual expression of this" (3a,63,1).[35] He goes on to say:

> It has been customary that whenever people are deputed to some defi-nite function they are marked off for it by means of some sign. Thus in ancient times it was usual for soldiers on enlistment for military service to be marked by some form of physical "character" in recognition of the fact that they were deputed for some function in the physical sphere. In the same way, therefore, when in the sacraments people are deputed for some function in the spiritual sphere pertaining to the worship of God, it naturally follows that as believers they are marked off by some form of spiritual character.[36]

Aquinas holds that sacramental character is given for the purpose of deput-ing people "to receive or to hand on to others the things pertaining to the worship of God" (3a,63,3).[37] He also assumes that sacramental character comes only with baptism, confirmation, and holy orders (3a,63,6). Baptism and confirmation, he says, empower one to receive other sacraments. Holy orders empower one to confer sacraments on others (3a,63,6). And he takes sacramental character to be something permanent or indelible (3a,63,5), not something lost by sins subsequently committed by those who receive it.

Aquinas, therefore, explicitly denies that sinful priests cannot validly celebrate sacraments (3a,64,5). In his view, sacramental character is a kind of office or ecclesial status, not a state of holiness. In 3a,63,2, he describes it as an instrumental "power" (*potentia*) "ordered to those things which pertain to divine worship."[38]

Aquinas also takes sacramental character to impart to the faithful "a certain kind of participation in the priesthood of Christ deriving from Christ himself" (3a,63,3; cf. 3a,63,5).[39] Character, he says, "is a kind of seal by which something is marked off as ordained to some end."[40] And there are two ends to which people of faith are ordained: the enjoyment of glory and the reception or handing on to others of what pertains to the worship of God. Putting these ideas together with the claim that Christians are members of Christ's body, and the view that the rites of the Christian religion derive from the priesthood of Christ, Aquinas concludes that all Christians share in Christ's priesthood simply by virtue of baptism. In 1 Peter 2:9 we read: "But you are a chosen race, a royal priesthood, a holy nation, God's own people." Aquinas does not quote this verse in 3a,63,3 or 63,5, but he clearly does want to say that all Christians share in Christ's priesthood. Unlike some Christians later than his time, however, he does not want to construe this conclusion as implying that there is not a genuine sacrament of holy orders conferring a status not had by all Christians. For Aquinas, the notion of all Christians sharing in Christ's priesthood is grounded in the notion that salvation comes from being at one with Christ in his saving work.

22.6 Causes of Sacraments (3a,64)

Given what I have just been explaining, you will realize that Aquinas takes sacraments and the grace they bring to derive from God. But given his insistence that sacraments bring about what they signify and that they involve rites, Aquinas also wants to say that people who administer them are causally involved in bringing about their effects. It is not, thinks Aquinas, that the grace received in a sacrament comes from the minister of the sacrament acting alone. But, says Aquinas, sacramental grace does come via ministers of sacraments, worthy or unworthy, acting as instruments of God (3a,64,1 and 2).

Aquinas does not deny that sinful ministers who administer sacraments act irreverently toward God and do wrong. He actually thinks that they sin gravely (3a,64,6). However, the sacraments they administer are valid since "an instrument acts not in virtue of its own form but through the power of the one by whom it is moved... [so,] it makes no difference to the instrument as instrument what form or power it may have over and above that which is required to give it its very nature as an instrument" (3a,64,5; cf. 3a,64,9).[41]

On the other hand, says Aquinas, ministers of sacraments can fail to celebrate them validly if they do not intend to celebrate them validly—if they do not intend to do what the Church has in mind concerning the celebration of sacraments and the manner in which they are to be celebrated (3a,64,8). His point here is best expressed by what he says while taking baptism as an example. He writes:

> The actions performed in the sacraments can be performed with various aims in view. Thus the act of washing with water, which takes place in Baptism, can be aimed at physical cleanliness or physical health, or be done in play, and there are many other reasons of this kind why this action should be performed. And because of this it is necessary to isolate and define the one purpose for which the action of washing is performed in baptism, and this is done through the intention of the minister. This intention in turn is expressed in the words pronounced in the sacraments, as when the minister says *I baptise you in the name of the Father* etc.[42]

In short, Aquinas thinks that sacraments are validly administered by ministers empowered to preside over them who intend to do what the Church means to do by celebrating the sacraments.

22.7 *Baptism (3a,66–71)*

When starting to write 3a, Aquinas intended to consider all of the Christian sacraments and then to turn to "the goal of life without end that we attain through Christ by our resurrection."[43] But the *Summa Theologiae* breaks off just a few questions into a discussion of the sacrament of penance. Still, Aquinas left us those questions, as well as a full discussion of baptism, confirmation, and the Eucharist. Much of that discussion reiterates points made by him in 3a,60–65, but it also advances a number of new claims. With respect to baptism, the main ones are as follows.

1. Baptism removes all sin, both original sin and individual sin committed in a person's lifetime. It makes its recipients beneficiaries of Christ's passion (3a,69,1) and also does away with the need for any punishment due to sin (3a,69,2). It is no magic cure for human ailments to which people after the fall of Adam are heirs (3a,69,3), but it does confer grace to those who by baptism become members of Christ's body (3a,69,4–8).
2. Water is essential to the celebration of baptism (3a,66,3–4) as are formulae used in validly celebrating the sacrament (3a,66,5 and 10). How much

water? Any amount (3a,66,7–8). However, we may analogically speak of "baptism by blood" and "baptism by desire." In the first, someone unbaptized sheds his or her blood in fidelity to Christ. In the second, someone knowing nothing of baptism or unable to be baptized is conformed to Christ by love and sorrow for sin. Baptism by blood and baptism by desire give one all the effects of baptism apart from its sacramental character. So they remove sin and give grace, though people "baptized" in this way should, if they survive and are able to, subsequently be formally baptized with water (3a,66,11).

3. The minister of baptism is normally a priest or bishop (3a,67,1–2). As needed, however, anyone (male, female, young, old, or even unbaptized) can baptize another person (3a,67,3–5).

4. "All are bound to be baptized and without it no one can be saved" (3a,68,1).[44] Aquinas's "proof text" here is John 3:5: "Jesus answered, 'Very truly, I tell you, no one can enter the kingdom of God without being born of water and Spirit.'" Whatever the author of John 3:5 had in mind, Aquinas's conclusion in 3a,68,1 seems somewhat sweeping, though he softens it slightly by saying that there were those before Christ who, though not baptized, were incorporated into Christ through faith in his future coming. Aquinas, however, is also clear that after the coming of Christ, salvation comes only through faith in Christ, which Aquinas takes to involve at least a desire for baptism (3a,68,2). "Those who are neither baptized nor wish to be baptized," he says, "cannot attain salvation because they are neither sacramentally nor intentionally incorporated into Christ through whom alone salvation is possible." But "desire for Baptism which comes from faith working through love" can "inwardly sanctify" someone since "the power of God is not restricted to visible sacraments."[45]

5. Given the importance of baptism, human beings should be baptized as quickly as possible (3a,68,3). Yet it would be wrong to baptize children below the age of reason who are born to Jewish parents or other non-Christians who do not wish them to be baptized. Those with the use of reason can decide for themselves whether to be baptized, but forcing baptism on children without the use of reason against the will of their parents is unjust (3a,68,10).

22.8 Confirmation (3a,72)

Over many centuries, the sacrament of confirmation has been celebrated in liturgically different ways by Eastern and Western Christians. In 3a,72, Aquinas writes about confirmation with little reference to this diversity. He talks about confirmation only as celebrated in the West during his time, and he has sometimes been taken to task for doing so.[46] He also takes sides on a debate current in his day concerning whether or not the sacrament of confirmation was instituted by Christ—contrary to people such as St. Bonaventure, Aquinas says in 3a,72,1, ad.1 that it had to be. In large part, though, his treatment of confirmation accords with his views about sacraments in general.

Thus, for example, Aquinas takes confirmation to be a natural stage in a Christian's growing in grace as a member of Christ's body since it celebrates a mature embracing of Christ's grace (3a,72,1) and gives grace to continue to embrace it (3a,72,5). He says, "As Baptism is a spiritual generation into Christian life, so Confirmation is a spiritual growth bringing people to spiritual maturity."[47] More specifically, Aquinas takes confirmation to give Christians "power for engaging in the spiritual battle against the enemies of the faith."[48] I presume that in saying this, Aquinas does not mean that confirmation automatically turns people into articulate theologians or philosophers. His idea seems to be that confirmation, by virtue of its character, marks one out as a spokesperson for Christ and, if received and continually acted on in faith, hope, and charity, can aid one to be just such a spokesperson as God sees fit (cf. what Aquinas says about courage in 2a2ae,123).

22.9 The Eucharist (3a,73–83)

Aquinas regards the Eucharist as the greatest sacrament. It is, he says, "the summit of the spiritual life and all the sacraments are ordered to it" (3a,73,3).[49] He writes in this way because he takes reception of the Eucharist by Christians to be the receiving of Christ himself as given to his followers for their salvation. Just as baptism and confirmation bring one to Christian birth and to maturity as a Christian, so the Eucharist, thinks Aquinas, nourishes one as a member of the Church. In 3a,73,1, he refers to the Eucharist as "spiritual food" and "spiritual refreshment."[50] In 3a,73,4, he speaks of it as commemorating the passion of Christ and as pointing to "the unity of the Church."[51] The Eucharist, he adds, also "prefigures that enjoyment of God which will be ours in Heaven" since "it keeps us on the way to Heaven" and "really contains Christ, who is full of grace."[52]

In approaching the Eucharist in this way, Aquinas is working from the view that Christ is truly present in the Eucharist and truly received by people when they consume it. Many Christian thinkers have defended a purely symbolic approach to the Eucharist—their idea being that the bread and wine used in the Eucharist merely represent Christ or stand for him somehow as, say, a flag might be thought to represent or stand for a country.[53] Or they have said that the Eucharist reminds us of Christ and allows us to witness to him. Aquinas, however, firmly rejects these ways of thinking.

"We could," he says, "never know by our senses that the real body of Christ and his blood are in this sacrament." But we know this "by our faith which is based on the authority of God" (3a,75,1).[54] In Aquinas's view, that Christ's body and blood are truly present in the Eucharist was taught by Christ himself, and to think of the Eucharist in merely symbolic or memorial terms is "contrary to the words of Christ."[55] In this sacrament, "we have the reality of Christ's body." In this sacrament, "the complete substance of the bread is converted into the complete substance of Christ's body, and the complete substance of the wine into the complete substance of Christ's blood" (3a,75,4).[56]

Aquinas grounds his thinking about the Eucharist on Matthew 26:26, Mark 14:22, and Luke 22:19. Preferring, as is usual with him, to read Scripture firstly in a literal sense, Aquinas takes these texts to mean that, at his last meal with his disciples before his death, Christ instituted the sacrament of the Eucharist while teaching that it is really his body and blood that is received in the sacrament. So in 3a,75,2, Aquinas argues that the words of consecration used when the Eucharist is celebrated ("This is my body" and so on) would just not be true on a symbolic understanding of the Eucharist, which Aquinas takes to hold that the substance of bread and wine remain present throughout the entire celebration of the Eucharist.

Aquinas maintains that after the words of consecration have been said by ministers who preside over the celebration of the Eucharist, there is *no* bread and *no* wine left. There is only the body and blood of Christ given to people for their salvation, every bit as much as it was given to them in the Incarnation. In holding to this view, Aquinas is not suggesting that when people receive the Eucharist they mangle Christ with their teeth. They mangle the appearances of bread and wine, he insists, but not the glorified Christ. How so? Because, says Aquinas, what is left of the bread and wine after the words of consecration are accidents that do not inhere in a substance.

That teaching of Aquinas is part of his claim that we should think of what happens in the celebration of the Eucharist as a unique case of transubstantiation. However, before I turn to that notion as developed by Aquinas, I should note some other things that he says about the Eucharist in general. Thus:

1. Aquinas does not say that reception of the Eucharist is necessary for people to be saved, as he takes baptism to be. Though Aquinas views the Eucharist as signifying "the unity of the mystical body of Christ which is an absolute requisite for salvation," and though he thinks of the Eucharist as the most

excellent of sacraments, he also holds that the Eucharist is not needed "for basic Christian living" (3a,73,3).[57] He means that baptism saves whether or not those who have been baptized go on to receive the Eucharist.

2. Aquinas takes the Eucharist to have been instituted by Christ before his death, and with this thought in mind he thinks of it as Christ's way of being present to his followers even though absent from them in obvious respects. So in 3a,73,5, he argues that "at the moment of his departure from his disciples in his natural presence, Christ left himself among them in sacramental presence" (3a,73,5).[58]

3. Since Aquinas thinks of Christ's death as a sacrifice, he also thinks of the Eucharist as a sacrifice in that he takes Christ, the crucified savior, to be given to people by means of it, and he takes the sacrificial aspect of the Eucharist to be prefigured in various Old Testament texts (3a,73,6).

4. Aquinas is emphatic that receiving the Eucharist brings grace to people who receive it worthily since it brings God to them. So in 3a,79,1, he says, "Just as by coming visibly into the world he brought the life of grace into it (cf. John 1:17), so by coming to people sacramentally he causes the life of grace (cf. John 6:58)."[59] Aquinas adds that by worthily receiving Christ in the Eucharist, Christians share in the effects of his passion (3a,79,2).[60] He even (you might think surprisingly) argues (3a,79,3) that receiving the Eucharist can forgive someone's sin even when the person in question "is in mortal sin, though not conscious of it or attached to it" as long as the person in question approaches the sacrament "reverently and devoutly" even if beforehand not being "sufficiently contrite."[61]

Now to Aquinas on transubstantiation, with which he is specifically concerned in 3a,75–77. His teaching can be summarized fairly quickly. It amounts to the following claims:

1. At the beginning of the celebration of the Eucharist, the (validly) presiding minister or ministers start with bread and wine on the altar before him or them.

2. At the words of consecration, the bread and wine cease to exist, though their appearances (their "species") remain.

3. At the words of consecration, the bread and wine become the body and blood of Christ.

4. This change can be expressed using the Aristotelian notions of substance and accident: After the words of consecration, the substance of bread and wine cease to exist and become the substance of Christ's body and blood; but the accidents of bread and wine remain after the words of consecration.

5. The right answer to the question "What is present before the words of consecration?" is "Bread and wine" and the right answer to the question "What is present after the words of consecration?" is "The body and blood of Christ."

6. The words of consecration miraculously lead to a change of substance—a "transubstantiation."

7. This change does not come about progressively but instantaneously.

8. The accidents of bread and wine that remain after the consecration are not the accidents of Christ's body and blood; they are not the accidents of any existing substance.

9. The whole of Christ as God incarnate is present after the consecration under the appearances of bread and wine, and Christ is wholly present in each particle of what remains in the accidents of bread and wine left behind after the consecration.

10. Christ's body and blood are not dimensively present after the consecration, as if one part of Christ's body were here and another part were there. They are present substantially as, for example, the substance of bread can be said to be present in every part of a loaf of bread.

11. Christ is not present in the Eucharist as a movable object is present in the world.

12. Christ in the Eucharist cannot be seen as something visible; he can be "seen" in the Eucharist only by virtue of faith.

That is the core of what Aquinas says about transubstantiation in 3a,75–77. I should, though, add some comments to accompany what I have just summarized. Thus:

1. The use of the word *transubstantiation* in connection with the Eucharist predates Aquinas, as does the belief that Christ really and not merely symbolically comes to be present in the Eucharist. The word *transubstantiation* was widely used in reference to the Eucharist in the twelfth century and the early thirteenth century. So Aquinas's appeal to transubstantiation was not something new. But Aquinas was one of the first theologians systematically to link the notion of Eucharistic change to the Aristotelian distinction between substance and accident.

2. Aquinas is clearly not trying to demystify the Eucharist by using Aristotelian terminology to talk about it. His discussion of the Eucharist inherits all the agnosticism when it comes to our knowledge of God that he has previously presented in the *Summa Theologiae* when talking about the divine nature, about God as Trinity, and about God incarnate. And Aqui-

nas never suggests that he has a philosophical proof that Christ is present in the Eucharist. Instead, he starts with what he takes to be the obvious (and, for him, received) reading of the New Testament accounts of the Last Supper. Then he seeks to explain how this reading can be restated in philosophical terms so as to preserve the idea that it is Christ who is really and truly received by those receiving the Eucharist. He is clearly aware that there is a miracle involved in the Eucharist. So, I suspect, he would have agreed with what Elizabeth Anscombe once said about transubstantiation. She notes that it would be wrong to think "that the thing can be understood, sorted out, expounded as a possibility with nothing mysterious about it. That is, that it can be understood in such a way as is perhaps demanded by those who attack it on the ground of its obvious difficulties."[62]

3. Aquinas employs Aristotelian terminology when writing about what happens in the Eucharist, but his claim that the Eucharist involves a change of substance leaving behind only accidents that are the accidents of no substance seriously departs from ways in which Aristotle writes about substance, accident, and change. Writing about Aquinas on the Eucharist, Martin Luther, who believed in the presence of Christ in the Eucharist, said that, as well as departing from the teaching of the Bible, Aquinas seems to know "neither his philosophy nor his logic" since "Aristotle speaks of subject and accidents so very differently from St Thomas." Luther goes on to pity Aquinas for "attempting to draw his opinions in matters of faith from Aristotle" while "building an unfortunate superstructure upon an unfortunate foundation."[63] And Luther is right to say that Aquinas departs from Aristotelian teaching when he writes about the Eucharist. It is, however, also worth noting that Aquinas, the theologian or exponent of *sacra doctrina*, frequently departs from Aristotelian teaching while drawing on what he takes to be insights and terminology of Aristotle, whom he certainly does not regard as presenting us with articles of Christian faith.[64] He does so, for example, when he writes about God as an agent cause whose effect is *esse* (cf. chapter 7.1–3). He does so again as he writes about happiness and virtue (cf. chapter 10.1 and 12.1–4). In response to Luther, therefore, one might observe that, in what he says about transubstantiation, Aquinas knows that he is using Aristotelian terminology and stretching it while trying to expound what he takes to be fundamentally beyond human understanding, as you might reasonably expect a revelation from God to be.[65] For Aquinas, if in the celebration of the Eucharist there is bread and wine to start with, then there is a substance of some kind. And if that substance is turned into another, as Aquinas believes that it is on New Testament grounds, then that substance no longer exists even if its accidents appear to

be there and can be dealt with as if they belonged to bread and wine. Furthermore, if that substance is changed into another, then there has occurred a change of substance, apparent accidents notwithstanding. As Aquinas is well aware, Aristotle thinks of substantial change as occurring when something perishes and turns into something else in the physical world. Aristotle would have said that a substantial change has occurred when, for example, a human being dies leaving but a corpse behind, a human corpse being something quite different from a living human being. As Herbert McCabe notes: "Aristotle could have made no sense of the notion of transubstantiation. It is not a notion that can be accommodated *within* the concepts of Aristotelian philosophy; it represents the breakdown of these concepts in face of a mystery."[66] But what if we believe on the authority of God that bread and wine cease to be bread and wine in the Eucharist and become the body and blood of Christ? Then, says Aquinas, we might say that in this case we have a miracle (not something that enters into Aristotle's view of the world) that can be talked about by saying that a unique and invisible change has occurred, one in which one substance turns into another while leaving its visible appearances behind in a particular location.[67]

22.10 Penance (3a,84–90)

As you are probably aware, some Christians practice a rite, which they take to be sacramental, by confessing their sins to a priest and by receiving absolution from the sins they confess as the priest says the equivalent of "I absolve you from your sins in the name of the Father, the Son, and the Holy Spirit." Such Christians would say that they are "going to confession" and thereby celebrating the sacrament of penance.[68] And it is penance, considered in this way, that Aquinas is concerned with in 3a,84–90. We should, however, note that the word *penance* was used before Aquinas in ways that differ from the way Aquinas understands it in 3a,84–90.

Christian talk about penance has its origins in New Testament texts such as John 20. Here Jesus is said to have appeared to his closest disciples after his resurrection, and in John 20:21–23 we read that Jesus, having said, "As the Father has sent me, so I send you," added, "Receive the Holy Spirit. If you forgive the sins of any, they are forgiven them." Again, James 5:16 reads: "Confess your sins to one another, and pray for one another, so that you may be healed." And Matthew 16:19 and 18:18 report Jesus as telling St. Peter that he (Peter) has been given "the keys of the kingdom of heaven" and that what he "binds" on earth will be "bound" in heaven, and then telling his disciples in general that the same applies to them. Texts such as these have frequently been taken to mean that Christians should confess their sins to a priest. I suspect that most contemporary New Testament scholars would not agree with this conclusion, and even if they do, the fact is that the Christian Church did not quickly embrace it.

During the second century there was discussion among Christians concerning whether some people should be formally excluded from the Church because of their sins. Some said that they should. Others were more lenient, arguing that repentant sinners could be readmitted to the Church, *though only once*. But we find various fourth- and fifth-century Christians readily allowing that Christians who have sinned can always be thought of as members of the Church, assuming that they repent of their sins and engage in certain activities as a sign of their repentance. What activities? They seem to have been various, but they also seem to have been public, as was the confession of sin. During this period, confession of sin by the sinner before the Church seems to have been something admitted before many people and forgiven with some severe conditions attached such as never engaging in sexual intercourse.

Views and practices concerning baptized Christians acknowledging that they had sinned after baptism continued to develop for many years and in ways that contemporary readers might find weird or positively inhuman.[69] What we need to note now, however, is that an official consensus had emerged a few years before Aquinas was born. In 1215, the Fourth Lateran Council decreed that "all the faithful of either sex, after they have reached the age of discernment, should individually confess their sins in a faithful manner to their own priest at least once a year."[70] It is against this background that Aquinas writes 3a,84–90, in which he says pretty much what you might expect him to say given his basic approach to sacraments.

He refers to penance using a text of St. Jerome (ca. 347–420), according to whom penance is a "second plank after shipwreck."[71] It is not, thinks Aquinas, essential for salvation as are baptism, confirmation, and the Eucharist since "unless people should actually sin, they would not need Penance" (3a,84,5).[72] But, says Aquinas, it is necessary for salvation given that one has sinned grievously.

Like other sacraments, says Aquinas, penance derives its power from Christ's death and resurrection (3a,84,7), though it also requires genuine sorrow for sin on the part of the penitent (3a,84,3 and 9). With this second thought in mind Aquinas speaks of there being a virtue of penance distinct from the sacrament of penance. This virtue is a disposition to grieve over past sins, to make satisfaction for them, and to avoid committing more sins (3a,85,1). "Penance as a virtue is seated in the will, and its proper act is a purpose of amendment for deeds committed against God" (3a,85,4).[73] Like faith, hope, and charity, which are bound up with it, penance is a supernatural virtue infused by God (3a,85,5 and 6).

Aquinas positively denies that the sacrament of penance is required for sins that are less than mortal (3a,87,2). When it comes to the effects of penance, his focus is on it as taking away mortal sin following God's gift of the virtue of penitence and following repentance on the part of the penitent (3a,86,2 and 87,1 and 2). Like other sacraments, he says, it involves ritual and can be discussed in terms of matter and form (3a,84,2 and 3), but the sacrament only "takes" if penitents are truly sorry for their sin (3a,86,3) and make amends in some way (3a,86,4).

Does the sacrament of penance have parts? Aquinas turns to this question in 3a,90. He argues that penance has parts in that we can think of it as involving contrition, confession, absolution, and satisfaction (3a,90,1 and 2). In 3a,90,4, he adds that "it is part of repentance to detest past sins, with the resolve to change one's life for the better."[74] Penitence involves a change of heart and here we can think of it as threefold.

The first is by rebirth to new life. That is the concern of the repentance preceding Baptism. The second is by reforming after a life that has been ruined by sin. This is the objective of repentance for mortal sins committed after Baptism. The third change is towards living a more holy life. This engages the repentance for venial sins, which are pardoned through any fervent act of charity.[75]

And with those thoughts the *Summa Theologiae* breaks off. Its conclusion might strike you as anticlimactic given so much of what comes before it. But it can hardly be said that Aquinas put down his pen on a pessimistic note.

23

Epilogue

THOMAS AQUINAS WAS canonized by Pope John XXII in 1325, though this was not because of his intellectual achievements. John XXII is reputed to have said of Aquinas, "As many miracles as articles."[1] The emphasis at the time of the canonization, however, was on Aquinas's holiness, not his theological or philosophical skills, which were called into question soon after he died.

In 1277, the bishop of Paris, Étienne Tempier, issued a condemnation of 219 propositions, some of which derived from the writings of Aquinas. A similar condemnation came from the archbishop of Canterbury, Robert Kilwardby, later the same year. Again, around 1278 the English Franciscan William de la Mare (d. ca. 1285) produced a text called *Correctorium Fratris Thomae* ("Corrective of Brother Thomas"), which castigated Aquinas's thinking in numerous ways and became highly influential among Franciscans. William's work led to some heated disputation between Dominicans and Franciscans that effectively lingered on for centuries.

In 1325, Tempier's condemnation was revoked by a later bishop of Paris "to the extent that it affects Saint Thomas," but many of Aquinas's views were criticized by ecclesiastical academics writing even in the wake of his canonization, and his prestige outside Dominican circles was not especially great until the fifteenth and sixteenth centuries.[2] Aquinas was a serious influence on the Council of Trent and the early years of the Society of Jesus (the Jesuits), whose founder, St Ignatius Loyola, directed that students in his society should study Aquinas as an authority.[3] During the Reformation period, however, Aquinas was a target of much criticism by Protestant theologians, as he has often been by Eastern Orthodox ones.[4] And in due course Aquinas often came to be ridiculed as a "medieval" figure rather than someone representing the kind of thinking associated with what is now commonly referred to as "the Enlightenment."

What is often referred to as "the Thomistic revival" began in the nineteenth century with Pope Leo XIII's encyclical *Aeterni Patris* (1879), which strongly commended the writings of Aquinas in reaction to philosophical trends then prevalent. But does Aquinas give us thoughts to embrace with good reason, and does he do so in the *Summa Theologiae*? Are its philosophical arguments cogent? Are its theological arguments sound? Leo XIII declared that Aquinas "reasoned in such a manner that in him there is wanting neither a full array of questions, nor an apt disposal of the various parts, nor the best method of proceeding, nor soundness of principles or strength of argument, nor clearness and elegance of style, nor a facility for explaining what is abstruse."[5] Is that verdict right, though?

The *Summa Theologiae* is clearly not lacking in questions. But questions are not arguments.[6] On the other hand, the *Summa Theologiae* ranges over much that surely needs to be asked concerning Christian doctrine. Because of the time and context in which it was written, it does not deal with a number of theological matters that strike many people today. Yet its scope is extensive, and it is a clearly written work. What one person finds clear, of course, another might take to be opaque, and much of the *Summa Theologiae* will strike many people as baffling at first reading. However, with some explanation of its most employed concepts, motivated readers will, I think, find it a lot easier to follow than the work of many theologians and philosophers. Readers turning to him now are, I suspect, likely to find him more immediately intelligible than medieval philosophers such as Duns Scotus (ca. 1266–1308) and William Ockham (ca. 1287–1347). They are also, I think, likely to find him more perspicuous than recent philosophical thinkers such as Martin Heidegger (1889–1976) or Alain Baidiou (b. 1937).

When evaluating the *Summa Theologiae*, therefore, everything really turns on whether or not it argues for its conclusions well, on whether its philosophical and theological moves are worth taking seriously. I have touched on these questions at various points in the present book, but I would like to conclude, as befits an epilogue, with some brief observations offered to the reader as aids for reflection.

23.1 *The Philosophy of the* Summa Theologiae

As we have seen, Aquinas draws a sharp distinction between what can be known by reason and what should be believed by faith, and he seems to suppose that in the *Summa Theologiae* he has established certain truths philosophically without relying on divine revelation. In doing so, he often depends on what we might call "deeper level" philosophical views such as those that come into play as he refers to substance, form, matter, and existence or being. These "deeper level" views are more presumed than argued for in the *Summa Theologiae*, and I have not said much about their philosophical value. One should, however, note that they are not uncontroversial. For example, while Aquinas's talk of things in the world proceeds on the assumption that there actually are such things, things that are not just ideas in our minds, some philosophers (even Christian ones) have challenged this assumption, while others have resisted the idea that we should think of the world as containing substances in Aquinas's sense, that we should think of what is common to them by using the language of "form" and "accident," or that individuality in things of a kind derives, as Aquinas says, from material factors.[7] Yet other philosophers (some of them Christian) have found Aquinas's talk of "being" to be confused. In particular, they have argued that it lacks logical insights defended by figures such as Frege and Russell.

Worries like these should, I think, at least nudge us into reflection on some very basic philosophical concepts without supposing that Aquinas is right about all of them or even any of them. Yet even supposing that we end up siding with the philosophical presuppositions underlying the *Summa Theologiae*, what are we to think of the conclusions that it arrives at while employing them? These chiefly amount to the following:

(1) God exists and is simple, perfect, good, limitless, actively present throughout the created order, unchangeable, eternal, providential, and omnipotent (1a,2–10, 1a,14–26, and 1a,44–49).
(2) One can truly speak of God using words that we normally employ when talking about what is not divine (1a,13).
(3) Without benefit of revelation, a certain view of human nature can be defended (1a,79–83).

One should also note that the *Summa Theologiae*'s discussions of what Aquinas takes to be matters of faith are shot through with philosophical arguments. Hence, for example, we find him defending what might be called the "coherence" of the doctrines of the Trinity and the Incarnation while employing such ideas as that distinction can amount to relation somehow (cf. Aquinas's notion that Father, Son, and Spirit are subsisting relations) or that sense can be made of one subject being both F and not F if it is *as such and such* F while *also* not F *considered under some other description* (cf. Aquinas's claim that Christ, *insofar as he is human*, is not omnipotent while, *insofar as he is divine*, is omnipotent). Ideas such as these also call for detailed philosophical evaluation. For now, though, I shall focus on what Aquinas says with respect to 1–3 above.

23.1.1 God

Many philosophers currently suppose that Aquinas's arguments for the truth of "God exists" in 1a,2 are all flawed. Maybe they are, but not for some reasons often advanced. For example, none of them abandon premises used in their support and thereby end up as self-contradictory.[8] It is often said that central to Aquinas's natural theology is some such reasoning as "everything requires a cause, so, there is a something (God) that does not." Yet the *Summa Theologiae* never employs that crude argument or anything like it. Rather, it typically notes that certain causal questions ought to lead us to ask related but different ones, the answer or answers to which do not raise the same questions. Aquinas's arguments for the truth of "God exists" never claim without reason that God is an exception to a universal rule. Instead, they argue that there are certain universal rules for which we need to account. In doing so, they deny the possibility of *a certain kind* of infinite regress—a point often stressed in criticism of them. As we have seen, though, they do not, as is frequently not appreciated, deny that *all* infinite regress is possible. Nor do they all depend on now outmoded scientific theories. The first of the Five Ways seems to conflict with Newton's first law of motion, but even Newton thought that some motion calls for a nonscientific explanation. It has been suggested that, contrary to what Aquinas supposes when arguing that God exists, we know on scientific grounds that some events come about without a scientifically detectable cause (or "agent cause" in Aquinas's terminology). It has also been suggested that something can come into existence without a cause in the spatiotemporal universe.[9] With respect to the first suggestion, however, not to be able to detect a cause (scientifically detectable or otherwise) is not to have established that there is none, and, in the light of his concept of God, Aquinas would actually have agreed with the second suggestion.

Given the way in which he argues that God must exist as the cause of things having (though not being) *esse*, Aquinas's natural theology in the *Summa Theologiae* evidently turns on the idea that nothing in the spatiotemporal world exists by nature and, therefore, everything in it cries out for a cause of its existing. His argument here is clearly not a scientific one. He would say that, even should we have the best possible understanding of what the universe is (what is in the world), there remains the question "How come any universe rather than nothing?"[10] So Aquinas's natural theology can, perhaps, be thought of as standing or falling on the legitimacy of this question, on the supposition that it has an answer, and on the idea that this answer lies in what is not part of the world.

Many philosophers have felt that the question need not be raised or that it is somehow confused.[11] Some have said that when you have explained what within the world accounts for what within the world needs to be explained, you have explained all that calls for explanation (a view that Aquinas notes in 1a,2,3). Others have said that there is no alternative to there being a world, that "there might have been nothing at all" is somehow nonsensical. Yet others, as I have noted, have held that Aquinas's talk of *esse* is riddled with mistakes concerning the logic of statements with "is" or "exists" in them.[12] And philosophers reasoning along these lines have done so in some detail and with a variety of careful arguments, so objections to Aquinas presented by them are not to be dismissed out of hand.

Yet neither are the many detailed responses to them coming even from other contemporary philosophers. You may think that I am now saying, "Oh well, there are good arguments in favor of Aquinas's natural theology, and there are good arguments against it, so we should deliver a verdict of 'Stalemate' with respect to it." That, though, is not my point. I am merely suggesting that Aquinas's basic argument in the *Summa Theologiae* for "God exists"—the "Why something rather than nothing?" argument—is still worthy of serious consideration, as many philosophers still believe it to be, even those arguing against it. Toward the end of his *Tractatus Logico-Philosophicus*, Wittgenstein said, "Not *how* the world is, is the mystical, but *that* it is."[13] In his "Lecture on Ethics" he observes, "*I wonder at the existence of the world.* And I am then inclined to use such phrases as 'how extraordinary that anything should exist' or 'how extraordinary that the world should exist.'"[14] Wittgenstein never went on to develop an account of God such as Aquinas provides. But is he talking nonsense in what I have just quoted him saying? Possibly, but not obviously.

When it comes to Aquinas's philosophically defended conclusions concerning the divine nature and the language we use to talk about God, these have had both friends and foes, and the debate between them continues. To some extent this is a debate concerning materialism (the view that only physical objects exist) and non-materialism (the idea that there is or might be something that is not physical). Considered as such, the debate goes back to ancient times and often continues with no reference to Aquinas. There are, however, plenty of critics of Aquinas on God's nature who are, like Aquinas, convinced that materialism is false, and many of these critics claim to share Aquinas's faith as a Christian. So why are they critical of his philosophical conclusions concerning the divine nature? The answer, of course, is "For many different reasons." Yet, I think, there is often something uniting religious believers hostile to what Aquinas says when developing his account of God in the *Summa Theologiae*.

In *The Coherence of Theism*, Richard Swinburne, one of the best known modern philosophers of religion, trenchantly maintains that belief in God's existence can be defended against many criticisms leveled against it. But what does he take the word *God* to mean? What does he mean by *theism*? He says that a theist is someone "who believes that there is a God." And by "God," he adds, the theist "understands something like a 'person without a body.'" "That God is a person, yet one without a body, seems," says Swinburne, "the most elementary claim of theism."[15] As he develops and defends the idea that God is a bodiless person, Swinburne seems to presume that a person is more or less what René Descartes (1596–1650) took himself to be when developing his famous argument "I think, therefore I am." Having concluded that he certainly exists, Descartes asks, "But what then am I?" He replies, "A thing that thinks." What is that, though? Descartes's answer is "A thing that doubts, understands, affirms, denies, is willing, is unwilling, and also imagines and has sensory perceptions."[16] Now Swinburne does not speak of God as having sensory perceptions, as doubting, or as denying. He does, however, suppose that "the most elementary claim of theism" is that God is an invisible center of consciousness, a mind with many and various thoughts, something having beliefs, and something to be strongly compared to us insofar as we subscribe to the distinction between mind and body defended by Descartes as he develops his account of what he takes himself to be.[17] And this is a view of what God is that is taken for granted by many philosophers, both theistic and nontheistic, and by many theologians.

Aquinas evidently does not share this view of what we should take ourselves to mean by the word *God*. Critics of his account of the divine nature, however, frequently fault him on just that count. Like Swinburne, they say that belief in God is most certainly belief in a particular person. They then frequently argue (as does Swinburne) that, for instance, if God is a person, then God cannot be simple, as Aquinas maintains.[18] Or they argue that if God is a person, then God cannot be immutable or outside time, as Aquinas believes God to be.[19] In short, critics of Aquinas's philosophy of God often take him not really to be talking about God or to be very wrong in his teachings concerning God.

Why do they think this? Once again, we may say, "For many different reasons."[20] In general, though, they tend to hold that the claim that "God is a person" sums up the biblical view of God and that elements of Aquinas's view of God conflict with what we can infer from this. But do they?

Arguably not. For one thing, the Bible never explicitly asserts "God is a person." For another, it seriously distinguishes between God and persons (taking "person" in Swinburne's sense). Of course, the Bible is full of anthropomorphic talk about God. It tells us, for example, that God once walked in a garden, that God talked to Moses "face to face, as one speaks to a friend," and that God has emotions such as hatred, joy, anger, and regret.[21] But the Bible also tells us that God created the universe, from which you might conclude that God is not seriously to be thought of as part of the universe. And as much as the Bible goes in for depicting God in human terms, it contains many passages that pull in the opposite direction. It talks of God's hiddenness.[22] It sometimes resists comparisons between God and creatures. A classic text here is Isaiah 40:18–26. You might think that when it comes to what we should mean by "God," biblical texts implying a serious likeness between God and creatures (especially people) should be favored over those noting the difference between God and creatures. But why? Taken as a whole, the Bible stresses the incomparability of God more than it does the similarity between God and creatures. Aquinas, commentator on the Bible as he was, is aware of this fact and, therefore, regards himself as "traditional" and "biblical" in what he says about the divine nature. Perhaps he was wrong to have done so, but it takes some argument to show that he was.

One may, of course, wish to argue that, since those who believe in God and talk about God inevitably employ words normally used to speak of what is not divine, we should conceive of God as if God were, after all, an inhabitant of the universe (so to speak). Aquinas, I have noted, argues otherwise. He does so in his account of divine simplicity, in his development of the view that words used when talking about God and creatures can be construed analogically, and in ways in which he appeals to this account when saying what cannot be true of God. Many have insisted that if language used to talk about God does not mean exactly what it means when talking of creatures (who are generally not, in Aquinas's sense, entirely simple), then it lacks meaning. So there is clearly matter for debate when it comes to Aquinas's philosophy of what we might call "talk about God." But this surely needs to be approached with careful attention to what Aquinas says in detail, not only in the *Summa Theologiae* but in other writings. I have the impression that it is not always so approached and that criticisms of Aquinas's discussions of God's nature often talk past him rather than at him. You, of course, might form a different impression.[23]

23.1.2 People

Aquinas's philosophical account of human nature in the *Summa Theologiae* raises as many questions as its philosophical account of God. Aquinas thinks that people are not essentially immaterial, as, for example, Descartes believed them to be. Yet Descartes was hardly an idiot (he is not referred to as the "father of modern philosophy" for nothing), and some contemporary thinkers favor a Cartesian account of human beings.[24] Others, however, hold that people are *nothing but* physical bodies in motion, while sometimes supposing that neuroscience is at least in principle exhaustively able to capture or describe what that amounts to.[25] Aquinas favors the view that people, though essentially material, have powers that allow us to think of them as operating at an immaterial level because of his view of human knowledge as being what occurs in us as we receive forms in an immaterial way, because he thinks that, for example, when understanding what a cat is, we have in us the form of a cat without actually being a cat. Is Aquinas thinking rightly here, however?

One might find his position attractive because it steers a middle course between a view of people as essentially immaterial and a view of them as nothing but physical. Against philosophers such as Descartes, one might want to stress that people are essentially material since to be alive as a human being is to be a thing of flesh and blood. However, against a purely materialistic account of people one might be struck, as many have, by the way in which consciousness seems to be something different from a series of physical processes, and different from an account of it given from a third-person perspective, since it is not empirically observable, even though one can sometimes, surely, observe people thinking just by looking at how they act.

What, though, of Aquinas's claim that people have souls that can survive the death of their bodies? His argument for the human soul being subsistent, immaterial, and naturally incorruptible has failed to convince some readers even though it has persuaded others.[26] Successful though it might actually be, however, it is not an easy argument to understand. Equally hard to construe is Aquinas's view that, after death, human souls continue to exist as remnants or parts of human beings waiting to be reunited with their bodies. That, I presume, is why it has been interpreted in some sharply conflicting ways.[27]

Aquinas's approach to human beings where ethics is concerned is also somewhat puzzling given the way in which it combines elements of Aristotelian thinking and beliefs about God that Aquinas takes to derive from divine revelation. Is he offering an account of morality that he thinks an atheist should be able to accept? Insofar as his account incorporates strictly religious beliefs, presumably he is not, but he does appear to think that what he says about ethics without relying on revelation should be acceptable to people with no belief in God. Do his purely philosophical ethical arguments work, however? Their drift is currently fashionable among moral philosophers since Aquinas is a proponent of virtue ethics and since virtue ethics is now somewhat popular in some circles, largely in the wake of Elizabeth Anscombe's seminal essay "Modern Moral Philosophy" and the writings of Philippa Foot.[28] Unlike some defenders of virtue ethics, however, Aquinas has views on what is and is not "reasonable" or "rational" in evaluating human behavior—views that will strike some people as reflecting Aquinas's religious beliefs rather than beliefs arrived at by philosophical reasoning. Aquinas is quick to tell us that this or that behavior accords with reason, or that this or that behavior does not. One might, however, wonder how well he justifies the verdicts he delivers on the reasonableness or naturalness of particular kinds of behavior, and many people have done so.[29]

23.2 *The Theology of the* Summa Theologiae

Aquinas's theology in the *Summa Theologiae* has frequently been denigrated because of the way in which he so obviously presents much philosophical argument even as he aims to write theology or, as he would have said, even as he aims to hand on *sacra doctrina*. Some have claimed that philosophy and theology do not mix and that Aquinas's theology is, therefore, infected by something alien. Others have suggested that it attempts to make theology subservient to philosophy in an unacceptable way. But the use of philosophical arguments when discussing theological topics has a long history and can be found in the writings of many indisputably theological authors both before and after Aquinas, and even the charge that philosophy and theology do not mix effectively amounts to a philosophical conclusion.

Yet the theology of the *Summa Theologiae* will still strike some readers as of little interest today. Why so?

Partly, perhaps, because of what modern standards would see as its non-feminist tone and the faulty biology lying behind it, and partly because of what Hans Küng calls its "court theology"—meaning its desire to stress the primacy of the papacy regarding right theological thinking. Küng says that Aquinas "put his theology at the service of dogmatic papolatry."[30] And, in a sense, this is true. I think that Küng's way of making the point is somewhat lacking in nuance and takes little note of what *sacra doctrina* meant to Aquinas and how it was engaged in by him not only in the *Summa Theologiae* but in many of his other writings. Yet Aquinas was indeed a defender of papal authority, and he took the pope to have ultimate authority when it comes to matters concerning Christian faith. As I noted in chapter 2, however, and in spite of what he says about the pope as he proceeds through the *Summa Theologiae*, Aquinas seems to give preference to the authority of biblical revelation over that of any human being.

Those approaching the *Summa Theologiae* today might also worry about its resolutely Christian focus. One might, of course, expect a Christian theologian to be talking to Christians while believing in the truth of Christianity. What, though, might we make of a theologian who seems uninterested in engaging with non-Christian religious believers while also saying things that appear to suggest that most of these have little or no hope of salvation? Perhaps not much. Yet Aquinas seems to be such a theologian. He often expresses

agreement with certain Jewish and Islamic authors, but the agreement seems
to be largely philosophical. When it comes to *sacra doctrina*, Aquinas appears
to be unequivocal. Salvation depends on explicitly accepting what he calls the
articles of faith. This is not a view that theologians today seem generally to
espouse, to say the least. Here one might, for example, note that the 1992 *Catechism of the Catholic Church*, promulgated by Pope John Paul II, accepts
(while citing the Second Vatican Council) that "those who, through no fault of
their own, do not know the Gospel of Christ or his Church, but who nevertheless seek God with a sincere heart, and, moved by grace, try in their actions to
do his will as they know it through the dictates of their conscience—those too
may achieve eternal salvation."[31] Even given what he says about the saints of
the Old Testament, Aquinas's take on non-Christians is, rightly or wrongly,
not as accommodating.[32]

23.2.1 Historical Assumptions

Another possible reason for worrying about the theology of the *Summa Theologiae* lies in what it takes to be historically true. In particular, can we really believe
that, as Aquinas supposed, theology should proceed on the assumption that the
Bible should be read as conveying history in the Genesis account of Adam and
Eve and in the New Testament accounts of the life and teaching of Jesus?

There are people who reject the idea that human beings are the product of
many millennia of evolution and hold that the Genesis story of Adam and Eve
can be read as historically accurate—you might be one of them. If so, though,
you are certainly in a minority, not only among biologists but also among
theologians. You might reply, "Why shouldn't those who believe in a historical
Adam be deemed theologians?" And that is a fair question. My point, however,
is that, like it or not, most professional theologians and religious leaders now
embrace some version of the Darwinian theory of evolution.[33] Even Pope John
Paul II, not noted for his theological liberalism, said that "new findings lead
us toward the recognition of evolution as more than an hypothesis."[34]

So, insofar as we agree with such a conclusion, how should we think of the
extent to which the *Summa Theologiae* proceeds at variance with it? We should
presumably have to say that it derives from mistakes. You will have noted by
now that quite a lot of the *Summa* presumes that Adam existed as a historical
individual and presents many inferences based on this presumption. Theologians respectful of Aquinas will, of course, try to see what can be salvaged of
the *Summa Theologiae's* treatment of Adam without subscribing to his historicity in the way that Aquinas did. But there would, I think, be a difficult work
of reconstruction involved in such an enterprise.

Perhaps an even more arduous work would be needed in order to cope with Aquinas's assumption that the Gospels accurately tell us what Jesus said and did. The *Summa Theologiae* always presupposes that this is the case. It does so, for example, in its account of Christ's life and in its treatment of the sacraments. It especially does so in its approach to the theological virtue of faith. Aquinas takes those with faith to believe, not in what philosophy can establish, but in what God has revealed in the teachings of Jesus, which, for Aquinas, include the doctrines of the Trinity and the Incarnation as understood by Church councils. So doubts about our access to what Jesus actually said and did strike at the heart of Aquinas's theology.

Many theologians, though, find them to be doubts that will not go away given New Testament scholarship in the last hundred years or so. As I have noted, skepticism concerning the historical value of the biblical portrait of Christ has been expressed by professional biblical exegetes for many years. As I write, some New Testament scholars seem confident that the Gospels present a basically reliable account of Jesus's teaching, but even among such scholars, remarkably different "portraits" of Jesus have emerged, and few present the picture that seems so important to the thinking of the *Summa Theologiae*. To say as much is not to suggest that this picture and all the conclusions that Aquinas draws from it should be cast aside. Yet readers of Aquinas should surely bear in mind that there is a problem for him here. Roman Catholic theologians who are less wedded to the historicity of the Gospels than Aquinas was might, perhaps, want to argue that what Aquinas says about Jesus and his teachings can be defended by appealing to the idea that the Church's reading of the New Testament should be preferred to what we would otherwise think about the Gospels proceeding only as historians. This view itself raises a lot of theological questions. One is: From where do we reliably derive the belief that the Church has the authority to comment on the New Testament? Aquinas seems to think that it comes from the teaching of Jesus.

In short, readers wanting to think about the theology of the *Summa Theologiae* today need to ask themselves: "Does it survive probing into the historicity of the Gospels? If it does not, how can it be seriously recommended in whole or in part? If it does, then how can this be shown to be the case?" Such readers might also like to consider the way in which Aquinas uses the word *conveniens* when trying to arrive at theological conclusions grounded, so he thinks, on biblical authority. As we have seen, at many points in the *Summa*, especially in 3a, Aquinas says that such and such is the case because it is *conveniens* ("fitting" or "appropriate"). But, one might ask, is what Aquinas takes to be *conveniens* really so? And if so, by what standard?

23.2.2 The Humanity of Christ

Another line of inquiry that some have pressed in criticism of the theology of the *Summa Theologiae* targets its presentation of Christ as a human being. Aquinas insists that Christ is both divine and human. Yet does his account of Christ effectively leave us with something not really human? Does it not effectively leave us with a view of Christ that accords with the heresy called "Docetism" condemned by the first Council of Nicaea in 325? Docetism holds that Christ only seemed to be human but was not really so, and it has been suggested that Aquinas, for all his claim to be orthodox, ends up falling into Docetism. Hence, for example, noting Aquinas's claim that Christ always enjoyed the beatific vision, Gerald O'Collins says that "the comprehensive grasp of *all* creatures and *all* they can do ... would lift Christ's human knowledge so clearly beyond the normal limits as to cast serious doubts on the genuineness of his humanity in one essential aspect."[35]

What O'Collins says is worthy of reflection. But it is hardly a knockdown argument against Aquinas's Christology unless O'Collins is suggesting (as I do not think he wants to) that one cannot have the beatific vision without ceasing to be human. And, in general, abilities that Aquinas ascribes to Christ, though unshared by other human beings, do not obviously amount to abilities that conflict with what seems to be essential to being human. Had Aquinas said that, for example, Christ, as human, was not able to occupy space, there would clearly be something to worry about. Yet he never says anything like this. Indeed, in the *Summa Theologiae* he corrects himself for having previously (in his *Commentary on the Sentences*) said something comparable when arguing that Christ lacked an agent intellect. In the *Summa Theologiae* he says that if Christ was human, he must have had an agent intellect.

You might, of course, still think that the Christ of the *Summa Theologiae* is a pretty unusual or abnormal human being. Surely, however, any account of Christ that holds that he is unequivocally both God and human is going to have to concede that, as incarnate, God is going to be a unique human being, one that might display what is possible for human beings even if they have not generally arrived at it. And any account of Christ as God and human might, perhaps, be advised to proceed on the side of caution when claiming to know in detail what something both divine and human would be like.

What is divine cannot, as divine, be killed. What is human cannot be reptilian. So much, for instance, seems clear. Can we, though, be sure that Christ, as Aquinas depicts him, cannot be human given that his humanity is the instrument of divinity in the way Aquinas takes it to be? In short, do we have any clear idea as to what a hypostatic union would look like? Do we, for that matter, have any clear idea as to what is and is not possible for a human being? "What or where is the common logical world that is occupied in exclusion by God and man?"[36] That God became incarnate in accordance with Aquinas's account of the Incarnation might be deemed to be so much mythology, as it was proclaimed to be in *The Myth of God Incarnate*, a volume that caused quite a stir in some quarters when it appeared.[37] If, however, we take mythology to be equivalent to fantasy, the case that Aquinas's view of the Incarnation is mythological needs to be argued. Maybe such a case can be made, but it will need to be as detailed, as philosophically sophisticated, and as argumentative as is Aquinas's case for the opposite conclusion.[38] And it will need to allow that Christian attempts to talk about the Incarnation in orthodox terms are always trying to capture a mystery in words that might be replaced as reflection continues, assuming that new formulations of the doctrine of the Incarnation do not positively contradict earlier ones.

Aquinas himself seems to have recognized that reformulating can be theologically appropriate. In the *Summa Theologiae*, he ranges over Christian doctrine, noting and appealing to early expressions of it (ways in which it was stated and defended before his time) while using Aristotelian and Platonic terminology in an attempt to make sense of it. I take this urge of Aquinas to make sense to be one of the great strengths of the *Summa*, and an indication of its theological sophistication. It indicates that Aquinas, though obviously a man of his times, believed that theologians need to draw on what is intellectually good while pressing forward and trying to express the mysteries of the Christian faith in new ways.

In this concluding chapter, I have tried to indicate critical questions that might be directed at the *Summa Theologiae*, and I am sure that Aquinas would have approved of me doing so because he obviously loved questions and disputation arising from them—another sign of his intellectual stature both as a philosopher and a theologian. But questions, of course, need answers. I have just tried to prompt you into asking some questions about the value of the *Summa Theologiae* or at least certain parts of it. To do justice to this work, you might now like to pursue them, to consider other ones, and to try to find answers to as many as you can.

Appendix

THE *SUMMA THEOLOGIAE* AT A GLANCE

Prima Pars

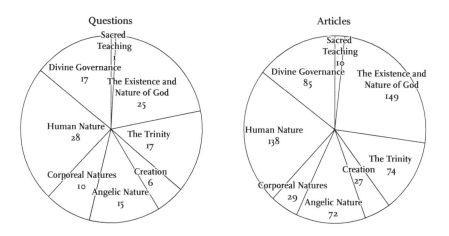

Prima Secundae

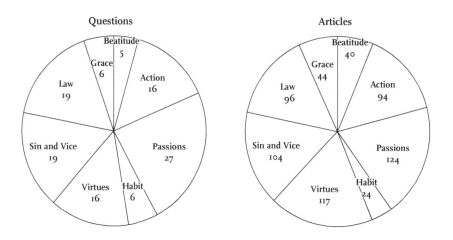

Secunda Secundae

Questions

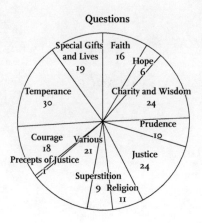

Special Gifts and Lives 19 · Faith 16 · Hope 6 · Temperance 30 · Charity and Wisdom 24 · Courage 18 · Various 21 · Prudence 10 · Precepts of Justice 1 · Justice 24 · Superstition 9 · Religion 11

Articles

Special Gifts and Lives 106 · Faith 78 · Hope 34 · Temperance 107 · Charity and Wisdom 150 · Courage 64 · Precepts of Justice 6 · Various 74 · Superstition 38 · Prudence 56 · Justice 106 · Religion 79

Tertia Pars

Questions

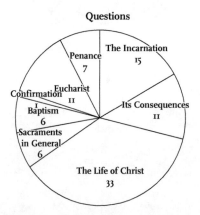

Penance 7 · The Incarnation 15 · Confirmation 1 · Eucharist 11 · Baptism 6 · Its Consequences 11 · Sacraments in General 6 · The Life of Christ 33

Articles

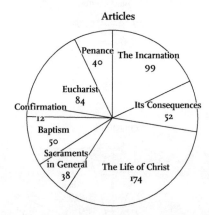

Penance 40 · The Incarnation 99 · Eucharist 84 · Confirmation 12 · Its Consequences 52 · Baptism 50 · Sacraments in General 38 · The Life of Christ 174

Notes

1. Introduction to *Summa Theologiae*, 1a,3.
2. For discussions of the date of Aquinas's birth, see James A. Weisheipl, *Friar Thomas D'Aquino* (Basil Blackwell: Oxford, 1975); Simon Tugwell, *Albert and Thomas: Selected Writings* (Paulist Press: New York and Mahwah, 1988); Jean-Pierre Torrell, *Saint Thomas Aquinas: The Person and His Work* (The Catholic University of America Press: Washington, D.C., 1996). Historians differ when it comes to providing a chronology for Aquinas's life. You should bear this in mind when reading the present chapter. If you look at the three works cited above, you will come to see where there is room for disagreement. For more on Aquinas's early life, see Adriano D'Oliva, *Les Débuts de l'enseignement de Thomas d'Aquin et sa Conception de la "Sacra Doctrina"* (Vrin: Paris, 2006). Also see Adriano Oliva, "Philosophy in the Teaching of Theology by Thomas Aquinas," *The Thomist* 76 (2012).
3. "Aquinas" in "Thomas Aquinas" seems to denote the name of his family (*de Aquino*), not the place of his birth. Aquinas was related to counts of that place. But these were flourishing long before Aquinas was born.
4. Books and articles on Aquinas sometimes refer to him as "Thomas." In this book I follow a standard convention of referring to him as "Aquinas."
5. The Benedictine Abbey of Monte Cassino was founded by St. Benedict of Nursia (ca. 480–ca. 550) himself. It was the abbey from which Benedictine monachism spread to become a presence in medieval society.
6. The University of Bologna was given a charter by Frederick I in 1158. But its origins preexist this charter. The University of Naples, however, was personally created by Frederick II. It has been referred to as the first "state" university.
7. See A. Robiglio, "Neapolitan Gold," *Bulletin de Philosophie Médievale* 44 (2002): xx–xx. Michael W. Dunne has replied to Robiglio in "Concerning 'Neapolitan Gold': William of Tocco and Peter of Ireland," *Bulletin de Philosophie Médiévale* 45

(2003): xx–xx. Robligio has, in turn, replied to Dunne in "*Et Petrum in insulam deportatur*. Concerning Michael Dunne's opinion on Peter of Ireland," *Bulletin de Philosophie Médiévale* 46 (2004).

8. For an account of ways in which Aquinas's writings on religious life (i.e., the life of those in religious orders) might give us an idea about his choice to become a Dominican, see Ulrich Horst, "Christ, *Exemplar Ordinis Fratrum Praedicantium*, According to Saint Thomas Aquinas," in Kent Emery Jr. and Joseph Wawrykow (eds.), *Christ Among the Medieval Dominicans* (University of Notre Dame Press: Notre Dame, 1998).

9. It is unlikely that Aquinas ever formally studied in the Faculty of Arts in Paris since his status as a member of a religious order meant that he was forbidden to do so.

10. Albert died in 1280. While he was working with Albert in Paris, Aquinas seems to have transcribed a copy of a text by Albert on *The Divine Names* by Dionysius the Areopagite.

11. Some scholars, however, date the *De Principiis Naturae* to a time shortly after Aquinas was living in Cologne.

12. If Aquinas did not deliver biblical lectures in Cologne, then he did so shortly having left Cologne for Paris sometime during or after 1251. A case for Aquinas lecturing on the Bible in Cologne is made by Weisheipl, op. cit. Reason for thinking that Aquinas started to lecture on the Bible in Paris rather than Cologne is provided by Adriano Oliva, op. cit.

13. For an introduction to Peter Lombard, see Philipp W. Rosemann, *Peter Lombard* (Oxford University Press: New York, 2004).

14. William was the author of *De Periculis Novissimorum Temporum* (*On the Dangers of Recent Times*). For a Latin and English edition of this, with some account of the secular/mendicant controversy, see *William of Saint-Amour, "De periculis novissimorum temporum*," edition, translation, and introduction by G. Geltner (Peeters: Paris, Leuven, Dudley, Mass., 2008).

15. It is not easy to provide a quick English translation of the title of this work of Aquinas. Here I am offering one that I hope not to be misleading given the work's contents.

16. Actually, it left him with other duties. See note 18 below.

17. Aquinas wrote commentaries on some of the Pauline Epistles, on the Gospels of John and Matthew, and on Isaiah, Jeremiah, Lamentations, Job, and the Psalms. For an introduction to Aquinas's biblical commentaries, see Thomas G. Weinandy, Daniel A. Keating, and John P. Yocum (eds.), *Aquinas on Scripture* (T&T Clark International: London and New York, 2005). Scriptural references abound in Aquinas's writings.

18. I offer a more detailed account (with relevant bibliography) of what *Quaestiones Disputatae* were in *Thomas Aquinas, On Evil*, translated by Richard Regan and edited with an introduction and notes by Brian Davies (Oxford University Press: New York, 2003), 8ff.

19. Masters of Theology at Paris were also required to preach. It is very difficult to date the "academic sermons" of Aquinas that are available for us to study. But you can get a sense of them from *Thomas Aquinas, The Academic Sermons*, translated by Mark-Robin Hoogland (The Catholic University of America Press: Washington, D.C., 2010).

20. It did not end because Aquinas was fired (or, in contemporary terminology, "refused tenure"). Eager to provide teachers for its students not working at a university, the Dominicans were then looking to have a series of Parisian masters. The time at Paris that Aquinas served when first being a master there was just the time then expected for a Dominican master to serve. His returning for a second time to Paris was exceptional.

21. For an English translation of this see *Thomas Aquinas: The Literal Exposition on Job*, translated by Anthony Damico (Scholars Press: Atlanta, 1989).

22. We cannot presume that "Summa Contra Gentiles" was the title given by Aquinas to the work we now know by that name. In some early manuscripts it goes by the name "*Liber de Veritate Catholicae Fidei Contra Errores Infidelium*" (*Book on the Truth of the Catholic Faith Against the Errors of Unbelievers*).

23. In chapter 2 of Book I of the *Summa Contra Gentiles*, Aquinas says that he is concerned with the truth of the Catholic faith. But, though quotations from the Bible abound in the first three books of the *Summa Contra Gentiles*, Aquinas does not get to specifically Christian doctrines until Book IV of the work. Up to that point he seems to be concerned with a notion of God that many of his Jewish and Muslim contemporaries would not have found problematic. Some readers of the *Summa Contra Gentiles* read it as an essay in the philosophy of religion, as does Norman Kretzmann in *The Metaphysics of Theism: Aquinas's Natural Theology in* Summa Contra Gentiles *I* (Clarendon: Oxford, 1997). Kretzmann persuasively argues that, in most of the *Summa Contra Gentiles*, Aquinas offers what would be thought of today as a purely philosophical (in no way appealing to divine revelation) treatise on God ("theology from the bottom up" in Kretzmann's words).

24. Did Aquinas think of what we now know as the *Summa Theologiae* as having that title? The text did not appear as a finished book during his lifetime. But the earliest manuscripts of its first part distributed in Paris bear the title "*Summa de Theologia*." For more on this matter, see A. Walz, "De genuino titulo *Summa theologiae*," *Angelicum* 18 (1941).

25. We do not know why Aquinas drafted his various commentaries on Aristotle. It was certainly not because he ever had to lecture formally on texts of Aristotle.

26. What I have just offered is but a sketch of Aquinas's life. Readers who want to study it in depth should consult the works by Oliva, Torrell, Tugwell, and Weisheipl mentioned above. For primary sources in Latin for the life of Aquinas, see Angelico Ferrua (ed.), *Thomae Aquinatis vitae fontes praecipuae* (Edizione Domenicane: Alba, 1968). For primary sources in English, see Kenelm

Foster (ed.), *The Life of Saint Thomas Aquinas: Biographical Documents* (Longmans, Green and Company: London, 1959).

27. Leonard Boyle observes that "Santa Sabina has the look of what I call a '*studium personale*,' a *studium* set up for or by a given master." I quote from Boyle, "The Setting of the *Summa Theologiae*," reprinted in Brian Davies (ed.), *Aquinas's "Summa Theologiae": Critical Essays* (Rowman and Littlefield: Boulder and London, 2006), 7. But the *studium* in Rome was obviously a provincial arrangement and was really a *studium* of Aquinas's province.

28. Cf. John Jenkins, *Knowledge and Faith in Thomas Aquinas* (Cambridge University Press: Cambridge, 1997), chapter 3.

29. I quote (with some emendation) from volume 1 of the Blackfriars edition of the *Summa Theologiae* (Eyre and Spottiswoode [London] and McGraw-Hill [New York], 1964), 1:3. This edition, with the same pagination, is now (since 2006) available from Cambridge University Press. All of my references to it can be taken as referring either to the Eyre and Spottiswoode printing or to the reprinting by Cambridge University Press. I shall therefore henceforth adopt the abbreviation "BLK/CUP" (followed by volume number and page number) when quoting from it. I sometimes, while noting that I do so, emend passages that I quote from BLK/CUP (mostly for reasons to do with clarity or inclusive language). My emendations, of course, are to be attributed to me, not to Eyre and Spottiswoode or Cambridge University Press. In 2006, Cambridge University Press published a revised version by me of part of the Blackfriars translation of the *Prima Pars*. See *Thomas Aquinas, "Summa Theologiae," Questions on God*, edited by Brian Davies and Brian Leftow (Cambridge University Press: Cambridge, 2006). When quoting from this text in the present volume (and while modifying it slightly so as to allow for inclusive language) I use the abbreviation "Davies and Leftow, 2006."

30. For an account of studies in the early years of the Dominican Order, see M. Michèle Mulchahey, *"First the Bow Is Bent in Study...": Dominican Education Before 1350* (Pontifical Institute of Medieval Studies: Toronto, 1998).

31. As well as having provincial chapters legislating for particular provinces (and consisting of friars from these provinces only), the Dominicans also have general chapters (composed of elected friars from all the provinces), which legislate for the order as a whole.

32. Preaching and hearing confessions were the tasks assigned to the Dominican Order by Pope Honorius III in 1217 and 1221.

33. Adriano Oliva dates the occurrence of this expression to the fourteenth century and not to the lifetime of Aquinas. See Adriano Oliva, "La *Somme de Theologie* de Thomas D'Aquin: Introduction Historique et Littéraire," *Chôra* 7–8 (2009–2010): 235. But what it referred to in the fourteenth century would seem more or less to match what Boyle has in mind when he speaks of *fratres communes*. I turn again to Boyle presently. In his article, Oliva notes that, in conventual

priories such as Orvieto, Aquinas could have been lecturing, not only to new-comers to the Dominican Order and to the study of theology but also to Domini-cans more advanced in their studies (and even to some non-Dominicans).

34. Note the occurrence of the word *incipientes* in the prologue to the *Summa*.

35. Boyle, op. cit., 3.

36. The Leonine Commission, established in 1880, is an organization devoted to producing critical editions of texts ascribed to Aquinas.

37. You will now see that I am echoing Boyle's title in my title for the present chap-ter of this book.

38. Boyle, op. cit., 20.

39. St. Dominic, who founded the Dominicans, was its first Master General. But he was not elected to be so since he founded the order and was not, therefore, elected to office in it. Subsequently, however, Dominicans elected individuals to preside over their order. Humbert of Romans was its fifth master.

40. This fact is well argued for by Adriano Oliva in "La *Somme de Theologie* de Thomas D'Aquin."

41. See *Thomas Aquinas, "Lectura romana in primum Sententiarum Petri Lombardi,"* edited by Leonard E. Boyle and John F. Boyle (Pontifical Institute of Medieval Studies: Toronto, 2006). The introduction to this book provides a case for thinking that Aquinas began again to comment on the *Sentences* while at Santa Sabina.

42. While teaching at Rome, Aquinas would have been dealing with Dominican students in formation and not all the people that Leonard Boyle (perhaps am-biguously) lumps together using the phrase *fratres communes*. Given Aquinas's career as a teacher, it is worth noting that he expresses his views about teaching and learning in a sermon delivered around 1268–1272. The text for the sermon is Luke 2:52 ("The boy Jesus advanced in age and wisdom and in grace with God and the people"). For an English translation of the sermon, see *Thomas Aquinas: The Academic Sermons*, translated by Mark-Robin Hoogland (The Catholic University of America Press: Washington, D.C., 2010). For an exposi-tion of the sermon, see Vivian Boland, "St. Thomas's Sermon *Puer Iesus*: A Neglected Source for His Understanding of Teaching and Learning," *New Blackfriars* 88 (2007).

43. Boyle, op. cit., 17.

44. It seems highly unlikely that Aquinas ever conceived of his *Summa Theologiae* as a substitute for Lombard's *Sentences* in the studies undertaken by Dominicans. The *Sentences* was an unstoppable force in Aquinas's day (though ways of lectur-ing on it developed—with the result that the structure of commentaries on the *Sentences* changed over time). When writing his text Aquinas might well have assumed that readers had the *Sentences* close at hand. But we really do not know.

45. Mark F. Johnson plausibly suggests that Aquinas might have written the *Summa* only for Dominican students destined themselves to become teachers of

Dominicans as lectors. See Mark F. Johnson, "Aquinas's *Summa theologiae* as Pedagogy," in Ronald B. Begley and Joseph W. Koterski, S.J. (eds.), *Medieval Education* (Fordham University Press: New York, 2005). My reservation with Johnson's suggestion is that it renders the *Summa*'s prologue somewhat misleading, though it does account for the way in which the *Summa* seems to make more demands on a reader than could have been met by the average Dominican in Aquinas's day.

46. Here you might also bear in mind what I say above about the deference given to Lombard's *Sentences* in and after Aquinas's day. Ideas thought to be those of Aquinas were condemned in Paris and Oxford in 1277, and you might think that this condemnation could have accounted for his province's not racing to adopt the *Summa* as a textbook for its students. But the Parisian/Oxford condemnation had no authority when it came to what Dominicans were about in their Roman province after the death of Aquinas. And from 1278 General Chapters of the Dominican Order insist that Aquinas's writings should be respected and taught.

47. By "theological treatise" I mean "a work written for believing Christians and in no way concerned to reflect on how Christianity might be defended philosophically." I accept that this definition is a crude one, but I am presently concerned to draw some (clearly real) distinctions in broad strokes.

48. For more on the *Summa Theologiae* in medieval times, see M.-D. Chenu, *Toward Understanding Saint Thomas* (Henry Regnery: Chicago, 1964), 298ff., 318. Also see Jean-Pierre Torrell, *Aquinas's* Summa: *Background, Structure and Reception* (The Catholic University of America Press: Washington, D.C., 2005), 69ff.

49. For an account of the structure of articles in the *Summa Theologiae*, see Otto Bird, "How to Read an Article in the *Summa*," *The New Scholasticism* 27 (1953). Note that not every article in the *Summa* conforms to the structure that I am outlining. Sometimes Aquinas accommodates objections that he raises. When citing passages in the *Summa Theologia* I use Arabic numerals following the practice of the Blackfriars edition. So, for example, 1a,2,3 means *Prima Pars*, question 2, article 3. Some authors favor using Roman numbers when quoting from the *Summa*.

50. For an amusing parody of a typical *Summa Theologiae* article, see http://www2.gsu.edu/~phltso/soap.html.

51. Chenu introduces the notion of the *Summa* having an *exitus-reditus* scheme in chapter 11 of *Toward Understanding Saint Thomas*.

52. Readers looking for good English translations of extracts from the writings of Aquinas in general might turn to *Thomas Aquinas: Selected Writings*, edited and translated with an introduction and notes by Ralph McInerny (Penguin: London, 1998), and *Aquinas: Selected Philosophical Writings*, selected and translated with an introduction and notes by Timothy McDermott (Oxford University Press: New York, 1993). McDermott's volume is arranged thematically and

presents texts that can be thought of as primarily philosophical. McInerny's book presents writings of Aquinas arranged by chronological order of composition and includes a number of his explicitly theological reflections.

53. Russell wrote: "There is little of the true philosophic spirit in Aquinas. He does not, like the Platonic Socrates, set out to follow wherever the argument may lead. He is not engaged in an inquiry, the result of which it is impossible to know in advance. Before he begins to philosophize, he already knows the truth; it is declared in the Catholic faith. If he can find apparently rational arguments for some parts of the faith, so much the better; if he cannot, he need only fall back on revelation. The finding of arguments for a conclusion given in advance is not philosophy, but special pleading. I cannot, therefore, feel that he deserves to be put on a level with the best philosophers either of Greece or of modern times." See Bertrand Russell, *History of Western Philosophy* (George Allen and Unwin: London, 1945), 484f. For a critique of Russell on Aquinas, see Mark T. Nelson, "What the Problem with Aquinas Isn't," *New Blackfriars* 87 (November 2006).

54. Anthony Kenny (ed.), *Aquinas: A Collection of Critical Essays* (University of Notre Dame Press: Notre Dame, 1976), 1.

55. In *Rewritten Theology: Aquinas After His Readers* (Blackwell: Oxford, 2006), Mark Jordan says that "Aquinas chose not to write philosophy" (155). Jordan's case makes sense if we think of what many people mean today by "philosophy" and if we also remember that in Aquinas's time the word *philosopher* was often thought of as basically equivalent to the phrase "pagan thinker." But Jordan's conclusion strikes me as an overstatement since Aquinas clearly did write some works that would easily pass as philosophical even in contemporary philosophical circles (analytical or continental) and since, even when writing on the assumption that certain "articles of faith" (as he calls them) are to be taken as given without philosophical demonstration, Aquinas often engages in philosophical discussions of questions that make the top 10 in any list of topics that philosophers have traditionally explored.

56. A decent Latin edition of the *Summa Theologiae* is available for free at http://www.corpusthomisticum.org/.

CHAPTER 2. SACRED TEACHING (IA,I)

1. Cf. 1a,1,7. The Apostles' Creed (ca. 180) is rendered thus in the English edition of the *Catechism of the Catholic Church* (1994): "I believe in God the Father almighty, creator of heaven and earth. I believe in Jesus Christ, his only Son, our Lord. He was conceived by the power of the Holy Spirit and born of the Virgin Mary. He suffered under Pontius Pilate, was crucified, died, and was buried. He descended to the dead. On the third day he rose again. He ascended into heaven and is seated at the right hand of the Father. He will come again to judge the living and the dead. I believe in the Holy Spirit, the holy catholic Church, the

communion of saints, the forgiveness of sins, the resurrection of the body, and the life everlasting." The same *Catechism* renders the Nicene Creed (325) as follows: "We believe in one God, the Father, the Almighty, maker of heaven and earth, of all that is, seen and unseen. We believe in one Lord, Jesus Christ, the only Son of God, eternally begotten of the Father, God from God, Light from Light, true God from true God, begotten, not made, of one Being with the Father. Through him all things were made. For us men and for our salvation, he came down from heaven: by the power of the Holy Spirit he became incarnate of the Virgin Mary, and became man. For our sake he was crucified under Pontius Pilate; he suffered death and was buried. On the third day he rose again in accordance with the Scriptures; he ascended into heaven and is seated at the right hand of the Father. He will come again in glory to judge the living and the dead, and his kingdom will have no end. We believe in the Holy Spirit, the Lord, the giver of life, who proceeds from the Father and the Son. With the Father and the Son he is worshiped and glorified. He has spoken through the prophets. We believe in one holy catholic and apostolic Church. We acknowledge one baptism for the forgiveness of sins. We look for the resurrection of the dead, and the life of the world to come." I quote these texts in their entirety so that readers of the present book might have a clear sense of what Aquinas took to be the core of what he calls *sacra doctrina*. He makes his position explicit in 2a2ae,1,8 where he says that the "articles of faith" are what the Nicene Creed proclaims.

2. For an English translation of Aquinas's inaugural lecture, see Simon Tugwell, *Albert and Thomas: Selected Writings*. In what I have just reported I am drawing on Tugwell's translation.

3. Davies and Leftow, 2006, 4.

4. Cf. Elizabeth Anscombe, "What Is It to Believe Someone?" in C.F. Delaney (ed.), *Rationality and Religious Belief* (University of Notre Dame Press: Notre Dame, 1979).

5. Davies and Leftow, 2006, 6.

6. Cf. Aquinas's Commentary on Boethius's *De Trinitate*, 2.2. Here we read: "The nature of science (*scientia*) consists in this, that from things already known conclusions about other matters follow of necessity. Seeing that this is possible in the case of divine realities, clearly there can be a science about them." I quote from *Aquinas on Faith and Reason*, edited with introductions by Stephen F. Brown (Hackett: Indianapolis/Cambridge, 1999), 30–31.

7. For more on Aquinas on "demonstration" see below (on 1a,2,2).

8. Davies and Leftow, 2006, 13. The phrase "origin and end" here, of course, supports the idea that Aquinas has an *exitus-reditus* scheme in mind when writing the *Summa Theologiae*.

9. Ibid., 15.

10. For a tool to help one search for Latin terms in the writings of Aquinas, see the *Index Thomisticus* (which runs to fifty-six printed volumes). For this work, which

is now indispensable for scholars of Aquinas, we are indebted to Fr. Roberto
Busa, S.J. (1913–2011). The *Index Thomisticus* is now available in some form
online at the *Corpus Thomisticum* site—http://www.corpusthomisticum.org/.

11. He writes of Mary: "It was necessary that she, as one conceived by sexual inter-
course, should have been conceived with original sin.... Also, were she not con-
ceived with original sin, she would not need to be redeemed by Christ, and so
Christ would not have been the universal redeemer of all human beings."
I quote from *"Compendium of Theology" by Thomas Aquinas*, translated by
Richard J. Regan (Oxford University Press: Oxford, 2009), 180.

12. For a good account of Barth on theology, see Christoph Schwöbel, "Theology,"
in John Webster (ed.), *The Cambridge Companion to Karl Barth* (Cambridge University Press: Cambridge, 2000), 17–36.

13. Davies and Leftow, 2006, 14.

14. Ibid., 14.

15. Ibid., 15.

16. Acts 17:28.

17. "No!" in Emil Brunner and Karl Barth, *Natural Theology* (Wipf and Stock:
Eugene, Ore., 2002), 75. Barth's essay was originally published in 1934.

18. For Vatican I on the matter, see its "Dogmatic Constitution on the Catholic
Faith" (*Dei Filius*), chapter 1. According to Vatican I, "God, the beginning and
end of all things, can be known, from created things, by the light of natural
human reason."

19. James Barr, *Biblical Faith and Natural Theology* (Clarendon: Oxford, 1993).

20. On the general question of whether reason should be thought not to be able to
give us any truths concerning God, see my "Is God Beyond Reason?" *Philosophical Investigations* 32, no. 4 (2009). There I go into more detail than I can here
concerning Barth and Barr.

21. Barr, *Biblical Faith and Natural Theology*, 104.

CHAPTER 3. KNOWING THAT GOD EXISTS (1A,1,2)

1. When I say "much-quoted" I am really thinking of 1a,2,3, in which Aquinas
provides five arguments for believing that God exists. The text of this article has
been reprinted in translation countless times. And it is often thought of as the
best that Aquinas has to offer when it comes to the question "Does God exist?"
In the present volume I try to introduce the text with an eye to its context.

2. Aquinas defends this position in Book I of his commentary on the *Sentences* and
Book I of his *Summa Contra Gentiles*.

3. This line of thinking can be found in the writings of some of Aquinas's contemporaries, notably St. Bonaventure (1217–1274). Cf. Question 1, Article 1 of his *De
Mysterio Trinitatis* (*Disputed Questions on the Mystery of the Trinity*). For an English
edition of this text, see *Saint Bonaventure's "Disputed Questions on the Mystery of the*

Trinity," introduced and translated by Zachary Hayes, OFM (The Franciscan Institute, St, Bonaventure University: New York, 1979). In this text, Bonaventure defends all of the positions discussed and rejected by Aquinas in 1a,2,1.

4. For an English translation of the *Proslogion*, see Brian Davies and G. R. Evans (eds.), *Anselm of Canterbury: The Major Works* (Oxford University Press: New York, 1998). For Anselm and the Ontological Argument, see my "Anselm and the Ontological Argument" in Brian Davies and Brian Leftow (eds.), *The Cambridge Companion to Anselm* (Cambridge University Press: Cambridge, 2004). For an account and discussion of the Ontological Argument from Anselm onward, see Graham Oppy, *Ontological Arguments and Belief in God* (Cambridge University Press: Cambridge, 1995).

5. Cf. Graham Oppy, *Ontological Arguments and Belief in God*.

6. Davies and Leftow, 2006, 20. Aquinas does not quote Anselm in connection with this argument, but he must have been familiar with Anselm's argument.

7. Gaunilo (a monk of the Abbey of Marmoutiers in France) replied to Anselm in a text called *Quid ad haec respondeat quidam pro insipiente* ("A Reply to the Foregoing by a Certain Writer on Behalf of the Fool"). Anselm replied to Gaunilo in *Quid ad haec respondeat editor ipsius libelli* ("A Reply to the Foregoing by the Author of the Book in Question"). To understand how Anselm conceived of his "ontological argument" one definitely needs to read his reply to Gaunilo. But this is something to which Aquinas never refers.

8. Cf. H. D. Lewis, *Philosophy of Religion* (The English Universities Press Ltd: London, 1965), chapter 14. Here Lewis speaks of knowing God on the basis of "cognition," "insight," and "intuition." He sums up his position by saying that God "is closer to all things than distinct finite things ever are to one another" while adding "This we see, not as inference, but in one insight or leap of thought" (146).

9. Cf. P. T. Geach, *Reason and Argument* (Basil Blackwell: Oxford, 1976), 18: "Bad logic books list 'begging the question' as a fallacy. This objection, however, is a mere confusion, and in the court of logic it should be denied a hearing: if the conclusion really is implicit in the premises, then the argument is logically as good as it can be—the conclusion really and indefeasibly follows from the premises." It might be suggested that people who know the premises of a valid argument can have no use for the argument since they already know its conclusion. As Geach observes, however: "This protest forgets that a man may know each premise, but never happen to think of the two premises together and draw the obvious conclusion." Moreover, even with the premises before them, people vary very much in their natural or acquired ability to derive conclusions from them; having the premises is no guarantee that they will know how to derive the right conclusion" (18–19).

10. I mention Barth again here since he is an especially famous modern theologian with whom some readers of this book might already be familiar. But in 1a,2,2,

Aquinas, of course, is writing with an eye to what he knew some of his predecessors and contemporaries thought.

11. With respect to not knowing what God is, Aquinas makes reference to St. John Damascene (ca. 676–749). I presume that he is alluding to Damascene's *De Fide Orthodoxa*, 1,4, which emphasizes the incomprehensibility of God. Aquinas definitely takes Damascene to be a Christian author to be read as authoritative.

12. Davies and Leftow, 2006, 23. For a text famously concluding that "it is wrong always, everywhere, and for anyone, to believe anything upon insufficient evidence," see W. K. Clifford, "The Ethics of Belief," in W. K. Clifford, *Lectures and Essays*, 2nd ed., edited by Leslie Stephen and Frederick Pollock (Macmillan: London, 1886). This essay has been frequently reprinted. It can be found in an edited form in my *Philosophy of Religion: A Guide and Anthology* (Oxford University Press: Oxford, 2000).

13. Davies and Leftow, 2006, 23 (with emendation).

14. For a good essay on Aquinas on "cause," see Michael Rota, "Causation," in Brian Davies and Eleonore Stump (eds.), *The Oxford Handbook of Thomas Aquinas* (Oxford University Press: Oxford, 2011), 104–114.

15. In all of the writings in which he discusses the matter, Aquinas takes arguments for the truth of "God exists" to be like this. To my knowledge, the best available account of Aquinas's many arguments for the truth of "God exists" is Fernand Van Steenberghen, *Le Problèm de l'existence de Dieu dans les Écrits de S. Thomas D'Aquin* (Éditions de l'institute supérieur de philosophie: Louvain-La-Neuve, 1980).

16. For a good account of the Five Ways, I would strongly recommend chapter 12 of John Wippel, *The Metaphysical Thought of Thomas Aquinas* (The Catholic University of America Press: Washington, D.C., 2000). An often-quoted critical discussion of the Five Ways is Anthony Kenny, *The Five Ways* (Routledge & Kegan Paul: London, 1969). For a helpful corrective to Kenny's book, see Lubor Velecky, *Aquinas' Five Arguments in the Summa Theologiae 1a 2,3* (Kok Pharos: Kampen, 1994); and C. F. J. Martin, *Thomas Aquinas: God and Explanation* (Edinburgh University Press: Edinburgh, 1997). All of the volumes just noted point readers in the direction of other secondary literature on the Ways.

17. This is the approach to God expressed by the claim "Something must have started it all." For a development of it, see William Lane Craig, *The Kalām Cosmological Argument* (Macmillan: London and Basingstoke, 1979).

18. Aquinas sometimes speaks of the effects of the first cause in a per se causal series as being "instruments" of it. Cf. his commentary on Aristotle's *Physics*, 8,9. Also cf. *De Veritate*, 27,4.

19. For a good account of Aquinas's distinction between causal series ordered per se and causal series ordered *per accidens*, see Scott MacDonald, "Aquinas's Parasitic Cosmological Argument" (*Medieval Philosophy and Theology*, vol. 1, 1991).

20. Davies and Leftow, 2006, 24–25.

21. By "real change" I mean a genuine modification of an existing thing (as, e.g., is someone's putting on weight or sailing from the United Kingdom to the United States). We sometimes seem to ascribe change to things where the change is not real change in this sense. Thus, for example, we may say "Mary came to be admired by Paul" without implying that Mary herself underwent any real change. This second sense of "change" is not what Aquinas is thinking of in the First Way.

22. This is not obvious from the text of the First Way (which only invokes an example of local motion). But note Aquinas's commentary on Book V of Aristotle's *Physics* (Lecture 2) in which the point is made clearly. The English word *change* can be rendered into (Aquinas's) Latin by both *motus* and *mutatio*. In his *Physics* commentary, Aquinas allows for *mutatio* that is not *motus* while referring to what he calls substantial change, which he thinks of, not as a change in an actually existing thing but as the coming into existence of something or the passing out of existence of it (e.g., the generation or death of a human being).

23. I use this example in order to bring out the fact that Aquinas does not in general think that all change in a subject is brought about by what is quite different from the subject. I might be frog-marched into my kitchen by someone, but my coming to be standing in my kitchen might also be explicable with reference to the movements of my legs, which are parts of me.

24. Davies and Leftow, 2006, 25.

25. In the Second Way Aquinas does not give any concrete examples of what he is thinking of when he speaks of efficient causes and effects ordered in series. But he is definitely thinking in terms of examples such as I give (while allowing that *a number* of efficient causes and effects of efficient causes might be observed *all together* [as it were])—as, when it comes, say, to a hand moving a stick that moves something else (an example that Aquinas *does* give in the First Way).

26. Anthony Kenny makes this point in his *The Five Ways* (Routledge & Kegan Paul: London, 1969), 35–36. In his *Thomas Aquinas: God and Explanations*, C. F. J. Martin speaks of the Second way as a "generalization" of the First Way (146).

27. Wippel, *The Metaphysical Thought of Thomas Aquinas*, 459.

28. Davies and Leftow, 2006, 25–26.

29. Basically, Aquinas takes a substance to be a naturally occurring thing, object, or being (as opposed to an artifact). This sense of "substance" can be found in the writings of Aristotle. According to this sense, dogs and cats, for example, would be substances (though computers or telephones would not). For more on this, see John F. Wippel, *The Metaphysical Thought of Thomas Aquinas* (cited above).

30. For a discussion of people wrongly interpreting Aquinas as saying that there has to be only one necessary being, see Patterson Brown, "St Thomas' Doctrine of Necessary Being," reprinted in Anthony Kenny (ed.), *Aquinas: A Collection of Critical Essays* (University of Notre Dame Press: Notre Dame, 1976).

31. When referring to contingency, some philosophers have said that there are statements that are contingently true because they are not true of logical

necessity. On this account, "the Eiffel Tower exists" is a logically contingent statement while "all triangles have three sides" is a logically necessary one. With this distinction in mind it has also been suggested that there is a corresponding difference when it comes to things that exist contingently and things that exist necessarily—the idea being that something existing contingently is something the existence of which can be denied without self-contradiction while the existence of something necessary cannot be denied without self-contradiction. As we have seen, Aquinas thinks that the proposition "God does not exist" can be denied without the person propounding it being guilty of self-contradiction.

32. An argument to this effect can be found in II,1 of *The Guide of the Perplexed* by Moses Maimonides (1135–1204). This is a text with which Aquinas was familiar.

33. The fallacy is sometimes called "the quantifier shift fallacy" and is illustrated by the argument "All roads lead somewhere, so there is some (one) place (e.g., Rome) to which all roads lead."

34. The interpretation of the Third Way to which I am now referring supposes that Aquinas is assuming that if the world has existed from infinity, perishable things in it would all have perished by now. For Aquinas clearly denying that philosophy can establish that the universe had a beginning, see John Wippel, *Metaphysical Themes in Thomas Aquinas*, chapter 8. Aquinas develops this case in his *De Aeternitate Mundi* (*On the Eternity of the World*). Cf. also *Summa Theologiae*, 1a,46,2.

35. I defend the second reading to which I here refer in "Aquinas's Third Way," *New Blackfriars* 82, no. 968 (October 2001). Note that in his *Summa Contra Gentiles* (I,15), Aquinas offers an argument strikingly similar to what we find in the Third Way. This argument is clearly concerned with things coming to be rather than things coming to pass away.

36. Davies and Leftow, 2006, 26.

37. I suspect that Aquinas would be happy to say that a badly behaved cat (by a criterion of being well behaved that we might have when thinking about cats) might be a very good cat (because it is healthy). Aquinas frequently takes "good" to be an adjective only understandable when it comes to the work it is doing as predicated of something in particular. We might ask "Is X good?" Abstracting from things that he wants to say about God's goodness, Aquinas would reply, "I cannot answer the question until I know to what you are referring by 'X.'" He would mean that we commend things as being good for different reasons and depending on what things we are talking about and under what category we place them—that, for example, we might say that Fred is a good parent but a bad doctor. When thinking about things in the world, Aquinas takes "good" to be an attributive adjective and not a predicative one. On this distinction, see P. T. Geach, "Good and Evil," *Analysis* 17 (1956).

38. One can see him doing so in, for example, *De Veritate*, 1,1. According to Aquinas, being, truth, and goodness are "convertible"—meaning that something exists only insofar as it is somehow true and good.

39. Again, cf. *De Veritate*, 1,1.

40. I quote here from Davies and Leftow, 2006, 26 (with some emendation).

41. Cf. William Paley, *Natural Theology* (1802), chapters 1–3.

CHAPTER 4. THE DIVINE NATURE: PART I (1A,3–13)

1. Davies and Leftow, 2006, 28.

2. In various writings Aquinas distinguishes between genuine substances, which he calls *entia per se* ("beings through themselves"), and things that are not such, which he refers to as *entia per accidens* ("beings by accident"). Things such as dogs or cats would, on this understanding, be genuine substances, while an artifact would not. When speaking of things being composite Aquinas is thinking of substances (*entia per se*)—naturally occurring things.

3. Aquinas distinguishes between "substantial form" and "accidental form." For him, a thing's substantial form amounts to what makes it what it is essentially or by nature (so he would say that the substantial form of a cat consists in what it takes for something simply to exist as a cat). But Aquinas also thinks that something with a distinct essence or nature might be described as having certain features or attributes that it can acquire or lose without ceasing to be what it is essentially. With this thought in mind, Aquinas will say, for example, that my cat can acquire the "accidental form" of weighing three pounds having previously weighed two pounds, but of course without ceasing to be the same cat.

4. For Aquinas discussing God's perfection and goodness in a text other than the *Summa Theologiae*, see *Summa Contra Gentiles* I,28 and I,37–41.

5. P. T. Geach, "Good and Evil," *Analysis* 17 (1956).

6. Davies and Leftow, 2006, 45.

7. A despairing teacher might say of a student that he or she is incapable of improvement. But Aquinas is not thinking of God as incapable of improvement in this sense. His point is that we cannot think of God as something that could possibly be better than it is.

8. Note that Aquinas distinguishes between being perfect and being good. Something can, he thinks, be good without being perfect. The distinction here explains why Aquinas devotes separate discussions to the questions "Is God perfect?" and "Is God good?" Aquinas's good/perfect distinction seems to be intelligible since we can, for instance, say that even a good such and such might be less than perfect.

9. Aquinas in general is fond of quoting Aristotle's *Nicomachean Ethics* I,1, 1094a3: "The good is what everything desires." He does so several times in 1a,5–6.

10. Davies and Leftow, 2006, 65.

11. Ibid., 68 (1a,6,4).

12. Cf. 1a,6,4. Whether or not Plato really did think of forms as Aquinas (influenced by Aristotle's reading of Plato) supposes that he did is, I should note, something about which contemporary Plato scholars disagree. For an introduction to the debate on this matter, see Gail Fine, *On Ideas: Aristotle's Criticism of Plato's Theory of Forms* (Oxford University Press: Oxford, 1995).

13. We shall later see that Aquinas does not take this idea to be incompatible with the belief that Jesus of Nazareth was divine.

14. For a critical account of this view, see Thomas G. Weinandy, *Does God Change?* (St. Bede's Publications: Still River, Mass., 1985). I note and comment on this view, and on variations of it, in chapter 6 of my *Thinking About God* (Wipf & Stock: Eugene, Ore., 2010).

15. Davies and Leftow, 2006, 93. At this point in the *Summa Theologiae* Aquinas is drawing especially on his reading of Boethius's *Consolation of Philosophy*. For a fine introduction to and discussion of this work (and to Boethius as a whole), see John Marenbon, *Boethius* (Oxford University Press: New York, 2003).

16. Cf. 1a,10,1, in which Aquinas agrees that "eternity" signifies duration of some sort.

17. In 1a,10,6 Aquinas asks whether there is only one aeviternity. As readers will see, he is somewhat agnostic on the matter, which is why I do not dwell on what he says about it.

18. In 1a,11, 1 and 2 Aquinas offers a number of complicated reflections on what number amounts to, reflections that I here pass over in silence. I cannot, however, resist noting that they are austerely philosophical reflections and count against the claim (which I have previously referenced) that Aquinas chose not to write philosophy.

19. First John 3:2 says of God: "We will be like him for we will see him as he is."

20. Most of what Aquinas says in 1a,12 is focused on our knowledge of God's essence. You should, however, note that in 1a,12,1–10 he is also (though largely by implication) concerned with knowledge of God's essence on the part of angels. This accounts for the recurrence in 1a,12 of the expression "created intellect/mind" (*intellectus creatus*). As we shall see, Aquinas has quite a lot to say about angels as the *Prima Pars* continues.

21. 1a,12,4 includes some comments by Aquinas on what knowledge amounts to in people and angels. These comments amount to previews (as it were) of some positions that Aquinas will defend later in the *Prima Pars*.

22. Actually, he does this briefly in 1a,12,1, ad.1.

23. 1a,12,11, like many passages in Aquinas's writings, makes it clear that, for Aquinas, there can be no direct perception or experience of God in the present life. For a sustained defense of a contrary position, see William P. Alston, *Perceiving God* (Cornell University Press: Ithaca, 1991).

24. Some words, of course, are not nouns or adjectives or verbs. "If," "then," "because," and "or" are examples.

25. Cf. Herbert McCabe, *God Still Matters* (Continuum: London and New York, 2002), 3: "We always do have to speak of our God with borrowed words; it is one of the special things about our God that...he is always dressed verbally in second-hand clothes that don't fit him very well." I am certain that Aquinas would have agreed with McCabe here.

26. Davies and Leftow, 2006, 140.

27. Cf. appendix 3 to volume 3 of the Blackfriars edition of the *Summa Theologiae*.

28. G. E. M Anscombe and P. T. Geach, *Three Philosophers* (Basil Blackwell: Oxford, 1961), 122.

29. Here Aquinas is reading Exodus 13 in the Latin Vulgate translation, according to which God tells Moses that God's name is *Qui Est*. Readers of contemporary commentaries on Exodus 13 will find scholars taking a variety of positions when it comes to explaining the Hebrew phrase that Aquinas read in Latin as *Qui Est*.

30. Davies and Leftow, 2006, 140 (with slight emendation).

CHAPTER 5. THE DIVINE NATURE: PART 2 (1A,14–26)

1. Philosophers sometimes distinguish between knowing *that* and knowing *how* (as in "I know that dogs are carnivorous" and "I know how to ride a bicycle"). In 1a,14 Aquinas is always concerned with knowledge as in knowledge of what something is, considered as a subcategory of "knowing that."

2. In *Summa Contra Gentiles* I,44, Aquinas also argues that God can hardly be perfect if God is something lacking the common, human perfection of having knowledge—if God's mode of being is that of being as restricted materially as, for example, that of a piece of coal.

3. Davies and Leftow, 2006, 187.

4. For an account of discussions of this question prior to the time of Aquinas, see Richard Sorabji, *Time, Creation and the Continuum* (Duckworth: London, 1983).

5. Note that while "John believes that-p" does not entail "p," "John knows that-p" does entail "p."

6. The line of argument in 1a,14,13 is, I think, presented with even greater clarity in 1:14 of Aquinas's commentary on Aristotle's *Peri Hermeneias*. For an English translation of this, see *Thomas Aquinas: Selected Philosophical Writings*, translated and edited by Timothy McDermott (Oxford University Press: New York, 1993), 277ff.

7. Davies and Leftow, 2006, 203.

8. Aquinas does not mean that one cannot know that, for example, my cat is not sleeping. He means that one cannot know a nonexistent cat whether conceived of as sleeping or awake.

9. Readers of Aquinas at this point should not assume that Aquinas would today be defending the death penalty for certain crimes. But he obviously had no

objection to capital punishment, in principle, in the society in which he lived, which did not have the ability that we have to contain violent criminals and to protect people from them. Note that in 1a,19,6, Aquinas alludes to the death penalty while referring to some people as being "public dangers" (Davies and Leftow, 2006, 229). In 2a2ae, 64, 2 and 3, he defends putting some people to death only with a view to the protection of others.

10. Davies and Leftow, 2006, 203.

11. Cf. Genesis 23:19 and Jeremiah 18:7-8.

12. In presenting what I am here calling (1), Aquinas does not pause to offer a detailed defense of the claim that some things that come about do not have to and that free human choices fall into this category. In 1a,19,8, however, he briefly notes an argument to which he will later return—the argument being that if everything comes about of necessity in the world then there is no room left for deliberation and free choice.

13. Davies and Leftow, 2006, 233.

14. This argument is expanded on by Aquinas in 1,14 of his commentary on Aristotle's *Peri Hermeneias*.

15. In 1a,20, Aquinas, though clearly thinking that to love is always to will the good of another, also wants to say that God's love differs from human love in two ways. First, Aquinas argues (1a,20,2), God wills the good of others by being the cause of that good and not by reacting to or promoting goodness considered as falling outside the causal activity of God. Second (1a,20,3), God's love does not admit to degrees of intensity in God (God being simple).

16. For Aristotle on commutative justice, see *Nichomachean Ethics*, 5,4, 1131b25.

17. Davies and Leftow, 2006, 263.

18. Ibid., 265.

19. Ibid.

20. One might ask, "To what extent do various Reformation authors agree or disagree with Aquinas when it comes to predestination?" That question, however, is not one I can engage with in this book.

21. Romans 8:28–30.

22. For Augustine on predestination, see, especially, his *De Gratia et Libero Arbitrio* (*On Grace and Free Choice*).

23. Cf. D. Z. Phillips, *The Problem of Evil and the Problem of God* (SCM: London, 2004), chapter 1.

24. Davies and Leftow, 2006, 274.

25. Ibid., 274–275.

26. As we have now seen, however, 1a,2–26 does not entirely abstract from specifically Christian teaching. Aquinas frequently quotes from the New Testament (considered by him as an authority) in this text. And in 1a,12 he is presupposing the notion of the beatific vision.

CHAPTER 6. THE DIVINE TRINITY (1A,27–43)

1. For a short introduction to the doctrine of the Trinity in Catholic thinking, see Gilles Emery, *The Trinity* (Catholic University of America Press: Washington, D.C., 2011).

2. For a detailed account of Aquinas on the Trinity, see Gilles Emery, *The Trinitarian Theology of Saint Thomas Aquinas* (Oxford University Press: Oxford, 2007). Also see Gilles Emery, *Trinity in Aquinas* (Sapientia: Ypsilanti, 2003). For a sensitive reading of the *Summa Theologiae*'s account of the Trinity written with an eye on some contemporary criticisms of it, see Rowan Williams, "What Does Love Know? St. Thomas on the Trinity," *New Blackfriars* 82, no. 964 (June 2001). For a discussion of Aquinas on the Trinity in its medieval context, see Russell L. Friedman, *Intellectual Traditions at the Medieval University: The Use of Philosophical Psychology in Trinitarian Theology Among the Franciscans and Dominicans* (Brill: Leiden and Boston, 2012); and Russell L. Friedman, *Medieval Trinitarian Thought from Aquinas to Ockham* (Cambridge: Cambridge University Press, 2010).

3. Some theologians have argued otherwise—notable examples being St. Anselm of Canterbury and St. Bonaventure. Both of these authors defend the claim that reason points inexorably to the notion of God as three in one.

4. BLK/CUP 6, 103.

5. Ibid.

6. At various points in his discussion of the Trinity in the *Summa Theologiae*, Aquinas tries to say why some accounts of what God is depart from what he takes to be orthodox Christian teaching. He makes it clear when he is doing this, and he specifies the authors whom he takes to be unorthodox (or, as Aquinas would say, heretical) when it comes to the Trinity. So I am not going to highlight what he says on this front. I shall leave it to you, should you be inclined, to chase down his references to Arius (ca. 250–ca. 356), Sabellius (early third century), and the other people to whom he alludes critically (as doctrinally suspect) in 1a,27 and following.

7. John's Gospel is hugely important as an influence on Aquinas's Trinitarian thinking. There is a good English translation of Aquinas's commentary on the Gospel of John. See *St. Thomas Aquinas: Commentary on the Gospel of St. John* (translated by Fabian R. Larcher). This (with contributions by James A. Weisheipl) comes in two volumes. The first was published by Magi Books (Albany, N.Y.) in 1980. The second was published by St. Bede's Publications (Petersham, Mass.) in 1998 (so far as I can gather, though, there is no publication date given in the printed work). This translation of Aquinas's commentary on John has been republished with a new introduction by Daniel Keating and M. Levering (Catholic University of America Press: Washington, D.C., 2010).

8. In speaking of knowing and loving as actions "in the spiritual world," Aquinas is thinking that knowing and loving are not simply material processes, even when it comes to knowing and loving in people, whom, as we shall see, he thinks of as essentially physical things.

9. BLK/CUP 6, 3, 4, 5, 7, 13.

10. In 1a,31,2, Aquinas indicates something of his outlook when it comes to discussions of the Trinity in general. These, he says, need to steer a middle course between denying that there is genuine distinction in God (that God really is Father, Son, and Spirit) and denying that God is simple.

11. 1a,28,1 (BLK/CUP 6, 23, 25).

12. 1a,28,1 (BLK/CUP 6, 25).

13. For an English translation of the *Categories*, see *Aristotle's "Categories" and "De Interpretatione,"* translated with notes by J. L. Ackrill (Clarendon: Oxford, 1963).

14. 1a,28,1 (BLK/CUP 6, 25).

15. 1a,28,2 (BLK/CUP 6, 29).

16. You might wish to reject this view as unintelligible since, you might say, relations cannot be *subsistent*, as Aquinas supposes in his discussion of the Trinity. For a modern philosophical defense of subsisting relations, however, see C. J. F. Williams, "Neither Confounding the Persons nor Dividing the Substance," in Alan Padgett (ed.), *Reason and the Christian Religion: Essays in Honour of Richard Swinburne* (Clarendon: Oxford, 1994).

17. 1a,28,2. I quote (with slight emendation) from BLK/CUP 6, 31.

18. 1a,28,3 (BLK/CUP 6, 35). In this article Aquinas seems to be concerned to rule out the approach to the Trinity sometimes referred to as modalism and commonly associated with the third-century theologian Sabellius.

19. 1a,29,3 (BLK/CUP 6, 53). Here Aquinas (cf. 1a,29,1) is drawing on a famous definition of *persona* offered by Boethius (*De Duabus Naturis*, 3). A person, Boethius says, is "an individual substance of a rational nature" (*Persona est rationalis naturae individua substantia*).

20. 1a,29,4 (BLK/CUP 6, 59).

21. 1a,29,4 (BLK/CUP 6, 61). In 1a,29 Aquinas discusses differences in meaning ascribed to the terms *"persona"* and *"hypostasis"* and asks whether we should take *"persona"* as used of the persons of the Trinity to be equivalent to *hypostasis*. Historical issues are driving this discussion. I pass over them in silence in the present chapter since in 1a,29, Aquinas actually explains them fairly clearly (or as clearly as I could) and since I am now trying to focus on what I take to be the essentials of Aquinas's teaching on the Trinity.

22. First Timothy 1:17 reads "To the King of the ages, immortal, invisible, the only God, be honor and glory forever and ever."

23. In 1a,32,2–4, Aquinas asks if we should posit characteristics in God (*utrum sint ponendae notiones in divinis*). Here he is asking whether or not we can use certain abstract terms (such as "fatherhood" or "sonship") when talking about the

Trinity (terms to be thought of as abstract by contrast to terms such as "Father" and "Son"). With the drift of 1a,13 in mind, Aquinas suggests that we can. But he notes that there are no articles of faith about the characteristics (1a,32,4). So I do not discuss what Aquinas says about divine characteristics while talking about what he says on the Trinity in the *Summa*—most of this being concerned with that with respect to which he thinks that there *are* articles of faith.

24. Obviously, each article in 1a,33–43 raises a question not previously explicitly discussed in the *Summa Theologiae*. So all of the answers to them that Aquinas gives add to what he has previously written. But some of them effectively only represent things that Aquinas has already said (the *corpus* of 1a,33,4 is a good example) while others seem to add what might not be naturally inferred from this. I am now concerned with what, in 1a,33–43, you might not immediately infer from what Aquinas said previously.

25. BLK/CUP 7, 15.

26. This point is rightly emphasized by Herbert McCabe in his essay "Aquinas on the Trinity" (in Herbert McCabe, *God Still Matters*, 51).

27. Ibid.

28. The Latin equivalent of the English verb "to send" is *mittere*. And the corresponding noun is *missio*. That explains why the title of 1a,43 is *de missione divinarum personarum* (which we can translate as "On the Mission or Sending of the Divine Persons").

29. McCabe, *God Still Matters*, 39.

30. Ibid., 39. McCabe goes on to talk of how contemporary physicists speak of matter in terms of both waves and particles without taking themselves to be talking nonsense even if they look forward to getting an understanding of the constituents of the universe while discarding the language of waves and particles.

31. BLK/CUP 6, 109.

CHAPTER 7. CREATION, GOOD, AND EVIL (1A,44–49)

1. BLK/CUP 8, 3.

2. Ibid., 7.

3. For some discussion of this notion, see Robert Pasnau and Christopher Shields, *The Philosophy of Aquinas* (Westview: Boulder and Oxford, 2004), 43–44. Also see my *Aquinas* (Continuum: London, 2002), 20ff.

4. BLK/CUP 8, 13.

5. Ibid., 21.

6. Ibid., 27.

7. Ibid., 31.

8. Ibid., 33.

9. Ibid., 37.

10. In 1a,45,4, Aquinas refines this conclusion slightly by saying that it is, properly speaking, only subsisting individuals that are created. Such individuals (things like a human being) will, of course, have accidental forms that creatively derive from God (if Aquinas's account of creation is correct). But, says Aquinas, accidental forms exist *in* subjects and do not exist independently of them. So Aquinas prefers to speak of them as "co-created" rather than as "created." He alludes to this notion again in 1a,45,8.

11. BLK/CUP 8, 45.

12. Ibid., 53.

13. Here I take Aquinas to be deferring to St. Augustine, who in *De Trinitate*, VI,10, speaks of there being a "trace" (*vestigium*) of the Trinity in the created world.

14. Aquinas turns to the question at some length in his *De Aeternitate Mundi* ("On the Eternity of the World") written around 1271.

15. Some biblical scholars would deny that Genesis says that the world had an absolute beginning in Aquinas's sense because it speaks of God working on a "formless void" when creating (Genesis 1:1-2). I am not, however, qualified to comment on this conclusion.

16. Cf. *Physics* 1,9 and *De Caelo* 1,3.

17. BLK/CUP 8, 99.

18. At this point you should also bear in mind Aquinas's view that "good" is a logically attributive adjective (cf. chapter 4 above). That is because he has exactly the same view when it comes to "bad."

19. BLK/CUP 8, 109.

20. You might say that someone is bad just because he or she does something that has bad consequences for other people. Yet, of course, bad consequences for people can arise without any badly acting person being involved. I can choose to kill you by braining you with the branch of a tree, but you might die because wind has caused the branch of a tree to fall on your head. We have the same consequence in each case, though only in the first do we have a case of moral evil or evil done.

21. If I murder you, then, Aquinas would say, I fail to act well. He recognizes, however, that my doing so might incidentally have welcome spin-offs (that, e.g., my heinous behavior might horrify people so that they end up devoting themselves to protecting potential murder victims).

CHAPTER 8. ANGELS AND THE DAYS OF CREATION (1A,50–74)

1. See note 3 below.

2. From the second half of the fifteenth century, Aquinas has often been referred to as "the angelic doctor." That is partly because of the attention he pays to angels in his writings and partly because of comparisons that some people seem to find between Aquinas and angels with respect to knowledge and to devotion to God.

3. Why is it the case that the topics discussed in 1a,50–74 are not at the forefront of contemporary theological discussion? One reason is that theologians for a long time now have thought that their business is to concentrate only on central doctrines of Christianity (these not generally taken by them to include belief in angels or in the conclusions that Aquinas defends in 1a,65–74). I strongly suspect that were Aquinas writing today, he would be writing little about angels. You have to remember, however, that Aquinas was a man of his time. You should also bear in mind that the *Summa Theologiae* belongs to a genre that has died out. It has been centuries since theologians wrote massive and comprehensive works like this text (or comparable medieval works such as the many commentaries on the *Sentences* of Peter Lombard).

4. BLK/CUP 9, 3 (with slight emendation).

5. It is an attempt to engage in what St. Anselm called "faith seeking understanding" (*Proslogion* 1).

6. 1a,50,1 might seem to present us with Aquinas seeking to demonstrate that angels exist. But the argument here assumes both the existence of God and that of angels while arguing that the universe would lack a possible way of being were there not something wholly immaterial but less exalted than God.

7. Aquinas speaks of angels as things that we need to believe in as existing. But the necessity here derives from premises that Aquinas takes to be revealed in biblical talk about angels. Cf. what he says about *sacra doctrina* as *scientia* in 1a,1.

8. Some of Aquinas's contemporaries (e.g., St. Bonaventure) thought of angels as composed of "spiritual matter" and form.

9. BLK/CUP 9, 23.

10. Ibid., 29.

11. Cf. what Aquinas says in 1a,8 about God being in places. Note, however, that in 1a,52,2 Aquinas denies that angels can be in all places as God is.

12. BLK/CUP 9, 57.

13. Cf. the discussion in 1a,14 and 19 of knowledge and will in God and bear in mind my comments on these questions.

14. Cf. my explanation of this kind of composition in my account of 1a,3.

15. This point is stressed again by Aquinas in 1a,61,1, in which he insists that the existence of angels is caused by God.

16. Aquinas thinks of anger and lust as involving an irreducible physical element. Cf. chapter 11 of the present book.

17. As an analogy to help understand why Aquinas thinks of Satan as originally the greatest of the angels, think along the following lines: Fred is a brilliant musician, mathematician, athlete, painter, and medical doctor; some of his children inherit some of his abilities; some inherit none of them; but Mary, Fred's daughter, has all the abilities and skills that her father has. With this scenario in mind, Aquinas would say that Mary is the greatest of all Fred's children (the one who most reflects what Fred is) and is, in this respect, like Satan when thought

of in relation to God. This analogy limps, however, since, as we have seen, Aquinas does not take individual angels to be members of a species and no creature has all of God's abilities.

18. Aquinas is thinking here that nothing that has a definite nature can want not to have that nature. He is thinking, for example, that much as I might admire the Grand Canyon, I could not want to be the Grand Canyon without willing my own nonexistence as a human being.

19. Cf. Jeffrey McCurry, "Why the Devil Fell: A Lesson in Spirituality from Aquinas's *Summa Theologiae*," *New Blackfriars* 87 (2006).

20. If you are interested in understanding the details of 1a,65–74 you might consider starting your research by consulting the very learned material provided by William A. Wallace, OP, in BLK/CUP 10. Wallace writes with considerable knowledge concerning medieval and pre-medieval scientific views.

21. For a fine translation of Augustine's *Confessions*, see *Saint Augustine Confessions*, translated with an introduction and notes by Henry Chadwick (Oxford University Press: Oxford, 1991).

22. BLK/CUP 10, 5, 7.

23. Ibid., 17.

CHAPTER 9. HUMAN BEINGS AND DIVINE GOVERNMENT (1A,75–119)

1. BLK/CUP 11, 3 (with slight emendation). In this chapter I am quoting from the BLK/CUP edition of the *Summa Theologiae*. But you might want to note that there are two good single-volume English translations of 1a,75–89 currently available. These are (1) *Thomas Aquinas: The Treatise on Human Nature, Summa Theologiae 1a 75–89*, translated with an introduction and commentary by Robert Pasnau (Hackett: Indianapolis/Cambridge, 2002); and (2) *Thomas Aquinas: Treatise on Human Nature*, translated by Alfred J. Freddoso (St. Augustine's Press: South Bend, Ind., 2010). I think that both of these translations are valuable and that they actually sometimes improve on the BLK/CUP translation. Pasnau's translation comes with an extremely helpful commentary.

2. Cf. BLK/CUP 11, 3: "Human nature demands distinct theological treatment precisely by virtue of the soul, not of its bodily character, except so far as soul bespeaks embodiment." Readers of 1a,75–89 should, however, note that this part of the *Summa* (rather like 1a,2–26) is very much a philosophical discussion, in spite of its many references to Christian authorities and in spite of the fact that 1a,89 assumes that people, in some sense, enjoy life after death. In saying this I mean that, though Aquinas writes 1a,75–89 as a teacher of *sacra doctrina*, the text relies heavily on what can be thought to be philosophical arguments as opposed to arguments based on divine revelation (as Aquinas thinks of this).

3. Although Aquinas is indebted to Aristotle when it comes to what he says about soul in the *Summa Theologiae*, his discussion of soul differs in many ways from what Aristotle says about it in *On Soul*, on which Aquinas wrote a commentary.

4. Aquinas would not say precisely this, since he would deny that a car is an individual in the sense that a human being is. He would think of a car as an artifact (and therefore as an *ens per accidens*) while he would think of a human being as a naturally occurring substance (an *ens* per se). But he would still agree that driver plus car = two distinguishable things in that it would be true to say that the car is not the driver and the driver is not the car.

5. Herbert McCabe, "The Immortality of the Soul," in *Aquinas: A Collection of Critical Essays* (University of Notre Dame Press: Notre Dame, 1976), 304.

6. Some commentators on Aquinas have suggested that we might read Aquinas (albeit somewhat anachronistically) as equating human understanding with the ability to use language. I have no comment to make on this reading of Aquinas. But it is interestingly developed by Herbert McCabe in *On Aquinas* (Continuum: London, 2008), which I commend to readers who want to try to connect Aquinas with what some famous linguistic philosophers have said, especially Ludwig Wittgenstein (1889–1951).

7. BLK/CUP 11, 11.

8. In 1a,76,2, Aquinas argues that there is not one soul for all human beings (as some of his contemporaries maintained to be the position of Aristotle). In this article he is denying that there is some single soul by which all people are animated. He claims that each human being is an individual with an individual soul animating it.

9. BLK/CUP 11, 19.

10. 1a,75,4, ad.2.

11. BLK/CUP 11, 49 (with slight emendation).

12. In 1a,78, Aquinas painstakingly lists the various powers of the soul that he takes to be found at the "vegetative" and sensory level.

13. In the *Summa Theologiae*, as elsewhere in his writings, Aquinas distinguishes understanding and reasoning. Reasoning, which he always takes to involve something presentable in the form of an argument from premises to conclusions, differs, in his view, from understanding, which he takes to be what we have as we grasp what something is or why the conclusion of a sound argument has to be true.

14. For a detailed defense of this reading of Aquinas, see Sheldon M. Cohen, "St. Thomas Aquinas on the Immaterial Reception of Sensible Forms," *Philosophical Review* 91 (April 1982).

15. For a clear and non-technical account of Aquinas on interior senses, see Herbert McCabe, *On Aquinas*, chapters 12 and 13.

16. Here one should remember how it is that Aquinas views human knowers as inferior to God and angels, who do not, he thinks, have to acquire knowledge as bodily individuals do.

17. Aquinas's notion of the agent intellect has sometimes been taken to be equivalent to that had by some philosophers who have said that we acquire concepts only as we pay attention to some sense data that we experience while ignoring others—a view sometimes referred to as "abstractionism." The philosophical problems of abstractionism are well highlighted by Peter Geach in his book *Mental Acts* (Routledge & Kegan Paul: London, 1957). But Aquinas is no defender of abstractionism as attacked by Geach. He does not think that the agent intellect is a power we have so as to focus on some sensations while filtering out other ones. He thinks of it as an ability to structure sense experiences so as to form a view of the world on the basis of which discussion of it can get started.

18. Anthony Kenny neatly sums up the essentials of Aquinas's teaching on agent intellect and possible intellect by saying that, for Aquinas, the former is "the human capacity to abstract universal ideas from particular sense-experience" while the latter is "the storehouse of those ideas once abstracted." See Anthony Kenny, *Aquinas* (Oxford University Press: Oxford, 1980), 69.

19. BLK/CUP 11, 187 (with slight emendation).

20. One can, for example, have knowledge that one does not act on in any way. One can also know while not being in any position to act.

21. The term "*synderesis*" entered medieval thinking from what St. Jerome (ca. 347–420) says in a commentary on the Old Testament book of Ezekiel.

22. Aquinas talks about *synderesis* at some length in Question 16 of his *De Veritate*.

23. For Aquinas's understanding of *per se nota quoad nos*, see chapter 3 above.

24. For more on Aquinas on *habitus*, see chapter 12.

25. Not innate since Aquinas takes it to depend on the operation of the agent intellect.

26. I quote from D. D. Raphael (ed.), *British Moralists 1650–1800* (Oxford University Press: Oxford, 1969), i, 351.

27. BLK/CUP 11, 193.

28. Submitting to dental treatment would be a good example.

29. 1a,83,1. I quote (with slight emendation) from BLK/CUP 11, 239.

30. One should realize that Aquinas is not claiming that people always act while having the power of *liberum arbitrium*. He is claiming that they sometimes do so when reasoning in a certain way and as having certain "appetites."

31. 1a,84,7. BLK/CUP 12, 43 (with slight emendation).

32. 1a,85,5. BLK/CUP 12, 77.

33. Pasnau, *Thomas Aquinas: The Treatise on Human Nature*, 357.

34. The view that Aquinas here ascribes to Averroes was a common one among philosophers in the ancient and medieval Islamic world.

35. 1a,88,2. BLK/CUP 12, 133.

36. 1a,89 should be read in conjunction with 1a,12.

37. 1a,89,1. BLK/CUP 12, 139.

38. Ibid.

39. 1a,89,6. BLK/CUP 12, 157.

40. That this is Aquinas's modest aim in 1a,89 is well emphasized by Robert Pasnau. Cf. *Thomas Aquinas: The Treatise on Human Nature*, 370–371.

41. 1a,89,8. BLK/CUP 12, 163.

42. Some contemporary readers will think that Aquinas is right to read the Genesis account of the origin of human beings as if it were literally true. Here I am not even going to try to comment on whether or not they are correct to do so. In 1a,102,1, Aquinas himself clearly indicates that he is reading the Genesis account literally. Speaking of Paradise (the garden of Eden), he observes: "What Scripture says about Paradise is set forth in the form of historical narrative, and in all matters that are so related in Scripture we must accept the truth of the history as our foundation and only build spiritual explanations on top of it" (BLK/CUP 13, 185).

43. 1a,93,6. BLK/CUP 13, 67.

44. 1a,105,8. BLK/CUP 14, 85.

45. Dionysius the Areopagite (sometimes known as Pseudo-Dionysius) was the unknown author of a collection of writings that were very influential in the thirteenth century because they were then presumed to have been written by the disciple of St. Paul mentioned in Acts 17:34. Aquinas quotes from these writings not only when talking about angels but also when discussing human knowledge of God (especially in 1a,13). Scholars today favor the view that the Dionysian writings come from the sixth century. For a fine introduction to them, see Paul Rorem, *Pseudo-Dionysius: A Commentary on the Texts and an Introduction to Their Influence* (Oxford University Press: New York, 1993).

46. So Aquinas does not equate causation with necessitation. He thinks that causes can sometimes act without bringing about what one might expect them to. He also thinks that some events lack a single cause even though their constituents do have causes. So in 1a,115,6 he allows for chance events that still have causal explanations of different kinds.

47. I elaborate on Aquinas's view of teaching in "Aquinas and the Academic Life," *New Blackfriars* 83 (July 2002).

CHAPTER 10. HAPPINESS, HUMAN ACTION, AND MORALITY
(1A2AE, 1–21)

1. I quote (with emendations) from BLK/CUP 16, 1.

2. 1a2ae,2,8. BLK/CUP 16, 55 (with emendation). Someone might say, "I do not aim at God when concerned with my happiness since I am an atheist." Aquinas's reply would, I presume, be that, whether atheist or not, one's ultimate happiness is to be found in union with God whether one recognizes this fact or not.

3. BLK/CUP 16, 85.

4. BLK/CUP 16, 129 (with slight emendation).

5. BLK/CUP 17, 9 (with slight emendation).

6. Here Aquinas seems to be concerned with thinking about actions from a theological perspective. Thus, 1a2ae,7,2 asks if theologians should take the circumstances of a human action into account. I am guessing that Aquinas's interest in writing for people hearing confessions is coming into play here.

7. BLK/CUP 17, 55 (with slight emendation).

8. Cf. Jennifer Hornsby, "Arm Raising and Arm Rising," *Philosophy* 55 (1980).

9. BLK/CUP 17, 89.

10. BLK/CUP 17, 95.

11. BLK/CUP 17, 103.

12. BLK/CUP 17, 105.

13. For a good account of Aquinas on human action aiming for an end, see Daniel Westberg, *Right Practical Reason: Aristotle, Action, and Prudence in Aquinas* (Clarendon: Oxford, 1994).

14. Herbert McCabe helpfully elaborates on this view of Aquinas by noting how it amounts to him thinking that "when we come to the field of human action there is no operation of the reason which is not also an operation of the will, and vice versa. There is an interweaving of understanding and being attracted that cannot be unraveled in practice. We think of what we are *attracted* to thinking of, and we are attracted to what we *think* of." See *On Aquinas*, 79. Cf. 1a2e,17,1, where Aquinas says that "acts of reason and will can bear on one another and interpenetrate" so that "you can reason about willing and will about reasoning." He adds that "an act of will [can be] charged with an element of reason" and "an act of reason [can be] charged with a quality of will-activity" (BLK/CUP 17, 185, with slight emendation).

15. Aquinas thinks that lots of things act while aiming for an end, but he does not think that everything acting for an end has reasons for doing what it does. He accepts that, say, a cat can act so as to preserve its offspring but not that it does so while thinking about what it is doing as, for example, I can and must think about what I am doing when I try to help my friends.

16. What Aquinas says here should be connected to what he says in 1a,79, 11–13.

17. Here Aquinas is following Aristotle. Cf. *Prior Analytics*, 25b37–40. In this text the pattern of reasoning for deductive theoretical reasoning is "If A is predicated of all B, and B is predicated of all C, then, necessarily, A is predicated of all C."

18. For defenses of Aquinas's thinking on the logic of practical and theoretical reasoning, see Anthony Kenny, "Practical Inference"; and P. T. Geach, "Dr. Kenny on Practical Inference," *Analysis* 26 (1966).

19. It might be better to say that Aquinas thinks that what is going on as we act voluntarily can in principle be presented as a piece of practical reasoning, for he does not claim that each time we act voluntarily we pause and take time to formulate what he would call a "practical syllogism," though he does not deny that

we might sometimes do just this as we, so to speak, "figure out" what to do in some context.

20. In 1a2ae,14,4, Aquinas acknowledges that we sometimes do not deliberate to any serious degree about means. Here he is thinking of cases where it does not matter whether we achieve a goal by doing this or something else and where the goal can be equally well obtained by doing either this or that. In this part of the *Summa Theologiae*, however, he is chiefly concerned with cases where what we do to achieve an end can matter very much.

21. BLK/CUP 17, 131.

22. Ibid., 153.

23. In this part of 1a2ae, Aquinas does not bluntly speak of "moral goodness" or "moral badness." His topic, however, is the goodness and badness of human actions, and he is concerned with them as subject to what I suppose we would now call moral praise or blame. One should also note that in 1a2ae,18,8, Aquinas speaks of a human act as being a "moral act" (*actus moralis*).

24. Cf. 1a,2ae,7,2.

25. Cf. 1a2ae,18,5. But Aquinas also seems to be aware that we can do what is a bad kind of thing while aiming at what is genuinely good and that we can do what is a good kind of thing with nefarious intentions.

26. Here Aquinas is supposing that human beings are essentially beings who act with reason or understanding and that the goodness or badness of their human actions should be evaluated with an eye on what perfects them considered as such.

27. Aquinas makes it clear in 1a2ae,18,8 that he takes stealing to be bad as a matter of definition. He is thinking that stealing is a bad kind of action regardless of circumstances (and I presume that his theological reason for doing so would lie in the biblical commandment "You shall not steal"). Many moral philosophers would not, of course, think in these terms, though they might thereby not really be disagreeing with Aquinas but might just be refusing to call certain actions examples of what Aquinas means by "stealing" (which he takes to amount to depriving someone of what belongs to them by what justice demands and by God's law). At this point you should also note that Aquinas's thinking concerning the goodness and badness of human acts does not depend on what we might call "consequentialist" considerations. He thinks that I might act well even if my action (perhaps for reasons beyond my control) has disastrous effects. He also thinks that I might act and by my action produce any number of good effects while still acting badly. In the *Summa Theologiae* Aquinas seems to think about goodness and badness in human action with an eye on the Ten Commandments (Exodus 20). He appears to think of these as positively ruling out certain actions as being good ones, as defining certain actions as bad kinds of action *period* (even though at various places in the *Summa*, and under the influence of Aristotle, he argues philosophically for them being so).

28. Here, of course, Aquinas is employing the "human act" and "act of a human being" distinction.

29. In 1a2ae,18,11, Aquinas observes that a circumstance *need* not render an action good or bad even though it can *sometimes* do so.

30. BLK/CUP 18, 53.

31. 1a2ae,19,3 (BLK/CUP 18, 55).

32. Cf. 1a2ae,91,1 and 93,1–6.

33. BLK/CUP 18, 63.

34. This line of thinking in Aquinas has sometimes been taken as holding that one's intellectual convictions can always excuse one when it comes to what one does. Aquinas does not seem to be saying quite this, however, since, while allowing that ignorance can sometimes render one non-culpable, he thinks that one can be blamed for not believing what one ought to believe. Thus, in 1a2ae,19,6 he (a) accepts that one might be blameless for having intercourse with someone else's spouse given that one was at the time convinced that the spouse in question was one's own (a rather fantastical example) but (b) denies that one is blameless for having intercourse with someone else's spouse just because one believes that this is a good thing to do. He says that in the second case here there is fault deriving from ignorance of something one ought to recognize (God's law forbidding adultery). I take it that (b) here commits Aquinas to the conclusion that one may be culpable for acting in accordance with what one takes to be true. His notion of excusable ignorance seems to be a fairly restricted one likely to get few honest thinkers off the hook.

35. What Aquinas says in 1a2ae about the voluntary, the involuntary, and the significance of ignorance when it comes to them strongly resembles what one can find in Aristotle. Cf. *Nicomachean Ethics,*Book III, chapter 1.

36. In this connection, Aquinas alludes to a judge willing good by condemning a man to death with an eye to what justice requires even though the condemned man's wife might be rightly horrified by the evil involved in the death of her husband.

37. Some people have suggested that God cannot be omnipotent if God cannot sin. Aquinas's view is that to be able to sin is to fail to be what God is.

38. Here Aquinas is thinking of "right" with a view to the phrase "acting rightly."

CHAPTER II. EMOTIONS (1A2AE,22–48)

1. There is no direct equivalent to the word *emotion* in thirteenth-century Latin. And what Aquinas counts as *passiones animae* might, for various reasons, be distinguished from what many people today mean by "emotions." For example, "emotion" in contemporary English is often used so as to suggest that an emotion is just a "feeling," while Aquinas has quite a complex account of *passiones animae* that includes the thought that their occurrence can involve cognition

and even moral worth. In this chapter, though, I largely stick with the thought that "emotions" is a good word to use when translating Aquinas's *passiones animae* into English (and while recognizing that "passion" in contemporary English commonly has overtones of vehemence or disturbance that Aquinas does not take to be essential to *passiones animae*). Anyway, readers of the present chapter will, I hope, get a sense of what Aquinas means by *passiones animae* regardless of what might be thought to be the best translation of that expression and regardless of the fact that emotion is a somewhat plastic, flexible, or ambiguous notion given present English usage of the word *emotion*. For some discussion of this matter, see Eric D'Arcy's introduction to volume 19 of the Blackfriars edition of the *Summa Theologiae*. For a provocative discussion of how medieval talk of "passions" gave way to talk about "emotions," see Thomas Dixon, *From Passions to Emotions* (Cambridge University Press: Cambridge, 2003).

2. That this is so is rightly noted by Peter King in chapter 16 of Brian Davies and Eleonore Stump (eds.), *The Oxford Handbook of Aquinas*. In this chapter King also provides a brief account of what Aquinas says about emotions in texts other than 1a2ae. In chapter 7 of *The Oxford Handbook of Philosophy of Emotion* (ed. Peter Goldie, Oxford University Press: Oxford, 2010), King offers a lucid account of emotions in medieval thought in general while noting how some medieval authors differ strongly from Aquinas when it comes to what an emotion is. For a fine book-length study of Aquinas on emotions (one that places Aquinas's thinking on emotions into a detailed historical context), see Nicholas Lombardo, *The Logic of Desire: Aquinas on Emotion* (Catholic University of America Press: Washington, D.C., 2011), which approaches Aquinas on emotions in primarily theological terms. Also see Robert Milner, *Thomas Aquinas on the Passions* (Cambridge University Press: Cambridge, 2009), which presents a fine philosophical account of Aquinas on *passiones animae*.

3. Here I use the phrase "bound up with" so as to avoid suggesting that Aquinas thinks that bodily states are caused by emotions and are to be thought of as connected to emotions by some kind of causal mechanism so that there is (a) an emotion, and (separately) (b) a physiological effect that can be understood apart from the emotion.

4. People sometimes speak of there being emotions that arise with no focus—for example, being in a state of fear for no reason. I think that Aquinas would take such cases to be nothing more than physiological states that resemble those that normally accompany certain emotions but that are not really emotions since they are not reactions to what is perceived. On this point, see Herbert McCabe, *On Aquinas*, 73.

5. As we shall see, Aquinas does not think of human emotions as simply matters of being drawn or repelled. For the moment, though, I am trying to paint his 1a2ae account of emotions in broad strokes.

6. A camera, like me, might physically register the presence of a bear. But it would not therefore have an emotion. If I see a bear before me, however, I might well

undergo an emotional reaction. What makes for the difference here? Aquinas thinks that it derives not only from my ability to understand but also from my sense appetites, my desires as a sensing thing, which is why he holds that emotions are not simply intellectual processes even if they depend on understanding in some sense.

7. One might perceive things *as* differently. You might perceive the Eiffel Tower as a blot on the Parisian landscape, or as a fine piece of architecture, or as something you must climb so as to get a good view of Paris, or as something you might throw yourself off when trying to commit suicide. Aquinas thinks that nonhuman animals can act on the basis of "perceiving *as*" (that, for example, a sheep can perceive a wolf as dangerous). He also thinks that we might perceive things as being such and such based on particular desires that we have.

8. Since we normally refer only to people and animals of different kinds as aggressive, it may seem odd that Aquinas speaks of there being aggressive emotions. But he wants to distinguish between emotions as reactions to what we perceive as good or bad and so on and emotions as responses to challenges.

9. In *The Logic of Desire* Nicholas Lombardo rightly emphasizes this point. Cf. 40ff.

10. Note, however, that in 1a2ae, Aquinas also argues that emotion cannot be severed from understanding or from how we think. Some philosophers have argued that human emotions are nothing but ways in which we "feel" as opposed to ways in which we understand. But Aquinas holds that understanding or thinking or perceiving is critical when it comes to having emotions. I might feel hot since the temperature outside is 100 degrees Fahrenheit. But Aquinas does not think of emotions as nothing but a collection of physical sensations to be identified by us through "introspection." He thinks that emotions are triggered by how, rightly or wrongly, we perceive the world to be, even if they also amount to us primarily being affectively drawn or repelled in some way based on that perception. So Aquinas has what is nowadays often referred to as a "cognitive" approach to emotions.

11. Aquinas is not here denying that one may first love and then hate one and the same thing (or that one and the same thing might be both seen and heard by us). His point is that, as one sees what is visible and hears what makes a noise, one loves what one reacts to in one way and hates what one reacts to in another.

12. One might suppose that we can will in the light of bad reasoning even if we take it to be good reasoning. Aquinas is aware of this fact, but wants to distinguish between right reasoning and bad reasoning as he understands it. Critics of Aquinas might, of course, challenge his understanding of what good and bad reasoning is. They might challenge him on his various 1a2ae verdicts concerning what is or is not reasonable. Aquinas, I presume, would reply to them by saying that reasonable action is action that aims at what he takes to be objectively good, what benefits us somehow as human beings.

13. Aquinas agrees that sight is a source of pleasure that is greater than that of touch, but only considered as a source of knowledge, not as a sensory pleasure.

14. BLK/CUP 20, 17 (with slight emendation).

15. This idea of Aquinas has been defended by many authors and criticized by others. For a sense of the debate here (together with what I take to be a cogent critique of Aquinas), see Gareth Moore, *A Question of Truth: Christianity and Homosexuality* (Continuum: London and New York, 2003), chapter 7.

16. Note the occurrence of the word *can* in this sentence. Aquinas is here talking about what might cause us pleasure but does not necessarily do so.

17. You should remember that Aquinas distinguishes between different kinds of causes, as I explained in chapter 3.

18. Note that Aquinas takes himself to be working on the basis of *admiratio* as he argues in 1a,2 and 3 for there being a cause (i.e., God) of there being something rather than nothing. "How come something rather than nothing?" is, for Aquinas, a legitimate question to press as we ask about the causes of things in the world, and of the world as a whole. Some philosophers would argue that there is no such thing as the world as a whole. I presume that Aquinas's answer to this point would run along the lines: "When I speak of the world as a whole, I do not mean to be understood as claiming that I can provide an inventory of all that exists in what we refer to as the universe. My point is that if you can think of what you take to exist, anything that you can take to be part of the universe, then you should consider asking how it comes to be *instead of there being nothing at all*, unless you think that its existence is inevitable given what it is."

19. Aquinas cites Stoic philosophers as holding that pleasure is intrinsically bad and Epicurean thinkers as holding that it is always good. He cites and disagrees with Plato as denying that there is pleasure that amounts to a supreme good. That is why 1a2ae,34,3 appears largely to be a critique of some lines of thinking to be found in Plato's dialogue *Philebus*.

20. For Aquinas on "contrary" and "contradictory," see 1a,17,4 (and chapter 5 above). One might wonder how to translate *tristitia* as Aquinas understands it. From what I have been saying you will see that I oscillate between "sorrow" and "sadness," which are, perhaps, not exactly synonymous in contemporary English usage since "sorrow" now tends to signify something more intense than sadness. Anyway, I take it that Aquinas regards *tristitia* as encompassing what we mean by both "sorrow" and "sadness."

21. One might *prefer* not to know something or other—prefer not to know that one has cancer, for example. But Aquinas denies that there is a *pleasure* of not knowing comparable to the pleasure of knowing.

22. I may be wrongly reading 1a2ae,37, but it seems to me that in this question Aquinas is seriously suggesting that pain or sorrow can frequently excuse us when it comes to our behavior.

23. BLK/CUP 21, 7.

24. Ibid., 11.
25. For a good account of the attention that Aquinas pays to the role of the body when it comes to human emotions, see appendix 6 to BLK/CUP 21.
26. BLK/CUP 21, 57.
27. Ibid.
28. BLK/CUP 21, 63. The physiology Aquinas is employing here is, doubtless, crude by contemporary standards. The same is true of what he says in 1a2ae, 44,1, ad.1 concerning the physiology of anger as involving "heat and spirits around the heart." Antique physiology notwithstanding, however, Aquinas is surely right in saying that fear and anger have physiological elements.
29. Aquinas thinks that we are angry because we think that there is wrong that ought to be made right somehow. You might say that some wrongs cannot be made right since they are past wrongs that cannot now be rectified. But Aquinas does not seem to be suggesting otherwise. His point seems to be that, while it would be absurd for me to be angry toward Hitler because of what he did (since there is nothing that I can now do to make him pay for this and since he did nothing to affect me), it does not follow that there is nothing I can do to try to make the effects of Hitler's actions conform to what is right and just. My anger toward Hitler might, I presume Aquinas to think, be what motivates me to do well by his victims. Aquinas seems to view anger as arising because of a perceived injury done to the one who becomes angry. But I take what he says about anger to allow him to concede that one might be angry because of injuries done to those one loves or respects in some way (injuries one might therefore take to be injuries to oneself in some sense).
30. Note, though, that in 1a2ae,48,3, Aquinas (while again relying on what we might take to be dubious physiology) says that anger can interfere with our use of reason more than other emotions.

CHAPTER 12. DISPOSITIONS, VIRTUES, GIFTS, BEATITUDES, AND FRUITS (IA2AE,49–70)

1. *Nicomachean Ethics*, 1106b. I quote from *Aristotle, "Nicomachean Ethics,"* edited by Roger Crisp (Cambridge University Press: Cambridge, 2000), 31.
2. 1a2ae,49–54 is another place in which Aquinas seems to be wearing a primarily philosophical hat as he writes. Only three references to the Bible occur in this text, but references to Aristotle abound, as do references to philosophical commentators on Aristotle. In this section of the present volume I am not going to dwell on ways in which Aquinas in 1a2ae,49–54 relates what he thinks to what he takes many other people to have thought. My aim is to give you a sense of what he takes the truth to be. BLK/CUP 22 provides much help to anyone wanting to concentrate on the (often somewhat difficult to understand) historical details influencing the text of 1a2ae,49–54.

3. For Aristotle on *hexis*, see *Categories*, 8b26–9a12 and 10b26–11a14. Also see *Metaphysics* Δ, 1022b2–14. In 1a2ae,49–54, Aquinas seems concerned to present an account of *habitus* that matches things that Aristotle says about *hexis* and related terms. I do not try to answer the question "Does he succeed in doing so?"

4. Anthony Kenny argues for this conclusion in BLK/CUP 22.

5. *Hexis* is a nominalization of the Greek verb "to have" (*echein*). *Habitus* is a nominalization of the Latin verb *habere* (to have).

6. BLK/CUP 22, xxi.

7. BLK/CUP 23, 11.

8. Ibid., 5. Notice that in his general treatment of virtue, Aquinas distances himself from the view that virtues amount to the possession of material states. One can already see him doing so in 1a2ae,50,1, in which he denies that, properly speaking, virtues are dispositions of the body. Aristotle speaks of health as a *hexis*. While not simply disagreeing with Aristotle on this point, Aquinas thinks it proper strongly to connect the notion of *habitus* to activity and to think of a *habitus* as "a state adapted to an activity" (BLK/CUP 22, 25).

9. BLK/CUP 23, 11.

10. "Virtus est bona qualitas mentis, qua recte vivitur, qua nullus male utitur, quam Deus in nobis sine nobis operatur."

11. BLK/CUP 23, 13.

12. Aquinas thinks of a genus as being general and a species as being particular within a genus. Thus, for example, he would have said that to call something an animal is to place it in a genus and that to call a human being a *rational* animal is to home in on a particular kind of animal. For a helpful account of Aquinas on genus and species, see appendix 4 to BLK/CUP 22. Note that in 1a2ae,55,4, Aquinas says that he would prefer to replace the word *quality* in the definition of virtue that he approves of by the word *habitus*. I take him to do this since he thinks of a virtue as something geared to action.

13. BLK/CUP 23, 15. In the ad.6 to 1a2ae,55,4, Aquinas draws a distinction between two possible senses of "God works in us without us." One of these would have us supposing that God forces us to act. The other would have us supposing that God works in us to make us to be freely acting creatures. In accordance with what we have now seen Aquinas to think about God and human freedom, in the ad.6 here Aquinas favors the second of these senses.

14. For a good account of Aquinas on intellectual virtues, see Tobias Hoffmann, "The Intellectual Virtues," in *The Oxford Handbook of Aquinas*, edited by Brian Davies and Eleonore Stump.

15. BLK/CUP 23, 31 (with slight emendation).

16. Ibid., 43.

17. Aquinas takes understanding to be a direct and non-inferential grasp of truth, a grasp of what he calls "principles." He takes science to be knowledge of truth as arrived at by reasoning and by means of principles. And he takes wisdom to be

knowledge of "the highest and deepest causes" (ibid., 45). For wisdom, science, and understanding as intellectual habits, see *Nicomachean Ethics* VI.

18. Ibid., 47.

19. For a development of this point, see Herbert McCabe, "Aquinas on Good Sense" in Herbert McCabe, *God Still Matters*. Cf. also Herbert McCabe, *On Aquinas*, chapter 11. In 1a2ae,57,6, Aquinas makes it clear that he grounds *prudentia* in right practical reasoning.

20. These virtues are lauded also by Plato and St. Augustine as well as virtually every author in the classical period and beyond.

21. I might inadvertently act well without having an ability to recognize what I should do. In that case, though, Aquinas would not take me to be displaying prudence. He would, I suppose, take me to be lucky (luck not being a virtue for Aquinas).

22. In 1 Corinthians 12, St. Paul turns to a discussion of "spiritual gifts" granted to Christians by God and inspired in them by God. In 1 Corinthians 13:3 he singles out faith, hope, and charity as the most significant of these. He writes: "And now faith, hope, and love abide, these three; and the greatest of these is love." The Greek word that Paul uses for "love" (γάπη) came to be translated into Latin as *caritas*.

23. For an account of Aristotle on the mean, I recommend J. O. Urmson, "Chapter Title," in *Aristotle's Ethics* (Basil Blackwell: Oxford, 1988).

24. In making these points, Aquinas goes in for a number of distinctions that I do not try to flag.

25. BLK/CUP 23, 211 (1a2ae,66,4).

26. Aquinas alludes to Isaiah 11 several times in 1a2ae,68. Isaiah 11:2–3 reads: "The spirit of the Lord shall rest on him, the spirit of wisdom and understanding, the spirit of counsel and might, the spirit of knowledge and the fear of the Lord. His delight shall be in the fear of the Lord."

27. This analogy is invoked in 1a2ae,68,1.

28. 1a,2ae,68,4. BLK/CUP 24, 21 (with slight emendation).

CHAPTER 13. SIN (1A2AE,71–85)

1. 1a2ae,71,6. The text of Augustine that Aquinas refers to in this article is *Contra Faustum* XXII, 27. For an English translation of this work, see *Answer to Faustus, a Manichean*, translated and introduced by Roland Teske (New City: Hyde Park, N.Y., 2007).

2. On *contra naturam*, cf. 1a2ae,31,7.

3. Aquinas distinguishes between mortal sin and venial sin. He elaborates on this distinction in 1a2ae,88 and 89.

4. BLK/CUP 25, 31.

5. Ibid., 71.

6. Here Aquinas understands excellence to include being virtuous, being well off, and having some dignity of office.

7. BLK/CUP 12, 109 (with slight emendation).

8. I say "probably" because Aquinas acknowledges that there have been different opinions on this matter.

9. Aquinas (more or less) thinks of diabolical possession along the lines in which it is depicted in films like *The Exorcist* (1973), and he thinks that such possession is not impossible. But he also thinks that it amounts to diabolical *coercion* that results in a *lack* of choice and, therefore, a lack of sin.

10. So I take it that Aquinas would be unsympathetic to the defense "I was only acting on orders" when it comes to sinful actions.

11. Romans 5:18–19.

12. Note that Aquinas has a discussion of original sin in question IV of his *De Malo*, the final form of which can be confidently dated to the period in which he was working on 1a2ae. Cf. my introduction to *On Evil*, 12–14, 43–49. I see no difference of perspective on original sin when it comes to the *Summa Theologiae* and the *De Malo*. For historical accounts of the development of thinking about original sin, see Tatha Wiley, *Original Sin: Origins, Developments, Contemporary Meaning* (Paulist: New York/Mahwah, N.J., 2002); and G. Vandervelde, *Original Sin* (Rodopi NV: Amsterdam, 1975).

13. 1a2ae,81,1 (BLK/CUP 26, 7). Note that Aquinas takes belief in original sin to derive from faith, not from philosophical or empirical investigation.

14. 1a2ae,81,1 (BLK/CUP 26, 11, with slight emendation).

15. Ibid. (with slight emendation).

16. Note that, unlike some famous theologians (Luther and St. Augustine come to mind here), Aquinas does not hold that belief in original sin should be taken to be belief that we are born with no ability to do great good or to be very good, or that human beings who die before getting the chance to make decisions (babies) inevitably end up damned to hell.

17. Note that Aquinas supposes that human generation derives primarily from men and not from women. This becomes clear in 1a2ae,81,5, in which he says that "the active causality in generation is from the father, the mother merely providing material" (BLK/CUP 26, 25). Here again we have a case of Aquinas relying on what would now generally be taken to be antiquated scientific notions.

18. BLK/CUP 44, 155, 157.

19. Cf. 1a2ae,85,1.

20. Cf. the distinction between *malum poenae* and *malum culpae* noted by Aquinas in 1a,48,5.

21. Can Aquinas's teaching on original sin and its effects survive reasons to suppose that Adam never existed as a historical person in the way Aquinas thinks him to have done? Not really, for the historicity of Adam, and what we might

now take to be erroneous views about what effects what in human procreation, are frequently appealed to by Aquinas as he develops his account of original sin. You might, though, wonder what Aquinas would be saying today about original sin if he were alive to talk to us and if he supposed that Adam never existed and that human procreation comes about differently from the way in which he thought of it given the science available to him in the thirteenth century. My guess (and it can only be a guess) is that he might say that what he says about original sin stands insofar as it depicts people as needing God's grace to raise them to a level higher than they can raise themselves without God's assistance. For Aquinas going into details about the notion of grace we have to wait until 1a2ae,106 and following, in which Aquinas hardly ever refers to original sin.

22. Note that Aquinas is explicit in 1a2ae,88,1 that "mortal" sin is only metaphorically mortal. It "kills" the soul not by making the soul not to exist but by being the reason why some people end up thoroughly estranged from God and God's goodness.

CHAPTER 14. LAW, OLD LAW, NEW LAW, AND GRACE (IA2AE,90–114)

1. So Aquinas approaches the topic of law by noting what he takes law to be when it is good law. You can assume that he acknowledges that some laws might be bad ones. But, he thinks, bad laws can only be deemed to be bad when thought of with a view to what laws should be.

2. 1a2ae,90,1 (BLK/CUP 28, 5, 7).

3. 1a2ae,90,4 (BLK/CUP 28, 17, with slight emendation).

4. Aquinas was not a democrat in the modern sense. He did not think that laws can (rightly) only be passed by people who have been elected by a popular vote or by a majority the lawful powers of which have been voted on. But 1a2ae 90, taken as it stands, is most definitely not anti-democratic. As Paul Sigmund observes, Aquinas's political and legal theory "combines traditional hierarchical and feudal views of the structure of society and politics with emerging community-oriented and incipiently egalitarian views of the proper ordering of society." Cf. Norman Kretzmann and Eleonore Stump (eds.), *The Cambridge Companion to Aquinas* (Cambridge University Press: Cambridge, 1993), 217. In 1a2ae,95,4, Aquinas lists different kinds of political regimes (governed by kingship, aristocracy, oligarchy, democracy, and tyranny) while speaking in favor of a regime in which law is what "people of birth together with the common people have sanctioned" (BLK/CUP 28, 117).

5. BLK/CUP 28, 19.

6. Ibid., 21 (with slight emendation).

7. Ibid., 23.

8. In 1a2ae,91,2, Aquinas seems to be heavily influenced by Romans 2:14 and 15 according to which "when the Gentiles, who do not possess the law [sc. the law of God as revealed in the Old Testament] do instinctively [by nature, or *naturaliter*, in the translation of Romans used by Aquinas] what the law requires, these, though not having the law, are a law to themselves." Aquinas reads this text as saying that the Gentiles "have the natural law whereby each understands and is aware of what is good and what is bad" (BLK/CUP 28, 23, with slight emendation).

9. Aquinas says that the first "precept" of natural law is that good should be done and evil avoided. But this precept does not tell how to act in particular circumstances. Indeed, it is not a precept at all but, rather, an observation concerning the meaning of the words *good* and *evil*.

10. BLK/CUP 28, 23.

11. Can there be biblical grounds for not reading a text of Scripture literally? We have seen that Aquinas thinks that there can be. He thinks, for example, that biblical talk about God having bodily parts should be read in the light of texts that teach that God is not a bodily individual.

12. In 2a2ae, Aquinas frequently cites various biblical texts as being the final word when it comes to what we should and should not do.

13. BLK/CUP 28, 53.

14. Ibid., 81.

15. Ibid., 89.

16. At this point in his discussion, Aquinas is thinking of human law at what he takes to be its best—as just law aiming to promote activity in accordance with eternal law and natural law.

17. BLK/CUP 28, 101.

18. *Etymologies*, 5,21. I quote from the translation of this text provided in BLK/CUP 28, 109. Isidore was archbishop of Seville for more than thirty years. His writings seriously influenced many medieval thinkers.

19. BLK/CUP 28, 119.

20. Ibid., 121.

21. Ibid., 125 (with slight emendation).

22. Ibid., 127.

23. Here Aquinas provides an example of what he has in mind. A city under siege might be ordered by its rulers to have its gates kept closed. But suppose that some of its citizens defending the city from outside its gates are seeking to get back into the city. In such a situation, thinks Aquinas, it might be right to open the gates to let them in.

24. Cf. BLK/CUP 28, 151. In connection with what Aquinas says at this point in 1a2ae you might reflect on the history of the United States's legislation concerning slavery and racial segregation.

25. Based on his reading of Galatians 3:19, Aquinas believes that the Old Law was promulgated by God through angels and via Moses (cf. 1a2ae,98,3).

26. Cf. 1a,1,1 for Aquinas arguing that divine teaching is needed for knowledge of truths about God's existence and nature.

27. BLK/CUP 29, 23.

28. 1a2ae,101–103 contains a long discussion of the ceremonial precepts of the Old Law. This discussion incorporates a significant amount of patristic teaching influencing Aquinas's reading of Old Testament texts. Its details need not concern us for purposes of the present volume, but, basically, they amount to arguments to the effect that certain Old Testament texts regulating the practice of divine worship were proper and fitting in their day but have now been rendered obsolete by the Incarnation and the grace of the Holy Spirit.

29. Cf. 1a2ae,98,4.

30. 1a2ae,99,4 (BLK/CUP 29, 43–45, with slight modification).

31. 1a2ae,98,1.

32. This fact should warn you not to pick on any particular passage in the *Summa Theologiae* as providing the last word from Aquinas when it comes to what he takes grace and the New Law to be.

33. Given that law is so often a matter of codified precepts or prohibitions, you might wonder how the presence of the Holy Spirit in someone can be spoken of as a law. Here, though, you need to remember that Aquinas thinks that law can be *in* something insofar as it acts in accordance with what can be codified. He argues, for example, that even natural inclinations in animals have the character of law (cf. 1a2ae,91,6). In his view, therefore, the New Law can be *in* us insofar as we are internally governed by the Holy Spirit. This aspect of Aquinas's teaching on law as internal is helpfully stressed by Michael Baur in "Law and Natural Law," in *The Oxford Handbook of Thomas Aquinas*.

34. BLK/CUP 30, 5.

35. As we shall see, Aquinas returns to the notion of justification in 1a2ae,113.

36. Aquinas is here rejecting the position of Joachim of Fiore (ca. 1130–1202), who looked forward to an age following that of Christ and the Church (an age of a New Law *Plus*, as it were, following the New Law as the New Law followed the Old Law). Joachim actually calculated that the age following that of Christ and the Church would begin in 1260. Aquinas does not mention Joachim by name in 1a2ae,106,4, but it is the teaching of Joachim that he has in mind in this article.

37. Here Aquinas seems to be thinking that while someone might labor to act virtuously in some respect (and succeed), another person might act so with joy and pleasure, this being something hard for someone who does not really have the virtue in question. Aquinas's notion of the New Law as "written in the heart" is coming into play at this point in his discussion.

38. Aquinas turns directly to the sacraments of the Church in 3a,60–90.

39. BLK/CUP 30, 43.

40. 1a2ae,108,2 (BLK/CUP 30, 47).

41. Here Aquinas is presuming that New Testament warrant can be given for think-
    ing of Christ as having instituted the sacraments to which Aquinas now refers
    (these being the sacraments of the Church as numbered by Roman Catholics,
    who, unlike some other Christians, take there to be seven of them).

42. 1a2ae,108,3 amounts to a short commentary by Aquinas on the text of Matthew
    5–7. Whether or not Aquinas's discussion of this text brings out what the author
    of Matthew 5–7 intended readers to understand by it is something you will need
    to consider for yourself (perhaps with the aid of various modern scholarly expo-
    sitions of the text). The interpretation of biblical texts in the Middle Ages is a
    subject to which a lot of work has been devoted. For an introduction to it, see
    Beryl Smalley, *The Study of the Bible in the Middle Ages*, 3rd ed. (Basil Blackwell:
    Oxford, 1984); and Beryl Smalley, *The Gospels in the Schools c.1100–c.1280* (Ham-
    bledon: London and Ronceverte, 1985).

43. BLK/CUP 30, 61.

44. Aquinas is here writing with an eye on Matthew 19:21 (dealing with poverty)
    and Matthew 19:10–12 (dealing with celibacy). The obedience that Aquinas has
    in mind as an evangelical counsel is obedience to people considered as speak-
    ing with the authority of Christ. The background to 1a2ae,108,4 is the existence
    of certain religious orders in the Catholic Church, members of which take vows
    of poverty, chastity, and obedience. Aquinas values such orders and thinks of
    those committed to them as doing what can help them to be more perfect than
    they might otherwise be. Note, though, that he is not claiming that a perfect
    Christian life cannot be led by people who have not taken religious vows of pov-
    erty, chastity, and obedience. He is saying that to live in accordance with such
    vows can be helpful even if it is not mandatory (hence his distinction between
    "precept" and "counsel").

45. In this connection, for example, 1a,12 and 23 should be borne in mind, as
    should what we find in 1a2ae concerning human acting for ends and what
    we find in 1a2ae concerning the difference between the Old Law and the
    New Law.

46. Arguably, Aquinas's views on grace developed throughout his lifetime. In this
    book I do not aim to flag such development, but to concentrate only what we
    find him saying about grace in the *Summa Theologiae*.

47. BLK/CUP 30, 111.

48. Ibid., 145.

49. 1a2ae,112,1 again (BLK/CUP 30, 146).

50. BLK/CUP 23, 137–139.

51. Cf. 1a2ae,112,1: "Just as it is impossible for anything to make fiery but fire alone,
    so it is necessary that God alone should make godlike, by communicating a
    share in his divine nature by participation and assimilation." In this connection
    also see my comments on 1a,2,3 (the Fourth Way).

52. BLK/CUP 23, 137–139 (with modifications).

53. In 1a2ae,109,4, Aquinas seems to be attacking the teaching of Pelagius (ca. 390–418). The writings of Pelagius have not survived in any serious form. Their contents have been reconstructed largely from the works of his detractors, especially St. Augustine of Hippo. Aquinas (rightly or wrongly, but certainly in accord with thirteenth-century norms) took Pelagius to have taught that human beings are able to choose to do good independently of God, good that can lead them to beatitude. Recent scholarship tends to favor an understanding of Pelagius according to which his theology is less susceptible to criticism than St. Augustine affirms it to be. Cf. John Ferguson, *Pelagius* (W. Heffer and Sons: Cambridge, 1956); and John Ferguson, "In Defence of Pelagius," *Theology* 83 (March 1980).

54. BLK/CUP 30, 93. Aquinas is here referring to what he calls justification, a topic he discusses directly in 1a2ae,113.

55. Ibid., 111 (with slight emendation).

56. Note that Aquinas's manner of making divisions of grace in 1a2ae,111 marks a development in his thinking (or, at least, his terminology) from the time that he wrote his commentary on the *Sentences*. In that work grace is spoken of as always being what in 1a2ae,111 Aquinas calls sanctifying grace.

57. BLK/CUP 30, 147.

58. Ibid., 171.

59. In the prologue to 1a2ae,112–113, Aquinas specifically calls "the justification of the unrighteous" an "effect of operative grace" (ibid., 163).

60. Romans 3:24.

61. BLK/CUP 30, 181–183.

62. 1a2ae,113,9.

63. BLK/CUP 30, 203 (with emendation).

64. Ibid. (with emendation).

65. Ibid. 30, 227.

66. Aquinas is clear that our freely doing good can lead us to the beatific vision, but he does not think that our doing good is meritorious except in terms decreed by God. We can merit as graced by God, he thinks, but we cannot merit grace as such. Here, of course, we need to remember that Aquinas thinks that our actions as brought about by the grace of God are always actions chosen by us. So, he thinks, we can merit because of them, though we cannot merit them. Cf. 1a2ae,114,3.

CHAPTER 15. FAITH, HOPE, AND CHARITY (2A2AE,1–46)

1. BLK/CUP 31, xxi.

2. Come the beatific vision, thinks Aquinas, we have no need for faith. Why he thinks this should be clear from what I go on to say in this chapter and from what I noted in chapter 4.

3. BLK/CUP 31, 29.

4. That God is one and that God is the creator are truths that Aquinas takes to be discoverable by human reasoning. So you might wonder why he lists them as articles of faith. But here Aquinas takes himself to be outlining the contents of the major Christian creeds that are, in his view, essential for Christian orthodoxy. Also note that Aquinas thinks that even what can be known by reason can fittingly be proposed to people as matters of faith. Cf. *Summa Contra Gentiles* I,4: "Beneficially, therefore, did the divine mercy provide that it should instruct us to hold by faith even those truths that the human reason is able to investigate. In this way, all people would easily be able to have a share in the knowledge of God, and this without uncertainty and error." I quote, with slight emendation, from the translation by Anton Pegis of *Summa Contra Gentiles* I (University of Notre Dame Press: Notre Dame, 1975). For this line of thinking in the *Summa Theologiae*, see 2a2ae,2,4.

5. BLK/CUP 31, 13.

6. Ibid., 9.

7. Hugh of St. Victor's definition of faith was influential in Aquinas's day. Hugh says that faith is a kind of mental certitude about absent realities, a certitude that is greater than opinion and less than that derived from knowledge (*Fides est certitudo quaedam animi de rebus absentibus supra opinionem et infra scientiam constituta*). See I, x, 2 of his *De Sacramentis*.

8. BLK/CUP 31, 63.

9. W. K. Clifford, *Lectures and Essays*, 2nd ed., edited by Leslie Stephen and Frederick Pollard (Macmillan: London, 1886). The quotation is the last sentence of "The Ethics of Belief" in this collection.

10. Cf. chapter 2 above.

11. Aquinas's point is not that believing without evidence is a virtue. He is not denigrating the gathering of evidence or reasons and the formulating of beliefs based on these things. But he does think that there can be occasions when believing without evidence is appropriate. For a development of this thought in recent philosophy, see G. E. M. Anscombe, "What Is It to Believe Someone?" (to which I refer in chapter 2, note 4).

12. BLK/CUP 31, 165.

13. Ibid., 167 (with slight emendation).

14. Ibid., 21.

15. Ibid., 17.

16. Ibid., 83.

17. What Aquinas means by believing explicitly at a remove can be illustrated with a contemporary example. Many people now believe that humans came to be as they are now by virtue of evolution. Yet how many of these people are evolutionary biologists? Few of them. People who believe in evolution are, for the most part, people who believe what they have been taught by evolutionary biologists.

18. 2a2ae,2,7–8 hardly squares with what contemporary biblical scholars would say about Old Testament teaching and its relation to Christian teaching following New Testament times. Here, though, one has to remember that Aquinas thinks of the Old Testament as pointing toward the New Testament and the Christian Church and, therefore, in various ways prophetically anticipating it and embracing it. In 2a2ae,1,7, Aquinas quotes Exodus 6:2 (where, as Aquinas read the Vulgate translation of this text, God says to Moses, "I am the God of Abraham, the God of Isaac, the God of Jacob,... And my name, Adonai, I did not show them"). Aquinas takes this text to indicate how believers at one time can share in the faith of believers at a later time without expressly using their ways of professing their faith.

19. BLK/CUP 31, 35, 37 (with slight emendation).

20. Ibid., 111 (with slight emendation).

21. Ibid., 125.

22. Ibid., 161, 163.

23. Aquinas's point here seems to be similar to what Antony Flew has in mind when talking about an atheist as possibly being someone who just does not believe that God exists, but not someone who positively asserts that God does not exist. Cf. Antony Flew, "The Presumption of Atheism," in Antony Flew, *The Presumption of Atheism and Other Essays* (Elek/Pemberton: London, 1976).

24. BLK/CUP 32, 47 (with slight emendation).

25. Ibid., 59. In 2a2ae,10,7, Aquinas seems to be commending debate with unbelievers that amounts to the giving of reasons and not just to a matter of arbitrarily ruling out what unbelievers say. He seems to do the same in 2a2ae,10,9.

26. By "heretic" Aquinas means "someone who claims to profess the truths of Christianity while not actually doing so." Aquinas is very disapproving of heresy, as should be obvious from 2a2ae,11.

27. BLK/CUP 32, 73.

28. BLK/CUP 33, 9 (with slight emendation).

29. Ibid., 23.

30. Ibid., 21 (with emendation).

31. Ibid. Note that Aquinas holds that Christ, being God, lacked the theological virtue of hope (2a2ae,18,2 ad.1). Christ could hope for immortality or relief from suffering, but not for the possession of God since this was already his by virtue of his divine nature.

32. BLK/CUP 33, 37. Many theologians have argued that everyone will eventually come to choose God and be united with God, that universal salvation is to be expected. Aquinas is not of their mind. He thinks (largely because of his reading of biblical texts such as Matthew 25:46) that some people (and some angels) are permanently estranged from God (cf. 3a,52,7). He does, though, believe in purgatory, considered as a state after death falling short of beatitude though

distinct from damnation, and he holds that there can be hope in those in this state just as there can be hope in people during their present life. Cf. 2a2ae,18,3.

33. BLK/CUP 33, 73.

34. Ibid., 77 (with slight emendation).

35. Ibid., 89 (with slight emendation).

36. Ibid., 107.

37. 2a2ae's treatment of charity seems to differ in its emphases from that which we find in Book III of Aquinas's *Commentary on the Sentences*, and it probably does so because of attention paid by Aquinas to Aristotle's *Ethics* between around 1265 and 1269–1272. For an illuminating discussion of 2a2ae's treatment on charity and its relation to the thinking of Aristotle, see Fergus Kerr, "Charity as Friendship" in Brian Davies (ed.), *Language, Meaning and God* (Wipf & Stock: Eugene, Ore., 2010).

38. BLK/CUP 34, 7.

39. Ibid., 165, 167 (with slight emendation).

40. Ibid., 39.

41. Ibid. (with slight emendation).

42. Ibid., 33.

43. 2a2ae,23,8, ad.1, 2, and 3.

44. BLK/CUP 34, 115, 117 (with slight emendation).

45. Ibid., 13.

46. Ibid., 29.

47. Ibid., 55, 57.

48. Ibid., 59.

49. In 2a2ae,26,11, we find Aquinas's medieval biological views coming into play. Here he argues that there is a case to be made for loving one's father more than one's mother since "the father, as the active partner [sc. in generation], is a principle in a higher way than the mother, who supplies the passive or material element" (BLK/CUP 34, 149).

50. BLK/CUP 34, 165 (with slight emendation).

51. For Aquinas in general, God as good is supremely lovable (cf. 1a,6). But he still maintains that sinners who are punished by God can hate God.

52. Cf. Book X of the *Institutes* of John Cassian (ca. 360–435).

53. This is Thomas Heath's neat rendition of what Aquinas takes *acedia* to be. Cf. BLK/CUP 35, 21.

54. For discussions of Aquinas and *acedia*, see Rebecca Konyndyk DeYoung, "Resistance to the Demands of Love: Aquinas on the Vice of *Acedia*," *The Thomist* 68 (2004): xx–xx; and Rebecca Konyndyk DeYoung, "Aquinas on the Vice of Sloth: Three Interpretive Issues," *The Thomist* 75 (2011).

55. BLK/CUP 35, 43.

56. Aquinas often says that what is against charity is "mortal of its kind" (*ex genera suo*) but might amount to venial sin depending on how much it is embraced by people.

57. BLK/CUP 35, 59, 61.
58. Ibid., 61.
59. 2a2ae,38,1, ad.1 (BLK/CUP 35, 61).
60. BLK/CUP 35, 69.
61. Ibid. Aquinas always upholds the primacy of the pope, the bishop of Rome, as governing the Church in the name of Christ. He has a strongly hierarchical approach to the Church and is convinced (on what he takes to be biblical grounds as well as non-biblical ones) that unity in the Church requires one person to lead it, this being the bishop of Rome (cf. 1a,36,2; 2a2ae,1,10; 2a2ae,11,2; 3a,8,6; *Summa Contra Gentiles* IV, 76; *Contra Errores Graecorum*, 32–38). But, living when he did, he never simply equates challenging the authority of the pope with heresy, as some have done since his time, especially since Vatican I's definition of papal infallibility. For Aquinas on the papacy, see Christopher Ryan, "Papal Primacy in Thomas Aquinas" in Christopher Ryan (ed.), *The Religious Roles of the Papacy: Ideals and Realities, 1150–1300* (Pontifical Institute of Mediaeval Studies: Toronto, 1989).
62. BLK/CUP 35, 81.
63. Ibid., 83.
64. Ibid., 83, 85. 2a2ae,40 is the only sustained discussion of war in the writings of Aquinas.
65. 2a2ae,40 echoes things that St. Augustine says about warfare. For some historical context to 2a2ae,40, see G. I. A. D. Draper, "The Origins of the Just War Tradition," *New Blackfriars* 46 (November 1964).
66. BLK/CUP 35, 99 (with slight modification). In 2a2ae,41,1, Aquinas cites Isidore of Seville for an etymological account of *rixosus* (quarrelsome) according to which it derives from *ricto canino* (the snarling of a dog).
67. Ibid., 97.
68. Ibid., 103, 105.
69. Ibid., 107. Aquinas's disapproval of tyrants emerges very sharply in his *De Regimine Principum* (ca. 1266 and, therefore, earlier than 2a2ae). For a translation of this text and related ones, see *St. Thomas Aquinas on Politics and Ethics*, translated and edited by Paul Sigmund (Norton: New York and London, 1958). In this connection I should note that Aquinas favored government by monarchy for a number of reasons.

CHAPTER 16. PRUDENCE, JUSTICE, AND INJUSTICE (2A2AE,47–79)

1. Notice that in 2a2ae Aquinas is saying that grace perfects nature and is not something that abolishes it or amounts to a declaration by God that imperfect human beings are saved regardless of how they behave or display what we might think of as goodness achieved by human effort (even effort supplemented by or raised to a higher level by God).

2. BLK/CUP 36, 43.

3. Ibid., 113.

4. Ibid., 47.

5. Ibid., 17.

6. Ibid., 25 (with slight emendation).

7. You may now be thinking that Aquinas thinks that only geniuses or scholars stand a chance of being prudent. But that is not his view. This point is nicely made by Herbert McCabe who argues that what Aquinas means by *prudentia* is basically what Jane Austen (not thinking about geniuses or scholars but of characters such as Elizabeth Bennett in *Pride and Prejudice*) meant by "good sense." See Herbert McCabe, "Aquinas on Good Sense" in Brian Davies (ed.), *Thomas Aquinas: Contemporary Philosophical Perspectives* (Oxford University Press: New York, 2002).

8. BLK/CUP 36, 129.

9. Ibid., 131–133.

10. Ibid., 135 (with slight emendation).

11. Ibid., 151 (with slight emendation).

12. Herbert McCabe, *On Aquinas*, 104.

13. Herbert McCabe, "Aquinas on Good Sense" in Brian Davies (ed.), *Thomas Aquinas: Contemporary Philosophical Perspectives*, 351. Aquinas notes some biblical texts in the Vulgate translation of the Bible that speak well of *astutia*. With an eye on them he argues that *astutia* primarily signifies something bad even if the word can sometimes be used to signify something good because of a resemblance between *prudentia* and *astutia* (cf. 2a2ae,55,3, ad.1).

14. BLK/CUP 36, 165 (with slight modification).

15. Aquinas's view of equality when it comes to justice should be connected with what he says about friendship and equality in his discussion of charity.

16. BLK/CUP 37, 5. Aquinas takes this definition of "justice" to square with that given by Aristotle in chapter 5 of Book V of the *Nicomachean Ethics*.

17. In 2a2ae,57,3, Aquinas (in reliance on some earlier authors, especially those influenced by Roman law) also acknowledges the existence of a right of the nations (*jus gentium*), an international law, as it were, which he takes to be a matter of universal custom. The notion of *jus gentium* faded away in European legal thinking (and European theological legal thinking) before the sixteenth century.

18. For Aquinas on *habitus*, see chapter 12 above.

19. BLK/CUP 37, 21 (with slight emendation).

20. Ibid., 49 (with slight emendation).

21. Ibid., 89.

22. Ibid.

23. Cf. 2a2ae,61,2.

24. BLK/CUP 37, 95.

25. Ibid., 103.
26. Ibid., 103, 104 (with slight emendation). Note that Aquinas takes lack of restitution to amount to sin. Cf. 2a2ae,62,2 and 62,8.
27. BLK/CUP 37, 59.
28. Aquinas is no philosophical vegetarian. Drawing on Genesis 1:29–30, he thinks that God has put animals under human dominion so that humans might eat them, as he thinks that God has put plants under the dominion of animals so that they might feed on them.
29. Aquinas does not discuss cases in which a person commits suicide because of what we now call pathological depression or, as the phrase goes, "not being of sound mind." That, I take it, is because he would consider such cases not to involve voluntary action. Note that in 2a2ae,64,5, ad.2 Aquinas says that what makes someone their own master is having the power of free choice (*liberum arbitrium*).
30. Aquinas countenances killing the innocent by divine order on the basis of Genesis 22:9ff. He clearly regards killing the innocent by divine order as an exception to a rule.
31. BLK/CUP 38, 37 (with slight emendation).
32. Ibid., 41.
33. For discussions of double effect, see P. A. Woodward (ed.), *The Doctrine of Double Effect* (University of Notre Dame Press: Notre Dame, 2001).
34. So Aquinas supports what is commonly called "retributive punishment" as inflicted on someone in accordance with how they have behaved. In doing so he is thinking as many societies do when imprisoning people on the principle that the punishment should fit the crime. Note that in 2a2ae,65,3, Aquinas seems to rely on the principle that what is unjust for an individual might be just for a king or a government. He invokes this principle several times over in 2a2ae. It derives from his general thinking about law, for which see chapter 14.
35. This distinction can be found in Aristotle (*Nicomachean Ethics* V,2) and in Isidore of Seville (*Etymologiae* X). It corresponds to a distinction commonly made in current U.S. state law.
36. Here Aquinas seems to be endorsing the view (clearly not upheld by everyone today) that punishment can only be justified on reformative or deterrent grounds.
37. The last clause here seems to have some potentially damaging implications for ways in which some legal trials are conducted today, with states or monarchs being the legal accusers. But Aquinas is not envisaging such a system of trial. He is thinking of accusers as parts within a whole that amounts to a body politic and not of the body politic as a possible accuser.
38. BLK/CUP 38, 151.
39. Ibid., 163.
40. Ibid., 187.

41. Ibid., 197.

42. In his teaching on charging for lending money, Aquinas is thoroughly in accord with the common ecclesiastical teaching of his day and with that of philosophers such as Aristotle. But Catholic moral theologians now tend to concede that usury, in Aquinas's understanding of it, is permissible. "Usury" is now commonly defined as demanding more payment for money loaned than is just. Note, though, that Aquinas is opposed on principle to demanding *any* interest for money loaned and seems unconcerned with how much loaners might gain from those to whom they have loaned money. Critics of Aquinas on usury typically argue that he fails to account for the fact that money loaned can increase in value as owned by a borrower and is not something consumed as a bottle of wine is.

CHAPTER 17. RELIGION AND OTHER MATTERS TO DO WITH JUSTICE (2A2AE,80–122)

1. BLK/CUP 39, 21 (with slight emendation).

2. Henry Fielding, *Tom Jones*, Book III, chapter 3.

3. People in Christian religious orders are commonly referred to as "religious" (used as a noun), meaning that they have a certain ecclesiastical status. When thinking of *religio* as displayed by religious people, however, Aquinas is thinking of it as something that should be displayed by all Christians, not just those who are members of religious orders. Cf. 2a2ae,81,1, ad.5 where he distinguishes between "religious" in a wide sense and "religious" in a restricted sense (BLK/CUP 39, 15).

4. BLK/CUP 39, 17.

5. Ibid., 25.

6. Ibid., 27.

7. Ibid., 29 (with slight emendation).

8. Ibid. (with slight emendation).

9. Ibid.

10. Aquinas uses the word *latria* to signify reverence due only to God, which I translate as "adoration." Reverence due to a holy creature he calls *dulia*.

11. Matthew 6:7ff; Luke 11:2ff.

12. The second view here seems to have been advanced in order to accommodate 1 Thessalonians 5:17 in which Christians are urged to "pray without ceasing." The view that petitionary prayer is second-grade prayer emerges in, for example, the writings of St. Bernard of Clairvaux (1090–1153) and William of St. Thierry (ca. 1085–1148).

13. Aquinas is not someone who changed his mind a lot during his writing career. But he does seem to have changed his mind when it comes to his approach to prayer. This fact is well documented by Simon Tugwell in *Albert and Thomas:*

Selected Writings. Also see Simon Tugwell, "Prayer, Humpty Dumpty and Thomas Aquinas," in Brian Davies (ed.), *Language, Meaning and God*, xx–xx. For an account of how Aquinas changed his mind on some other matters, see Giorgio Pini, "The Development of Aquinas's Thought," in Brian Davies and Eleonore Stump (eds.), *The Oxford Handbook of Aquinas.*

14. BLK/CUP 39, 49.
15. Ibid., 77 (with emendation).
16. Ibid., 53 (with some emendation).
17. Ibid. (with slight emendation). For a good modern rendition of Aquinas's teaching on prayer, see Herbert McCabe, "Prayer," in Herbert McCabe, *God Still Matters.*
18. One of my favorite characters in the *Harry Potter* novels is Professor Sybill Trelawney, who is professor of divination at Hogwarts School of Witchcraft and Wizardry. The *Harry Potter* novels have sometimes been attacked as being grounded in views contrary to Christianity, and I have no doubt that Sybill Trelawney would have been thought of by Aquinas as a victim of superstition had she been a real person. But she is, of course, not a real person, and I suspect that Aquinas, were he alive today, would have enjoyed the way Rowling depicts her in the entertaining novels that compose the collection of *Harry Potter* books, while noting that they are to be recognized as entertainment and not as a profession of belief as to how things operate under the providence of God.
19. BLK/CUP 40, 121.
20. When it comes to the definition of "simony," Aquinas has in mind Acts 8:18–24 in which a character described as a magician (Acts 8:9) is said to have asked that he be allowed to impart the Holy Spirit for a price.
21. "Prudentially governed," thinks Aquinas (2a2ae,101,4), since one may sometimes need to decide whether, say, piety due to one's parents should be neglected in favor of piety due to God, or vice versa. Note that in 2a2ae,121, and in addition to what he says in 2a2ae,101, Aquinas speaks of there being piety that is a gift of the Holy Spirit that leads us to offer filial piety toward God and to worship God as God ought to be worshiped. This gift of piety, he adds, corresponds to the meekness referred to in Matthew 5:4.
22. Aquinas is here thinking that it might (with the emphasis on *might*) be right to be respectful in word and deed to, say, political leaders (regardless of their moral standing and whether or not one agrees with their views or policies) and to people set over one (regardless of their moral standing) should one happen to be a cleric or a member of a religious order.
23. BLK/CUP 41, 73. In 2a2ae,104, the emphasis falls on obedience to those *rightly* in authority over one and acting *rightly* in that capacity.
24. Ibid., 91 (with slight emendation).
25. Ibid. Aquinas's use of the "so far as possible" clause is important here. He does not think that when you give me a Christmas present I am automatically obliged

to give you a gift that is better than what you have given me. If you agree with nothing else in the *Summa Theologiae*, you may, perhaps, agree with Aquinas on this conclusion.

26. Ibid., 125.

27. In my account of Aquinas on lying, I do not provide references to articles in 2a2ae,110 since I intend to provide a general account of this question taken as a whole.

28. BLK/CUP 41, 177. When it comes to what Aquinas says about deception, you might wonder about spies and double agents going undercover to promote what they take to be a good end. Such people, I presume, infiltrate organizations precisely as deceivers (or even as hypocrites). Would Aquinas therefore take them to be vicious rather than virtuous? The question is hard to answer since Aquinas does not talk about spies and double agents and since he had no idea of what these might amount to today. That said, however, I suspect that he would be unsympathetic to people trying to do the best by their country by positively and intentionally lying. My guess is that he would say that countries should do the best they can to defend themselves so long as they commission the agents representing them to act justly in accordance with his understanding of justice. What this might mean in practice would for Aquinas doubtless fall under what he calls the virtue of prudence. It is, I think, important to note that one can read through both 1a2ae and 2a2ae without finding a specific instruction as to what to do in various circumstances in which one might find oneself. I mean, for example, if your question is "Should I pay the invoice I have just received?" the *Secunda Pars* offers you no answer. Instead, it seeks to indicate what virtue and vice are in general and in particular while continually making qualifications when it comes to how sinful this or that action might be in context. The *Secunda Pars* does not provide a list along the lines "Definitely do A, B, and C right now," though it does provide a list of what should generally be done and what should never be done.

29. Aquinas is clearly working with a slightly different understanding of "irony" than we find used when people talk about the irony in Jane Austen novels or the irony involved in saying exactly the opposite of what one means for rhetorical effect.

30. In his discussion of avarice and prodigality, Aquinas is saying that one needs to strike a mean when it comes to property. He thinks that one can rightly acquire property so as to put it to good use. But he also thinks that one's attitude to it can be wrongly acquisitive and unreflective.

31. Aquinas is depending on Aristotle in his use of the term *epieikeia*. Cf. *Nicomachean Ethics* V,10 and *Rhetoric* I,13.

32. Here Aquinas is using terminology and argument to be found in Aristotle's *Nicomachean Ethics* V,10.

CHAPTER 18. COURAGE AND TEMPERANCE (2A2AE,123–170)

1. Cf. chapter 11.
2. BLK/CUP 42, 9.
3. Ibid., 9, 11.
4. Ibid., 21.
5. Ibid., 37.
6. In 2a2ae,123,12, Aquinas ranks the cardinal virtues in terms of excellence. He gives first place to prudence, second place to justice, third place to courage, and fourth place to temperance. This ranking corresponds to the order in which Aquinas discusses the cardinal virtues in 2a2ae and is found again in 2a2ae,141,8.
7. When turning to the topic of martyrdom, Aquinas does not discuss the case of non-Christians being prepared to die in defense of some cause they believe in. I presume that he would want to evaluate each instance of such preparedness separately in order to determine whether the cause for which the people involved are prepared to die is a good and just one.
8. For example, he takes a disordered fear of losing one's possessions to be present in avarice.
9. BLK/CUP 42, 99.
10. BLK/CUP 42, 103 (with slight emendation).
11. In *On Aquinas* (167), Herbert McCabe suggests that James Murray, who was the primary editor of the *Oxford English Dictionary*, might have been considered by Aquinas as someone displaying magnanimity. Certainly, when embarking on his task as editor of the *OED*, Murray was facing a serious challenge. And his perseverance and success seems to have led to a good that is recognized worldwide.
12. When discussing magnificence, Aquinas is primarily thinking of it as a virtue displayed by wealthy people. Note, though, that in 2a2ae,134,3, ad.4 Aquinas agrees that even non-wealthy people can act in a spirit of magnificence by trying to support a project that, though it might be thought small by comparison with what can be supported by a lot of money, is still great when considered in the light of the income available to the poor but magnificent person.
13. In 2a2ae,135,2, Aquinas says that stinginess as a vice can be compared with "wastefulness" (*consumptio*). He takes both stinginess and wastefulness to be vices in opposition to each other. Stingy people are unwilling to spend money. Wasteful people want to spend more than they should.
14. One might today encourage someone to be patient while waiting for a train that is a few minutes late. In his discussion of patience, however, Aquinas seems to be thinking of it as bearing up in the face of serious difficulties or evils, not matters as trivial as having to wait for a slightly late train.
15. BLK/CUP 43, 5, 7 (with some emendation).
16. Ibid., 15.

17. Ibid., 193.
18. Cf. *Reproductive BioMedicine on Line* 43(2011): 205–211 (available online at http://www.sciencedirect.com/science/article/pii/S1472648310620378).
19. For some criticism of Aquinas on this matter, see chapters 4 and 5 of Gareth Moore, *The Body in Context* (Continuum: London and New York, 2001).
20. BLK/CUP 43, 13.
21. You might think that we can be sensually engaged with more than food, drink, and sex. For what about, say, preoccupation with beautiful works of art? In his discussion of temperance, however, Aquinas does not discuss aesthetic appreciation (even should it be thought to be excessive).
22. BLK/CUP 43, 23.
23. Ibid., 43.
24. Ibid., 69.
25. The Catholic Church in Aquinas's day imposed on the faithful certain regulations concerning fasting. Aquinas does nothing to try to criticize them in 2a2ae,146 and 147, in which he actually defensively indicates what some of these regulations amount to.
26. BLK/CUP 43, 121 (with slight emendation).
27. Ibid., 141 (with slight emendation).
28. Ibid., 149.
29. I doubt that any moral theologian today would argue along these lines. But maybe some would. However, the issue of whether or not, or to what extent, the inebriated are guilty for what they end up doing while drunk is very much a live one today (and not only for moral theologians).
30. Aquinas does not say so, but the same point can be made with respect to people who engage in homosexual sex.
31. BLK/CUP 43, 197.
32. Ibid., 207 (with slight emendation). Note that the order in which Aquinas goes on to consider lustful sins in 2a2ae,154 does not correspond to the order in which he cites them in 2a2ae,154,1. In what follows I abide by the order in which he discusses sins of lust after 2a2ae,154,1.
33. Ibid., 211.
34. Ibid., 213. Aquinas's valuing of men above women seems to be at work in this quotation. So, perhaps, also at work is a view of what good child rearing depended on in the thirteenth century rather than a view of what it can depend on today (in some countries, anyway).
35. So in 2a2ae,154,6, Aquinas seems to assume that only a man can be a seducer. He does not allow for the possibility of a woman seducing a man, or of a man seducing a man, or of a woman seducing a woman. What Aquinas does *not* discuss when it comes to seduction should, perhaps, alert you to the fact that his approach to sexual relations comes with assumptions about the sociology of sexual behavior that he might not have were he living today.

36. Since the time of Aquinas, various countries have tried legally to define how close is too close when it comes to incest. Aquinas is obviously unaware of distinctions thrown up by such definitions. When thinking of incest as bad he is thinking of such obvious cases as mothers having sex with their sons, or fathers having sex with their daughters, or men or boys having sex with their sisters. I say this with some caution, however, since in 2a2ae,154,9 Aquinas seems to take the victim of incest always to be female.

37. BLK/CUP 43, 254.

38. He also says that there is unnatural vice "if the natural style of intercourse is not observed, as regards the proper organ or according to other rather beastly and monstrous techniques" (ibid.). Since he does not explain exactly what he has in mind here, one will have to engage in guesswork when interpreting this passage.

39. Ibid., 247.

40. BLK/CUP 44, 119.

41. Ibid., 151.

42. Aquinas is relying here on a literal reading of Genesis 3:5. In 2a2ae,163,4, he goes on to say that Eve's sin was worse than Adam's since, while like Adam, Eve aspired to a kind of equality with God, her doing so sprang from trust in the Devil, while Adam's sin did not.

43. Is Aquinas here offering a theodicy, an attempt to explain why human death and suffering is permitted by God for a good moral reason? I do not think so since Aquinas does not think of God as something subject to moral evaluation, and, of course, he thinks that sin occurs only as God fails to give grace. At the same time, though, one needs to remember that Aquinas holds that when people freely sin, it is they who sin, that human freedom is not obliterated by God making or not making us saints. So he takes sin to be what people chose to engage in, and he takes refraining from sin by God's grace to amount to the same thing. These points should be remembered when reading 2a2ae,164, if only so that one might explain why its account of the effects of Adam's sin might be thought to be open to question.

44. BLK/CUP 44, 211.

45. This is how it is translated in BLK/CUP 44.

46. Ibid., 197.

CHAPTER 19. FREELY GIVEN GRACES, KINDS OF LIFE, AND STATES OF LIFE (2A2AE,171–189)

1. Cf. the introduction to 2a2ae,171 and following (BLK/CUP 45, 3).

2. For two good introductions to Aquinas's ecclesiology, both of which are helpful for reading the *Summa Theologiae*, see "The Idea of the Church in St. Thomas

Aquinas," in Yves Congar, *The Mystery of the Church* (Helicon: Baltimore, 1960), xx–xx; and "The Church According to Thomas Aquinas," in Avery Dulles, *A Church to Believe In* (Crossroad: New York, 1982).

3. In some contemporary theology, what Aquinas means by a freely given grace is referred to as a "charism." I do not know why that usage has come about. "Charism" derives from the Greek word for "grace" or "favor," but Aquinas distinguishes between grace of different kinds, *gratia gratis data* being only one of them (as we saw in chapter 14).

4. In 1a2ae, Aquinas presents gratuitous grace as possibly amounting to nothing more than grace given to a teacher so as to present the truths of faith effectively to a student. In 2a2ae (though in a way that coheres with what he says in 1a2ae), he homes in on graces given that are less common than this.

5. BLK/CUP 45, 5, 7 (with slight emendation).

6. For Aquinas on falseness in *cognitio*, cf. 1a,17,3.

7. BLK/CUP 45, 97.

8. 1 Corinthians 14:2–3.

9. Acts 2:1–11.

10. BLK/CUP 45, 133.

11. Ibid., 139.

12. Ibid.

13. For a helpful discussion of "contemplation" in authors earlier than Aquinas, and for a helpful discussion of Aquinas on contemplation and action, see Simon Tugwell, *Albert and Thomas: Selected Writings*, 279–286.

14. For an argument to this effect, see ibid.

15. In *Nicomachean Ethics* X,7, Aristotle praises the contemplative life. Aristotle's thinking about contemplation is also something that influences Aquinas's discussion of it, as is evident from 2a2ae,182,1.

16. For example, in 2a2ae,189,4, he roundly declares that someone who makes a solemn commitment to become a member of a religious order is bound to remain in that order until death. Current Roman Catholic thinking, however, seems to allow for such a person leaving a religious order without guilt (given certain processes, anyway).

17. Here Aquinas is defending the existence of the mendicant orders in the Church of his day.

CHAPTER 20. GOD INCARNATE (3A,1–26)

1. BLK/CUP 48, 3.

2. Aquinas takes the New Testament to provide us with a reliable account of what Jesus of Nazareth said and did. Contemporary New Testament scholars, however, do not generally share his confidence on this matter. For a sense of contemporary conclusions when it comes to our knowledge of Jesus, see James

K. Beilby and Paul Rhodes (eds.), *The Historical Jesus: Five Views* (IVP Academic: Downers Grove, Ill., 2009). For a much more comprehensive sense, see Tom Holmen and Stanley E. Porter (eds.), *Handbook for the Study of the Historical Jesus*, 4 vols. (Brill: Leiden, 2011).

3. In 3a,1–26, Aquinas is frequently concerned to identify and refute what he takes to be heretical views about the Incarnation. In what I say about Aquinas on the Incarnation, I do not report and document his comments on these views. For solid accounts of views about the Incarnation that Aquinas takes to be heretical, see J. N. D. Kelly, *Early Christian Doctrines*, 5th ed. (A. C. Black: London, 1977); and Aloys Grillmeier, *Christ in Christian Tradition*, vol. 1, 2nd ed. (Mowbray: London, 1975).

4. Norman P. Tanner (ed.), *Decrees of the Ecumenical Councils* (Sheed and Ward/ Georgetown University Press: London and Washington, D.C., 1990), 1:86.

5. BLK/CUP 48, 145.

6. Aquinas thinks that we can understand what Christ is insofar as he is human and insofar as we have a grasp of what it is to be human. He does not, however, think that we can grasp what the Incarnation is insofar as it involves a union of divinity and humanity.

7. Some people do find what Aquinas says in discussing the Incarnation to be nonsensical largely because they take it to be attributing incompatible properties to one and the same thing. For a recent philosophical defense of Aquinas on the Incarnation in general, see Eleonore Stump, *Aquinas* (Routledge: London and New York, 2003), chapter 14. For an account of Aquinas on the Incarnation coming with discussion of the Incarnation as written about by a number of other medieval authors, see Richard Cross, *The Metaphysics of the Incarnation: Thomas Aquinas to Duns Scotus* (Oxford University Press: Oxford, 2002).

8. BLK/CUP 48, 45 (with slight emendation). By "the Word" here Aquinas means the second person of the Trinity. The allusion is to John 1:14.

9. Here Aquinas is relying on the notion of relative identity: the idea that something can be thought of as both X and Y even though "X" and "Y" seem to be different. For a defense of this notion, with reference to other literature on it, see Peter Van Inwagen, "And Yet They Are Not Three Gods but One God" in Thomas V. Morris (ed.), *Philosophy and the Christian Faith* (University of Notre Dame Press: Notre Dame, 1988).

10. Herbert McCabe, *God Still Matters*, 107.

11. The Latin word that I here render by "fitting" is *conveniens*, which can also be translated as "appropriate" or "right." Aquinas makes much use of the word *conveniens* in 3a.

12. BLK/CUP 48, 5.

13. Aquinas here distinguishes between two senses of "necessary." Something may be necessary (a) absolutely speaking since some end just cannot be obtained without it, or (b) conditionally in that it is a particularly good way of obtaining

some end. Aquinas denies that the Incarnation is necessary in the first sense, but accepts that it is necessary in the second one.

14. BLK/CUP 48, 11 (with slight emendation).

15. In 3a,1,2, Aquinas also says that the Incarnation is fitting since it resulted in Christ making "satisfaction." He returns to this claim in 3a,48.

16. BLK/CUP 50, 9.

17. Ibid., 19.

18. Ibid., 33.

19. Aquinas is here taking "person" to mean something that exists as an individual in some sense while bearing in mind his 1a discussion of what "person" means when it comes to discussions of the Trinity.

20. BLK/CUP 49, 11.

21. Aquinas returns to the notion of Christ's beatific knowledge in 3a,10.

22. BLK/CUP 49, 21.

23. Ibid., 25.

24. So Aquinas's view of Christ's grace belongs to his ecclesiology as well as his Christology.

25. BLK/CUP 49, 59 (with slight emendation).

26. Ibid., 85 (with slight emendation).

27. Aquinas clearly thinks that people can be brought to beatitude by God in more than one way (cf. 3a,1,2). On the other hand, he places great emphasis on his belief that God has graciously chosen to draw us to beatitude by sending God the Son to live among us in order to declare God's love for human beings as God incarnate teaching us about God and urging us to be one with God. So Aquinas thinks of human beatitude as causally connected with Christ and, therefore, thinks that Christ must have enjoyed the beatific vision as able to bring it about in us (on the principle that one cannot give what one does not have).

28. BLK/CUP 49, 89 (with slight emendation).

29. Ibid., 93. Here Aquinas seems to be thinking that what human beings arrive at when knowing what things in the world are must have been known to Christ. One might wonder if even two human beings can know what each other knows given that there are indexical terms like "here" and "there." I might know that it is raining *here* (in Paris, say) since I am here and know that it is raining where I am as I speak. But you cannot truly claim to know that it is raining *here* if you are not where I am when I claim to know that it is raining where I am. Note, though, that sensitive as he is to matters of time and place when it comes to presenting true-or-false propositions, Aquinas primarily thinks of human knowledge as arising as we encounter the world at a sensory level (cf. chapter 9 above). By "infused knowledge" Aquinas means knowledge not derived from personal and sensory experience though equivalent to this by the grace of God.

30. Aquinas, of course, does not refer to atomic physics. But what I note here seems to be entailed by what he says about the knowledge of Christ.

31. BLK/CUP 49, 97 (with slight emendation). In his *Commentary on the Sentences*, Aquinas denies that Christ gained knowledge by means of an agent intellect. So 3a,9,4 represents a change of mind on Aquinas's part, one evidently prompted by a desire to make Christ seem more human than his previous view might appear to do.

32. Ibid., 139.

33. Ibid., 103 (with slight emendation).

34. Ibid., 123.

35. Ibid. (with slight emendation).

36. Aquinas will, therefore, go on to say that the crucifixion of Christ was possible because of what he was as human.

37. Aquinas is not saying in 3a,19,2 that Christ continually decided how his bodily functions should proceed from moment to moment. His point seems to be that Christ's bodily functions were voluntary in the sense that he could have made them work other than he allowed them to do. The main idea he is pushing here is that all of Christ's activity is the activity of a single subject in control of it.

38. BLK/CUP 50, 111.

39. Notice that in 3a,21, Aquinas is following the line of thought found in 2a2ae,83.

40. BLK/CUP 50, 123.

41. Ibid., 138, 139.

42. We shall see more from Aquinas on this theme in chapter 21.

43. BLK/CUP 50, 213 (with slight emendation).

CHAPTER 21. THE LIFE, DEATH, RESURRECTION, AND ASCENSION OF CHRIST (3A,27–59)

1. BLK/CUP 51, 3 (with slight emendation).

2. Aquinas also discusses Mary in Book 3 of his *Commentary on the Sentences*, Book 4 of the *Summa Contra Gentiles*, his commentaries on the Gospel of Matthew and John, and his *Compendium Theologiae*. There is also a record (*reportatio*) of one or more sermons of Aquinas on Mary dating from around 1273.

3. For a detailed account of Mary in theological discussions, the classic text is Hilda Graef, *Mary: A History of Doctrine and Devotion*, 2 vols. (Sheed and Ward: London, 1963). For more recent accounts, see Sarah Jane Boss (ed.), *Mary: The Complete Resource* (Oxford University Press: New York, 2007).

4. With respect to Jeremiah and John, Aquinas appeals to Jeremiah 1:5 and Luke 1:15.

5. For an excellent account of Aquinas's thinking on embryology, see Fabrizio Amerini, *Aquinas on the Beginning and End of Human Life* (Harvard University Press: Cambridge, Mass., 2013).

6. BLK/CUP 51, 11.

7. Aquinas's position here differs from current Roman Catholic teaching.

8. BLK/CUP 51, 37.

9. Ibid., 55.

10. "Christ" renders the title term "Messiah," so is not a proper name, though people regularly talk as if "Christ" were the proper name of Jesus. In 3a,37,2, Aquinas is rightly making a distinction between the title "Christ" and the proper name "Jesus."

11. That Christ's death is of saving significance is emphasized in Romans 3, in which St. Paul notes how both Jews and Gentiles fall short before God in various ways while adding that God has provided a means of redemption for them through Christ and his death "effective through faith." But the idea that Christ's death brings people to God is one to be found pretty much throughout the New Testament, even though New Testament authors, with the possible exception of St. Paul and the author of Hebrews, do not engage in lengthy theological or philosophical discussions as to how this is so. We have a commentary on Romans by Aquinas. It has not been critically edited by the Leonine Commission, but for an English translation of it, see John Mortensen and Enrique Alarcón (eds.), Fabian R. Lacher, trans., *Commentary on the Letter of Saint Paul to the Romans* (The Aquinas Institute for the Study of Sacred Doctrine: Lander, Wyo., 2012). Commentaries on Romans in English are legion. I continue to think that one of the best among them is C. H. Dodd, *The Epistle of Paul to the Romans* (Collins: London, 1932). Dodd has a sense of Paul as *arguing* and is, therefore, of a mind with Aquinas, who often takes Paul to be arguing and to have arguments on which one can comment.

12. New Testament authors sometimes speak of Christ as redeeming people. In doing so they seem to be thinking that Christ liberates people in some way.

13. BLK/CUP 54, 9 (with slight emendation).

14. Ibid., 79.

15. For two good discussions of Aquinas on satisfaction, see Rik Van Nieuwenhove, "'Bearing the Marks of Christ's Passion': Aquinas's Soteriology," in Rik Van Nieuwenhove and Joseph Wawrykow (eds.), *The Theology of Thomas Aquinas* (University of Notre Dame Press: Notre Dame, 2005), xx–xx; and chapter 15 of Eleonore Stump, *Aquinas* (Routledge: London and New York, 2003). See also Romanus Cessario, "Aquinas on Christian Salvation," in Thomas Weinandy, Daniel Keating, and John Yocum (eds.), *Aquinas on Doctrine* (T&T Clark International: London and New York, 2004).

16. 3a,48,2 (BLK/CUP 54, 79, with some emendation).

17. So Christ's passion, for Aquinas, is not any old suffering you might care to mention. It is suffering willingly accepted on behalf of a certain cause (and is not comparable to, say, being accidentally eaten alive by wild animals).

18. BLK/CUP 54, 105.

19. Ibid., 7 (with slight emendation).

20. Ibid., 77 (with slight emendation).

21. BLK/CUP 52, 43.
22. Ibid.
23. The Gospel of John has no account of Christ being tempted by Satan. Perhaps this is due to the fact that from its first verse it presents Jesus as the Word incarnate in a way that closely corresponds to how Aquinas generally thinks of Christ given his understanding of the hypostatic union.
24. BLK/CUP 53, 71 (with slight emendation).
25. Ibid., 121.
26. Ibid., 117.
27. Ibid.
28. Note, however, that Aquinas frequently uses *probare* in a weak sense—as meaning something like "to indicate."
29. The translators of BLK/CUP 53 can, I think, be criticized for their rendering of 3a,43,4 since they translate Aquinas as claiming that Christ's miracles *demonstrate* that Christ was God.
30. The same argument occurs in *Summa Contra Gentiles* IV,55. But as I said in a previous note, Aquinas frequently uses *probare* in a weak sense as meaning something like "to indicate."
31. BLK/CUP 53, 157 (with slight emendation).
32. Ibid., 161.
33. BLK/CUP 54, 121.
34. In 3a,52,2, Aquinas holds that Christ's descent into hell had an effect on the damned (as emphasizing to them their rejection of God) but did not amount to him being present to them as their savior.
35. BLK/CUP 55, 19.
36. Ibid., 71, 73 (with slight emendation).
37. Aquinas thinks that the resurrection of Christ took him beyond the possibility of perishing physically, but he seems to think of Christ's ascension as adding something to his resurrection in terms of place. On the other hand, in 3a,57, Aquinas does not offer any developed metaphysical or physical account of how this is so. Instead, he contents himself with continually drawing a contrast between bodies being in places as we are familiar with them and Christ now being in a place with which we are not familiar.

CHAPTER 22. THE SACRAMENTS OF THE CHRISTIAN
CHURCH (3A,60–90)

1. BLK/CUP 56, 3. The Latin word *sacramentum* came to be used by some people as equivalent to the Greek word for "mystery" (the word used for "sacrament" in the Eastern Church). So perhaps Aquinas is indulging in a play on words when connecting the mysteries of the Word incarnate and the sacraments of the

Church. He certainly thinks that the sacraments have the significance that they do precisely because of the mystery of the Incarnation.

2. *Sentences*, 4.2.1.

3. There are some differences between Aquinas's treatment of sacraments in 3a and his earlier treatment in his commentary on the *Sentences*. For discussion of this, together with accounts of Aquinas's approach to sacraments in 3a, see John Yocum, "Sacraments in Aquinas," in Thomas Weinandy, Daniel Keating, and John Yocum (eds.), *Aquinas on Doctrine*; and Liam Walsh, "Sacraments," in Rik Van Nieuwenhove and Joseph Wawrykow (eds.), *The Theology of Thomas Aquinas*. See also Marilyn McCord Adams, *Some Later Medieval Theories of the Eucharist: Thomas Aquinas, Giles of Rome, Duns Scotus, and William Ockham*, chapters 4 and 8.

4. That sacraments are saving signs is emphasized by St. Augustine in texts such as *De Civitate Dei* X,3 and Book 2 of *De Doctrina Christiana*.

5. Suppose that two people in love with each other choose to symbolize this while acting out a wedding ceremony though not actually marrying each other. Their behavior would be purely symbolic. By contrast, consider two people saying "I do" or "With this ring I thee wed" at a real wedding service. When saying this, the couple are not symbolizing a wedding or reporting on one. They are actually marrying each other. When speaking of sacraments as signs, Aquinas is thinking of them as bringing something about every bit as much as does saying "I do" or "With this ring I thee wed" at a real wedding. The analogy I am drawing here (and it is only an analogy) rests on the notion of performative utterance commonly associated with the philosopher J. L. Austin (1911–1960). Apart from saying "I do" or whatever at a wedding, examples of performative utterances include someone naming a ship by saying "I name this ship '*Victory*'" or someone saying "I bet you $400 that Jim will win the election." For Austin on performative utterance, see J. L. Austin, *How to Do Things with Words* (Harvard University Press: Cambridge, Mass., 1962).

6. Cf. Herbert McCabe, *The Teaching of the Catholic Church* (Darton, Longman & Todd: London, 2000). McCabe is picking up on a slogan familiar to Aquinas according to which sacraments *efficunt quod figurant* ("do what they signify"). Aquinas cites this slogan in 3a,62,1, ad.1.

7. BLK/CUP 56, 13.

8. This view has been developed at length by Edward Schillebeeckx in *Christ the Sacrament of the Encounter with God* (Sheed and Ward: London, 1963).

9. BLK/CUP 56, 67.

10. Aquinas will sometimes speak of the "matter" and "form" of a sacrament. By "matter" he means the physical elements used in celebrating a sacrament, for example, water in the case of baptism. By "form" he means the words used in the celebration of the sacrament. Just as he takes form to make material things intelligible, Aquinas takes sacramental form to proclaim what they actually are.

11. BLK/CUP 56, 39 (with slight emendation).

12. Ibid. (with slight emendation). In 3a,61,1, ad.3, Aquinas backs up what he says by appealing to Romans 6:3.

13. Timothy McDermott, *St Thomas Aquinas, "Summa Theologiae," A Concise Translation* (Eyre and Spottiswoode: London, 1989), 543. This view of Aquinas obviously presupposes that we get to God not only because God has come to save us but also because we respond to God's offer of salvation in an appropriate way.

14. I do not know how a theologian might today develop an account of human salvation along Aquinas's lines so as to include among the saved those who know nothing of Christ and believe in things that Christians take to be false. But any such account will have to take seriously the way in which Aquinas's thoughts on salvation are tied to his thinking about Christ as God incarnate while also, perhaps, drawing on his claim that God can save people without becoming incarnate and without sacraments.

15. The reference is to *De Civitate Dei* X,5.

16. In 3a,60, 1, Aquinas uses the same examples of analogy as he gives in 1a,13,5.

17. BLK/CUP 56, 9.

18. Ibid. (with slight emendation).

19. BLK/CUP 56, 11, 13.

20. Ibid., 15.

21. Ibid., 9.

22. Ibid., 15 (with slight emendation).

23. Ibid., 45 (with slight emendation).

24. Ibid., 47, 49 (with slight emendation).

25. I am tempted to summarize this teaching of Aquinas by saying that he thinks that sacraments are fun; things that we can enjoy.

26. BLK/CUP 56, 39.

27. Here I am trying to put together what Aquinas has in mind in the objections and replies in 3a,61,1.

28. BLK/CUP 56, 69.

29. Ibid., 53 (with emendation). In this connection, Aquinas invokes the authority of Galatians 3:27.

30. Ibid. (with slight emendation).

31. 3a,62,1, ad.1 (BLK/CUP 56, 55).

32. Ibid., 57.

33. Ibid., 59.

34. Augustine, like Aquinas, recognizes that someone might celebrate a sacrament while intending to bring about something quite at odds with the will of God or what the Church understands by the sacrament in question. In such a case, both of them agree that the sacrament has not been validly celebrated and is just a fake sacrament, rather as counterfeit money is fake money. See below regarding 3a,64,8.

35. BLK/CUP 56, 79.
36. Ibid.
37. BLK/CUP 56, 87.
38. Ibid., 83.
39. Ibid., 87.
40. Ibid.
41. BLK/CUP 56, 117 (with slight emendation).
42. Ibid., 127.
43. Foreword (*Prologus*) to 3a (BLK/CUP 48, 3).
44. BLK/CUP 57, 83.
45. Ibid., 85, 87. As I have noted, apart from acknowledging that there were Old Testament saints, Aquinas has nothing to say about salvation when it comes to members of religions other than Judaism (as it was in Old Testament times) and Christianity in what Aquinas takes to be its orthodox form. However, a careful reading of what he says about baptism by desire, about conscience, and about divine omnipotence surely ought to leave one feeling that this contains the seeds for a development of Aquinas's thinking about salvation that might seem less exclusive than the teaching of 3a,68,2 appears to be at first reading.
46. Cf. appendix 5 to BLK/CUP 57.
47. Ibid., 205 (with slight emendation).
48. Ibid.
49. BLK/CUP 58, 11.
50. Ibid., 5.
51. Ibid., 15.
52. Ibid., 15, 17.
53. Two famous exponents of this approach to the Eucharist are Berengarius of Tours (ca. 1040–1080) and Ulrich Zwingli (1484–1531). Aquinas refers to Berengarius in 3a,75,1. For Zwingli on the Eucharist, see W. P. Stephens, *The Theology of Huldrych Zwingli* (Oxford University Press: Oxford, 1986), 180ff.
54. BLK/CUP 58, 55, 57.
55. Ibid., 57.
56. Ibid., 71, 73.
57. Ibid., 11.
58. Ibid., 19 (with slight emendation).
59. BLK/CUP 59, 5.
60. What, according to Aquinas, would it be to receive the Eucharist *unworthily*? It would be to receive it by not really wanting what it signifies, or to receive it in a state of sin, or to receive it only to suit one's purposes given one's status in society. Cf. 3a,79,3.
61. BLK/CUP 59, 13.
62. Elizabeth Anscombe, "On Transubstantiation," in G. E. M. Anscombe, *Collected Philosophical Papers* (Basil Blackwell: Oxford, 1981), 3:109.

63. I quote from Abdel Ross Wentz (ed.), *Luther's Works* (Muhlenberg: Philadelphia, 1959), 6:29. The quotes come from Luther's *The Babylonian Captivity of the Church*.

64. Aquinas is not an Aristotelian as Aristotle was. He is someone who used the philosophy of Aristotle to defend views that did not even occur to Aristotle. I have tried to draw attention to this fact several times in the present volume.

65. As I have noted, Aquinas thinks that all our attempts to talk about God inevitably lead us to stretch the meanings of words. Cf. chapter 4.7 above.

66. Herbert McCabe, *God Matters*, 146.

67. For some philosophical criticism of Aquinas on transubstantiation, see (1) Anthony Kenny, "The Use of Logical Analysis in Theology," in John Coulson (ed.), *Theology and the University* (Helicon: Baltimore, 1964), xx–xx; and (2) Michael Dummett, "The Intelligibility of Eucharistic Doctrine," in William J. Abraham and Steven W. Holtzer (eds.), *The Rationality of Religious Belief* (Oxford University Press: Oxford, 1987), xx–xx. In my *The Thought of Thomas Aquinas* (Clarendon: Oxford, 1992), I note how Aquinas in 3a seems to anticipate and reply to the criticisms leveled by Kenny and Dummett against his teaching on transubstantiation (cf. 374–376).

68. Roman Catholics would say this, as would, for example, many Anglicans and Eastern Orthodox.

69. For a concise account of all this, see Frank O'Loughlin, *The Future of the Sacrament of Penance* (Paulist: New York/Mahwah, N.J., 2007).

70. Cf. Norman P. Tanner, *Decrees of the Ecumenical Councils*, 1:245.

71. *Commentary on Isaiah*, 2.

72. BLK/CUP 60, 27 (with slight emendation).

73. Ibid., 63.

74. Ibid., 173.

75. Ibid.

CHAPTER 23. EPILOGUE

1. John XXII clearly read a fair amount of Aquinas. He bought copies of Aquinas's works and annotated some of them. Cf. A. Dondaine, "La Collection des Oeuvres de Saint Thomas dite de Jean XXII et Jacquet Maci," *Scriptorium* 27 (1975).

2. For a discussion of the circulation of Aquinas's writings in the years after his death, see J. N. Hilgarth, *Who Read Thomas Aquinas?* (Pontifical Institute of Mediaeval Studies: Toronto, 1992).

3. St. Ignatius Loyola was born in 1491 and died in 1556. There is a long-standing tradition, going back to the seventeenth century, according to which the *Summa Theologiae* was placed for veneration on an altar during the Council of Trent. But I cannot find any serious historical support for this tradition. For an account of how Aquinas has been an influence over the years, see Romanus Cessario,

A Short History of Thomism (The Catholic University of America Press: Washington, D.C, 2005); and Christopher Upham, "The Influence of Aquinas," in Brian Davies and Eleonore Stump (eds.), *The Oxford Handbook of Aquinas*.

4. For a good account of Aquinas and Orthodox theologians, see Markus Plested, *Orthodox Readings of Aquinas* (Oxford University Press: Oxford, 2012).

5. I quote from the English translation of *Aeterni Patris* as it currently appears on the Vatican's website.

6. A student (Huw Price) of one of Wittgenstein's friends (Rush Rhees) once told me that Wittgenstein, referring to the *Summa Theologiae*, said that he liked Aquinas's questions but did not think much of his answers. This is hearsay, of course, but it is, I think, interesting hearsay. And—more hearsay—one of Wittgenstein's surviving friends (Peter Geach) tells me that a copy of the *Summa Theologiae* was on Wittgenstein's bookshelf even though Wittgenstein was not much of a book collector.

7. For a famous development of the view that the world amounts to ideas that we have, see George Berkeley (1685–1753), especially his *Treatise Concerning the Principles of Human Knowledge* (1710); and his *Three Dialogues Between Hylas and Philonous* (1713). For some history and discussion of philosophical approaches to the term "substance," see E. J. Lowe, *A Survey of Metaphysics* (Oxford University Press: Oxford, 2002); P. M. S. Hacker, *Human Nature: The Categorial Framework* (Blackwell: Oxford, 2007); and the entry "Substance" in the online *Stanford Encyclopedia of Philosophy*. Criticisms of Aquinas's view of being (and, correspondingly, of sentences with the verb "to be" in them) have been developed in the wake of something that Immanuel Kant (1724–1804) said in his *Critique of Pure Reason* (1781). He argued that "being is obviously not a real predicate," while seeming to mean that to say that something exists is not to say what it is or to give us information about it. This conclusion, easier to state than to understand or refute, has been defended at length and with much logical dexterity by C. J. F. Williams in *What Is Existence?* (Clarendon: Oxford, 1981). For criticisms of it, see, among other citable works, Colin McGinn, *Logical Properties* (Clarendon: Oxford, 2000); and (with explicit reference to Aquinas) Barry Miller, *A Most Unlikely God* (University of Notre Dame Press: Notre Dame, 1996).

8. This point is well emphasized by C. J. F. Williams in "Neither Confounding the Persons nor Dividing the Substance" (cited in chapter 6).

9. This conclusion is famously argued for by David Hume (1711–1776) in Book I, Section III of his *A Treatise of Human Nature* (1739–1740). Here Hume suggests that "the separation...of the idea of a cause from that of a beginning of existence, is plainly possible for the imagination; and consequently the actual separation of these objects is so far possible, that it implies no contradiction nor absurdity." For a critique of Hume's argument, see G. E. M. Anscombe, "'Whatever Has a Beginning of Existence Must Have a Cause': Hume's Argument Exposed," in Volume 1 of Anscombe's *Collected Philosophical Papers* (Blackwell: Oxford, 1981).

10. Aquinas does not baldly raise the question "Why is there something rather than nothing?" Allowing for various qualifications that he would wish to make concerning words like *thing* and *nothing*, however, this question is central to Aquinas's philosophy of God. For more on this, see John F. Wippel, "Thomas Aquinas on the Ultimate Why Question: Why Is There Anything at All Rather Than Absolutely Nothing?" in John F. Wippel (ed.), *The Ultimate Why Question: Why Is There Anything at All Rather Than Absolutely Nothing?* (Catholic University of America Press: Washington, D.C., 2011).

11. Cf. Bede Rundle, *Why There Is Something Rather Than Nothing* (Clarendon: Oxford, 2004).

12. I have mentioned C. J. F. Williams's *What Is Existence?* but also note Anthony Kenny, *Aquinas on Being* (Clarendon: Oxford, 2002), which is critical of Aquinas on being in general; and C. J. F. Williams, "Being," in Philip L. Quinn and Charles Taliaferro (eds.), *A Companion to Philosophy of Religion* (Blackwell: Oxford, 1997), which targets Aquinas's view of divine simplicity. I discuss Kenny's book in my article "Kenny on Aquinas on Being," *The Modern Schoolman* 82 (2005).

13. Ludwig Wittgenstein, *Tractatus Logico-Philosophicus*, translated by C. K. Ogden (Routledge & Kegan Paul: London, 1922).

14. I quote from *Ludwig Wittgenstein, Philosophical Occasions 1912–1951*, edited by James Klagge and Alfred Norman (Hackett, Indianapolis and Cambridge, 1993), 41.

15. Richard Swinburne, *The Coherence of Theism*, rev. ed. (Clarendon: Oxford, 1993), 1.

16. I quote from *The Philosophical Writings of Descartes*, vol. 2, translated by John Cottingham, Robert Stoothhoff, and Dugold Murdoch (Cambridge University Press: Cambridge, 1984), 19.

17. Descartes holds that we are essentially incorporeal minds connected to bodies in a way that allows for interaction between our minds and our bodies. This view of ourselves (sometimes referred to as "substance dualism") is defended by Swinburne in *The Evolution of the Soul*, rev. ed. (Clarendon: Oxford, 1997).

18. Cf. Alvin Plantinga, *Does God Have a Nature?* (Marquette University Press: Milwaukee, 1980), 47.

19. Cf. Nicholas Wolterstorff, "God Everlasting" in J. Orlebeke and Lewis B. Smedes (eds.), *God and the Good* (Eerdmans: Grand Rapids, 1975). For a defense of divine immutability written with an eye on Aquinas and other theologians, see Thomas G. Weinandy, *Does God Change?* (St. Bede's : Still River, Mass., 1985). For a defense of divine timelessness, see Paul Helm, *Eternal God* (Clarendon: Oxford, 1988). For a critique of the view that God is not in time, see Nelson Pike, *God and Timelessness* (Routledge & Kegan Paul: London, 1970).

20. I try to explain some of them in my *An Introduction to the Philosophy of Religion*, 3rd ed. (Oxford University Press: Oxford, 2004), chapters 1 and 8.

21. Cf. Genesis 3:8; Genesis 8:21; Exodus 33:11; Psalm 2:4; Psalm 38:13; and Isaiah 7:18.

22. Cf. Samuel Ballantine, *The Hidden God: The Hiding of the Face of God in the Old Testament* (Oxford University Press: Oxford, 1983). For some philosophical reflections on the hiddenness of God, see Daniel Howard Snyder, and Paul Moser (eds.), *Divine Hiddenness* (Cambridge University Press: Cambridge, 2002).

23. For good accounts of criticisms of Aquinas on divine simplicity, see James E. Dolezal, *God Without Parts: Divine Simplicity and the Metaphysics of God's Absoluteness* (Pickwick: Eugene, Ore., 2011); and Peter Weigel, *Aquinas on Simplicity* (Peter Lang: Bern, 2008). Dolezal and Weigel offer detailed discussions of the criticisms on which they report.

24. Cf. Mark Baker and Stewart Goetz (eds.), *The Soul Hypothesis* (Continuum: London, 2011); John Hawthorne, "Cartesian Dualism," in Peter Van Inwagen and Dean Zimmerman (eds.), *Persons Human and Divine* (Oxford University Press: Oxford, 2007); and E. J. Lowe, *Subjects of Experience* (Cambridge University Press: Cambridge, 1996). For earlier defenses of the claim that we are really immaterial substances, see H. D. Lewis, *The Elusive Mind* (George Allen and Unwin: London, 1969); and H. D. Lewis, *Persons and Life After Death* (Macmillan: London, 1978).

25. For an account of this view, see (among many other works that I could recommend) William Jaworski, *Philosophy of Mind: A Comprehensive Introduction* (Wiley-Blackwell: Oxford, 2011); and Jaegwon Kim, *Philosophy of Mind* (Westview: Boulder, Col. and Oxford, 1998). For an interesting discussion of what people are as they know, think, believe, and have emotions, see M. R. Bennett and P. M. S. Hacker, *Philosophical Foundations of Neuroscience* (Blackwell: Oxford, 2003).

26. The argument is criticized by, for example, Anthony Kenny in chapter 12 of his *Aquinas on Mind* (Routledge: London and New York, 1993). It is presented sympathetically by Herbert McCabe in Anthony Kenny (ed.), *Aquinas: A Collection of Critical Essays* (University of Notre Dame Press: Notre Dame, 1969).

27. For conflicting interpretations, see Patrick Toner, "Personhood and Death in St. Thomas Aquinas," *History of Philosophy Quarterly* 26 (2009); and Eleonore Stump, *Aquinas* (Routledge: London, 2003), chapter 1, especially 51–54.

28. "Modern Moral Philosophy" first appeared in *Philosophy* 33 (1958). It has been reprinted a number of times. For Philippa Foot and virtue ethics, see Philippa Foot, *Virtues and Vices* (University of California Press: Berkeley, 1978); and *Natural Goodness* (Clarendon: Oxford, 2001).

29. Cf. Gareth Moore, *A Question of Truth*, chapter 7; and Gareth Moore, *The Body in Context*.

30. Hans Küng, *Great Christian Thinkers* (Continuum: New York, 2002), 120.

31. *Catechism of the Catholic Church*, 847. I quote from the edition of the *Catechism* published by Geoffrey Chapman (London, 1994).

32. Note, though, that Aquinas's Jewish and Islamic contemporaries would have been equally unaccommodating concerning Christian believers. What is perhaps most interesting is that thinkers during the medieval period, while being absolutely sure that those of other religions were damned to hell, nonetheless engaged in dialogue.

33. For favorable discussion of theories of evolution written with an eye on certain religious beliefs, see Michael Ruse, *Darwinism and Its Discontents* (Cambridge University Press: Cambridge, 2006); and Robert Pennock and Michael Ruse (eds.), *But Is It Science? The Philosophical Question in the Creation/Evolution Controversy*, 2nd ed. (Prometheus: Buffalo, 2008).

34. *Message to the Pontifical Academy of Sciences*, October 1996.

35. Gerald O'Collins, *Christology: A Biblical, Historical, and Systematic Study of Jesus* (Oxford University Press: New York, 1995), 207.

36. Here I am quoting from Herbert McCabe, *God Matters*, 57.

37. John Hick (ed.), *The Myth of God Incarnate* (SCM: London, 1977).

38. Cf. Herbert McCabe, *God Matters*. Here McCabe reviews *The Myth of God Incarnate* and engages in a discussion of the volume with Maurice Wiles (1923–2005), who contributed to it. In my view, the conversation between Wiles and McCabe is a model of what a theological debate should be (and often was in Aquinas's day).

Bibliography

Abraham, William J., and Holtzer, Steven W. (eds.), *The Rationality of Religious Belief* (Oxford University Press: Oxford, 1987).

Ackrill, J. L. (trans.), *Aristotle's "Categories" and "De Interpretatione"* (Clarendon Press: Oxford, 1963).

Adams, Marilyn McCord, *Some Later Medieval Theories of the Eucharist: Thomas Aquinas, Giles of Rome, Duns Scotus, and William Ockham* (Oxford University Press: Oxford, 2010).

Aertsen, Jan, *Nature and Creature: Thomas Aquinas's Way of Thought* (Brill: Leiden, 1988).

Alston, William P., *Perceiving God* (Cornell University Press: Ithaca, 1991).

Amerini, Fabrizio, *Aquinas on the Beginning and End of Human Life* (Harvard University Press: Cambridge, Mass., 2013).

Anscombe, Elizabeth, *Collected Philosophical Papers* (Basil Blackwell: Oxford, 1981).

———, "What Is It to Believe Someone?" in Delaney, C. F. (ed.), *Rationality and Religious Belief* (University of Notre Dame Press: Notre Dame, 1979).

Austin, J. L., *How to Do Things with Words* (Harvard University Press: Cambridge, Mass., 1962).

Baker, Mark, and Goetz, Stewart (eds.), *The Soul Hypothesis* (New York: London, 2011).

Ballantine, Samuel, *The Hidden God: The Hiding of the Face of God in the Old Testament* (Oxford University Press: Oxford, 1983).

Barr, James, *Biblical Faith and Natural Theology* (Clarendon: Oxford, 1993).

Barton, Stephen C. (ed.), *The Cambridge Companion to the Gospels* (Cambridge University Press: Cambridge, 2006).

Bauerschmidt, Frederick Christian, *Holy Teaching: Introducing the "Summa Theologiae" of St. Thomas Aquinas* (Brazos: Grand Rapids, 2005).

Beilby, James K., and Rhodes, Paul (eds.), *The Historical Jesus: Five Views* (IVP Academic: Downers Grove, Ill., 2009).

Bennett, M. R., and Hacker, P. M. S., *Philosophical Foundations of Neuroscience* (Blackwell: Oxford, 2003).

Berkeley, George, *The Principles of Human Knowledge and Other Writings* (edited and introduced by G. J. Warnock) (Collins: Glasgow, 1962).

Bird, Otto, "How to Read an Article in the *Summa*," *The New Scholasticism* 27 (1953).

Boland, Vivian, "St. Thomas's Sermon *Puer Iesus*: A Neglected Source for His Understanding of Teaching and Learning," *New Blackfriars* 88 (2007).

Boss, Sarah Jane (ed.), *Mary: The Complete Resource* (Oxford University Press: New York, 2007).

Boyle, Leonard, "The Setting of the *Summa Theologiae*" in Davies, Brian (ed.), *Aquinas's "Summa Theologiae": Critical Essays* (Rowman and Littlefield: Boulder and London, 2006).

Boyle, Leonard E., and Boyle, John (eds.), *Thomas Aquinas, "Lectura romana in primum Sententiarum Petri Lombardi"* (Pontifical Institute of Mediaeval Studies: Toronto, 2006).

Brown, Patterson, "St. Thomas' Doctrine of Necessary Being" in Kenny, Anthony (ed.), *Aquinas: A Collection of Critical Essays* (University of Notre Dame Press: Notre Dame, 1976).

Brown, Stephen F. (ed.), *Aquinas on Faith and Reason* (Hackett: Indianapolis and Cambridge, 1999).

Brunner, Emil, and Barth, Karl, *Natural Theology: Comprising "Nature and Grace" by Professor Dr. Emil Brunner and the Reply "No!" by Dr. Karl Barth* (Wipf and Stock: Eugene, Ore., 2002).

Burrell, David B., *Freedom and Creation in Three Traditions* (University of Notre Dame Press: Notre Dame, 1993).

———, *Knowing the Unknowable God: Ibn-Sina, Maimonides, Aquinas* (University of Notre Dame Press: Notre Dame, 1986).

Catechismus Catholicae Ecclesiae (*Catechism of the Catholic Church*) (Libreria Editrice: Vatican City, 1994 [English edition, Geoffrey Chapman: London, 1994]).

Cessario, Romanus, "Aquinas on Christian Salvation" in Weinandy, Thomas, Keating, Daniel, and Yocum, John (eds.), *Aquinas on Doctrine* (T&T Clark International: London and New York, 2004).

———, *A Short History of Thomism* (The Catholic University of America Press: Washington, D.C., 2005).

Chenu, M.-D., *Aquinas and His Role in Theology* (The Liturgical Press: Collegeville, Minn., 2002).

———, *Toward Understanding Saint Thomas* (Henry Regnery: Chicago, 1964).

Clifford, W. K., "The Ethics of Belief," in *Lectures and Essays*, 2nd ed., edited by Leslie Stephen and Frederick Pollock (Macmillan: London, 1886).

Cohen, Sheldon, "St. Thomas Aquinas on the Immaterial Reception of Sensible Forms," *Philosophical Review* 91 (April 1982).

Congar, Yves, *The Mystery of the Church* (Helicon: Baltimore, 1960).

Coulson, John (ed.), *Theology and the University* (Helicon: Baltimore, 1964).

Craig, William Lane, *The Kalām Cosmological Argument* (Macmillan: London and Basingstoke, 1979).

Damico, Anthony (trans.), *Thomas Aquinas: The Literal Exposition on Job* (Scholars Press: Atlanta, 1989).

Davies, Brian, "Anselm and the Ontological Argument," in Davies, Brian, and Leftow, Brian (eds.), *The Cambridge Companion to Anselm* (Cambridge University Press: Cambridge, 2004).

———, *Aquinas* (Continuum: London, 2002).

———, "Aquinas and Atheism" in Bullivant, Stephen, and Ruse, Michael (eds.), *The Oxford Handbook of Atheism* (Oxford University Press: Oxford, 2013).

———, "Aquinas and the Academic Life," *New Blackfriars* 83 (July 2002).

——— (ed.), *Aquinas's "Summa Theologiae": Critical Essays* (Rowman and Littlefield: Boulder and London, 2006).

———, "Aquinas's Third Way," *New Blackfriars* 82 (October 2001).

———, "God" in McCosker, Philip, and Turner, Denys (eds.), *The Cambridge Companion to the "Summa Theologiae"* (Cambridge University Press: Cambridge, 2014).

———, *An Introduction to the Philosophy of Religion*, 3rd ed. (Oxford University Press: Oxford, 2004).

———, "Is God Beyond Reason?" *Philosophical Investigations* 32, no. 4 (2009).

———, "Kenny on Aquinas on Being," (*The Modern Schoolman* 82 (2005).

——— (ed.), *Language, Meaning and God* (Wipf & Stock: Eugene, Ore., 2010).

———, *Philosophy of Religion: A Guide and Anthology* (Oxford University Press: Oxford, 2000).

———, "Simplicity" in Taliaferro, Charles, and Meister, Chad (eds.), *The Cambridge Companion to Christian Philosophical Theology* (Cambridge University Press: Cambridge, 2010).

———, *Thinking About God* (Wipf & Stock: Eugene, Ore., 2010).

——— (ed.), *Thomas Aquinas: Contemporary Philosophical Perspectives* (Oxford University Press: New York, 2002).

——— (ed.), *Thomas Aquinas, "On Evil,"* translated by Richard Regan (Oxford University Press: New York, 2003).

———, *Thomas Aquinas on God and Evil* (Oxford University Press: Oxford, 2011).

———, *The Thought of Thomas Aquinas* (Clarendon: Oxford, 1992).

Davies, Brian, and Evans, G. R. (eds.), *Anselm of Canterbury: The Major Works* (Oxford University Press: New York, 1998).

Davies, Brian, and Leftow, Brian (eds.), *The Cambridge Companion to Anselm* (Cambridge University Press: Cambridge, 2004).

———, *Thomas Aquinas, "Summa Theologiae," Questions on God* (Cambridge University Press: Cambridge, 2006).

Davies, Brian, and Stump, Eleonore (eds.), *The Oxford Handbook of Thomas Aquinas* (Oxford University Press: Oxford, 2011).

Delaney, C. F. (ed.), *Rationality and Religious Belief* (University of Notre Dame Press: Notre Dame, 1979).

Descartes, René, *Selected Philosophical Writings*, translated by Cottingham, John, Stoothoff, Robert, and Murdoch, Dugald (Cambridge University Press: Cambridge, 1988).

DeYoung, Rebecca Konyndyk, "Aquinas on the Vice of Sloth: Three Interpretive Issues," *The Thomist* 75 (2011).

————, "Resistance to the Demands of Love: Aquinas on the Vice of *Acedia*," *The Thomist* 68 (2004).

Dixon, Thomas, *From Passions to Emotions* (Cambridge University Press: Cambridge, 2003).

Dodd, C. H., *The Epistle of Paul to the Romans* (Collins: London, 1932).

Dolezal, James E., *God Without Parts: Divine Simplicity and the Metaphysics of God's Absoluteness* (Pickwick: Eugene, Ore., 2001).

Dondaine, A., "La Collection des Oeuvres de Saint Thomas dite de Jean XXII et Jacquet Maci," *Scriptorium* 29 (1975).

Draper, G. I. A. D., "The Origins of the Just War Tradition," *New Blackfriars* 46 (November 1964).

Dulles, Avery, *A Church to Believe In* (Crossroad: New York, 1982).

Dummett, Michael, "The Intelligibility of Eucharistic Doctrine," in Abraham, William J., and Holtzer, Steven (eds.), *The Rationality of Religious Belief* (Oxford University Press: Oxford, 1987).

Dunne, Michael, "Concerning 'Neapolitan Gold': William of Tocco and Peter of Ireland," *Bulletin de Philosophie Médiévale* 45 (2003).

Elders, Leo J., *The Philosophical Theology of St. Thomas Aquinas* (Brill: Leiden, 1990).

Emery, Gilles, *The Trinitarian Theology of Saint Thomas Aquinas* (Oxford University Press: Oxford, 2007).

————, *The Trinity* (The Catholic University of America Press: Washington, D.C., 2011).

————, *Trinity in Aquinas* (Sapientia: Ypsilanti, 2003).

Evans, G. R. (ed.), *The Medieval Theologians* (Blackwell: Oxford, 2001).

Ferguson, John, "In Defence of Pelagius," *Theology* 83 (March 1980).

————, *Pelagius* (W. Heffer and Sons: Cambridge, 1956).

Ferrua, Angelico (ed.), *Thomae Aquinatis vitae fontes praecipuae* (Edizione Domenicane: Alba, 1968).

Fine, Gail, *On Ideas: Aristotle's Criticism of Plato's Theory of Forms* (Oxford University Press: Oxford, 1995).

Flew, Antony, *The Presumption of Atheism and Other Essays* (Elek/Pemberton: London, 1976).

Foot, Philippa, *Natural Goodness* (Clarendon: Oxford, 2001).

————, *Virtues and Vices* (University of California Press: Berkeley, 1978).

Foster, Kenelm (ed.), *The Life of Saint Thomas Aquinas: Biographical Documents* (Longmans, Green and Company: London, 1959).

Freddoso, Alfred J. (trans.), *Thomas Aquinas: Treatise on Human Nature* (St. Augustine's: South Bend, Ind., 2010).

Friedman, Russell L., *Intellectual Traditions at the Medieval University: The Use of Philosophical Psychology in Trinitarian Theology Among the Franciscans and Dominicans* (Brill: Leiden, 2012).

————, *Medieval Trinitarian Thought from Aquinas to Ockham* (Cambridge University Press: Cambridge, 2010).

Geach, P. T., "Dr. Kenny on Practical Inference," *Analysis* 26 (1966).

————, *God and the Soul* (Routledge & Kegan Paul: London, 1969).

————, "Good and Evil," *Analysis* 17 (1956).

————, *Mental Acts* (Routledge & Kegan Paul: London, 1957).

————, *Reason and Argument* (Basil Blackwell: Oxford, 1976).

Geltner, G. (ed. and trans.), *William of Saint-Amour, "De periculis novissimorum temporum"* (Peeters: Paris, Leuven, Dudley, Mass., 2008).

Glenn, Paul J., *A Tour of the Summa* (Tan Books and Publishers: Rockford, Ill., 1978).

Goldie, Peter (ed.), *The Oxford Handbook of Philosophy of Emotion* (Oxford University Press: Oxford, 2010).

Graef, Hilda, *Mary: A History of Doctrine and Devotion*, 2 vols. (Sheed and Ward: London, 1963).

Gratsch, Edward J., *Aquinas's Summa: An Introduction and Interpretation* (Theological Publications in India: Bangalore, 1990).

Hacker, P. M. S., *Human Nature: The Categorial Framework* (Blackwell: Oxford, 2007).

Hawthorne, John, "Cartesian Dualism" in Van Inwagen, Peter, and Zimmerman, Dean (eds.), *Persons Human and Divine* (Oxford University Press: Oxford, 2007).

Hayes, Zachary (trans.), *Saint Bonaventure's 'Disputed Questions on the Mystery of the Trinity* (The Franciscan Institute, St. Bonaventure University: New York, 1979).

Helm, Paul, *Eternal God* (Clarendon: Oxford, 1988).

Hick, John (ed.), *The Myth of God Incarnate* (SCM Press: London, 1977).

Hilgarth, Jocelyn, *Who Read Thomas Aquinas?* (Pontifical Institute of Mediaeval Studies: Toronto, 1992).

Holmen, Tom, and Porter, Stanley E. (eds.), *Handbook for the Study of the Historical Jesus*, 4 vols. (Brill: Leiden, 2011).

Hood, John Y. B., *Aquinas and the Jews* (University of Pennsylvania Press: Philadelphia, 1995).

Hoogland, Mark-Robin (trans.), *Thomas Aquinas, "The Academic Sermons"* (Catholic University of America Press: Washington, D.C., 2010).

Hornsby, Jennifer, "Arm Raising and Arm Rising," *Philosophy* 55 (1980).

Horst, Ulrich, "Christ, *Exemplar Ordinis Fratrum Praedicantium*, According to Saint Thomas Aquinas" in Emery, Kent, and Wawrykow, Joseph (eds.), *Christ Among the Medieval Dominicans* (University of Notre Dame Press: Notre Dame, 1998).

Hume, David, *Enquiries Concerning Human Understanding and Concerning the Principles of Morals*, edited by L. A. Selby-Bigge, 3rd ed. (Clarendon: Oxford, 1975).

Jaworski, William, *Philosophy of Mind: A Comprehensive Introduction* (Wiley-Blackwell: Oxford, 2011).

Jenkins, John, *Knowledge and Faith in Thomas Aquinas* (Cambridge University Press: Cambridge, 1997).

Jordan, Mark, *Rewritten Theology: Aquinas After His Readers* (Blackwell: Oxford, 2006).

Kant, Immanuel, *Critique of Pure Reason*, translated and edited by Paul Guyer and Allen W. Wood (Cambridge University Press: Cambridge, 1998).

Kenny, Anthony, *Aquinas* (Oxford University Press: Oxford, 1980).

———— (ed.), *Aquinas: A Collection of Critical Essays* (University of Notre Dame Press: Notre Dame, 1976).

————, *Aquinas on Being* (Clarendon: Oxford, 2002).

————, *Aquinas on Mind* (Routledge: London and New York, 1993).

————, *Essays on the Aristotelian Tradition* (Clarendon: Oxford, 2001).

————, *The Five Ways* (Routledge & Kegan Paul: London, 1969).

————, "Practical Inference," *Analysis* 26 (1966).

Kerr, Fergus, *After Aquinas: Versions of Thomism* (Blackwell: Oxford, 2002).

Kim, Jaegwon, *Philosophy of Mind* (Westview: Boulder, Col., 1998).

Kretzmann, Norman, *The Metaphysics of Creation: Aquinas's Natural Theology in "Summa Contra Gentiles II"* (Clarendon: Oxford, 1999).

————, *The Metaphysics of Theism: Aquinas's Natural Theology in "Summa Contra Gentiles I"* (Clarendon: Oxford, 1997).

Kretzmann, Norman, and Stump, Eleonore (eds.), *The Cambridge Companion to Aquinas* (Cambridge University Press: Cambridge, 1993).

Küng, Hans, *Great Christian Thinkers* (Continuum: New York, 2002).

Larcher, Fabian (trans.), *Commentary on the Letter of Saint Paul to the Romans*, edited by John Mortensen and Enrique Alarcón (The Aquinas Institute for the Study of Sacred Doctrine: Lander, Wyo., 2012).

————, *St. Thomas Aquinas: Commentary on the Gospel of St. John*, edited by Daniel Keating and Matthew Levering (Catholic University of America Press: Washington, D.C., 2010).

Lewis, H. D., *The Elusive Mind* (George Allen and Unwin: London, 1969).

————, *Persons and Life After Death* (Macmillan: London, 1978).

————, *Philosophy of Religion* (The English Universities Press: London, 1965).

Lombardo, Nicholas, *The Logic of Desire: Aquinas on Emotion* (Catholic University of America Press: Washington, D.C., 2011).

Loughlin, Stephen J., *Aquinas's Summa Theologiae* (T & T Clark: London and New York, 2010).

Lowe, E. J., *Subjects of Experience* (Cambridge University Press: Cambridge, 1996).

————, *A Survey of Metaphysics* (Oxford University Press: Oxford, 2002).

MacDonald, Scott, "Aquinas's Parasitic Cosmological Argument" (*Medieval Philosophy and Theology* 1, 1991).

Marenbon, John, *Boethius* (Oxford University Press: New York, 2003).

———— (ed.), *Medieval Philosophy* (Routledge: London and New York, 1998).

Martin, C. F. J., *Thomas Aquinas: God and Explanations* (Edinburgh University Press: Edinburgh, 1997).

McCabe, Herbert, "Aquinas on Good Sense" in Davies, Brian (ed.), *Thomas Aquinas: Contemporary Philosophical Perspectives* (Oxford University Press: New York, 2002).

————, *God Matters* (Geoffrey Chapman: London, 1987).

————, *God Still Matters* (Continuum: London and New York, 2002).

————, "The Immortality of the Soul" in Kenny, Anthony (ed.), *Aquinas: A Collection of Critical Essays* (University of Notre Dame Press: Notre Dame, 1976).

————, *On Aquinas* (Continuum: London and New York, 2008).

————, *The Teaching of the Catholic Church* (Darton, Longman, and Todd: London, 2000).

McCosker, Philip, and Turner, Denys (eds.), *The Cambridge Companion to the "Summa Theologiae"* (Cambridge University Press: Cambridge, 2014).

McDermott, Timothy (ed. and trans.), *Aquinas: Selected Philosophical Writings* (Oxford University Press: New York, 1993).

———, *St. Thomas Aquinas, "Summa Theologiae," A Concise Translation* (Eyre and Spottiswoode: London, 1989).

McGinn, Colin, *Logical Properties* (Clarendon: Oxford, 2000).

McGrade, A. S. (ed.), *The Cambridge Companion to Medieval Philosophy* (Cambridge University Press: Cambridge, 2003).

McInerny, Ralph (ed. and trans.), *Thomas Aquinas: Selected Writings* (Penguin: London, 1998).

Miller, Barry, *A Most Unlikely God* (University of Notre Dame Press, Notre Dame, 1996).

Milner, Robert, *Thomas Aquinas on the Passions* (Cambridge University Press: Cambridge, 2009).

Moore, Gareth, *The Body in Context: Sex and Catholicism* (Continuum: London and New York, 2001).

———, *A Question of Truth: Christianity and Homosexuality* (Continuum: London and New York, 2003).

Mulcahey, M. Michèle, *"First the Bow Is Bent in Study…": Dominican Education Before 1350* (Pontifical Institute of Mediaeval Studies: Toronto, 1998).

Nelson, Mark T., "What the Problem with Aquinas Isn't," *New Blackfriars* 87 (2006).

Nieuwenhove, Rik Van, "'Bearing the Marks of Christ's Passion': Aquinas's Soteriology" in Van Nieuwenhove, Rik, and Wawrykow, Joseph (eds.), *The Theology of Thomas Aquinas* (University of Notre Dame Press: Notre Dame., 2005).

Nieuwenhove, Rik Van, and Wawrykow, Joseph (eds.), *The Theology of Thomas Aquinas* (University of Notre Dame Press: Notre Dame, 2005).

O'Collins, Gerald, *Christology: A Biblical, Historical and Systematic Study of Jesus* (Oxford University Press: Oxford, 1995).

Oliva, Adriano, "La *Somme de Théologie* de Thomas D'Aquin: Introduction Historique et Littéraire," *Chôra* 7–8 (2009–2010).

———, *Les Débuts de l'enseignement de Thomas d'Aquin et sa Conception de la "Sacra Doctrina"* (Vrin: Paris, 2006).

O'Loughlin, Frank, *The Future of the Sacrament of Penance* (Paulist: New York and Mahwah, N.J., 2007).

Oppy, Graham, *Ontological Arguments and Belief in God* (Cambridge University Press: Cambridge, 1995).

Pasnau, Robert, *Thomas Aquinas on Human Nature: A Philosophical Study of "Summa Theologiae" Ia 75–89* (Cambridge University Press: Cambridge, 2002).

——— (trans.), *Thomas Aquinas, The Treatise on Human Nature, Summa Theologiae 1a 75–89* (Hackett: Indianapolis, 2002).

Pasnau, Robert, and Shields, Christopher, *The Philosophy of Aquinas* (Westview: Boulder and Oxford, 2004).

Pegis, Anton (trans.), *Summa Contra Gentiles, Book One: God* (University of Notre Dame Press: Notre Dame, 1975).

Pennock, Robert, and Ruse, Michael (eds.), *But Is It Science? The Philosophical Question in the Creation/Evolution Controversy*, 2nd ed. (Prometheus: Buffalo, 2008).

Persson, Per Erik, *"Sacra Doctrina": Reason and Revelation in Aquinas* (Fortress: Philadelphia, 1970).

Phillips, D. Z., *The Problem of Evil and the Problem of God* (SCM Press: London, 2004).

Pike, Nelson, *God and Timelessness* (Routledge & Kegan Paul: London, 1970).

Pini, Giorgio, "The Development of Aquinas's Thought" in Davies, Brian, and Stump, Eleonore (eds.), *The Oxford Handbook of Aquinas* (Oxford University Press: Oxford, 2011).

Plantinga, Alvin, *Does God Have a Nature?* (Marquette University Press: Milwaukee, 1980).

Plested, Markus, *Orthodox Readings of Aquinas* (Oxford University Press: Oxford, 2012).

Pope, Stephen J. (ed.), *The Ethics of Aquinas* (Georgetown University Press: Washington, D.C., 2002).

Raphael, D. D. (ed.), *British Moralists 1650–1800* (Oxford University Press: Oxford, 1969).

Regan, Richard J. (trans.), *"Compendium of Theology" by Thomas Aquinas* (Oxford University Press: Oxford, 2009).

Robiglio, A., *"Et Petrum in insulam deportatur.* Concerning Michael Dunne's Opinion on Peter of Ireland," *Bulletin de Philosophie Médiévale* 46, 2004.

———, "Neapolitan Gold," *Bulletin de Philosophie Médiévale* 44 (2002).

Rogerson, J. W., and Lieu, Judith M., *The Oxford Handbook of Biblical Studies* (Oxford University Press: New York, 2006).

Rorem, Paul, *Pseudo-Dionysius: A Commentary on the Texts and an Introduction to Their Influence* (Oxford University Press: New York, 1993).

Rosemann, Philip W., *Peter Lombard* (Oxford University Press: New York, 2004).

Rota, Michael, "Cause" in Davies, Brian, and Stump, Eleonore (eds.), *The Oxford Handbook of Thomas Aquinas* (Oxford University Press: Oxford, 2011).

Rundle, Bede, *Why There Is Something rather than Nothing* (Clarendon: Oxford, 2004).

Ruse, Michael, *Darwinism and Its Discontents* (Cambridge University Press: Cambridge, 2006).

Russell, Bertrand, *History of Western Philosophy* (George Allen and Unwin: London, 1945).

Ryan, Christopher, "Papal Primacy in Thomas Aquinas" in Ryan, Christopher (ed.), *The Religious Roles of the Papacy: Ideals and Realities, 1150–1300* (Pontifical Institute of Mediaeval Studies: Toronto, 1989).

——— (ed.), *The Religious Roles of the Papacy: Ideals and Realities, 1150–1300* (Pontifical Institute of Mediaeval Studies: Toronto, 1989).

Schillebeeckx, Edward, *Christ the Sacrament of the Encounter with God* (Sheed and Ward: London, 1963).

Schwöbel, Christoph, "Theology" in Webster, John (ed.), *The Cambridge Companion to Karl Barth* (Cambridge University Press: Cambridge, 2000).

Shanley, Brian J., *Thomas Aquinas: The Treatise on the Divine Nature, "Summa Theologiae 1 1–13"* (Hackett: Indianapolis and Cambridge, 2006).

Sigmund, Paul (trans.), *St. Thomas Aquinas on Politics and Ethics* (W. W. Norton: New York and London, 1958).

Smalley, Beryl, *The Gospels in the Schools c.1100–c.1280* (Hambledon: London and Ronceverte, 1985).

———, *The Study of the Bible in the Middle Ages*, 3rd ed. (Basil Blackwell: Oxford, 1984).

Snyder, Daniel Howard, and Moser, Paul (eds.), *Divine Hiddenness* (Cambridge University Press: Cambridge, 2002).

Sorabji, Richard, *Time, Creation and the Continuum* (Duckworth: London, 1983).

Stephens, W. P., *The Theology of Huldrych Zwingli* (Oxford University Press: Oxford, 1986).

Stump, Eleonore, *Aquinas* (Routledge: London and New York, 2003).

Swinburne, Richard, *The Coherence of Theism*, rev. ed. (Clarendon: Oxford, 1993).

———, *The Evolution of the Soul*, rev. ed. (Clarendon: Oxford, 1997).

Taliaferro, Charles, and Meister, Chad (eds.), *The Cambridge Companion to Christian Philosophical Theology* (Cambridge University Press: Cambridge, 2010).

Tanner, Norman P. (ed.), *Decrees of the Ecumenical Councils* (Sheed and Ward and Georgetown University Press: London and Washington, D.C., 1990).

Teske, Roland (trans.), *Answer to Faustus, a Manichean* (New City: Hyde Park, N.Y., 2007).

Toner, Patrick, "Personhood and Death in St. Thomas Aquinas," *History of Philosophy Quarterly* 26 (2009).

Torrell, Jean-Pierre, *Aquinas' Summa: Background, Structure and Reception* (Catholic University of America Press: Washington, D.C., 2005).

———, *Saint Thomas Aquinas: The Person and His Work* (Catholic University of America Press: Washington, D.C., 1996).

Tugwell, Simon, *Albert and Thomas: Selected Writings* (Paulist: New York and Mahwah, N.J., 1988).

———, "Prayer, Humpty Dumpty and Thomas Aquinas" in Davies, Brian (ed.), *Language, Meaning and God* (Wipf & Stock: Eugene, Ore., 2010).

Turner, Denys, *Thomas Aquinas: A Portrait* (Yale University Press: New Haven, 2013).

Urmson, J. O., *Aristotle's Ethics* (Basil Blackwell: Oxford, 1988).

Vandervelde, G., *Original Sin* (RodopiNV: Amsterdam, 1975).

Van Steenberghen, Fernand, *Le problèm de l'existence de Dieu dans les écrits de S. Thomas d'Aquin* (Éditions de l'institute supérieur de philosophie: Louvain-La-Neuve, 1980).

Velde, Rudi A. te, *Aquinas on God: The "Divine Science" of the "Summa Theologiae"* (Ashgate: Aldershot and Burlington, Vt., 2006).

Velecky, Lubor, *Aquinas' Five Arguments in the Summa Theologiae 1a 2,3* (Kok Pharos: Kampen, 1994).

Walsh, Liam, "Sacraments" in Van Nieuwenhove, Rik, and Wawrykow, Joseph (eds.), *The Theology of Thomas Aquinas* (University of Notre Dame Press: Notre Dame, 2005).

Walz, A., "De genuino titulo *Summa theologiae*," *Angelicum* 18 (1941).

Webster, John (ed.), *The Cambridge Companion to Karl Barth* (Cambridge University Press: Cambridge, 2000).

Weigel, Peter, *Aquinas on Divine Simplicity* (Peter Lang: Oxford and New York, 2008).

Weinandy, Thomas G., *Does God Change?* (St. Bede's: Still River, Mass., 1985).

Weinandy, Thomas G., Keating, Daniel A., and Yocum, John P. (eds.), *Aquinas on Scripture* (T&T Clark International: London and New York, 2005).

Weisheipl, James, *Friar Thomas D'Aquino* (Basil Blackwell: Oxford, 1975).

Wentz, Abdel Ross (ed.), *Luther's Works* (Muhlenberg: Philadelphia, 1959).

Westberg, Daniel, *Right Practical Reason: Aristotle, Action, and Prudence in Aquinas* (Clarendon: Oxford, 1994).

Wiley, Tatha, *Original Sin: Origins, Developments, Contemporary Meaning* (Paulist: New York and Mahwah, N.J., 2002).

Williams, C. J. F., "Being" in Quinn, Philip L., and Taliaferro, Charles (eds.), *A Companion to Philosophy of Religion* (Blackwell: Oxford, 1997).

———, "Neither Confounding the Persons nor Dividing the Substance" in Padgett, Alan G. (ed.), *Reason and the Christian Religion* (Clarendon: Oxford, 1994).

———, *What Is Existence?* (Clarendon: Oxford, 1981).

Williams, Rowan, "What Does Love Know? St. Thomas on the Trinity," *New Blackfriars* 82 (2001).

Windass, Stanley, "Saint Augustine and the Just War," *New Blackfriars* 43 (1962): xx–xx.

Wippel, John, *The Metaphysical Thought of Thomas Aquinas* (Catholic University of America Press: Washington, D.C., 2000).

——— (ed.), *The Ultimate Why Question: Why Is There Anything At All rather than Absolutely Nothing?* (Catholic University of America Press: Washington, D.C., 2011).

Wittgenstein, Ludwig, *Philosophical Occasions 1912–1951*, edited by James Klagge and Alfred Norman (Hackett: Indianapolis, 1993).

———, *Tractatus-Logico Philosophicus*, translated by C. K. Ogden (Routledge & Kegan Paul: London, 1922).

Wolterstorff, Nicholas, "God Everlasting" in Orlebeke, J., and Smedes, Lewis B. (eds.), *God and the Good* (Eerdmans: Grand Rapids, 1975).

Woodward, P. A. (ed.), *The Doctrine of Double Effect* (University of Notre Dame Press: Notre Dame, 2001).

Index

9 780199 380633